ACCESS

Building Literacy Through Learning™

Math

60°

Great Source Education Group

a division of Houghton Mifflin Company

Wilmington, Massachusetts

www.greatsource.com

AUTHORS

Dr. Elva Duran holds a Ph.D. from the University of Oregon in special education and reading disabilities. Duran has been an elementary reading and middle school teacher in Texas and overseas. Currently, she is a professor in the Department of Special Education, Rehabilitation, and School Psychology at California State University, Sacramento, where she teaches beginning reading and language and literacy courses. Duran is co-author of the Leamos Español reading program and has published two textbooks, *Teaching Students with Moderate/Severe Disabilities* and *Systematic Instruction in Reading for Spanish-Speaking Students*.

Jo Gusman grew up in a family of migrants and knows firsthand the complexities surrounding a second-language learner. Gusman's career in bilingual education began in 1974. In 1981, she joined the staff of the Newcomer School in Sacramento, California. There she developed her brain-based ESL strategies. Her work has garnered national television appearances and awards, including the Presidential Recognition for Excellence in Teaching. Gusman is the author of *Practical Strategies for Accelerating the Literacy Skills and Content Learning of Your ESL Students*. She is a featured video presenter, including "Multiple Intelligences and the Second Language Learner." Currently, she teaches at California State University, Sacramento, and at the Multiple Intelligences Institute at the University of California, Riverside.

Dr. John Shefelbine is a professor in the Department of Teacher Education, California State University, Sacramento. His degrees include a Master of Arts in Teaching in reading and language arts, K–12, from Harvard University and a Ph.D. in educational psychology from Stanford University. During his 11 years as an elementary and middle school teacher, Shefelbine has worked with students from linguistically and culturally diverse populations in Alaska, Arizona, Idaho, and New Mexico. Shefelbine was a contributor to the California Reading Language Arts Framework, the California Reading Initiative, and the California Reading and Literature Project and has authored a variety of reading materials and programs for developing fluent, confident readers.

EDITORIAL: Developed by Nieman Inc. with Phil LaLeike
DESIGN: Ronan Design

International Standard Book Number -13: 978-0-669–50904–5
International Standard Book Number -10: 0–669–50904–3

7 8 9   2266   20 19 18 17
4500643657

CONSULTANTS

Shane Bassett
Mill Park Elementary School
David Douglas School District
Portland, OR

Jeanette Gordon
Senior Educational Consultant
Illinois Resource Center
Des Plaines, IL

Dr. Aixa Perez-Prado
College of Education
Florida International University
Miami, FL

Dennis Terdy
Director of Grants
   and Special Programs
Newcomer Center
   Township High School
Arlington Heights, IL

RESEARCH SITE LEADERS

Carmen Concepción
Lawton Chiles Middle School
Miami, FL

Andrea Dabbs
Edendale Middle School
San Lorenzo, CA

Daniel Garcia
Public School 130
Bronx, NY

Bobbi Ciriza Houtchens
Arroyo Valley High School
San Bernardino, CA

Portia McFarland
Wendell Phillips High School
Chicago, IL

TEACHER GROUP REVIEWERS

Sara Ainsworth
Hannah Beardsley Middle School
Crystal Lake, IL

Walter A. Blair
Otis Elementary School
Chicago, IL

Vincent U. Egonmwan
Joyce Kilmer Elementary School
Chicago, IL

Anne Hopkins
Arie Crown School
Skokie, IL

Heather Pusich
Field Middle School
Northbrook, IL

Dana Robinson
Prairie Crossing Charter School
Grayslake, IL

Nestor Torres
Chase Elementary School
Chicago, IL

RESEARCH SITE MATH REVIEWERS

Maritza Baez
Lawton Chiles Middle School
Miami, FL

Andrew Dunbar, Jr.
M.S. 201 STAR Academy
Bronx, NY

Elizabeth Heckman
Edendale Middle School
San Lorenzo, CA

Teri Paine
Martin Luther King, Jr.
   Middle School
San Bernardino, CA

Geraldine Wilson
Warren Elementary School
Chicago, IL

MATH TEACHER REVIEWERS

Anita Bright
Fairfax County Public Schools
Fairfax, VA

Bridgette Calloway-Hall
O'Farrell Community School
San Diego, CA

Renée Crawford
O'Farrell Community School
San Diego, CA

Roberta Girardi
Howard County Public Schools
Ellicott City, MD

Velia Gomez
Gilmore Middle School
Racine, WI

Abdullahi Mohamed
Sanford Middle School
Minneapolis, MN

Steve Paterwic
High School of Science
   and Technology
Springfield, MA

Mario Perez
Newcomer Center/
   School District 214
Arlington Heights, IL

Cristina Sanchez-Lopez
Illinois Resource Center
Des Plaines, IL

TABLE OF

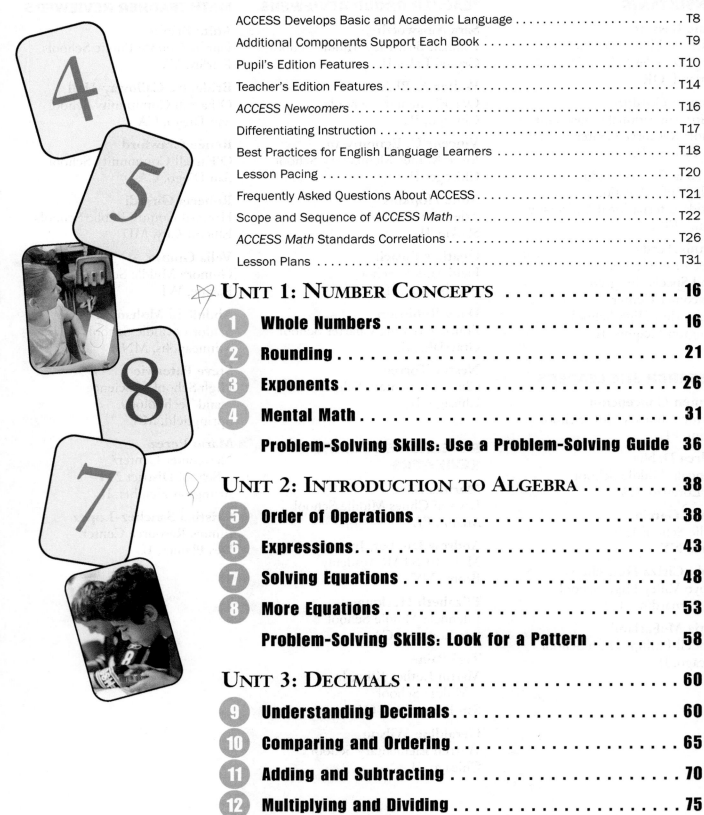

CONTENTS

TABLE OF

CONTENTS

ACCESS Develops Basic and Academic Language

The ACCESS program is a standards-based middle-school program for English language learners. It builds students' understanding of the big ideas in English, math, science, and American history while developing language proficiency in English. The *Newcomers* program gives beginning students survival language and starts them on their way to success in school.

Additional Components Support Each Book

With ACCESS, you have the components you need to support your teaching.

The **Teacher's Edition** provides succinct, informative notes, along with activity ideas and suggestions for ways to differentiate instruction based on students' language proficiency.

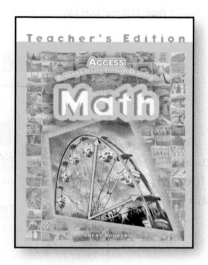

The **Practice Book** helps students master problem-solving skills, build academic vocabulary, and write about what they have learned.

Overhead Transparencies provide students with 36 forms and graphic organizers for practicing math concepts and help to focus students' writing and oral presentations. Transparencies can also be used as copy masters for forms, such as number lines or grids, for students' work.

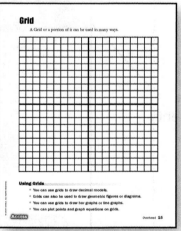

The **Assessment Book** provides tests for each lesson, which assess students' growth in both language development and mathematics content.

The **Assessment Folder** helps you track students' language development over the school year.

Pupil's Edition Features

Each ACCESS Pupil's Edition is organized around lessons specifically designed to meet the needs of English language learners. Each lesson has three parts.

1. Talk and Explore
2. Look and Read
3. Develop Language

1. Talk and Explore

Gives students the **Big Idea** of the lesson

Connects with students

Introduces **Key Concepts** needed to understand the lesson

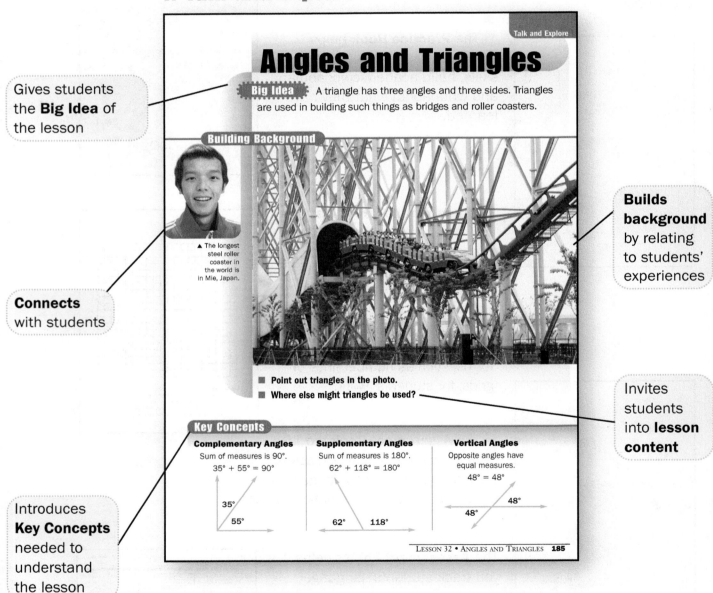

Builds background by relating to students' experiences

Invites students into **lesson content**

2. Look and Read

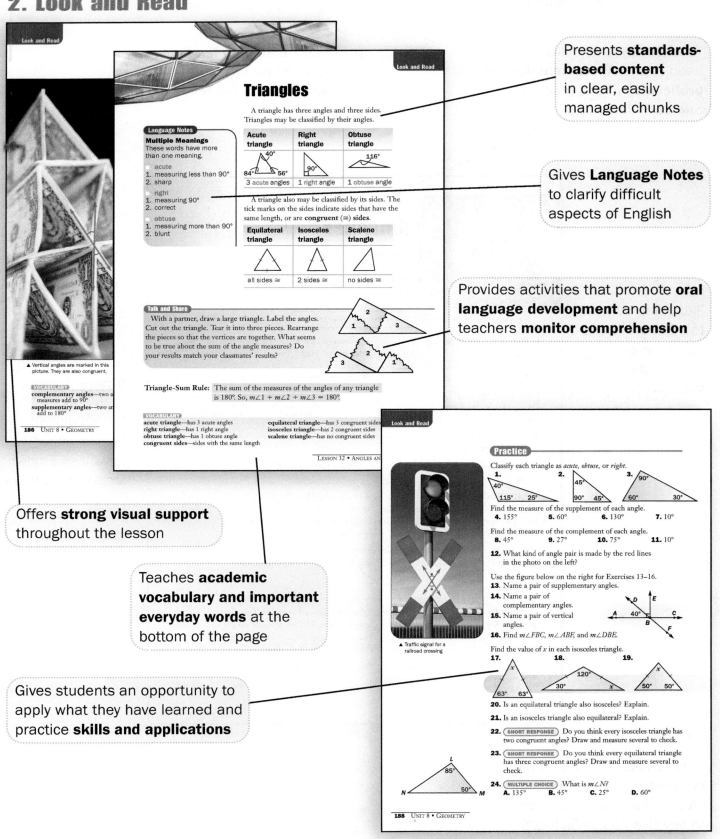

Presents **standards-based content** in clear, easily managed chunks

Gives **Language Notes** to clarify difficult aspects of English

Provides activities that promote **oral language development** and help teachers **monitor comprehension**

Offers **strong visual support** throughout the lesson

Teaches **academic vocabulary and important everyday words** at the bottom of the page

Gives students an opportunity to apply what they have learned and practice **skills and applications**

Triangles

A triangle has three angles and three sides. Triangles may be classified by their angles.

Language Notes

Multiple Meanings
These words have more than one meaning.

☐ acute
1. measuring less than 90°
2. sharp

☐ right
1. measuring 90°
2. correct

☐ obtuse
1. measuring more than 90°
2. blunt

Acute triangle	Right triangle	Obtuse triangle
40° 84° 56°	90°	116°
3 acute angles	1 right angle	1 obtuse angle

A triangle also may be classified by its sides. The tick marks on the sides indicate sides that have the same length, or are **congruent** (≅) **sides**.

Equilateral triangle	Isosceles triangle	Scalene triangle
all sides ≅	2 sides ≅	no sides ≅

Talk and Share

With a partner, draw a large triangle. Label the angles. Cut out the triangle. Tear it into three pieces. Rearrange the pieces so that the vertices are together. What seems to be true about the sum of the angle measures? Do your results match your classmates' results?

▲ Vertical angles are marked in this picture. They are also congruent.

VOCABULARY
complementary angles—two a... measures add to 90°
supplementary angles—two a... add to 180°

Triangle-Sum Rule: The sum of the measures of the angles of any triangle is 180°. So, $m\angle 1 + m\angle 2 + m\angle 3 = 180°$.

VOCABULARY
acute triangle—has 3 acute angles
right triangle—has 1 right angle
obtuse triangle—has 1 obtuse angle
congruent sides—sides with the same length

equilateral triangle—has 3 congruent sides
isosceles triangle—has 2 congruent sides
scalene triangle—has no congruent sides

186 UNIT 8 • GEOMETRY

LESSON 32 • ANGLES AN...

Practice

Classify each triangle as *acute*, *obtuse*, or *right*.
1. 40° 115° 25°
2. 45° 90° 45°
3. 90° 60° 30°

Find the measure of the supplement of each angle.
4. 155°   5. 60°   6. 130°   7. 10°

Find the measure of the complement of each angle.
8. 45°   9. 27°   10. 75°   11. 10°

12. What kind of angle pair is made by the red lines in the photo on the left?

Use the figure below on the right for Exercises 13–16.
13. Name a pair of supplementary angles.
14. Name a pair of complementary angles.
15. Name a pair of vertical angles.
16. Find $m\angle FBC$, $m\angle ABF$, and $m\angle DBE$.

Find the value of x in each isosceles triangle.
17. x 63° 63°
18. 120° 30° x
19. x 50° 50°

20. Is an equilateral triangle also isosceles? Explain.
21. Is an isosceles triangle also equilateral? Explain.
22. (SHORT RESPONSE) Do you think every isosceles triangle has two congruent angles? Draw and measure several to check.
23. (SHORT RESPONSE) Do you think every equilateral triangle has three congruent angles? Draw and measure several to check.
24. (MULTIPLE CHOICE) What is $m\angle N$?
A. 135°   B. 45°   C. 25°   D. 60°

▲ Traffic signal for a railroad crossing

188 UNIT 8 • GEOMETRY

---

3. Develop Language

Teaches students skills they need to achieve **communicative proficiency** and to produce **authentic language**

Uses **academic language needed for critical thinking and high-stakes tests**

Illustrates how to organize ideas using helpful **graphic organizers**

Differentiates **activities** for beginning and intermediate/ advanced English language learners

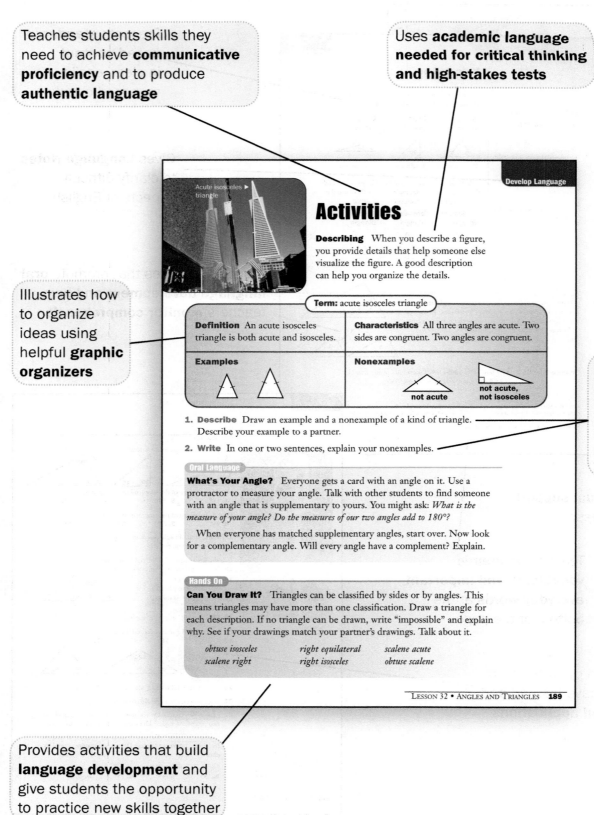

Provides activities that build **language development** and give students the opportunity to practice new skills together

Problem-Solving Skills

Solve a Simpler Problem

Each unit ends with a **problem-solving lesson.** Twelve strategies are taught throughout the book.

Sometimes you can understand how to solve difficult problems by solving a simpler problem first.

Problem: Find the sum of the measures of the angles in a hexagon.

Hexagon

Read and Understand

Need to find: Sum of the measures of the angles in a hexagon

You know: There are six sides and six angles in a hexagon.

Key fact: The sum of the angle measures in a triangle is 180°.

Diagonal

Quadrilateral

Four skills—**Read and Understand, Plan and Solve, Answer,** and **Look Back**—are taught in each problem-solving lesson.

Plan and Solve
Solve a simpler problem first. Find the sum of the measures of the angles in a quadrilateral and in a pentagon. Then look for a pattern.

Draw a diagonal of the quadrilateral to divide it into two triangles. The sum of the angle measures is $2 \times 180° = 360°$.

Draw two diagonals from a vertex of a pentagon to divide it into three triangles. The sum of the angle measures is $3 \times 180° = 540°$.

Pentagon

Put the information in a table and look for a pattern.

	Triangle	Quadrilateral	Pentagon	Hexagon
Number of sides	3	4	5	6
Number of triangles	1	2	3	4
Sum of angle measures	$1 \times 180° = 180°$	$2 \times 180° = 360°$	$3 \times 180° = 540°$	?

Answer   The sum of the angle measures in a hexagon is $4 \times 180° = 720°$.

Look Back   The pattern in the table shows that the sum of the angle measures is (number of sides − 2) × 180°. Then $(6 − 2) \times 180° = 4(180°) = 720°$.

Talk and Share
Work with a partner. Explain how you could solve a simpler problem to help you find the height of a stack of 100 pennies.

210   UNIT 8 • GEOMETRY

Practice

1. If the sum of the angle measures of a figure is 540°, what kind of figure is it?

2. What is the sum of the angle measures of a square?

3. Find the sum of the angle measures of a decagon (a 10-sided figure).

Use the strategy *solve a simpler problem.*

4. Find the sum of the whole numbers 1 through 50.

5. The seats in a theater are numbered 1 through 200. How many seats have a 3 in the number?

6. Six volleyball players on a team all shake hands with one another. How many handshakes take place?

Choose a strategy and solve each problem.

7. Juan is drawing a border around his bedroom walls using the pattern shown. Will the 36th figure be a triangle or a square?

8. Half of Nadine's books are about candle making. One-fourth of her books are about sailing. The remaining two books are about birds. How many books does she have?

9. For lunch, you choose a meat, a vegetable, and a fruit from the menu on the right. How many different lunches are possible?

~LUNCH MENU~
* Jerk Chicken
* Mongolian Beef
* Red Beans
* Black-eyed Peas

* Banana
* Mango
* Orange

Highlights a different aspect of English in each problem-solving lesson through **Grammar Spotlights**

Grammar Spotlight

Imperatives   Imperatives are verbs that express a command or a request. They sometimes are followed by exclamation points.

Common Imperatives	Imperatives in This Lesson
Go at once!	*Find* the sum.
Please *do* it now!	*Solve* a simpler problem.
Tell me why you were late.	*Look* for a pattern.
Wash your hands before dinner.	*Choose* a strategy.

1. Think of a sentence with an imperative. Say it aloud and have your partner write it down. Check to see if your partner wrote it correctly.

2. Write down an imperative sentence as your partner speaks one. Have your partner check to see if you wrote it correctly.

3. Talk with your partner about times when imperatives often are used.

SOLVE A SIMPLER PROBLEM   **211**

Teacher's Edition Features

The Teacher's Edition provides page-by-page support for planning and instruction.

Both mathematical and language **standards** drive each lesson.

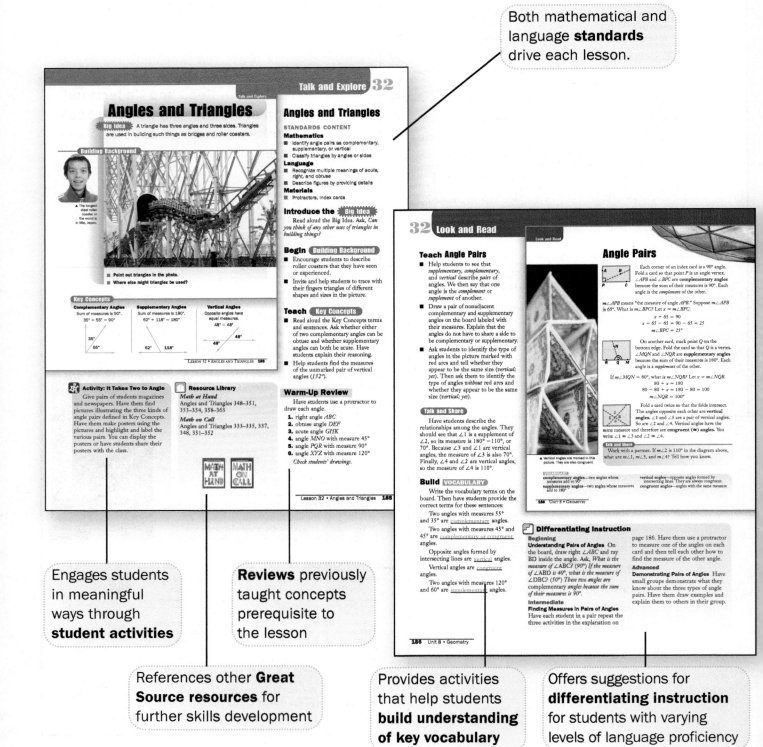

Engages students in meaningful ways through **student activities**

Reviews previously taught concepts prerequisite to the lesson

References other **Great Source resources** for further skills development

Provides activities that help students **build understanding of key vocabulary**

Offers suggestions for **differentiating instruction** for students with varying levels of language proficiency

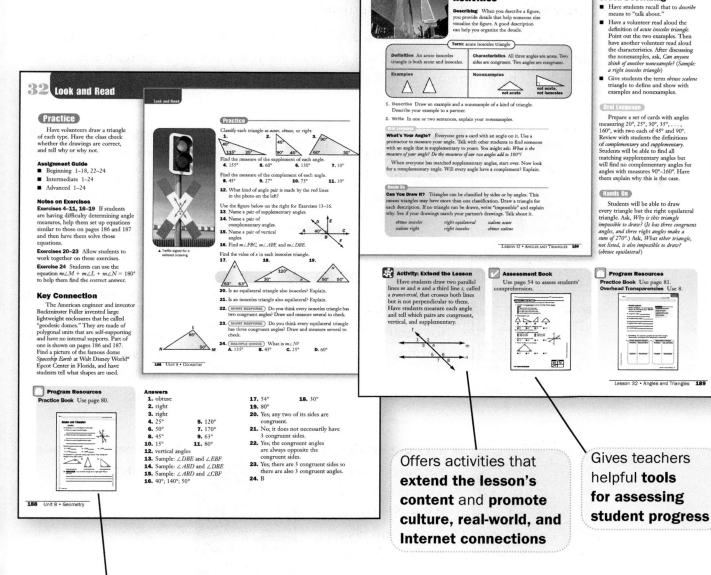

Offers activities that **extend the lesson's content** and **promote culture, real-world, and Internet connections**

Gives teachers helpful **tools for assessing student progress**

References relevant pages in the **Practice Book** for additional practice and language development

ACCESS Newcomers

ACCESS Newcomers is a multi-level program for beginning English language learners. The program offers three progressive stages: Starting Out, Getting Ready, and School Readiness, plus an introductory Readiness unit for those newcomers who arrive with little educational background.

ACCESS Newcomers introduces 2,487 high-frequency vocabulary words, including important academic terms that will get students ready for their content-area subjects. The program includes:

■ **320-page Pupil's Edition** for whole-class instruction

■ **Word Tiles** for hands-on learning

■ **Assessment Folder** for tracking students' language development over the school year

■ **120 Lesson Cards** for pull-out programs and small-group instruction. *Overhead Transparencies* are available for each lesson card.

■ **CD of additional resources,** including printable Word Tiles, Sentence Strips, and take-home activities

■ **Assessment Book** to document student progress

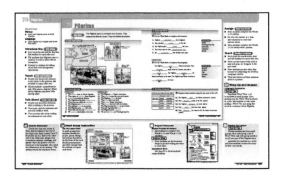

■ **Teacher's Edition** with a four-step lesson plan for giving students practice listening, speaking, reading, and writing vocabulary words in sentence contexts. Additional activities develop students' understanding of English.

Differentiating Instruction

A typical classroom of English language learners includes students at varying levels of language proficiency. ACCESS helps teachers differentiate their instruction to meet these different students' needs. In each of the three lesson parts—Talk and Explore, Look and Read, and Develop Language—you can support your students, as the chart below shows. In addition, teaching notes on every two-page spread give specific activity suggestions for Differentiating Instruction. You can also use the *Assessment Folder* to track students' progress over the course of the year.

Language Proficiency	Talk and Explore	Look and Read	Develop Language
Beginning An effective teaching method for beginning students is to pair them with more proficient partners or with partners who speak the same first language.	Build background by naming objects in the introductory picture. Write key words on the board. Read aloud and have students repeat with you.	Use the introductory paragraph, heads, picture captions, and summaries to help students get a broad overview of the lesson.	Invite students to draw and pantomime to show what they know. Encourage one-word and short-phrase responses.
Intermediate To facilitate learning for intermediate students, you may want to change student partners and form small groups with different combinations of students.	Build background with the picture and encourage students to draw on their own experiences, using short sentences, pantomime, and labels to show what they know.	Have students use headings and picture captions to predict what they will learn. Encourage note-taking and K-W-L Charts. Let partners help each other. Over time, raise your expectations for language use.	Relate lesson content to academic expectations in other classes, in assignments, and on tests. Assign the Write activity. Work gradually through lists and numbered sentences to complete paragraph responses.
Advanced At times, pair advanced students to help them challenge each other.	Build background through a discussion of the picture and how it introduces key ideas of the lesson. Use the questions to stimulate a class or group discussion.	Help students use reading skills, such as predicting, finding main ideas, and comparing and contrasting. Expect silent reading, but check comprehension through the Talk and Share activities.	Encourage written responses. Ask that role-plays be scripted. Help students write descriptive, persuasive, and explanatory paragraphs.

Best Practices for English Language Learners

1. Every lesson opens with a Big Idea that introduces the content.

Big Idea Lines and angles are all around you. They form the basic shapes of many things

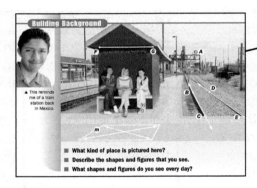

2. An introductory photo helps students connect to the lesson and build language.

3. Key Concepts establish content and academic vocabulary and break down the fundamental concepts of each lesson.

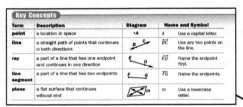

4. Content is continually reinforced with strong visual presentation.

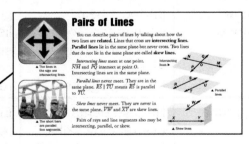

5. Talk and Share activities promote oral language development and help teachers monitor comprehension.

VOCABULARY

related—having something in common
intersecting lines—lines in the same plane that meet at one point
parallel lines—lines in the same plane that never cross
skew lines—lines that lie in different planes

6. Vocabulary support is given throughout each lesson and in a comprehensive glossary.

Language Notes

Verb Phrases
These phrases have special meanings.

- **line up:** make straight or put in the right position
- **make up:** form or compose

7. Language Notes teach and help clarify difficult aspects of the English language.

8. Develop Language activities build students' communicative abilities and academic vocabulary for high-stakes tests.

Activities

Classifying The figures on the left are triangles. You can classify or sort triangles by the size of their angles. The size of the largest angle determines whether the triangle is acute, right, or obtuse. Copy the table below to record your findings.

1. **Classify** Use a protractor to measure the largest angle of each triangle shown. Then write the measure of that angle and the name of each triangle in the table to classify it as acute, right, or obtuse.
2. **Draw** Draw an acute triangle, a right triangle, and an obtuse triangle. Ask a partner to classify your triangles.
3. **Explain** Tell how you decided to classify each triangle.

Acute Triangle	Right Triangle	Obtuse Triangle
		130° △ ABC

Grammar Spotlight

Imperatives Imperatives are verbs that express a command or a request. They sometimes are followed by exclamation points.

Common Imperatives	Imperatives in This Lesson
Go at once!	*Find* the sum.
Please *do* it now!	*Solve* a simpler problem.
Tell me why you were late.	*Look* for a pattern.
Wash your hands before dinner.	*Choose* a strategy.

1. Think of a sentence with an imperative. Say it aloud and have your partner write it down. Check to see if your partner wrote it correctly.
2. Write down an imperative sentence as your partner speaks one. Have your partner check to see if you wrote it correctly.
3. Talk with your partner about times when imperatives often are used.

9. Ongoing, consistent instruction in grammar helps students make progress in understanding English.

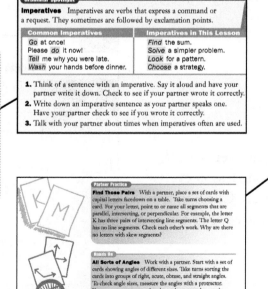

Partner Practice
Find Those Pairs With a partner, place a set of cards with capital letters facedown on a table. Take turns choosing a card. For your letter, point to or name all segments that are parallel, intersecting, or perpendicular. For example, the letter K has three pairs of intersecting line segments. The letter Q has no line segments. Check each other's work. Why are there no letters with skew segments?

Hands On
All Sorts of Angles Work with a partner. Start with a set of cards showing angles of different sizes. Take turns sorting the cards into groups of right, acute, obtuse, and straight angles. To check angle sizes, measure the angles with a protractor. Your partner must agree that the cards are sorted correctly.

10. A variety of activities promotes oral communication and increases the amount of time students are producing and practicing language.

ACCESS gives English language learners the tools they need to develop literacy and build content knowledge in all their school subjects.

Lesson Pacing

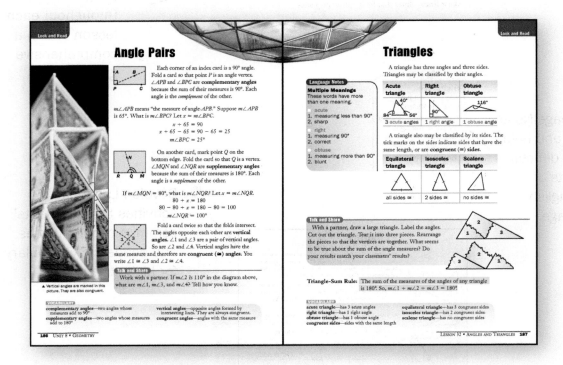

One-year Course

1. The program can be taught in one school year by covering each lesson in one and a half weeks. To complete ACCESS in one year, cover *two pages every day*.

Two-year Course

2. The program can be taught over two school years by covering one lesson every three weeks. To complete ACCESS in two years, move at the pace of *one page per day*.

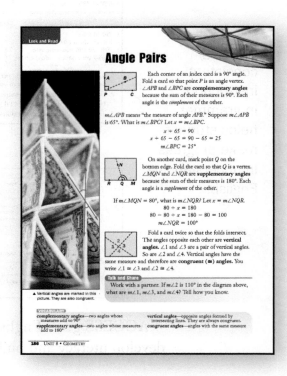

Frequently Asked Questions About ACCESS

Q: How can ACCESS work for all my English language learners?

A: ACCESS can work for many levels of learners because it targets intermediate and advanced students and offers *Newcomers* for beginners. ACCESS is also a great resource for students who are transitioning from ESL programs into mainstream classes but who need sheltered content instruction.

Q: How does ACCESS compare to our basal text?

A: ACCESS shelters the content of the subject. It covers the topics and standards of a content area, but with about 10% of the words. Students need to read texts that are on their reading level. They need comprehensible text, as opposed to frustrating tomes that have considerably more information and complexity than they can currently handle. ACCESS gives ESL students access, or an entry point, making content ACCESSible.

Q: Does this mean teachers have to teach both math and English?

A: No. But, in order to reach ESL students, math teachers often find themselves having to make key terms and the language underlying concepts more accessible. *ACCESS Math* helps teachers by presenting key concepts and academic vocabulary through highly visual presentations of the ideas. The result is a resource that supplements what math teachers are trying to accomplish in their regular classes and saves them hours of preparation.

Q: How can ACCESS help my students who have little or no educational background?

A: *ACCESS Newcomers* has a readiness unit that covers the basics, such as the alphabet, addition and subtraction, colors, countries of the world, and places in America. The three levels in *ACCESS Newcomers* become gradually more sophisticated as students are challenged to accelerate their learning and transition into the next proficiency level.

Q: How does ACCESS prepare my students for high-stakes tests and help me show annual yearly progress?

A: ACCESS is a standards-based program. It teaches the language and skills integral to test-taking as well as the standards-based content on the tests themselves. ACCESS gives students the academic language required to understand school assignments and teacher explanations and models how to produce written responses for successful test taking.

Lesson	Big Idea	Key Concepts	Language Notes	Develop Language (or Grammar Spotlight)
Lesson 1: Whole Numbers	You can use whole numbers to compare many real-world things when you understand how the numbers are written.	standard form, short-word form, word form	Multiple Meanings: *order*	Comparing
Lesson 2: Rounding	You don't always need an exact number. Often an estimated number is more useful. You can find an estimated number by rounding.	exact number, estimate, rounded	Multiple Meanings: *estimate, round*	Interpreting
Lesson 3: Exponents	You can use exponents to write some numbers in a convenient short form.	standard form, expanded form, exponential form	Multiple Meanings: *factor, base, power, square, cube*	Predicting
Lesson 4: Mental Math	You don't always need paper and pencil to compute. You can do it in your head. This is called "mental math."	mental math, compensation	Multiple Meanings: *property, operation*	Explaining
Problem Solving: Use a Problem-Solving Guide				Form Plural Nouns
Lesson 5: Order of Operations	Mathematics is a language that means the same thing all over the world. This lesson explains some of the rules for understanding the language of math.	order of operations, parentheses	Signal Words: Time Order	Choosing an Operation
Lesson 6: Expressions	To solve word problems, it sometimes helps to write a mathematical expression first.	rule, variable	Multiple Meanings: *rule*	Evaluating
Lesson 7: Solving Equations	Many problems involving addition and subtraction can be solved more easily if you use equations.	equation, Addition Property of Equality, balance		Describing
Lesson 8: More Equations	In the last lesson, you solved addition and subtraction equations by doing the same thing to both sides of them. You can solve multiplication and division equations the same way.	Division Property of Equality		Explaining
Problem Solving: Look for a Pattern				Phrasal Verbs
Lesson 9: Understanding Decimals	You can't always use whole numbers to tell *how much*. Decimal numbers, such as 0.5 or 34.65, show amounts that are between whole numbers.	decimal number, digits, decimal point	Confusing Word Pairs: *tenths, hundredths, thousandths/ tens, hundreds, thousands*	Identifying
Lesson 10: Comparing and Ordering	The number with the most digits is not always the greatest number. Place value is an important clue to decimal numbers.	is less than, is greater than	Signal Words: Compare/ Contrast	Organizing
Lesson 11: Adding and Subtracting	Dollars and cents use decimal numbers to the hundredths place. Adding or subtracting amounts of money is the same as adding or subtracting decimals.	regroup		Summarizing
Lesson 12: Multiplying and Dividing	Travelers often need to change money used in one country to money used in another country. You can change money by multiplying or dividing with decimals.	currency		Demonstrating

Lesson	Big Idea	Key Concepts	Language Notes	Develop Language (or Grammar Spotlight)
Problem Solving: Guess, Check, and Revise				Using *too* and *very*
Lesson 13: Divisibility	When a number divides another number with no remainder, you can use that information to solve problems involving the two numbers.	divisible, factor, multiple		Analyzing
Lesson 14: Prime and Composite	Divisibility rules can help you decide whether a number has factors other than 1 and itself.	composite number, factor tree, prime number	Multiple Meanings: *prime*	Describing
Lesson 15: Greatest Common Factor	Every number has factors. Every pair of numbers has at least one factor that is common to both numbers.	Venn Diagram, common factors, greatest common factors	Idioms: return the favor	Responding
Lesson 16: Least Common Multiple	Every number has many multiples. Every pair of numbers has multiples that are common to both numbers. The least common multiple will help you find out when events might happen at the same time.	multiples, common multiples, least common multiple	Signal Words for Importance: *least, greatest*	Persuading
Problem Solving: Make an Organized List				The Word *the*
Lesson 17: Understanding Fractions	Fractions represent parts. They may represent a number of equal-sized parts of a whole or a number of items in a set. Fractions show division.	decimal, fraction	Signal Words for Location: *denominator*	Interpreting
Lesson 18: Mixed Numbers	Some fractions are equal to or greater than 1. You can write these fractions in several ways.	fractions, mixed numbers, proper fractions, improper fractions	Multiple Meanings: *proper, improper*	Describing
Lesson 19: Comparing and Ordering	You can compare things in many ways. You can put some things next to each other to see how they are different. To compare fractions, you first write fractions with a common denominator.	compare, least, greatest		Comparing
Lesson 20: Adding Fractions	The skills used for adding whole numbers and decimals also work for adding fractions and mixed numbers.	common denominators, rename	Multiple Meanings: *like, check*	Comparing and Contrasting
Lesson 21: Subtracting Fractions	You subtract fractions and mixed numbers by using the same skills you use for adding fractions and mixed numbers.	whole numbers, decimals, mixed numbers		Demonstrating
Lesson 22: Multiplying and Dividing	You always should use mental math to do a computation when you can. When you cannot, then you should use the skills you have learned.	model, fraction model, quotient		Clarifying
Problem Solving: Work Backward				Simple Sentence
Lesson 23: Ratios and Proportions	Ratios describe relationships between two quantities. Ratios often are expressed as fractions. When two ratios are equal, you can write them in a proportion.	ratio, proportion, rate	Multiple Meanings: *term*	Evaluating
Lesson 24: Understanding Percent	A percent is a special kind of ratio in which a part is compared to one hundred. Percents are useful in making comparisons.	fractions, decimals, percents		Predicting

Lesson	Big Idea	Key Concepts	Language Notes	Develop Language (or Grammar Spotlight)
Lesson 25: Percent of a Number	Percents can be less than 1% and greater than 100%. There are several ways to find a percent of a number.	less than 1%, from 1% to 100%, more than 100%	Idioms: give 110%	Persuading
Lesson 26: Applications of Percent	Percents are used in many everyday situations. Discounts, sales tax, and interest earned on savings accounts all involve percents.	percent, commission, discount, sales tax, interest, tip	Homophones: *principal, principle*	Summarizing
Problem Solving: Use Logical Reasoning				Adjectives: Using *some, any, many, every, each,* and *neither/nor*
Lesson 27: Organizing Data	We organize and show data in graphs, charts, and other kinds of pictures.	survey, data, line plot	Confusing Word Pairs: *choose, choice*	Gathering Data
Lesson 28: Analyzing Data	There are many ways to display data. Stem-and-leaf plots are useful displays because they show how data fall into groups.	stem-and-leaf plot, stem, leaf	Multiple Meanings: *leaf, stem*	Analyzing
Lesson 29: Bar and Line Graphs	Graphs show trends and differences in data that tables do not show. Bar graphs can give a quick comparison of quantities. Line graphs can show how data change over time.	table, line graph, bar graph	Multiple Meanings: *scale*	Interpreting
Lesson 30: Double Bar Graphs	Graphs can show a comparison of two or more quantities. Some graphs can give false impressions. Be careful when you draw one. Be critical when you read one.	double bar graph	Homophones: *break, brake*	Contrasting
Problem Solving: Make a Table				Using Numbers with Nouns
Lesson 31: Lines and Angles	Lines and angles are all around you. They form the basic shapes of many things.	point, line, ray, line segment, plane	Verb Phrases: *line up, make up*	Classifying
Lesson 32: Angles and Triangles	A triangle has three angles and three sides. Triangles are used in building such things as bridges and roller coasters.	complementary angles, supplementary angles, vertical angles	Multiple Meanings: *acute, right, obtuse*	Describing
Lesson 33: Polygons	Plane figures can have three or more straight sides. Some four-sided figures have shapes that you have seen many times.	polygon, side, angle, vertex	Multiple Meanings: *figure, regular*	Synthesizing
Lesson 34: Congruent Figures	Often when figures are congruent, they fit together. Many objects and designs are made from congruent polygons.	congruent, corresponding sides, corresponding angles	Multiple Meanings: *corresponding*	Summarizing
Lesson 35: Similar Figures	You can draw a figure that is the same as another figure in all ways but size. The new figure will be similar to the original. The new size may be easier to work with.	similar figures, proportional	Multiple Meanings: *model*	Identifying
Lesson 36: Transformations	Geometry studies shapes and sizes. It also studies movement. This lesson explores ways to move a figure.	transformation, pre-image, image		Explaining
Problem Solving: Solve a Simpler Problem				Imperatives
Lesson 37: Perimeter and Area	There are two measurements that relate to plane figures. One is the distance around. The other is the space inside.	perimeter, area	Multiple Meanings: *base*	Connecting

Lesson	Big Idea	Key Concepts	Language Notes	Develop Language (or Grammar Spotlight)
Lesson 38: Circles	A circle is a special shape with no straight sides. It is a set of points in a plane that are the same distance from the center point. There are special formulas related to circles.	circle, center, radius	Confusing Word Pairs: *circle, sphere*	Organizing
Lesson 39: Surface Area	Packages and containers come in many different shapes. Sometimes you need to find the total area of all the outside surfaces of a package or container.	solid figure, edge, vertex, faces	Multiple Meanings: *net*	Persuading
Lesson 40: Volume	Volume is a measure of how much space a solid takes up. That measure is based on the dimensions of the solid.	volume, cubic unit	Multiple Meanings: *volume*	Comparing and Contrasting
Problem Solving: Draw a Diagram				*Fewer Than/Less Than*
Lesson 41: What Is Probability?	Before an event happens, you may be able to measure how likely it is to occur. That measure is called the *probability* of the event.	outcome, event, equally likely outcomes, probability	Confusing Word Pairs: *chance, change*	Interpreting
Lesson 42: Making Predictions	When a game or an experiment involves probability, you can gather and use data to help you make a prediction.	experiment, trial, success		Predicting
Lesson 43: Counting	You can use special methods to find and to count all possible outcomes. The methods are useful for finding a large number or only a small number of outcomes.	tree diagram	Signal Words: Time Order	Persuading
Lesson 44: Arrangements	When you list the outcomes for a compound event, the way you order them may be important.	arrangement, permutation, combination	Signal Words: Time Order	Clarifying
Problem Solving: Simulate a Problem				*Who* or *What*
Lesson 45: What Are Integers?	Many situations cannot be represented by whole numbers. You may need negative numbers to show a loss, a temperature below zero, or an opposite direction.	integers, positive integers, negative integers	Signal Words: Positive/Negative; Multiple Meanings: *positive, negative*	Identifying
Lesson 46: Adding and Subtracting Integers	You can add or subtract integers by modeling the operations with colored chips or by using rules.	model, zero pair		Summarizing
Lesson 47: Multiplying and Dividing Integers	In many real-life situations, you need to multiply or divide with negative integers. Often patterns will help you discover rules and keep you on the right track.	patterns	Idioms: on the right track	Organizing
Lesson 48: The Coordinate Plane	A coordinate plane helps to show how an area is laid out. Integers can be used to locate points on the plane.	y-axis, x-axis, coordinates, coordinate plane	Multiple Meanings: *coordinate, graph*	Explaining
Problem Solving: Write an Equation				*More, Less, Fewer,* and *Than*
Lesson 49: Solving Equations	Sometimes it takes more than one step to solve an equation, even if it has only one variable.	simple equation, two-operation equation	Homophones: *way, weigh*	Justifying
Lesson 50: Inequalities	Many times you need to compare two quantities that are not equal. You can use mathematical sentences to make these comparisons.	mathematical sentence, equation, inequality	Multiple Meanings: *solution*	Comparing
Problem Solving: Make a Model				*Some* and *Any*

Lesson	National Mathematics Standards
Lesson 1: Whole Numbers	Students should understand the place-value structure of the base-ten number system and be able to represent and compare whole numbers.
Lesson 2: Rounding	Students should develop and use strategies to estimate the results of whole-number computations and to judge the reasonableness of such results.
Lesson 3: Exponents	Students should develop an understanding of large numbers and recognize and appropriately use exponential notation.
Lesson 4: Mental Math	Students should identify such properties as commutativity, associativity, and distributivity and use them to compute with whole numbers; use the associative and commutative properties of addition and multiplication and the distributive property of multiplication over addition to simplify computations with integers.
Problem Solving: Use a Problem-Solving Guide	Students should build new mathematical knowledge through problem solving; solve problems that arise in mathematics and in other contexts.
Lesson 5: Order of Operations	Students should understand the meaning and effects of arithmetic operations with integers.
Lesson 6: Expressions	Students should use symbolic algebra to represent situations and to solve problems, represent, analyze, and generalize a variety of patterns with tables, words, and symbolic rules.
Lesson 7: Solving Equations	Students should recognize and generate equivalent forms for simple algebraic expressions and solve linear equations.
Lesson 8: More Equations	Students should recognize and generate equivalent forms for simple algebraic expressions and solve linear equations.
Problem Solving: Look for a Pattern	Students should represent, analyze, and generalize a variety of patterns; build new mathematical knowledge through problem solving; solve problems that arise in mathematics and in other contexts; apply and adapt a variety of appropriate strategies to solve problems.
Lesson 9: Understanding Decimals	Students should understand the place-value structure of the base-ten number system and be able to represent decimals.
Lesson 10: Comparing and Ordering	Students should compare and order decimals efficiently and find their approximate locations on a number line.
Lesson 11: Adding and Subtracting	Students should develop and analyze algorithms for computing with decimals and develop fluency in their use.
Lesson 12: Multiplying and Dividing	Students should develop and analyze algorithms for computing with decimals and develop fluency in their use.
Problem Solving: Guess, Check, and Revise	Students should build new mathematical knowledge through problem solving; solve problems that arise in mathematics and in other contexts; apply and adapt a variety of appropriate strategies to solve problems.
Lesson 13: Divisibility	Students should use factors and multiples to solve problems.
Lesson 14: Prime and Composite	Students should use factors, multiples, and prime factorization to solve problems.
Lesson 15: Greatest Common Factor	Students should use factors, multiples, and prime factorization to solve problems.
Lesson 16: Least Common Multiple	Students should use factors, multiples, and prime factorization to solve problems.
Problem Solving: Make an Organized List	Students should build new mathematical knowledge through problem solving; solve problems that arise in mathematics and in other contexts; apply and adapt a variety of appropriate strategies to solve problems.
Lesson 17: Understanding Fractions	Students should develop understanding of fractions as parts of unit wholes, as parts of a collection, as locations on number lines, and as divisions of whole numbers.
Lesson 18: Mixed Numbers	Students should develop understanding of fractions as parts of unit wholes, as parts of a collection, as locations on number lines, and as divisions of whole numbers.
Lesson 19: Comparing and Ordering	Students should compare and order fractions and decimals efficiently and find their approximate locations on a number line.
Lesson 20: Adding Fractions	Students should develop and analyze algorithms for computing with fractions and develop fluency in their use.
Lesson 21: Subtracting Fractions	Students should develop and analyze algorithms for computing with fractions and develop fluency in their use.
Lesson 22: Multiplying and Dividing	Students should develop and analyze algorithms for computing with fractions and develop fluency in their use.
Problem Solving: Work Backward	Students should build new mathematical knowledge through problem solving; solve problems that arise in mathematics and in other contexts; apply and adapt a variety of appropriate strategies to solve problems.
Lesson 23: Ratios and Proportions	Students should understand and use ratios and proportions to represent quantitative relationships; develop, analyze, and explain methods for solving problems involving proportions, such as finding equivalent ratios.
Lesson 24: Understanding Percent	Students should work flexibly with fractions, decimals, and percents to solve problems.
Lesson 25: Percent of a Number	Students should develop meaning for percents greater than 100 and less than 1; work flexibly with fractions, decimals, and percents to solve problems.

TESOL Standards

1.1 Social Interactions, **1.2** Personal expression, **1.3** Extend communicative competence, **2.1** Interact in a classroom, **2.2** Provide subject matter information, **2.3** Apply academic knowledge, **3.1** Use appropriate language, **3.2** Use nonverbal communication, **3.3** Extend sociolinguistic competence

1.1 Social interactions, **1.2** Personal expression, **1.3** Extend communicative competence, **2.1** Interact in a classroom, **2.2** Provide subject matter information, **2.3** Apply academic knowledge, **3.1** Use appropriate language, **3.2** Use nonverbal communication, **3.3** Extend sociolinguistic competence

1.1 Social interactions, **1.3** Extend communicative competence, **2.1** Interact in a classroom, **2.2** Provide subject matter information, **2.3** Apply academic knowledge, **3.1** Use appropriate language, **3.2** Use nonverbal communication, **3.3** Extend sociolinguistic competence

1.1 Social Interactions, **1.2** Personal expression, **1.3** Extend communicative competence, **2.1** Interact in a classroom, **2.2** Provide subject matter information, **2.3** Apply academic knowledge, **3.1** Use appropriate language, **3.2** Use nonverbal communication, **3.3** Extend sociolinguistic competence

1.1 Social Interactions, **1.2** Personal expression, **1.3** Extend communicative competence, **2.1** Interact in a classroom, **2.2** Provide subject matter information, **2.3** Apply academic knowledge, **3.1** Use appropriate language, **3.2** Use nonverbal communication, **3.3** Extend sociolinguistic competence

1.1 Social interactions, **1.2** Personal expression, **1.3** Extend communicative competence, **2.1** Interact in a classroom, **2.2** Provide subject matter information, **2.3** Apply academic knowledge, **3.1** Use appropriate language, **3.2** Use nonverbal communication, **3.3** Extend sociolinguistic competence

1.1 Social interactions, **1.2** Personal expression, **1.3** Extend communicative competence, **2.1** Interact in a classroom, **2.2** Provide subject matter information, **2.3** Apply academic knowledge, **3.1** Use appropriate language, **3.2** Use nonverbal communication, **3.3** Extend sociolinguistic competence

1.1 Social Interactions, **1.2** Personal expression, **1.3** Extend communicative competence, **2.1** Interact in a classroom, **2.2** Provide subject matter information, **2.3** Apply academic knowledge, **3.1** Use appropriate language, **3.2** Use nonverbal communication, **3.3** Extend sociolinguistic competence

1.1 Social Interactions, **1.2** Personal expression, **1.3** Extend communicative competence, **2.1** Interact in a classroom, **2.2** Provide subject matter information, **2.3** Apply academic knowledge, **3.2** Use nonverbal communication, **3.3** Extend sociolinguistic competence

1.1 Social Interactions, **1.2** Personal expression, **1.3** Extend communicative competence, **2.1** Interact in a classroom, **2.2** Provide subject matter information, **2.3** Apply academic knowledge, **3.1** Use appropriate language, **3.2** Use nonverbal communication, **3.3** Extend sociolinguistic competence

1.1 Social interactions, **1.3** Extend communicative competence, **2.1** Interact in a classroom, **2.2** Provide subject matter information, **2.3** Apply academic knowledge, **3.1** Use appropriate language, **3.2** Use nonverbal communication, **3.3** Extend sociolinguistic competence

1.1 Social interactions, **1.2** Personal expression, **1.3** Extend communicative competence, **2.1** Interact in a classroom, **2.2** Provide subject matter information, **2.3** Apply academic knowledge, **3.1** Use appropriate language, **3.2** Use nonverbal communication, **3.3** Extend sociolinguistic competence

1.1 Social interactions, **1.2** Personal expression, **1.3** Extend communicative competence, **2.1** Interact in a classroom, **2.2** Provide subject matter information, **2.3** Apply academic knowledge, **3.1** Use appropriate language, **3.2** Use nonverbal communication, **3.3** Extend sociolinguistic competence

1.1 Social interactions, **1.3** Extend communicative competence, **2.1** Interact in a classroom, **2.2** Provide subject matter information, **2.3** Apply academic knowledge, **3.1** Use appropriate language, **3.2** Use nonverbal communication, **3.3** Extend sociolinguistic competence

1.1 Social interactions, **1.2** Personal expression, **1.3** Extend communicative competence, **2.1** Interact in a classroom, **2.2** Provide subject matter information, **2.3** Apply academic knowledge, **3.1** Use appropriate language, **3.2** Use nonverbal communication, **3.3** Extend sociolinguistic competence

1.1 Social interactions, **1.3** Extend communicative competence, *See also* **2.1, 2.2, 2.3, 3.1, 3.2, 3.3.**

1.1 Social interactions, **1.2** Personal expression, **1.3** Extend communicative competence, **2.1** Interact in a classroom, **2.2** Provide subject matter information, **2.3** Apply academic knowledge, **3.1** Use appropriate language, **3.2** Use nonverbal communication, **3.3** Extend sociolinguistic competence

1.1 Social interactions, **1.3** Extend communicative competence, **2.1** Interact in a classroom, **2.2** Provide subject matter information, **2.3** Apply academic knowledge, **3.1** Use appropriate language, **3.2** Use nonverbal communication, **3.3** Extend sociolinguistic competence

1.1 Social interactions, **1.2** Personal expression, **1.3** Extend communicative competence, **2.1** Interact in a classroom, **2.2** Provide subject matter information, **2.3** Apply academic knowledge, **3.1** Use appropriate language, **3.2** Use nonverbal communication, **3.3** Extend sociolinguistic competence

1.1 Social interactions, **1.3** Extend communicative competence, **2.1** Interact in a classroom, **2.2** Provide subject matter information, **2.3** Apply academic knowledge, **3.1** Use appropriate language, **3.2** Use nonverbal communication, **3.3** Extend sociolinguistic competence

1.1 Social Interactions, **1.2** Personal expression, **1.3** Extend communicative competence, **2.1** Interact in a classroom, **2.2** Provide subject matter information, **2.3** Apply academic knowledge, **3.2** Use nonverbal communication, **3.3** Extend sociolinguistic competence

1.1 Social interactions, **1.2** Personal expression, **1.3** Extend communicative competence, **2.1** Interact in a classroom, **2.2** Provide subject matter information, **2.3** Apply academic knowledge, **3.1** Use appropriate language, **3.2** Use nonverbal communication, **3.3** Extend sociolinguistic competence

1.1 Social interactions, **1.3** Extend communicative competence, **2.1** Interact in a classroom, **2.2** Provide subject matter information, **2.3** Apply academic knowledge, **3.1** Use appropriate language, **3.2** Use nonverbal communication, **3.3** Extend sociolinguistic competence

1.1 Social Interactions, **1.2** Personal expression, **1.3** Extend communicative competence, *See also* **2.1, 2.2, 2.3, 3.1, 3.2, 3.3.**

1.1 Social interactions, **1.2** Personal expression, **1.3** Extend communicative competence, **2.1** Interact in a classroom, **2.2** Provide subject matter information, **2.3** Apply academic knowledge, **3.1** Use appropriate language, **3.2** Use nonverbal communication, **3.3** Extend sociolinguistic competence

1.1 Social interactions, **1.2** Personal expression, **1.3** Extend communicative competence, **2.1** Interact in a classroom, **2.2** Provide subject matter information, **2.3** Apply academic knowledge, **3.1** Use appropriate language, **3.2** Use nonverbal communication, **3.3** Extend sociolinguistic competence

1.1 Social Interactions, **1.2** Personal expression, **1.3** Extend communicative competence, **2.1** Interact in a classroom, **2.2** Provide subject matter information, **2.3** Apply academic knowledge, **3.2** Use nonverbal communication, **3.3** Extend sociolinguistic competence

1.1 Social interactions, **1.2** Personal expression, **1.3** Extend communicative competence, **2.1** Interact in a classroom, **2.2** Provide subject matter information, **2.3** Apply academic knowledge, **3.1** Use appropriate language, **3.2** Use nonverbal communication, **3.3** Extend sociolinguistic competence

1.1 Social interactions, **1.2** Personal expression, **1.3** Extend communicative competence, **2.1** Interact in a classroom, **2.2** Provide subject matter information, **2.3** Apply academic knowledge, **3.1** Use appropriate language, **3.2** Use nonverbal communication, **3.3** Extend sociolinguistic competence

1.1 Social interactions, **1.2** Personal expression, **1.3** Extend communicative competence, **2.1** Interact in a classroom, **2.2** Provide subject matter information, **2.3** Apply academic knowledge, **3.1** Use appropriate language, **3.2** Use nonverbal communication, **3.3** Extend sociolinguistic competence

Lesson	National Mathematics Standards
Lesson 26: Applications of Percent	Students should work flexibly with fractions, decimals, and percents to solve problems.
Problem Solving: Use Logical Reasoning	Students should build new mathematical knowledge through problem solving; solve problems that arise in mathematics and in other contexts; apply and adapt a variety of appropriate strategies to solve problems.
Lesson 27: Organizing Data	Students should formulate questions that can be addressed with data and collect, organize, and display relevant data to answer them; represent data using tables and graphs such as line plots.
Lesson 28: Analyzing Data	Students should find, use, and interpret measures of center and spread, including mean; discuss and understand the correspondence between data sets and their graphical representations, especially stem-and-leaf plots; represent data using tables and graphs such as line plots.
Lesson 29: Bar and Line Graphs	Students should represent data using tables and graphs.
Lesson 30: Double Bar Graphs	Students should represent data using tables and graphs.
Problem Solving: Make a Table	Students should build new mathematical knowledge through problem solving; solve problems that arise in mathematics and in other contexts; apply and adapt a variety of appropriate strategies to solve problems.
Lesson 31: Lines and Angles	Students should precisely describe, classify, and understand relationships among types of two-dimensional objects using their defining properties; understand, select, and use units of appropriate size and type to measure angles.
Lesson 32: Angles and Triangles	Students should identify, compare, and analyze attributes of two-dimensional shapes and develop vocabulary to describe the attributes.
Lesson 33: Polygons	Students should identify, compare, and analyze attributes of two- and three-dimensional shapes and develop vocabulary to describe the attributes; classify two-dimensional shapes according to their properties and develop definitions of classes of shapes such as triangles.
Lesson 34: Congruent Figures	Students should create and critique inductive and deductive arguments concerning geometric ideas and relationships, such as congruence.
Lesson 35: Similar Figures	Students should understand relationships among the angles and side lengths of similar objects; create and critique inductive and deductive arguments concerning geometric ideas and relationships, such as congruence and similarity.
Lesson 36: Transformations	Students should describe sizes, positions, and orientations of shapes under informal transformations such as flips, turns, and slides.
Problem Solving: Solve a Simpler Problem	Students should build new mathematical knowledge through problem solving; solve problems that arise in mathematics and in other contexts; apply and adapt a variety of appropriate strategies to solve problems.
Lesson 37: Perimeter and Area	Students should understand, select, and use units of appropriate size and type to measure perimeter and area.
Lesson 38: Circles	Students should develop and use formulas to determine the circumference of circles and the area of triangles, parallelograms, trapezoids, and circles and develop strategies to find the area of more complex shapes.
Lesson 39: Surface Area	Students should develop strategies to determine the surface area of selected prisms and cylinders.
Lesson 40: Volume	Students should develop strategies to determine the volume of selected prisms and cylinders.
Problem Solving: Draw a Diagram	Students should build new mathematical knowledge through problem solving; solve problems that arise in mathematics and in other contexts; apply and adapt a variety of appropriate strategies to solve problems.
Lesson 41: What Is Probability?	Students should understand and apply basic concepts of probability.
Lesson 42: Making Predictions	Students should use a basic understanding of probability to make and test conjectures about the results of experiments; develop and evaluate inferences and predictions that are based on data.
Lesson 43: Counting	Students should compute probabilities for simple compound events, using such methods as organized lists and tree diagrams.
Lesson 44: Arrangements	Students should compute probabilities for simple compound events, using such methods as organized lists and area models.
Problem Solving: Simulate a Problem	Students should build new mathematical knowledge through problem solving; solve problems that arise in mathematics and in other contexts; apply and adapt a variety of appropriate strategies to solve problems.
Lesson 45: What Are Integers?	Students should develop meaning for integers and represent and compare quantities with them.
Lesson 46: Adding and Subtracting Integers	Students should develop and analyze algorithms for computing with integers and develop fluency in their use.
Lesson 47: Multiplying and Dividing Integers	Students should develop and analyze algorithms for computing with integers and develop fluency in their use.
Lesson 48: The Coordinate Plane	Students should use symbolic algebra to represent situations and to solve problems, especially those that involve linear relationships; model and solve contextualized problems using various representations, such as graphs, tables, and equations.
Problem Solving: Write an Equation	Students should build new mathematical knowledge through problem solving; solve problems that arise in mathematics and in other contexts; apply and adapt a variety of appropriate strategies to solve problems.
Lesson 49: Solving Equations	Students should use symbolic algebra to represent situations and to solve problems, especially those that involve linear relationships.
Lesson 50: Inequalities	Students should represent and analyze mathematical situations using algebraic symbols.
Problem Solving: Make a Model	Students should build new mathematical knowledge through problem solving; solve problems that arise in mathematics and in other contexts; apply and adapt a variety of appropriate strategies to solve problems.

Lessons 1–50

Whole Numbers

STANDARDS CONTENT

Mathematics
- Read and write large whole numbers
- Compare and order numbers

Language
- Recognize multiple meanings of *order*
- Compare whole numbers using a number line

Introduce the Big Idea
- Read aloud the Big Idea. Ask students to give examples of whole numbers (*0, 1, 2, 3, . . .*).
- Point out that the distances in the picture are very large whole numbers.

Begin Building Background
- Invite students to share what they know about this country's space-exploration program. Ask someone to point to the Sun and to name each planet. Ask a volunteer to demonstrate how the planets travel around the Sun.
- Ask, *Which planet is closest to the Sun?* (Mercury) *Which planet is farthest from the Sun?* (Pluto)

Teach Key Concepts

Read the terms aloud. Ask, *What do you notice about the three forms?* (All show the same number.) Discuss how the terms vary. Then give extra examples.

Warm-Up Review

Write the following numbers on the board. Have students read each one aloud and have volunteers write the numbers on the board in standard form.

1. seventeen *(17)*
2. thirty-nine *(39)*
3. sixty *(60)*
4. three hundred forty-two *(342)*
5. eight hundred three *(803)*
6. one thousand, five hundred one *(1,501)*

Whole Numbers

Big Idea You can use whole numbers to compare many real-world things when you understand how the numbers are written.

Building Background

▲ I'd like to be an astronaut and fly to Mars.

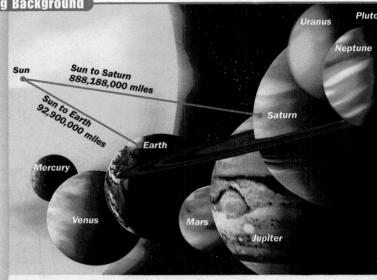

Sun

Sun to Saturn 888,188,000 miles

Sun to Earth 92,900,000 miles

Uranus   Pluto
Neptune
Saturn
Earth
Mercury
Venus   Mars
Jupiter

- **What do you see here?**
- **How many miles is it from the Sun to Earth?**
- **Look at the distances from the Sun to Earth and from the Sun to Saturn. Which distance is greater?**

Key Concepts

Standard form shows the number using digits 0 through 9. **Short-word form** shows the number using both digits and words. **Word form** shows the number using only words.

Standard Form		Short-word Form
85,310		85 thousand 310

Word Form
eighty-five thousand three hundred ten

16 UNIT 1 • NUMBER CONCEPTS

Activity: Post Those Numbers

Provide students with magazines and newspapers. Have them find examples of numbers in the three forms discussed. Have them work in pairs to make posters with their examples, identifying each with its form.

Resource Library

Math at Hand
Whole Numbers 003–006, 008–010

Math on Call
Whole Numbers 003–009

Reader's Handbook (red)
Reading Math 117–131

Reader's Handbook (yellow)
Reading Math 88–100

Understanding Whole Numbers

In 1958, the spacecraft *Pioneer I* traveled 72,765 miles. This number is shown in the place-value table below.

Digits in a **whole number** are grouped into periods. A **period** has three digits. Each digit has both a **place** and a **value.**

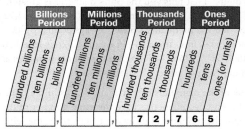

Billions Period			Millions Period			Thousands Period			Ones Period		
hundred billions	ten billions	billions	hundred millions	ten millions	millions	hundred thousands	ten thousands	thousands	hundreds	tens	ones (or units)
		,				7	2	,	7	6	5

The digit 2 in the number above is in the thousands place. So its value is 2 thousands, or 2,000. The 6 is in the tens place, so its value is 6 tens, or 60.

The numbers you see on these pages are written in **standard form.** The commas separate every three digits to make the number easy to read.

Standard Form   7 2 , 7 6 5

Word Form   seventy-two thousand   seven hundred sixty-five

Talk and Share

Tell your partner how the first and second 7s are different in 708,741. Then tell what the zero in 708,741 means.

VOCABULARY

digit—any one of these 10 symbols used to write numbers:
0, 1, 2, 3, 4, 5, 6, 7, 8, 9
whole number—a number in the set 0, 1, 2, 3, 4, . . .
period—a group of 3 digits in a number
place—the position of a digit in a number
value—the quantity represented by a digit based on its position
standard form—a number written with only digits and with commas between the periods

▲ *Pioneer I* was America's first spacecraft.

In 1992, Mae Jemison became the first African-American woman to go into space. ▼

Teach Understanding Whole Numbers

■ Ask, *Why do you think the solar system, a spaceship, and an astronaut are pictured in a math lesson?* (*Distances in space are large whole numbers.*)

■ Focus on the place-value table and the names of the places and periods. Say, *Try to find a pattern in the place names.* (*Each place is 10 times the place to its right.*) Read the number aloud as you point to and say each place. Provide other numbers as examples and ask students to name the place and value of each digit.

■ Explain that a comma is used to separate periods in a whole number.

■ Point out how the period names help to write a number in word form.

Talk and Share

Ask students to share their answers. They should understand that the zero in 708,241 shows that there are no ten thousands.

Build VOCABULARY

Be sure that students know the ten digits in our number system—0, 1, 2, 3, 4, 5, 6, 7, 8, and 9—and that these ten digits can be used to name any whole number.

Ask students to begin a vocabulary word card file of words that appear in the lesson Vocabulary. Also, students should begin a math journal to keep track of the concepts that they learn in each unit.

Differentiating Instruction

Beginning

Identifying Place Value Give four or five students each a number card from 0 through 9. Line the students up in front of the group. Have other group members identify the place and the value of each number.

Intermediate

Using Place-Value Tables Have partners take turns picking one of the numbers in the table on page 18. Have the other partner read the number aloud. Then have partners use place-value tables and work together to name the place and value of each digit for several numbers.

Advanced

Working with Large Numbers Have students work in small groups to find large numbers in their other textbooks. Have them practice reading several numbers aloud, giving the place and the value of each digit.

Teach Comparing Whole Numbers

- Display a paper circle and a ball. Invite someone to show or explain what a *diameter* is (*the distance across a circle or a sphere through its center*).

- Ask, *How are the planet names listed?* (*by distance from the Sun*)

- Explain that we compare two numbers by telling which is greater or less. With whole numbers, the number with more digits is greater.

- Write the inequality symbols on the board and ask students to tell what each one stands for.

- Discuss what to "order" numbers means. Lead students in ordering the four diameters.

Talk and Share

Ask pairs to explain how they ordered the diameters.

Answers: 1,423; 3,032; 4,194; 7,519; 7,926; 30,775; 32,193; 74,978; 88,736; 865,400; greatest, Jupiter; least, Pluto

Language Notes

Point out how the word *order* is used in the reading. Give students example sentences for meanings 2 and 3, for instance: *I order you to sit down. Let's order a pizza.*

Build VOCABULARY

Discuss with students the three symbols <, >, and =. Ask, *How are they alike?* (*Each is used to compare two numbers.*) Stress that each of the two inequality symbols, < and >, *points to the lesser number.*

The inequality symbols can be thought of as the end arrows of a number line.

less   greater

Comparing Whole Numbers

Planets and Sun	Diameter (in miles)
Sun	865,400
Mercury	3,032
Venus	7,519
Earth	7,926
Mars	4,194
Jupiter	88,736
Saturn	74,978
Uranus	32,193
Neptune	30,775
Pluto	1,423

This table gives the **diameter** in miles for each planet and the Sun. To compare the diameters of Earth and the Sun, decide which diameter is greater. The Sun's diameter has 6 digits, and Earth's diameter has 4 digits. That tells you the Sun's diameter is greater. You write "865,400 is greater than 7,926" as "865,400 > 7,926." Notice that the **inequality symbol** always points to the number that is less. You also can write "7,926 is less than 865,400" or "7,926 < 865,400." If two whole numbers are the same, you use an equals sign (=).

Look at the diameters of Earth and Venus in the table on the left. The two diameters have the same number of digits. Compare the numbers digit by digit, starting at the left.

7,926   The thousands digits are the same,
7,519   so compare the hundreds digits. The
          9 is greater than 5, so 7,926 > 7,519.

To order the diameters of Earth, Mars, Mercury, and Venus from least to greatest, compare digits, starting at the left.

	Order thousands.	Order hundreds.	Complete the numbers.
least	3,■■■	3,032	3,032
↓	4,■■■	4,194	4,194
	7,■■■	7,5■■	7,519
greatest	7,■■■	7,9■■	7,926

The diameters in order are 3,032; 4,194; 7,519; and 7,926.

Talk and Share

With your partner, order all 10 diameters from least to greatest. Talk about which planet has the greatest diameter. Which has the least?

VOCABULARY

diameter—the distance from one side of a circle to the other through the center
inequality symbol (> or <)   a symbol showing that two numbers are not equal
< a symbol showing that the first number is less than the second
> a symbol showing that the first number is greater than the second

Language Notes

Multiple Meanings
This word has more than one meaning.

■ order
1. arrange
2. tell someone what to do
3. buy something

Differentiating Instruction

Beginning
Comparing Heights Have two students stand up. Ask, *Who is taller?* Say, *(Name) is taller, so her height is greater.* Give two other students cards containing a < and a > symbol. Ask the person with the correct card to stand between the original two. Have the two students switch positions, and have the correct card inserted. Have students practice saying the comparisons. Then have the entire group arrange themselves in order by height.

Intermediate
Writing Comparisons Ask each student to choose two diameters from the table and write both a mathematical sentence and an English sentence comparing the two numbers. (*Check students' work.*)

Advanced
Comparing Planet Sizes Have pairs of students write several sentences about the sizes of the planets, for instance, which is largest, which is smallest, and which are about the same size.

Practice

For each of these numbers, tell the place and the value of each 5.

1. 35,002   **2.** 579,000   **3.** 66,315

4. 852,442,309   **5.** 44,500   **6.** 178,653

Read each number aloud and then write it in word form.

7. 902   **8.** 1,047   **9.** 83,120

10. 22,009   **11.** 800,440   **12.** 936,000,000

Write each number in standard form.

13. four hundred two thousand, eight hundred seventy-one

14. five hundred ninety-two million, six hundred thousand, thirty-four

15. six hundred fifty million, ninety-eight

Use $<$, $>$, or $=$ to compare the numbers in each pair.

16. 55,679,802 ▨ 55,678,802

17. 49,889 ▨ 49,898

Order the numbers from least to greatest.

18. 43,502   43,520   42,503   42,350

19. 99,850   110,359   98,905   101,962

Complete this table so that each number is written in standard form and in word form. The numbers are from the "cover story" on the right.

COVER STORY

On October 18, 1989, the spacecraft *Galileo* left Earth on its 6-year journey to Jupiter, about two billion, four hundred million miles away. Jupiter is our solar system's largest planet. If you could fill the planets, Jupiter would hold 1,316 times as much as Earth. When *Galileo* reached Jupiter, *Galileo* was traveling at a speed of 106,000 miles an hour. At that rate, you could travel to Earth's moon and back in 5 hours.

	Standard Form	Word Form
20.	18	?
21.	1989	?
22.	?	two billion, four hundred million
23.	1,316	?
24.	106,000	?

25. A very old planet has been discovered in a system with a different sun. The planet is about 13 billion years old. Write this number in standard form.

26. (EXTENDED RESPONSE) Is it easier to compare numbers in standard form or in word form? Explain your answer.

Practice

You may wish to have students read aloud the numbers in Exercises 1–6 to be sure they are reading them correctly. Discuss again the use of periods in writing numbers in word form, and writing 2-digit numbers with hyphens.

Assignment Guide

- Beginning 1–13 odd, 20–26 even
- Intermediate 2–14 even, 16–26
- Advanced 1–25 odd, 26

Notes on Exercises

Exercises 20–24 Have a volunteer read aloud the article about the spacecraft *Galileo*. Tell the class that Galileo was a mathematician and astronomer who discovered in 1610 that Jupiter has four moons.

Exercise 26 Share with students your standards for grading extended-response questions. For example you might use a 4-point rubric like this one:

4: Full credit—correct answer, complete explanation

3: Partial credit—correct answer, incomplete explanation

2: Partial credit—incorrect answer, correct explanation; or correct answer, incorrect explanation

1: Partial credit—incorrect answer, explanation partially correct

0: No credit—both answer and explanation incorrect or missing

Answers

1. thousands; 5,000

2. hundred thousands; 500,000

3. ones; 5

4. ten millions; 50,000,000

5. hundreds; 500   **6.** tens, 50

7. nine hundred two

8. one thousand, forty-seven

9. eighty-three thousand, one hundred twenty

10. twenty-two thousand, nine

11. eight hundred thousand, four hundred forty

12. nine hundred thirty-six million

13. 402,871   **14.** 592,600,034

15. 650,000,098   **16.** $>$ **17.** $<$

18. 42,350; 42,503; 43,502; 43,520

19. 98,905; 99,850; 101,962; 110,359

20. eighteen

21. one thousand, nine hundred eighty-nine

22. 2,400,000,000

23. one thousand, three hundred sixteen

24. one hundred six thousand

25. 13,000,000,000

26. Sample: Standard form; it's easier to compare digits than words.

Program Resources

Practice Book Use page 4.

Teach Comparing

- Demonstrate how to set up a number line. Point out the difference between the tick marks and the points that are marked, or *plotted*, on the number line.

- Label a number line 10–20 (Overhead Transparency 28). Emphasize that of two numbers on a number line, the one farther to the right is greater. Ask students to identify two numbers on the line. Ask, *Which is greater?*

Oral Language

You may wish to have students play a practice round to ensure that they understand the activity.

Partner Practice

Say, *The number of students who attend our school is the* population. *Try to estimate this number.* Explain that many towns and cities post population numbers on highway signs to tell how many people live there. Tell them that the sign shown on page 20 uses "POP" as an abbreviation for "population." Have a volunteer read the population sign. Ask, *Why are the listings funny?*

Develop Language

Activities

Comparing When you compare two numbers in math, you tell which is greater. Work with a partner. Copy the number line below. Each of you think of a number between 500,000 and 800,000. Mark your numbers on the number line. Whose number is greater? How do you know?

500,000	600,000	700,000	800,000
550,000	650,000	750,000	

1. **Draw** Create a number line from 45,000 to 70,000, marked off by 5,000s. Each of you think of a number between 45,000 and 70,000. Mark your numbers on the number line.

2. **Explain** Tell how you know whose number is greater.

Oral Language

Which Is Greatest? Work in a small group with a set of number cards, labeled 0 through 9. Each person draws a line for each place-value position of a 7-digit number, like this.

_____ , _____ _____ _____ , _____ _____ _____

Place the cards face down. One person draws a card and reads the digit aloud. Then each person writes that digit in one of the place-value positions. Continue drawing and placing new digits until you have placed 7 digits. Next, each person reads his or her number aloud, and the group compares numbers. The person with the greatest number is the winner. Play again, but this time the winner has the least number.

Partner Practice

People, People, Everywhere! Look up how many people live in your town or a favorite city. Use the key word **population** to help you. Discuss your findings with a partner. Write the population numbers in standard form as well as in word form. Draw a picture and write a few sentences about the area.

VOCABULARY
population—all the people and/or animals who live in an area

Program Resources

Practice Book Use page 5.
Overhead Transparencies Use 28.

Assessment Book

Use page 23 to assess students' comprehension.

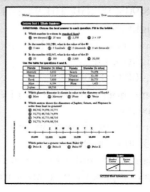

Activity: Culture Connection

The ancient Egyptians did not use a place-value numbering system such as ours. Instead, they used pictures, or *hieroglyphics*, to represent numbers. They added the values of the pictures. Sticks were 1s, upside-down Us were 10s, and coils were 100s. Show students the number 243:

Have students use the symbols to show 32 + 110 = 142 (∩∩∩|| + ⌒∩ = ⌒∩∩∩∩||).

Rounding

Big Idea You don't always need an exact number. Often an estimated number is more useful. You can find an estimated number by rounding.

Building Background

▲ We read about a volcano in the newspaper. It was amazing!

- What is happening in this picture?
- How much of the mountain do you think will be lost?
- How could you estimate the damage it might cause?

Key Concepts

An **exact number** is one that has been counted. An **estimate** is a number that stands for data that have been **rounded** or that cannot be counted accurately.

Exact Number
585 students

Estimate
600 students. The number 585 is **rounded** to the nearest hundred.

LESSON 2 • ROUNDING **21**

Activity: Find the Numbers

Have students work in small groups to find examples of exact and estimated numbers in their other textbooks. Have them make a list of exact and estimated numbers and explain how they decided in which list to put each number.

Resource Library

Math at Hand
Rounding Whole Numbers 095

Math on Call
Rounding Whole Numbers 010

Rounding

STANDARDS CONTENT

Mathematics
- Round to make an estimate
- Use a number line to round

Language
- Recognize multiple meanings of *estimate* and *round*
- Use a Web to interpret mathematical data

Materials
- Number line (Overhead Transparency 28)

Introduce the **Big Idea**

Read aloud the Big Idea. Have volunteers tell how many sisters and brothers they have. Explain that these numbers are *exact* numbers. Then give an approximation for the population of your school using the term *about*. Explain that this is an *estimated* number.

Begin **Building Background**

Tell students that flowing lava can reach temperatures of more than 2,000 °F, while the temperature of a hot day might be 100 °F. Then discuss the questions below the picture.

Teach **Key Concepts**

Explain the two diagrams. Ask, *Is 585 closer to 500 or 600? (600) How do you know?* Ask, *How would the second diagram change if the exact number had been 504? (There would be only 5 groups of 100.)*

Warm-Up Review

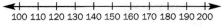
100 110 120 130 140 150 160 170 180 190 200

Draw the number line shown above (Overhead Transparency 28). Have volunteers mark each of the following numbers on the number line and tell whether the number is closer to 100 or 200.

1. 145 *(100)*   **2.** 112 *(100)*
3. 198 *(200)*   **4.** 139 *(100)*
5. 101 *(100)*   **6.** 175 *(200)*
7. 152 *(200)*   **8.** 180 *(200)*

Teach Rounding

- To help students prepare to read this lesson, explain that large numbers can be used to describe a volcano's eruptions.

- Ask a volunteer to read the definition of *eruptions* in Vocabulary at the bottom of the page. Have students tell what they know about damage from eruptions. Ask, *Why do you think people use estimates to describe the damage?*

- Discuss the meanings of rounding up and rounding down. Be sure students understand that all digits to the right of the rounding place should become zeros. Then have students round 2,851 to the nearest thousand (*3,000*).

Language Notes

Point out the red words in the reading. Explain that the first definition for *round* is the mathematical use, while the second definition represents the word in common English usage. Have volunteers name things that are round.

Talk and Share

Students should notice that the rounded numbers are the same. Have them check their partner's numbers by using the steps for rounding.

Rounding

The Tambora volcano in Sumbawa, Indonesia, had one of its worst **eruptions** in 1815. More than 50,000 people were killed. The height of the volcano dropped from 4,300 meters to 2,851 meters as a result of the eruption.

The number 50,000 is an **estimate** of a number, while 2,851 is an exact number. The most common method for finding an estimate is to **round**. The table below shows the steps to round the number 2,851 to the nearest hundred and to the nearest ten.

▲ This building was nearly buried by a volcanic eruption.

	Nearest 100	Nearest 10
Underline the rounding place. Circle the digit to its right.	2,851 / 2,851	2,851 / 2,851 The digit is 1. Do not change the rounding place. 2,85
■ If the circled digit is less than 5, do not change the digit in the rounding place. This is called "rounding down."		
■ If the circled digit is 5 or greater, add 1 to the digit in the rounding place. This is called "rounding up."	The digit is 5. Add 1 to the digit in the rounding place. 2,9	
Change the remaining digits to 0.	2,900	2,850

We can write 2,851 ≈ 2,900 or 2,851 ≈ 2,850. The symbol ≈ means "is about equal to."

Language Notes

Multiple Meanings These words have more than one meaning.

■ estimate
1. an approximate value
2. an educated guess

■ round
1. change a number to give an estimate
2. shaped like a ring or a circle

Talk and Share

Work with a partner. Round 586,992 to the nearest hundred and then to the nearest thousand. Say the numbers aloud. Tell what you notice. Name two different numbers that become 587,000 when rounded to the nearest thousand. Explain how you got your answer.

VOCABULARY
eruptions—sudden, violent outbursts. During the eruption of a volcano, hot, melted rock pours down the side of a mountain.
estimate—an approximate value
round—change a number to give an estimated value

Activity: Diameters in the Round

Have students copy the list of diameters on page 18. Then have them round each diameter to the nearest hundred and nearest thousand (*865,400, 865,000; 3,000, 3,000; 7,500, 8,000; 7,900, 8,000; 4,200, 4,000; 88,700, 89,000; 75,000, 75,000; 32,200, 32,000; 30,800, 31,000; 1,400, 1,000*).

Differentiating Instruction

Beginning
Talking About Pictures Ask student pairs to examine the photographs on pages 21 and 22. Then have them work together to generate a list of words that describe what they see.

Intermediate
Discussing the Terms Have students return to the paragraph about the Tambora volcano eruption. Ask them to skim for the terms *estimate* and *round*. Then have them take turns telling a partner what the terms mean.

Advanced
Using Multiple Meanings Have students refer to the definitions of *estimate* and *round* in Language Notes. Then have them write sentences that demonstrate both definitions of each word.

Rounding on a Number Line

Hurricane Andrew hit Florida in 1992. It caused a lot of damage. Repair costs were huge. News reports said that 742,580 families asked for **insurance money** to fix things that Hurricane Andrew destroyed.

You can use a number line to round 742,580 to the nearest thousand. Remember that the numbers on a number line become greater from left to right. To **plot** a number on a number line, you first locate the spot where the number belongs. Then you draw a point at that spot and write the number above it.

Notice that 742,500 is plotted halfway between 742,000 and 743,000. Because 742,580 is closer to 743,000 than to 742,000, it rounds to 743,000.

Talk and Share

With a partner, decide whether 742,200 is less than or greater than the halfway number, 742,500. How does knowing this help you to round 742,200 to the nearest thousand?

▲ This weather photograph shows the state of Florida outlined in pink. The green areas show where the winds are strongest.

Hurricane Andrew caused about $26 billion in damages.

VOCABULARY

insurance money—the money an insurance company pays to people affected by a disaster

plot—place a point on a number line

LESSON 2 • ROUNDING **23**

Teach Rounding on a Number Line

■ Have someone read aloud the photo captions. Invite students to tell about other areas that have hurricanes.

■ Ask, *Do you think 742,580 is a great number of families?* Have them compare this number with the population of their town or city.

■ Draw a number line labeled *2,000*, *2,500*, and *3,000* on the board. Plot 2,580 on the line and have students note that it rounds to 3,000. Then work through the example on the page. Have students suggest other numbers that would round up to 743,000 and numbers that would round down to 742,000.

Talk and Share

Students can tell from the number line that 742,200 is less than 742,500. This means that 742,200 is closer to 742,000 than to 743,000.

Build VOCABULARY

Discuss with students the types of insurance that are common (*medical, automobile, homeowners', life*). Ask, *What does insurance pay for?*

Differentiating Instruction

Beginning
Pronouncing Large Numbers Have students practice reading large numbers aloud. Model for the class: *Seven hundred forty-two thousand, five hundred eighty.* Ask partners to read the following aloud: *742,500, 742,000, 743,000.* Then ask them to write and say three large numbers of their own.

Intermediate
Making Key Concept Notes Have small groups of students reread the first three paragraphs on page 23.

Then have them make a set of key concept notes that explore the most important terms and ideas. For example:

Key Concept	Notes
Insurance money	What a company pays out after a disaster

Advanced
Explaining the Steps in Rounding
Have partners work together to list the series of steps to follow when using a number line to round numbers.

Activity: Round It Out

Have pairs of students list all the 3-digit numbers ending in 7 that round to 300 when rounded to the nearest hundred (*257, 267, 277, 287, 297, 307, 317, 327, 337, 347*). Then have them tell which of these numbers rounds to 320 when rounded to the nearest ten (*317*). Ask which other numbers round to 320 when rounded to the nearest ten (*315, 316, 318, 319, 320, 321, 322, 324*). Ask why they should not include 325 in this list. (*325 rounds to 330.*)

Practice

Before they begin Exercises 1–6, students should name the digit in the rounding place of each number. Then have them tell what number they will look at to help them decide how to round.

Assignment Guide
- Beginning 1–15 odd, 19, 20
- Intermediate 2–16 even, 17–20
- Advanced 2–16 even, 17–20

Notes on Exercises

Exercise 17 Be sure students see that there are many possible answers.

Exercise 18 Students must round 58 to the nearest ten. Then they must divide by 10.

Exercise 19 Juan should be able to go 396 miles on 18 gallons of gas. However, he would probably stop for gas because the gauge would be very close to "empty" before he arrived.

Exercise 20 Students will encounter multiple-choice questions on standardized tests. Frequently, one or more answers can be rejected because they are not reasonable. In this exercise, students may need to round all four numbers to determine the correct choice.

Look and Read

Practice

Round each number to the underlined place. Tell how you do it.
1. 56,292
2. 36,002
3. 449,992
4. 475,448
5. 803,565
6. 80,005,000

Copy the number line below. Read each number and plot it on the number line. Then round each number to the nearest hundred thousand.
7. 356,780
8. 101,998
9. 250,000
10. 148,675
11. 283,005
12. 302,561

Draw a number line. Label it and use it to round each number to the nearest hundred.
13. 375
14. 501
15. 59
16. 848

17. Give two numbers that would be 385,000 when rounded to the nearest thousand. One should be less than 385,000 and the other should be greater than 385,000.

18. Sue Lin has some $10 bills. She needs $58 to buy a jacket. How many $10 bills should Sue Lin take to the store? Explain.

19. Juan's car gets 22 miles to a gallon of gas. The gas tank holds 18 gallons of gas. Juan plans to take a 390-mile trip. If he starts with a full tank, will he have to stop for more gas along the way? Explain.

20. **MULTIPLE CHOICE**
Which number is 600 when rounded to the nearest ten?
A. 579
B. 609
C. 596
D. 615

Program Resources
Practice Book Use page 6.
Overhead Transparencies Use 28.

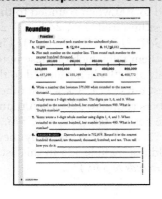

Answers
1. 57,000
2. 36,000
3. 400,000
4. 475,400
5. 804,000
6. 80,010,000
7–12. Check students' number-line points.
7. 400,000
8. 100,000
9. 300,000
10. 100,000
11. 300,000
12. 300,000

13–16.

59   375 501   848

0 100 200 300 400 500 600 700 800 900

13. 400
14. 500
15. 100
16. 800
17. Samples: 385,421; 384,862
18. 6 $10 bills; 58 rounds to 60, which is 6 × 10; if she takes only 5 $10 bills, she won't have enough money.
19. 18 × 22 = 396; Juan should plan to stop for gas before the end of the trip. 396 is very close to 390, and he should not risk running out of gas.
20. C

Activities

Interpreting When you interpret something, you say what it means. When you interpret **data,** you tell what the information means to you. You might interpret the data about Hurricane Andrew to mean that hurricane damage is very costly. You also might interpret the data to mean that hurricanes are very dangerous to people and property.

Work in a small group to find a very large number in a newspaper or magazine.

1. **Draw** Make a Web like the one shown here. Put your number in the center.

2. **Write** Describe in the outer ovals any data that relate to the number.

3. **Interpret** Work together to interpret the number. Share your findings with the class.

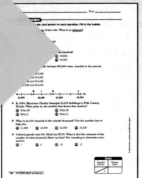

Web

- about $26 billion in damages
- families ask for insurance money
- in Florida
- in 1992
- **742,580 homes**
- hit by Hurricane Andrew

Oral Language

How Close Is It? Work in a small group with 3 sets of number cards, labeled 0 through 9. Take turns being the leader. The leader calls out a 3-digit number. Three group members form the number by standing in order with the correct number cards. Then the leader says, "Round to the nearest hundred." The student in the hundreds place raises her hand and looks at the card to her left. Then she decides whether to keep her number card or exchange it for the next higher one. Next, she explains her decision. All students with cards to her left then trade their cards for zero cards.

Partner Practice

Round and Tell Write a 6-digit number on a piece of paper and trade with a partner. Read aloud your partner's number. Then round it to the nearest hundred thousand. Tell the steps you used to do the rounding. Then have your partner round your number.

VOCABULARY
data—facts; information

Teach Interpreting

- Invite students to discuss the sample Web. Have students read the items aloud. Ask, *How does each item relate to the central item? (Each helps to explain or tells more about the item, in this case a number, in the center.)*

- After students find their large numbers, stress that they must read the article very carefully to create a Web. Have them work in pairs to interpret various terms in their articles.

- Have students take turns suggesting terms to place in the outer ovals. Be sure that every student has an opportunity to contribute an idea.

Oral Language

Have students vary the activity by rounding their numbers to the nearest ten. Students can extend the activity by using four number cards and rounding to the nearest thousand and to the nearest hundred.

Partner Practice

For extra practice, have students round their numbers to the nearest ten thousand, thousand, hundred, and ten.

Activity: Culture

Mount Saint
south of Sea
violently
and hu
damage.
than 1,000
created a hug
Helens had bee.
The volcano beca.
in the fall of 2004.
research other active
report their findings to

Assessment Book

Use page 24 to assess students' hension.

Program Resources

Practice Book Use page 7.
Overhead Transparencies Use 33.

Exponents

STANDARDS CONTENT

Mathematics
■ Use exponents to make an estimate
■ Simplify numbers with exponents

Language
■ Recognize multiple meanings of *factor, base, power, square,* and *cube*
■ Predict by looking at patterns

Materials
■ Large pieces of paper, such as tissue

Introduce the **Big Idea**

Read aloud the Big Idea. Write $4 \times 4 \times 4 \times 4 \times 4 \times 4$ on the board. Explain that this expression can be written in a short form using an *exponent* and write 4^6.

Begin **Building Background**

Ask a volunteer to describe a chessboard. If possible, display a chessboard or a checkerboard. Ask, *How can you find the number of squares?* (*Multiply 8 times 8.*) Say, *This number, too, can be written in a short form, 8^2.*

Teach **Key Concepts**

Explain that numbers are generally written in *standard form* using the digits 0 through 9. Explain that the *expanded,* or "spread-out," *form* uses multiplication to write a number. Stress the terms *base* and *exponent.* Explain that the word *exponential* comes from the word *exponent.*

Warm-Up Review

Have students find each product.
1. $2 \times 2 \times 2 \times 2$ (*16*)
2. $2 \times 2 \times 2 \times 2 \times 2$ (*32*)
3. $2 \times 2 \times 2 \times 2 \times 2 \times 2$ (*64*)
4. $3 \times 3 \times 3$ (*27*)
5. 8×8 (*64*)
6. $5 \times 5 \times 5$ (*125*)
7. $10 \times 10 \times 10$ (*1,000*)
8. $10 \times 10 \times 10 \times 10 \times 10$ (*100,000*)

Talk and Explore

Exponents

Big Idea You can use exponents to write some numbers in a convenient short form.

Building Background

▲ I've watched people play a game like this.

■ **What game are these people playing?**
■ **What games have you played that use a square game board?**
■ **Explain how to play your favorite game.**

Key Concepts

A number in **standard form** is written using the digits 0 through 9. A number in **expanded form** is a product of *factors.* A factor is any number multiplied by another number. A number in **exponential form** is written with an *exponent.*

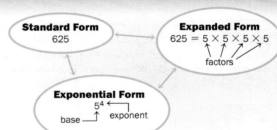

Standard Form
625

Expanded Form
$625 = 5 \times 5 \times 5 \times 5$
factors

Exponential Form
5^4
base — exponent

26 UNIT 1 • NUMBER CONCEPTS

 Activity: Use Those Exponents

Have partners work together to make a table with the following heads: *Expanded Form, Base, Exponent, Exponential Form,* and *Standard Form.* Give students the eight products in the Warm-Up Review to fill in the table. (*Check students' tables.*)

Resource Library

Math at Hand
Exponents 006–007, 065–066

Math on Call
Exponents 005–006, 071–072, 075–076, 080

Exponents

The number of small squares on a chessboard can be found by multiplying: 8 rows × 8 squares per row = 64. Any number multiplied by another number is called a **factor.** When the factors are the same, the number can be written in a short form using an exponent: 8 × 8 = 64 and 8^2 = 64. The **exponent** (^{2}) tells you how many times the base (8) is used as a factor. This activity will help you understand exponents.

Activity

Work with a partner. Cut a large piece of paper in half. Stack the two pieces of paper and cut them in half again. Repeat the process two more times. Each cut gives twice as many pieces of paper as the previous cut. How

Number of Cuts	Pieces of Paper	Number of 2s
1	2 = 2	1
2	4 = 2 × 2	2
3	8 = 2 × 2 × 2	3
4	?	?
5	?	?
6	?	?
7	?	?
8	?	?

many pieces of paper will you have after these 4 cuts? How many pieces of paper would you have if you could make 7 cuts? 8 cuts? Copy and complete the table shown above.

A short way to write 2 × 2 × 2 is 2^3. The **exponential form** of 2 × 2 × 2 is 2^3. Also, 2^3 can be read "2 to the third **power**" or "2 cubed."

$$2 \times 2 \times 2 \quad = \quad 2^3$$

Expanded form
3 factors of 2

Exponent or power;
the number of times the base is used as a factor

Base
the repeated factor

VOCABULARY

factor—a number that is multiplied
exponent—a number that tells how many times another number (the base) is used as a factor
base—a number raised to a power
exponential form—a number written with an exponent
power—an exponent

Language Notes

Multiple Meanings
These words have more than one meaning.

■ factor
1. a number that is multiplied
2. something that produces a result

■ base
1. a repeated factor
2. the part on which an object stands; the bottom

■ power
1. an exponent
2. strength or force

■ **square**
1. the second power of a number
2. a flat figure with 4 equal angles and 4 equal sides

■ **cube**
1. the third power of a number
2. a solid figure with 6 square sides

Talk and Share

With a partner, add a fourth column to your table. Write the exponential form of each number from the second column.

Teach Exponents

■ Relate the boldface terms in the first paragraph to the terms in the Key Concepts. Have students use the numbers to draw a graphic organizer like that on page 26.

■ Check to make sure that students understand the directions for the activity. Use tissue paper for this activity because seven or eight cuts are difficult on firmer paper.

Answers: 16 and four 2s, 32 and five 2s, 64 and six 2s, 128 and seven 2s, 256 and eight 2s

Language Notes

Have students point out the terms *factor, base,* and *power* in the reading. Discuss their math meanings. Have volunteers describe and give examples to illustrate these terms' English meanings. *Squared* and *cubed* are found on page 28.

Talk and Share

Have students title the fourth column *Using Exponents.* The entries should be: $2^1, 2^2, 2^3, 2^4, 2^5, 2^6, 2^7, 2^8$.

Build VOCABULARY

Discuss the vocabulary terms, and have students note that *power* is the same as *exponent.*

Differentiating Instruction

Beginning

Understanding Exponents Reread the Big Idea aloud. Then write $6 \times 6 \times 6 \times 6 = 6^4$. Say, *The exponent 4 is used to write 6 × 6 × 6 × 6 in a more convenient way.* Have students point to the *factors (the 6s)*, base (6), and *exponent (4).*

Intermediate

Identifying Terms Refer students to the table they completed in Talk and Share. Ask questions such as: *What is the base in the fourth row? What is the*

exponent in the sixth row? What is the standard form in the fifth row? What is the expanded form in the seventh row?

Advanced

Switching Forms Have partners write three numbers with repeated factors and three with an exponent. Have them exchange papers and write the exponential form and expanded form, respectively, for each number. Have them explain their reasoning.

Activity: Exponential Power

Have students copy these sentences and fill in the blanks with vocabulary terms from pages 26 and 27.

In the multiplication 4 × 4 × 4, each 4 is a <u>factor</u>. 4 × 4 × 4 is a number in <u>expanded</u> form. In the number 6^3, 6 is the <u>base</u> and 3 is the <u>exponent</u>, or <u>power</u>. In <u>standard</u> form, 6^3 is 216.

Teach Exponential Form

- Point out that an exponent is smaller and raised so that it does not look like a factor.

- Relate the vocabulary words *squared* and *cubed* to the corresponding words in the Language Notes on page 27. On the board, sketch a 4-by-4 square and a 4-by-4-by-4 cube. Label the diagrams *Area of square = 4 × 4 = 4²* and *Volume of cube = 4 × 4 × 4 = 4³*, respectively. Point to the labels and say, *This shows why we read* four to the second power *as* four squared *and* four to the third power *as* four cubed.

- Have students explore and share how their calculators evaluate powers. Not all calculators are programmed like the one shown on page 28.

Talk and Share

Have students note that on this page, they are doing the reverse of what they did on page 27. Have students check their standard forms by using their calculators and the exponent feature.

Answers: 7 × 7, 49; 3 × 3 × 3 × 3 × 3, 243; 5 × 5 × 5, 125; 8, 8

Look and Read

Exponential Form

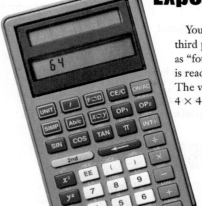

▲ Calculator

You read 4^1 as "4 to the first power." The second and third powers of a number have special names. 4^2 is read as "four to the second power" or "four **squared**," and 4^3 is read as "four to the third power" or "four **cubed**." The value of 4^2 is 4×4, or 16. The value of 4^3 is $4 \times 4 \times 4$, or 64.

To check the value of 4^3, you can use a calculator like this:

It is easy to confuse the base and the exponent. Notice that 2^3 and 3^2 are not the same number. Writing numbers in expanded form will help you see why.

$$2^3 = \underbrace{2 \times 2 \times 2}_{\text{3 factors of 2}} = 8 \qquad 3^2 = \underbrace{3 \times 3}_{\text{2 factors of 3}} = 9$$

Notice that a base is never multiplied by its exponent. $3^2 \neq 6$.

Talk and Share

With a partner, look at the table below. Find the standard form of each number by first writing the number in expanded form. Talk about how to do this.

Exponential Form	Expanded Form	Standard Form
4^3	$4 \times 4 \times 4$	64
7^2	?	?
3^5	?	?
5^3	?	?
8^1	?	?

VOCABULARY
squared—raised to the second power
cubed—raised to the third power

 Activity: Which Is Greater?

Have students use calculators to write the numbers in each pair below in standard form and then tell which is greater. Have them try to find a pattern to decide which is greater without computing.

2^7 and 7^2 *(128 and 49, $2^7 > 7^2$)*
3^4 and 4^3 *(81 and 64, $3^4 > 4^3$)*
2^5 and 5^2 *(32 and 25, $2^5 > 5^2$)*
6^3 and 9^3 *(216 and 729, $6^3 < 9^3$)*

The number with the greater base is less except when the exponents are the same.

Differentiating Instruction

Beginning
Reading Exponents On the board, write a variety of numbers raised to different powers. Be sure to include some with 2 or 3 as the exponent. Have students read aloud each number and then name the base and the exponent. For those with 2 or 3 as the exponent, ask students to read the number using *cubed* or *squared*.

Intermediate
Using Exponents Have partners each prepare a list of six numbers to different powers less than 10. Have them exchange lists, and write their partners' numbers in words. Have them identify the base and the exponent of each number.

Advanced
Explaining an Exponent Have students explain in writing why 3^4 is *not* 12. (*Sample: 3^4 is the product of four factors of 3: $3 \times 3 \times 3 \times 3$, or 81. 12 is the product of 3 and 4.*)

Practice

Write each product in exponential form.
1. $8 \times 8 \times 8 \times 8 \times 8$ 2. $15 \times 15 \times 15 \times 15$
3. $100 \times 100 \times 100$ 4. $32 \times 32 \times 32 \times 32 \times 32 \times 32$

Write each number in expanded form.
5. 16^2 6. 13^5 7. 7^7 8. 20^6

Find the value of each number.
9. 7^3 10. 6^3 11. 20^3 12. 2^5

13. What is the value of any number to the first power? Explain.

14. What is the value of 1 to any power? Explain.

Maria is saving her pennies. Each day she saves 3 times the number of pennies she saved the day before. On day 1, Maria saved 3 pennies. Copy and fill in the table to find how many pennies she will save on the seventh day.

	Day	Pennies, Expanded Form	Pennies, Exponential Form	Pennies, Standard Form
	1	3	3^1	3
15.	2	3×3	?	?
16.	3	?	?	?
17.	4	?	?	?
18.	5	?	?	?
19.	6	?	?	?
20.	7	?	?	?

21. Find the total amount of money Maria will have saved in the first 7 days.

22. (EXTENDED RESPONSE) To be clever, Terry told Jamal that he has 4^5 cents. Jamal said that he has 5^4 cents. Janine thinks the boys have the same amount of money. Is Janine correct? How do you know? Write the two numbers in expanded form and in standard form to explain your answer.

Practice

Tell students to imagine that they have to decide on a plan of payment for doing chores. One plan gives them $5 a week. The other gives them $2 the first week, 2 × $2 the second week, 2 × 2 × $2 the third week, and so on. With which plan would they have a greater *total* amount of money at the end of 2 weeks? (*the first plan, $10 and $6*) 3 weeks? (*the first plan, $15 and $14*) 4 weeks? (*the second plan, $20 and $30*) Ask which plan they prefer, and why. Have them relate the second plan to powers of 2.

Assignment Guide
■ Beginning 1–13 odd, 15–17, 21
■ Intermediate 2–14 even, 15–22
■ Advanced 2–14 even, 15–22

Notes on Exercises
Exercises 5–8 Remind students that 16^2 does *not* mean 16 × 2. You might have them read aloud each number and tell the base and the exponent. Have students use calculators to find the *standard form* of each number.

Exercises 9–12 You may wish to have students use calculators.

Exercises 13 and 14 Give students several examples to make sure they understand the concepts.

Answers
1. 8^5 2. 15^4
3. 100^3 4. 32^6
5. 16×16
6. $13 \times 13 \times 13 \times 13 \times 13$
7. $7 \times 7 \times 7 \times 7 \times 7 \times 7 \times 7$
8. $20 \times 20 \times 20 \times 20 \times 20 \times 20$
9. 343   10. 216
11. 8,000   12. 32
13. That number; the number is used as a factor only once.
14. 1; the repeated factors all are 1s, so the product is 1.

15. 3^2; 9
16. $3 \times 3 \times 3$; 3^3; 27
17. $3 \times 3 \times 3 \times 3$; 3^4; 81
18. $3 \times 3 \times 3 \times 3 \times 3$; 3^5; 243
19. $3 \times 3 \times 3 \times 3 \times 3 \times 3$; 3^6; 729
20. $3 \times 3 \times 3 \times 3 \times 3 \times 3 \times 3$; 3^7; 2,187
21. $32.79
22. Janine is incorrect.
$4^5 = 4 \times 4 \times 4 \times 4 \times 4$
= 1,024 cents or $10.24,
and $5^4 = 5 \times 5 \times 5 \times 5$
= 625 cents, or $6.25.

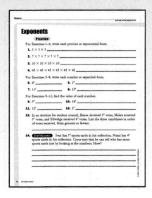

Teach Predicting

- Ask students to describe some situations in which predicting is used (*weather forecasting, predicting winners in sports contests,* and so on).

- The values in the 2nd through 5th rows in the table are 100; 1,000; 10,000; and 100,000. Ask, *How is the number of zeros in each standard form related to the power of 10?* (*The number of zeros in each entry is the same as the exponent of 10.*)

- Students should extend this pattern to predict the 8th and 9th powers (*100,000,000 and 1,000,000,000*).

- Say, *Use the pattern in the table to predict the value of 10 to the zero power (1).* If students realize that each power is 10 times the power before, they can divide 10 by 10 to get 1. Tell them that mathematicians have agreed that any number to the zero power is 1.

Partner Practice

Have group members discuss the meanings. Invite volunteers to use the words in sentences that reveal the meanings.

Oral Language

Students should realize that using the greater number as the exponent gives a greater value. This value could be used as a score.

Develop Language

Activities

Predicting When you predict, you say what you think will happen. To help you predict in math, you look for a pattern. Then you say what number will come next in the pattern. Copy the table. Work with a partner to find the 2nd, 3rd, 4th, and 5th powers of 10. Write them in your table.

1. **Describe** What pattern do you notice?

2. **Predict** Predict the values of the 8th and 9th powers of 10.

3. **Verify** Check your predictions by using your calculator.

Powers of 10	Standard Form
10^1	10
10^2	?
10^3	?
10^4	?
10^5	?
⋮	⋮
10^8	?
10^9	?

4. **Talk** With a partner, discuss the powers of 10. Tell how the number of zeros in standard form is related to the exponent.

Partner Practice

What's the Difference? Use a dictionary to find different meanings of *power* and *base*. Discuss the meanings with a partner. Draw pictures or diagrams to help you remember the meanings.

Oral Language

Lots of Language Work with a small group. Take turns tossing two number cubes that are different colors. Each time, use the number on one cube as a base and the number on the other cube as the exponent. Find the value of the base raised to the exponent.

Program Resources
Practice Book Use page 9.

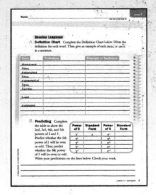

Assessment Book
Use page 25 to assess students' comprehension.

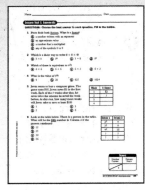

Activity: Real-world Connection
Remind students that each place in the base-ten number system is 10 times the place to its right. Say, *Computers can recognize only two levels of electrical charges, so they use the binary, or base two, system. With only the digits 0 and 1, it is constructed in the same manner as the base-ten system, using powers of 2.* Help students to write 3, 5, and 9 in the binary system ($11_{base\ two}$, $101_{base\ two}$, $1001_{base\ two}$).

Mental Math

Big Idea You don't always need paper and pencil to compute. You can do it in your head. This is called "mental math."

Building Background

▲ I've seen contests like this on TV.

■ What games or contests do you enjoy?
■ In what games do you use mental math?

Key Concepts

You can use **mental math** to solve problems in your head without using paper and pencil. **Compensation** is one mental math method. You choose numbers that you can compute easily. They need to be close to the numbers in the problem. Then you compensate, or make up for, the difference between your numbers and the problem's numbers.

12 × 59

Paper and Pencil

```
      1
     59
  ×  12
  ─────
    118
     59
  ─────
    708
```

Mental Math Using Compensation

60 is easier to work with than 59. I'll find 12 × 60. Then I'll subtract 12 × 1 to compensate for using 60.

12 × 60 = 720
12 × 1 = 12
720 − 12 = 708!

LESSON 4 • MENTAL MATH **31**

Mental Math

STANDARDS CONTENT

Mathematics
■ Use properties of operations to rewrite mathematical phrases
■ Use compatible numbers and the mental math strategy of compensation

Language
■ Recognize multiple meanings of *property* and *operation*
■ Explain to support a decision

Introduce the **Big Idea**

Read aloud the Big Idea. Write a variety of problems on the board, including some that can be solved using mental math. Ask students to identify and talk about which problems they can do "in their heads" and which problems require paper and pencil or a calculator.

Begin **Building Background**

Have students describe their experiences participating as contestants in or watching an academic bowl.

Teach **Key Concepts**

Discuss the ideas in Key Concepts. Stress that *compensate* means to "make up for." In compensation, when a number is changed to make computation easier, an amount must then be added or subtracted from the result to make up for the change.

Warm-Up Review

Have students find each answer.
1. 40 + 60 (*100*)
2. 85 − 35 (*50*)
3. 6 × 8 (*48*)
4. 6 × 80 (*480*)
5. 60 × 80 (*4,800*)
6. 35 ÷ 5 (*7*)
7. 350 ÷ 5 (*70*)
8. 350 ÷ 50 (*7*)

Activity: In Your Head!

On the board, write exercises similar to those in the Warm-Up Review. Have partners give each other at least five problems like these to solve using mental math. Encourage them to use all four operations. Have them explain their strategies.

Resource Library

Math at Hand
Mental Math 073–088
Properties 216–225

Math on Call
Mental Math 088–091, 093, 117–121, 143–148
Properties 212–221

Teach **Properties and Mental Math**

■ Discuss the properties one by one. Have students compute to verify the answers given. Reinforce with extra examples.

■ Ask, *Does the Commutative Property work for subtraction and division?* (*no*) Have students check these examples with their calculators: $23 - 8$ and $8 - 23$; $8 \div 4$ and $4 \div 8$ (*15, −15; 2, 0.5*).

■ Ask, *Does the Associative Property work for subtraction and division?* (*no*) Stress that operations within parentheses must be done first. These examples show that the property does not work for subtraction or division:

$(16 - 4) - 2 = 10$
$16 - (4 - 2) = 14$
$80 \div (20 \div 2) = 8$
$(80 \div 20) \div 2 = 2$

Talk and Share

Two ways to calculate $5 \times 8 \times 2$ mentally are $(5 \times 8) \times 2 = 40 \times 2 = 80$ and $(5 \times 2) \times 8 = 10 \times 8 = 80$.

Answers: Distributive, Associative, Commutative, Commutative

Language Notes

Point out the terms *operation* and *property* in the reading. Have volunteers describe their experiences with the terms.

Build VOCABULARY

Ask, *Does anyone in your family commute to work?* Relate this to "going both ways," which is similar to the Commutative Property. Tell students that their friends are *associates*; that is, they "go around together." This is similar to the Associative Property. Then tell them that you *distribute* books, or "give one to each." In the Distributive Property, a factor is multiplied times each addend in a sum.

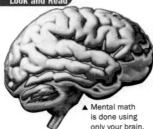

▲ Mental math is done using only your brain.

Properties and Mental Math

Properties are special qualities of something. The math operations of addition and multiplication have special qualities that help you solve problems mentally. Some of these properties are given in the table below.

Commutative Properties	**Associative Properties**	**Distributive Property**
You can add numbers in any order and get the same sum.	You can group numbers in different ways and get the same sum.	You can multiply a sum by a factor by finding two separate products and adding the products.
$8 + 5 = 13$ $5 + 8 = 13$	$4 + (6 + 17) = 27$ $(4 + 6) + 17 = 27$	$8 \times (10 + 2) = 96$ $(8 \times 10) + (8 \times 2) = 96$
You can multiply numbers in any order and get the same product.	You can group numbers in different ways and get the same product.	$(20 + 5) \times 3 = 75$ $(20 \times 3) + (5 \times 3) = 75$
$4 \times 9 = 36$ $9 \times 4 = 36$	$2 \times (5 \times 13) = 130$ $(2 \times 5) \times 13 = 130$	

Talk and Share

Tell or show your partner two different ways to compute $5 \times 8 \times 2$ mentally. Then tell which property is shown by each of the following sentences.

$7 \times (5 + 62) = (7 \times 5) + (7 \times 62)$
$(15 + 7) + 3 = 15 + (7 + 3)$
$58 \times 79 = 79 \times 58$
$34 + 66 = 66 + 34$

Language Notes

Multiple Meanings
These words have more than one meaning.

☐ property
1. a quality that makes something special
2. something that is owned, such as a house or land

☐ operation
1. something done to numbers to get an answer
2. the way a thing works

VOCABULARY

properties—the special qualities of something
operations—the things done to numbers according to certain rules. The four basic operations are addition, subtraction, multiplication, and division.
Commutative Properties—properties that say changing the order of addends or factors does not change a sum or product
Associative Properties—properties that say changing the grouping of addends or factors does not change a sum or product
Distributive Property—a property that says you can break apart numbers into smaller numbers for calculating

---

Differentiating Instruction

Beginning
Understanding the Properties On the board, write: $8 + 7$; $(2 + 9) + 6$; $5 \times (3 + 6)$; 6×4; $5 \times (2 \times 4)$; $7 + 8$; $2 + (9 + 6)$; $(5 \times 3) + (5 \times 6)$; 4×6; and $(5 \times 2) \times 4$. Have a volunteer find two expressions that have the same answer. Ask, *How do you know?* Then say, *That is an example of the Commutative (or Associative or Distributive) Property.* Repeat until all matching pairs have been identified.

Intermediate
Identifying the Properties After students read each part of the properties table on page 32, have pairs discuss the property illustrated and suggest other examples for each.

Advanced
Using Properties After students read through the properties table on page 32, have pairs take turns writing a phrase and having the partner supply a matching phrase and name the property used.

Mental Math Strategies

Kim works in the school bookstore. He needs to know how many pencils are in 5 boxes. Each box holds 24 packages, and each package holds 20 pencils. Kim needs to find the product $5 \times 24 \times 20$. He uses a mental math **strategy**. He knows that 5 and 20 are easy to multiply in his head. They are **compatible numbers**. The Commutative Property tells him that $5 \times 24 \times 20 = 5 \times 20 \times 24$. Mathematically his thinking looks like this:

$$5 \times 24 \times 20 = 5 \times 20 \times 24 = 100 \times 24 = 2,400$$

There are 2,400 pencils in the 5 boxes.

Lupe wants to buy three 29¢ notebooks. Kim uses the Distributive Property and mental math to find the total cost. He breaks apart 29.

$$3 \times 29 = 3 \times (30 - 1) = 3 \times 30 + (3 \times (-1)) = 90 - 3 = 87$$

The 3 notebooks together cost 87¢.

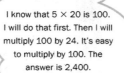

I know that 5×20 is 100. I will do that first. Then I will multiply 100 by 24. It's easy to multiply by 100. The answer is 2,400.

Kim uses **compensation** to find answers mentally. He had 58 math books in the store. Then Mr. Poe returned 93 math books. How many math books are there now? Kim thinks:

$$58 + 93 = (58 + 3) + (93 - 3) = 61 + 90 = 151$$

He keeps things balanced by adding 3 to one number and subtracting 3 from the other number. There are 151 books now.

Talk and Share

Work with a partner. Tell how to find each answer by using mental math.

$200 \times 36 \times 5$ $25 + 634 + 75$ $352 - 49$

VOCABULARY

strategy—a plan for how to do something
compatible numbers—pairs of numbers that can be computed easily
compensation—something that makes up for a difference. In mental math, you use compatible numbers close to those in a problem and *compensate* for, or make up for, the changes.

LESSON 4 • MENTAL MATH   **33**

Teach Mental Math Strategies

- You might want to draw a diagram of the pencil situation on the board.

- Say, *Tell me pairs of numbers that are easy to add or multiply using mental math.* Write students' suggestions on the board and discuss why the numbers are compatible.

- After discussing the Distributive Property, demonstrate breaking apart with addition. For instance, $58 + 79 = (50 + 8) + (70 + 9) = 120 + 17 = 137$. Review how to find sums of 10 when adding a column of numbers.

- Explain, *Usually in addition, the same number is added and then subtracted as in the book's example. In subtraction, the same number generally is added to each number, as in $58 - 39 = (58 + 1) - (39 + 1) = 59 - 40 = 19$. Give students extra examples using compensation.*

Talk and Share

Ask, *What properties could you use with the first exercise?* (*Commutative and Associative*) Have students explain how to do it. For $25 + 634 + 75$, ask students to identify compatible numbers (*25 and 75*). For $352 - 49$, ask, *What number can you add to 49 and 352 to solve using mental math?* (*1*)

See Additional Answers, page T39.

Differentiating Instruction

Beginning
Identifying Compatible Numbers
Have volunteers explain *compatible numbers*. Invite students to suggest compatible numbers they find easy to work with. Encourage them to consider all four operations (*Samples: addition: 4 and 6, 70 and 30; subtraction: 56 and 50, 79 and 9; multiplication: 20 and 5, 25 and 40; division: 40 and 4, 60 and 30*).

Intermediate/Advanced
Explaining How to Use Mental Math
Give pairs of students these problems, and have them take turns telling their partner how they can solve them using mental math.

$4 \times 31 \times 25$; $200 \times 16 \times 5$;
$398 + 56$; $572 + 299$;
8×39; 7×63;
$81 - 58$; $492 - 179$

(*See Additional Answers, page T39.*)

Activity: Quick as a Wink

Give small groups a set of thirty cards, each containing an arithmetic problem that can be solved using mental math. Students take turns drawing a card and giving the answer within five seconds. If the student answers correctly within the time limit, the card is kept. If not, the card is returned to the bottom of the deck. The student with the most cards at the end of the playing time is the winner of the game.

Practice

Have students review the properties by completing these sentences:

The Commutative Property has <u>two</u> numbers and uses the operation of <u>addition</u> or <u>multiplication</u>. The <u>Associative</u> Property has parentheses and <u>three</u> numbers but uses only addition or multiplication. The <u>Distributive</u> Property has parentheses and uses the operations of <u>addition</u> and <u>multiplication</u>.

Assignment Guide
- Beginning 1–8, 13–17, 19, 20
- Intermediate 1–20
- Advanced 1–22

Notes on Exercises
Exercises 9–16 Have students describe how they found each answer.

Exercises 19 and 20 Remind students to do the work in parentheses first. Discuss the properties with students to make sure they arrive at the correct conclusions. For Exercise 20, have them describe when the property works.

Exercises 21 and 22 If students have trouble with these exercises, review the teaching notes on page 32. Have students share their examples and conclusions with the class.

Practice

Find each missing number. Tell which property or properties are shown.
1. $(38 \times 12) \times 63 = 38 \times (\blacksquare \times 63)$
2. $82 + 58 = 58 + \blacksquare$
3. $(5 \times 12) + (\blacksquare \times 18) = 5 \times (12 + 18)$
4. $58 + (79 + 142) = (58 + \blacksquare) + 79$

Find each answer by using mental math. Tell which property or properties you used.
5. 67×4
6. $40 \times 13 \times 5$
7. $30 + 562 + 70$
8. $(40 \times 17) + (40 \times 3)$

Find each answer by using mental math.
9. $598 + 239$
10. $75 + 561 + 25$
11. 8×62
12. $5 \times 681 \times 20$
13. $743 - 298$
14. $(83 \times 8) + (83 \times 2)$
15. 50×46
16. $56 + 239$

17. Desi knows that there are 3 feet in a yard and 12 inches in a foot. Show two ways he can find the number of inches in 5 yards. Find the number of inches mentally.

18. Yuko bought 5 T-shirts at $8 each and 5 pairs of jeans at $22 each. Show two ways she can find the total cost. Then find the total cost. Which way is easier?

19. (EXTENDED RESPONSE) Does the Distributive Property work with multiplication and subtraction? Try it with $8 \times (10 - 7)$ and $9 \times (5 - 3)$. Show your work.

20. (EXTENDED RESPONSE) Does the Distributive Property work with division and addition? Try it with $(40 + 8) \div 4$ and $100 \div (20 + 5)$. Show your work.

21. (EXTENDED RESPONSE) Does the Commutative Property work with division? Give an example to support your answer.

22. (EXTENDED RESPONSE) Does the Associative Property work with subtraction and division? Give examples to support your answer.

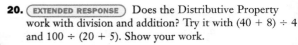
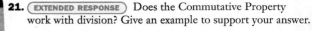

Program Resources
Practice Book Use page 10.

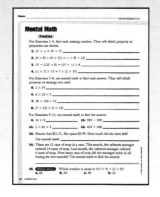

Answers
1. 12; Assoc., Mult.
2. 82; Comm., Add.
3. 5; Distr.
4. 142; Comm., Assoc., Add.
5. 268; Distr.
6. 2,600; Comm., Assoc., Mult.
7. 662; Comm., Assoc., Add.
8. 800; Distr.
9. 837
10. 661
11. 496
12. 68,100
13. 445
14. 830
15. 2,300
16. 295

17. *Sample:* $(3 \times 12) \times 5$ or $3 \times (12 \times 5)$; 180 in.
18. $(5 \times 8) + (5 \times 22)$ or $5 \times (8 + 22)$; $150; the second way
19. Yes; $8 \times (10 - 7) = (8 \times 3) = 24$, $(8 \times 10) - (8 \times 7) = 80 - 56 = 24$; $9 \times (5 - 3) = 9 \times 2 = 18$, $(9 \times 5) - (9 \times 3) = 45 - 27 = 18$
20. Sometimes; $(40 + 8) \div 4 = 48 \div 4 = 12$, $(40 \div 4) + (8 \div 4) = 10 + 2 = 12$; $100 \div (20 + 5) = 100 \div 25 = 4$, $(100 \div 20) + (100 \div 5) = 5 + 20 = 25$, $4 \neq 25$

See Additional Answers, page T39.

Activities

Explaining When you explain something, you make it clearer. You also give reasons to support what you think. In the problem below, make your decision and then give your reasons for it.

Alexander's mother showed him two expressions: $(3 \times 4) + 2$ and $3 \times (4 + 2)$. She said he could choose one amount to spend at the fair.

1. Decide Which amount should Alexander choose?

2. Explain Tell how you decided.

3. Justify Show the computation that helped you decide.

Partner Practice

Name That Property Talk with your partner about each property. Find a word to help you and your partner remember how each property works. For example, *regroup* is a good word for the Associative Property.

Associative Property
$7 + (3 + 8) = (7 + 3) + 8$ $4 \times (25 \times 7) = (4 \times 25) \times 7$

Commutative Property
$18 + 9 + 12 = 18 + 12 + 9$ $5 \times 188 \times 2 = 5 \times 2 \times 188$

Distributive Property
$5 \times 13 = 5 \times (10 + 3) = (5 \times 10) + (5 \times 3)$

Find the value of each quantity above. Compare your answers with your partner's.

Oral Language

Rap About It Talk with a partner about mental math strategies and about properties. Write a rap, a poem, or a rhyme about one of them to share with the class. To get you started, read these aloud.

Compensation
When I get something
I give something away.
That's how I compensate
Every day.

Commutative Property
When I take time to multiply
It does not matter whether I
Do 20 times 12 or 12 times 20
Because both ways, I get plenty.

Develop Language

Teach Explaining

Remind students that they often are asked to explain their work. Sometimes the explanation involves simply showing computations and giving reasons, and sometimes it involves describing steps in a process.

Answers:

1. $3 \times (4 + 2)$

2. $3 \times (4 + 2) = 18$; $(3 \times 4) + 2 = 14$; $18 > 14$

Partner Practice

If students have difficulty finding descriptive words for the properties, have them refer to the table on page 32.

Answers: 18; 700; 39; 1,880; 65

Oral Language

Invite students to read their examples aloud and explain what they mean.

Key Connection

Write 0 and 1 on the board. Have volunteers write examples using 0 or 1 with each addition and multiplication. Ask, *What special properties do these numbers have?* (*Any number plus 0 is that number. Any number times 0 is 0. Any number times 1 is that number.*) Introduce the Identity Property: *Adding 0 or multiplying by 1 leaves any number unchanged.*

Activity: Extend the Lesson

Write the following on the board:

$6 \times 1 = 6$

$6 \times 10 = 60$

$6 \times 100 = 600$

$6 \times 1,000 = 6,000$

Ask, *What pattern do you notice?* (*The number of zeros in the product is the same as the number of zeros in the second factor.*) Have partners write problems like these for each other to solve.

Assessment Book

Use page 26 to assess students' comprehension.

Program Resources

Practice Book Use page 11.

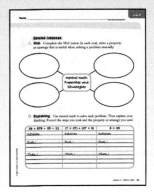

Use a Problem-Solving Guide

STANDARDS CONTENT
Mathematics
- Solve problems using a Problem-Solving Guide

Language
- Form plural nouns

Teach Use a Problem-Solving Guide

- Begin a class discussion by having volunteers describe special summertime activities or trips they have taken.

- Work through the four steps of the guide. Tell students that this guide will be used in every problem-solving lesson in the text to help them organize information, solve problems, and check answers.

- Stress that the Look Back step is very important. Students should always check to see if their solution answers the question and is reasonable. They can sometimes solve the problem in another way to check.

Talk and Share

After partners have had time to discuss the four steps, give volunteers the opportunity to describe the steps in their own words.

Problem-Solving Skills

Use a Problem-Solving Guide

Problem solving is easier if you have a plan for getting started. Always read the problem carefully. Think of a strategy or method you can use. You might have to try more than one.

You can use the Problem-Solving Guide presented here. It has four steps.

Problem: Several families traveled during their summer vacations. The Patels drove 3,078 miles. The O'Neils drove 7,590 miles. The Coxes drove 2,722 miles. The Lees drove 889 miles more than the Patels and Coxes drove altogether. How many miles did the Lees drive?

1. Read and Understand

What are you asked to find? The number of miles the Lees drove

What facts do you know? The distances that the Patels, O'Neils, and Coxes drove

What key idea relates the question and the facts? The Lees drove more miles than the Patels and Coxes drove together.

2. Plan and Solve
What strategy or operation could you use to solve the problem? Add to find the distance the Patels and Coxes drove together: $3,078 + 2,722 = 5,800$. Then add to that sum the extra distance that the Lees drove: $5,800 + 889 = 6,689$.

3. Answer
Write your answer clearly, using labels as needed. Your answer should be a complete sentence. The Lees drove 6,689 miles.

4. Look Back
Does your answer make sense? Does it answer the question asked in the original problem? You can round the distances to the nearest thousand and add. The estimated sum is close to the distance the Lees drove. The answer agrees with the question in the original problem.

Talk and Share
Talk with a partner. Describe the four steps of the problem-solving guide.

Activity: Solve It

Have partners write two simple problems for each other to solve. One should include extra information and the other should not have enough information. The partner should identify the extra information and tell what information is still needed to solve the problem. Have students relate their problems to the steps in the Problem-Solving Guide and solve the problems, supplying information for the problem that does not have enough.

Differentiating Instruction

Beginning
Drawing Diagrams Draw these two diagrams on the board. Ask students how they would find the missing information.

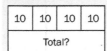

10	10	10	10
Total?			

(Add or multiply)

18	Amount Left?
32	

(Subtract)

Intermediate
Solving a Problem Say aloud several simple problems involving one operation. After each, ask students what operation would solve the problem. Ask what words helped them decide.

Advanced
Exploring the Solution Have partners write and exchange problems that involve more than one operation. The partner should solve the problem, explaining each step in writing.

Practice

Follow the *problem-solving guide* to help you solve each problem. Show your work.

	22 years	
Amy's age	Amy's age	4 years

Bret's age

1. Bret Lee is 4 years older than his sister Amy. The sum of their ages is 22 years. How old are Amy and Bret? The diagram at the right shows how the facts are related. The first row equals the sum of the items in the second row. Use the diagram to help you solve the problem.

a. What are you asked to find?   **b.** What facts are given?

c. Give the answer in a complete sentence. Explain how your answer makes sense.

2. The Patels planned to drive 600 miles on the last day of their trip. By noon they had driven 247 miles. How many more miles did they need to drive?

3. On a social studies test, true-false questions are worth 4 points. Multiple-choice questions are worth 3 points. Marta had 12 true-false questions correct and 15 multiple-choice questions correct. What was her total score?

4. Erin bought a can of tennis balls for $2.98, a sun hat for $12.25, and a shirt for $18.50. Her change was $6.27. How much money had Erin given the cashier?

Grammar Spotlight

Singular and Plural Nouns   A noun is plural if it refers to more than one thing. Usually, you add *s* to a noun to make it plural, but sometimes you add *es*.

If the noun ends in *sh*, *ch*, *x*, *s*, or *z*, you need to add *es* to make it plural. If you are not sure how to spell the plural form of a word, look it up in the dictionary.

Singular Noun	Plural Noun
mile	miles
dish	dishes
box	boxes
party	parties
monkey	monkeys
miss	misses

Work with a small group.

1. Look for plural forms of words in the practice problems and in your answers.

2. Work with a partner to form the plural of the last name of each student in your class.

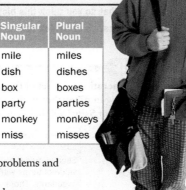

USE A PROBLEM-SOLVING GUIDE   **37**

Practice

Frequently, information in a problem can be pictured in a diagram. For instance, the problem on page 36 could be pictured like this:

3,078 mi	2,722 mi	889 mi
Total Distance		

Assignment Guide
- Beginning 1–4
- Intermediate 1–4
- Advanced 1–4

Notes on Exercises
Exercise 1 Help students to see that if 4 is subtracted from 22, the difference is two times Amy's age. They might use a guess-and-check strategy to look back.

Exercise 2 Suggest this diagram:

247 mi	Need to Drive
600 mi	

Grammar Spotlight

Point to objects in the room. Ask students to spell the name of each object and then to form the plural. Students might need to use their dictionaries to find words that fit each category in the exercises.

Answers
1. a. Amy's and Bret's ages
b. The sum of the ages is 22 years; Bret is 4 years older than Amy.
c. Amy's age: 9 years; Bret's age: 13 years
2. The Patels need to drive 353 more miles.
3. Marta's total score was 93 points.
4. $40.00

Activity: Identify the Cue Words
Discuss cue words in problem questions and how they often indicate which operation to use. The following may indicate addition or multiplication: *How many (much) <u>in all</u>? How many (much) <u>altogether</u>? What is the <u>total</u>?* Subtraction may be indicated by these: *How many (much) <u>more than</u>? What is the <u>difference</u> between?* Division may be indicated by: *How many (much) <u>in each equal part</u>?* Have students share ideas for other cue words or phrases.

Program Resources
Practice Book Use pages 12 and 13.

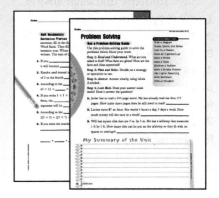

Order of Operations

STANDARDS CONTENT

Mathematics
- Apply the order of operations to solve problems
- Translate words into mathematical expressions

Language
- Recognize signal words for time order
- Choose an appropriate operation

Introduce the **Big Idea**

Read aloud the Big Idea. Explain that word usage in math may be different from everyday English usage. However, the terms and symbols in math are accepted and understood all over the world.

Begin **Building Background**

Ask volunteers to describe situations in which they or someone in their family had to put something together. Ask, *Did the person follow the directions or was he or she able to complete the project without directions?*

Teach **Key Concepts**

Review with students the meanings of *operation* and *order* that they learned in Unit 1. Say, *In this lesson, you will learn in what order to compute when a problem involves more than one operation.* Point out the parentheses in the examples. Students should enjoy the mnemonic and may wish to make up their own.

Warm-Up Review

Have students find each answer.
1. 5^2 *(25)*
2. 3^3 *(27)*
3. $5 \times (3 + 4)$ *(35)*
4. $18 - (5 + 6)$ *(7)*
5. $13 \times (20 \times 5)$ *(1,300)*
6. $145 + (75 + 25)$ *(245)*
7. $23 \times (8 + 2)$ *(230)*
8. $31 + (2 \times 3)$ *(37)*

Talk and Explore

Order of Operations

Big Idea Mathematics is a language that means the same thing all over the world. This lesson explains some of the rules for understanding the language of math.

Building Background

▲ I never have seen a bicycle that looks like this!

- What's wrong with this bicycle?
- What do you think this bicycle has to do with math?
- What do you think about the way this bicycle was put together?

Key Concepts

The **order of operations** is a set of rules that tell you how to simplify a numerical expression. Anything in **parentheses** always is done first. A phrase such as, "**P**lease **E**xcuse **M**y **D**ear **A**unt **S**ally" will help you remember what to do first, next, and so on.

(Please) parentheses	(Excuse) exponents	(My Dear) multiplication or division	(Aunt Sally) addition or subtraction
$112 - 4 \times (\mathbf{15 + 8})$ $112 - 4 \times \mathbf{23}$ First, calculate inside the parentheses.	$112 - 4 \times 23$ Second, find the value of terms with exponents. There are none, so go on.	$112 - \mathbf{4 \times 23}$ $112 - \mathbf{92}$ Third, multiply.	$112 - 92$ 20 Last, subtract.

38 UNIT 2 • INTRODUCTION TO ALGEBRA

 Activity: What to Do! What to Do!

Ask partners to write several problems similar to the one in Key Concepts. Have them exchange problems and explain to each other what must be done first in each problem. Encourage students to refer to the rules for order of operations in their explanations.

Resource Library

Math at Hand
Order of Operations 212–214
Expressions 235–239

Math on Call
Order of Operations 207–210
Expressions 203–206

Reader's Handbook (red)
Reading Math 117–131

Order of Operations

A mathematical **expression** has numbers and one or more operations. The expression $32 + 11 \times 5$ has two operations, addition and multiplication. Which should you do first?

Activity

With a partner, simplify $6^2 + 24 - 7 \times 3$. What did you do *first? second? next? last?* Did your classmates and you get the same answers? Why or why not?

To make sure we all get the same value for an expression, mathematicians have agreed on rules for the **order of operations**.

Rules for Order of Operations

1. Work inside **p**arentheses before doing anything else.
2. Simplify any terms with **e**xponents.
3. **M**ultiply and **d**ivide from left to right.
4. **A**dd and **s**ubtract from left to right.

Use the rules to simplify this expression: $6^2 + 24 - 7 \times 3$.

$6^2 + 24 - 7 \times 3$ There are no parentheses, so do exponents first. $6^2 = 6 \times 6 = 36$

$36 + 24 - 7 \times 3$ Next, multiply. $7 \times 3 = 21$ There is no division.

$36 + 24 - 21$ Last, add and subtract in order from left to right.

$60 - 21$

39

Talk and Share

Tell your partner how to simplify $40 - 7 \times 5 + 2^3$. You should get 13. Now use your calculator. It should follow the rules if it is a *scientific* calculator.

VOCABULARY

expression—a mathematical phrase with numbers and operation symbols
order of operations—a set of rules for simplifying numerical expressions
parentheses—two curved lines used to enclose a quantity. In $2 \times (3 + 1)$, the parentheses enclose $3 + 1$.

Language Notes

Signal Words:
Time Order
These words are clues to the order in which things happened.

☐ first
☐ second
☐ next
☐ last

▲ *Please Excuse My Dear Aunt Sally* is called a *mnemonic device.* It uses easy words that begin with the same letters as something you need to remember. Can you make up another mnemonic device?

Teach Order of Operations

■ Ask students to explain how they arrived at their Activity answers.

■ Point out that each student had a logical way to simplify the expression, but everyone must use the same rules to get the same answer. Have volunteers read aloud the four steps in the table. Call attention to the underlined words and bold initial letters, and relate them to the mnemonic on page 38.

■ Finally, work through the example on the board, using this format:

$6^2 + 24 - 7 \times 3$
$36 + 24 - 7 \times 3$
$36 + 24 - 21$
$60 - 21$
39

Language Notes

Have someone read aloud the signal words and point to them in the text. On the board, write three steps for brushing teeth, in the wrong order:

• Squeeze toothpaste onto brush.
• Remove cap from tube of toothpaste.
• Wet toothbrush.

Ask students to tell which step should come *first*, *next*, and *last*.

Talk and Share

Explain that some calculators do not follow the order of operations. You may need to help students adjust their key sequences to get the correct answer.

Build VOCABULARY

To help students understand the concept of *expression*, write on the board, *Mary did well on her math test.* Underline "on her math test." Explain that this is a *phrase*, or part of the sentence. Tell students that an *expression* is a mathematical phrase, or part of a mathematical sentence.

Differentiating Instruction

Beginning
Simplifying Expressions Write $8 \times 5 - (12 \div 3) + 2^2$ on the board. Have students copy the expression and underline what part they should evaluate first and tell why. Have them compute that part. Have them repeat this process until they get the final answer, *40*.

Intermediate
Explaining Order Write $8 \times 5 - (12 \div 3) + 2^2$ on the board. Have partners take turns telling each other what steps to follow to simplify the expression and why. Then have them simplify the expression *(40)*.

Advanced
Writing the Reasons Write $8 \times 5 - (12 \div 3) + 2^2$ on the board. Have partners copy the expression and evaluate it in the same way as the example on page 39. Have them write reasons for each step, using the words *first, second, last,* and the rules for the order of operations.

Teach Expressions with Variables

- Have a volunteer read the first paragraph. Write examples of arithmetic and algebraic expressions on the board, and have students identify each type.

- Discuss the terms in the table. Stress the words *sum*, *difference*, *product*, and *quotient* as the answers to problems involving addition, subtraction, multiplication, and division, respectively. Point out the different ways to express each operation in words. Also point out the different ways to express multiplication and division using symbols. Explain that the phrase *the difference of 13 and* q means "13 − q," not "q − 13" and that the phrase *the quotient of 24 and* x means "24 divided by x," not "x divided by 24."

- Work with the class to make a poster listing various terms that relate to each operation.

Talk and Share

For further practice, have partners tell each other various expressions involving one operation and a variable. Have partners write the expressions.

Build VOCABULARY

Stress the connection between *variable* and *vary.* Let students suggest things that vary, such as the time the sun rises, the temperature, and the price of gasoline. Have them evaluate a simple expression for several values of the variable.

Point out that the word *algebraic* is derived from the word *algebra.* Ask, *Do you know anyone who is studying algebra in high school? What do you think is studied in algebra class?*

Expressions with Variables

In the activity on page 39, you simplified an **arithmetic expression.** An arithmetic expression is a **phrase** that has numbers and operation symbols. An **algebraic expression** is a phrase containing numbers, operation symbols, and *variables.* A **variable** is something that can change. It usually is shown by a letter that stands for one or more numbers.

Operation	Algebraic Expressions	Can Be Read
Addition	$25 + a$	the **sum** of 25 and a
	$a + 19$	a plus 19
	$4 + a$	4 increased by a
	$16 + a$	16 more than a
Subtraction	$13 - q$	the **difference** of 13 and q
	$q - 22$	q minus 22
	$q - 8$	8 less than q
	$40 - q$	40 decreased by q
Multiplication	$5 \times n$	the **product** of 5 and n
	$10(n)$	10 times n
	$18n$	18 times n
	$16 \cdot n$	16 multiplied by n
Division	$24 \div x$	the **quotient** of 24 and x
	$\frac{x}{20}$	x divided by 20

The table suggests that any expression may be described in several different ways. For example, $25 + a$ could be read as "25 plus a," "25 increased by a," or "25 more than a."

Talk and Share

Work with a partner. Take turns reading each expression two different ways: $25 \div a$, $15 - m$, $60n$, $c + 36$. Describe a situation suggested by $c + 36$.

VOCABULARY

arithmetic expression—an expression with numbers and operations
phrase—a group of words and symbols with meaning. It has a subject but no verb.
algebraic expression—a phrase containing variables as well as numbers and operations

variable—a quantity that can have different values
sum—the result of adding
difference—the result of subtracting
product—the result of multiplying
quotient—the result of dividing

Differentiating Instruction

Beginning
Matching Words and Symbols On the board, write the words *plus, minus, times, divided by, sum, difference, product,* and *quotient.* Have students tell what operation is indicated by each word. Have volunteers write after each word its corresponding mathematical symbol and then use the word in a sentence.

Intermediate
Creating a Web Have students make a Web with *operations* in the center and *addition, subtraction, multiplication,* and *division* in four surrounding circles. Then have them add words, symbols, and examples to further explain each operation.

Advanced
Describing Operations Have students describe in writing what it means to *add,* to *subtract,* to *multiply,* and to *divide.*

Practice

Use the rules for the order of operations to simplify each expression.

1. $80 \div 10 \times 4 - 1$ **2.** $80 \div (10 \times 4) - 1$

3. $(16 - 7) \times (5 + 6)$ **4.** $(8 - 3)2 + 24 \div 3$

5. $8^2 \div 4 - 2 \times 8$ **6.** $(12 - 3^2) \times 4 + 2$

7. $28 \div (4 + 3) \times 9$ **8.** $(6 \cdot 7 + 8) \div 2$

Tell or write two different word phrases for each algebraic expression.

9. $s - 20$ **10.** $30x$

11. $\frac{16}{n}$ **12.** $49 + d$

Many people eat with chopsticks. ▼

Write an algebraic expression for each word phrase.

13. 32 more than a

14. 40 less than x

15. y divided by 9

16. the product of 25 and c

17. the quotient of 18 and n

18. 8 Asian dinners increased by m Asian dinners

Use each of the numbers 3, 4, 5, and 6 once to make the sentence true.

19. ■ + ■ × (■ − ■) = 17

20. ■ × (■ − ■) + ■ = 19

Use parentheses to make each sentence true.

21. $8 + 5 \times 6 - 3 = 39$

22. $7 - 2 \times 8 \div 4 = 10$

Read aloud each expression. Describe a situation suggested by each. For example, "$d + 3$" is "d plus 3" and could be "the number of dogs increased by 3."

23. $c \div 100$ **24.** $3y$ **25.** $m + 100$ **26.** $37 - n$

27. (MULTIPLE CHOICE) Simplify $24 \div (2 \times 6) + 6$.
    A. 144   **B.** 78   **C.** 8   **D.** 1

28. (MULTIPLE CHOICE) Simplify $3 \times 4^2 \div (12 - 4)$.
    A. 0   **B.** 6   **C.** 8   **D.** 18

LESSON 5 • ORDER OF OPERATIONS   **41**

Practice

Write $3 \times (7^2 + 27 \div 9)$ on the board. Have students tell which operation to do first, second, and so on, to simplify the expression. Then have them simplify the expression (*156*).

Assignment Guide
■ Beginning 1–23 odd
■ Intermediate 1–27 odd
■ Advanced 2–28 even

Notes on Exercises
Exercises 1–8 You may want to have volunteers read each expression aloud and to explain the order in which to evaluate the expression before students begin the exercises.

Exercises 9–12 Be sure that students use the correct vocabulary with these phrases.

Exercises 19–22 Students will probably need to use a guess-and-check strategy for these exercises. You may wish to let them work in groups or pairs.

Answers
1. 31   **2.** 1   **3.** 99

4. 18   **5.** 0   **6.** 14

7. 36   **8.** 25

9–12. Samples are given.

9. s minus 20; s decreased by 20

10. 30 times x; x multiplied by 30

11. 16 divided by n; the quotient of 16 and n

12. the sum of 49 and d; d more than 49

13. $a + 32$ **14.** $x - 40$

15. $\frac{y}{9}$ **16.** $25c$

17. $\frac{18}{n}$ **18.** $8 + m$

19. $5 + 4 \times (6 - 3) = 17$

20. $5 \times (6 - 3) + 4 = 19$

21. $(8 + 5) \times (6 - 3) = 39$

22. $(7 - 2) \times 8 \div 4 = 10$

23–26. Samples are given.

23. the number of dollars in c cents

24. the number of feet in y yards

25. m mugs increased by 100

26. n nails less than 37

27. C   **28.** B

Program Resources
Practice Book Use page 14.

Teach Choosing an Operation

Point out the key words in italic type in each problem. You might suggest that students draw a diagram to help them visualize each situation.

Answers:

a. *subtraction*

b. *multiplication or addition*

c. *division*

d. *division*

Partner Practice

Encourage pairs to use a guess-and-check strategy to find the phrases that work.

Sample answers: 8 + 3 × 3 + 4 = 21; 6 ÷ 3 × 5 = 10; 7 × 4 − 9 = 19

Oral Language

Have partners verify that their partner's expressions are correct. Ask volunteers to share their stories with the class.

Develop Language

Ben

Susanne

Activities

Choosing an Operation To solve problems, you need to identify key words. Key words usually tell you which operations to use with the numbers in a problem. For instance, to find *how many in all*, you probably would add or multiply.

Choose Try to visualize each problem first. Then work with a partner to tell what operation you would use in each situation. Discuss why you chose each operation.

a. *How much taller* is Ben than Susanne?

b. Each box has 9 books. How many books are there *in all*?

c. Sondra has a basket of apples to *share equally* among her friends. How many apples will each friend get?

d. A piece of fabric is to be *cut into pieces* of a certain length. How many pieces can be cut from the fabric?

Partner Practice

Express Yourself Work with a partner. Choose numbers and symbols from the circle to write an expression equal to the green number. Some numbers and symbols may be used more than once or not at all. The first one is done. Compare answers with your partner. Then make up a new problem for your partner.

| 4 7 2 5
 × ÷ + | 8 3 4
 + − × | 6 3 5
 × ÷ | 9 8 7 4
 − × |

$4 \times 2 + 7 \times 5 = 43$ ____ $= 21$ ____ $= 10$ ____ $= 19$

Oral Language

Meet Our Pet Write a story that uses numbers to tell about a pet you would like the class to adopt. Replace each number with an expression. Instead of "He eats 2 pounds of food a day," write, "He eats $5 - 9 \div 3$ pounds of food a day." Read the story to the class. Then trade stories with your partner and simplify the expressions.

This hungry pet is a puppy. ▶

📖 **Program Resources**

Practice Book Use page 15.

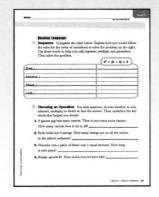

✔ **Assessment Book**

Use page 27 to assess students' comprehension.

Activity: Technology Connection

Have groups of students work together to use their calculators to create key sequences to evaluate the expressions in Exercises 1–8 on page 41. They may use parentheses and memory keys.

Expressions

Big Idea To solve word problems, it sometimes helps to write a mathematical expression first.

Building Background

▲ I like to scuba dive near colorful coral reefs.

- Tell what you know about scuba diving.
- If you rented equipment, what questions would you ask?
- How could you find the cost of renting equipment?

Key Concepts

Renting a boat costs $25 plus $10 an hour. You can write the cost as an algebraic expression, or **rule**. The **variable** in the rule stands for a number that can change. In this example, the variable (h) stands for the number of hours. The cost of renting a boat for h hours is $25 + 10h$. Note that $10h$ means 10 times h. Also,

$$10h = \underbrace{h + h + h + h + h + h + h + h + h + h.}_{10h}$$

Cost for 3 hours = $25 + 3($10) = $55
Cost for h hours = $25 + h($10) = $25 + 10h$

variable   rule

LESSON 6 • EXPRESSIONS   **43**

Activity: Give Me a Rule!

Have partners tell each other various rules involving a variable, such as "Subtract n from 25." Have them try to give rules involving a variable and two operations, such as "Add 6 to the quotient of 8 and x." The partner should write an expression for each rule.

Resource Library

Math at Hand
Expressions 237–239

Math on Call
Expressions 202–208, 210

Reader's Handbook (red)
Focus on Word Problems 143–154

Expressions

STANDARDS CONTENT

Mathematics
- Write and evaluate algebraic expressions
- Write algebraic expressions based on patterns

Language
- Recognize multiple meanings of *rule*
- Evaluate to make a judgment

Introduce the **Big Idea**

- Have someone read aloud the Big Idea. Explain that an expression shows how quantities are related.
- Some expressions are *arithmetic*, with only numbers and operations. Others are *algebraic*, with numbers, operations, and one or more variables.

Begin **Building Background**

To explain the term *scuba*, write this on the board: **s**elf-**c**ontained **u**nderwater **b**reathing **a**pparatus. Discuss the words' meanings. Ask, *Have any of you scuba dived? Tell us about it.*

Teach **Key Concepts**

- Explain that a rule can be stated in words or as an algebraic expression.
- Point out the difference between the times sign ($\times$) and the variable x. Then discuss the different forms of showing multiplication: 3×5, $3 \cdot 5$, $3(5)$, and $3n$.

Warm-Up Review

Have students write an expression for each situation.

1. 18 plus n $(18 + n)$
2. the product of 4 and x $(4x)$
3. 5 less y $(5 - y)$
4. 5 less than y $(y - 5)$
5. the quotient of 15 and m $\left(\frac{15}{m}\right)$
6. the quotient of m and 15 $\left(\frac{m}{15}\right)$
7. the number of pennies in d dimes $(10d)$

Teach Algebraic Expressions

- Point out how the expression above the numbers in the first table relates to the numbers and operations below it. Have students find the costs for 4 and 5 days ($4 \times \$105 + \$75 = \$495$; $5 \times \$105 + \$75 = \$600$). Guide students to write an algebraic expression for finding the cost for any number of days.

- Present this example to the class: *The rental fee for cross-country skis and boots is $10 plus $5 an hour* (h). Have them make and present a table showing the number of hours (*h*) from 1 through 5 and the rental cost (10 + 5*h*) for those five hours.

- Explain that the diagram relating to Jarod's bowling costs can help them write an algebraic expression, which in turn will help them solve a problem involving the costs.

Talk and Share

Ask volunteers to share and explain their results.

Answer: If Jarod has his own shoes and he bowls before noon, the cost expression is $2(c - 1)$.

Look and Read

Algebraic Expressions

An air tank holds compressed air for breathing while underwater. ▼

To find the cost to rent scuba gear, you need to know how many days you plan to rent it. The sign below on the left shows the costs. You multiply the cost per day by the number of days and add $75 for the cost of the deposit.

Number of Days	×	Daily Cost	+	Deposit	=	Total Cost
1	×	$105	+	$75	=	$105 + $75 = $180
2	×	$105	+	$75	=	(2 × $105) + $75 = $285
3	×	$105	+	$75	=	(3 × $105) + $75 = $390

How much would the cost be for 4 days? for 5 days?

This algebraic expression gives the cost for any number of days: $105d + 75$. The **variable** *d* stands for the number of days and $105d$ means $105 \times d$. To find the cost for 8 days, replace the variable with 8 and **evaluate** the expression.

$$105d + 75 = (105 \times 8) + 75 = 840 + 75 = 915$$

The cost for 8 days is $915.

*Air Tank
$75 deposit
$105 per day*

When Jarod bowls, he pays $2.50 to rent bowling shoes. He always bowls 2 games. Write an expression to show Jarod's total cost to bowl. Use *c* for the cost of 1 game.

The diagram shows that the total cost in the top row is equal to the sum of the parts in the bottom row. The total cost for 2 games and shoe rental is $2c + 2.50$.

Total Cost		
Game 1	Game 2	Shoes
c	c	$2.50

Talk and Share

Work with a partner. Suppose Jarod has his own shoes and gets $1 off per game for bowling before noon. Talk about and then write an algebraic expression to show Jarod's cost to bowl 2 games before noon.

VOCABULARY
variable—a letter that stands for a number that can change. Having a *variable* in a problem is what makes algebra different from arithmetic.
evaluate—find the value of an algebraic expression

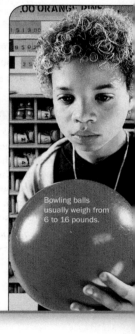

Bowling balls usually weigh from 6 to 16 pounds.

 Activity: Express Yourself!

Give pairs of students a spinner labeled 1–10 and a set of six cards, each containing an algebraic expression involving two operations and a variable. For each card drawn, the pair spins two different numbers and evaluates the expression by replacing the variable with each of the numbers. Remind students to use the rules for the order of operations. Partners should check each other's work.

 Differentiating Instruction

Beginning
Understanding Expressions On the board, write these expressions: $x + 5$, $n - 4$, $6a$, $12 \div c$. Have volunteers read each expression. Then ask students to take turns replacing the variables with numbers less than 20 and evaluate the expressions.

Intermediate
Exchanging Expressions Ask students to write six simple algebraic expressions. Have them exchange expressions with a partner. Have partners read the

expressions aloud, replace variables with numbers, and simplify.

Advanced
Writing Expressions Write this situation on the board: *Cathy bought 3 pairs of jeans. The tax was $5.29.* Say, *Draw a diagram and write an expression for the total cost.*

Sample:

J	J	J	$5.29
	3J + $5.29		

Expressions and Patterns

Tables A, B, and C contain a variable and a **rule** that tells you what to do to the variable. The first column gives values for the variable. The second column shows the value of the expression. The rule is written as an algebraic expression.

In table A, for example, the rule is $a + 27$. If the value of the variable a is 5, then the value of the expression $a + 27$ is $5 + 27$, or 32.

Table B has a variable d and values but no rule. Study the columns of numbers. Each number in the Rule column is the sum of 6 and the number in the Variable column. So the rule is "Add 6," written $d + 6$.

In table C, each number in the Rule column is the number in the Variable column divided by 2. The rule is "Divide by 2," or $\frac{x}{2}$.

To write expressions, you first find a **pattern.** Find how the value changes from one number to the next. Each number is a **term.**

Find the rule and give the next 3 terms for this pattern.

The rule is "Subtract 4." The next 3 terms are 24, 20, and 16.

VOCABULARY
rule—an expression that tells you what to do to a variable
pattern—a group of numbers related by a rule
term—a number, variable, product, or quotient in an expression. Terms are separated by a plus or minus sign.

A

Variable	Rule
a	$a + 27$
5	32
13	40
18	45
35	62

B

Variable	Rule
d	?
32	38
50	56
61	67
74	80

C

Variable	Rule
x	?
18	9
24	12
40	20
74	37

Language Notes

Multiple Meanings
This word has more than one meaning.

☐ rule
1. a statement that tells how to do something or what may not be done
2. a way to do something

Talk and Share

Talk with your partner and look for a numerical pattern for these terms: 2, 6, 18, 54. Find a rule and give the next 3 terms for the pattern.

Teach Expressions and Patterns

■ Work through table A with the class. Be sure that all students understand how values have replaced the variable in each line. Then have students give several more values to use as replacements. Tell them that they are *evaluating* the expression for the given value.

■ For tables B and C, ask, *What has been done to the first number in each row to get the second number?* Tell students that finding this pattern will help them to write the rule. The rule must work for every row.

■ Work through the pattern showing "Subtract 4." Have students write an expression for this rule $(n - 4)$.

Language Notes

Discuss the two meanings given for the word *rule.* Suggest these other meanings: to "govern" and to "mark with lines."

Talk and Share

Have partners set up a diagram like the pattern of subtracting 4s to help them. Be sure they have the same rule for each succeeding number in the pattern. Let volunteers present their findings.

Answers: The rule is "Multiply by 3."
The terms are 162, 486, and 1,458.

Build VOCABULARY

Review the vocabulary words and write them on the board. Have students look up other meanings for the word *term.* Then read these sentences and have students insert the appropriate word.

A president's term lasts four years.

A king or queen rules a country.

A rule can be written as an algebraic expression.

Each number in a pattern is called a term.

Differentiating Instruction

Beginning
Evaluating Expressions Give each student a set of four cards labeled *2, 3, 4,* and *6.* Write on the board: $2n + 8$, $25 - 3n$, $8 \times n$, and $36 \div n$. Have students take turns placing a number card over the variable in one of the expressions. Have the other students evaluate the resulting expressions.

Intermediate
Telling the Rule On the board, write several tables similar to table A. Have students show in the Rule column the

indicated computation and value for each row. For instance, for the rule $8n$ and variable value 3, they should write $8 \times 3 = 24$.

Advanced
Discovering Patterns Have students write how the number patterns in each pair below are the same and different: 2, 4, 6, 8, . . . and 2, 4, 8, 16, . . . ; 50, 45, 40, 35, . . . and 144, 72, 36, 18, . . . *(Same: Numbers increase or decrease; different: operations are addition/multiplication and subtraction/division.)*

Practice

Before assigning the exercises, ask students to explain the rules for the order of operations. Then have small groups work together to create a pattern of four-number exchange patterns, and write both a rule and an algebraic expression for the pattern. Ask students to give the next three terms.

Assignment Guide
- Beginning 1–13 odd, 16–20 even
- Intermediate 2–20 even
- Advanced 2–12 even, 13–20

Notes on Exercises
Exercises 9–12 Students may need calculators for some of these exercises.

Exercises 13–15 Work through these as a class and help students see that there is no single operation that leads from one term to the next.

Exercise 20 Short-response questions usually have more than one part and require that work be shown. Each answer is awarded from 0 to 2 points. You might use a rubric such as this one:

2: Full credit—correct answer, complete explanation

1: Partial credit—incorrect answer, correct explanation; or correct answer, incorrect explanation

0: No credit—both answer and explanation incorrect or missing

Look and Read

Practice

Copy and fill in the tables to evaluate each expression for the given values.

1.

n	$50 - n$
5	
13	
22	
47	

2.

x	$7x$
5	
9	
12	
125	

3.

m	$2m + 8$
2	
5	
16	
32	

4.

y	$3y - 2$
8	
12	
20	
30	

Find the rule for each table. Then write an expression for the rule.

5.

a	?
6	30
8	40
11	55
15	75

6.

x	?
9	24
15	30
23	38
34	49

7.

y	?
34	21
42	29
50	37
65	52

8.

n	?
96	12
64	8
48	6
24	3

Find the rule and give the next 3 terms for each pattern.

9. 5 10 15 20

10. 1,024 512 256 128

11. 2 8 32 128

12. 150 133 116 99

EXTENDED RESPONSE Describe each pattern. Then find the next 3 terms. Can you write a rule for the pattern? Tell why or why not.

13. 1 2 5 10 17 26

14. 1 4 9 16 25 36

15. 1 5 3 7 5 9 7 11

A go-cart race ▼

For Exercises 16–19, read aloud each phrase. Then tell or write a mathematical expression for each.

16. The number of quarters in d dollars

17. The number of pounds in z ounces

18. The number of eggs in d dozen

19. The number of tons in p pounds

20. **SHORT RESPONSE** The cost to rent a go-cart track for parties is $40 plus $150 an hour. Write an expression to find the total cost to rent the track. Use h for the number of hours. Find the cost to rent the track for 5 hours.

Program Resources
Practice Book Use page 16.

Answers
1. 45, 37, 28, 3
2. 35, 63, 84, 875
3. 12, 18, 40, 72
4. 22, 34, 58, 88
5. Multiply by 5; $5a$
6. Add 15; $x + 15$
7. Subtract 13; $y - 13$
8. Divide by 8; $\frac{n}{8}$
9. Add 5; 25, 30, 35
10. Divide by 2; 64, 32, 16
11. Multiply by 4; 512, 2,048, 8,192
12. Subtract 17; 82, 65, 48

13. Add 1, then 3, then 5, and so on; 37, 50, 65; no, the rule is not the same for each step.
14. The numbers are the squares of the counting numbers 1, 2, 3, . . . ; 49, 64, 81; no, each number does not depend on the number before it.
15. Add 4, then subtract 2; 9, 13, 11; no, the rule is not the same for each step.
16. $4d$ **17.** $\frac{z}{16}$ **18.** $12d$
19. $\frac{p}{2000}$ **20.** $40 + 150h$; $790

Activities

Evaluating When you evaluate mathematical expressions, you find their values. In another kind of evaluating, you make a judgment. You decide whether something has everything it needs to have. Does it *meet the criteria?*

Is the figure at the left a square? The Criteria and Evaluation Chart can help you decide. *Evaluation:* The figure is not a square.

Criteria and Evaluation Chart

Criteria for a Square	Evaluation
Figure has 4 sides.	Yes
Sides are straight.	Yes
Sides are all the same length.	No
Angles are all the same size.	No

1. Evaluate Give the steps for finding the value of the expression $5 \times (7 - 4)^2 + 12$. Have your partner evaluate your method. You must name each operation in the correct order.

2. Evaluate Have your partner give the steps for rounding 568,993 to the nearest ten thousand. Your partner must tell each step in the correct order. Evaluate your partner's method.

Oral Language

Words Have Roots The root of the word *variable* is *var*. It means "different." Work with a group to tell how *variable* means "different" in math. Name other words that have *var* in them. Make up sentences with those words. Use a dictionary. If you can, name some *var* words in other languages and tell their meanings.

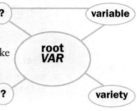

Partner Practice

Tic-Tac-Math One partner marks with an X. The other partner marks with an O. Take turns choosing a square from the game board. Read the expression aloud and name the operation. If your partner agrees with your answer, then put your mark over that square. The first person to mark 3 squares across, down, or on a diagonal is the winner. Create a new game board for another pair. Trade and play the game.

n plus 35	23 divided by *x*	5 less than 4*a*
w less 10	product of *w* and 15	13 times *y*
quotient of *w* and 7	19 more than *x*	sum of *k* and 12

Teach Evaluating

- Make sure students understand the meaning of *criteria*.

- Have students describe a square. Be sure that they all have the same correct criteria. Then have them evaluate the figure on page 47. They should find that two sides are a bit longer than two other sides and that the angles are not all the same size.

- Draw a circle and an oval on the board. Have students talk about what makes the circle a circle and why the oval is *not* a circle.

- Have partners set up charts like the one shown in order to evaluate each other's work.

Oral Language

- Explain that many words in the English language have Latin or Greek roots. Have them refer to dictionary entries to find several words with each origin.

- Ask students to give examples and meanings of words using the numerical prefixes *bi-*, *tri-*, *quad-*, *penta-*, *oct-*, and *dec-*. Again, they may use their dictionaries.

Partner Practice

Students need to know that a diagonal is a line from one corner to a nonadjacent corner. You may have to explain the basic idea of tic-tac-toe.

Activity: Extend the Lesson

Have students research the many fees and rental costs that are given as a base price plus a price per time usage. They can find examples in grocery, hardware, or sporting-goods stores (for instance, rates for rug-shampooer rental). Have them make a list of the rates and supply an algebraic expression for each rate.

Assessment Book

Use page 28 to assess students' comprehension.

Program Resources

Practice Book Use page 17.

Solving Equations

STANDARDS CONTENT

Mathematics
- Solve equations by subtracting
- Solve equations by adding

Language
- Describe a method for solving an equation

Materials
- Algebra tiles, balance scale

Introduce the Big Idea

Read aloud the Big Idea. Write several simple arithmetic equations. Explain that an equation is a mathematical sentence in which the equals sign is the verb.

Begin Building Background

Explain that the photo shows a Japanese Kabuki theater play. Invite students to share their experiences with plays or puppet shows.

Answer: $82 − $38 = $44

Teach Key Concepts

Help students to see the similarities between a balance scale and an equation. Use a balance scale to illustrate the Addition Property of Equality. Place the same number of weights in each pan, and write the equation on the board. Add the same number of weights to each pan to show that the balance is maintained. Write the resulting equation.

Warm-Up Review

Have students find each missing number and verify the equality.

1. $5 + 8 + 7 = 13 + \blacksquare$ (7)
2. $12 + 6 = 9 + 3 + \blacksquare$ (6)
3. $18 + \blacksquare = 9 + 9 + 4$ (4)
4. $22 − 8 = 20 + 2 − \blacksquare$ (8)
5. $15 − 12 = 9 + 6 − \blacksquare$ (12)
6. $5 + 8 + \blacksquare = 13 + \blacksquare$
   (any number)
7. $15 − \blacksquare = 9 + 6 − \blacksquare$
   (any number 0–15)

Solving Equations

Big Idea Many problems involving addition and subtraction can be solved more easily if you use equations.

Building Background

▲ I was in a play last year. I got to play a dancer.

- **What is happening here? Tell about a play that you've seen.**
- **You have $38. How much more money do you need for an $82 ticket to the play?**

Key Concepts

An **equation** is like a balance scale. It must always have equal quantities on both sides. The **Addition Property of Equality** says that adding the same thing to both sides of an equation does not change the equality. The equation is still in **balance**.

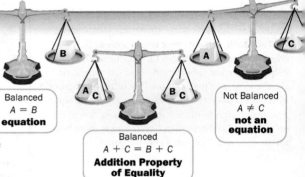

Balanced
$A = B$
equation

Balanced
$A + C = B + C$
Addition Property of Equality

Not Balanced
$A \neq C$
not an equation

Activity: Keep It Balanced!

Have partners each write a list of six equations involving addition, such as $6 + 14 = 8 + 12$. Have them exchange lists and show that adding the same number to each side of an equation keeps the equation balanced. Then have them repeat the activity but subtract the same number from each side of the equations.

Resource Library

Math at Hand
Addition Property of Equality 232–233
Variables and Equations 236, 240–242

Math on Call
Addition Property of Equality 228
Variables and Equations 202–203, 205, 241–242

Solving Equations by Subtracting

An **equation** is a mathematical **sentence** that says two quantities are equal. The first equation shown below is true because $25 + 5 = 30$ and $6 \times 5 = 30$. The second equation is false because $48 \div 8 = 6$ but $16 - 8 = 8$. What value of x will make the third equation true? **Solve the equation** to find the correct value. Use mental math: What number plus 8 equals 15? $7 + 8 = 15$, so $x = 7$.

$25 + 5 = 6 \times 5$ T $48 \div 8 = 16 - 8$ F $x + 8 = 15$?

$x + 8 = 15$
$x = 7$

The algebra tiles at the right model the solution. The green stick stands for x and the black line stands for an equals sign.

To solve $n + 38 = 82$, you need to get the variable alone on one side of the equation. Because subtraction *undoes* addition, you can subtract 38 from the left side of the equation to get n alone. To keep the equation balanced, you also must subtract 38 from the right side.

$$n + 38 = 82$$
$$n + 38 - 38 = 82 - 38 \quad \leftarrow \text{Subtract 38 from both sides.}$$
$$n = 44 \quad \leftarrow \text{Compute.}$$
$$\text{Check: } 44 + 38 \stackrel{?}{=} 82 \quad \leftarrow \text{Use 44 for } n.$$
$$82 = 82 \quad \leftarrow \text{The solution makes the statement true.}$$

This method works because of the **Subtraction Property of Equality**. It says that if two quantities are equal, subtracting the same number from both quantities does not change the equality.

Talk and Share

Work with a partner. Discuss when to use mental math to solve an equation. Tell how you check a solution. For each equation, tell why the number given for n is, or is not, a solution.

$18 + n = 12, n = 30$; $22 = n + 10, n = 12$; $n + 13 = 13, n = 0$

VOCABULARY

equation—a mathematical sentence stating that two quantities are equal. The expressions on both sides of the equals sign (=) have the same value.
sentence—a group of words or symbols that express a complete idea
solve the equation—find values that make the equation true
Subtraction Property of Equality—the property that says subtracting the same number from both sides of an equation does not change the equality

LESSON 7 • SOLVING EQUATIONS   **49**

Teach Solving Equations by Subtracting

- Help students recognize that any number but 7 will result in a false statement if the number replaces the variable in $x + 8 = 15$. So 7 is the only *solution*. It makes the equation true, or *solves the equation*.

- If you have a balance scale, repeat the activity in the Key Concepts notes, using subtraction to illustrate the Subtraction Property of Equality.

- Work through the algebra tile diagram. Each green rectangle represents the variable x, and each yellow tile represents 1. Use tiles or diagrams to demonstrate some simple addition equations. Have students tell what equation is being modeled and model the solution.

- Finally, work through the symbolic solving of the second example. Write other equations on the board and have volunteers explain their reasoning as they show how to solve them.

Talk and Share

Students may use a guess-and-check strategy. They should find that the solution to the first equation is not correct: *18 + 30 = 48, not 12*; the solutions to the other two are correct: *22 = 12 + 10 and 0 + 13 = 13*.

Differentiating Instruction

Beginning
Using Algebra Tiles with Addition Equations Give students algebra tiles. Help pairs to model and solve simple addition equations, such as $x + 6 = 13$ and $x + 12 = 24$ (x = 7; y = *12*). For each equation, have students demonstrate how they solved the equation.

Intermediate
Modeling Addition Equations Have pairs draw diagrams like that of the algebra tile model on page 49 and

exchange them with their partners to solve. Have the partner write the equation modeled, show how to remove tiles, and then write the solution.

Advanced
Writing Directions for Solving Addition Equations Have students pretend that they have to tell someone how to solve the equation $15 + n = 64$. Have them write the directions, beginning with how to tell what was done to the variable and ending with the solution (n = *49*).

Activity: Tile Away Your Time!

Give each pair of students an envelope marked with an x and a pile of tiles or counters. Have them take turns modeling addition equations and having their partners solve them by removing tiles. For example, one student places 12 tiles and the envelope containing 8 tiles on one side of the desk and 20 tiles on the other side. The partner solves by removing 12 tiles from each side of the desk and finds that there are 8 tiles in the envelope.

Teach Solving Equations by Adding

- Discuss the first example, stressing the thought processes used. Write several simple subtraction equations on the board. Ask, *How can you solve the equations using mental math?* Have volunteers share their reasoning.

- Work through the second example. Ask, *How can you get the variable alone on one side of the equation?* Refer students to the Addition Property of Equality they explored with the balance scale on page 48.

- Give students more examples of subtraction equations, and have them verbalize the solutions and reasons for each step.

- Explain that *inverse* operations are operations that undo each other. Relate the term *inverse* to *reverse* or *opposite*. Ask volunteers to describe these two terms and how they relate to the term *undo*.

Talk and Share

Students should recognize that for the seesaw to remain balanced, the same-weight person needs to get on or off both ends. This situation models the two properties of equality introduced in this lesson.

Solving Equations by Adding

Solve the equation $y - 9 = 8$. You probably can use mental math: What number minus 9 equals 8? $17 - 9 = 8$, so $y = 17$.

To solve the equation $m - 47 = 78$, think about getting the variable m alone on one side of the equation. How can you undo subtracting 47? Because addition *undoes* subtraction, you can add 47 to the left side of the equation to get m alone. To keep the equation balanced, you also must add 47 to the right side of the equation.

$$m - 47 = 78$$
$$m - 47 + 47 = 78 + 47 \quad \leftarrow \text{Add 47 to both sides.}$$
$$m = 125 \quad \leftarrow \text{Compute.}$$
$$\text{Check: } 125 - 47 \overset{?}{=} 78 \quad \leftarrow \text{Use 125 for } m.$$
$$78 = 78 \quad \leftarrow \text{The solution checks.}$$

You can use this method because of the **Addition Property of Equality**. It says that if two quantities are equal, adding the same number to both quantities does not change the equality.

To solve these equations, you use the idea that subtraction undoes addition and addition undoes subtraction. Because they undo each other, addition and subtraction are **inverse operations.**

Talk and Share

Tell your partner how the Addition and Subtraction Properties of Equality are like the seesaw shown.

VOCABULARY
Addition Property of Equality—a property that says adding the same number to both sides of an equation does not change the equality
inverse operations—operations that undo each other. Addition and subtraction are *inverse operations.*

 Activity: Back Up!

Review the terms *inverse* and *undo*. Then have partners find examples of four pairs of actions that are inverses of each other. Encourage them to be creative, and allow them to share their examples with the class.

 Differentiating Instruction

Beginning
Understanding Subtraction Equations
Write a variety of simple addition and subtraction equations on the board. Write some of them with the variable on the right side of the equals sign. Have students tell what operation was done to the variable in each equation and how to undo that operation.

Intermediate
Solving Subtraction Equations Have students prepare a list of six subtraction equations for their partner to solve and

to check. Have the solver explain how to solve each equation.

Advanced
Writing Directions for Solving Subtraction Equations Have students pretend that they have to tell someone else how to solve $42 = x - 29$. Have them write the directions, beginning with how to tell what was done to the variable and ending with the solution ($x = 71$).

Practice

In each exercise, tell whether the value given for the variable is a solution. Explain why or why not.

1. $18 + n = 35, n = 53$ **2.** $20 - x = 15, x = 5$

3. $m + 14 = 14, m = 28$ **4.** $17 = 32 - n, n = 15$

Tell a partner how to get the variable alone on one side of the equation. The first one is done for you.

5. $k - 8 = 23$ *Add 8 to both sides.* **6.** $x + 14 = 39$ **7.** $z - 21 = 19$

8. The solution to $x + 6 = 10$ is modeled on the right with algebra tiles. What is the solution?

$x + 6 = 10$

Solve each equation. Check your solutions.

9. $45 = b - 18$ **10.** $k - 24 = 19$

11. $16 + p = 25$ **12.** $z + 15 = 92$

13. $n + 58 = 102$ **14.** $b - 40 = 72$

15. $n - 58 = 102$ **16.** $81 = s + 45$

Write the equation shown by each diagram. Then solve the equation. The first one is started for you.

17.

n	10
23	

$n + 10 = 23$
$n + 10 - 10 = 23 - 10$
$n = \blacksquare$

18.

n	15
30	

19.

23	n
76	

20. Clothes & More had a sale on shoes. Every pair was $15 off. Sonia paid $27 for her shoes. Write and solve an equation to find the original price of the shoes.

21. Luz ordered a printer from a computer company. The price of the printer was $129. If Luz paid $141 including shipping fees, what was the cost of shipping? Write and solve an equation to find the cost of shipping.

22. (EXTENDED RESPONSE) Explain how to solve the equation $19 - a = 6$.

LESSON 7 • SOLVING EQUATIONS **51**

Practice

For Exercises 9–16, have students tell whether the solution for each will be greater than or less than the number being added to or subtracted from the variable. Have them tell how they know.

Assignment Guide
■ Beginning 1–7 odd, 8, 9–19 odd, 20
■ Intermediate 2–18 even, 19–21
■ Advanced 2–20 even, 21, 22

Notes on Exercises
Exercises 1–4 Be sure students understand that they must replace the variable with the value given to determine whether the sentence is true.

Exercises 17–19 Remind students that the two rows of the diagrams represent equal quantities.

Exercise 22 Students may try to explain a procedure for solving this equation using one of the properties of equality. It is possible to add a to both sides and then subtract 6 from both sides. But many students probably will use a guess-and-check strategy.

Answers

1. No; $18 + 53 = 71$, not 35
2. Yes; $20 - 5 = 15$
3. No; $28 + 14 = 42$, not 14
4. Yes; $17 = 32 - 15$
5. Add 8 to both sides.
6. Subtract 14 from both sides.
7. Add 21 to both sides.
8. $x = 4$ **9.** $b = 63$
10. $k = 43$ **11.** $p = 9$
12. $z = 77$ **13.** $n = 44$
14. $b = 112$ **15.** $n = 160$
16. $s = 36$
17. $n + 10 = 23; n = 13$

18. $n + 15 = 30; n = 15$
19. $23 + n = 76; n = 53$
20. $s - 15 = 27;$ $42
21. $129 + c = 141;$ $12
22. Sample: I would think: 19 minus what number equals 6? Then I would try numbers between 1 and 19 and find that 13 works.

Program Resources
Practice Book Use page 18.

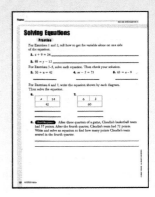

7 Develop Language

Teach Describing

- Have students tell in their own words what it means to *describe* something. They may refer to writing about something or to drawing a picture to represent it. Tell them that the suffix *-scribe* comes from the Latin word *scribere*, which means "to write."

- Have partners repeat the activity with several more diagrams that they have drawn.

Hands On

If you do not have access to algebra tiles, you may substitute envelopes and paper clips or counters, and have students do the activity as it is described in "Tile Away Your Time!" on page 49.

Partner Practice

Encourage students to be creative with their sentences. Have them share their more amusing examples with the class. Have them draw diagrams like the one at the top of the page to represent their equations.

Oral Language

Have students share their observations. Some might say that Patty hasn't bothered to solve the problem. Others might say that she doesn't realize *x* and *w* are *variables* and can stand for different numbers.

Develop Language

Activities

Describing When you describe something, you tell about it.

1. **Describe** Describe the diagram at the right.

n	8
25	

2. **Tell** Have your partner tell what equation is shown by the diagram.

3. **Describe** List the steps you would use to solve your partner's equation.

Hands On

Model That Materials: algebra tiles
Work with a partner. Take turns using algebra tiles to model an equation, such as $x + 9 = 14$. Each partner must show how to solve the equation and tell how to get x alone on one side.

$x + 9 = 14$

Partner Practice

My Story Take turns writing an equation. Make up a story of two or three sentences to go with your partner's equation. Solve the equation. Then have your partner make up sentences and solve your equation. A sample for $x + 11 = 27$ is shown.

(Answer: The brother is 16.)

> $x + 11 = 27$
> The ages of my brother and my sister add to 27. My sister is 11. How old is my brother?

Oral Language

Very Variable Read the comic strip and tell why the little girl is wrong.

—Charles M. Schulz ©1971

52 Unit 2 • Introduction to Algebra

Program Resources

Practice Book Use page 19.

Assessment Book

Use page 29 to assess students' comprehension.

Activity: Culture Connection

The photo on page 48 depicts Kabuki theater, which has its origins in 17th-century Japan. It features melodramatic presentations of historical or domestic events. The costumes and makeup are colorful, the scenery is spectacular, and the acting is lively and exaggerated.

Interested students can find the current cost of plays on Broadway in New York City at http://www.nyc. com/theatre. Ask, *How much would it cost for the class to attend a play?*

Talk and Explore

More Equations

Big Idea In the last lesson, you solved addition and subtraction equations by doing the same thing to both sides of them. You can solve multiplication and division equations the same way.

Building Background

▲ I have been to the San Diego Wild Animal Park. There are no cages there!

■ **What would you do if you visited a zoo?**

■ **What is your favorite zoo animal?**

■ **Tell how you might find the number of pounds of food needed for a herd of elephants each day. What would you need to know first?**

Key Concepts

The properties of equality are statements that describe how to work with equations. The **Division Property of Equality** helps you solve an equation that involves multiplication.

Division Property of Equality

$40x = 120$ ← This equation is read, "40 times x equals 120."

$40x \div 40 = 120 \div 40$ ← To get the variable x alone, divide both sides of the equation by 40.

$x = 3$ ← x stands alone on one side, and the solution to the equation is on the other. The value of the variable x is 3.

variable   value

LESSON 8 • MORE EQUATIONS **53**

Activity: Balance That Equation!

Have partners each write a list of six equations involving multiplication, such as $6 \times 2 = 4 \times 3$. Have students exchange lists and show that dividing both sides of an equation by the same nonzero number keeps the equation balanced. Then have them repeat the activity but multiply both sides of the equations by the same number.

Resource Library

Math at Hand
Multiplication Property of Equality 232, 234
Equations 243

Math on Call
Multiplication Property of Equality 229
Equations 241–242

More Equations

STANDARDS CONTENT
Mathematics
■ Solve equations by dividing
■ Solve equations by multiplying
Language
■ Explain how to solve an equation
Materials
■ Pan balance, envelopes, pennies

Introduce the **Big Idea**

Read aloud the Big Idea. Review the Addition and Subtraction Properties of Equality. This lesson shows how to solve multiplication and division equations using similar properties.

Begin **Building Background**

■ Have volunteers describe their favorite zoo animal or favorite trip.

■ To find the amount of food needed for a herd of elephants, students must find the number of elephants and how much food an elephant eats in a day. A grown elephant can consume 330 pounds of food and 40 gallons of water in one day.

Teach **Key Concepts**

Ask, *How can you get the variable alone?* Whatever they do to one side, they must also do to the other side to keep the equation balanced.

Warm-Up Review

Have students find each missing number and verify the equality.

1. $5 \times (4 + 3) = \blacksquare \times 7$ (5)
2. $(6 + 2) \times 3 = 8 \times \blacksquare$ (3)
3. $10 \times \blacksquare = (5 + 5) \times 8$ (8)
4. $(10 + 4) \div 7 = 14 \div \blacksquare$ (7)
5. $(8 + 12) \div 4 = 20 \div \blacksquare$ (4)
6. $(8 + 2) \div \blacksquare = 10 \div \blacksquare$ (*any nonzero number*)
7. $10 \times \blacksquare = (5 + 5) \times \blacksquare$ (*any number*)

Teach Solving Equations by Dividing

- After discussing the first example, write several simple multiplication equations on the board. Ask, *How can you use mental math to solve these equations?* Have volunteers share their reasoning.

- Then work through the algebra-tile diagram. Point out that each *x* tile has the same value as one of the equal groups of 1s tiles, so the solution is $x = 9$. Use algebra tiles or diagrams on the board to demonstrate some simple division equations. Ask students to tell what equation is being modeled and to model the solution.

- Finally, work through the symbolic solving of the second equation. Point out the reasons for each step. Write other examples on the board, and have volunteers tell their reasoning as they show how to solve the equations. Explain that they are using the Division Property of Equality.

Talk and Share

Students should multiply 8 and 18 to check if 18 is the solution to the first equation. For the equation $9a = 108$, you might want to have students write out the steps as shown on page 54.

Answers: Divide both sides by 9; a = 12

Solving Equations by Dividing

▲ A giraffe's tongue can be 21 inches long! This helps the giraffe eat hard-to-reach leaves on trees.

A zookeeper feeds 150 pounds of food to two giraffes every day. How much food is this for each giraffe? Solve the equation $2x = 150$ to find out.

Remember that $2x$ means $2 \times x$. Then use mental math if possible. Think, "What number multiplied by 2 equals 150?" $2 \times 75 = 150$, so $x = 75$.

You can use algebra tiles to *see* a solution to a simple equation. On the left is the variable *x*, 4 times. On the right is 36: $4x = 36$. Split each side into 4 groups. You see that each *x* is equal to 9.

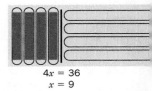

$4x = 36$
$x = 9$

When you can't use mental math or algebra tiles, use inverse operations. Multiplication and division are inverse operations because they undo each other. To solve the equation $15n = 120$, divide the left side of the equation by 15. This undoes the multiplication and gets *n* alone. To keep the equality, you also must divide the right side by 15.

$15n = 120$	← **This means 15 times *n* equals 120.**
$15n \div 15 = 120 \div 15$	← **Divide both sides by 15.**
$n = 8$	← **Compute.**
Check: $15 \times 8 \stackrel{?}{=} 120$	← **Use 8 for *n*.**
$120 = 120$	← **The solution checks.**

You can use this method because of the **Division Property of Equality.** It says that if two quantities are equal, dividing both quantities by the same nonzero number does not change the equality.

Talk and Share

Work with a partner. For $8n = 144$, does $n = 18$? Explain. Tell how to solve $9a = 108$. Show your check.

VOCABULARY

Division Property of Equality—the property that says if two quantities are equal, dividing both quantities by the same nonzero number does not change the equality

---

Activity: Piles of Tiles

Give each pair of students six envelopes marked with an *x* and a pile of tiles or counters. Have them take turns modeling multiplication equations and having the partner solve by separating the tiles into equal piles. For instance, one student places 4 tiles into each of 5 envelopes on one side of the desk and 20 tiles on the other side. The partner solves by separating the 20 tiles into 5 equal piles and finds that there are 4 tiles in each envelope.

Differentiating Instruction

Beginning

Using Algebra Tiles with Multiplication Equations Give students algebra tiles. Help pairs to model and solve simple multiplication equations such as $5x = 30$ and $8x = 32$ (*x = 6; x = 4*). For each equation, have students show how they solved the equation.

Intermediate

Modeling Multiplication Equations Have students draw diagrams like that of the algebra-tile model and exchange them with a partner to solve.

Have the partner write the equation modeled, show how to group the tiles, and then write the solution.

Advanced

Writing Directions for Solving Equations Have students pretend that they have to tell someone else how to solve the equation $35 = 7n$. Have them write the directions, beginning with how to tell what was done to the variable and ending with the solution (*n = 5*).

Solving Equations by Multiplying

The zookeeper has found that if he divides his bags of peanuts equally among 5 elephants, he can give each one 9 bags of peanuts. How many bags of peanuts does he have?

Solve the equation $\frac{b}{5} = 9$. Remember that $\frac{b}{5}$ means $b \div 5$. You probably can use mental math: What number divided by 5 equals 9? $45 \div 5 = 9$, so $b = 45$.

To solve the equation $\frac{a}{24} = 8$, think about getting the variable alone on one side of the equation. How can you undo dividing by 24? You can multiply the left side of the equation by 24 to get a alone. To keep the equation balanced, you also must multiply the right side of the equation by 24.

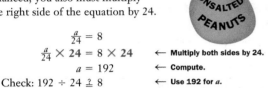

▲ Adult elephants eat about 330 pounds of food a day. They spend about 16 hours feeding and only 4 to 5 hours sleeping.

$$\frac{a}{24} = 8$$
$$\frac{a}{24} \times 24 = 8 \times 24 \qquad \leftarrow \text{ Multiply both sides by 24.}$$
$$a = 192 \qquad \leftarrow \text{ Compute.}$$
Check: $192 \div 24 \overset{?}{=} 8 \qquad \leftarrow \text{ Use 192 for } a.$
$$192 = 192 \qquad \leftarrow \text{ The solution checks.}$$

You can use this method because of the **Multiplication Property of Equality**: It says that if two quantities are equal, multiplying both quantities by the same nonzero number does not change the equality.

Talk and Share

Have your partner tell how to solve $\frac{c}{12} = 360$. Show how to check your answer.

Tell your partner how you know the solution to $\frac{x}{10} = 50$ is *not* $x = 5$.

VOCABULARY

Multiplication Property of Equality—the property that says if two quantities are equal, multiplying both quantities by the same nonzero number does not change the equality

Teach Solving Equations by Multiplying

- After discussing the first example, write several simple division equations on the board. Ask, *How can you solve the equations using mental math?* Have volunteers explain their reasoning.

- Work through the symbolic solving of the second example. Ask, *How can you get the variable alone on one side of the equation?* Explain that this procedure works because multiplication *undoes* division. Point out the reasons for each step, and explain how to check the equation. Write other examples on the board, and have volunteers explain their reasoning as they show how to solve the equations. Explain that here they are using the Multiplication Property of Equality to solve equations.

Talk and Share

- Have students write out the steps as shown on the page for solving and checking $\frac{c}{12} = 360$. They may use calculators.

- Watch for students who divide 50 by 10 and think 5 is the solution. Have them use calculators if necessary to verify that $\frac{5}{10}$ is not 50 but 0.5.

  Answers: Multiply both sides by 12; c = 4,320; substitute 4,320 for c in the equation and simplify. $\frac{5}{10} = 0.5 \neq 50$

Differentiating Instruction

Beginning
Understanding Division Equations
Write a variety of simple multiplication and division equations on the board. Write some of them with the variable on the right side of the equals sign. Have students tell what operation was done to the variable in each equation and how to undo the operation.

Intermediate
Solving Division Equations Have students prepare a list of six division equations for a partner to solve and

check. Have the solver explain how he or she solved the equation.

Advanced
Writing Directions for Solving Division Equations Have students pretend that they have to tell someone else how to solve the equation $12 = \frac{a}{7}$. Have them write the directions, beginning with how to tell what was done to the variable and ending with the solution ($a = 84$).

 Activity: Post the Equality Properties

Have students work in small groups to make a poster listing the four properties of equality. Have them give an example illustrating each property and an example of how to use that property to solve an equation.

Look and Read

Practice

For Exercises 9–16, have students tell whether the solution for each will be greater than or less than the number multiplying or dividing the variable. Have them tell how they know.

Assignment Guide
■ Beginning 1–7 odd, 8, 9–19 odd, 20

■ Intermediate 2–18 even, 19, 20

■ Advanced 2–18 even, 19–21

Notes on Exercises
Exercises 1–4 Students must replace the variable with the given value to determine whether the sentence is true. They may want to use calculators to verify their answers.

Exercises 9–16 You may wish to allow students to use calculators for these exercises. Emphasize the importance of checking solutions.

Exercises 17 and 18 Remind students that the two rows of the diagram represent equal quantities.

Exercise 20 Have students explain why the divisor in the equation is 6 rather than 5. (*Jon plus 5 friends makes 6.*)

Exercise 21 Students will probably have to use a guess-and-check strategy to solve this equation.

Practice

In each exercise, use mental math to answer the question. Explain your answer.

1. If $x = 1$, does $\frac{x}{8} = 8$?

2. If $y = 3$, does $18y = 54$?

3. If $n = 35$, does $1 = \frac{n}{35}$?

4. If $x = 50$, does $5x = 10$?

Tell how to get the variable alone on one side of the equation. The first one is done for you.

5. $8k = 56$ *Divide both sides by 8.*

6. $\frac{x}{10} = 10$

7. $42 = 14y$

8. The solution to $2x = 24$ is modeled on the right with algebra tiles. What is the solution?

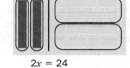

$2x = 24$

For Exercises 9–16, tell which property of equality you need to use to solve the equation. Then solve each equation and check your solutions.

9. $117 = 9s$

10. $\frac{r}{5} = 55$

11. $15 = \frac{t}{7}$

12. $8m = 96$

13. $\frac{a}{18} = 9$

14. $63 = 63c$

15. $3n = 102$

16. $\frac{x}{12} = 12$

Tell or write the equation shown by each diagram. Then explain how to solve the equation. Remember that $n + n + n + n + n = 5n$.

17.
n	n	n	n	n
45				

18.
x	x	x	x	x	x	x
63						

19. Fumi paid $85 for 5 sessions at Fit and Trim Exercise. Write and solve an equation to find the cost per session.

20. Jon and his 5 friends shared the cost of lunch at Buddy's Diner. Each person's share was $12. Use the equation $\frac{c}{6} = 12$ to find the total cost of the lunch.

21. (**EXTENDED RESPONSE**) Explain how you would solve the equation $\frac{84}{m} = 7$.

Program Resources
Practice Book Use page 20.

Answers
1. No; $1 \div 8 = 0.125$, not 1

2. Yes; $18 \times 3 = 54$

3. Yes; $35 \div 35 = 1$

4. No; $5 \times 50 = 250$, not 10

5. Divide both sides by 8.

6. Multiply both sides by 10.

7. Divide both sides by 14.

8. $x = 12$

9. Div. Prop. Eq., $s = 13$

10. Mult. Prop. Eq., $r = 275$

11. Mult. Prop. Eq., $t = 105$

12. Div. Prop. Eq., $m = 12$

13. Mult. Prop. Eq., $a = 162$

14. Div. Prop. Eq., $c = 1$

15. Div. Prop. Eq., $n = 34$

16. Mult. Prop. Eq., $x = 144$

17. $5n = 45$; divide both sides by 5; $n = 9$

18. $7x = 63$; divide both sides by 7; $x = 9$

19. $5x = 85$; $17

20. $72

21. Sample: I would think: 84 divided by what number equals 7? Then I would try various numbers and find that 12 works.

Activities

Explaining When you explain, you make something clear. To explain a math problem, you tell how to solve it and give reasons for what you do.

a	a	a	a	a	a
		36			

1. **Write** Write the equation represented by the diagram.

2. **Explain** Tell your partner how to solve the equation using mental math and then by using a property of equality. Have your partner check your solution.

3. **Draw** Make a diagram of a different equation. Have your partner explain how to solve it. Check your partner's solution.

Oral Language

Keeping All Things Equal State the Properties of Equality for Addition, Subtraction, Multiplication, and Division. Give an example of each property and tell how the property is used.

Hands On

What's My Number? Materials: small envelopes, pennies, balance scale

With a partner, take turns choosing 1, 2, or 3 envelopes. Choose a number and put that number of pennies into each envelope. Label each envelope X. Place the envelopes on one side of the scale. Your partner then must place pennies on the other side of the scale until it balances. Then have your partner count the pennies and tell how many pennies are in each envelope.

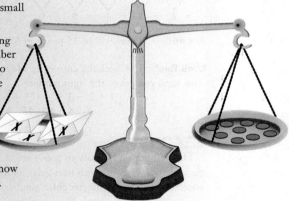

Teach Explaining

Have volunteers *explain* a simple process, such as how to set the table for dinner or how to mow the lawn. Then have students work through the math activity. For the Explain step, you may want to have them write the steps in their solution.

Oral Language

You may wish to have volunteers write their examples of the properties on the board for the class to verify.

Hands On

If students have difficulty weighing out the correct number of loose pennies, have them place the same number of empty envelopes as X envelopes on the loose-penny side. The weights should then be more accurate.

Key Connection

In the 1600s, Frenchman René Descartes decided that the letters a, b, and c should represent known numbers and that the letters x, y, and z should be used for unknown numbers. He also began to write numbers in exponential form, that is, x^2 for xx, x^3 for xxx, and so on.

Activity: Culture Connection

In 1650 B.C., Ahmes, an Egyptian scribe, copied a 200-year-old document. Thirty-five hundred years later, in 1858, it was bought by Scottish collector Alexander Henry Rhind. The "Rhind Papyrus" is one of the oldest mathematical documents in the world.

Have students solve this problem, similar to one from the Rhind Papyrus: A bag of grain is enough for 8 loaves of bread. How many loaves can be baked from 8 bags of grain? (*64 loaves*)

Assessment Book

Use page 30 to assess students' comprehension.

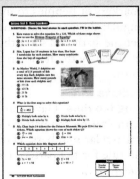

Program Resources

Practice Book Use page 21.

Look for a Pattern

STANDARDS CONTENT

Mathematics
- Solve problems by looking for a pattern

Language
- Recognize phrasal verbs

Teach Look for a Pattern

- As you work through the example, remind students of the problem-solving plan they learned in the first unit. Stress the various parts of the Read and Understand step.

- Ask, *How does each row of pearls in the diagrams compare with the row below it?* (*Every row in the pearl pattern has one more pearl than the row below it.*) Students can use that information to check the answer in Look Back.

- Be sure students know that *at least 60* means "60 or more" and that they should stop when they reach a number at or beyond 60.

Talk and Share

Encourage partners to copy and extend the pattern of numbers in the Plan and Solve step or the addition in the Look Back step. Have them find the fifteenth triangular number. Either method should yield the answer (*120*).

Problem-Solving Skills

Look for a Pattern

Sometimes numbers form a pattern. Finding a pattern can help you solve a problem.

Problem: Angelina has 60 pearls to use to decorate the front of her costume. She wants the pearls in a triangle with the same number of pearls on each side. What is the greatest number of pearls Angelina can use in her triangle?

Read and Understand

Need to find: The greatest number of pearls Angelina can use in her triangle

You know: She wants the same number of pearls on each side of the triangle.

Key fact: Angelina has 60 pearls.

Plan and Solve
Draw a diagram of how the pearls will be sewn onto the costume. The diagram shows how the first five triangles will look.

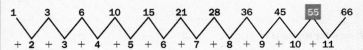

1   3   6   10   15

Study the pattern of pearls. Then extend the pattern until there are at least 60 pearls. 66 is too many. 55 is the right number.

1 $\xrightarrow{+2}$ 3 $\xrightarrow{+3}$ 6 $\xrightarrow{+4}$ 10 $\xrightarrow{+5}$ 15 $\xrightarrow{+6}$ 21 $\xrightarrow{+7}$ 28 $\xrightarrow{+8}$ 36 $\xrightarrow{+9}$ 45 $\xrightarrow{+10}$ 55 $\xrightarrow{+11}$ 66

Answer
There will be 55 pearls in Angelina's triangle.

Look Back
Check the answer by adding the numbers of pearls in each row until you get to the right number:

$1 + 2 + 3 + 4 + 5 + 6 + 7 + 8 + 9 + 10$
3   6   10   15   21   28   36   45   55

Talk and Share

The numbers in the pattern above are called *triangular numbers* because of their shapes. 55 is the 10th triangular number. Discuss with your partner how you could find the 15th triangular number.

 Activity: Extend the Lesson

Rectangular numbers are modeled by rectangular arrays: 1×2, 2×3, 3×4, ... Have students draw at least the first six or seven of them and find a pattern in the numbers. Have them extend the pattern to find the tenth rectangular number, 110 (*10 × 11*).

Students might wish to investigate pentagonal and hexagonal numbers and to make a poster to illustrate these numbers, which are called *figurate numbers.*

 Differentiating Instruction

Beginning
Verifying a Pattern Give students round markers or pennies to make the triangular designs. Have them construct the sixth and seventh triangles to verify the numbers in the pattern.

Intermediate
Describing the Rule Have students describe in writing the pattern shown by the triangular numbers. Have them write the rule for the pattern (*Add 2, add 3, add 4, . . .*).

Advanced
Explaining a Pattern Have students write several sentences telling how they found the fifteenth triangular number in Talk and Share.

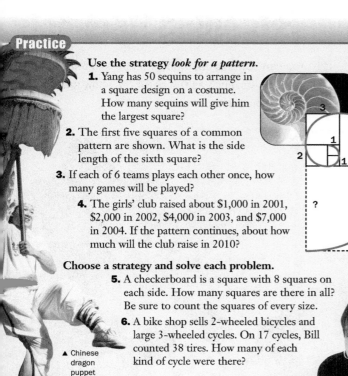

Use the strategy *look for a pattern.*

1. Yang has 50 sequins to arrange in a square design on a costume. How many sequins will give him the largest square?

2. The first five squares of a common pattern are shown. What is the side length of the sixth square?

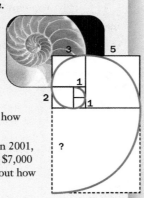

3. If each of 6 teams plays each other once, how many games will be played?

4. The girls' club raised about $1,000 in 2001, $2,000 in 2002, $4,000 in 2003, and $7,000 in 2004. If the pattern continues, about how much will the club raise in 2010?

Choose a strategy and solve each problem.

5. A checkerboard is a square with 8 squares on each side. How many squares are there in all? Be sure to count the squares of every size.

6. A bike shop sells 2-wheeled bicycles and large 3-wheeled cycles. On 17 cycles, Bill counted 38 tires. How many of each kind of cycle were there?

▲ Chinese dragon puppet

Grammar Spotlight

Phrasal Verbs Phrasal verbs are verbs that make sense only when used with a preposition, such as *into*, *out*, or *at*. Usually the verb phrase can be replaced by a single verb.

Example	Meaning
Jane ran into Joe yesterday.	met
Firemen put out fires.	extinguish
Look into the problem.	examine

1. Work with your partner to find examples of different phrasal verbs. You will find two examples on page 52.

2. Take turns writing sentences using the phrasal verbs you find.

3. Try to find a single verb that has the same meaning as each phrasal verb on your list.

LOOK FOR A PATTERN **59**

Tell students that the numbers on page 58 are called *triangular* numbers and the numbers in Exercise 1 on this page are called *square* numbers. Ask, *Why are these numbers called triangular and square numbers?* (They can be modeled with triangular and square patterns.)

Assignment Guide
- Beginning 1–6
- Intermediate 1–6
- Advanced 1–6

Notes on Exercises
Exercise 2 Have students extend the diagram to verify the side length of the eighth square (*21*). Be sure they recognize that the first and second squares both have a side length of 1.

Exercise 3 Tell students to be careful not to count any one game twice.

Exercise 5 Students should count squares that are 1 by 1, 2 by 2, 3 by 3, and so on. If they list the numbers of each size square, starting with the largest, they will find the square numbers in order from 1 through 64.

Grammar Spotlight

Have volunteers read aloud the sentences in the table. Have them identify the verb and the preposition in each sentence. Ask if the sentences make sense without the prepositions.

Answers
1. 49 sequins
2. 8
3. 15 games
4. $46,000
5. 204 squares
6. 13 bicycles, 4 three-wheelers

Activity: Extend the Lesson
The number pattern in Exercise 2 is the *Fibonacci Sequence*, named after Italian mathematician Leonardo Fibonacci, who originated it. He lived around 1170 to 1250. This pattern is found in the numbers of flower petals, the branching of trees, and the spirals of pinecones and pineapples.

Have students describe the pattern of the Fibonacci Sequence and find the next five terms: 1 1 2 3 5 8 . . . (*Add the previous two numbers; 13, 21, 34, 55, 89*).

Program Resources
Practice Book Use pages 22 and 23.

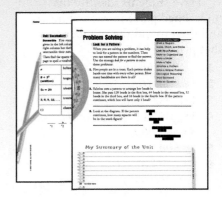

Understanding Decimals

STANDARDS CONTENT

Mathematics
- Read decimals in words and write decimals in digits
- Round decimals

Language
- Recognize confusing word pairs
- Identify steps in a process

Materials
- 10-by-10 grids (Overhead Transparency 15)

Introduce the Big Idea

Read aloud the Big Idea. On the board, draw a number line. Ask students to point out whole and decimal numbers from 0 to 3.

Begin Building Background

Tell students that the Iditarod Trail Sled-Dog Race is an annual event. The trail was a dog-sled mail route in the early 1900s. See http://www.iditarod.com.

Teach Key Concepts

- Tell students that the prefix *dec-* means "ten." Ask, *Why is our number system a* decimal *system?* (*It is based on the number 10.*)
- Point out that the digits to the left of the decimal point are read as a whole number and the digits to the right are read as a fraction.

Warm-Up Review

Have students identify the underlined place in each number and then round the number to that place.

1. 1,<u>3</u>75 (*hundreds, 1,400*)
2. 58,9<u>0</u>6 (*tens, 58,910*)
3. 146,<u>2</u>82 (*hundreds, 147,000*)
4. 35,<u>6</u>04,811 (*hundred thousands, 35,600,000*)
5. 48,<u>5</u>00,000 (*millions, 49,000,000*)
6. 526,3<u>2</u>4,025 (*ten thousands, 526,390,000*)

Understanding Decimals

Big Idea You can't always use whole numbers to tell *how much*. Decimal numbers, such as 0.5 or 34.65, show amounts that are between whole numbers.

Building Background

▲ Sometimes my dad lets me help him train our dogs.

- Tell what you think it would be like to ride on a dogsled.
- How could you find out about the annual Iditarod dogsled race in Alaska?
- What kinds of numbers would you use to tell how fast a dogsled can travel?

Key Concepts

A **decimal number** is made up of **digits** and a **decimal point**. When you read a decimal number, you say *and* for the decimal point. The number 143.572 is read *one hundred forty-three <u>and</u> five hundred seventy-two thousand<u>ths</u>.*

Decimal Number

digits

1 4 3 . 5 7 2

└ decimal point

Activity: Finding Decimals

Have small groups of students find examples of decimal numbers in their other textbooks. Ask them to make a list of the numbers and to take turns reading the numbers aloud.

Resource Library

Math at Hand
Decimals 011–014, 096

Math on Call
Decimals 011–014, 021

Reader's Handbook (red)
Reading Math 117–131

Reader's Handbook (yellow)
Reading Math 88–100

Reading and Writing Decimals

▲ An Iditarod dogsled can be pulled by up to 16 dogs. The driver is called a *musher*.

Robert Sorlie won the 2003 Iditarod Race. His **average speed** for the 1,100 miles was 4.62 miles per hour.

To model the **decimal number** 4.62, divide one unit into 100 equal parts. Each part is one **hundredth,** or 0.01, of one unit. The hundredth **grids** below show 4 wholes and 62 hundredths, or 4.62. The decimal number 4.62 is read *four <u>and</u> sixty-two hundredths*. The **decimal point** separates the whole-number part from the **decimal part.**

If you have trouble reading a decimal, you may wish to put it in a place-value table first. The part before the decimal point is 1 or greater. The part after the decimal point is less than 1.

Janke is a race fan, but he lives 148.25 miles from the starting point in Anchorage. To say 148.25 in words, follow these steps.

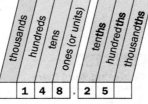

1. Say the part that is before the decimal point. → *one hundred forty-eight*
2. Say *and* for the decimal point. → *and*
3. Say the part that follows the decimal point. → *twenty-five*
4. Say the place for the part after the decimal point. → *hundredths*

Talk and Share

With a partner, say aloud the number modeled at the right. Write the number in words. How many digits should be to the right of the decimal point? Explain.

VOCABULARY

average speed—the approximate speed that something moves over a period of time
decimal number—a number written with digits and a decimal point
hundredth—1 of 100 equal parts
grid—a pattern of evenly-spaced lines running across and up and down
decimal point—the symbol in a decimal number that separates the whole-number part from the decimal part
decimal part—the part of a number that follows the decimal point

LESSON 9 • UNDERSTANDING DECIMALS   **61**

Teach Reading and Writing Decimals

■ As you discuss the model, ask *How many hundredths are in one column? How many columns are there?* Help them to see that a column is *one tenth*, or *0.1*, of 1.

■ Discuss the meaning of and how to write *one thousandth*.

■ Work through the place-value example with the students. Be sure they understand that the name for the part after the decimal point uses the name above the last digit.

■ Relate this place-value table to a whole-number place-value table, like that on page 17. Ask, *How is each place related to the place at its right?* (*Each place is 10 times the place to its right.*)

■ Write more examples on the board. Have volunteers read the numbers and tell the place of indicated digits. Explain that for numbers less than 1, we usually write a zero to the left of the decimal point.

Talk and Share

The number modeled is 2.79, read and written "two and seventy-nine hundredths." Tell students to imagine that 30 hundredths in the third square are not colored. Have them tell two ways to read the new number (*2 and 70 hundredths, 2 and 7 tenths*).

Build VOCABULARY

Point out that *average speed* is found by dividing the total distance by the total time. Ask, *Do you think Sorlie went exactly 4.62 miles an hour for the whole race? Why or why not?*

Discuss again the three places after the decimal point in the place-value chart. Relate *tenths* to *tens*, *hundredths* to *hundreds*, and *thousandths* to *thousands*. Show how each decimal part ends in *-th*.

Differentiating Instruction

Beginning
Modeling Decimals Give students 10-by-10 grids (Overhead Transparency 15). Read decimal numbers and have them shade the grids to show each number. Have them explain how they decided to shade each grid and write the number under each model.

Intermediate
Using a Place-Value Table Give each student a place-value table from thousands to thousandths, like the one on page 61, with vertical lines

extended so there is room to write five or more numbers. Have volunteers say a decimal number with five to seven digits. Have the other students write that number in their tables. Check that the numbers have been written correctly.

Advanced
Writing Numbers in Words Write four or five decimal numbers on the board. Have a volunteer read each number aloud. Then have students write each number in words.

Teach **Rounding Decimals**

■ As you discuss rounding 0.64 to the nearest tenth, be sure students remember that 0.60 and 0.70 are the same as 0.6 and 0.7, respectively. Ask, *Why is 0.65 the halfway point?* (*There are as many tenths above it as below it.*) They might want to relate the decimal numbers to the whole numbers 60, 64, 65, 69, and 70 to better understand the relationships.

■ Write a whole number on the board, and have students explain how to round it to a given place. Tell them that they will use the same steps to round decimal numbers.

■ Write 29.0483 on the board and work through the rounding, having volunteers supply the steps.

▲ Sometimes as little as 0.64 second separates first and second place winners.

Language Notes

Remind students that the places to the right of a decimal point correspond to the places to the left, but that the places to the right end in *-th*. These places represent parts of a unit, or numbers less than 1.

Language Notes

Confusing Word Pairs
These words are easily mixed up.

■ tenths, hundredths, thousandths
names of decimal numbers ending in *ths*, located to the right of the decimal point

■ tens, **hundreds, thousands**
names of whole numbers to the left of the decimal point

Talk and Share

The rounded number is 29.1. Tell students that it is customary to talk about "decimal places," and that this term refers to the number of digits to the right of the decimal point.

Rounding Decimals

Round 0.64, 0.69, and 0.65 to the nearest tenth. On a number line, look to see whether each number is to the left, to the right, or at the halfway point. Notice that 0.64 is to the left of the halfway point 0.65, so it rounds to 0.6. But 0.69 is to the right of 0.65, so it rounds to 0.7. Because 0.65 is the halfway point, it rounds to 0.7.

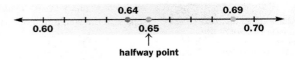

halfway point

Without a number line, look at two digits: the digit to be rounded and the digit on its right. In each case, the digit 6 is in the tenths place. It will stay the same or change to the next greater number. All digits to the right of the tenths place will be dropped.

4 < 5, so the 6 stays the same.	9 > 5 and 5 = 5, so the 6 becomes 7.
0.6④ ↓ 0.6	0.6⑨　0.6⑤ ↓　　↓ 0.7　　0.7

Round 29.0483 to the nearest hundredth.

29.0483
↓
29.04⑧
↓
29.05

Step 1: Underline the digit in the hundredths place, 4.

Step 2: Circle the digit to the right of the hundredths place, 8.

Step 3: 8 ≥ 5, so change the digit in the rounding place from 4 to 5. Drop all digits after the hundredths place.

The symbol ≈ means "is about equal to." 29.0483 ≈ 29.05

Talk and Share

Work with a partner to round 29.05 to the tenths place.

VOCABULARY

round—change a number to give an estimated value
≈　is about equal to

Activity: Round It Off!

Have partners each make a list of six numbers with at least six digits each and containing a decimal point. Each number should have one digit from the thousands to the thousandths place underlined. Have partners exchange lists and orally explain how to round the numbers to the place specified.

Differentiating Instruction

Beginning
Rounding Decimals Give students sheets of paper, each with a number from 1 to 9 on the front and 0 on the back and a sheet with a decimal point. Have five or six students line up and display a decimal number. Name a place in the number, and have students form the rounded number with the sheets. Repeat with other numbers.

Intermediate
Plotting Decimals Have students each draw a number line labeled *0, 0.5, 1,*

1.5, 2. Have pairs take turns naming decimal numbers, with some to thousandths, between 0 and 2. The partner should mark that number on his or her line and explain why the number is in the correct position.

Advanced
Explaining Rounding Have students write several sentences explaining how to round 54.698 to the nearest hundredth. Have them explain why there should be two decimal places.

Practice

Use the diagram at the right for Exercises 1–4.
1. What number is modeled?
2. Write the number in words.
3. Round the number to the nearest tenth.
4. Between what two whole numbers is the decimal number?

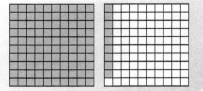

5. How many tens are in 100?   6. How many ones are in 10?
7. How many tenths are in 1?   8. How many hundredths are in one tenth?
9. How many thousandths are in one tenth?

Name the place of the underlined digit. Then round the number to that place.
10. 17.4<u>8</u>7   11. 235.<u>0</u>91   12. 1<u>2</u>.751
13. 0.35<u>4</u>9   14. 1<u>0</u>.036   15. 2.09<u>9</u>8

In 2004, Lance Armstrong won the Tour de France bicycle race for the sixth year in a row. His average speed was about 25.91 miles per hour.
16. Name the digit in the tenths place in 25.91.
17. Name the digit to the right of the tenths place.
18. To round 25.91 to the tenths place, will you change the digit in the tenths place or not? Explain your answer.

For Exercises 19–21, write the value of each set of coins as a decimal part of a dollar.
19. 3 dimes, 1 nickel
20. 1 quarter, 2 dimes, 4 nickels
21. the amount of change if an item costs $0.39 and you pay with 2 quarters

penny   dime   quarter   nickel

35.5 cm
11.3 cm

22. (MULTIPLE CHOICE) If you divide the distance around a circle by the distance across, you get about 3.1415929. This number is called pi and is written π. What is the value of π to the nearest hundredth?
A. 3.1   B. 3.14   C. 3.1416   D. 3.15

LESSON 9 • UNDERSTANDING DECIMALS   **63**

Practice

Draw a number line from 0 through 3 on the board. Mark 0, 0.5, 1, 1.5, 2, 2.5, and 3 on the line. Give students various decimals between 0 and 3, and have volunteers mark the numbers on the number line. Then have them round each number to the nearest whole number.

Assignment Guide
■ Beginning 1–8, 13–19, 21, 22
■ Intermediate 1–19, 21, 22
■ Advanced 1–22

Notes on Exercises
Exercises 5–9 Students may need to refer to the place-value table.

Exercises 10–15 It may help students to copy each number, showing the underlining and circling the digit to the right of the underlined number.

Exercise 15 This number is 2.100 when rounded. The zeros should be retained to indicate the rounding place.

Exercises 19–21 If students are having difficulty, have them change each coin to the correct number of cents. Then remind them that a cent is *one hundredth* of a dollar.

Exercise 22 The value calculated here is the number π. The actual value of π is a nonterminating, nonrepeating decimal.

Answers
1. 1.09
2. one and nine hundredths
3. 1.1
4. 1 and 2
5. 10 tens
6. 10 ones
7. 10 tenths
8. 10 hundredths
9. 100 thousandths
10. hundredths, 17.49
11. tenths, 235.1
12. ones, 13
13. thousandths, 0.355
14. ones, 10
15. thousandths, 2.100
16. 9
17. 1
18. No; 1 is less than 5.
19. $0.35
20. $0.65
21. $0.11
22. B

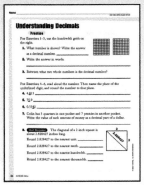

Program Resources
Practice Book Use page 24.
Overhead Transparencies Use 15.

Teach Identifying

Have volunteers explain a simple process, such as how to wash dishes after a meal. Have them write each step, including the words *first*, *second*, *third*, *fourth*, and so on. Then have them complete the math activity.

Partner Practice

For each number in a list, you may wish to have partners underline the digit specified and circle the digit to its right to help them round correctly.

Oral Language

Ask, *What happens to the value of a number as the decimal moves to the right and to the left? (The value of the number increases; the value of the number decreases.)*

Key Connection

It is believed that the written numerical symbols for 1–9 originated with the Hindus around 500 A.D. They are called Hindu-Arabic numerals. By the year 650 A.D., zero was also being used in Indian mathematics.

Among the first people to use a symbol for zero were the Mayans of Central America in the seventh century and earlier.

Develop Language

▲ When you build or create something, you do it in steps.

Activities

Identifying When you identify steps in a process, you list in order everything needed for the process. The words *first*, *second*, *third*, *fourth*, and so on tell you the order in which you do things.

On page 62, you learned 3 steps to round the number 29.0483 to the nearest hundredth. Use those steps to help you and your partner do the following.

1. **Write** First, write a number with 4 decimal places. Second, trade numbers with your partner.

2. **Identify** Then, list in order the steps for rounding your partner's number to the nearest thousandth.

Partner Practice

Round and Round Write 5 numbers with decimal places. Next to each number, write the place to which the number should be rounded. Trade lists with a partner. Read each number aloud. Read the place to which you should round. Then tell whether the digit in that place stays the same or changes to the next greater number. Write down the rounded number. Make sure you and your partner agree on the answers.

Oral Language

Move That Point! Work in a small group. Each group needs two sets of number cards, labeled 0 through 9, and one card with a decimal point. Use 4 of your number cards and the decimal point card to form a decimal number. Talk about how to read the number. Read the number aloud. Then change the position of the decimal point card and discuss how to read the new number. After you make and read several different numbers with the same cards, pick 4 new number cards and repeat the activity.

🎁 Program Resources
Practice Book Use page 25.

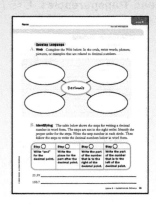

✓ Assessment Book
Use page 31 to assess students' comprehension.

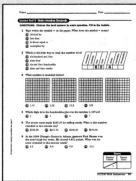

🏃 Activity: Culture Connection

The decimal point was first used in a book by a Scotsman, John Napier, in 1617. Some cultures, however, use a raised dot or comma rather than a decimal point.

Napier invented a mechanical device for multiplying numbers called "Napier's Bones." Find out and then show the class how to use a paper-and-pencil method that replicates multiplying with Napier's Bones. See http://www.johnnapier.com_rods.htm.

Comparing and Ordering

Talk and Explore

Big Idea The number with the most digits is not always the greatest number. Place value is an important clue to decimal numbers.

Building Background

▲ I would like to see the crown jewels up close sometime!

- **What do you see in this photo?**
- **What palace or great place have you visited?**
- **Would you prefer to visit the British Museum or the Tower of London?**

Key Concepts

You use the same words when you compare decimals as you do when you compare whole numbers. Read the number sentence from left to right. The inequality symbol points to the number whose value is less.

2.5 < 5.5
is less than

5.5 > 2.5
is greater than

Place in London, England	Number of Visitors in a Year
Tower of London	2.5 million
British Museum	5.5 million

LESSON 10 • COMPARING AND ORDERING **65**

Activity: Rounding Tic-Tac-Toe

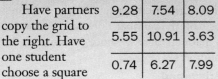

Have partners copy the grid to the right. Have one student choose a square and round the number to the nearest tenth. If the answer is correct, the student takes the square. Otherwise, the partner gets a chance to answer correctly and take the square. To win, a student takes three squares in a row, a column, or a diagonal.

9.28	7.54	8.09
5.55	10.91	3.63
0.74	6.27	7.99

Resource Library

Math at Hand
Equivalent Decimals 015
Comparing and Ordering Decimals 016–018

Math on Call
Equivalent Decimals 017
Comparing and Ordering Decimals 018–020

Comparing and Ordering

STANDARDS CONTENT
Mathematics
- Compare decimals
- Order decimals

Language
- Identify signal words for comparing and contrasting
- Organize information

Materials
- 10-by-10 grids (Overhead Transparency 15), centimeter rulers

Introduce the **Big Idea**
Read aloud the Big Idea. On the board, write *2,980; 13,021;* and *15.* Ask, *Which is least? (15) Which is greatest? (13,021)* Point out that comparing the *numbers* of digits works for these whole numbers.

Begin **Building Background**
Jewels, which are often measured in decimals, are the context for this lesson. Invite students to share what they know about famous jewels. Ask, *Where could you go to see famous jewels?*

Teach **Key Concepts**
Suggest that students think of each inequality symbol as an arrow that points to the number with the lesser value.

Warm-Up Review
Have students use < or > to compare the numbers in Exercises 1–4 and order the numbers from least to greatest in Exercises 5 and 6.

1. 1,503 ■ 1,530 (<)
2. 44,561 ■ 44,498 (>)
3. 506,678 ■ 507,786 (<)
4. 98,999 ■ 99,000 (<)
5. 3,556 3,665 3,565 3,655
   (*3,556; 3,565; 3,655; 3,665*)
6. 9,820 8,092 9,802 8,902
   (*8,092; 8,902; 9,802; 9,820*)

Teach Comparing Decimals

■ Draw students' attention to the grid model showing 0.7 and 0.63 and call attention to the number line. Explain that these models are visual but not very practical. Remind students that 0.7 is the same as 0.70. To convince them, explain that $8 and $8.00 name the same amount.

■ Work through the example. Ask, *Why do you have to line up the decimal points?* (*to keep the places of the digits lined up*) You might have students read aloud the two numbers so they can tell that 75 thousandths is greater than 9 thousandths.

■ Work through the next example, stressing the importance of lining up the decimal points. Students may need help rounding because these two numbers involve *ten thousandths*.

Talk and Share

■ Ask if students can write these numbers and the numbers in Key Concepts in standard form. If not, give them the numbers 1,750,000; 1,550,000; 2,500,000; and 5,500,000 so that they realize their magnitude.

■ Distribute 10-by-10 grids for students to use.

Answer: Because a greater area is shaded, 1.75 is greater than 1.55.

Look and Read

Comparing Decimals

0.7   0.63

Jaime has a ring with 0.7 carat of diamonds. Her necklace has 0.63 carat. Use grids to compare the number of carats. A greater area is shaded for 0.7 than for 0.63. So 0.7 > 0.63. This is read *seven tenths is greater than sixty-three hundredths.*

Another way to compare 0.7 and 0.63 is to plot each point on a number line. The number whose point is to the right of the other is the greater number.

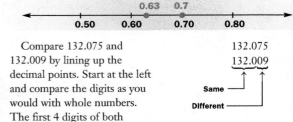

Compare 132.075 and 132.009 by lining up the decimal points. Start at the left and compare the digits as you would with whole numbers. The first 4 digits of both numbers are the same. But the digits in the hundredths place are different. Because 7 > 0, you know 132.075 > 132.009.

132.075
132.009
Same
Different

Compare 0.008 and 0.0103. Line up the decimal points. Put a zero after the 8 so that the number of decimal places is the same for both numbers. In the first two places, the digits are alike. But the digits in the hundredths place are different. 0 < 1, so 0.008 < 0.0103.

Insert zero.
0.0080↵
0.0103
Same
Different

Diamonds are weighed in *carats*. The Star of Africa is one of the crown jewels. It weighs 530.2 carats and is the world's largest diamond. The Hope Diamond, below, weighs $112\frac{3}{16}$ carats. ▼

Talk and Share

Work with a partner. Using 10-by-10 grids, shade in 1.75 for the number of people (in millions) who visited Westminster Abbey in one year. Shade grids to show 1.55 for the number of people (in millions) who visited Windsor Castle that year. Tell which number is greater. Explain how you know.

Activity: Grid and Bear It!

Give pairs of students several copies of 10-by-10 grids (Overhead Transparency 15). Have one partner tell the other a pair of decimals between 0 and 3. The partner should shade grids to show each number and then write two sentences comparing the numbers. Have partners discuss how they would compare the numbers without grids. Then have them switch roles and repeat the activity.

Differentiating Instruction

Beginning
Comparing Decimals Using Grids
Give students 10-by-10 grids. On the board, write pairs of decimals less than 1, some in tenths, some in hundredths, and some in tenths and hundredths. Have students shade their grids and write a mathematical sentence comparing the numbers in each pair.

Intermediate
Comparing Decimals on a Number Line Have partners tell each other pairs of decimals between 0 and 3. Have

them draw number lines and mark the pair on the number line, and then write a mathematical sentence to compare the numbers.

Advanced
Comparing Decimals Have partners give each other a pair of decimal numbers to thousandths. Each partner should explain how to compare the two numbers and then write two comparison sentences.

Ordering Decimals

For comparison, one student measured his fingers. He measured the length of each finger and the distance around each finger in centimeters (cm).

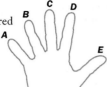

Finger	Length	Distance Around
A	6.9 cm	5.8 cm
B	7.6 cm	6.9 cm
C	7.9 cm	7.1 cm
D	6.8 cm	6.5 cm
E	6.0 cm	7.6 cm

Then the class organized the information by ordering the lengths from shortest to longest. For each group of numbers, they started by comparing digits from left to right. First they compared the digits in the ones place and then in the tenths place. The ordered numbers are shown.

Length (cm) (shortest to longest)	Distance Around (cm) (shortest to longest)
6.0 Finger E	5.8 Finger A
6.8 Finger D	6.5 Finger D
6.9 Finger A	6.9 Finger B
7.6 Finger B	7.1 Finger C
7.9 Finger C	7.6 Finger E

Language Notes

Signal Words: Compare/Contrast
These words point to ways things are alike and different.

- ☐ same/different
- ☐ alike/**not like**
- ☐ shortest/longest

Talk and Share

Trace your hand and your partner's hand. Use a centimeter ruler to measure the length of each finger in your tracings to the nearest tenth of a centimeter. Then list the lengths of your and your partner's fingers from shortest to longest.

Teach Ordering Decimals

■ Begin by reviewing how to order whole numbers. Write several sets of four or five whole numbers on the board, and have volunteers explain how to order them. Ask, *How should you line up the numbers?* (by their last digits) *Where should you begin comparing digits?* (at the left)

■ Next, tell students that ordering decimal numbers is done the same way, except that the numbers are lined up by the decimal points.

■ Have the class work through ordering the finger lengths and distances around to verify that the two ordered lists are correct.

Talk and Share

Be sure that students are measuring correctly to the nearest tenth of a centimeter, or *millimeter*. Students also may enjoy measuring the distances around their own fingers. They can use a piece of string and then measure the string using their ruler.

Differentiating Instruction

Beginning
Using Number Cards to Order Decimals Give each of four students three number cards from 1–9, a 0 card, and a decimal-point card. Have students make four different numbers less than 1, placing the 0 card before the decimal point. Have them tell which number is least and which is greatest and then order them from least to greatest.

Intermediate
Ordering Decimals On separate slips of paper, have each student write four different decimals less than 1 with four digits after the decimal place. Have students place the slips facedown and mix them up. Ask each student to choose four numbers and tell how to order them from least to greatest.

Advanced
Ordering Decimals Have students brainstorm a list of 3- and 4-digit numbers less than 10 and make a class poster explaining how to order the numbers.

Activity: Using Hand Spans to Measure

Have students measure their hand spans, the distance from the tip of the little finger to the tip of the thumb when the hand is spread wide. Tell them that they can use this measure to estimate lengths when they have no measuring tool. Invite them to use their hand spans to estimate measures of their desks, books, and so on. They can check their estimates by measuring the items with a ruler.

Practice

For Exercises 2–7, ask students to tell which place they need to consider when comparing the numbers in each pair.

Assignment Guide
- Beginning 1–7, 8–14 even
- Intermediate 1–7, 9–13 odd, 14
- Advanced 1–10, 12–14

Notes on Exercises
Exercise 7 Be sure that students recognize that inserting zeros at the end of a number after the decimal point does not change the value of the number.

Exercises 8–10 Point out that even though baseball statistics are called "percentages," which literally imply hundredths ("per hundred"), the numbers are actually expressed as decimals to the nearest *thousandth*, not hundredth.

Exercise 9 Be sure students know that to find a number between 0.537 and 0.463, they will need to find a number greater than 0.463 and less than 0.537.

Exercise 14 Ask, *How do you know which answer is correct?* Listen for correct use of vocabulary.

Look and Read

Practice

1. Write a decimal number for each grid on the left. Then compare the two decimal numbers.

Use <, =, or > to compare the numbers in each pair.

2. 153.072 and 151.8   **3.** 0.0307 and 0.0316
4. 12.052 and 12.0503   **5.** 78.01 and 70.81
6. 0.0053 and 0.00503   **7.** 25.17 and 25.170

The list below shows the winning percentages for 6 baseball teams near the end of a season. The percentages are written as decimals. Use the list for Exercises 8–11.

Chicago Cubs	0.543
Cincinnati Reds	0.426
Houston Astros	0.537
Milwaukee Brewers	0.420
Pittsburgh Pirates	0.463
St. Louis Cardinals	0.525

8. Which team had the greatest winning percentage?
9. Which team(s) had a winning percentage that was between those of the Astros and the Pirates?
10. List the percentages in order, from least to greatest.
11. Which team had the least percentage of wins?

Use the nutrition information shown in the table on the left.
12. Tell how you can find the least and greatest numbers.
13. Compare the numbers for sodium and for potassium. Tell which place lets you compare the two numbers. Does the cereal have more potassium or more sodium?
14. (MULTIPLE CHOICE) Which number is *not* between 45.72 and 45.8?
A. 45.726   **B.** 45.797   **C.** 45.09   **D.** 45.778

▲ Philadelphia Phillies' Jimmy Rollins swings during a game against the St. Louis Cardinals.

Chompo Oat Cereal (1 serving) Ingredients (in grams)	
Total Fat	1.5
Cholesterol	0.3
Sodium	0.350
Potassium	0.360
Carbohydrates	38

Program Resources
Practice Book Use page 26.
Overhead Transparencies Use 15.

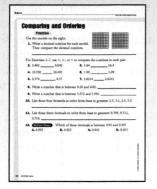

Answers
1. 0.4, 0.04; 0.4 > 0.04
2. >
3. <
4. >
5. >
6. >
7. =
8. Chicago Cubs
9. St. Louis Cardinals
10. 0.420, 0.426, 0.463, 0.525, 0.537, 0.543
11. Milwaukee Brewers
12. Sample: Write the numbers in order from least to greatest. Then choose the first and the last.
13. hundredths place; potassium
14. C

Activities

Organizing When you organize information, you arrange it in a way that is easy to use. Sometimes you do this in a table. Work with a partner to complete the sales table on the right.

In the year 2000, *TIME* sold about 4.07 million copies of each issue, *Reader's Digest* sold about 12.61 million copies of each issue, and *Smithsonian Magazine* sold about 2.06 million copies of each issue. In 2003, the number of copies sold were 4.10 million for *TIME*, 11.07 million for *Reader's Digest*, and 2.03 million for the *Smithsonian*.

1. **Make** Set up a table to organize the information above. Use the columns for years and use the rows for different magazines. Copy the table shown to help you.

2. **Explain** Tell how you can use your table to show how sales changed from the year 2000 to the year 2003.

3. **Describe** Talk about a magazine you like. Tell what you like about it.

Hands On

Line 'Em Up! Work in small groups. Each person in the group should use one or more grids to shade a decimal number. As a group, list all the numbers represented on the grids. Make sure the decimal points are lined up. Finally, order the numbers in the list from least to greatest.

Partner Practice

Order in the Library Some libraries use the Dewey Decimal System to assign decimal numbers to books. This is how they organize the books. The books on the right are in order by decimals, least to greatest, but the decimal labels have fallen off. Work with a partner to match each book to its label.

792.3   156.2   431.77   278.51   311.0

129.86 598.43

Develop Language

Teach Organizing

- You may want to work with students as they construct their tables. Suggest that they draw both vertical and horizontal rules to make sure that they write all the information in the correct places.

- Ask volunteers to write the number of copies as standard-form numbers. These numbers might be more meaningful to the class.

- You might want to have copies of each of the magazines available for the students to see.

Hands On

Suggest that the numbers students shade in the grids be no greater than 2. Encourage them to give numbers to both tenths and hundredths.

Partner Practice

You might suggest that students choose from the school library several nonfiction books in different areas that interest them. Have them compare the decimal numbers on the spines and order the numbers from least to greatest.

Answer: 129.86, 156.2, 278.51, 311.0, 431.77, 598.43, 792.3

Activity: Culture Connection

The Dewey Decimal System is used in many libraries. This system organizes nonfiction books into ten main groups and uses decimal numbers to categorize topics. For an animated tour, further explanations, and activities, have students check out:

- http://www.oclc.org/dewey/resources/tour
- http://library.thinkquest.org/5002

Assessment Book

Use page 32 to assess students' comprehension.

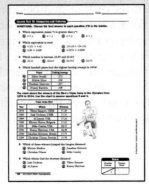

Program Resources

Practice Book Use page 27.

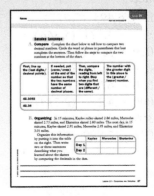

Adding and Subtracting

STANDARDS CONTENT

Mathematics
- Add decimals
- Subtract decimals

Language
- Summarize information

Introduce the Big Idea

Read aloud the Big Idea. On the board, write different amounts of money, some less than $1 and some more. Ask, *Which digits represent ones? Tenths? Hundredths?* Then have students talk about how these places are related to dollars, dimes, and cents. Ask volunteers to show how they would add or subtract several of the money amounts.

Begin Building Background

Explain that this group of young people is camping. Here, they are roasting marshmallows. Ask volunteers to describe their camping experiences.

Teach Key Concepts

Ask a volunteer to tell how to line up the digits and compute 4,289 − 865 (*3,424*). Point out any regrouping that is necessary. Then tell the class that adding and subtracting decimals is done in the same way, after lining up the decimal points.

Warm-Up Review

Have students find each sum or difference.

1. 562 + 6,495 (*7,057*)
2. 8,887 − 3,521 (*5,366*)
3. 4,029 + 558 (*4,587*)
4. 782 − 359 (*423*)
5. 5,000 + 678 (*5,678*)
6. 7,000 − 4,286 (*2,714*)
7. 2,309 + 3,865 (*6,174*)
8. 8,021 − 7,889 (*132*)

Adding and Subtracting

Big Idea Dollars and cents use decimal numbers to the hundredths place. Adding or subtracting amounts of money is the same as adding or subtracting decimals.

Building Background

▲ When I go camping with my family, I take my guitar.

- Describe what these people are doing.
- Do you like to go camping? Where do you go?
- Tell some of the items you would need on a camping trip.

Key Concepts

When you add or subtract whole numbers, you sometimes need to **regroup** by writing a number in a different form. Regrouping to add or subtract decimal numbers is like regrouping to add or subtract whole numbers.

Operation	Example	Regrouping
Add	$\overset{11}{25.7}$ $+18.9$ $\overline{44.6}$	7 + 9 = 16 **Regroup** 16 as 10 + 6. 1 + 5 + 8 = 14 **Regroup** 14 as 10 + 4.
Subtract	$\overset{6\ 15}{4.75}$ -1.38 $\overline{3.37}$	75 = 70 + 5 **Regroup** 75 as 60 + 15

 Activity: Three's a Regroup

Give pairs of students a set of number cards 0–9. Have them choose three or four number cards and make a 3- or 4-digit number. Have partners take turns renaming the numbers to regroup a 10 as 1s, a 100 as 10s, and a 1,000 as 100s. For example, 572 with a 10 regrouped as 1s is 500 + 60 + 12. Partners should check each other's regrouping.

Resource Library

Math at Hand
Adding and Subtracting Decimals
101, 118–126, 129–133, 135

Math on Call
Adding and Subtracting Decimals
91, 96–99, 101–103, 125–129, 131

Adding Decimals

Your cousin is going to day camp. You are shopping with her. What is the total cost of a canteen ($3.50), a backpack ($6.39), and a camp T-shirt ($9.95)?

The costs of the items are given in decimal numbers. To add decimal numbers, *first write the numbers so the decimal points line up.* Then write another decimal point, also lined up, in the sum.

```
   3.50      Line up the
   6.39      decimal points.
 + 9.95
            Write another
   .    ←   decimal point
            for the sum.
```

To add, start with the column all the way to the right. Then work to the left, one column at a time. Add as with whole numbers. The total cost of the 3 items is $19.84.

```
   1 1
   3.50
   6.39
 + 9.95
  19.84
```

- 0 + 9 + 5 = 14
- **Regroup 14 as 4 + 10.**
- 1 + 5 + 3 + 9 = 18
- **Regroup 18 as 8 + 10.**
- 1 + 3 + 6 + 9 = 19

Items for Day Camp
- Canteen $3.50
- Backpack $6.39
- Camp T-shirt $9.95
- Insect Spray $2.59
- Bandages $1.98

▲ Bandages

When you add decimal numbers, always start by lining up the decimal points and the columns of digits. For example, to add 8.06, 14.283, and 1.2, line up the decimal points. Write extra zeros so that each number has the same number of decimal places. Then add.

```
  1 1
  8.060      Write extra zeros so
 14.283      that all 3 numbers
+ 1.200      have the same number
 23.543      of decimal points.
```

Talk and Share

Discuss the items for day camp with your partner. Which would cost more, the insect spray, bandages, and a T-shirt, or two canteens and a backpack? Agree on a plan to answer the question, and then follow your plan. Why do you need to line up the decimal points before you add decimal numbers?

VOCABULARY
regroup—rewrite a number as a sum of different numbers

◀ Backpack

Teach Adding Decimals

- Ask a volunteer to read aloud the camp-supply list so that students know which prices are being added in the example.
- Have students round each number to the nearest whole number and estimate the sum before you address the worked-out examples.
- Work through the first example on the board, pointing out how the decimal points have been lined up. Discuss the two regroupings.
- Ask, *In the second example, why can you write zeros at the end of 8.06 and 1.2? (Adding zeros at the end does not change the numbers' value.)*
- Ask volunteers to choose different combinations of items from the camp-supply list. Have them write the prices on the board and find the sums.

Talk and Share

- Be sure that students realize that the second group of items involves *two* canteens. Ask, *How many numbers will you add? (3 numbers)*
- The first group of items ($14.52) costs more than the second group ($13.39). Ask volunteers to show the sums and to find their difference ($1.13).

Differentiating Instruction

Beginning
Using Grids to Add Decimals Give students 10-by-10 grids (Overhead Transparency 15). On the board, write addition problems such as *0.8 + 0.32* and *0.52 + 0.73.* Ask students to shade their grids, using a different color for each number. Have them write each sum.

Intermediate
Adding Decimals Have each student write three different numbers with two or three decimal places on three small slips of paper. Place the slips of paper facedown and mix. Have each student choose three slips of paper, find the sum, and explain his or her procedures.

Advanced
Explaining Addition of Decimals On the board, write *0.86 + 7.93 + 8.995.* Have students write several sentences explaining how to find the sum. They should rewrite the problem in vertical format and address the necessary regroupings. Have them compare their explanations.

 Activity: Add 'Em Up!

Give each small group a set of cards with names and prices of beach items, such as *sunglasses, $12.95; towel, $9.49; bathing suit, $49.99; sun-block lotion, $6.95;* and *sandals, $3.98.* Have each member of the group select a card and read aloud the name and the price. Have them work together to find the total price of the items. They can use estimation and/or calculators to check their totals. Have them mix the cards and repeat the activity several times.

Teach Subtracting Decimals

- For each example, have students estimate the difference before discussing the procedure.

- Stress again the necessity of lining up the decimal points before computing. Ask, *What is the first step in subtracting?* Then ask, *Can you subtract 8 from 5? What must you do?* Show on the board that the 7 tenths 5 hundredths must be regrouped as 6 tenths 15 hundredths in order to subtract.

- With the second example, be sure students understand why they can rewrite 34.6 as 34.60. In this example, two different numbers have to be regrouped.

- In the third example, the two zeros represent cents. Point out that the zero in the tenths place cannot be regrouped, so the 10 ones are regrouped as 9 ones 10 tenths. Then the 10 tenths can be regrouped as 9 tenths 10 hundredths.

Talk and Share

Students may notice that because the more expensive item is the same in each combination (*the backpack*), they merely need to compare the costs for the insect spray and the canteen.

Answer: backpack and canteen

Build VOCABULARY

On the board, write a variety of addition and subtraction problems involving decimals. Be sure to include types that involve regrouping. Then give students completion sentences referring to the problems. Here are some examples: When I add 8 tenths, 9 tenths, and 7 tenths, I regroup the sum as <u>4</u> tenths <u>2</u> ones. When I subtract 48 hundredths from 80 hundredths, I have to regroup <u>8</u> tenths as <u>7</u> tenths <u>10</u> hundredths.

Look and Read

Subtracting Decimals

How much more does a tent cost than a sleeping bag? To answer this question, subtract the decimal numbers.

Tent $29.75
Sleeping Bag   14.68

Line up the decimal points and write one for the difference.	$29.75 \\ -14.68 \\ \hline $	$\overset{6\,15}{29.7\cancel{5}} \\ -14.68 \\ \hline 15.07$	Start at the right. Regroup so you can subtract.

The tent costs $15.07 more than the sleeping bag. For this problem, you regrouped by moving a 10 from the 7 to the 5 to get 15. Then you could subtract the 8.

Write in extra zeros as needed so the columns of numbers line up. Remember, you may write in zeros at the *end* of a decimal number without changing its value.

In a science class project, one watermelon grew to be 34.6 cm long and another was 29.42 cm long. What is the difference in the lengths of the two watermelons?

Line up the decimal points and write one for the difference.	Write a zero so the numbers have the same number of decimal places.	Now regroup and subtract.
$34.6 \\ -29.42 \\ \hline $	$34.60 \\ -29.42 \\ \hline $	$\overset{2\,14\,5\,10}{3\cancel{4}.\cancel{6}\cancel{0}} \\ -29.42 \\ \hline 5.18$

▲ Watermelons

The difference in the two lengths is 5.18 cm.

If you buy the insect spray and pay with a $10 bill, what is your change? Now you will have to regroup several times.

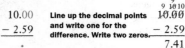

Insect Spray $2.59

$10.00 \\ -2.59 \\ \hline $	Line up the decimal points and write one for the difference. Write two zeros.	$\overset{9}{}\overset{9\,\,10\,10}{1\cancel{0}.\cancel{0}\cancel{0}} \\ -2.59 \\ \hline 7.41$	Start at the right. Now regroup and subtract.

The change from $10 is $7.41.

Talk and Share

Work with a partner. Look back at the list on page 71. Find which is less, the difference in cost between the insect spray and the backpack, or the difference in cost between the backpack and the canteen.

Canteen ▶

◢ Differentiating Instruction

Beginning
Using Grids to Subtract Decimals
Give students 10-by-10 grids and subtraction problems such as 0.84 − 0.41, 0.5 − 0.39, and 1.2 − 0.73. Have students shade the first number in each pair, *X* out small squares to show the number being subtracted, and write the difference.

Intermediate
Subtracting Decimals Have each student write two different numbers with several decimal places on two

small slips of paper. Then have students place the slips of paper facedown and mix them up. Have students choose two slips of paper, find the difference, and explain the regrouping.

Advanced
Explaining Subtraction Steps On the board, write *7.01 − 3.885*. Have students talk about how to do subtraction and then write several sentences explaining the procedure. Tell them to be sure to explain the regrouping.

Practice

Find each sum or difference.
1. $23.75 + $98.86
2. 3.025 − 1.98
3. 101.1 + 101.01 + 101.099
4. $42 − $15.77
5. 618 + 0.618 + 618.618
6. 123.5 − 87.062

Use mental math to find each sum or difference.
7. 10.5 − 8
8. 1.1 + 2.2 + 3.3
9. 0.1 + 0.02 + 0.003
10. 19.47 − 12.47

For Exercises 11–12, use the list of items at the right.
11. What is the total cost of all 4 items on the list?
12. What is your change if you buy the first-aid kit and the towel and pay with a $20 bill?

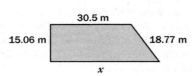

Also needed for Camp
First-aid kit $4.98
Towel   5.19
Swim suit   22.50
Sun block   3.49

13. A student added 0.8 and 0.5 and got a sum of 0.13. What did that student do wrong?

The sum of the lengths of the sides of the field below is 115 meters. Use that information for Exercises 14–16.
14. Write an expression for the sum of the lengths of all sides of the field.
15. Find the length of the side labeled x.
16. What is the difference between the lengths of the two shortest sides?

30.5 m
15.06 m   18.77 m
x

17. (EXTENDED RESPONSE) One triangle has side lengths that are 15.2 units, 11.08 units, and 13.59 units. Another triangle has side lengths that are 16.97 units, 16.23 units, and 9.6 units. Find the sum of the lengths of the sides of each triangle. Then find the difference of the sums for the two triangles.

18. (SHORT RESPONSE) Denzel paddled his kayak for 5 days. His daily distances in miles were 3.4, 4.7, 5.1, 4.4, and 3.5. Round each distance to the nearest whole number. Then add to estimate how many miles he paddled altogether.

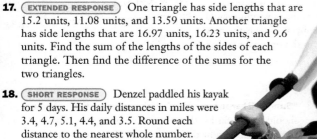
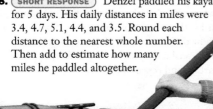

Practice

Before students begin the assignment, have volunteers read Exercises 1–6 aloud and supply an estimate for each answer.

Assignment Guide
- Beginning 1–12, 14–18 even
- Intermediate 1–18
- Advanced 1–18

Notes on Exercises
Exercise 12 Have students use play money to act out making change with some of the items in this exercise and those on page 71. For instance, ask, *How much change would you get if you gave $10 for a towel?* Have the students practice adding back the change: $5.19, $5.20, $5.25, $5.50, $5.75, $6.00, $7.00, $8.00, $9.00, $10.00.

Exercise 17 Suggest that students draw a diagram of each triangle and label each diagram with the dimensions before they find the sums.

Exercise 18 Have students find Denzel's actual distance (*21.1 mi*) for comparison.

Answers
1. $122.61
2. 1.045
3. 303.209
4. $26.23
5. 1,237.236
6. 36.438
7. 2.5
8. 6.6
9. 0.123
10. 7.00
11. $36.16
12. $9.83

13. Sample: He added 8 tenths and 5 tenths and wrote the answer as 13 hundredths. He should have regrouped the tenths to get 1.3.
14. 15.06 + 30.5 + 18.77 + x
15. 50.67 m
16. 3.71 m
17. 39.87 units; 42.8 units; 2.93 units
18. 21 mi

Program Resources
Practice Book Use page 28.

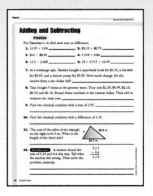

Teach Summarizing

■ Tell students that the word *summarize* means "to give a summary." The word *summary* comes from the Latin *summa*, which means "sum." So when students *summarize*, they should include all the important ideas.

■ Have students follow the pattern shown for "Adding Decimals" to write their summaries.

Partner Practice

The new sum is always twice the greater addend. The new difference is always twice the lesser addend.

Oral Language

You will need to prepare a set of decimal cards for this activity, or have students prepare them. The numbers should have no more than three digits so that students are able to talk about them.

Develop Language

Adding Decimals

Terms/ideas sum; regroup; line up the decimal points

Skill adding columns of numbers

Steps

1. Line up decimal points.
2. Write zeros after the decimal part so the numbers have the same number of decimal places.
3. Write a decimal point for the sum.
4. Starting at the right, add columns of digits.

Activities

Summarizing When you summarize mathematics information, you should list the key terms and ideas, describe the ideas and skills involved, and list the steps you should follow. At the left is one way to summarize adding decimals.

Work with a partner.

1. **Explain** Tell why it is important to summarize information as you read or study.

2. **Summarize** Make a list like the one shown to summarize the information you learned about subtracting decimals. Compare your list with your partner's.

Partner Practice

How Does It Work? Work with a partner. Each partner should write a decimal number. One partner should find the sum of the two numbers, and the other partner should find the difference of the two numbers.

Then find both the sum and the difference of your two results. How is the new sum related to one of the original numbers? How is the new difference related to one of the original numbers?

Sample

Your number: 7.35
Partner's number: 6.19
Sum: $7.35 + 6.19 = 13.54$
Difference: $7.35 - 6.19 = 1.16$
New sum: $13.54 + 1.16 = 14.70$
New difference: $13.54 - 1.16 = 12.38$

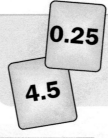

Oral Language

"Sum" Differences Work with a partner. Each of you should have a card with a decimal number. One of you should describe how to find the sum of the two numbers. The other should describe how to find the difference. Choose a new partner and repeat the activity.

Program Resources

Practice Book Use page 29.

Assessment Book

Use page 33 to assess students' comprehension.

Activity: Extend the Lesson

A *palindrome* is a word, sentence, or number that reads the same in both directions, such as "dad." Two famous ones are "Madam, I'm Adam" and "Able was I ere I saw Elba."

Give students these steps to make a palindrome from 125: reverse the digits, 521; add the numbers, 125 + 521 = 646. If this does not give a palindrome, repeat the procedure as many times as necessary. Have partners try the procedure with several numbers.

Talk and Explore

Multiplying and Dividing

Big Idea Travelers often need to change money used in one country to money used in another country. You can change money by multiplying or dividing with decimals.

Building Background

▲ I like to collect coins from the United States and from Chile.

■ What do you think this table is used for?

■ Money has different names in different countries. What different names for money do you know?

■ Where can you change one currency for another?

Key Concepts

Currency is another name for money. To change currency of one country to that of another, you usually multiply or divide by decimal numbers.

If:	$1	=	8.28 yuan
Then:	$30	=	30 × 8.28
		≈	248 yuan

LESSON 12 • MULTIPLYING AND DIVIDING **75**

 Activity: Money Exchange

Give pairs of students cards marked *dollar, half dollar, quarter, dime, nickel,* and *penny* and a number cube. Have them choose one or more cards and take turns explaining how to exchange the greater-value coin for the lesser-value coin. Then have them choose two cards and toss the number cube. They should tell how many of the lesser-value coins could be exchanged for the tossed number of the greater-value coin.

 Resource Library

Math at Hand
Multiplying and Dividing Decimals
107, 113, 121, 137–140, 142–155

Math on Call
Multiplying and Dividing Decimals
152–155, 158–159, 179–181, 184–186

Reader's Handbook (red)
Focus on Math Tests 593–597

Multiplying and Dividing

STANDARDS CONTENT
Mathematics
■ Multiply decimals
■ Divide decimals
Language
■ Demonstrate a procedure

Introduce the **Big Idea**

Read aloud the Big Idea. Discuss with the class whether foreign money can be used in this country. Invite students to share their experiences exchanging one country's money for that of another.

Begin **Building Background**

■ Ask, *Does anyone collect coins? If so, from what countries?*

■ Point out that the photo shows a currency-exchange table used to show how to change one currency to another. *Currency* is the coins and paper money used by a country.

Teach **Key Concepts**

Be sure the students understand why they need to *multiply* to change the yuan to dollars. (*There are more yuan in a dollar than dollars in a yuan.*) Remind students that the symbol ≈ means "is about equal to."

Warm-Up Review

Have students find each answer.
1. 18 × 15 (*270*)
2. 352 ÷ 4 (*88*)
3. 25 × 14 (*350*)
4. 783 ÷ 3 (*261*)
5. 500 × 6 (*3,000*)
6. 420 ÷ 20 (*21*)
7. 657 × 9 (*5,913*)
8. 1,728 ÷ 12 (*144*)

Teach Multiplying Decimals

- Work through the whole-number example on the board, pointing out the factors and the product. Show the regrouping numbers. Be sure the students understand the procedure.

- Have students round the numbers in the second example to the nearest hundred and nearest whole number to estimate the product (*300 × 9 = 2,700*). Then work through the example on the board. Remind students that *decimal places* refers to the number of digits after the decimal point.

- In the third example, students can verify that the decimal point is in the correct position by estimating.

- For the last example, ask, *Why do you need to write two zeros before the 9? (to have 5 decimal places)*

- On the board, write a variety of multiplication problems involving decimals. Provide the products and have students tell or show where to place the decimal points and insert zeros.

Talk and Share

Suggest that students choose numbers greater than 1 with two or three digits. Have them estimate and then compute the answer. They can check by using calculators.

Multiplying Decimals

Do you remember how to multiply whole numbers? You write the two **factors** so they line up on the right side. Then you find the **product**.

$$\begin{array}{r} 437 \\ \times\ 24 \\ \hline 1748 \\ 874 \\ \hline 10{,}488 \end{array}$$

Line up the digits of the factors from the right. ← Factors ← Find the product.

You follow the same steps to multiply a decimal number by a whole number. But after you multiply, you find the sum of the decimal places in all the decimal factors. Then you write the product so it has the same number of decimal places.

Dillon is going to China and wants to **convert** $275 to Chinese yuan. If, on the day he leaves, one U.S. dollar equals 8.68 yuan, he will multiply 275 by 8.68.

$$\begin{array}{r} 275 \\ \times\ 8.68 \\ \hline 2200 \\ 1650 \\ 2\,200 \\ \hline 2{,}387.00 \end{array}$$

275 ← No decimal places
× 8.68 ← 2 decimal places
2,387.00 ← 2 decimal places in all

In the examples below, both factors are decimal numbers. After you multiply, find the total number of decimal places in the factors. Then write the product so that it has that number of decimal places. Notice that you may have to insert zeros at the left to write the product with the correct number of decimal places.

$$\begin{array}{r} 2.37 \\ \times\ 1.24 \\ \hline 948 \\ 474 \\ 237 \\ \hline 2.9388 \end{array}$$

2.37 ← 2 decimal places
× 1.24 ← 2 decimal places
2.9388 ← 4 decimal places

$$\begin{array}{r} 0.054 \\ \times\ 0.17 \\ \hline 378 \\ 54 \\ \hline .00918 \end{array}$$

0.054 ← 3 decimal places
× 0.17 ← 2 decimal places
.00918 ← 5 decimal places

Insert zeros on the left to write the product with 5 decimal places.

Talk and Share

Work with a partner. Each of you should write a decimal number. Discuss how to find the product of the two decimal numbers. Then find the product.

VOCABULARY
factors—numbers that are multiplied
product—the result of multiplying
convert—change, switch, or trade

Activity: How Many Places?

Have pairs of students each write a decimal number. Then have them tell how many decimal places will be in the product of the two numbers. Have them repeat the activity at least ten times.

Differentiating Instruction

Beginning
Using Grids to Multiply Decimals
Give students problems such as 5 × 0.7 and 4 × 0.24. Help students use the repeated-addition concept to shade 10-by-10 grids (Overhead Transparency 15) to find each product.

Intermediate
Describing Decimal Multiplication
On the board, write problems such as *2 × 0.3* and *3 × 0.22*. Ask students to read each aloud; give its product mentally, for instance, *2 times 3 tenths*

equals 6 tenths; and write the product (*0.6*).

Advanced
Modeling Decimal Multiplication
Explain this model to students. Use two different shadings. Then have them model 0.3 × 0.6 and 0.5 × 0.6. Have them tell how they did it.

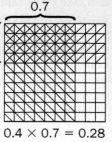

0.4 × 0.7 = 0.28

Dividing Decimals

Do you know the math terms for the parts of a division problem? You divide the **dividend** by the **divisor**. The result is the **quotient**. The same terms are used when you divide with decimals.

$$7)\overline{350} \quad \begin{matrix} 50 \leftarrow \text{quotient} \\ \overline{350} \leftarrow \text{dividend} \end{matrix}$$
divisor

To divide a decimal by a whole number, first write a decimal point for the quotient *directly* above the decimal point in the dividend. Then complete the steps of the division. The quotient is 11.5.

$$5)\overline{57.5}$$
Write a decimal point for the quotient.

To divide a decimal by a decimal, you need to complete one more step *before* you write a decimal point in the quotient.

$$\begin{array}{r} 11.5 \\ 5\overline{)57.5} \\ -5 \\ \hline 7 \\ -5 \\ \hline 25 \\ -25 \\ \hline 0 \end{array}$$

Look at the problem below. There are two decimal places in the divisor, 0.17. Change both the divisor and the dividend by moving the decimal points two places to the right. When you move decimal points two places to the right, you have multiplied both numbers by 100. It does not change the quotient.

$$0.17)\overline{7.157} \rightarrow 0.17)\overline{7.15.7}$$

0.17 has 2 decimal places. So move both decimal points 2 places to the right.

$$17)\overline{715.7} \rightarrow \begin{array}{r} 42.1 \\ 17\overline{)715.7} \\ 68 \\ \hline 35 \\ 34 \\ \hline 17 \\ 17 \\ \hline 0 \end{array}$$

The divisor is now a whole number. Write the decimal point in the quotient and finish the division.

The quotient is 42.1.

LESSON 12 • MULTIPLYING AND DIVIDING **77**

Differentiating Instruction

Beginning
Using Grids to Divide Decimals
Give students problems with a whole-number divisor, such as 0.8 ÷ 2 and 0.25 ÷ 5. Give students 10-by-10 grids and ask them to shade a grid to show the dividend. Then have them draw loops to show the division and write the quotient.

Intermediate
Describing Decimal Division On the board, write problems with a whole-number divisor, such as 0.6 ÷ 2 and

0.18 ÷ 3. Ask students to read each aloud and give its product mentally, for instance, *6 tenths divided by 2 equals 3 tenths.* Then have them write the quotient (*0.3*).

Advanced
Explaining Decimal Division Give students the division problem 0.8704 ÷ 0.34 (*2.56*). Have them explain in several sentences how they would find the quotient. Have them show their work.

Teach Dividing Decimals

- Have students estimate the quotient in the second example to convince them that the procedure is correct.

- Before you begin the third example, write this pattern on the board:

  $8 \div 4 = 2$

  $80 \div 40 = 2$

  $800 \div 400 = 2$

  $8{,}000 \div 4{,}000 = 2$

  Say, *Look at the four division problems. How is the second one different from the first? (Both parts have been multiplied by 10.) Has the answer changed? (no)* Repeat with the remaining divisions to help students understand that if they multiply both the divisor and the dividend by the same power of 10, the quotients are the same.

- Then write this pattern on the board to show how to use mental math to multiply by powers of 10:

  $0.5 \times 1 \qquad = 0.5$

  $0.5 \times 10 \qquad = 5$

  $0.5 \times 100 \qquad = 50$

  $0.5 \times 1{,}000 = 500$

Talk and Share

Encourage students to choose numbers greater than 1 so that they can estimate their quotients. Then have them compute. They can check by using a calculator.

Build **VOCABULARY**

On the board, write a variety of multiplication and division problems with decimals. Then give students completion sentences referring to the problems. Here are some examples: When I multiply two factors, the answer is the <u>product</u>. To divide 56 by 1.4, I have to first multiply both numbers by <u>10</u>. The product of 8.29 and 6.2 will have <u>three</u> decimal places.

Practice

Ask volunteers to supply estimates for the answers to Exercises 1–13 before you make the assignment. With some exercises, for instance Exercise 4, they will be able to say only that the product is less than 1. After students complete these exercises, you may wish to let them check their answers by using a calculator.

Assignment Guide
- Beginning 1–14, 16
- Intermediate 1–16, 18
- Advanced 1–18

Notes on Exercises

Exercise 3 Students will need to insert a zero at the right in the quotient before placing the decimal point.

Exercise 4 Students will need to insert zeros at the left in the product before placing the decimal point.

Exercise 10 Be sure students know they will have to insert zeros to the right of 3,200 in order to divide.

Look and Read

Practice

Rewrite each answer with a decimal point in the correct position.

1. $27.1 \times 1.42 = 38482$ **2.** $67.5 \div 54 = 125$

3. $465 \div 0.31 = 150$ **4.** $0.22 \times 0.007 = 154$

Copy the problem and replace each ■ with the correct digit. Then write the product with the correct number of decimal places.

5.
$$\begin{array}{r} 20.5 \\ \times\ 8.1 \\ \hline 2\blacksquare\blacksquare \\ 1\blacksquare 4\ 0 \\ \hline \blacksquare\blacksquare\blacksquare\blacksquare \end{array}$$

6.
$$\begin{array}{r} 0.67 \\ \times\ 0.03 \\ \hline \blacksquare\blacksquare\blacksquare\blacksquare \end{array}$$

7.
$$\begin{array}{r} 1,358 \\ \times\ 0.29 \\ \hline 1\blacksquare\blacksquare\blacksquare 2 \\ \blacksquare 7\blacksquare\blacksquare \\ \hline \blacksquare\blacksquare\blacksquare\blacksquare\blacksquare \end{array}$$

Find each quotient or product.

8. $81\overline{)86.67}$ **9.** $0.07\overline{)0.238}$ **10.** $1.28\overline{)3,200}$

11. 243×9.5 **12.** 0.047×3.8 **13.** 6.76×1.21

14. In Mexico, the Guyer family spent 475 pesos at a restaurant. One Mexican peso is 0.098 U.S. dollar. Multiply 475 by 0.098 to find the cost in U.S. dollars.

15. Pony Express riders delivered mail in the 1860s. A rider often carried about 1,000 letters. If each letter weighed about 0.6 ounce, find the weight of the mail.

For Exercises 16–18, use these exchange values.
  1 U.S. dollar = 8.28 Chinese yuan
  1 U.S. dollar = 6.18 Egyptian pounds

16. What is the value in U.S. dollars of 345.69 Chinese yuan? Calculate the answer by dividing 345.69 by 8.28.

17. What is the value in U.S. dollars of 930.09 Egyptian pounds? Calculate the answer by dividing 930.09 by 6.18.

18. (EXTENDED RESPONSE) What is the total value in U.S. dollars of 293.94 Chinese yuan and 219.39 Egyptian pounds? Explain how you found your answer.

Program Resources

Practice Book Use page 30.

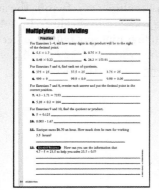

Answers

1. 38.482
2. 1.25
3. 1,500
4. 0.00154
5. 205, 1640, 166.05
6. 0.0201
7. 12222, 2716, 393.82
8. 1.07
9. 3.4
10. 2,500
11. 2,308.5
12. 0.1786
13. 8.1796

14. $46.55
15. 600 oz
16. $41.75
17. $150.50
18. $71.00; I divided 293.94 by 8.28 to find the value of the yuan ($35.50) and 219.39 by 6.18 to find the value of the pounds ($35.50); then I added the two quotients.

Activities

Demonstrating When you demonstrate, you show how something is done. Work with a partner to demonstrate how to convert currencies. Find a list of the latest currency exchange rates in a newspaper.

Sometimes a table shows the number of U.S. dollars in one unit of another country's money. For example, on the day this table was printed, one U.S. dollar was equal to 3.47 Peruvian sols.

1. **Demonstrate** Show how to convert $78 to sols by multiplying the dollars by 3.47.

2. **Demonstrate** One U.S. dollar is equal to 107.305 Japanese yen. Show how to convert $250 to Japanese yen by multiplying the number of dollars by 107.305.

3. **Explain** You multiply to change dollars to yen. Tell what you must do to convert Japanese yen to U.S. dollars.

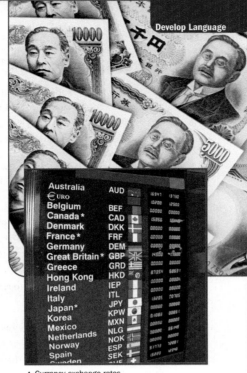

▲ Currency exchange rates

Oral Language

Are You Close? Work with a partner. Each of you should have a card with a decimal number on it. Read the number on your partner's card. *Estimate* the product of your two numbers while your partner *computes* the product. Compare answers. If your answers are not close, discuss why not and then compute the product again. Repeat the activity with a new partner.

Partner Practice

Pony Express Back in the 1860s, mail was carried by riders on horseback. One system was called the Pony Express. In those days, it cost $5 to send a letter by Pony Express, and that was a lot of money! One 1860 dollar would be worth about $21.28 today. How much, in today's dollars, did it cost to send a letter by Pony Express?

LESSON 12 • MULTIPLYING AND DIVIDING **79**

Teach Demonstrating

■ Tell students that to *demonstrate* something is to show or to tell clearly how it is done. In this activity, students' demonstrations will probably involve only paper and pencil.

■ Students should realize that if they multiply to change dollars to a foreign currency, they should divide to change that foreign currency to dollars.

■ Students might want to follow the daily changes in currency rates by consulting the Internet.

Oral Language

For easier estimating, students should choose numbers greater than 1.

Partner Practice

It would cost $106.40 to send a letter by Pony Express in today's dollars. Have partners discuss whether they think that is a great deal of money to send a letter by Pony Express, considering the time, distances, dangers, and so on.

Key Connection

The Pony Express was established in 1860 and dissolved in 1861 after the transcontinental telegraph came into being. The trail ran 1,966 miles from St. Joseph, MO, to Sacramento, CA. The trip took about ten days.

Activity: Extend the Lesson

Have students find products of numbers and powers of 10. Then have them find quotients of whole or decimal numbers divided by powers of 10. Have them write two mental math rules for multiplying when one factor is a power of 10 and dividing when the divisor is a power of 10. (*To multiply, move the decimal point to the right as many places as there are zeros. To divide, move the decimal point to the left as many places as there are zeros.*)

Assessment Book

Use page 34 to assess students' comprehension.

Program Resources

Practice Book Use page 31.

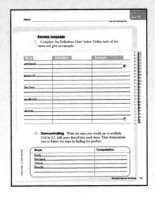

Guess, Check, and Revise

STANDARDS CONTENT

Mathematics
■ Solve problems by guessing, checking, and revising

Language
■ Know when to use *too* and *very*

Teach Guess, Check, and Revise

■ Have a volunteer read aloud the first paragraph. Ask, *Do you think this is a good problem-solving method? Have you ever used it?*

■ Work through the solution to the problem. Encourage students to make "educated" guesses when they solve this type of problem. Here they might round $5.50 to $6 and divide 44 by 6. In this case, their first guess would be 7.

Talk and Share

■ Students should recognize that any odd number times $5.50 will give an amount with $0.50, so the number must be even.

■ If they try 10 as their first guess, students can use mental math to multiply and find that $55 is too much.

Build VOCABULARY

Discuss the three terms in the title. Tell students that to *guess*, they should think first and then make an *educated* guess. Ask, *If I tell you my secret number has only one digit, will you guess 45? Why or why not?*

Ask, *What does it mean to* check? (*see if something is correct*) They should be familiar with checking answers.

The word *revise* means to "see again" in order to improve or correct.

Problem-Solving Skills

Guess, Check, and Revise

One way to solve a problem is to guess the answer and check to see if it works. If it doesn't, you revise your guess and check again.

Problem: You want a new skateboard that costs $140. You have $96 and can save $5.50 each week. How many weeks will it take for you to save enough money for the skateboard?

Read and Understand

Need to find: The number of weeks you need to save money for the skateboard

You know: The cost of the skateboard is $140. You have $96. You can save $5.50 each week.

Key fact: You need to save $140 – $96, or $44.

Plan and Solve

Guess: Try 6 weeks as a solution.

Check: 6 weeks at $5.50 per week is $33. You know that you need to save $44, so the guess of 6 weeks is too low.

Revise: Try 7 weeks.

Check: 7 weeks at $5.50 per week is $38.50. This is still too low, but closer.

Revise: Try 8 weeks as a solution.

Check: 8 weeks at $5.50 per week is $44. Yes!

Answer At $5.50 a week, you need to save for 8 weeks.

Look Back For the Revise step, you check to see if the current guess gives you number that is too small or too large. That helps you make your next guess.

Guess Select a value.

Chec Does that solve th probler

Revise Was your value too high or too low?

Talk and Share

Talk with a partner and decide whether the number 6 was a good first try. Tell how you know after a couple of guesses that the number of weeks has to be an even number. Would 10 be a good first guess? Explain.

Differentiating Instruction

Beginning
Explaining Strategies Play "Guess My Number" with students, giving simple clues such as, *My number is between 10 and 20. It can be divided by 2, 3, and 6. It does not end in 2.* Have students explain their strategies as they try to guess your number (*18*).

Intermediate
Writing Riddles Have pairs of students take turns making up riddles. They should think of a number, perform several operations using that number,

and give their partner the final result. The partner should use a guess-and-check strategy to find the number.

Advanced
Creating a Magic Square Give students the square shown below. Have them create a "magic square" using the numbers 1–9 once each. The sum in each row, column, and diagonal is the same (*15*). One solution is given.

4	9	2
3	5	7
8	1	6

Bottle caps ▶

Use the strategy *guess, check, and revise.*

1. You have $42.50 and can save $8.50 each week. How many weeks will you need to save for shoes that cost $85? What would your first guess be? Why?

2. Your class saves bottle caps for a charity drive. Your class has 4,000 bottle caps and plans to save 175 more each week. How soon will you have more than 8,000 bottle caps?

3. You have 42 feet of paper for two banners. One banner should be 4 feet longer than the other. How long will each banner be?

4. Adult tickets for a dance were $6 each and student tickets cost $3 each. The value of the 370 tickets sold is $1,560. How many adults bought tickets? How many students?

Choose a strategy and solve the problem.

5. A rectangular pool is 25 feet by 60 feet. Around the pool is a path that is 7 feet wide. How many feet of fencing does it take to go around the outside of the path?

Grammar Spotlight

Using too and very Use *very* when you want to emphasize or stress a description. Use *too* when you want to show that you made a decision.

Example	Purposes
This tea is very *hot.*	You want to stress that the tea is hot.
This tea is too *hot.*	The decision: It is so hot that you can't drink it.
That movie is very *long.*	You want to emphasize that the movie is long.
That movie is too *long.*	The decision: It is so long that you don't want to watch it.

1. Think of two sentences, one with *too* and one with *very*. Say both sentences aloud. Have your partner write them. Check to see if your partner wrote them correctly.

2. Tell your partner why you used *too* and *very* in each sentence.

3. Talk with your partner about how *too* and *very* are used differently.

GUESS, CHECK, AND REVISE **81**

Practice

Have students use a guess, check, and revise strategy to solve some simple equations, such as $5n = 120$, $\frac{96}{x} = 8$, and $35 - a = 18$ (n = *24*, x = *12*, a = *17*). Have them explain their thinking.

Assignment Guide

■ Beginning 1–5

■ Intermediate 1–5

■ Advanced 1–5

Notes on Exercises

Exercises 3 and 5 Encourage students to draw a diagram for each of these exercises so that they can better visualize the problem situation.

Grammar Spotlight

■ Discuss the words *too* and *very* and then read through the examples in the chart.

■ Before assigning the exercises, have students orally finish sentences such as these:

• It is very cold. It is too cold to _____ .

• She ran very slowly. She ran too slowly to _____ .

Answers

1. 5 weeks; answers will vary.

2. 23 weeks

3. 23 ft, 19 ft

4. 150 adults, 220 students

5. 226 ft

Program Resources

Practice Book Use pages 32 and 33.

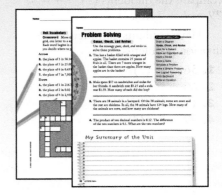

Divisibility

STANDARDS CONTENT

Mathematics
- ■ Tell whether one whole number is divisible by another
- ■ Learn divisibility rules

Language
- ■ Analyze a family of math facts

Introduce the Big Idea

- ■ Read aloud the Big Idea. Ask, *Who can tell me what a* remainder *is?*
- ■ Write *8 ÷ 4, 8 ÷ 3,* and *8 ÷ 2* on the board. Ask, *Which solution has a remainder?* (*8 ÷ 3 = 2 R2*)

Begin Building Background

Have students name events at which a marching band may play. Discuss how the marchers are arranged.

Teach Key Concepts

- ■ Discuss the terms *divisible, factor,* and *multiple.* Students may recall using the term *factor* to name numbers multiplied to find a product.
- ■ Point out that the diagram shows three ways to describe the relationship between 3 and 15.
- ■ Have students describe situations in which they might use the relationships between 3 and 15.

Warm-Up Review

Review division with and without remainders. Write *28 ÷ 4 =* and *29 ÷ 4 =* on the board. Have students complete each number sentence and compare the quotients (*28 ÷ 4 = 7; 29 ÷ 4 = 7 R1*).

Have students complete these division problems.

1. 56 ÷ 8 (*7*)
2. 60 ÷ 7 (*8 R4*)
3. 19 ÷ 8 (*2 R3*)
4. 99 ÷ 9 (*11*)

Divisibility

Big Idea When a number divides another number with no remainder, you can use that information to solve problems involving the two numbers.

Building Background

▲ I love to see the marching bands at football games.

- ■ What are these people doing?
- ■ Describe another way to arrange the band members in equal rows.
- ■ Tell why you cannot arrange the band members in equal rows of 8.

Key Concepts

The number 15 is **divisible** by 3 because there is no remainder from the division. Being divisible by 3 also means that 3 is a **factor** of 15 and that 15 is a **multiple** of 3.

$3 \times 5 = 15$
So 15 is a **multiple** of 3 and a **multiple** of 5.

$15 = 3 \times 5$
So 3 is a **factor** of 15. So is 5.

$3\overline{)15}$
15 is **divisible** by 3 and by 5.

82 Unit 4 • Number Theory

Activity: Is There a Remainder?

Have students list the numbers from 10 through 40 that do *not* have a remainder when divided by 2. Have them describe the pattern of the listed numbers. (*They are even numbers.*)

Point out that another way to say "divided with no remainder" is to say "divisible." Explain that 8 is divisible by 2, but 9 is *not* divisible by 2.

Have students use the word *divisible* as they repeat the activity, dividing by 5 and then by 10. (*They end in 5 or 0; they end in 0.*)

Resource Library

Math at Hand
Divisibility 062

Math on Call
Divisibility 069

Reader's Handbook (red)
Reading Math 117–131

Reader's Handbook (yellow)
Reading Math 88–100

Divisibility

Mr. Mills is trying to decide how to arrange the 18 members of his school band. The diagram shows all the ways he can arrange them in equal rows.

A **factor** of a number divides that number without a **remainder**. The tall, thin rectangle at the right illustrates that every whole number can be divided by 1 and by itself, so 1 and 18 are factors of 18. The other two rectangles show that the numbers 3, 6, 2, and 9 also are factors of 18. So these are all the factors of 18.

$$1, 2, 3, 6, 9, 18$$

Two ideas that are closely related to factors are *multiple* and *divisible*. A **multiple** of a number is the product of that number and another whole number greater than zero. A whole number is **divisible** by a second number if there is no remainder after dividing.

Factors of 18

3×6

1×18

2×9

For the statement $18 \div 9 = 2$, we have the following relationships:

18 is a *multiple* of 9.   18 is a *multiple* of 2.
18 is *divisible* by 9.   18 is *divisible* by 2.
9 is a *factor* of 18.   2 is a *factor* of 18.

Talk and Share

Work with a partner to find the missing numbers for each sentence.

21 is a multiple of 3, so ___ is a factor of ___ and ___ is divisible by ___ .

39 is divisible by 13, so ___ is a factor of ___ and ___ is a multiple of ___ .

VOCABULARY

factor—a whole number that divides another whole number without a remainder
remainder—the amount left after division. When you divide 7 by 2, you get 3 with a remainder of 1.

multiple—the product of a factor and a whole number greater than zero. 35 and 21 are multiples of 7.
divisible—able to be divided without a remainder. 10 is divisible by 5 because $10 \div 5$ is 2 with no remainder.

LESSON 13 • DIVISIBILITY   **83**

Teach Divisibility

■ Elicit the response that all whole numbers have at least two factors and that some whole numbers may have many factors.

■ Demonstrate how to find all factors of 18 by listing the numbers 1–18 on the board. Ask, *Is 1 a factor of 18?* (*yes*) Write *yes* next to the 1. Then ask, *What number times 1 equals 18?* (*18*) Write *yes* next to the 18. Continue from 2 through 6. Ask, *Why can you stop at 6?* (*It has already been identified as a factor.*)

■ Ask students to state the relationships for $18 \div 3$ and explain their reasoning. For example, 18 is divisible by 3 because after dividing there is no remainder.

Talk and Share

Have students work in pairs. As a class, discuss how students know which numbers to use to complete each sentence.

Answers: 3, 21, 21, 3; 13, 39, 39, 13

Build **VOCABULARY**

Point out that a *multiple* of a number results from *multiplying* that number by a number greater than zero. Have students suggest other word clues to help them remember the meanings of *factor* and *divisible*.

Differentiating Instruction

Beginning
Using Rectangular Models Have students use the pictures of rectangles as models to determine divisibility. Point out that each rectangle has exactly 18 small squares. Have them write number sentences to describe each rectangle ($1 \times 18 = 18$, $2 \times 9 = 18$, $3 \times 6 = 18$). Then have pairs of students explain each relationship in the example $18 \div 9$ to reinforce their understanding of the vocabulary terms. For example, *18 is a multiple of 9 because $9 \times 2 = 18$.*

Intermediate
Writing Number Sentences Have student pairs draw a 2-by-3 rectangle and write number sentences to describe the rectangle. Ask them to use the terms *multiple, factor,* and *divisible* to describe the relationships between the numbers 2 and 6.

Advanced
Describing Terms Have students use the terms *multiple, divisible, factor,* and *remainder* to describe the relationships between 10 and 100.

 Activity: Xs Mark the Spots

Have pairs of students draw sixteen *Xs* in equal groups in as many different ways as they can. Have them use the terms *divisible, factor,* and *multiple* to explain their results. (*16 is a multiple of 1, 16, 2, 8, and 4; 16 is divisible by 1, 2, 4, 8, and 16; 1, 2, 4, 8, and 16 are factors of 16.*)

Teach Divisibility Rules

- Students should know that they can divide to see if one number is divisible by another, but that it is faster to use divisibility rules.

- Suggest that students apply the divisibility rules in any order that makes sense to them.

- Ask, *Did you find all of the factors of 96 by using divisibility rules?* (*No; the factors are 1, 2, 3, 4, 6, 8, 12, 16, 24, 32, 48, and 96.*) Have them explain how divisibility rules can help them find factors. (*If a rule finds a factor, look for a number that can be multiplied by that factor to get the product. 3 is a factor of 51; 51 ÷ 3 gives you another factor, 17.*)

Talk and Share

Point out that every whole number is divisible by 1 and by itself, and that these numbers should be included when listing *all* factors.

Answers: 3 and 9; it is also divisible by 1 and the number itself, 27; more information is needed to determine other factors.

Build VOCABULARY

Have students complete these sentences. Every whole number is divisible by 1 and by itself . The numbers 1, 3, 13, and 39 are the only factors of 39 . If a number is divisible by 7, then 7 is a factor of that number.

Divisibility Rules

$$20 = 5 \times 4$$
$$35 = 5 \times 7$$
$$50 = 5 \times 10$$

5 is a factor of 20, 35, and 50.

Are the numbers 20, 35, and 50 divisible by 5? Yes, because each number has 5 as a factor. In fact, if any number has 0 or 5 as the ones digit, then it is divisible by 5.

A **divisibility rule** is a quick way to tell when one number is divisible by another.

Divisibility Rules

A whole number is divisible by	Examples
2 if the ones digit is 0, 2, 4, 6, or 8.	6; 82; 960 (The ones digits are 6, 2, and 0.)
3 if the sum of the digits is divisible by 3.	15; 237 (For 15, 1 + 5 = 6 and 6 is divisible by 3. For 237, 2 + 3 + 7 = 12 and 12 is divisible by 3.)
5 if the ones digit is 0 or 5.	20; 35; 50 (The ones digits are 0, 5, and 0.)
9 if the sum of the digits is divisible by 9.	72; 387 (For 72, 7 + 2 = 9 and 9 is divisible by 9. For 387, 3 + 8 + 7 = 18 and 18 is divisible by 9.)
10 if the ones digit is 0.	10; 170; 12,000 (The ones digits are all 0.)

How do the divisibility rules apply to the number 96?

Is 96 divisible by 2?	Yes; the ones digit is 6.
Is 96 divisible by 3?	Yes; 9 + 6 = 15 and 15 is divisible by 3.
Is 96 divisible by 9?	No; 9 + 6 = 15 and 15 is NOT divisible by 9.
Is 96 divisible by 5?	No; the ones digit is NOT 0 or 5.
Is 96 divisible by 10?	No; the ones digit is NOT 0.

Talk and Share

Work with a partner. The sum of the digits of a number is 27, so that number is divisible by what two numbers? Could the number be divisible by other numbers as well? Explain.

VOCABULARY

divisibility rule—a quick way to tell when one number is divisible by another number

---

Activity: *Div* as a Root

Tell students that the root for *divisibility* is *div*, meaning "separate." Have students list other words that have *div* as the root (*Samples: divide, dividend, divisor, divider, divvy, divert*).

Differentiating Instruction

Beginning

Choosing the Rules Have pairs of students look at the table of divisibility rules on page 84. Have them each write a 2-digit number and circle the ones digit. Ask, *Which divisibility rules use the number in the ones digit?* (*rules for 2, 5, and 10*) *Which divisibility rules use the sum of the digits?* (*rules for 3 and 9*)

Intermediate

Discussing Divisibility Have students work in pairs and take turns telling each other how to use divisibility rules to see if 2, 3, 5, 9, or 10 people can evenly share $60 (*2, 3, 5, or 10 people*).

Advanced

Finding a New Rule Have students refer to the table of divisibility rules on page 84. Challenge pairs of students to find and write a divisibility rule for 6. Have them share the rule with the class. (*A whole number is divisible by 6 if it is divisible by 2 and by 3. The ones digit is an even number and the sum of its digits is divisible by 3.*)

Practice

List all the factors of each number.
1. 12   **2.** 35   **3.** 25   **4.** 48   **5.** 60   **6.** 100

Write 3 sentences using the words *factor*, *multiple*, and *divisible* to describe each pair of numbers.
  7. 8 and 32   **8.** 10 and 90   **9.** 5 and 45

10. Describe the different ways 20 baton twirlers can arrange themselves in equal rows.

Tell whether the first number is divisible by the second number. State the divisibility rule that you use.
11. 150 and 5   **12.** 2,163 and 3   **13.** 2,163 and 9
14. 40,001 and 2   **15.** 22,222 and 3   **16.** 18,360 and 9

Tell whether each number is divisible by 2, 3, 5, 9, or 10.
17. 72   **18.** 84   **19.** 90   **20.** 120   **21.** 125   **22.** 144

23. How do you know that 34 is NOT divisible by 3?

24. (EXTENDED RESPONSE) The Yoshidas are planning to install ceramic floor tiles in a small hallway. The hallway measures 4 feet by 12 feet. Tiles are squares measuring 3, 6, 9, or 12 inches on each side. Which tiles can the Yoshidas use without having to cut any of them to fit?

25. List all whole numbers less than 75 that are divisible by 10. What is a quick way to tell if a number is divisible by 10?

26. (SHORT RESPONSE) Tell why a number divisible by 9 is also divisible by 3.

27. (SHORT RESPONSE) If a number is divisible by 5, is it also divisible by 10? Explain.

28. (EXTENDED RESPONSE) The school dance teams will march in a parade. Each team will be arranged in equal rows. Which team can be arranged in more ways, a team of 20 members or a team of 25? Tell why.

▲ Baton twirlers

LESSON 13 • DIVISIBILITY   **85**

Practice

Review the terms *multiple*, *factor*, *divisible*, and *remainder*. Write *30* on the board. Say, *Use divisibility rules to find if 30 is divisible by 2, 3, 5, 9, or 10 (2, 3, 5, 10)*. Ask, *Are there other factors of 30?* (*yes; 1, 6, 15, 30*) Have a volunteer explain how to find the other factors (*Sample: 30 ÷ 1 = 30, 30 ÷ 2 = 15, 30 ÷ 5 = 6*).

Assignment Guide
■ Beginning 4–12, 16–22 even, 25–27
■ Intermediate 2–22 even, 23–27
■ Advanced 1–23 odd, 24–28

Notes on Exercises
Exercise 10 Model a response such as ____ *rows with* ____ *baton twirlers each* for students to use in the answer, or encourage them to draw pictures.

Exercises 17–22 Remind students to use the divisibility rule for each of the five numbers 2, 3, 5, 9, and 10.

Exercise 24 Have students change 4 ft to 48 in. and 12 ft to 144 in. and then find which tile sizes are factors of both 48 and 144.

Exercise 28 Suggest that students first list all pairs of factors that give a product of 20 and of 25.

Answers
1. 1, 2, 3, 4, 6, 12
2. 1, 5, 7, 35
3. 1, 5, 25
4. 1, 2, 3, 4, 6, 8, 12, 16, 24, 48
5. 1, 2, 3, 4, 5, 6, 10, 12, 15, 20, 30, 60
6. 1, 2, 4, 5, 10, 20, 25, 50, 100
7. 8 is a factor of 32; 32 is a multiple of 8; 32 is divisible by 8.
8. 10 is a factor of 90; 90 is a multiple of 10; 90 is divisible by 10.
9. 5 is a factor of 45; 45 is a multiple of 5; 45 is divisible by 5.
10. 1 by 20, 20 by 1; 2 by 10, 10 by 2; 4 by 5, 5 by 4
11. Yes; the ones digit is 0.
12. Yes; 2 + 1 + 6 + 3 = 12 and 12 is divisible by 3.
13. No; 2 + 1 + 6 + 3 = 12 and 12 is not divisible by 9.
14. No; the ones digit is not 0, 2, 4, 6, or 8.

See Additional Answers, page T39.

Program Resources
Practice Book Use page 34.

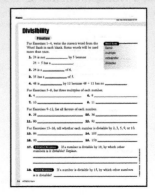

Teach Analyzing

- Explain to students that to *analyze* is to study and then describe the relationships among two or more numbers, objects, or concepts. One way to analyze and show relationships is to use a Web.

- Ask, *What words or phrases were used to describe relationships among numbers in this lesson?* (*multiple, factor, divisible*) Point out that the Web shown describes the relationships among the number sentences in the center. Note the new sentence "18 is the product of 3 and 6."

- After pairs finish their Webs, have volunteers share the ways they stated the relationships among 6, 9, and 54.

Oral Language

- Give each of five students a card labeled 2, 5, 3, 9, or 10. Be sure that numbers are not repeated within a group.

- You may want to model how to state the divisibility rule for a card: *A whole number is divisible by my number if its ones digit is zero.*

Partner Practice

Each pair of students will need twenty number cards to complete the activity as written. You may have students make the cards as part of the activity.

Develop Language

Activities

6 × 3 = 18
18 ÷ 6 = 3
18 ÷ 3 = 6

- 18 is a multiple of 6.
- 18 is a multiple of 3.
- 3 is a factor of 18.
- 18 is the product of 3 and 6.
- 6 is a factor of 18.
- 18 is divisible by 3.
- 18 is divisible by 6.

Analyzing When you analyze numbers, you try to describe how the numbers are related. There are many ways to describe a product and the division statements related to it.

Some of the statements for the numbers 6, 3, and 18 are shown in the Web at the left.

1. **Draw** Draw a Web like the one shown. Fill in the circles with the same sentences but use the numbers 6, 9, and 54.

2. **Analyze** Work with a partner to write sentences that describe how the words *factor*, *product*, *divisible*, and *multiple* are related. Check each other's work.

Oral Language

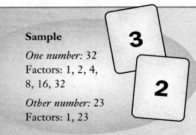

What's My Number? Work with four other students. Each of you should have a card labeled with one of the numbers 2, 3, 5, 9, or 10. Talk to other students. Tell a student the divisibility rule for your number. Then see if that student can identify your number. Switch roles. Let the student tell you his or her divisibility rule. See if you can identify his or her number.

Partner Practice

Sample

One number: 32
Factors: 1, 2, 4, 8, 16, 32

Other number: 23
Factors: 1, 23

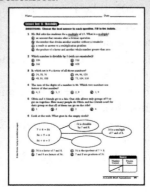

3

2

Factor It In Work with a partner. Place two sets of number cards labeled 0 through 9 into a bag. Take turns selecting two cards. Form a two-digit number and name all the factors of your number. If the two digits are different, switch them to form a new number. Then name the factors of this new number. Your partner should check that you named all the factors of each number. A sample is shown.

Program Resources

Practice Book Use page 35.
Overhead Transparencies Use 33.

Assessment Book

Use page 35 to assess students' comprehension.

Activity: Extend the Lesson

Ask students how many days are in a leap year (*366 days*). Point out that leap years are divisible by 4, so 1964 is a leap year.

Century years are years ending with two zeros, such as 1900. Century years are leap years only if they are divisible by 400. Ask students if 1900 is a leap year (*no; 1900 ÷ 400 = 4.75*).

Have students find which years from 2010 through 2020 are leap years (*2012, 2016, 2020*).

Talk and Explore

Prime and Composite

Big Idea Divisibility rules can help you decide whether a number has factors other than 1 and itself.

Building Background

▲ I have a code that I use with my friends to exchange secret messages.

■ **What are these soldiers doing?**

■ **Give an example of a code for secret messages.**

■ **Why do you think the U.S. army used Navajo speakers to send secret messages during World War II?**

Key Concepts

A **composite number** is a whole number with more than two factors. A **factor tree** shows a way to factor a composite number, such as 30. This tree has branches leading down from 30 to a pair of factors.

If a factor is a composite number, like 6, you break it down into new factors. If a factor is *prime*, like 5, you are finished with that branch. A **prime number** has no factors other than itself and 1. Continue writing factors until all factors are prime numbers.

Factor Tree

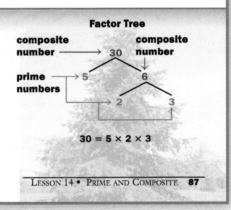

composite number → 30 ← composite number

prime numbers → 5   6

2   3

$30 = 5 \times 2 \times 3$

LESSON 14 • PRIME AND COMPOSITE **87**

Prime and Composite

STANDARDS CONTENT
Mathematics
■ Identify a number as prime or composite
■ Write the prime factorization for a number

Language
■ Recognize multiple meanings of *prime*
■ Describe by providing details

Introduce the **Big Idea**

Read aloud the Big Idea. Ask students what types of problems could be solved using divisibility rules (*grouping, sharing*).

Begin **Building Background**

Read the caption below the student photograph. Tell students that many codes are based on the special qualities of numbers.

Teach **Key Concepts**

Introduce the terms *composite, prime,* and *factor tree*. Tell students that a *factor tree* is a type of graphic organizer used to show the factors of a composite number. Ask, *Why do the branches of this tree end with 5, 2, and 3? (The ends of the branches are the prime factors.)*

Warm-Up Review

Have students find all factors for each number.

1. 16 (*1, 2, 4, 8, 16*)
2. 42 (*1, 2, 3, 6, 7, 14, 21, 42*)
3. 50 (*1, 2, 5, 10, 25, 50*)
4. 65 (*1, 5, 13, 65*)
5. 36 (*1, 2, 3, 4, 6, 9, 12, 18, 36*)
6. 48 (*1, 2, 3, 4, 6, 8, 12, 16, 24, 48*)

 Activity: Arrange the Desks!

Have students draw a diagram to show all the different ways 20 desks can be arranged in rows with an equal number of desks in each row. Then have them list the factors (*1 × 20, 2 × 10, 4 × 5; factors: 1, 2, 4, 5, 10, 20*). Ask, *Is 20 a prime or composite number? (Composite; it has more than two factors.)*

Repeat for 11 desks. (*1 × 11; factors: 1, 11; prime; it has only two factors.*) Ask, *Is this arrangement a practical one?*

 Resource Library

Math at Hand
Prime and Composite Numbers
053–056

Math on Call
Prime and Composite Numbers
058–061, 542

Reader's Handbook (red)
Focus on Math Tests 593–597

Teach Prime and Composite

- Before discussing the Prime/Composite table, point out that prime numbers have exactly two factors. Stress that composite numbers have more than two factors, although the exact number of factors varies.
- Ask, *Why do you think 1 is neither prime nor composite? (It has only one factor, 1.)*
- Discuss how to read the code. Point out that each letter corresponds to a different number.

Talk and Share

Have students work in pairs. Encourage students to expand the key provided on the page or make a key of their own using other symbols. Have students share their codes and messages with the class.

Build VOCABULARY

Have students create a Two-column Chart (Overhead Transparency 29) for the words *prime* and *composite*. Have them write a brief definition and give three examples.

Look and Read

Prime and Composite

Some numbers, such as 3, 11, or 29, have only two factors: 1 and the number itself. Such numbers are called **prime numbers,** or primes. If a number is not prime, then it has more than two factors and is a **composite number.** In the examples below, the number 4 has three factors, and the number 24 has eight factors.

Prime Numbers	Composite Numbers
3: factors are 1 and 3	4: factors are 1, 2, and 4
11: factors are 1 and 11	15: factors are 1, 3, 5, and 15
29: factors are 1 and 29	24: factors are 1, 2, 3, 4, 6, 8, 12, and 24

If you have enough time, you can always break, or solve, a **code** and read the secret message. A code based on very large prime numbers can take a computer years to solve!

Number	Factors	Type
1	1	---
2	1, 2	prime
3	1, 3	prime
4	1, 2, 4	composite
5	1, 5	prime
6	1, 2, 3, 6	composite
7	1, 7	prime

The table on the left lists all the factors of the numbers 1 through 7 and tells whether each number is prime or composite. Note that the number 1 is *neither prime nor composite.*

Here is a simple coded message that uses primes: 3 29 3 23 31

Here is the key to **decode,** or solve, the code:

2 3 5 7 11 13 17 19 23 29 31 37 ...
A E I O U   R   S   T   M   N   Y   H ...

So 3 29 3 23 31 = ENEMY.

Talk and Share

With a partner, write a simple coded message using the key above. Trade messages with other pairs of students and decode.

VOCABULARY

prime numbers—whole numbers greater than 1 whose only factors are 1 and the number itself
composite number—a whole number with more than two factors
code—a system of secret writing
decode—solve a code to read a message

Activity: What Kind of Rectangle?

Have pairs use grid paper (Overhead Transparency 15) to make as many 28-square rectangles as they can. Have them list the factors for 28, classify 28 as composite or prime, and explain their reasoning. Repeat for 17 squares (*28: 1, 2, 4, 7, 14, 28; composite, because it has more than two factors; 17: 1, 17; prime, because it has only two factors*).

Differentiating Instruction

Beginning
Finding a Prime Pattern Ask students to focus on the second table. Have them look for the pattern between the number of factors and the classification as *prime* or *composite.* Then have them state or show that relationship.

Intermediate
Explaining Prime and Composite Ask pairs of students to explain how to tell whether a number is *prime* or *composite.* (*Sample: Try dividing it by 2, 3, 5, 7, 9, and 10.*) Then have them share how they would determine whether 49 is a prime or a composite number (*Divide by 7; composite*).

Advanced
Extending the Prime Table Have pairs of students extend the second table to include the numbers 8–30. Have students list the prime numbers from 2 through 30 (*2, 3, 5, 7, 11, 13, 17, 19, 23, 29*) and explain how they found them.

Prime Factorization

You can use a **factor tree** to find the prime factors of a number. Here are two different factor trees for 180. To make a factor tree, keep drawing branches for the tree until the factor at the end of each branch is a prime number.

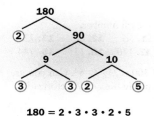

Break each composite number into 2 factors.

Circle the prime number at the bottom of each branch.

A dot centered between 2 numbers is another way to show multiplication.

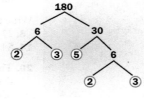

$180 = 2 \cdot 3 \cdot 3 \cdot 2 \cdot 5$

$180 = 2 \cdot 3 \cdot 5 \cdot 2 \cdot 3$

Notice that both sets of prime factors of 180 contain two 2s, two 3s, and one 5. To write the **prime factorization** of a number, write the number as a product of prime numbers. Then use an **exponent** to show factors that repeat.

$180 = 2 \cdot 2 \cdot 3 \cdot 3 \cdot 5$

Write the factors in order, from least to greatest.

$2 \cdot 2 = 2^2$

$3 \cdot 3 = 3^2$

Use exponents to show repeated factors.

So $180 = 2 \cdot 2 \cdot 3 \cdot 3 \cdot 5$
$= 2^2 \cdot 3^2 \cdot 5$

Braille is a code that uses raised dots on paper for letters. Blind people read by feeling the dots. ▼

Talk and Share

Work with a partner. Talk about how you can tell that a prime factorization is correct. Tell whether $225 = 3^2 \cdot 5^2$. Explain your thinking.

VOCABULARY

factor tree—a diagram that shows the prime factors of a number
prime factorization—a product of prime numbers
exponent—a number that tells how many times another number (the base) is used as a factor

Language Notes

Multiple Meanings
This word has more than one meaning.

- prime
1. a number with only two factors, 1 and the number itself
2. of good quality
3. prepare or make ready

Teach Prime Factorization

- Any two factors with a product of 180 can be used as the first branches of the tree, but the prime factorization at the end always will be the same. Two examples are shown.

- On the board, draw a factor tree for 180 with 10 and 18 as the first branches. Ask volunteers to show how to complete the factor tree.

- Be sure students understand that each time they find a prime factor, they should list that number in the prime factorization. Ask, *How can you be sure you have listed all the prime factors?* (Sample: Before using exponents, make sure every circled number is listed.)

Talk and Share

Ask volunteers to share the ways they found to check that the prime factorization is correct.

Sample answer: Check that the numbers are prime numbers. Then multiply the factors in the prime factorization. The product must equal the starting number.

Language Notes

Point out how the word *prime*, shown in red type, is used in the reading. Ask someone to read aloud the other meanings in Language Notes.

Differentiating Instruction

Beginning
Drawing a Factor Tree Ask students to look at the factor tree in the example. Help them to draw a factor tree for 180 starting with 5 and 36 as the first branches. (*Check students' factor trees.*)

Intermediate
Finding a Prime Factorization Have pairs of students explain how to draw a factor tree and how to use that tree to find the prime factorization of 75.

(*Factor trees can begin with 3 and 25 or 5 and 15; $3 \cdot 5^2$.*)

Advanced
Discussing the Differences Have partners explain why two factor trees for the same number can look different. Have them draw two factor trees for 48. (*Sample: Factor trees can begin with 2 and 24, 3 and 16, 4 and 12, or 6 and 8. All end with the prime numbers 2, 2, 2, 2, 3.*)

Activity: It's Not So Prime

Have each student in a pair roll a number cube two times to make a 2-digit number and find the prime factorization for that number. The student with more prime factors in his or her prime factorization scores one point. The first student to score five points wins.

Practice

Review the terms *prime*, *composite*, and *prime factorization*. Have each student write an example of a prime number and a composite number. Then have students explain how to find the prime factorization for the composite number.

Assignment Guide
- Beginning 1–7, 9–21 odd, 23, 26–29
- Intermediate 1–7, 8–26 even, 27–29
- Advanced 1–7, 14–29

Notes on Exercises
Exercises 8–19 Remind students to list the prime factors in order from least to greatest using the prime numbers, not the exponent numbers.

Exercise 22–24 Students should assume that all the tiles are the same size. Remind students that the dimensions of a rectangle are its *length* and its *width*. Review how to state dimensions using *by* or the symbol ×. Some students may find it helpful to model the exercise using grid paper or congruent paper squares.

Exercise 28 Suggest that students use a counterexample such as 121 as part of their explanation. 121 is not divisible by these numbers, but is divisible by 11.

Practice

Tell whether each number is prime or composite.
1. 31   **2.** 39   **3.** 54   **4.** 81   **5.** 97   **6.** 99

7. What prime number is even? Tell why no other even numbers are prime.

Write the prime factorization for each number.
8. 27   **9.** 45   **10.** 49   **11.** 56   **12.** 60   **13.** 72
14. 84   **15.** 96   **16.** 100   **17.** 120   **18.** 125   **19.** 144

20. The prime factorization of 300 is $2^2 \cdot 3 \cdot 5^2$. Can you use that information to write quickly the *prime* factorization of 600? Explain.

21. One factorization of a number is $3 \cdot 5^2 \cdot 14$. What is the *prime* factorization of that number?

22. Reid has 36 small square tiles left over from tiling a floor. He is going to use them to make a rectangular design for a table top. How many different rectangles can he form? Give the dimensions of each rectangle.

23. (SHORT RESPONSE) Can you form a rectangle using any number of small squares? Explain.

24. (SHORT RESPONSE) The number of small squares you have is a prime number. How many different rectangles can you form using all the squares?

Copy and complete each factor tree. Then write the prime factorization for each number.

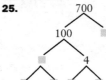   

25. 700 / 100 / 4   **26.** 2,250 / 225 / 25 9

27. (EXTENDED RESPONSE) Draw a factor tree for the prime factorization of 112.

28. (EXTENDED RESPONSE) If a number is not divisible by 2, 3, 4, 5, 6, 9, or 10, is it a prime number? Explain.

29. (MULTIPLE CHOICE) Which number has $2 \cdot 3 \cdot 5^2$ as its prime factorization?
A. 15   **B.** 60   **C.** 150   **D.** 900

Program Resources
Practice Book Use page 36.

Answers
1. prime   **2.** composite
3. composite   **4.** composite
5. prime   **6.** composite
7. 2; all other even numbers have at least three factors: 1, 2, and the number itself.
8. 3^3 **9.** $3^2 \cdot 5$
10. 7^2 **11.** $2^3 \cdot 7$
12. $2^2 \cdot 3 \cdot 5$ **13.** $2^3 \cdot 3^2$
14. $2^2 \cdot 3 \cdot 7$ **15.** $2^5 \cdot 3$
16. $2^2 \cdot 5^2$ **17.** $2^3 \cdot 3 \cdot 5$
18. 5^3 **19.** $2^4 \cdot 3^2$
20. 600 is $2 \cdot 300$, so the prime factorization of 600 has one more factor of 2; so $600 = 2^3 \cdot 3 \cdot 5^2$.
21. $2 \cdot 3 \cdot 5^2 \cdot 7$
22. 5 rectangles: 1 by 36, 2 by 18, 3 by 12, 4 by 9, 6 by 6
23. Yes; the squares match up by sides and you can always make a row of single squares.
24. 1 rectangle
See Additional Answers, page T39.

Activities

Describing When you describe, you tell about the details of something. Here you and a partner each will create a code and write a secret message. Then you will describe your codes to each other and decode your partner's message.

1. **Create** Make up a code by matching numbers with letters.

2. **Write** Provide a key to organize your code. The key shows what number represents each letter.

3. **Describe** Explain your code as you give your partner your secret message and key.

4. **Decode** Solve the codes and read the messages. Check to see if they are correct.

Oral Language

Prime Time Work with a small group. Take turns choosing a number from 25 through 50 and telling the group all the factors of your number. If your number is composite, you also should tell or write the prime factorization.

Partner Practice

Sift Them Out Eratosthenes was a Greek mathematician who lived around 200 B.C. He created a *method*, or way, of finding prime numbers. This method is called the "Sieve of Eratosthenes." A sieve is like a strainer.

Work with a partner to complete a hundred chart like the one on the right. Cross out 1, because it is neither prime nor composite. Circle 2, the first prime. Cross out all other multiples of 2. Then circle 3, the next prime. Cross out all other multiples of 3. Continue this procedure with 5, 7, and 11. The numbers not crossed out are the prime numbers between 1 and 100. Tell what patterns in your chart helped you.

Sieve of Eratosthenes

X	②	3	A	5	6	7	8	9	10
11	12	13	14	15	16	17	18	19	20
21	22	23	24	25	26	27	28	29	30
31	32	33	34	35	36	37	38	39	40
41	42	43	44	45	46	47	48	49	50
51	52	53	54	55	56	57	58	59	60
61	62	63	64	65	66	67	68	69	70
71	72	73	74	75	76	77	78	79	80
81	82	83	84	85	86	87	88	89	90
91	92	93	94	95	96	97	98	99	100

Develop Language

Teach Describing

- Review the meaning of *describe*. Remind students that in addition to using words to write a description, they can also use pictures, diagrams, or photographs.

- Ask students why each code must have a key (*to decipher coded messages*). Be sure students understand that the code they will create should use numbers for letters.

- You may wish to review the code on page 88 with students so that they understand what is expected. Stress that students should write their own key and not use the partial code printed on the page.

Oral Language

Have students work in small groups. Point out that there are multiple parts to the activity. Suggest that students make a list of what is expected and use the list to make sure they cover all points in their discussions.

Partner Practice

- Give each pair of students a hundred chart for this activity.

- Encourage students to list the prime numbers below their "sieves."

See Additional Answers, page T39.

Activity: What Is It?

Tell students that Christian Goldbach, in about 1742, made two guesses. One was that every even number greater than 2 is the sum of two prime numbers. The other was that every odd number greater than 5 is the sum of three prime numbers. Have students test Goldbach's ideas with numbers less than 50 and share their sums.

Assessment Book

Use page 36 to assess students' comprehension.

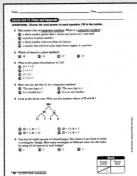

Program Resources

Practice Book Use page 37.

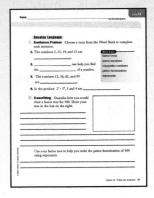

Greatest Common Factor

STANDARDS CONTENT

Mathematics
- Find all common factors of two or more numbers
- Find the greatest common factor (GCF) of two or more numbers

Language
- Recognize the meaning of the idiom *return the favor*
- Respond to an invitation

Materials
- Venn Diagram (Overhead Transparency 31)

Introduce the **Big Idea**

Have a volunteer read aloud the Big Idea. Discuss what *common* means in this context (*shared*). Ask students what one factor is common to all numbers (*1*).

Begin **Building Background**

- Discuss the questions below the picture. Point out that some recycling programs accept parts of computers and other equipment.
- Ask, *What things do you know that are made from recycled items?*

Teach **Key Concepts**

Introduce the vocabulary as you discuss how to use this graphic organizer. Ask, *What does this Venn Diagram show?* (*factors and common factors of 24 and 30*)

Warm-Up Review

Have students list all the factors for each number.

1. 21 (*1, 3, 7, 21*)
2. 31 (*1, 31*)
3. 80 (*1, 2, 4, 5, 8, 10, 16, 20, 40, 80*)
4. 44 (*1, 2, 4, 11, 22, 44*)
5. 97 (*1, 97*)
6. 92 (*1, 2, 4, 23, 46, 92*)

Talk and Explore

Greatest Common Factor

Big Idea Every number has factors. Every pair of numbers has at least one factor that is common to both numbers.

Building Background

▲ Our class at school has a recycling project.

- **What do you see in the picture?**
- **What kinds of things can be reused to make new items?**
- **What kinds of things does your family or school recycle?**

Key Concepts

A **Venn Diagram** is an organizer that shows what two sets have in common. The Venn Diagram here shows all the factors of 24 and 30. The overlap shows the **common factors**, numbers that are factors of 24 and of 30. Of the common factors, 6 is the **greatest common factor (GCF).**

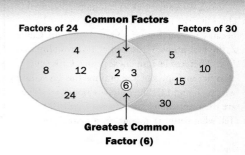

Activity: What's in Common?

Label the outer ovals of a Venn Diagram (Overhead Transparency 31) *boys* and *girls*. Label the overlap *white shoes*. Have students write their names in the appropriate section of the diagram. Then point to the overlap and ask, *What do these students have in common?* (*white shoes*)

Resource Library

Math at Hand
Factors 050–051, 053–058

Math on Call
Factors 056, 058–061, 065–066

Common Factors

A **common factor** of two or more numbers is a factor they share. For example, 1 is a common factor of any pair of numbers.

The sixth grade at Murphy Middle School has 56 students. The seventh grade has 48 students. The students want to form teams to collect materials to recycle. Each team should have the same number of sixth-grade students and the same number of seventh-grade students. How many teams can they form?

To start, find all the common factors of 48 and 56. To do this, list all the factors of each number and then circle the numbers that appear on both lists.

Factors of 48:   ①, ②, 3, ④, 6, ⑧, 12, 16, 24, 48

Factors of 56:   ①, ②, ④, 7, ⑧, 14, 28, 56

These steps show that the common factors of 48 and 56 are 1, 2, 4, and 8. The classes can have 1, 2, 4, or 8 teams. For example, each of the 8 teams would have 7 sixth-grade students and 6 seventh-grade students.

▲ To *recycle* means to take something old and make it useful again.

Find all the common factors of 8 and 33.

Factors of 8:   ①, 2, 4, 8
Factors of 33:   ①, 3, 11, 33

The only common factor is 1.

Find all the common factors of 15, 45, and 75.

Factors of 15:   ①, ③, ⑤, ⑮
Factors of 45:   ①, ③, ⑤, 9, ⑮, 45
Factors of 75:   ①, ③, ⑤, ⑮, 25, 75

The common factors are 1, 3, 5, and 15.

Talk and Share

With your partner, name at least three numbers with a common factor of 6. What number is a common factor of every pair of numbers?

▲ Objects made of rubber, glass, paper, wood, plastic, and metal can be recycled.

VOCABULARY
common factor—a factor that two or more numbers share

Teach Common Factors

■ Show students this other way to show common factors:

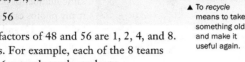
48: ① ② 3 ④ 6 ⑧ 12 16 24 48
56: ① ② ④ 7 ⑧ 14 28 56

■ If students have difficulty finding common factors, suggest that they list all the factors of the lesser number and see if any of those numbers are also factors of the greater number.

Talk and Share

Ask, *How did you find three numbers with a common factor of 6? (Sample: We multiplied 6 by three different whole numbers 12, 18, 24, 36, ...) Why will two numbers always have 1 as a common factor? (Every number is divisible by 1.)*

Sample answers: 12, 18, 24; 1

Build VOCABULARY

Point out that the word *common* has multiple meanings. Stress that *common* in mathematics usually means "shared," not "ordinary."

Differentiating Instruction

Beginning
Understanding Common Factors On the board, write two numbers less than 40. Have volunteers list the factors of each number and show how they found the factors. Have another volunteer circle pairs of common factors. Repeat the activity several more times, giving each student a chance to share.

Intermediate
Finding Common Factors Have pairs of students alternate choosing two or three numbers less than 40 and having the partner list the factors of each number and then tell which are common factors. Have them talk about how they found the factors.

Advanced
Telling How to Find Common Factors Have students choose two or three numbers less than 40 and explain orally or in writing how to find the factors and the common factors of their numbers.

 Activity: Factor It In

Have partners give each other two numbers less than 50. Have them list the common factors, explaining their procedures. Then have partners repeat the activity with three numbers between 50 and 100.

Teach Greatest Common Factor

- Encourage students to use their vocabulary skills to define *common prime factors* (*the prime factors that two or more numbers share*).

- After discussing both examples, demonstrate on the board how to find the GCF in the first example using prime factorization, and the GCF in the second example by listing factors.

Talk and Share

Have pairs share their responses with the class.

Answers: 13; the lesser number, because the greater number can never be a factor of the lesser number

Language Notes

Draw students' attention to the Language Notes. Invite volunteers to use a dictionary to find various meanings of *return*. Ask, *Which one helps you to understand this idiom?*

Build VOCABULARY

Ask students to discuss and then write their own definitions for *greatest common factor* and *common prime factors*.

Look and Read

Greatest Common Factor

Once you know the common factors of two numbers, you can find the **greatest common factor (GCF)**. The GCF is simply the *greatest* of the common factors. In the first problem on page 93, the GCF is 8. The greatest number of teams that can be formed with an equal number of sixth graders and seventh graders is 8.

Dan's father helped him with an art project. To return the favor, Dan is organizing photos of his father's artwork into an album. He has 8 photos of wood carvings for one section, 36 photos of paintings for another section, and 12 photos of drawings for the last section. Dan wants the same number of photos on each page of the album. How many photos can he put on each page? The answer is the GCF of 8, 12, and 36.

Factors of 8: (1),(2),(4), 8
Factors of 12: (1),(2), 3,(4), 6, 12
Factors of 36: (1),(2), 3,(4), 6, 9, 12, 18, 36

Common factors: 1, 2, 4
Greatest Common Factor (GCF): 4

You can find the prime factorization of each number first. Then multiply the common prime factors to find the GCF. Find the GCF of 24 and 60.

$24 = (2) \cdot (2) \cdot 2 \cdot (3)$ ← **Find all common prime factors.**
$60 = (2) \cdot (2) \cdot (3) \cdot 5$
$2 \cdot 2 \cdot 3 = 12$ ← **Multiply the common prime factors.**

The GCF of 24 and 60 is 12.

Language Notes

Idioms
This saying doesn't mean what it seems.

- **return the favor**
  Do something kind for someone who has helped you.

Talk and Share

Work with a partner. Find the GCF of 13 and 26. Can the GCF of two numbers be one of the numbers? If so, which is the GCF, the lesser number or the greater number? Talk about it and explain why.

VOCABULARY
greatest common factor (GCF)—the greatest factor common to two or more numbers

---

Activity: Factor the Web

Have small groups write *factor* in the center of a Web (Overhead Transparency 33) and then use phrases from this unit that include *factor* to complete the Web (*factor tree, prime factorization, common factor, greatest common factor, common prime factors*).

Differentiating Instruction

Beginning
Using Two Ways to Find a GCF On the board, write *24* below *18*. Have volunteers list all factors, circle the common factors, and identify the GCF (*6*). Then say, *You can also use prime factorization to find the GCF.* Write each prime factorization. Ask volunteers to circle common factors. Say, *The GCF is the product of the common prime factors, 2 times 3.* Repeat with other examples.

Intermediate
Comparing Ways to Find a GCF Have pairs work together to find the GCF of 24 and 84 using the directions for the Beginning activity (*12*). Have pairs talk with other pairs about which method they prefer and why.

Advanced
Explaining Ways to Find a GCF Have students find the GCF of 36 and 108 using the directions for the Beginning activity (*36*). Have them describe the two methods in writing.

Practice

Find all the common factors for each group of numbers.

1. 12, 15   **2.** 21, 42   **3.** 6, 15
4. 9, 11   **5.** 24, 45   **6.** 14, 35
7. 36, 60   **8.** 24, 80   **9.** 12, 18, 24
10. 20, 30, 50   **11.** 27, 45, 72   **12.** 18, 27, 81

Find the GCF for each group of numbers.

13. 4, 6   **14.** 15, 20   **15.** 12, 17   **16.** 21, 35
17. 27, 45   **18.** 9, 17   **19.** 18, 48   **20.** 30, 75
21. 12, 18, 23   **22.** 16, 20, 24   **23.** 36, 60, 84   **24.** 40, 48, 80

25. What is the largest square Betsy can use to make a quilt that measures 72 inches by 99 inches?

26. Pedro is making stools. He has three wooden sticks that are 36, 40, and 48 inches long. What is the length of the longest legs that he can cut without any wood left over?

27. Marty and Fred work for the same hourly wage. One day, Marty earned $117 dollars and Fred earned $91. What is their hourly wage?

28. Manuel has a stamp collection of 144 U.S. stamps and 120 foreign stamps. He wants to separate them into two stamp albums with the same number of stamps on each page. What is the greatest number of stamps he can put on each page?

29. (SHORT RESPONSE) The GCF of 12, 18, and 24 cannot be greater than 12. Explain why.

30. (SHORT RESPONSE) Of the numbers from 1 to 25, which number has the most factors? List all the factors of that number.

31. (SHORT RESPONSE) If two different numbers are both prime numbers, what is their GCF? Explain.

32. (MULTIPLE CHOICE) Which pair of numbers has a GCF of 12?
   A. 12 and 18   **B.** 24 and 42   **C.** 1 and 12   **D.** 24 and 36

LESSON 15 • GREATEST COMMON FACTOR   **95**

Practice

Ask, *What words are indicated by the initials GCF?* (*greatest common factor*) Write 10, 25, and 30 on the board. After students find the GCF (5), have volunteers explain how they found their answer.

Assignment Guide
- Beginning 1–21 odd, 27, 29, 30, 32
- Intermediate 1–29 odd, 32
- Advanced 2–28 even, 29–32

Notes on Exercises
Exercises 1–24 Suggest that students work in pairs. They can help each other and check each other's work.

Exercises 25–28 Help students realize that they are looking for the GCF in each exercise. Extend the practice by having students find how many squares are needed in Exercise 25, small pegs they will have in Exercise 26, hours each person will work in Exercise 27, and the number of pages in each album in Exercise 28 (*88 squares; 31 pegs; Marty: 9 hours, Fred: 7 hours; U.S.: 6 pages, foreign: 5 pages*).

Exercise 31 Ask students if there are any factors, other than 1, that are common to two prime numbers (*no*).

Answers
1. 1, 3   **2.** 1, 3, 7, 21
3. 1, 3   **4.** 1
5. 1, 3   **6.** 1, 7
7. 1, 2, 3, 4, 6, 12
8. 1, 2, 4, 8   **9.** 1, 2, 3, 6
10. 1, 2, 5, 10   **11.** 1, 3, 9
12. 1, 3, 9   **13.** 2
14. 5   **15.** 1
16. 7   **17.** 9
18. 1   **19.** 6
20. 15   **21.** 1
22. 4   **23.** 12
24. 8   **25.** 9 in. by 9 in.
26. 4 in.   **27.** $13
28. 24 stamps
29. Sample: The greatest factor a number can have is the number itself.
30. 24; 1, 2, 3, 4, 6, 8, 12, 24
31. 1; a prime number has only itself and 1 as factors.
32. D

Program Resources
Practice Book Use page 38.
Overhead Transparencies Use 31.

Teach Responding

■ Explain that to *respond* means to answer a question and that the noun form of *respond* is *response*.

■ Have a volunteer read aloud the first paragraph. Then discuss the two headings in the chart. Be sure students understand that if 6 people attend the party, they should prepare 1 pan of lasagna. For 12 people, they need 2 pans. For 24 people, they need 4 pans.

■ Discuss what it means to write a polite response, mentioning use of courtesy words such as *thank you*.

■ Ask volunteers to read their responses aloud.

Partner Practice

Have students restate the problem before they start following the steps.

Answers:

1. *60: 1, 2, 3, 4, 5, 6, 10, 12, 15, 20, 30, 60; 45: 1, 3, 5, 9, 15, 45*

2. *1, 3, 5, 15*

3. *15; each woman can get 4 loaves of bread and 3 pies.*

Hands On

■ Instead of cards, you may want to have students count off to assign the numbers 24, 30, 36, 40, 42, and 48.

■ Ask volunteers to draw their diagrams on the board and to show or tell how they set them up.

Develop Language

Number of people	Amount to prepare one pan
6	
12	?
24	?

Activities

Responding When you respond, you answer a question someone has asked. Imagine that you have been asked to make lasagna for a party. Before you respond, you want to figure out how much lasagna you need to make.

1. **Plan** Copy the table on the left and complete it to help you decide how much lasagna to prepare. Use your table to help you plan for a party of 12 people and 24 people.

2. **Respond** Write a polite response. Write that you will attend the party and make lasagna. Also, ask how many people will be there.

Partner Practice

It Takes Teamwork! Work with a partner. Read this problem aloud. A local baker gave a women's club 60 loaves of bread and 45 pies. Each member gets the same number of loaves and the same number of pies. What is the greatest number of women who can get bread and pies?

1. Find all the factors of 60 and of 45.

2. Find all the common factors of 60 and 45.

3. Which common factor is the greatest common factor? Show how this number solves the problem.

Hands On

Diagram It Each of you in class has a card with 24, 30, 36, 40, 42, or 48 on it. Find a student who has a number different from yours. Together, draw a Venn Diagram. In one circle, list the factors of your number. In the other circle, list the factors of your partner's number. Put the common factors in the part where the circles overlap. Identify the greatest common factor. Pair up with another student and repeat the activity. A sample is shown.

Factors of 16 — Factors of 20

8, 16 | 2, 4, 1 | 5, 10, 20

Greatest Common Factor (4)   Common Factors

🎁 **Program Resources**

Practice Book Use page 39.
Overhead Transparencies Use 31.

✓ **Assessment Book**

Use page 37 to assess students' comprehension.

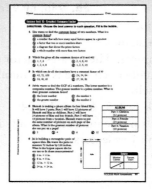

Activity: Extend the Lesson

Tell students that pairs of numbers such as 9 and 10 or 21 and 28 are said to be *relatively prime* because their only common factor is 1. Ask, *Are the numbers prime?* (*no*) Challenge students to list as many pairs of relatively prime numbers as they can in one minute.

Have students describe the methods they used to make their lists.

Least Common Multiple

Big Idea Every number has many multiples. Every pair of numbers has multiples that are common to both numbers. The least common multiple will help you find out when events might happen at the same time.

Building Background

▲ Every summer, I hear the buzzing of cicadas. They are really loud!

- When have you heard the buzzing of a cicada?
- What other kinds of insects make sounds?
- How do you think insects make sounds?

Key Concepts

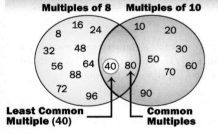

Multiples of 8   Multiples of 10

8 16 24   10 20
32 48   30
56 64 40 80 50 60
88   70
72 96   90

Least Common Multiple (40)   **Common Multiples**

The numbers 8 and 10 have many **multiples.** Listed here are their multiples less than 100. The **common multiples** less than 100 are 40 and 80. Because 40 is less than 80, 40 is the **least common multiple (LCM)** of 8 and 10.

LESSON 16 • LEAST COMMON MULTIPLE **97**

Activity: Show Me the Multiple

On the board, write the first four multiples of 2, 3, 4, 5, and 6. Have volunteers write the next four numbers in each list to extend the pattern. Ask, *What does the first row show? (multiples of 2)* Repeat with the remaining rows.

Then name two or three sets of multiples and ask volunteers to circle numbers common to the sets.

Resource Library

Math at Hand
Multiples 050, 059–061

Math on Call
Multiples 067–068

Least Common Multiple

STANDARDS CONTENT

Mathematics
- Find common multiples of two or more numbers
- Find the least common multiple (LCM) of two or more numbers

Language
- Recognize signal words referring to order of importance
- Persuade a person by giving reasons

Introduce the **Big Idea**

Ask, *What is a* multiple *of a number? (the product of that number and a whole number greater than zero)* Then ask a volunteer to read aloud the Big Idea.

Begin **Building Background**

As students discuss the questions below the picture, point out that there is a name for words such as *buzz,* that sound like what they name—*onomatopoeia.*

Teach **Key Concepts**

- Introduce the vocabulary terms *common multiples* and *least common multiple.*
- Remind students that they used a Venn Diagram to show factors and common factors in the last lesson. Then ask, *What is shown in this Venn Diagram? (multiples and common multiples of 8 and 10)*

Warm-Up Review

Have students complete each pattern.
1. 2 4 6 ▦ 10 ▦ ▦ *(8, 12, 14)*
2. 3 ▦ 9 ▦ 15 18 ▦ *(6, 12, 21)*
3. 5 10 15 20 ▦ ▦ ▦ *(25, 30, 35)*
4. ▦ ▦ 12 16 20 ▦ 28 *(4, 8, 24)*
5. 10 ▦ 30 ▦ 50 ▦ 70 *(20, 40, 60)*

Teach Common Multiples

- As part of a discussion about cicadas, make sure students know that the insects are mostly harmless and short-lived, but people may want to prepare for the large number of insects that might appear.

- Draw a timeline to help students visualize the hatching cycles of the two types of cicadas.

- For a hands-on approach, have pairs of students use cubes or counters to show the first five multiples of 2 and of 4. Ask which stacks are the same heights and if there are any common multiples. Encourage partners to use vocabulary words to describe their models. (*Sample: We used cubes to model multiples of 2 and of 4. We compared the heights of the stacks and found that 4 and 8 are common multiples.*)

Talk and Share

Partners should list the common multiples of 3 and 6 and look for a pattern.

Answer: Multiply the multiple by 2, 3, 4, ...

Build VOCABULARY

Ask students to describe how the words *multiple* and *multiply* are related. Ask, *How does knowing the meaning of* multiply *help you remember the meaning of* multiple?

Common Multiples

The insect shown here is a *dog-day cicada*. This type of cicada is very common in North America. It takes 4 to 7 years to develop. If a 4-year cicada and a 7-year cicada hatch in the same year, their buzzing is very loud. When is the next time they both will hatch in the same year? You can use common multiples to find out.

A **common multiple** of two or more numbers is a multiple all the numbers share. You always can find a common multiple of two or more numbers by finding their product. The product of 4 and 7 is 28, so every 28 years the two kinds of cicadas again will hatch at the same time.

You also could list the multiples of each number and circle the common multiples.

Multiples of 4: 4, 8, 12, 16, 20, 24, ㉘, 32, 36, 40, 44, 48, 52, ㊲, . . .

Multiples of 7: 7, 14, 21, ㉘, 35, 42, 49, ㊲, . . .

These lists show that 28 and 56 are the first two common multiples of 4 and 7. Both kinds of cicadas will hatch in the same year every 28 years, in 56 years, and so on.

The dog-day cicada also is called the *annual cicada,* or the *harvestfly.* ▶

Find the first two common multiples of 5, 10, and 15. Start by listing the multiples of 5, 10, and 15.

Multiples of 5:   5, 10, 15, 20, 25, ㉚, 35, 40, 45, 50, 55, ㊿, . . .

Multiples of 10: 10, 20, ㉚, 40, 50, ㊿, . . .

Multiples of 15: 15, ㉚, 45, ㊿, . . .

The first two common multiples of 5, 10, and 15 are 30 and 60.

Talk and Share

Talk with a partner. If you know a common multiple for two numbers, how can you easily find more common multiples for the same pair of numbers? Explain your thinking.

VOCABULARY
common multiple—a number that is a multiple of two or more numbers

---

Activity: Multiples on a Number Line

Use Overhead Transparency 28, number-line, to draw the following diagram.

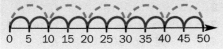

Have students identify sets of multiples and common multiples (*sets of multiples: 5, 10, 15, 20, 25, 30, 35, 40, 45, 50; 10, 20, 30, 40, 50; common multiples: 10, 20, 30, 40, 50*).

Differentiating Instruction

Beginning
Understanding Common Multiples On the board, write two numbers less than 12. Have volunteers list the first ten multiples of each number and tell how they found them. Have other volunteers circle pairs of common multiples.

Intermediate
Finding Common Multiples Have pairs of students alternate choosing two or three numbers less than 12. Have the partner list the first ten multiples of each number and then tell which are common multiples. Have them tell how they found the multiples.

Advanced
Finding a Quick Method Challenge students to find a quick method for finding the first common multiple of two or more prime numbers and the first common multiple of two or more numbers that have no common factors other than 1. Have them write a sentence or two about their methods. In each case, the common multiple is the product of the two numbers.

Least Common Multiple

The **least common multiple (LCM)** of two or more numbers is the least of the common multiples. Note that the product of 4 and 6 gives a common multiple, 24. But the product of two numbers is not always the LCM. The LCM of 4 and 6 is 12.

One way to find the LCM is to look at the common multiples of the numbers. The lists below show how to find the LCM of 9, 12, and 36.

List the multiples of each number. Circle the common multiples.

Multiples of 9:   9, 18, 27, ㊱, 45, 54, 63, ㊲, 81, . . .

Multiples of 12:   12, 24, ㊱, 48, 60, ㊲, 84, . . .

Multiples of 36:   ㊱, ㊲, 108, . . .

The first two common multiples are 36 and 72. The least of these two multiples is 36. So the LCM is 36.

Another way to find the LCM is to start with the prime factorizations of each number. Here are the prime factorizations of 20 and 35.

$$20 = 2 \cdot 2 \cdot 5 \qquad 35 = 5 \cdot 7$$

Choose the *most* times a factor appears in either number. You need two 2s, one 5, and one 7. The LCM is the product of these prime factors.

$$2 \cdot 2 \cdot 5 \cdot 7 = 140$$

The LCM of 20 and 35 is 140.

Talk and Share

Work with a partner. Suppose you have lists of multiples for two numbers. Explain how you can use the lists to find the least common multiple of the two numbers.

VOCABULARY

least common multiple (LCM)—the least multiple common to two or more numbers

Language Notes

Signal Words for Importance
These words give clues about what is important.

■ **least:** less than any other

■ **greatest:** more than any other

▲ Periodical cicadas live underground 13 to 17 years before coming out.

Teach Least Common Multiple

■ Point out that when the multiples are listed in numerical order, the least common multiple is the first common multiple.

■ Suggest that students align *like* factors as shown below to make sure all the needed factors are included when using the prime factorization method.

$$20 = 2 \cdot 2 \cdot 5$$
$$35 = \qquad\quad 5 \cdot 7$$
$$\text{LCM} = 2 \cdot 2 \cdot 5 \cdot 7$$

Language Notes

Discuss how *greatest* and *least* are used to describe greatest common factor and least common multiple. Point out that *about*, *all*, and *never* also are signal words for importance. Ask, *Can you name other signal words for importance?* (*Samples: every, none*)

Talk and Share

Ask volunteers to share their explanations with the class.

Answer: Circle pairs of common multiples and then identify the least.

Build VOCABULARY

Have partners take turns using a vocabulary word from Unit 4 in a sentence, while the other gives a definition or an example.

Differentiating Instruction

Beginning
Using Two Ways to Find the LCM On the board, write *12* below *8*. Have volunteers list the first six multiples, circle the common multiples, and identify the LCM (*24*). Then say, *You can also use prime factorization to find the LCM.* On the board, write each prime factorization. Ask, *What is the greatest number of times 2 is a factor? 3?* Say, *The LCM is the product of three 2s and one 3.* Repeat with other examples.

Intermediate
Comparing Ways to Find the LCM
Have pairs work together to find the LCM of 12 and 16 using the directions for the Beginning activity (*48*). Have pairs talk with other pairs about which method they prefer and why.

Advanced
Explaining Ways to Find the LCM
Have students find the LCM of 24 and 36 using the directions for the Beginning activity (*72*). Have them describe the two methods in writing.

Activity: Toss the Multiples

Give pairs of students two or three number cubes. Have them take turns tossing two or three numbers and find their least common multiple. They could also toss two cubes for a 2-digit number and the third cube for a 1-digit number.

Practice

Ask, *What is the difference between the GCF and the LCM? (The GCF is the greatest number that is a factor of two or more numbers. The LCM is the least number that is a multiple of two or more numbers.)*

Ask a volunteer to show how to find the GCF of 12 and 15 (*3*). Ask another volunteer to show how to find the LCM of 12 and 15 (*60*).

Assignment Guide
■ Beginning 1–5, 10–26 even
■ Intermediate 1–21 odd, 24–26
■ Advanced 2–20 even, 21–26

Notes on Exercises
Exercises 1–12 Remind students to look for the first three *common multiples* for each pair of numbers and not just the first three multiples.

Exercise 21 Discuss Cate's method for finding the LCM.

Exercise 23 Students should understand that they must find the LCM of 2, 3, and 5 and then add 1.

Practice

Find the first 3 common multiples for each group of numbers.
1. 1, 19   **2.** 9, 10   **3.** 4, 10   **4.** 3, 6
5. 10, 25   **6.** 4, 6   **7.** 3, 11   **8.** 12, 20
9. 2, 5, 6   **10.** 2, 3, 7   **11.** 6, 8, 9   **12.** 6, 10, 12

Find the LCM for each group of numbers.
13. 4, 20   **14.** 15, 25   **15.** 24, 30   **16.** 12, 18
17. 10, 15, 20 **18.** 3, 8, 16 **19.** 4, 9, 12 **20.** 12, 18, 27

21. Cate uses another method to find the LCM. She lists multiples of the greatest number in the group until she finds one that is a multiple of the other numbers. Use Cate's method to find the LCM of 6, 8, and 16.

22. Trisha eats lunch at the Cafe every 3 days. Mimi eats there every 5 days. If Trisha meets Mimi at lunch today, in how many days will they meet at lunch again?

23. When Ms. Chavez divides her class into groups of 2, 3, or 5, there is always one student left over. Her class has more than 20 students. How many students are in the class?

Here are the prime factorizations of some numbers. Use them to find the LCM of the numbers in Exercises 24 and 25.
$18 = 2 \cdot 3 \cdot 3$ $20 = 2 \cdot 2 \cdot 5$
$45 = 3 \cdot 3 \cdot 5$ $54 = 2 \cdot 3 \cdot 3 \cdot 3$
24. 18 and 20   **25.** 20, 45, and 54

26. (EXTENDED RESPONSE) A package of hot dogs has 9 hot dogs. A package of buns has 12 buns. Follow the steps to find how many packages you should buy to have the same number of hot dogs and buns.
  a. Find the first six multiples of 9.
  b. Find the first six multiples of 12.
  c. What is the least common multiple of 9 and 12?
  d. How many packages of hot dogs and how many packages of buns do you need to have the same number of hot dogs as buns?

Program Resources
Practice Book Use page 40.

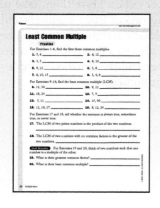

Answers
1. 19, 38, 57
2. 90, 180, 270
3. 20, 40, 60
4. 6, 12, 18
5. 50, 100, 150
6. 12, 24, 36
7. 33, 66, 99
8. 60, 120, 180
9. 30, 60, 90
10. 42, 84, 126
11. 72, 144, 216
12. 60, 120, 180
13. 20
14. 75
15. 120
16. 36
17. 60
18. 48
19. 36
20. 108

21. 16, 32, 48; 48 is the LCM; it is the least multiple of 16 that is also a multiple of 6 and 8.
22. in 15 days
23. 31 students
24. $2^2 \cdot 3^2 \cdot 5 = 180$
25. $2^2 \cdot 3^3 \cdot 5 = 540$
26. a. 9, 18, 27, 36, 45, 54
   b. 12, 24, 36, 48, 60, 72
   c. 36
   d. 4 packages of hot dogs
      3 packages of buns

Activities

Persuading When you persuade, you give reasons to convince someone else to accept your ideas. You might be able to persuade your friend to come to the baseball games in your park on certain days if you knew when the snow-cone cart would be there. The games are played every 3 days. The cart is there every 4 days. Work with a partner to find out how often you can see a baseball game and also buy snow cones at the park.

1. **Find** Find the LCM of 3 and 4. Show your work.

2. **Explain** Tell your partner how you found the LCM.

3. **Persuade** Write a short paragraph of 3 or 4 sentences to persuade your friend to go with you every 12 days.

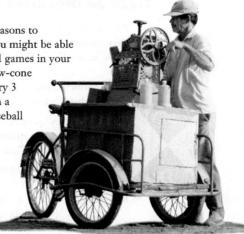

▲ Snow-cone cart

Hands On

Find the Least Work with a partner. Place a set of number cards labeled 4, 6, 12, 15, 18, 20, 24, 25, and 30 face down. Each of you should draw one card. Find the least common multiple of the two numbers. Replace the cards and repeat the activity.

Oral Language

And the LCM Is . . . Work in small groups. Each group should select a different number from this list: 24, 30, 36, 40, 48, and 60. As a group, find two other numbers for which your group's number is the least common multiple. Compute the LCM of your group's three numbers. Tell the other groups what you found and explain what you did.

LESSON 16 • LEAST COMMON MULTIPLE **101**

Develop Language

Teach Persuading

■ Explain to students that when they *persuade*, they convince someone to accept their ideas. Give students examples of persuading, such as persuading a parent to let them go to the movies with a friend. Discuss ways to persuade someone. Ask, for instance, *How would you persuade a classmate to vote for you as class president?*

■ Be sure students understand the problem, especially the inference that the friend is more likely to come to the game when the snow-cone cart is there. Then have students work in pairs to find that the LCM is 12.

Hands On

Have students make the cards. Remind students that partners should share the responsibilities as they work together.

Oral Language

Have students share their methods of solving and then choose a different number and repeat the exercise using another group's method. Students should notice that the number on the card will always be the LCM of all three numbers.

 Activity: Persuade Me

Present this situation to students: Sara is going to the store to buy hot dogs and buns. There are 8 hot dogs in a package. There are 10 buns in a package. She wants to have the same number of hot dogs as buns.

Ask small groups of students to write a paragraph to persuade their classmates that Sara needs to buy 5 packages of hot dogs and 4 packages of buns.

 Assessment Book

Use page 38 to assess students' comprehension.

Program Resources

Practice Book Use page 41.

Make an Organized List

STANDARDS CONTENT

Mathematics
■ Solve problems by making an organized list

Language
■ Understand how to use the word *the* with places and names

Teach Make an Organized List

■ Read aloud the name of the strategy. Ask students what *organized* means (*arranged according to some order*).

■ Ask a volunteer to read aloud the first paragraph. Point out that the code words do not correspond to actual words.

■ Ask, *How can you make sure that all the possible code words are listed for each starting letter?*

  Talk and Share

This problem is similar to the one above, but it has fewer possibilities. Encourage a pair of students to go to the board and list all the different code words. Ask one of them to explain how they found them.

Answer: 6 code words: 123, 132, 213, 231, 312, 321

Problem-Solving Skills

Make an Organized List

Problem: Suppose you and a friend are going to create a secret code for personal messages. How many different 4-letter code words can you make using the letters W, X, Y, and Z?

Read and Understand Read the problem carefully to make sure you understand what is asked.

Need to find: All possible different arrangements of the 4 letters W, X, Y, and Z

You know: Each code word uses all 4 letters.

Key fact: The code word WXYZ is different from the code word WXZY.

Plan and Solve Make an organized list of all the possibilities. Here is a list that groups the code words by their first letters.

Code words that start with W	Code words that start with X	Code words that start with Y	Code words that start with Z
WXYZ, WXZY, WYXZ, WYZX, WZXY, WZYX	XWYZ, XWZY, XYWZ, XYZW, XZWY, XZYW	YWXZ, YWZX, YXWZ, YXZW, YZWX, YZXW	ZWXY, ZWYX, ZXWY, ZXYW, ZYWX, ZYXW

Answer For each letter, there are 6 code words that start with that letter. The total number of code words is 24.

Look Back The pattern for listing words starting with X, Y, and Z is the same as that for words starting with W. So check to see that you have 6 different words starting with each of the 4 letters: 4 · 6 = 24 code words. Make sure no two words are exactly the same.

Talk and Share

Work with a partner. Suppose you want to make 3-digit code words using the digits 1, 2, and 3. How many different code words can you make?

 Activity: How Many Choices?

Write this table on the board.

Monitor	Hard Drive	Proc. Speed
17 in.	40 GB	2.8 GHz
19 in.	80 GB	3.06 GHz
21 in.	120 GB	

Have students make an organized list to find how many different computers they could order using these options (*18 different computers*).

Differentiating Instruction

Beginning
Comparing Codes Have small groups of students look at the code words that start with *W* to see how all words differ. Then have students compare the list with the code words that start with *Y* to see how that list was written. (*It is the same list as for W except that the letter Y was written for the letter W, and vice versa.*) Encourage students to look for other patterns in the lists.

Intermediate/Advanced
Explaining the Steps Encourage students to explain why the number of words listed is the same for each start letter. Ask them to explain how this could help them check to make sure that all possible code words are listed.

Practice

Use the strategy *make an organized list.*

1. How many different 5-letter code words can you make?

2. At an art fair, Sue Lin was given 36 feet of rope to outline an area where she and her friends could sit. How many different rectangular areas can she outline so the sides of the rectangles are whole numbers? List the dimensions.

3. The baseball team at the University of Rafael has 5 pitchers and 2 catchers. How many pitcher-catcher pairs are possible?

Choose a strategy to solve each problem.

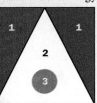

4. The target at the left shows the number of points you get for hitting each part. If you hit the target with two darts, how many different total scores can you get?

5. Tamika went shopping for her Kwanzaa celebration. She spent one-third of her money at a candle shop, $18 at a CD store, and half her remaining money at a bookstore. She had $6 left. How much money did Tamika start with?

Grammar Spotlight

The Word *the* The word *the* is used in special ways with places and names.

Usage	Examples
Use *the* in a phrase that contains the word *of*.	The baseball team at the University of Rafael has 5 pitchers and 2 catchers.
Use *the* with some country names but not with others.	We live in the United States, and we also live in America. Colin is from the United Kingdom, but Colin is also from Britain. Jan is from the Netherlands, but Jan is also from Holland.
Use *the* before the plural name of a whole family.	The Becks live in Seattle. The Olsons moved to Redmond.

1. Think of a sentence that uses the word *the* with a place or a name. Say it aloud and have your partner write it. Check to see if your partner wrote it correctly.

2. Talk with your partner about sentences that use *the* with places and names.

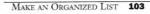

Practice

Say, *Coaches sometimes need to make an organized list to see possible arrangements of players. Can you think of other situations that would require an organized list?*

Assignment Guide
- Beginning 2–5
- Intermediate 1–5
- Advanced 1–5

Notes on Exercises

Exercise 1 Suggest that students work in pairs for this exercise.

Exercise 3 Students can assign each pitcher a number and each catcher a letter to help them organize the list.

Exercise 4 Be sure students understand that the total score is the sum for the two hits. Point out that the problem asks for different total scores, not different ways to score.

Grammar Spotlight

- Read aloud the table showing how the word *the* is used to name places and people. Use last names that are familiar to the students.

- Ask students how the example involving names of countries differs from the other two. (*The usage varies depending on the country. In the other examples, the usage is a constant.*)

Answers
1. 120 words

2. 9 areas; 1 by 17, 2 by 16, 3 by 15, 4 by 14, 5 by 13, 6 by 12, 7 by 11, 8 by 10, 9 by 9

3. 10 pairs

4. 5 different scores are possible: 6, 5, 4, 3, 2

5. $45

Activity: Where Is It?

Ask students to cut out examples that show how the word *the* is used to name places in local newspapers. Have them place a map of their town in the center of a poster and then paste the cut-out examples around the map. They should use string to connect the name in each cut-out example with its geographical location on the map.

Program Resources

Practice Book Use pages 42 and 43.

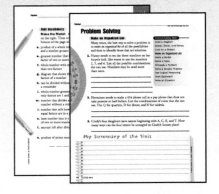

Understanding Fractions

STANDARDS CONTENT

Mathematics
- Use fractions to represent parts of a whole or a set
- Write equivalent fractions

Language
- Recognize the prefix *de-*
- Interpret results involving a group of fractions

Introduce the **Big Idea**

Ask, *What kinds of numbers show equal-sized parts of a whole?* (*decimals, fractions*) Then read aloud the Big Idea.

Begin **Building Background**

Invite students to share their thoughts about hot-air balloons. Ask students to explain how they answered the third question (*6 of 15*).

Teach **Key Concepts**

- Discuss the terms *decimal*, *part*, and *fraction*. Review how to read the fraction names. Tell students that denominators other than *half*, *third*, and *fifth* are formed by adding the *th* sound to the number name.

- Have students name situations in which they have used fractions, such as measuring when cooking.

Warm-Up Review

Have students find each product or quotient.

1. $35 \div 5$ (*7*)
2. 7×6 (*42*)
3. 9×8 (*72*)
4. $48 \div 12$ (*4*)
5. $45 \div 15$ (*3*)
6. $63 \div 7$ (*9*)
7. 8×7 (*56*)
8. 9×6 (*54*)

Talk and Explore

Understanding Fractions

Big Idea Fractions represent parts. They may represent a number of equal-sized parts of a whole or a number of items in a set. Fractions show division.

Building Background

▲ I've always wanted to go up in a hot-air balloon. It would be amazing to look at the ground from up in the air!

- **What do you know about hot-air balloons?**
- **What would you look at from high in the air?**
- **If 9 of 15 balloons are still on the ground, tell what part of the set of balloons is in the air.**

Key Concepts

A **decimal** expresses a quantity that is part of a whole or part of a **set** of items. A **fraction** is another way of showing a part.

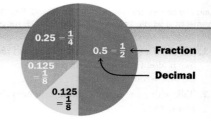

$0.25 = \frac{1}{4}$
$0.5 = \frac{1}{2}$ ← **Fraction** / **Decimal**
$0.125 = \frac{1}{8}$
$0.125 = \frac{1}{8}$

104 UNIT 5 • FRACTIONS AND MIXED NUMBERS

 Activity: Coin Fractions

Draw a table with these headings on the board: *Coin, Number of Cents, Decimal Part of $1, Fraction Part of $1.*

Remind students that coins represent parts of a dollar, with a cent being $\frac{1}{100}$ of a dollar.

Have students complete the table for these coins: penny, nickel, dime, quarter, and half dollar. Allow students to use a fraction calculator to help. (*See Additional Answers, page T39.*)

Resource Library

Math at Hand
Fractions 028–031, 033, 035, 037

Math on Call
Fractions 030–031, 036–037

Reader's Handbook (red)
Reading Math 117–131

Reader's Handbook (yellow)
Reading Math 88–100

Modeling Fractions

A **fraction** is a number that describes part of a whole or part of a **set.** The top number of a fraction is the **numerator.** The bottom number is the denominator. Suppose 9 hot-air balloons are on the ground and there are 15 balloons altogether. Write a fraction to tell what portion of the balloons is on the ground.

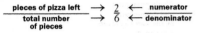

$$\frac{\text{number of balloons on the ground}}{\text{total number of balloons}} \rightarrow \frac{9}{15} \leftarrow \begin{array}{l}\text{numerator}\\ \leftarrow \text{denominator}\end{array}$$

$\frac{9}{15}$ tells you that 9 of the 15 balloons are on the ground.

The pizza at the right was cut into 6 slices, and 2 slices are left. Write a fraction to show what part of the pizza is left.

$$\frac{\text{pieces of pizza left}}{\text{total number of pieces}} \rightarrow \frac{2}{6} \leftarrow \begin{array}{l}\text{numerator}\\ \leftarrow \text{denominator}\end{array}$$

The fraction $\frac{2}{6}$ tells what part of the pizza is left.

A fraction also indicates division. Three-fifths means 3 divided by 5.

$$\frac{3}{5} = 3 \div 5 = 5\overline{)3}$$

Language Notes

Signal Words for Location
This word gives a clue about where things are.

- denominator
  de sometimes means "down" or "lower" and *nom* means "name." A denominator names the lower, or bottom, number in a fraction.

Talk and Share

Work with a partner to write a fraction that shows how much pizza was eaten from the pizza shown above. Write another fraction to show how much pizza there was before any was eaten. Finally, write a fraction to show how much pizza there was after all of it had been eaten.

VOCABULARY

fraction—a number that describes part of something
set—a group of items
numerator—the number above the fraction bar that tells the number of equal parts or objects being considered
denominator—the number below the fraction bar that tells the number of equal parts or objects in all

Teach Modeling Fractions

- Use plain language to review the parts of a fraction. The *numerator* is the top number. It tells the number of parts being considered. The *denominator* is the bottom number. It tells the total number of parts.

- Draw a circle on the board and shade $\frac{5}{8}$. Draw eight *X*s on the board and circle five of them. Ask students how the models are alike and how they are different. (*Both show $\frac{5}{8}$. One is a whole, and the other is a set.*)

- Point out that the parts of the whole are of equal size.

Language Notes

Read aloud the word clues that can help students remember which number in a fraction is the *denominator*.

Talk and Share

Help students see that $\frac{6}{6} = 1$, the whole pizza.
Answers: $\frac{4}{6}, \frac{6}{6}, \frac{0}{6}$

Build VOCABULARY

Ask students to define *fraction, numerator,* and *denominator*. Have students write a fraction and label the *numerator* and the *denominator*.

Differentiating Instruction

Beginning
Drawing Fraction Models Have volunteers explain the three ways fractions were used in the examples (*as part of a whole, part of a set, and division*). Have each student choose a way, draw a model on the board, and explain it.

Intermediate
Describing Fraction Situations
In pairs, have students find three situations that can be described by $\frac{1}{4}$. One situation should be part of a whole, one part of a set, and the third division.

Advanced
Writing About Fractions Have students look at the pizza diagram on page 105 and write an explanation of why the fraction $\frac{1}{3}$ describes the amount of pizza left. (*Sample: Two slices together make a third of the pizza, so the amount left is 1 of 3 equal parts.*) Ask them to give two fractions for the amount eaten ($\frac{4}{6}$ and $\frac{2}{3}$).

Activity: Model the Fractions

Have students carefully sketch models for three different fractions. Have them trade models with a partner, write the fractions shown, identify the numerators and denominators, and explain what each number represents.

Teach Equivalent Fractions

- Point out that for each example of equivalent fractions, the two models are the same size.

- Stress that the numerator and the denominator must be multiplied or divided by the *same* nonzero number. Explain that this action is the same as multiplying or dividing by 1, which changes the *form* of the fraction but not its *value*.

- Ask, *How do you know that $\frac{9}{12}$ is equal to $\frac{3}{4}$?* (Sample: If I divide the numerator and the denominator of $\frac{9}{12}$ by 3, I get $\frac{3}{4}$.)

- Show students how to find a fraction equivalent to $\frac{24}{36}$ in several steps ($\frac{24 \div 6}{36 \div 6} = \frac{4}{6}$; $\frac{4 \div 2}{6 \div 2} = \frac{2}{3}$) Ask, *Why is it a good idea to use the GCF to write a fraction in simplest form?* (so you need only one step)

Talk and Share

Students should see that the fractions $\frac{2}{3}$ and $\frac{4}{6}$ are equivalent because $\frac{2}{3} \times \frac{2}{2} = \frac{4}{6}$. Since $\frac{8}{9}$ is in simplest form, it cannot be simplified to $\frac{2}{3}$ or $\frac{4}{6}$.

Sample answer: $\frac{3}{5}$ and $\frac{18}{30}$ are equivalent to $\frac{12}{20}$.

Build VOCABULARY

Point out that *equal* and *equivalent* both mean "same."

Equivalent Fractions

Equivalent fractions are fractions that name the same amount. The models below show pairs of equivalent fractions.

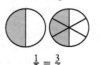

$$\frac{1}{2} = \frac{3}{6} \qquad \frac{8}{10} = \frac{4}{5} \qquad \frac{9}{12} = \frac{3}{4}$$

You also can use multiplication or division to find equivalent fractions.

$$\frac{1 \times 3}{2 \times 3} = \frac{3}{6} \quad \leftarrow \quad \text{Multiply numerator and denominator by the same nonzero number, 3.}$$

$$\frac{8 \div 2}{10 \div 2} = \frac{4}{5} \quad \leftarrow \quad \text{Divide numerator and denominator by the same nonzero number, 2.}$$

The fraction $\frac{3}{4}$ is in **simplest form,** sometimes called in *lowest terms*. This is because the only common factor of the numerator and denominator is 1.

To write $\frac{24}{36}$ in simplest form, you can use division. You could divide both numbers by 6 and then again by 2, but it is faster to divide by the greatest common factor. The greatest common factor (GCF) of 24 and 36 is 12.

$$\frac{24 \div 12}{36 \div 12} = \frac{2}{3} \quad \leftarrow \quad \text{Divide numerator and denominator by the GCF, 12.}$$

The simplest form of $\frac{24}{36}$ is $\frac{2}{3}$.

Talk and Share

Work with a partner. Tell which fraction is NOT equivalent to the other two: $\frac{2}{3}, \frac{4}{6}, \frac{8}{9}$. Explain your thinking. Then find two fractions equivalent to $\frac{12}{20}$. Use multiplication or division.

VOCABULARY
equivalent fractions—fractions that name the same amount
simplest form—a fraction whose numerator and denominator have no common factor other than 1, sometimes called *lowest terms*.

 Activity: Folding Fraction Models

Have students fold a sheet of paper in half and then unfold the paper. Ask students how many equal parts are shown (*2 equal parts*). Have them label one part $\frac{1}{2}$. Then have students fold the same paper to show fourths, eighths, and sixteenths. Finally, have students identify the equivalent fractions.

Differentiating Instruction

Beginning
Comparing the Fraction Models Have small groups of students compare the pictures of the models on page 106. Ask them which fraction in each pair is in simplest form and tell why they chose that fraction.

Intermediate
Finding Fractions on a Ruler Have students work in small groups to find equivalent fractions on an inch ruler. Have one student point to a tick mark between 0 and 1 inch. The other

students should name as many fractions as they can for that tick mark. Tell them that any mark that can be named by only one fraction represents a fraction in simplest form.

Advanced
Modeling Equivalent Fractions Have pairs of students alternate drawing a fraction model and having the partner draw a model of an equivalent fraction and explain how he or she found the equivalent fraction.

Practice

Name the fraction for each colored portion.

1.   **2.**   **3.**   **4.** ★★★★ ★★★☆

Name the fraction for each point on the number line.

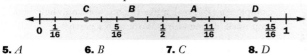

5. A **6.** B **7.** C **8.** D

Write three fractions equivalent to each fraction.

9. $\frac{5}{6}$ **10.** $\frac{3}{10}$ **11.** $\frac{25}{40}$ **12.** $\frac{18}{24}$

Find each missing number.

13. $\frac{5}{12} = \frac{\blacksquare}{48}$ **14.** $\frac{18}{30} = \frac{\blacksquare}{5}$ **15.** $\frac{9}{10} = \frac{36}{\blacksquare}$ **16.** $\frac{16}{24} = \frac{2}{\blacksquare}$

Write each fraction in simplest form.

17. $\frac{3}{9}$ **18.** $\frac{6}{10}$ **19.** $\frac{14}{16}$ **20.** $\frac{13}{26}$

21. $\frac{18}{45}$ **22.** $\frac{36}{48}$ **23.** $\frac{24}{60}$ **24.** $\frac{25}{75}$

A clown at Terri's birthday party made 18 animal balloons for the guests: 5 rabbits, 6 elephants, 4 dogs, and 3 fish. Tell what fraction of the total number of balloons is represented by each animal. Give each fraction in simplest form.

25. rabbits **26.** elephants
27. dogs **28.** fish

29. What fraction of the whole numbers from 1 to 100 are odd numbers?

30. What fraction of the whole numbers from 1 to 20 are composite? prime?

▲ Balloons can be blown up and twisted into shapes such as animals, necklaces, and even hats.

31. (EXTENDED RESPONSE) Yomi ate $\frac{2}{3}$ of her egg roll. Kyoshi ate $\frac{4}{6}$ of his. The egg rolls were the same size. Did they eat the same amount? Show or tell how you know.

32. (MULTIPLE CHOICE) Choose the fraction equivalent to $\frac{22}{33}$.

A. $\frac{1}{1}$ **B.** $\frac{1}{3}$ **C.** $\frac{2}{3}$ **D.** $\frac{11}{12}$

Practice

Draw a model showing $\frac{4}{8}$ on the board. Have students name the fraction, give the fraction in simplest form, and name two other equivalent fractions ($\frac{4}{8}$, $\frac{1}{2}$; *samples:* $\frac{2}{4}$, $\frac{8}{16}$).

Assignment Guide
- Beginning 1–27 odd, 31, 32
- Intermediate 1–5, 6–28 even, 29–32
- Advanced 1–12, 14–28 even, 29–32

Notes on Exercises
Exercises 5–8 Remind students that all points on this number line are the same distance apart. Ask what fraction each point between zero and 1 represents ($\frac{1}{16}$). Name the first tick mark on the number line, $\frac{1}{16}$, to get students started.

Exercises 25–28 Suggest that students draw pictures if they need help writing the fractions. Remind them to write the final answer in simplest form.

Exercise 29 Ask students to explain the meanings of even (*divisible by 2*) and odd (*not divisible by 2*).

Exercise 30 Review the meanings of *composite* and *prime*. Encourage students to make lists of the composite and prime numbers.

Answers
1. $\frac{4}{6}$ or $\frac{2}{3}$ **2.** $\frac{5}{12}$
3. $\frac{3}{8}$ **4.** $\frac{7}{8}$
5. $\frac{10}{16}$ or $\frac{5}{8}$ **6.** $\frac{6}{16}$ or $\frac{3}{8}$
7. $\frac{3}{16}$ **8.** $\frac{14}{16}$ or $\frac{7}{8}$
9. Sample: $\frac{10}{12}, \frac{15}{18}, \frac{20}{24}$
10. Sample: $\frac{6}{20}, \frac{9}{30}, \frac{12}{40}$
11. Sample: $\frac{5}{8}, \frac{50}{80}, \frac{75}{120}$
12. Sample: $\frac{9}{12}, \frac{3}{4}, \frac{36}{48}$

13. 20 **14.** 3
15. 40 **16.** 3
17. $\frac{1}{3}$ **18.** $\frac{3}{5}$ **19.** $\frac{7}{8}$
20. $\frac{1}{2}$ **21.** $\frac{2}{5}$ **22.** $\frac{3}{4}$
23. $\frac{2}{5}$ **24.** $\frac{1}{3}$ **25.** $\frac{5}{18}$
26. $\frac{1}{3}$ **27.** $\frac{2}{9}$ **28.** $\frac{1}{6}$
29. $\frac{1}{2}$ **30.** $\frac{11}{20}; \frac{8}{20}$
31. Yes; $\frac{2}{3} = \frac{2 \times 2}{3 \times 2} = \frac{4}{6}$
32. C

Program Resources
Practice Book Use page 44.

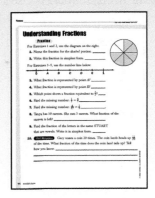

Teach Interpreting

- Explain to students that to *interpret* means to "explain the meaning of." In this activity, students will interpret the value of pairs of fractions.

- Some students may find shortcuts when comparing fractions. They may recognize that if $a = b$ and $b = c$, then $a = c$. You may want to have students compare $\frac{3}{5}$, $\frac{4}{8}$, and $\frac{4}{5}$ with each of the other fractions.

- Let students work independently, but have partners evaluate their models.

  Answers: $\frac{3}{5} = \frac{12}{20}$; $\frac{4}{8} = \frac{5}{10} = \frac{20}{40}$; $\frac{4}{5} = \frac{8}{10} = \frac{12}{15}$

Partner Practice

Suggest that students find the hourly pay for each pay scale.

Answers: $\$7/\frac{1}{2}h = \$14/hour$; $\$9/\frac{2}{3}h = \$13.50/hour$

Oral Language

You could also have students use other models to complete this activity.

Develop Language

Activities

Interpreting When you interpret results, you use your own words to describe what the information means.

1. **Interpret** Take two fractions at a time from the list below and rewrite them with common denominators. Interpret the results by telling which fractions are equivalent. Each of the fractions shown will be equivalent to $\frac{3}{5}$, $\frac{4}{8}$, or $\frac{4}{5}$. Complete a table or list like the one shown to help you keep track of your work. Work with a partner.

$$\frac{3}{5} \quad \frac{4}{8} \quad \frac{4}{5} \quad \frac{5}{10} \quad \frac{8}{10} \quad \frac{12}{15} \quad \frac{12}{20} \quad \frac{20}{40}$$

Fraction	Fraction	Equivalent?
$\frac{3}{5}$	$\frac{12}{20}$; $(\frac{12}{20} \div 4 = \frac{3}{5})$	yes

2. **Write** Write two or three sentences to explain how you compared the fractions.

3. **Draw** Show a pair of equivalent fractions by drawing circle models like the ones at the top of page 106. Have your partner check your work.

Partner Practice

Paychecks With a partner, decide which pay rate is better. Would it be better to earn $7 for each $\frac{1}{2}$ hour worked or $9 for each $\frac{2}{3}$ hour worked? Explain your answer.

Oral Language

Make It Simplest Work with a partner. Shade a 10-by-10 grid to represent a fraction. Your partner should say the fraction and then tell what the fraction is in simplest terms. Take turns shading a grid to represent a fraction. Tell how you find the simplest form of a fraction.

Program Resources

Practice Book Use page 45.
Overhead Transparencies Use 15.

Assessment Book

Use page 39 to assess students' comprehension.

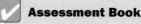

Activity: Extend the Lesson

To help students recognize fractional parts beyond the traditional circle models, have them draw several 4-by-4 squares on grid paper. Have them divide the squares into two equal parts in as many different ways as they can. Encourage them to use colors to make their designs into mathematical artwork. Display the designs when students are finished.

$\left(\textit{Samples:} \right.$ 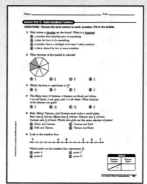 $\left. \right)$

Mixed Numbers

Talk and Explore

Big Idea Some fractions are equal to or greater than 1. You can write these fractions in several ways.

Building Background

▲ I like to help with craft projects. I enjoy measuring things.

- **What are these girls doing?**
- **What items have you tie-dyed?**
- **How can you measure $\frac{1}{2}$ cup of salt for the dye if you have only a $\frac{1}{4}$ cup measuring cup?**

Key Concepts

Fractions can be classified by how they compare to 1.

Fractions

Mixed Numbers	**Proper Fractions**	**Improper Fractions**
are greater than 1.	are less than 1.	are greater than or equal to 1.
$2\frac{1}{5}$, $31\frac{4}{9}$, $5\frac{6}{7}$	$\frac{99}{100}$, $\frac{1}{3}$, $\frac{14}{29}$	$\frac{100}{89}$, $\frac{9}{9}$, $\frac{23}{19}$
Each is the sum of a whole number and a fraction.	The numerator is less than the denominator.	The numerator is greater than or equal to the denominator.

LESSON 18 • MIXED NUMBERS **109**

Activity: Proper or Not?

Create this number line (Overhead Transparency 28).

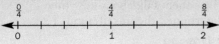

Have students copy the number line and extend it to 3. Have them plot $\frac{1}{2}$, $1\frac{3}{4}$, $2\frac{1}{4}$, and $\frac{11}{4}$ on the number line.

Have them classify each number as a mixed number, a proper fraction, or an improper fraction (*proper:* $\frac{1}{2}$; *improper:* $\frac{11}{4}$; *mixed:* $1\frac{3}{4}$, $2\frac{1}{4}$).

Resource Library

Math at Hand
Fractions and Mixed Numbers
029, 034

Math on Call
Fractions and Mixed Numbers
033–034

Mixed Numbers

STANDARDS CONTENT
Mathematics
- Write improper fractions as mixed numbers
- Write mixed numbers as improper fractions

Language
- Recognize multiple meanings of *proper* and *improper*
- Describe fractions

Introduce the **Big Idea**

Read aloud the Big Idea. Ask students to give examples of fractions greater than 1 ($\frac{3}{2}$, $\frac{19}{8}$).

Begin **Building Background**

Demonstrate how to use two $\frac{1}{4}$-cup measuring cups to measure $\frac{1}{2}$ cup of salt. Ask, *How could you draw a picture to help you find the number of $\frac{1}{4}$-cup measures needed?*

Teach **Key Concepts**

- Introduce the terms *mixed number*, *proper fraction*, and *improper fraction* as ways to classify fractions. Have students describe what is unique about each classification.
- Ask students to name other fractions that could be included in each group.

Warm-Up Review

Have students evaluate each expression.

1. $6 \times 3 + 2$ (*20*)
2. $9 \times 8 + 7$ (*79*)
3. $2 \times 5 + 1$ (*11*)
4. $7 \times 4 + 3$ (*31*)
5. $3 \times 5 + 4$ (*19*)
6. $2 \times 6 + 5$ (*17*)
7. $5 \times 9 + 1$ (*46*)
8. $1 \times 8 + 5$ (*13*)

Teach Writing Improper Fractions as Mixed Numbers

- Have volunteers read each of the first three paragraphs and explain why each model fits the definition.
- Ask, *Why do five batches of dye need $\frac{5}{2}$ cup of salt?* (5 times a half is 5 halves.)

Language Notes

Discuss the multiple meanings of *proper* and *improper.* Point out that the words are also *antonyms,* or opposites.

Talk and Share

Have partners share their explanations with the class.

Answers: No, proper fractions are always less than 1; when the numerator is divisible by the denominator; you can divide without a remainder.

Build VOCABULARY

Point out that the prefix *im-* can mean "not," and *improper* means "not proper." A fraction that is not proper is greater than or equal to 1. Its numerator is greater than or equal to the denominator. Any improper fraction can be written as a mixed number or a whole number.

Language Notes

Multiple Meanings
These words have more than one meaning.

☐ proper
1. a fraction whose numerator is less than its denominator
2. right or correct

☐ improper
1. a fraction whose numerator is greater than or equal to its denominator
2. wrong or incorrect

Writing Improper Fractions as Mixed Numbers

A **proper fraction** is a fraction less than 1. The numerator is less than the denominator.

An **improper fraction** is greater than or equal to 1. The numerator is greater than or equal to the denominator.

 $\frac{5}{6} \leftarrow$ proper fractions $\rightarrow \frac{3}{10}$

   $\frac{19}{8} \leftarrow$ improper fraction

A **mixed number** is greater than 1. Each is the sum of a whole number and a proper fraction.

 $1\frac{3}{4} \leftarrow$ mixed number

If you want to make 5 batches of dye, how much salt will you need? You need $\frac{1}{2}$ cup for each batch, so you need $\frac{5}{2}$ cups of salt. You can write $\frac{5}{2}$ as a mixed number. Remember that a fraction can indicate division.

$$\frac{5}{2} = \begin{array}{r} 2\frac{1}{2} \leftarrow \text{remainder} \\ 2\overline{)5} \leftarrow \text{divisor} \\ -4 \\ \hline 1 \end{array}$$

You will need $2\frac{1}{2}$ cups of salt.

Talk and Share

Talk with a partner. Tell whether a proper fraction ever can be written as a whole number. Tell when an improper fraction can be written as a whole number. Explain your thinking.

VOCABULARY

proper fraction—a fraction whose numerator is less than its denominator
improper fraction—a fraction whose numerator is greater than or equal to its denominator
mixed number—a number with a whole-number part and a fraction part

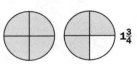

Tie-Dye
4 quarts warm water
$\frac{1}{2}$ cup salt
$\frac{1}{2}$ cup water softener
$\frac{3}{4}$ cup dry dye **or**
$1\frac{1}{2}$ cups liquid dye
$\frac{1}{2}$ cup urea

Activity: Don't Be Improper!

Have students list ten fractions, some proper and some improper. Have partners classify each fraction as *proper* or *improper* and show how to write each improper fraction as a mixed number.

Differentiating Instruction

Beginning
Drawing Fraction Models Have students write *proper fraction, improper fraction,* and *mixed number* on a sheet of paper. Have them read through the examples on page 110 and then draw a model to illustrate each term.

Intermediate
Discussing Improper Fractions and Mixed Numbers Have students reread the examples on page 110. Then have pairs take turns. One partner draws a

model of an improper fraction and the other labels it with a mixed number. Have them talk about how they determined the mixed number.

Advanced
Naming Mixed Numbers by Dividing Have students reread the examples on page 110. Have pairs of students alternate writing an improper fraction and having the partner use division to find the corresponding mixed number. Have students explain how they did it.

Writing Mixed Numbers as Improper Fractions

To write $3\frac{1}{4}$ as an improper fraction, you can use a model.

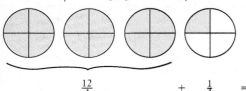

$$\frac{12}{4} \qquad + \qquad \frac{1}{4} \qquad = \qquad \frac{13}{4}$$

You also can use multiplication and addition.

Step 1	**Step 2**	**Step 3**
Each of the 3 yellow circles has 4 parts, or 12 total parts.	The 4th circle has 1 yellow part, so add it to the 12.	Write the sum 13 as the numerator. Keep the same denominator.
$4 \times 3 = 12$	$12 + 1 = 13$	$\frac{(12 + 1)}{4} = \frac{13}{4}$

Write $5\frac{2}{3}$ as an improper fraction.

$$5\frac{2}{3} = \frac{(3 \times 5) + 2}{3} = \frac{15 + 2}{3} = \frac{17}{3}$$

Write 6 as an improper fraction with a denominator of 3.

$$6 = \frac{6}{1} \qquad \leftarrow \text{Write the whole number as a fraction over 1.}$$

$$\frac{6 \times 3}{1 \times 3} = \frac{18}{3} \qquad \leftarrow \text{Multiply numerator and denominator by 3.}$$

$$6 = \frac{18}{3}$$

1/4 cup

Talk and Share

Work with a partner to answer these questions. If you have only a $\frac{1}{2}$-cup measure, how can you measure $1\frac{1}{2}$ cups of liquid? How can you measure $1\frac{1}{2}$ cups of liquid if you have only a $\frac{1}{4}$-cup measure?

Teach Writing Mixed Numbers as Improper Fractions

■ Use the models to explain why the whole number and the denominator are multiplied in Step 1. Point out that there are 3 wholes, each with 4 equal parts. So there are 12 fourths, which is the same as 3×4, or 12, written over the denominator, 4. The 1 fourth in the fractional part is added to the 12 fourths in the whole-number part for a total of 13 fourths.

■ An alternate approach is to rewrite $3\frac{1}{4}$ as $3 + \frac{1}{4}$. Change 3 to $\frac{12}{4}$ and add $\frac{1}{4}$ ($\frac{12}{4} + \frac{1}{4} = \frac{13}{4}$).

Talk and Share

You may want to use 2-c, $\frac{1}{2}$-c, and $\frac{1}{4}$-c measuring cups to model students' responses. Encourage students to explain how they decided on their answers. ($1\frac{1}{2} = \frac{3}{2}$, *so use three $\frac{1}{2}$ cups; $1\frac{1}{2} = 1\frac{2}{4} = \frac{6}{4}$, so use six $\frac{1}{4}$ cups*)

Build VOCABULARY

Write *proper fraction, improper fraction,* and *mixed number* on the board. Have volunteers draw a model to illustrate each term.

Differentiating Instruction

Beginning

Rewriting Mixed Numbers Have students use an inch ruler to draw a 6-in. line. Have them mark and label points on the line for measures greater than 1 in., such as $1\frac{3}{4}$ in., $3\frac{5}{8}$ in., and $4\frac{1}{2}$ in. Then have them relabel each point in fourths, eighths and halves, respectively ($\frac{7}{4}, \frac{29}{8}, \frac{9}{2}$).

Intermediate

Using Fraction Vocabulary Have pairs of students reread the three steps on page 111. Then have them use the terms *mixed number, improper fraction, numerator,* and *denominator* to talk about these steps in rewriting $2\frac{5}{6}$: $2\frac{5}{6} = \frac{(2 \times 6) + 5}{6} = \frac{17}{6}$.

Advanced

Telling Why in Writing Have pairs of students explain in writing how to write $2\frac{5}{6}$ as an improper fraction. Have them explain *why* they multiply the whole number by the denominator.

Activity: Use a Word Cube

Have pairs write the vocabulary words from Build Vocabulary (above) on a large version of the cube pattern shown below and then form the cube. Have students alternate tossing the cube, defining the word shown, and giving an example.

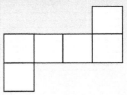

Practice

Have students write *20 sixths* in simplest form and as a mixed number. Ask a volunteer to explain how to write the fraction in each number in simplest form. ($\frac{20}{6} = \frac{10}{3}$; $3\frac{2}{6} = 3\frac{1}{3}$; *divide the numerator and the denominator by 2.*)

Assignment Guide
- Beginning 2–22 even, 23, 24, 27, 28
- Intermediate 1–23 odd, 24–28
- Advanced 1–6, 7–23 odd, 24–28

Notes on Exercises

Exercises 1–6 Have students write the fraction part of their answers in simplest form.

Exercise 24 This exercise asks students how to measure the amount of beans by using a $\frac{1}{2}$-c measuring cup.

Exercises 24–26 Ask volunteers to explain how they solved these problems. Remind students that *triple* means "multiply by three."

Exercises 27 and 28 These exercises preview Lesson 19, comparing and ordering fractions with unlike denominators. Have students sketch models or a number line if they need help.

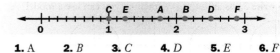

Practice

Give a mixed or whole number and an improper fraction for each point on the number line.

1. A   **2.** B   **3.** C   **4.** D   **5.** E   **6.** F

Write each improper fraction as a mixed or whole number. Give fractions in simplest form.

7. $\frac{4}{3}$ **8.** $\frac{11}{2}$ **9.** $\frac{18}{4}$ **10.** $\frac{12}{2}$

11. $\frac{21}{3}$ **12.** $\frac{32}{8}$ **13.** $\frac{16}{6}$ **14.** $\frac{48}{12}$

Write each mixed number as an improper fraction.

15. $6\frac{1}{2}$ **16.** $8\frac{2}{3}$ **17.** $7\frac{2}{5}$ **18.** $9\frac{9}{10}$

19. $4\frac{3}{7}$ **20.** $6\frac{2}{9}$ **21.** $8\frac{3}{8}$ **22.** $11\frac{1}{6}$

23. Write 12 as an improper fraction.

Use the recipe for Exercises 24–26. Assume you have only a $\frac{1}{2}$-cup measure.

24. How will you measure the beans for the dip?

25. Write a mixed number for the amount of onions you will need if you triple the dip recipe.

26. How many $\frac{1}{2}$ cups of salsa will you need if you triple the recipe?

27. (EXTENDED RESPONSE) Kurasawa has $2\frac{3}{4}$ pounds of rice. Morito has $\frac{10}{4}$ pounds of rice. Who has more rice? Explain.

28. (MULTIPLE CHOICE) Which mixed number is greater than $\frac{15}{6}$?

   A. $2\frac{4}{6}$ **B.** $2\frac{3}{6}$ **C.** $2\frac{2}{6}$ **D.** $2\frac{1}{6}$

Cinco de Mayo Dip

2 cups refried beans
1 cup sour cream
$\frac{1}{2}$ cup taco meat
1 cup shredded cheese
$\frac{1}{2}$ cup chopped onion
1 cup shredded lettuce
$1\frac{1}{2}$ cups salsa
seasoned salt

Combine beans, meat, onion, and salt in bottom of 9" pan. Top with sour cream and cheese. Bake for 25 minutes in 350° oven. Sprinkle lettuce over cheese. Top with salsa. Serve with tortilla chips.

Program Resources

Practice Book Use page 46.

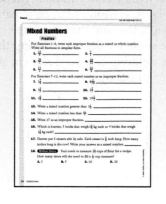

Answers

1. $1\frac{3}{4}, \frac{7}{4}$ **2.** $2\frac{1}{8}, \frac{17}{8}$

3. $1, \frac{8}{8}$ **4.** $2\frac{1}{2}, \frac{5}{2}$

5. $1\frac{1}{4}, \frac{5}{4}$ **6.** $2\frac{7}{8}, \frac{23}{8}$

7. $1\frac{1}{3}$ **8.** $5\frac{1}{2}$

9. $4\frac{1}{2}$ **10.** 6

11. 7   **12.** 4

13. $2\frac{2}{3}$ **14.** 4

15. $\frac{13}{2}$ **16.** $\frac{26}{3}$

17. $\frac{37}{5}$ **18.** $\frac{99}{10}$

19. $\frac{31}{7}$ **20.** $\frac{56}{9}$

21. $\frac{67}{8}$ **22.** $\frac{67}{6}$

23. Samples: $\frac{12}{1}, \frac{24}{2}$

24. Use four $\frac{1}{2}$-c measures.

25. $1\frac{1}{2}$, or $\frac{3}{2}$, c

26. Nine $\frac{1}{2}$ cups

27. Kurasawa; he has $\frac{11}{4}$ lb, which is more than Morito's $\frac{10}{4}$ lb.

28. A

Activities

Describing Describe the relationship among the words in the circle shown at the right. Do this by telling how the three types of numbers are alike and how they are different. Work with a partner.

Mixed Number

Improper Fraction

Proper Fraction

1. **Explain** Tell what each term means by giving two examples of each.

2. **Draw** Draw a picture with circles or grids to show one example of each term.

3. **Describe** Tell how proper fractions, improper fractions, and mixed numbers are alike.

4. **Describe** Tell how proper fractions, improper fractions, and mixed numbers are different.

Hands On

What's the Rule(r)? Take turns with a partner. On an inch ruler, point to a tick mark to the right of 1. Have your partner say the mixed number and the improper fraction for the tick mark. Each of you should take at least five turns.

Oral Language

The Great Fraction Divide Take turns giving your partner a division problem to solve. The dividend should have two digits and the divisor should have one digit. Have your partner find the quotient. It will be a whole number or a mixed number. Fraction answers should be in simplest terms.

Sample: You say, "15 divided by 6." Your partner does the division and says, "The quotient is $2\frac{3}{6}$. That is $2\frac{1}{2}$ in simplest terms."

Develop Language

Teach Describing

■ Remind students that to *describe* is to "tell about the details" of something. For this activity, they will describe mixed numbers, improper fractions, and proper fractions.

■ Have students work in pairs to complete the activity. Then have the students come together to share their results.

Hands On

Review how to pronounce a mixed number. Write several mixed numbers on the board and have volunteers read the numbers aloud. Be sure that students know that they must say *and* between the whole number and the fraction.

Oral Language

■ Review the terms *dividend, divisor,* and *quotient.* Ask two volunteers to read the sample problem and two other volunteers to model another problem before student pairs begin their work.

■ Encourage students to use mental math to find each quotient.

Activity: No Peeking!

Have students draw a model of a mixed number and write the mixed number and improper fraction that is shown by the model. Ask them to keep their drawing a secret.

Ask each student to describe the model to a partner while the partner draws the model based on the oral description. When the model is drawn correctly, the partner writes the mixed number and improper fraction shown by the model.

Assessment Book

Use page 40 to assess students' comprehension.

Program Resources

Practice Book Use page 47.

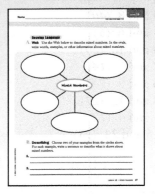

Comparing and Ordering

STANDARDS CONTENT

Mathematics
- Compare and order fractions and decimals
- Compare and order mixed numbers and fractions

Language
- Compare fractional parts using models

Materials
- Number lines (Overhead Transparency 28)

Introduce the Big Idea

Read aloud the Big Idea. Tell students that they can compare fractions by rewriting the fractions with the same denominator.

Begin Building Background

Ask volunteers to describe shells (or other items) they like to collect. Ask, *How could you compare two shells? (Samples: by size, shape, type, color)*

Teach Key Concepts

- Review the symbols for *is equal to, is less than,* and *is greater than.* Have students share ways to remember the symbols' meanings. (*Sample: The inequality symbol points to the lesser number.*)

- Ask, *Can you think of times when you might need to compare fractions?*

Warm-Up Review

Have students find the LCM for each pair of numbers.

1. 5 and 8 (*40*)
2. 3 and 6 (*6*)
3. 4 and 10 (*20*)
4. 2 and 7 (*14*)
5. 6 and 8 (*24*)
6. 8 and 12 (*24*)
7. 3 and 4 (*12*)
8. 16 and 24 (*48*)

Comparing and Ordering

Big Idea You can compare things in many ways. You can put some things next to each other to see how they are different. To compare fractions, you first write the fractions with a common denominator.

Building Background

▲ When I go to the beach, I look for pretty shells.

- **What is happening in the photo?**
- **Where can you find shells or coral or sharks' teeth?**
- **How would you arrange these shells?**

▲ The tooth on the left is a shark's tooth. The other tooth belonged to a dinosaur!

Key Concepts

When you **compare** sizes of small things, you may have to compare fractions. On a number line from 0 to 1, the fraction closest to 0 has the **least** value. The fraction closest to 1 has the **greatest** value. Of the fractions shown below, $\frac{1}{8}$ is the least and $\frac{7}{8}$ is the greatest.

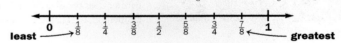

least ⟶ 0 $\frac{1}{8}$ $\frac{1}{4}$ $\frac{3}{8}$ $\frac{1}{2}$ $\frac{5}{8}$ $\frac{3}{4}$ $\frac{7}{8}$ 1 ⟵ greatest

---

Activity: Which Price Is More?

Give small groups of students catalogs or grocery ads from several different stores. Have them compare prices for several items.

Ask, *Why do you need to make sure you are comparing the same product and the same size of that item? (The comparison doesn't mean anything if the items are not alike.)*

Have students list each item and use mathematical symbols to show the comparisons.

Resource Library

Math at Hand
Comparing and Ordering Fractions
038–042

Math on Call
Comparing and Ordering Fractions
039–041

***Reader's Handbook* (red)**
Focus on Math Tests, 593–597

Comparing and Ordering Fractions

▲ The jaws of a great white shark can have about 3,000 teeth.

To compare and order the lengths of a shark's teeth shown on the right, first rewrite the fractions using their least common denominator. The **least common denominator (LCD)** is the least common multiple of the denominators. When you use the LCD, the numerators and denominators are as small as possible, and it is easier to compare the fractions. Compare $\frac{7}{8}$, $\frac{3}{4}$, and $\frac{15}{16}$.

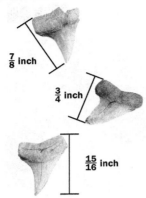

$\frac{7}{8}$ inch

$\frac{3}{4}$ inch

$\frac{15}{16}$ inch

$$\frac{7}{8} = \frac{14}{16}, \quad \frac{3}{4} = \frac{12}{16}, \quad \frac{15}{16} = \frac{15}{16}$$

← 16 is the LCD for 8, 4, and 16.

Now the fractions have the same denominator. You can use the numerators to compare them.

$$\frac{14}{16} > \frac{12}{16}, \text{ so } \frac{7}{8} > \frac{3}{4}. \qquad \frac{15}{16} > \frac{14}{16}, \text{ so } \frac{15}{16} > \frac{7}{8}.$$

You also can change the fractions to decimals by dividing. You then can compare and order the decimals.

$$\frac{7}{8} = 7 \div 8 = 0.875$$
$$\frac{3}{4} = 3 \div 4 = 0.75$$
$$\frac{15}{16} = 15 \div 16 = 0.9375$$

◄ Great white shark

Because $0.75 < 0.875 < 0.9375$, the fractions in order from least to greatest are $\frac{3}{4}$, $\frac{7}{8}$, and $\frac{15}{16}$. The lengths of a shark's teeth in order from least to greatest are $\frac{3}{4}$ inch, $\frac{7}{8}$ inch, and $\frac{15}{16}$ inch.

Talk and Share

Work with a partner to compare $\frac{2}{3}$ and $\frac{7}{12}$. One of you should use fractions and the other should first change the fractions to decimals. Round the decimals to the nearest hundredth. Compare your results. Then tell which way of comparing is easier for you.

VOCABULARY

least common denominator (LCD)—the least common multiple of the denominators of two or more fractions

---

Teach Comparing and Ordering Fractions

- Review the term *least common multiple*. Review how to find the LCM of two numbers. Tell students that the *least common denominator* of two fractions is the LCM of the fractions' denominators.

- You may wish to have students use models to help them compare and order fractions. Fraction strips can be laid next to one another to compare fractions. Circle models can be overlaid to compare the fractional parts. Number lines show relative value.

Talk and Share

Discuss what denominators students used to write each fraction. Ask students who used 36, the product of the two denominators, to share their work. Point out that the method is correct but because students are working with greater numbers, it is easier to make errors.

Answers: $\frac{2}{3} = \frac{8}{12}$, $\frac{8}{12} > \frac{7}{12}$, *so* $\frac{2}{3} > \frac{7}{12}$; *or* $\frac{2}{3} \approx 0.67$, $\frac{7}{12} \approx 0.58$; $0.67 > 0.58$, *so* $\frac{2}{3} > \frac{7}{12}$

Build VOCABULARY

Have students write the term *least common denominator* in their math journals. Have them use their own words to write a definition and show the LCD for $\frac{3}{8}$ and $\frac{3}{4}$ (*8*).

Differentiating Instruction

Beginning
Ordering Fractional Line Segments
Have pairs of students draw line segments measuring $\frac{1}{2}$, $\frac{7}{8}$, $\frac{5}{8}$ and $\frac{1}{4}$ in. Ask them to visually compare the lengths and write the order from least to greatest. Then have them order the fractions using either method on page 115 ($\frac{1}{4}$, $\frac{1}{2}$, $\frac{5}{8}$, $\frac{7}{8}$).

Intermediate
Ordering Fractions Have students reread the examples on page 115. Then have them order these fractions from least to greatest: $\frac{1}{2}$, $\frac{3}{8}$, $\frac{9}{16}$, $\frac{1}{4}$ ($\frac{1}{4}$, $\frac{3}{8}$, $\frac{1}{2}$, $\frac{9}{16}$). Have them talk about how they found the order.

Advanced
Using Patterns to Order Fractions
Have pairs of students mentally order, from least to greatest, fractions that have the same denominator, such as $\frac{5}{12}$, $\frac{11}{12}$, $\frac{7}{12}$, and $\frac{1}{12}$, and fractions with the same numerator, such as $\frac{1}{8}$, $\frac{1}{2}$, $\frac{1}{4}$, and $\frac{1}{6}$. Have them write two sentences that explain how to order these two types of fractions. (*If fractions have the same denominator, order their numerators from least to greatest. If fractions have the same numerator, order their denominators from greatest to least.*)

Teach Comparing and Ordering Mixed Numbers

- Stress the sequence of the steps used to compare mixed numbers. Students should compare the fractional parts of $1\frac{3}{16}$, $1\frac{1}{2}$, and $1\frac{1}{8}$ because the whole-number parts are the same. To do this, they should write the fractions with their LCD.

- If models were used to compare fractions, the same models can be used to compare mixed numbers.

Talk and Share

You may wish to have partners use both mixed numbers and improper fractions to order mixed numbers before they discuss their preferences.

Answers: $3\frac{5}{6} = 3\frac{10}{12}$, $3\frac{1}{2} = 3\frac{6}{12}$, $3\frac{7}{12}$, $3\frac{3}{4} = 3\frac{9}{12}$; $3\frac{5}{6} = \frac{23}{6} = \frac{46}{12}$, $3\frac{1}{2} = \frac{7}{2} = \frac{42}{12}$, $3\frac{7}{12} = \frac{43}{12}$, $3\frac{3}{4} = \frac{15}{4} = \frac{45}{12}$; *either way,* $3\frac{1}{2} < 3\frac{7}{12} < 3\frac{3}{4} < 3\frac{5}{6}$

Build VOCABULARY

Discuss how the phrases *least to greatest* and *greatest to least* are used to show different order.

Comparing and Ordering Mixed Numbers

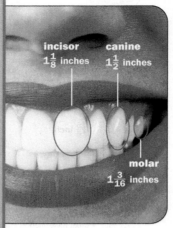

incisor $1\frac{1}{8}$ inches canine $1\frac{1}{2}$ inches

molar $1\frac{3}{16}$ inches

Human teeth, with their roots, can be more than an inch long. Typical lengths for adult teeth, with roots, are shown at the left. Write the lengths in order from least to greatest.

$1\frac{3}{16}$ $1\frac{1}{2}$ $1\frac{1}{8}$ ← The whole-number parts are the same, so order the fractions.

$1\frac{3}{16} = 1\frac{3}{16}$
$1\frac{1}{8} = 1\frac{2}{16}$ ← Write the fractions with their least common denominator, 16.
$1\frac{1}{2} = 1\frac{8}{16}$

$1\frac{2}{16} < 1\frac{3}{16} < 1\frac{8}{16}$ ← Write the mixed numbers in order by their fraction parts.
↓ ↓ ↓
$1\frac{1}{8} < 1\frac{3}{16} < 1\frac{1}{2}$

The lengths of these teeth in order from least to greatest are $1\frac{1}{8}$ inches, $1\frac{3}{16}$ inches, and $1\frac{1}{2}$ inches.

You also can compare and order mixed numbers by first writing them as improper fractions with their least common denominators. Write $2\frac{3}{8}$, $1\frac{3}{4}$, $2\frac{1}{4}$, and $1\frac{7}{8}$ in order from least to greatest.

$2\frac{3}{8} = \frac{19}{8}$ $1\frac{3}{4} = \frac{7}{4} = \frac{14}{8}$ $2\frac{1}{4} = \frac{9}{4} = \frac{18}{8}$ $1\frac{7}{8} = \frac{15}{8}$

$\frac{14}{8} < \frac{15}{8} < \frac{18}{8} < \frac{19}{8}$
↓ ↓ ↓ ↓
$1\frac{3}{4} < 1\frac{7}{8} < 2\frac{1}{4} < 2\frac{3}{8}$

You can check by picturing the numbers on a number line.

$1\frac{3}{4}$ $1\frac{7}{8}$ $2\frac{1}{4}$ $2\frac{3}{8}$

0 1 2 3

Talk and Share

Discuss with a partner how to order $3\frac{5}{6}$, $3\frac{1}{2}$, $3\frac{7}{12}$, and $3\frac{3}{4}$ from least to greatest. Each of you should order the numbers. One of you should use mixed numbers. The other should use improper fractions. Talk about which way you find easier.

Activity: I'm the Greatest!

Have pairs of students write a proper fraction, an improper fraction, a decimal, or a mixed number on each of twenty cards. Have them mix up the cards and each place ten cards facedown on the desk. Have students turn over their top card and compare the numbers. The partner with the greater number gets both cards. The game continues until all cards are taken. The student with more cards is the winner.

Differentiating Instruction

Beginning
Ordering Measures Have small groups of students align their pencils on a sheet of paper from shortest to longest. Then have them measure each pencil and write its length next to it. Have them write the lengths from least to greatest and note that some of the order depends on only the whole-number part.

Intermediate
Using Improper Factions to Order Have pairs of students follow the directions for the Beginning activity.

But have them write each measure as an improper fraction to order the lengths from least to greatest.

Advanced
Writing Steps to Order Have pairs of students write the steps used to order mixed numbers by writing them as improper fractions. (*Sample: 1: Write mixed numbers as improper fractions with the same denominator. 2: Compare numerators. 3: Put in order by numerators.*)

Practice

Compare the numbers in each pair using $<$, $=$, or $>$.

1. $\frac{5}{6}$ ▪ $\frac{3}{4}$ **2.** $\frac{7}{9}$ ▪ $\frac{5}{6}$ **3.** $\frac{7}{12}$ ▪ $\frac{5}{8}$ **4.** $\frac{5}{7}$ ▪ $\frac{11}{14}$

5. $\frac{4}{8}$ ▪ $\frac{12}{24}$ **6.** $\frac{1}{5}$ ▪ $\frac{2}{15}$ **7.** $\frac{3}{8}$ ▪ $\frac{2}{5}$ **8.** $\frac{5}{7}$ ▪ $\frac{4}{5}$

9. $6\frac{1}{6}$ ▪ $5\frac{5}{6}$ **10.** $3\frac{5}{12}$ ▪ $3\frac{1}{3}$ **11.** $5\frac{5}{8}$ ▪ $5\frac{7}{10}$ **12.** $4\frac{1}{4}$ ▪ $3\frac{9}{10}$

13. $2\frac{11}{12}$ ▪ $2\frac{1}{8}$ **14.** $4\frac{3}{16}$ ▪ $4\frac{1}{8}$ **15.** $3\frac{2}{5}$ ▪ $3\frac{4}{9}$ **16.** $2\frac{12}{16}$ ▪ $2\frac{9}{12}$

Order the numbers from least to greatest.

17. $\frac{2}{3}, \frac{3}{5}, \frac{1}{2}, \frac{2}{5}$ **18.** $\frac{7}{32}, \frac{1}{4}, \frac{3}{16}, \frac{3}{8}$

Violins, violas, cellos, and basses are all in the string section of an orchestra. ▼

19. $\frac{3}{5}, \frac{2}{3}, \frac{5}{6}, \frac{5}{8}$ **20.** $3\frac{1}{3}, \frac{3}{3}, 3\frac{2}{3}, \frac{2}{3}$

21. $\frac{5}{8}, 0.375, \frac{3}{4}, \frac{7}{10}$ **22.** $2.5, 2\frac{3}{5}, 2\frac{3}{8}, 2.25$

23. It took Ayisha $\frac{3}{5}$ hour to complete her homework and $\frac{7}{12}$ hour for Sam to complete his. Who worked longer?

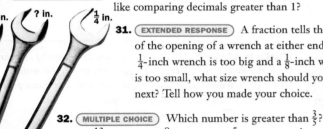

An orchestra string section has 32 violins, 10 violas, 12 cellos, and 6 string basses. What fraction of the string section are

24. violins? **25.** violas?

26. cellos? **27.** string basses?

28. Write the fractions of strings in order from least to greatest in simplest form.

29. (EXTENDED RESPONSE) To order $3\frac{1}{2}$, $5\frac{5}{6}$, $4\frac{2}{3}$, and $2\frac{3}{8}$, do you need to write the fractions with their least common denominator? Explain.

30. (EXTENDED RESPONSE) How is comparing mixed numbers like comparing decimals greater than 1?

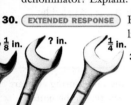

$\frac{1}{8}$ in.   ? in. $\frac{1}{4}$ in.

31. (EXTENDED RESPONSE) A fraction tells the size of the opening of a wrench at either end. If a $\frac{1}{4}$-inch wrench is too big and a $\frac{1}{8}$-inch wrench is too small, what size wrench should you try next? Tell how you made your choice.

32. (MULTIPLE CHOICE) Which number is greater than $\frac{3}{5}$?

A. $\frac{13}{25}$ B. $\frac{8}{15}$ C. $\frac{5}{10}$ D. $\frac{4}{6}$

Practice

Review the symbols for *is less than* and *is greater than*. Ask students to use symbols to compare $\frac{1}{4}$ and $\frac{2}{5}$. Have them explain how they made the comparison. ($\frac{1}{4} < \frac{2}{5}$ or $\frac{2}{5} > \frac{1}{4}$; *sample: I wrote the fractions with their LCD*.)

Assignment Guide
- Beginning 1–13, 15–23 odd, 24–30, 32
- Intermediate 1–14, 16–22 even, 23–30, 32
- Advanced 1–14, 16–22 even, 24–32

Notes on Exercises
Exercises 1–8 Encourage students to use calculators to check their answers.

Exercises 17–22 Ask volunteers to tell which exercise is the easiest and to explain why. (*Sample: Exercise 20 is easiest because all the fraction parts have the same denominator.*)

Exercises 24–27 Some students might find it helpful to make a table first.

Exercise 31 You may want to list some wrench sizes or accept any fraction that is greater than $\frac{1}{8}$ and less than $\frac{1}{4}$. Some possible wrench sizes are $\frac{3}{16}$ in., $\frac{5}{32}$ in., and $\frac{7}{32}$ in.

Answers

1. $>$ **2.** $<$ **3.** $<$

4. $<$ **5.** $=$ **6.** $>$

7. $<$ **8.** $<$ **9.** $>$

10. $>$ **11.** $<$ **12.** $>$

13. $>$ **14.** $>$ **15.** $<$

16. $=$ **17.** $\frac{2}{5}, \frac{1}{2}, \frac{3}{5}, \frac{2}{3}$

18. $\frac{3}{16}, \frac{7}{32}, \frac{1}{4}, \frac{3}{8}$

19. $\frac{3}{5}, \frac{5}{8}, \frac{2}{3}, \frac{5}{6}$ **20.** $\frac{2}{3}, \frac{3}{3}, 3\frac{1}{3}, 3\frac{2}{3}$

21. $0.375, \frac{5}{8}, \frac{7}{10}, \frac{3}{4}$

22. $2.25, 2\frac{3}{8}, 2.5, 2\frac{3}{5}$

23. Ayisha **24.** $\frac{8}{15}$

25. $\frac{1}{6}$ **26.** $\frac{1}{5}$

27. $\frac{1}{10}$ **28.** $\frac{1}{10}, \frac{1}{6}, \frac{1}{5}, \frac{8}{15}$

29. No; you need to compare only the whole numbers.

30. Sample: In both, it may be enough to compare the whole-number parts.

31. Sample: $\frac{3}{16}$ in.; on a ruler $\frac{3}{16}$ in. is between $\frac{1}{8}$ in. and $\frac{1}{4}$ in.

32. D

19 Develop Language

Teach Comparing

- Remind students that to *compare* numbers is to put them in order by size.

- Be sure students understand that they are to draw four same-sized circle models showing $\frac{2}{3}$, $\frac{2}{6}$, $\frac{2}{8}$, and $\frac{2}{10}$.

- Most students will be able to sketch the circles accurately enough to order the fractions. Students who have difficulty can use fraction strips to make the comparisons.

  Answers:
  1. $\frac{2}{10}$, $\frac{2}{8}$, $\frac{2}{6}$, $\frac{2}{3}$
  3. *is less than*

Hands On

Small groups will need twenty cards for the fraction part of this activity, twenty cards for the mixed-number part of the activity, and approximately ten additional cards for the decimal and fraction parts.

Partner Practice

Suggest that students write equivalent fractions with the same denominator to help them order the labels. You can show students a set of measuring cups to help them quantify the amounts. This activity could also be done with measuring spoons $(\frac{1}{4}, \frac{1}{3}, \frac{1}{2}, \frac{2}{3}, \frac{3}{4})$.

Develop Language

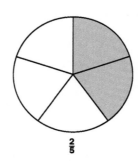
$\frac{2}{5}$

Activities

Comparing One way to compare numbers is to put them in order by size.

Work with a partner to compare thirds, sixths, eighths, and tenths. Together, draw circles and shade them to show two thirds, two sixths, two eighths, and two tenths. Label each circle with the fraction it shows. Make sure your circles are all the same size. The sample drawing shows two fifths.

1. **Compare** Compare the fractions by looking at the circles. Write the fractions in order from least to greatest.

2. **Explain** Tell what you wrote. Use the words *is greater than* and *is less than*.

3. **Complete** If two fractions have the same numerator, the fraction with the greater denominator is _____ than the other fraction.

4. **Check** See if your conclusion works with other pairs of fractions, such as $\frac{4}{5}$ and $\frac{4}{6}$.

Hands On

Come to Order! Work in a small group. In a bag, place a set of 20 cards labeled with fractions less than 1. Draw four cards and order the fractions from least to greatest.

To check each other's work, change the fractions to decimals and see if they are in order. Use a calculator to help you. For example, to change $\frac{5}{8}$ to a decimal, press 5 ÷ 8 =. The display will show 0.625.

Partner Practice

What's in a Label? Work with a partner. Measuring cups are stacked with the largest cup, a 1-cup measure, on the bottom. Order the fractions from least to greatest so that you can put the correct labels on the other five cups.

$\left(\frac{2}{3}\right)$ $\left(\frac{1}{2}\right)$ $\left(\frac{3}{4}\right)$ $\left(\frac{1}{3}\right)$ $\left(\frac{1}{4}\right)$

118 UNIT 5 • FRACTIONS AND MIXED NUMBERS

Program Resources
Practice Book Use page 49.

Assessment Book
Use page 41 to assess students' comprehension.

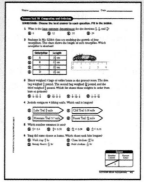

Activity: Internet Connection

Have students use these sites for interactive practice with comparing and ordering fractions. The visual-fractions site has two options: circle models and number lines.

- http://www.visualfractions.com
- http://www.shodor.org/interactivate

Adding Fractions

Big Idea The skills used for adding whole numbers and decimals also work for adding fractions and mixed numbers.

Building Background

▲ In my house, we speak both Arabic and English.

- **What do you see in the picture?**
- **How many languages do you think are spoken in the world?**
- **Which languages do you think are spoken by the most people?**

Key Concepts

When you add whole numbers and decimals, you add by place value. That is, you add thousands, hundreds, tens, ones, tenths, hundredths, and so on. When you add fractions, you must have fractions with denominators that are alike, or **common denominators**. Sometimes with whole numbers, decimals, and fractions you need to rewrite the numbers, or **rename** them.

Whole Numbers

$$\begin{array}{r} {\scriptstyle 1\,1} \\ 567 \\ + 378 \\ \hline 945 \end{array}$$

Add ones. Rename.
Add tens. Rename.

Decimals

$$\begin{array}{r} {\scriptstyle 1\,1} \\ 47.9 \\ + 66.8 \\ \hline 114.7 \end{array}$$

Add tenths. Rename.
Add ones. Rename.

Fractions

Common denominator →

$\frac{3}{4} + \frac{1}{2}$ Rename $\frac{1}{2}$ as $\frac{2}{4}$.

$\frac{3}{4} + \frac{2}{4} = \frac{5}{4}$ Add.

$\frac{5}{4} = 1\frac{1}{4}$ Rename $\frac{5}{4}$.

LESSON 20 • ADDING FRACTIONS **119**

Activity: By Any Other Name

Write 1.7 + 1.8 on the board in vertical form. Ask students how the 15 tenths are renamed to find the sum (*as 1 one and 5 tenths*).

Write $2\frac{15}{10}$ on the board. Elicit that the 15 tenths can be renamed as 1 and 5 tenths, so $2\frac{15}{10} = 2 + 1\frac{5}{10} = 3\frac{5}{10} = 3\frac{1}{2}$.

Ask volunteers to show how to rename these numbers: $2\frac{8}{6}$ ($3\frac{2}{6} = 3\frac{1}{3}$), $4\frac{5}{3}$ ($5\frac{2}{3}$), $1\frac{6}{4}$ ($2\frac{2}{4} = 2\frac{1}{2}$), and $2\frac{14}{8}$ ($3\frac{6}{8} = 3\frac{3}{4}$).

Resource Library

Math at Hand
Common Denominators 036
Adding with Fractions 158–161

Math on Call
Common Denominators 038
Adding with Fractions 104–107

Adding Fractions

STANDARDS CONTENT

Mathematics
- Add fractions
- Add mixed numbers

Language
- Recognize multiple meanings of *like* and *check*
- Compare and contrast adding fractions and mixed numbers

Introduce the **Big Idea**

Read aloud the Big Idea. Ask, *How are fractions and mixed numbers like decimals? (Sample: They can have whole-number parts and parts less than 1.)*

Begin **Building Background**

After asking the questions below the photo, take a poll to see what languages are spoken by the students and teachers in your class. Ask students what other languages they would like to learn.

Teach **Key Concepts**

- Discuss the vocabulary words *place value*, *common denominators*, and *rename*.
- Ask students to name some common denominators for $\frac{1}{2}$ and $\frac{3}{4}$ (*Sample: 4, 8, 12, 16*).

Warm-Up Review

Have students find the least common denominator for each pair of fractions.

1. $\frac{2}{3}$ and $\frac{3}{5}$ *(15)*
2. $\frac{1}{2}$ and $\frac{7}{8}$ *(8)*
3. $\frac{5}{8}$ and $\frac{10}{12}$ *(24)*
4. $\frac{1}{3}$ and $\frac{1}{2}$ *(6)*
5. $\frac{7}{8}$ and $\frac{5}{6}$ *(24)*
6. $\frac{3}{4}$ and $\frac{6}{10}$ *(20)*
7. $\frac{3}{10}$ and $\frac{1}{2}$ *(10)*

Teach **Adding Fractions**

- For the second example, you may want to show the addition in vertical form to emphasize that the fractions are renamed.

$$\frac{3}{50} = \frac{6}{100}$$
$$+ \frac{1}{20} = + \frac{5}{100}$$

- Students need to understand that before they can add fractions, they must make sure that the denominators are the same. Then they add the numerators, write the sum over the denominator, and write the fraction in simplest form.

- Remind students that *LCD* means "least common denominator."

Language Notes

Discuss the multiple meanings of *check* shown in Language Notes. Have students tell how the word is used on pages 120 and 121.

Talk and Share

After pairs of students have found the first two sums, encourage them to find each sum before drawing the models. Have them draw the model to check that their addition is correct.

Answers:

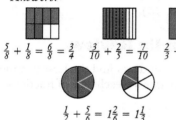

$$\frac{5}{8} + \frac{1}{8} = \frac{6}{8} = \frac{3}{4} \qquad \frac{3}{10} + \frac{2}{5} = \frac{7}{10} \qquad \frac{2}{3} + \frac{1}{3} = 1$$

$$\frac{1}{2} + \frac{5}{6} = 1\frac{2}{6} = 1\frac{1}{3}$$

Build VOCABULARY

On the board, write *LCD*, *numerator*, *denominator*, *improper fraction*, *simplest form*, and *mixed number*. Have students say a term and give a definition and example.

Adding Fractions

Language	Fraction (to nearest $\frac{1}{100}$)
Mandarin	$\frac{7}{50}$
Hindustani	$\frac{7}{100}$
Spanish	$\frac{3}{50}$
English	$\frac{1}{20}$
Bengali	$\frac{3}{100}$
Arabic	$\frac{3}{100}$
Portuguese	$\frac{3}{100}$
Russian	$\frac{3}{100}$
Japanese	$\frac{1}{50}$
German	$\frac{1}{50}$

The table on the left gives the fraction of the world's population that speaks each of the 10 most common languages. Mandarin is spoken by about 874,000,000 people, or by 7 out of every 50 people on Earth. Fewer than half that many people—about 358,000,000—speak Spanish. To find what fraction of the world population speaks either Mandarin or Spanish, find $\frac{7}{50} + \frac{3}{50}$.

Step 1

$\frac{7}{50} + \frac{3}{50}$ The fractions have common, or *like*, denominators.

$\frac{7 + 3}{50}$ Add the numerators. Keep the denominators.

Step 2

$\frac{7 + 3}{50} = \frac{10}{50}$ Add.

$\frac{10}{50} = \frac{1}{5}$ Write in simplest form.

One-fifth of the world's population speaks Mandarin or Spanish. To find the fraction of the world's population that speaks Spanish or English, find $\frac{3}{50} + \frac{1}{20}$.

$$\frac{3}{50} + \frac{1}{20} = \frac{6}{100} + \frac{5}{100} = \frac{11}{100} \quad \leftarrow \text{Write the fractions with their least common denominator, 100. Then add.}$$

$\frac{11}{100}$ of the world's population speaks Spanish or English.

The circle models show $\frac{3}{4} + \frac{3}{4}$.

$$\frac{3}{4} + \frac{3}{4} = \frac{6}{4} = 1\frac{2}{4} = 1\frac{1}{2}$$

You also can add $\frac{3}{4} + \frac{3}{4}$ without a model.

$$\frac{3}{4} + \frac{3}{4} = \frac{3 + 3}{4} = \frac{6}{4} \quad \leftarrow \text{Add the numerators. Keep the denominator.}$$

$$\frac{3}{4} + \frac{3}{4} = \frac{6}{4} = 1\frac{2}{4} = 1\frac{1}{2} \quad \leftarrow \text{Write the improper fraction as a mixed number in simplest form.}$$

Talk and Share

Work with a partner. Draw circle or grid models to show each sum. Give sums in simplest form. Check your work.

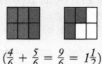

$$\frac{5}{8} + \frac{1}{8} \qquad \frac{3}{10} + \frac{2}{5} \qquad \frac{2}{3} + \frac{1}{3} \qquad \frac{1}{2} + \frac{5}{6}$$

Language Notes

Multiple Meanings
These words have more than one meaning.

☐ **like**
1. similar
2. enjoy something

☐ **check**
1. make sure something is correct
2. the bill for a restaurant meal
3. a written order to a bank for money from an account

Differentiating Instruction

Beginning

Modeling Fraction Addition On the board, draw this model and help students identify the fractions being added. Have them give the sums in simplest form.

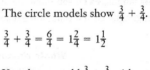

$$\left(\frac{4}{6} + \frac{5}{6} = \frac{9}{6} = 1\frac{1}{2}\right)$$

Intermediate

Using a Number Line to Add Fractions Have pairs of students use a number line from 0–1 marked in eighths (Overhead Transparency 28) and work together to demonstrate how to find sums such as $\frac{1}{8} + \frac{3}{8}$, $\frac{1}{2} + \frac{1}{8}$, and $\frac{7}{8} + \frac{5}{8}$. Tell them to give sums in simplest form $\left(\frac{1}{2}, \frac{5}{8}, 1\frac{1}{2}\right)$.

Advanced

Finding the Total Have students copy the Language table on page 120 and add a column titled *In Hundredths*. Have them complete the table and find the total fraction of the world's population that speaks the ten languages $\left(\frac{12}{25}\right)$.

Adding Mixed Numbers

To find how much soy sauce and water are used in the recipe for Mandarin spareribs, find $1\frac{1}{4} + 1\frac{1}{4}$.

Step 1		Step 2		Step 3	
$1\frac{1}{4}$ $+ 1\frac{1}{4}$ $\overline{\frac{2}{4}}$	Add the fractions.	$1\frac{1}{4}$ $+ 1\frac{1}{4}$ $\overline{2\frac{2}{4}}$	Add the whole numbers.	$2\frac{2}{4} = 2\frac{1}{2}$	Write the fraction in simplest form.

There are $2\frac{1}{2}$ cups of soy sauce and water in the recipe.

Find $5\frac{1}{2} + 2\frac{1}{3}$.

Step 1		Step 2	
$5\frac{1}{2} = 5\frac{3}{6}$ $+ 2\frac{1}{3} = + 2\frac{2}{6}$	Write the fractions with their least common denominator, 6.	$5\frac{3}{6}$ $+ 2\frac{2}{6}$ $\overline{7\frac{5}{6}}$	Add the fractions. Add the whole numbers.

Find $2\frac{11}{12} + 1\frac{11}{12}$.

Step 1		Step 2	
$2\frac{11}{12}$ $+ 1\frac{11}{12}$ $\overline{3\frac{22}{12}}$	Add the fractions. Add the whole numbers.	$\frac{22}{12} = 1\frac{10}{12} = 1\frac{5}{6}$ $3 + 1\frac{5}{6} = 4\frac{5}{6}$	Write the sum as a mixed number in simplest form.

You can check your answer by estimating.

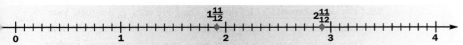

The number line shows that $2\frac{11}{12}$ is close to 3 and $1\frac{11}{12}$ is close to 2. You know $3 + 2 = 5$, so $4\frac{5}{6}$ is a reasonable answer because it is close to 5.

Talk and Share

Work with a partner to find $4\frac{2}{3} + 3\frac{5}{12}$. Check your answer by estimating on a number line.

Mandarin Spareribs

8 pounds spareribs, cut into serving size, precooked
$2\frac{1}{2}$ cups brown sugar
$1\frac{1}{4}$ cups soy sauce
$1\frac{1}{4}$ cups water
$\frac{1}{4}$ cup rice vinegar
Arrange ribs in shallow pan.
Mix together the other items and pour over ribs.
Let rest for 4 hours.
Roast in greased roasting pan in oven set at 325° for 1 hour.
Baste ribs with liquid.
Serves 10.

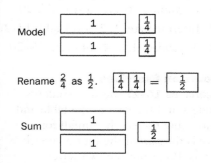

Teach Adding Mixed Numbers

■ Students may use models to add mixed numbers. Have them draw a grid model or use fraction strips to show $1\frac{1}{4} + 1\frac{1}{4}$.

Model

Rename $\frac{2}{4}$ as $\frac{1}{2}$.

Sum

■ Ask volunteers to recap the steps for adding mixed numbers:
  • Rewrite the fractions with the LCD, if needed.
  • Add fractions.
  • Add whole numbers.
  • Write the sum in simplest form.

■ Explain that students could write the mixed numbers as improper fractions and then add. Then they will have to rewrite the sum as a mixed number in simplest form.

■ Show how to estimate sums by rounding fractions to the nearest whole number. Have students estimate $2\frac{1}{3} + 1\frac{3}{4}$ and $\frac{1}{8} + \frac{1}{8}$. Ask students what it means if the estimated sum is 0. (*4, 0; the fraction is close to 0.*)

Talk and Share

This activity provides an opportunity to assess how well students understand the value of mixed numbers in relation to other numbers.

Answer: $4\frac{2}{3} + 3\frac{5}{12} = 8\frac{1}{12}$

Differentiating Instruction

Beginning
Modeling Mixed-Number Addition On the board, draw mixed-number addition models. Have volunteers identify the numbers being added and tell how to get the sum. (*Sample: Add the whole-number parts and the fraction parts separately and then combine the two sums.*)

Intermediate
Measuring to Add Mixed Numbers
Have pairs draw a line across a sheet of paper. Have one student mark off and label a mixed-number measure. Have

the partner add and label a mixed-number measure. Ask the students to write the addition, find the total length marked, and check by measuring.

Advanced
Adding Three Mixed Numbers Have pairs of students work together to find how much brown sugar is needed for three recipes of Mandarin spareribs on page 121. Have them write the numbers vertically and talk about how to find the sum ($7\frac{1}{2}$).

Practice

Write $1\frac{1}{5} + 1\frac{9}{10}$ on the board. Have a volunteer find the sum and explain each step $(3\frac{1}{10})$.

Assignment Guide
- Beginning 1–11, 13–19 odd, 20
- Intermediate 1, 2, 3–13 odd, 14–20
- Advanced 1, 2, 4–14 even, 15–20

Notes on Exercises

Exercises 14–17 Be sure students understand the data in the table and know that the yearly rainfall for each city is the *sum* of the four 3-month totals. Point out the two-letter abbreviations for the states' names.

Exercise 18 You may wish to remind students that all of Jaime's CDs are considered an entire set.

Exercise 20 Suggest that students estimate the missing number to eliminate answer choices before finding the exact answer.

Practice

Write the addition sentence shown in each model. Give answers in simplest form.

1.   **2.**

Find each sum. Give the answer in simplest form.

3. $\frac{7}{20} + \frac{9}{20}$ **4.** $\frac{11}{16} + \frac{5}{16}$ **5.** $\frac{3}{10} + \frac{1}{6}$ **6.** $\frac{2}{3} + \frac{4}{5}$

7. $\frac{5}{8} + \frac{7}{12}$ **8.** $8\frac{8}{9} + 7\frac{4}{9}$ **9.** $4\frac{2}{3} + 5\frac{1}{6}$ **10.** $\frac{7}{12} + \frac{5}{6}$

11. $4\frac{1}{10} + 2\frac{1}{10} + 4\frac{3}{10}$ **12.** $\frac{3}{4} + \frac{7}{8} + \frac{5}{24}$ **13.** $1\frac{2}{3} + \frac{5}{6} + 3\frac{1}{4}$

The table below lists average total rainfall amounts, in inches, for 3-month periods for 3 different cities.

City	January through March	April through June	July through September	October through December
Albuquerque, NM	$1\frac{3}{10}$	$2\frac{4}{10}$	$3\frac{7}{10}$	$1\frac{8}{10}$
Houston, TX	$9\frac{2}{10}$	$13\frac{9}{10}$	$11\frac{9}{10}$	$10\frac{8}{10}$
Mobile, AL	16	16	$21\frac{1}{10}$	$11\frac{7}{10}$

For each city, find the total yearly rainfall.
14. Albuquerque **15.** Houston **16.** Mobile
17. List the cities in order from least to greatest yearly rainfall.

18. (EXTENDED RESPONSE) Of Jaime's CDs, $\frac{3}{8}$ are salsa, $\frac{3}{16}$ are rock, $\frac{1}{4}$ are country, and $\frac{1}{8}$ are blues. Of what kind of music does she have the most? Does she have any CDs that are *not* in one of these groups? Explain.

19. (EXTENDED RESPONSE) Explain how to add $\frac{5}{6}$ and $\frac{1}{4}$. Could you use a denominator of 24? Why or why not?

20. (MULTIPLE CHOICE) Complete this number sentence: $5\frac{2}{3} + \blacksquare = 8\frac{7}{12}$.
A. $3\frac{11}{12}$ **B.** $3\frac{3}{4}$ **C.** $2\frac{11}{12}$ **D.** $2\frac{3}{4}$

Program Resources
Practice Book Use page 50.

Answers

1. $\frac{7}{10} + \frac{9}{10} = \frac{16}{10} = 1\frac{3}{5}$

2. $\frac{5}{8} + 2\frac{1}{8} = 2\frac{6}{8} = 2\frac{3}{4}$

3. $\frac{4}{5}$ **4.** 1

5. $\frac{7}{15}$ **6.** $1\frac{7}{15}$

7. $1\frac{5}{24}$ **8.** $16\frac{1}{3}$

9. $9\frac{5}{6}$ **10.** $1\frac{5}{12}$

11. $10\frac{1}{2}$ **12.** $1\frac{5}{6}$

13. $5\frac{3}{4}$ **14.** $9\frac{1}{5}$ in.

15. $45\frac{4}{5}$ in. **16.** $64\frac{4}{5}$ in.

17. Albuquerque, Houston, Mobile

18. Salsa; yes; $\frac{3}{8} + \frac{3}{16} + \frac{1}{4} + \frac{1}{8} = \frac{15}{16}$, so $\frac{1}{16}$ is not in one of the groups.

19. Write $\frac{5}{6}$ as $\frac{10}{12}$ and $\frac{1}{4}$ as $\frac{3}{12}$; $\frac{10}{12} + \frac{3}{12} = \frac{13}{12} = 1\frac{1}{12}$. Yes; the answer in simplest form will be the same regardless of the common denominator used.

20. C

Activities

Comparing and Contrasting When you compare things, you tell what is the same about them. When you contrast, you tell what is different.

For example, compare and contrast $\frac{8}{6}$ and $\frac{5}{6}$.

Compare: Both fractions have a denominator of 6.

Contrast: $\frac{8}{6}$ is an improper fraction and greater than 1;

$\frac{5}{6}$ is a proper fraction and less than 1.

$\frac{5}{6} < \frac{8}{6}$

Compare and Contrast Work with a partner to compare and contrast the pairs of numbers given.

1. $\frac{25}{32}, \frac{25}{48}$ **2.** $8\frac{3}{8}, 6\frac{3}{8}$ **3.** $1\frac{3}{4}, 1\frac{7}{8}$ **4.** $3\frac{3}{2}, 4\frac{1}{2}$

Hands On

Use the Ruler Work in a small group. Put cards showing fractions and mixed numbers less than 6 into a bag. The fractions should have denominators of 8, 4, or 2. Take turns drawing two cards. Use two rulers to find the sum of the two numbers. The picture shows how to find the sum of $1\frac{1}{2}$ and $4\frac{3}{4}$.

$$1\frac{1}{2} + 4\frac{3}{4} = 6\frac{1}{4}$$

$4\frac{3}{4}$

$1\frac{1}{2}$ **Sum** $6\frac{1}{4}$

Partner Practice

Test Me Work with a partner. Each of you should prepare a quiz of five items involving addition of fractions and mixed numbers. Do not use denominators greater than 12. Trade quizzes and solve the problems. Check your work.

LESSON 20 • ADDING FRACTIONS **123**

Teach Comparing and Contrasting

Discuss the example and then have pairs of students compare and contrast the number pairs listed. Remind students to finish each exercise by telling which number is greater and why.

Answers:

1. *Same numerator, different denominator;* $\frac{25}{32} > \frac{25}{48}$

2. *Same fraction part, different whole-number part;* $8\frac{3}{8} > 6\frac{3}{8}$

3. *Same whole-number part, different fraction part;* $1\frac{3}{4} < 1\frac{7}{8}$

4. *Same fraction part,* $3\frac{3}{2}$ *incorrectly has an improper fraction as the fraction part;* $3\frac{3}{2} = 4\frac{1}{2}$

Hands On

■ Discuss how to use the rulers to model addition. Have students use rulers to find $1\frac{1}{2} + 4\frac{3}{4}$ as shown in the picture to make sure they understand how to complete the activity.

■ Save the cards to use for a similar activity in Lesson 21.

Partner Practice

Encourage students to include at least one word problem in their quizzes.

Activity: Extend the Lesson

Draw the magic square below on the board, without the red answers. Explain that the sums of the numbers in each row, column, and diagonal should be equal. Have students complete the square and find the common sum ($1\frac{7}{8}$).

1	$\frac{1}{8}$	$\frac{3}{4}$
$\frac{3}{8}$	$\frac{5}{8}$	$\frac{7}{8}$
$\frac{1}{2}$	$1\frac{1}{8}$	$\frac{1}{4}$

Assessment Book

Use page 42 to assess students' comprehension.

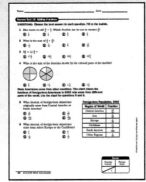

Program Resources

Practice Book Use page 51.

Subtracting Fractions

STANDARDS CONTENT

Mathematics
- Subtract fractions
- Subtract mixed numbers

Language
- Demonstrate how to subtract fractions

Materials
- Paper plates, scissors, rulers

Introduce the Big Idea

Read aloud the Big Idea. Ask students to use what they know about adding and subtracting whole numbers and adding fractions to predict how to subtract fractions.

Begin Building Background

Invite students to imagine that they are among the people in the picture. Ask them to describe what they hear and what they feel. Then ask the questions below the photo.

Teach Key Concepts

- Discuss *place value*, *common denominators*, and *rename*. Write $500 - 450$ on the board. Ask students to name the place of each digit. Have a volunteer explain how to perform the subtraction.

- Have five volunteers stand. Ask, *What fraction of the set does each person represent?* ($\frac{1}{5}$) Have two students sit. Ask, *What part of the set is left standing?* ($\frac{3}{5}$)

Warm-Up Review

Have students find the least common denominator of each pair of fractions.

1. $\frac{5}{12}$ and $\frac{1}{3}$ *(12)*   2. $\frac{2}{5}$ and $\frac{1}{12}$ *(60)*
3. $\frac{4}{6}$ and $\frac{1}{4}$ *(12)*   4. $\frac{3}{8}$ and $\frac{1}{3}$ *(24)*
5. $\frac{3}{4}$ and $\frac{1}{8}$ *(8)*   6. $\frac{1}{12}$ and $\frac{7}{8}$ *(24)*
7. $\frac{1}{9}$ and $\frac{5}{6}$ *(18)*   8. $\frac{2}{7}$ and $\frac{1}{5}$ *(35)*

Subtracting Fractions

Big Idea You subtract fractions and mixed numbers by using the same skills you use for adding fractions and mixed numbers.

Building Background

▲ Every year, millions of monarch butterflies travel south to spend the winter in Mexico.

- Describe what you see in the picture.
- Tell what kinds of butterflies you have seen.
- How could you compare the size of different butterflies?

Key Concepts

When you subtract whole numbers and decimals, you subtract by place value. When you subtract fractions, your fractions must have common denominators. Sometimes you need to rename or rewrite numbers in order to subtract.

Whole Numbers		Decimals		Mixed Numbers	
$\begin{array}{r} {}^{8\,12}\\ 392\\ -\;189\\ \hline 203 \end{array}$	You can't subtract ones. Rename. Now subtract ones, tens, and hundreds.	$\begin{array}{r} {}^{1\,10}\\ 20.7\\ -\;16.5\\ \hline 4.2 \end{array}$	Subtract tenths. You can't subtract ones. Rename. Then subtract.	$\begin{array}{r} 4\frac{1}{3} = \\ -\;2\frac{2}{3} = \end{array}\begin{array}{r} 3\frac{4}{3}\\ -\;2\frac{2}{3}\\ \hline 1\frac{2}{3} \end{array}$	Rename $4\frac{1}{3}$ as $3\frac{4}{3}$. Then subtract.

Activity: We Are Family

Have small groups of students write an addition sentence that has two different fractions as addends. Encourage them to use math vocabulary to explain how they found the sum.

Then have students write a related addition sentence and two related subtraction sentences using the same numbers. Have them explain how they know their sentences are correct.

Resource Library

Math at Hand
Subtracting with Fractions 163–166

Math on Call
Subtracting with Fractions 132–135

Subtracting Fractions

The Western **pygmy** blue butterfly is the smallest butterfly in the United States. Find the difference in wingspreads for the Western pygmy and the Arctic skipper. Find $\frac{7}{8} - \frac{3}{8}$.

 Western pygmy blue $\frac{3}{8}$ inch

Arctic skipper $\frac{7}{8}$ inch ↗ **Wingspread**

Step 1		**Step 2**	
$\frac{7}{8} - \frac{3}{8}$	The fractions have like denominators.	$\frac{7-3}{8} = \frac{4}{8}$	Subtract.
$\frac{7-3}{8}$	Subtract the numerators. Keep the denominator.	$\frac{4}{8} = \frac{1}{2}$	Write in simplest form.

The difference in wingspreads is $\frac{1}{2}$ inch.

The Karner blue is an **endangered** butterfly. How much greater is the wingspread of the Karner blue than that of the Western pygmy? Find $\frac{3}{4} - \frac{3}{8}$.

Karner blue $\frac{3}{4}$ inch

Step 1		**Step 2**	
$\frac{3}{4} = \frac{6}{8}$ $-\frac{3}{8} = -\frac{3}{8}$	Write the fractions with their LCD, 8.	$\frac{3}{4} = \frac{6}{8}$ $-\frac{3}{8} = -\frac{3}{8}$ $\frac{3}{8}$	Subtract.

The wingspread of the Karner blue is $\frac{3}{8}$ inch greater than that of the Western pygmy.

Talk and Share

Work with a partner. Tell what subtraction sentence is shown by the model. Then draw models to show each of the differences below. Give differences in simplest form.

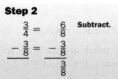

$\frac{5}{6} - \frac{1}{6}$ $\frac{11}{12} - \frac{1}{12}$ $\frac{7}{8} - \frac{3}{4}$

VOCABULARY

pygmy—very small
endangered—so few in number that it is likely to become *extinct*, or disappear

Teach Subtracting Fractions

- Ask students how they would find the size of a butterfly. Explain that the size depends on the *wingspread*, or the distance from the tip of one wing to the tip of the other when the wings are spread out.

- An alternate approach to using algorithms is to have students use models such as fraction strips, area models, or number lines to show subtraction. To use fraction strips, have students model each fraction and then compare the strips. The difference is the part of the strips that do not match up.

Talk and Share

Have students write subtraction sentences for their models. Encourage them to find the differences before they draw the models.
Answers: Model shows $\frac{11}{16} - \frac{5}{16} = \frac{6}{16}$.

$\frac{5}{6} - \frac{1}{6} = \frac{2}{3}$ $\frac{11}{12} - \frac{1}{12} = \frac{5}{6}$ $\frac{7}{8} - \frac{3}{4} = \frac{1}{8}$

Build VOCABULARY

Introduce the words *pygmy* and *endangered* along with their definitions. Have students list as many synonyms as possible for *pygmy* and *endangered*. Then have them brainstorm antonyms and share their lists.

Differentiating Instruction

Beginning
Understanding Fraction Subtraction
Have students complete the sentences and supply the missing numbers.

$\frac{5}{6} - \frac{1}{2} = \frac{5}{6} - \frac{3}{6}$ Write fractions with their LCD.

$\frac{(5 - 3)}{6}$ Subtract the numerators.

$\frac{1}{3}$ Keep the denominator.

$\frac{1}{3}$ Write in simplest form.

Intermediate
Telling How to Subtract Fractions
Have pairs of students supply the missing numbers and tell each other the steps to find the difference $\frac{7}{8} - \frac{3}{4}$.

$\frac{7}{8} - \frac{3}{4} = \frac{7}{8} - \frac{6}{8} = \frac{7-6}{8} = \frac{1}{8}$

(*See Beginning activity for steps.*)

Advanced
Describing How to Subtract Fractions
Have pairs of students each choose a fraction with a denominator of 12 or less. Have them determine which is greater and then find the difference. Have them describe each step of the process in writing.

Teach Subtracting Mixed Numbers

- Spend a few minutes talking about the birds pictured and which of them students recognize.

- Ask, *Why should you subtract the fraction part first?* (Sample: *I might need to rename the top fraction in order to subtract, and that would change the whole-number part.*)

- When discussing the third example, ask, *Why was 3 renamed as $2\frac{10}{10}$ instead of $2\frac{2}{2}$, $2\frac{3}{3}$, or $2\frac{5}{5}$ when finding $3 - 2\frac{7}{10}$?* (*The denominators must be the same before fractions can be subtracted.*)

Talk and Share

You may want to discuss how to change mixed numbers to decimals: Divide the numerator by the denominator and add the quotient to the whole number.

Answers: Change fractions to have the same denominator; $3\frac{3}{10}$, $1\frac{7}{20}$; $4\frac{2}{5} - 1\frac{1}{10} = \frac{44}{10} - \frac{11}{10} = \frac{33}{10} = 3\frac{3}{10}$; $4\frac{2}{5} - 1\frac{1}{10} = 4.4 - 1.1 = 3.3 = 3\frac{3}{10}$; $1\frac{3}{5} - \frac{1}{4} = 1\frac{12}{20} - \frac{5}{20} = \frac{32}{20} - \frac{5}{20} = \frac{27}{20} = 1\frac{7}{20}$; $1\frac{3}{5} - \frac{1}{4} = 1.6 - 0.25 = 1.35$; $1\frac{7}{20} = 1.35$

Subtracting Mixed Numbers

Look at the photos of the birds. To find how much heavier the Steller's jay is than the Eastern bluebird, find $3\frac{7}{10} - 1\frac{1}{10}$. Their weights are given in ounces (oz).

Eastern bluebird $1\frac{1}{10}$ oz

Step 1	Step 2	Step 3
$3\frac{7}{10}$ Subtract the fractions. $-1\frac{1}{10}$ $\frac{6}{10}$	$3\frac{7}{10}$ Subtract the whole numbers. $-1\frac{1}{10}$ $2\frac{6}{10}$	$2\frac{6}{10} = 2\frac{3}{5}$ Write the fraction in simplest form.

The Steller's jay is $2\frac{3}{5}$ ounces heavier than the Eastern bluebird.

Find the difference in the weights of the Mexican jay and the cardinal. Find $4\frac{2}{5} - 1\frac{3}{5}$.

Cardinal $1\frac{3}{5}$ oz

Steller's jay $3\frac{7}{10}$ oz

Step 1	Step 2
$4\frac{2}{5}$ You can't subtract the fractions, so rename $4\frac{2}{5}$. $-1\frac{3}{5}$ $4\frac{2}{5} = 3 + 1\frac{2}{5} = 3\frac{7}{5}$	$3\frac{7}{5}$ Subtract the fractions. $-1\frac{3}{5}$ Subtract the whole numbers. $2\frac{4}{5}$

The difference in weights is $2\frac{4}{5}$ ounces.

How much heavier is the Blue jay than the American robin? Find $3 - 2\frac{7}{10}$.

Mexican jay $4\frac{2}{5}$ oz

Step 1	Step 2
3 You can't subtract, so rename 3 to show tenths. $-2\frac{7}{10}$ $3 = 2 + 1 = 2\frac{10}{10}$	$2\frac{10}{10}$ Subtract the fractions. $-2\frac{7}{10}$ Subtract the whole numbers. $\frac{3}{10}$

American robin $2\frac{7}{10}$ oz

The Blue jay is $\frac{3}{10}$ ounce heavier than the robin.

Blue jay 3 oz

Talk and Share

Talk with a partner about how you could find $4\frac{2}{5} - 1\frac{1}{10}$ and $1\frac{3}{5} - \frac{1}{4}$. Then find the differences. One of you should check your answers by changing the mixed numbers to improper fractions. The other should check answers by using a calculator to change the mixed numbers to decimals.

Activity: Rename Me

Have students "rename" these scrambled words to form mathematical terms:

- cidalme (*decimal*)
- uneamrrot (*numerator*)
- laecp ualve (*place value*)
- ctionfar (*fraction*)
- emitodnonar (*denominator*)
- quvleentia (*equivalent*)

Differentiating Instruction

Beginning
Understanding Mixed-Number Subtraction Using the format from the Beginning activity on page 125, give students the subtraction example $5\frac{2}{5} - 3\frac{7}{10}$. Have them supply the steps for finding the difference and the solution ($1\frac{7}{10}$).

Intermediate
Telling How to Subtract Mixed Numbers Give students a subtraction problem similar to that in the Beginning activity, without the

sentences. Have them fill in the missing numbers and write the steps.

Advanced
Writing How to Subtract Mixed Numbers Have pairs of students each choose a mixed number with fraction denominator 12 or less. Have them find the difference and write each step of the process.

Practice

Write the subtraction sentence shown in each exercise. Give answers in simplest form.

1.

2.

Find each difference. Give answers in simplest form.

3. $\frac{5}{8} - \frac{1}{8}$ **4.** $\frac{7}{9} - \frac{2}{9}$ **5.** $\frac{5}{8} - \frac{1}{3}$

6. $\frac{4}{11} - \frac{3}{22}$ **7.** $\frac{5}{8} - \frac{1}{6}$ **8.** $15\frac{3}{4} - 11\frac{1}{2}$

9. $5\frac{5}{6} - \frac{1}{6}$ **10.** $4\frac{7}{10} - 4\frac{1}{10}$ **11.** $3\frac{5}{12} - 2\frac{11}{12}$

12. $7\frac{1}{6} - 4\frac{5}{6}$ **13.** $8\frac{3}{10} - 2\frac{4}{5}$ **14.** $6 - 4\frac{2}{3}$

There are about 300,000 species of beetles in the world. They range in length from $\frac{1}{50}$ inch for a feather-winged beetle to 5 inches for the African Goliath beetle. Pictured on the right are some of the beetles in Julio's insect collection.

15. Write the names of the click beetle, the stag beetle, and the unicorn beetle in order by their lengths from longest to shortest.

16. How much longer is the stag beetle than the unicorn beetle?

17. How much longer is the click beetle than the June bug?

18. How much longer is the ladybug than a feather-winged beetle?

19. How much longer is a Japanese beetle than a ladybug?

20. (**EXTENDED RESPONSE**) Tell or show how to subtract $4\frac{4}{5}$ from $6\frac{1}{2}$.

21. (**MULTIPLE CHOICE**) Complete this number sentence: $4\frac{5}{12} - \blacksquare = \frac{2}{3}$.

 A. $4\frac{1}{4}$ **B.** $3\frac{3}{4}$ **C.** $3\frac{1}{4}$ **D.** 2

22. (**MULTIPLE CHOICE**) In which expression would you need to rename before you subtract?

 A. $\frac{9}{10} - \frac{1}{10}$ **B.** $1\frac{4}{5} - \frac{2}{5}$ **C.** $4\frac{5}{6} - 3$ **D.** $6\frac{3}{7} - 2\frac{6}{7}$

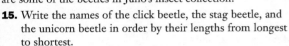

Click beetle
$1\frac{2}{5}$ inches

Stag beetle
$1\frac{3}{5}$ inches

Japanese beetle
$\frac{2}{5}$ inch

Ladybug
$\frac{3}{10}$ inch

June bug
$\frac{9}{10}$ inch

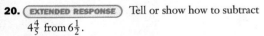

Unicorn beetle
$1\frac{1}{2}$ inches

African Goliath beetle
5 inches

Practice

Have students explain why they might need to rename a number before they subtract mixed numbers. (*The number being subtracted has a greater fraction part than the number being subtracted from, so the lesser fraction must be renamed.*)

Offer these tips for finding a common denominator before subtracting:

- The greater denominator is the LCD if it is a multiple of the lesser denominator, for instance, 12 for $\frac{5}{6}$ and $\frac{7}{12}$.
- If each fraction is in simplest form and the two denominators have 1 as their only common factor, the LCD is the product of the two denominators, for instance, 6 for $\frac{1}{2}$ and $\frac{1}{3}$.

Assignment Guide
- Beginning 1–11, 15–17, 21, 22
- Intermediate 1–7, 11–18, 20–22
- Advanced 1–5, 10–22

Notes on Exercises
Exercises 15–19 Students can find most of the information needed in the captions for the pictures. However, the length for a feather-winged beetle is in the paragraph above Exercise 15.

Exercise 21 Suggest that students add to check their subtraction.

Answers

1. $\frac{9}{10} - \frac{3}{10} = \frac{6}{10} = \frac{3}{5}$

2. $1\frac{3}{8} - \frac{5}{8} = \frac{6}{8} = \frac{3}{4}$

3. $\frac{1}{2}$ **4.** $\frac{5}{9}$

5. $\frac{7}{24}$ **6.** $\frac{5}{22}$

7. $\frac{11}{24}$ **8.** $4\frac{1}{4}$

9. $5\frac{2}{3}$ **10.** $\frac{3}{5}$

11. $\frac{1}{2}$ **12.** $2\frac{1}{3}$

13. $5\frac{1}{2}$ **14.** $1\frac{1}{3}$

15. stag, unicorn, click

16. $\frac{1}{10}$ in.   **17.** $\frac{1}{2}$ in.

18. $\frac{7}{25}$ in.   **19.** $\frac{1}{10}$ in.

20. $6\frac{1}{2} - 4\frac{4}{5} = 6\frac{5}{10} - 4\frac{8}{10} = 5\frac{15}{10} - 4\frac{8}{10} = 1\frac{7}{10}$

21. B   **22.** D

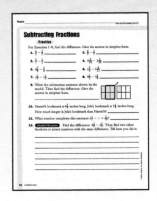

Teach Demonstrating

- Introduce the meaning of the word *demonstrate* by having volunteers show how to perform an action such as tying shoes. Then tell students that the word *demonstrate* means "to show how to do something," as when the volunteer demonstrated how to tie shoes.

- Demonstrate how to use paper plates to subtract $\frac{1}{3}$ from $\frac{5}{6}$; or model the activity while students use paper plates to demonstrate this subtraction.

- Although students should independently demonstrate how to subtract $\frac{1}{4}$ from $\frac{7}{8}$, you may want to have students work in pairs to talk about how they used the model to do the subtraction.

Hands On

- Suggest that students use the cards they made for the ruler activity in Lesson 20.

- Some students may need to use a straightedge to help them align the original mixed numbers.

Partner Practice

Encourage students to include at least one word problem for their partners to solve.

Develop Language

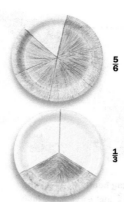

$\frac{5}{6}$

$\frac{1}{3}$

Activities

Demonstrating When you demonstrate, you show how to do something. Demonstrate how to subtract $\frac{1}{3}$ from $\frac{5}{6}$.

Start with paper plates. Shade $\frac{5}{6}$ of one plate and shade $\frac{1}{3}$ of the other plate. Cut out the $\frac{1}{3}$. Place the cut part over the shaded part of the other plate. Cut off the part that is $\frac{1}{3}$. How much of the $\frac{5}{6}$ is left?

1. Demonstrate Show how to subtract $\frac{1}{4}$ from $\frac{7}{8}$ with paper plates or by drawing models on paper.

2. Explain Tell how you used the model to do the subtraction.

Hands On

Use a Ruler Work in a small group. Put cards showing fractions and mixed numbers into a bag. Numbers should be less than 10. Denominators should be 16, 8, 4, or 2. Take turns choosing two cards. Use rulers as shown to find the difference of the two numbers. The picture shows how to find the difference of $2\frac{3}{8}$ and $4\frac{1}{4}$.

$$4\frac{1}{4} - 2\frac{3}{8} = 1\frac{7}{8}$$

$1\frac{7}{8}$ $4\frac{1}{4}$

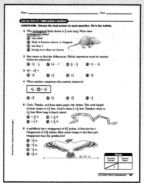

$2\frac{3}{8}$

Partner Practice

Test Me Work with a partner. Each of you should prepare a quiz of 5 items involving subtraction of fractions and mixed numbers. Do not use denominators greater than 25. Trade quizzes and solve the problems. Check your partner's work.

Program Resources
Practice Book Use page 53.

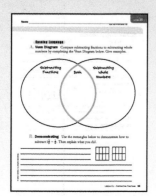

Assessment Book
Use page 43 to assess students' comprehension.

Activity: Extend the Lesson
Ask students to describe the pattern and then write the next three numbers in the following pattern.

$$\frac{1}{2} \quad \frac{5}{6} \quad \frac{7}{12} \quad \frac{11}{12} \quad \frac{2}{3} \quad 1 \quad \frac{3}{4}$$

(Pattern is add $\frac{1}{3}$, subtract $\frac{1}{4}$; $1\frac{1}{12}, \frac{5}{6}, 1\frac{1}{6}$)

Challenge students to write their own patterns.

Multiplying and Dividing

Big Idea You always should use mental math to do a computation when you can. When you cannot, then you should use the skills you have learned.

Building Background

▲ I have a quilt that my grandmother gave me when I was a baby.

- Do you know someone who sews quilts? If so, who?
- How do you think the patterns are put together?
- How can you easily cut all the pieces before you start sewing?

Key Concepts

This **model** is a **fraction model.** It shows a **quotient.** The model shows the number of quilt pieces, $\frac{3}{4}$ inch wide, that can be cut from a 6-inch piece of fabric.

You can cut 8 pieces that are each $\frac{3}{4}$ inch wide. The quotient of $6 \div \frac{3}{4}$ is 8.

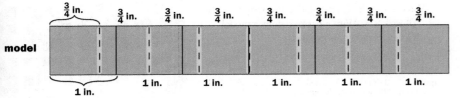

LESSON 22 • MULTIPLYING AND DIVIDING **129**

Multiplying and Dividing

STANDARDS CONTENT
Mathematics
- Multiply with fractions and mixed numbers
- Divide with fractions and mixed numbers

Language
- Clarify how to divide by a fraction

Introduce the **Big Idea**

Have students multiply 5 and 105 (*525*). Ask them how they could use mental math to find the product $(5 \times (100 + 5) = (5 \times 100) + (5 \times 5) = 500 + 25 = 525)$. Then read aloud the Big Idea.

Begin **Building Background**

Display a quilt to the class and identify the pattern. Ask students to describe the quilts in the picture.

Teach **Key Concepts**

- Walk students through the fraction model. Be sure students understand that the solid lines are 1-in. marks and that the dashed lines show $\frac{3}{4}$-in. marks, or where to cut each $\frac{3}{4}$-in. piece.
- Ask students to suggest other problems that could be solved using this fraction model.

Warm-Up Review

Have students write each improper fraction as a mixed number in simplest form.

1. $\frac{11}{2}$ $(5\frac{1}{2})$
2. $\frac{20}{6}$ $(3\frac{1}{3})$
3. $\frac{42}{5}$ $(8\frac{2}{5})$
4. $\frac{62}{4}$ $(15\frac{1}{2})$
5. $\frac{52}{3}$ $(17\frac{1}{3})$
6. $\frac{100}{12}$ $(8\frac{1}{3})$
7. $\frac{42}{8}$ $(5\frac{1}{4})$

Activity: Draw a Fraction Model

Write $2 \div \frac{1}{2} = 4$ and $2 \div \frac{2}{3} = 3$ on the board. Have students identify the quotients (*4, 3*).

Have small groups of students draw fraction models to show the division sentences written on the board. Encourage them to discuss how they should draw the models before putting pencil to paper.

$$\left(\begin{array}{cc} \text{▯▯▯} & \text{▯▯▯} \\ 2 \div \frac{1}{2} = 4 & 2 \div \frac{2}{3} = 3 \end{array} \right)$$

Resource Library

Math at Hand
Multiplying with Fractions 167–170, 450–451
Dividing with Fractions 171–176

Math on Call
Multiplying with Fractions 160–163, 165, 169
Dividing with Fractions 187–192, 198–199

Teach Multiplying with Fractions and Mixed Numbers

- Point out that the word *of* in the phrase $\frac{1}{3}$ *of 4* means "times."

- Before discussing the second example, show how to draw a model to find $\frac{1}{2} \times \frac{1}{4}$. On the board, draw a rectangle with a vertical line to show halves. Shade one half. Draw horizontal lines to show fourths and shade one fourth using a different shading. Ask, *What is the product of $\frac{1}{2}$ and $\frac{1}{4}$?* ($\frac{1}{8}$)

- Work through the remaining examples. Stress that to multiply fractions, multiply the numerators *and* the denominators.

Talk and Share

Remind students of the Commutative Property of Multiplication: The order in which two numbers are multiplied does not affect the product. After students draw a model showing $4 \times \frac{1}{3}$, have them look for similarities and differences between their models and the model at the top of page 130.

Answer:

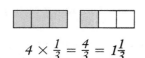

$$4 \times \frac{1}{3} = \frac{4}{3} = 1\frac{1}{3}$$

Multiplying with Fractions and Mixed Numbers

$$\frac{1}{3} \times 4 = \frac{4}{3}$$

Draw a model to help you multiply with fractions. Find $\frac{1}{3} \times 4$, or $\frac{1}{3}$ of 4. In the model on the left, 4 wholes have been divided into thirds. One third of 4 is colored. $\frac{1}{3}$ of 4 is $\frac{4}{3}$, or $1\frac{1}{3}$.

Find $\frac{1}{4} \times \frac{2}{5}$, or $\frac{1}{4}$ of $\frac{2}{5}$.

The blue part shows $\frac{2}{5}$.

The red part shows $\frac{1}{4}$. The overlapping part shows $\frac{1}{4}$ of $\frac{2}{5}$.

$$\frac{1}{4} \times \frac{2}{5} = \frac{2}{20}$$

You also can find $\frac{1}{4} \times \frac{2}{5}$ without a model.

$$\frac{1}{4} \times \frac{2}{5} = \frac{1 \times 2}{4 \times 5} = \frac{2}{20} = \frac{1}{10} \quad \longleftarrow \text{Multiply the numerators and denominators. Simplify.}$$

Each row of a **quilt** has 4 squares. Each square is $9\frac{1}{2}$ inches wide. How long is one row? Find $4 \times 9\frac{1}{2}$.

$$4 \times 9\frac{1}{2} = \frac{4}{1} \times \frac{19}{2} \quad \longleftarrow \text{Write both numbers as improper fractions.}$$

$$\frac{4 \times 19}{1 \times 2} = \frac{76}{2} = 38 \quad \longleftarrow \text{Multiply the numerators and denominators. Simplify.}$$

Each row is 38 inches long.

Now find $\frac{1}{5} \times 2\frac{1}{2}$. To multiply a fraction and a mixed number, first change the mixed number to an improper fraction. Then multiply the numerators and denominators.

$$\frac{1}{5} \times 2\frac{1}{2} = \frac{1}{5} \times \frac{5}{2} \quad \longleftarrow \text{Write } 2\frac{1}{2} \text{ as an improper fraction.}$$

$$\frac{1 \times 5}{5 \times 2} = \frac{5}{10} = \frac{1}{2} \quad \longleftarrow \text{Multiply the numerators and denominators. Simplify.}$$

Talk and Share

You can use the Commutative Property to write $\frac{1}{3} \times 4$ as $4 \times \frac{1}{3}$. With a partner, draw a model with grids to show this product.

VOCABULARY
quilt—a kind of blanket for a bed. A quilt has a soft pad in the middle and many designs made with stitches.

 Activity: To Simplify or Not

Have partners take turns tossing a number cube four times and using the four numbers to write two fractions. Have students multiply the fractions and tell if the product is in simplest form. If it is not, they should explain how to simplify the fraction.

 Differentiating Instruction

Beginning
Understanding Fraction Multiplication
Give students several whole-number/fraction products to find. They can use the repeated-addition concept with an inch ruler or a number line (Overhead Transparency 28). Have them talk about how the blue and red model on page 130 shows $\frac{1}{4}$ of $\frac{2}{5}$.

Intermediate
Modeling Fraction Multiplication
Have pairs of students read the examples on page 130. Then have

them draw models for $\frac{3}{4} \times \frac{2}{3}$ and $2 \times 3\frac{1}{2}$. Have pairs talk about how their models show the multiplication. Then have them perform the multiplication without the models ($\frac{1}{2}$, 7).

Advanced
Writing About Fraction Multiplication Have pairs of students read the examples on page 130. Then have one student choose a fraction and the other choose a mixed number. Have them find the product and supply the steps for doing so in writing.

Dividing with Fractions and Mixed Numbers

You know how to multiply with fractions and mixed numbers. Now you will learn to divide by them. Find $4 \div \frac{1}{2}$.

$4 \div \frac{1}{2}$ means "How many halves ($\frac{1}{2}$s) are in 4?" The model shows that there are 8 halves in 4. $4 \div \frac{1}{2} = 8$.

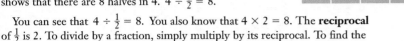

You can see that $4 \div \frac{1}{2} = 8$. You also know that $4 \times 2 = 8$. The **reciprocal** of $\frac{1}{2}$ is 2. To divide by a fraction, simply multiply by its reciprocal. To find the reciprocal of any fraction, switch the numerator and the denominator.

Find $\frac{7}{8} \div 2$.

Step 1
Write both numbers as fractions.

$\frac{7}{8} \div 2$
$\downarrow$
$\frac{7}{8} \div \frac{2}{1}$

Step 2
Replace the division with multiplication. Replace the divisor with its reciprocal.

$\frac{7}{8} \div \frac{2}{1}$
$\downarrow \quad \downarrow$
$\frac{7}{8} \times \frac{1}{2}$

Step 3
Multiply.

$\frac{7}{8} \times \frac{1}{2} = \frac{7 \times 1}{8 \times 2}$
$= \frac{7}{16}$

A strip quilt is made with narrow strips of fabric. How many $1\frac{1}{2}$-inch strips can be cut from fabric that is 36 inches wide? Find $36 \div 1\frac{1}{2}$.

$36 \div 1\frac{1}{2} = \frac{36}{1} \div \frac{3}{2}$ ← Write both numbers as improper fractions.

$\frac{36}{1} \div \frac{3}{2} = \frac{36}{1} \times \frac{2}{3}$ ← Change the division to multiplication. Change $\frac{3}{2}$ to its reciprocal, $\frac{2}{3}$.

$\frac{36}{1} \times \frac{2}{3} = \frac{36 \times 2}{1 \times 3} = \frac{72}{3} = 24$ ← Multiply and simplify.

Twenty-four $1\frac{1}{2}$-inch strips can be cut from fabric that is 36 inches wide.

Talk and Share

Work with a partner. Notice that the product of the reciprocals $\frac{3}{4}$ and $\frac{4}{3}$ is $\frac{12}{12}$, or 1. Will the product of two reciprocals always be 1? Give a couple of examples to support your answer.

VOCABULARY

reciprocal—The number by which another is multiplied to get a product of 1. The reciprocal of $\frac{a}{b}$ is $\frac{b}{a}$ because $\frac{a}{b} \times \frac{b}{a} = \frac{ab}{ab} = 1$, where $a \neq 0$, $b \neq 0$.

Teach Dividing with Fractions and Mixed Numbers

- Summarize the division concepts by providing some context. Remind students that dividing any number by a fraction is the same as finding how many fractional parts are in that number. Dividing a fraction by a whole number can be thought of as separating the fraction into that number of equal parts.

- Draw this model to reinforce the second example, showing $\frac{7}{8}$ separated into two equal parts.

Talk and Share

Have students work in pairs and share their answers with the class. You might point out that the same numbers are multiplied in the numerator as in the denominator but in a different order.

Answers: yes; samples: $\frac{5}{8} \times \frac{8}{5} = \frac{40}{40} = 1$; $2\frac{1}{3} \cdot \frac{3}{7} = \frac{7}{3} \cdot \frac{3}{7} = \frac{21}{21} = 1$

Build VOCABULARY

Explain that the *reciprocal* of any fraction can be found by switching the numerator and the denominator. Ask, *How can you find the reciprocal of a mixed number?* (*Write the mixed number as an improper fraction; then switch the numerator and the denominator.*)

Differentiating Instruction

Beginning
Understanding Fraction Division On the board, draw models of $2 \div \frac{1}{2}$ and $\frac{3}{5} \div 2$. Have students talk about how the models show the division. Then show them that $2 \div \frac{1}{2}$ gives the same answer as 2×2 and that $\frac{3}{5} \div 2$ gives the same answer as $\frac{3}{5} \times \frac{1}{2}$.

Intermediate
Explaining Fraction Division After students read the examples on page 131, refer them to the Key Concepts model on page 129 that shows $6 \div \frac{3}{4}$. Have pairs of students talk about how to find the quotient without using the model (*Sample: Change division to multiplication; switch numbers in the fractions; multiply*).

Advanced
Writing About Fraction Division Have pairs of students choose a fraction and a mixed number and write a division problem. Ask, *Can you draw a model for your problem?* (probably not) Have them talk about how the quotient will relate to the two numbers. Then have them use the steps outlined on page 131 to find the quotient and verify that the procedure is correct.

Practice

Have students summarize the steps needed to multiply a fraction and a mixed number. (*Write the mixed number as an improper fraction. Multiply the numerators and the denominators. Simplify, if possible.*)

Ask students to summarize the steps needed to divide a fraction by a mixed number. (*Write the mixed number as an improper fraction. Change the division to multiplication and write the reciprocal of the improper fraction. Multiply. Simplify, if possible.*)

Assignment Guide
- Beginning 1–36
- Intermediate 1–37
- Advanced 1–38

Notes on Exercises

Exercise 15 Multiplying two numbers by the same number does not change their relationship, so students need to compare only $\frac{6}{7}$ and $\frac{8}{7}$.

Exercises 22–29 Encourage students to show each step as they complete the division. Remind them to use the reciprocal of the second number (the divisor), not the reciprocal of the first number (the dividend), when dividing.

Exercise 38 Show students how to use this shortcut to multiply two fractions.

$$\frac{1}{4} \times 8 = \frac{1}{\cancel{4}_1} \times \frac{\cancel{8}^2}{1} = \frac{2}{1} = 2$$

Look and Read

Practice

Find each product. Give answers in simplest form.

1. $\frac{1}{3} \times \frac{4}{5}$ **2.** $\frac{3}{5} \times 2$ **3.** $\frac{2}{3} \times \frac{3}{4}$

4. $\frac{5}{8} \times 6 = \frac{5}{8} \times \frac{6}{1} = $ ■   **5.** $\frac{1}{3} \times 4\frac{1}{2} = \frac{1}{3} \times \frac{9}{2} = $ ■

6. $\frac{3}{4} \times \frac{5}{8}$ **7.** $\frac{1}{5} \times \frac{5}{9}$ **8.** $\frac{2}{5} \times \frac{7}{8}$ **9.** $\frac{5}{7} \times 9$

10. $\frac{5}{6} \times 18$ **11.** $\frac{3}{4} \times 3\frac{1}{5}$ **12.** $2\frac{1}{2} \times \frac{7}{10}$ **13.** $4\frac{1}{2} \times 1\frac{1}{3}$

Use mental math to compare. Use <, =, or >.

14. $\frac{1}{3} \times \frac{5}{1}$ ■ $\frac{3}{4} \times \frac{4}{3}$ **15.** $\frac{1}{2} \times \frac{6}{7}$ ■ $\frac{8}{7} \times \frac{1}{2}$

Give the reciprocal of each number.

16. $\frac{2}{5}$ **17.** $\frac{5}{12}$ **18.** 8   **19.** $4\frac{2}{3}$

Find each quotient. Give answers in simplest form.

20. $\frac{5}{8} \div 2\frac{1}{3} = \frac{5}{8} \times \frac{3}{7} = $ ■   **21.** $\frac{8}{15} \div \frac{4}{5} = \frac{8}{15} \times \frac{5}{4} = $ ■

22. $6 \div \frac{2}{3}$ **23.** $\frac{9}{10} \div 3$ **24.** $\frac{1}{3} \div \frac{1}{2}$ **25.** $\frac{9}{16} \div \frac{3}{8}$

26. $2\frac{1}{2} \div \frac{2}{3}$ **27.** $\frac{3}{8} \div 1\frac{1}{2}$ **28.** $\frac{1}{2} \div 4\frac{1}{4}$ **29.** $1\frac{3}{4} \div 2\frac{1}{2}$

Copy and complete each sentence with *is equal to*, *is less than*, or *is greater than*.

30. The product $8 \times \frac{2}{3}$ ___ 8.   **31.** The quotient $8 \div \frac{2}{3}$ ___ 8.

32. The product $3\frac{1}{3} \times \frac{3}{10}$ ___ 1. **33.** The product $\frac{3}{8} \times \frac{4}{9}$ ___ 1.

34. The quotient $6 \div 3\frac{1}{2}$ ___ 6. **35.** The quotient $5\frac{1}{2} \div \frac{3}{4}$ ___ $5\frac{1}{2}$.

36. Each square of a quilt is $7\frac{1}{2}$ inches wide. How many squares are in a row that is 60 inches long?

37. (EXTENDED RESPONSE) Maddy needs 16 squares of fabric for the width of her quilt and 24 squares for the length. Each square is $3\frac{1}{2}$ inches on a side. How long and how wide is her quilt? Explain.

38. (EXTENDED RESPONSE) C. J. uses this shortcut to find $\frac{3}{4} \times 8$: Divide 8 by 4 and then multiply by 3. Will this method work with every product of a fraction and a whole number? Explain. Try it with several examples.

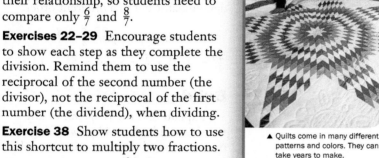

▲ Quilts come in many different patterns and colors. They can take years to make.

Program Resources

Practice Book Use page 54.

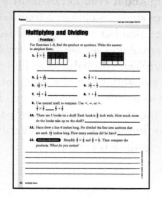

Answers

1. $\frac{4}{15}$ **2.** $\frac{6}{5} = 1\frac{1}{5}$ **19.** $\frac{3}{14}$ **20.** $\frac{15}{56}$

3. $\frac{6}{12} = \frac{1}{2}$ **4.** $3\frac{3}{4}$ **21.** $\frac{2}{3}$ **22.** 9

5. $1\frac{1}{2}$ **6.** $\frac{15}{32}$ **23.** $\frac{3}{10}$ **24.** $\frac{2}{3}$

7. $\frac{1}{9}$ **8.** $\frac{7}{20}$ **25.** $1\frac{1}{2}$ **26.** $3\frac{3}{4}$

9. $6\frac{3}{7}$ **10.** 15   **27.** $\frac{1}{4}$ **28.** $\frac{2}{17}$

11. $2\frac{2}{5}$ **12.** $1\frac{3}{4}$ **29.** $\frac{7}{10}$ **30.** is less than

13. 6   **14.** =   **31.** is greater than

32. is equal to   **33.** is less than

15. <   **16.** $\frac{5}{2}$ **34.** is less than   **35.** is greater than

17. $\frac{12}{5}$ **18.** $\frac{1}{8}$ *See Additional Answers, page T39–T40.*

Activities

Clarifying *To clarify* means to make something clear or easy to understand. You can clarify how to divide one fraction by another by listing all the steps in order. This example shows the steps in dividing $\frac{7}{12}$ by $\frac{2}{3}$.

1. **Describe** Copy the example. Work with a partner to describe each step of the division.

2. **Explain** Tell what steps are needed to find $\frac{7}{12} \div 1\frac{2}{3}$.

$$\frac{7}{12} \div \frac{2}{3} = \frac{7}{12} \times \frac{3}{2}$$
$$= \frac{7 \times 3}{12 \times 2}$$
$$= \frac{21}{24}$$
$$= \frac{7}{8}$$
$$\frac{7}{12} \div \frac{2}{3} = \frac{7}{8}$$

Hands On

Calculate It You can find products or check answers by using a calculator. The answers you get will be decimals.

Find $\frac{3}{8} \times \frac{4}{5}$.

Press: (3 ÷ 8) STO▶
Press: (4 ÷ 5) = × RCL =
Display: 0.3
(Note: On some calculators, STO▶ is M+ and RCL is MR.) Now find $\frac{13}{25} \times \frac{3}{20}$.

Oral Language

Distribute the Whole Many times you can multiply a whole number and a mixed number using mental math and the Distributive Property. Remember that a mixed number is the sum of a whole number and a fraction. Here is an example.

$$8 \times 4\frac{1}{2} = 8 \times (4 + \frac{1}{2}) = (8 \times 4) + (8 \times \frac{1}{2}) = 32 + 4 = 36$$

Take turns with a partner telling how to use the Distributive Property to find each product below.

$6 \times 4\frac{1}{3}$ $12 \times 2\frac{1}{2}$ $10 \times 3\frac{2}{5}$ $16 \times 1\frac{3}{8}$

LESSON 22 • MULTIPLYING AND DIVIDING   **133**

Teach Clarifying

■ Point out that when a teacher or student answers questions, he or she is often *clarifying* something about the lesson.

■ Have students work in pairs to write the clarification. You may want to work with students first to show how to find $\frac{5}{6} \div \frac{1}{3}$ and write the appropriate steps.

Answers:

1. *Rewrite $\frac{2}{3}$ as $\frac{3}{2}$ and change division to multiplication; Find 7×3 and 12×2; Simplify $\frac{21}{24}$ as $\frac{7}{8}$.*

2. *Rewrite $1\frac{2}{3}$ as $\frac{5}{3}$ and change division to multiplication; Find 7×3 and 12×5; Simplify $\frac{21}{60}$ as $\frac{7}{20}$.*

Hands On

Review how to use a calculator to multiply two fractions. Some students may prefer direct input using parentheses: $(3 \div 8) \times (4 \div 5) = 0.3$ ($\frac{13}{25} \times \frac{3}{20} = 0.078$). Have students suggest multiplication problems, and have pairs find the products.

Oral Language

Review the Distributive Property with whole numbers before students read the activity.

Activity: Could You Clarify?

Have small groups of students write an invitation to a party, but have them omit some important information, such as the name of the host. They should also replace all numbers for dates, times, and addresses with multiplication or division problems with fractions.

Have groups trade invitations, find the correct numbers, and *clarify* any other questions about the party.

Assessment Book

Use page 44 to assess students' comprehension.

Program Resources

Practice Book Use page 55.

Work Backward

STANDARDS CONTENT

Mathematics
■ Solve problems by working backward

Language
■ Identify *subject* and *verb*

Teach Work Backward

■ Introduce the strategy *work backward.* Point out that *backward* means "from back to front" or "from end to beginning." Working backward requires "undoing" what has been done.

■ Read aloud the problem at the top of the page. Discuss any vocabulary, such as *tasks (chores or work that has to be done)* that students may not understand.

■ Point out that the needed data are listed separately from the problem. Suggest that when students solve problems, they select a way to organize information and keep track of the data as they learn more. Ask them to name ways to keep track of data (*Samples: diagrams, timelines, flow charts, area models, tables*).

Talk and Share

Suggest that students use a timeline to help them organize the information.

Answer: 23 students

Problem-Solving Skills

Work Backward

When you know how something ends, you may need to work backward to find out the beginning parts.

Problem: Ursula earned $\frac{1}{3}$ of her money by picking berries and $\frac{1}{6}$ of her money by watering plants. She earned the rest by mowing the lawn. Ursula made $5 watering plants. How much did she earn for each of the other tasks?

Read and Understand   Read the problem carefully. Make sure you understand what is being asked.

Need to find: The amount earned for each task

You know: Ursula earned $\frac{1}{3}$ for picking berries, $\frac{1}{6}$ for watering plants, and the rest by mowing the lawn.

Key fact: She made $5 for watering plants.

Plan and Solve   Start with what you know and work backward.

$5 is $\frac{1}{6}$ of her earnings. How much were Ursula's total earnings?

Plants: $\frac{1}{6}$ of the total is $5. If $\frac{1}{6}$ is $5, then $\frac{6}{6}$ is $30.

Berries: She earned $\frac{1}{3}$ of the total for picking berries. $\frac{1}{3} \times 30 = \frac{1}{3} \times \frac{30}{1} = \frac{30}{3} = 10$. For this she earned $10.

Mowing: She earned $5 for watering plants and $10 for picking berries, for a total of $15. $30 − $15 = $15, so Ursula earned $15 for mowing the lawn.

Answer   Ursula earned $10 for picking berries and $15 for mowing the lawn.

Look Back   She earned $15 for mowing the lawn, $10 for picking berries, and $5 for watering plants. $15 + $10 + $5 = $30. The answer checks.

Talk and Share

Discuss this question with a partner. A class had 29 students at the end of the school year. Four new students joined the class in December. In March, two new students entered the class. How many students were in the class at the start of the school year?

Activity: Find the Number

Present these problems:

• One fourth of a number added to 8 is 28. What is the number? (*80*)

• A number divided by $\frac{2}{3}$, and then multiplied by 4 is 180. What is the number? (*30*)

Have students explain how they solved each problem. Then have pairs of students write similar number riddles that can be solved by working backward. Have them trade with another pair and solve.

Differentiating Instruction

Beginning
Using a Model   Provide pairs of students with a model showing the known data. Point out that the total amount of money earned is the whole. Have students use information in the Plan and Solve section to find the dollar value for each part of the model and for the whole. Have them identify each part of the model.

Mowing → Plants $5
$ <u>15</u>   Berries $ <u>10</u>

Intermediate
Using an Organizer   Have students use an organizer of their choice to record the data in the problem. The organizer can be as simple as a list of the known data with dollar amounts earned written next to each item on the list.

Advanced
Using a Different Method   Ask students to find and explain a different way to work backward and solve the problem.

(See Additional Answers, page T40.)

1. In the problem about Ursula, what piece of information did you start with in order to begin solving the problem?

2. What fraction of Ursula's earnings came from mowing the lawn? How can you check your answer?

Use the strategy *work backward.*

3. At a card-trading show, Angel bought 16 cards and won 7 cards. When he left, he had 108 cards. How many cards did he have before he went to the card-trading show?

4. Zehra cleaned the kitchen in 45 minutes, the bathroom in 15 minutes, the bedroom in 25 minutes, and the living room in 40 minutes. She took a 30-minute lunch break. If she finished working at 1:30 p.m., when did she begin?

Choose a strategy and solve each problem.

5. If Shankar enjoys the rain in Mumbai, during which three months should he visit? Explain your answer.

6. Together, Debbie, Karen, and Wendy have $160. Debbie has half as much as Karen. Wendy has $85. How much money does Debbie have? How much does Karen have?

Mumbai, India	
MONTH	AVERAGE RAINFALL (IN INCHES)
January	0.0
February	0.0
March	0.0
April	0.0
May	0.5
June	22.3
July	25.6
August	19.2
September	14.0
October	3.5
November	0.2
December	0.0

Grammar Spotlight

Simple Sentence A sentence has a subject and a verb and expresses a complete thought. The *subject* is what acts or is acted upon. The *verb* shows action or a state of being.

Denny threw the ball.   *Subject:* Denny *Verb:* threw

Simple Sentences	Simple Sentences in this Lesson
Maria and Bob ran to school.	Ursula made $5 watering plants.
Cooking is Papa's favorite thing to do.	Angel bought 16 cards.
The telephone rang.	Wendy has $85.

1. Work with a partner. Take turns acting out something, such as running. Say a simple sentence to tell what you are doing. Your partner should identify the subject and the verb.

2. Write three simple sentences to tell what some of your classmates are doing. Identify the subject and the verb of each sentence.

Ask, *What types of problems can be solved using the strategy* work backward? Students should understand that this strategy is used when they know how things in the problem end and need to find out what happened earlier.

Assignment Guide
- Beginning 1–6
- Intermediate 1–6
- Advanced 1–6

Notes on Exercises
Exercise 1 Remind students that the problem about Ursula is the problem on page 134.

Exercise 5 Read aloud, and have students repeat, the names for the months in the table.

Grammar Spotlight

- Define a simple sentence as a sentence with one main *clause*. Tell students that a *clause* is a group of related words that has both a subject and a verb.

- Have volunteers read aloud the examples and identify the subjects and verbs. Then have students work in pairs to complete the activity.

Answers
1. $5 for watering plants
2. $\frac{1}{2}$; $\frac{1}{2} \times 30 = 15$, which works in the problem
3. 85 cards
4. 10:55 a.m.
5. June, July, and August; that's when the most rain falls.
6. $25, $50

 Activity: Solve It Two Ways

Give students this problem: It takes Tony 35 minutes to get ready for work, 20 minutes to eat lunch, and 45 minutes to get to work. If he has to be at work at 1:30 p.m., what time should he start to get ready?

Have students work backward to solve the problem and then solve the problem a different way. (*11:50 a.m.; Samples: Refer to a clock; add the times and subtract from 1:30 p.m.*)

 Program Resources

Practice Book Use pages 56 and 57.

Ratios and Proportions

STANDARDS CONTENT

Mathematics
- Use ratios to compare quantities
- Write and solve proportions

Language
- Recognize multiple meanings of *term*
- Evaluate real-world situations by comparing ratios

Materials
- Counters in two colors

Introduce the Big Idea

Read the Big Idea aloud. Then write *4 quarters/10 dimes* on the board. Explain that this is a *ratio* that shows a relationship between quarters and dimes.

Begin Building Background

Ask, *How many dogs could 2, 3, and 4 people walk if each person walked 6 dogs?* (*12 dogs, 18 dogs, 24 dogs*)

Focus students' attention on the photo. Discuss the questions below the photo to elicit the following answers: *A man is walking 6 dogs; 6 dogs, 1 man; sample: 1 to 6*

Teach Key Concepts

- Discuss the terms *ratio, proportion,* and *rate.* Explain that all of the ratios are read using the word *to:* 3 *to* 4, 10 *to* 8, 4.8 *to* 9.6.

- Point out that the slash sign in a rate, (/), is read as *per* or *for.*

Warm-Up Review

Have students write two equivalent fractions for each fraction. (*Sample answers are given.*)

1. $\frac{1}{2}$ $\left(\frac{2}{4}, \frac{3}{6}\right)$ 5. $\frac{12}{7}$ $\left(\frac{24}{14}, \frac{36}{21}\right)$

2. $\frac{4}{3}$ $\left(\frac{8}{6}, \frac{12}{9}\right)$ 6. $\frac{5}{6}$ $\left(\frac{10}{12}, \frac{15}{18}\right)$

3. $\frac{20}{30}$ $\left(\frac{2}{3}, \frac{4}{6}\right)$ 7. $\frac{60}{24}$ $\left(\frac{10}{4}, \frac{5}{2}\right)$

4. $\frac{3}{10}$ $\left(\frac{6}{20}, \frac{9}{30}\right)$

Talk and Explore

Ratios and Proportions

 Big Idea   Ratios describe relationships between two quantities. Ratios often are expressed as fractions. When two ratios are equal, you can write them in a proportion.

Building Background

▲ I like walking my dog Scruffy. It's good exercise for both of us.

- **What is happening in the picture?**
- **How many dogs are there? How many people are walking dogs?**
- **How might you describe the relationship between the number of people and the number of dogs?**

Key Concepts

ratio	proportion	rate
a comparison of two quantities by division	a statement that two ratios are equal	a ratio with different units of measure
3:4 10 to 8 $\frac{4.8}{9.6}$	$\frac{2}{3} = \frac{8}{12}$ $\frac{25}{100} = \frac{1}{4}$	\$3/hour 26 miles/gallon

---

 Activity: Ratio or Proportion?

Have students complete these sentences.

1. A proportion has two equal <u>b</u>.
   a) terms   b) ratios
   c) decimals d) variables
2. A <u>d</u> is a type of a ratio.
   a) proportion b) numerator
   c) term   d) rate
3. A <u>a</u> is a comparison of two quantities by division.
   a) ratio   b) noun
   c) symbol d) part

Resource Library

Math at Hand
Ratios and Proportion 181–187

Math on Call
Ratios and Proportion 423–426, 429–435, 438–439

Reader's Handbook (red)
Circle Graph, 558

Ratios

A **ratio** is a comparison of two quantities by division. Each number in a ratio is called a **term.** In the photo on the opposite page, the ratio of dogs to people is 6 to 1. The terms of the ratio are 6 and 1.

An animal shelter has 5 staff members. The ratio of staff members to dogs at the shelter can be written as 5:14, 5 to 14, or $\frac{5}{14}$. Most of the time, we write ratios as fractions.

Ratio of rabbits to dogs: $\frac{9 \text{ rabbits}}{14 \text{ dogs}}$, or $\frac{9}{14}$

Ratio of cats to rabbits: $\frac{13 \text{ cats}}{9 \text{ rabbits}}$, or $\frac{13}{9}$

Ratio of dogs to the total number of pets available for adoption: $\frac{14 \text{ dogs}}{36 \text{ animals}}$ or $\frac{14}{36}$

Gavin has 3 gerbils and 5 goldfish. The ratio of gerbils to goldfish is $\frac{3}{5}$. Find four ratios equal to this ratio. You can find ratios equal to a given ratio by multiplying or dividing each term of the given ratio by the same nonzero number.

	2×3	3×3	4×3	5×3
Gerbils 3	6	9	12	15
Goldfish 5	10	15	20	25
	2×5	3×5	4×5	5×5

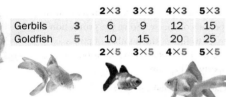

Talk and Share

Volunteer Vets   With a partner, think about a group of 6 girls, 4 boys, and 1 adult leader who volunteer at an animal shelter. How many children are in the group? How many leaders are there? How many people are there in all? What is the ratio of leaders to children? What is the ratio of children to leaders? Tell how the answers to the last two questions are different.

VOCABULARY
ratio—a pair of numbers compared by division
term—one of the two parts of a ratio

Look and Read

Adopt me!

Choose from
14 Dogs
13 Cats
9 Rabbits

Language Notes

Multiple Meanings
This word has more than one meaning.

- term
1. one of the parts in a ratio
2. a part of an algebraic expression containing numbers and/or variables
3. a number in a pattern
4. a set period of time, as in *school term*

LESSON 23 • RATIOS AND PROPORTIONS   **137**

Look and Read

Teach Ratios

- Point out that a ratio has two terms and is never written as a whole number or a mixed number.

- Explain that the first word in a comparison tells which term to write as the *first term* in the ratio.

- Suggest that students draw pictures or use counters to help them understand the situations described on page 137. For the adoption problem, they can use abbreviations for each type of animal or draw a simple sketch.

- Elicit that finding equal ratios is like finding equivalent fractions.

Language Notes

Draw students' attention to the Language Notes. Discuss the meanings of the word *term*. Point out how this word is used in the reading.

Talk and Share

Identify each of the six questions in the exercise before pairs begin their work.

Answers: 10 children; 1 leader; 11 in all; $\frac{1}{10}$, $\frac{10}{1}$; the terms are the same but in opposite order.

Build **VOCABULARY**

Review the meaning of *ratio* and *term*. Have students add each word, its definition, and examples of each term to their vocabulary card file. Have them show ratios in three different ways.

Differentiating Instruction

Beginning
Describing the Ratio Have pairs of students draw a row with 3 squares and a row with 2 circles. Have them write a ratio of squares to circles and use their own words to describe the relationship. (*3:2; sample: For every 3 squares there are 2 circles.*)

Intermediate
Writing a Ratio Have pairs of students write a ratio. Ask them to name items that can be described by the ratio, and to explain their reasoning (*Sample: $\frac{1}{4}$;*

1 car for every 4 tires). Have each pair find three equal ratios and talk about what they mean ($\frac{2}{8}$, $\frac{3}{12}$, $\frac{4}{16}$).

Advanced
Explaining Ratios Follow the directions for the Intermediate activity, but have students also explain how to find the equal ratios. (*Sample: Multiply or divide the first and second terms by the same nonzero number.*)

Lesson 23 • Ratios and Proportions   **137**

Teach **Proportions**

- Ask students to compare the units in the terms of each ratio in the pizza proportion. (*They are the same for the first terms and for the second terms of both ratios.*) Explain that the two ratios in a proportion must compare items in the same order.

- Show that using cross products is a shortcut for multiplying both sides of a proportion by 1 so that the ratios have a common denominator: $\frac{6}{7} \times \frac{21}{21} = \frac{18}{21} \times \frac{7}{7}$. Then compare the numerators: 6×21 and 18×7, which are the cross products.

- Suggest that students circle the terms to multiply when finding cross products:

- Have students solve these proportions: $\frac{a}{16} = \frac{2}{8}$ and $\frac{35}{7} = \frac{175}{b}$. Ask students why the first proportion can be solved using mental math. (a = 4, b = 35; *the numbers are small and 32 divided by 8 = 4 is a basic fact.*)

Talk and Share

Ask students to name the two methods to find whether two ratios form a proportion. (*Look for equal ratios; use cross products.*)

Answers: Yes, find cross products. 3 · 15 = 5 · 9 = 45; multiply 3 and 5 by 3 to get $\frac{9}{15}$. Yes, 6 · 18 = 12 · 9 = 108. No, 5 · 30 = 150, 12 · 15 = 180, and 150 ≠ 180.

Build VOCABULARY

Define *proportion*. Explain that some crosses look like a multiplication symbol, ×. Suggest that students remember that cross products are found by multiplying the numbers at opposite ends of each line segment forming the "×."

Proportions

▲ In Italian, the word *pizza* means "pie." Pizza originally came from Italy and usually has cheese and tomato sauce. What do you like on your pizza?

Carmen is making large pizzas. She needs 2 pounds of cheese for 3 pizzas. How many pounds of cheese does she need for 6 pizzas? By using mental math, you know that she will need 4 pounds of cheese. The two ratios can be written as a **proportion**. A proportion is an equation stating that two ratios are equal. The ratios must compare quantities in the same way.

$$\frac{2 \text{ lb}}{3 \text{ pizzas}} = \frac{2 \times 2}{3 \times 2} = \frac{4 \text{ lb}}{6 \text{ pizzas}} \quad \leftarrow \text{pounds of cheese} \atop \leftarrow \text{number of pizzas}$$

Do the ratios $\frac{6}{7}$ and $\frac{18}{21}$ form a proportion? $\frac{6 \times 3}{7 \times 3} = \frac{18}{21}$ The ratios are equal, so they do form a proportion.

Another way to tell if ratios form a proportion is to use **cross products**.

$$\frac{6}{7} \overset{?}{=} \frac{18}{21}$$

To find the cross products, multiply the blue terms together and the purple terms together. The cross products are equal, so the ratios form a proportion.

6×21 and 7×18
$126 = 126$
So, $\frac{6}{7} = \frac{18}{21}$.

How many pizzas can Carmen make with 30 pounds of cheese? Solve the proportion $\frac{2}{3} = \frac{30}{p}$ to find p, the number of pizzas. Use cross products and the Division Property of Equality.

$\frac{2}{3} = \frac{30}{p}$
$2 \times p = 3 \times 30$
$2p = 90$
$p = 45$

Carmen can make 45 pizzas.

Talk and Share

Work with a partner to describe two ways to find out if the ratios $\frac{3}{5}$ and $\frac{9}{15}$ form a proportion. Do $\frac{3}{5}$ and $\frac{9}{15}$ form a proportion? Is $\frac{6}{12} = \frac{9}{18}$ a true statement? Is $\frac{5}{12} = \frac{15}{30}$ a true statement? Tell how you determined your answers.

VOCABULARY
proportion—a statement that two ratios are equal
cross products—in a proportion, the products of the first term of one ratio and the second term of the other ratio

---

Differentiating Instruction

Beginning
Using Ratio Vocabulary Have partners each write a proportion, exchange papers, and label the parts using *term*, *ratio*, *proportion*, and *cross products*. Have them check each other's work.

Intermediate
Deciding About Ratios Have a small group make a poster for the class showing ways to tell if two ratios form a proportion. Their poster should include labeled examples.

Advanced
Determining Proportions Give partners these two pairs of ratios: $\frac{15}{25}, \frac{3}{5}$ and $\frac{7}{8}, \frac{21}{32}$. Have them test whether the ratios form a proportion and explain why or why not. (*Samples: $\frac{15}{25} = \frac{3}{5}$, because 15 ÷ 3 = 5 and 25 ÷ 5 = 5; $\frac{7}{8} \neq \frac{21}{32}$, because 7 × 32 = 224 and 8 × 21 = 168.*)

Practice

Read the ratio aloud. Then find two ratios equal to the one given.

1. $\frac{18}{12}$ **2.** $\frac{5}{8}$ **3.** $\frac{48}{12}$ **4.** $\frac{6}{9}$ **5.** $\frac{1.5}{4.5}$ **6.** $\frac{40}{100}$

Tell whether the ratios in each exercise form a proportion. Explain why or why not.

7. $\frac{10}{25} \overset{?}{=} \frac{2}{5}$ **8.** $\frac{20}{12} \overset{?}{=} \frac{50}{30}$ **9.** $\frac{4}{5} \overset{?}{=} \frac{5}{6}$

10. $\frac{54}{45} \overset{?}{=} \frac{60}{50}$ **11.** $\frac{0.5}{4} \overset{?}{=} \frac{0.8}{7}$ **12.** $\frac{13}{39} \overset{?}{=} \frac{26}{81}$

13. Explain why the ratios $\frac{12}{18}$ and $\frac{24}{16}$ are not equal.

Solve each proportion.

14. $\frac{n}{72} = \frac{5}{6}$ **15.** $\frac{24}{40} = \frac{m}{10}$ **16.** $\frac{3}{x} = \frac{7.5}{10}$

17. $\frac{64}{100} = \frac{96}{c}$ **18.** $\frac{a}{1.6} = \frac{4.5}{2.4}$ **19.** $\frac{n}{2.7} = \frac{0.8}{2.4}$

20. Ricardo needs 8 pounds of cheese to make 5 pans of lasagna. How many pounds of cheese does he need for 20 pans of lasagna?

Use the circle graph for Exercises 21–24. It shows the number of instruments in each section of an orchestra.

21. What is the total number of instruments?

22. What is the ratio of strings to brass instruments?

23. How many woodwinds would there be in a 144-piece orchestra?

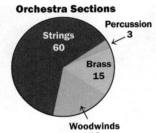

Orchestra Sections

Strings 60 · Percussion 3 · Brass 15 · Woodwinds 18

▲ A violin is a string instrument.

24. How many percussion instruments would there be in a 64-piece orchestra?

25. Pause for Pets has a ratio of 5 staff members to 36 pets. How many staff members must be added to have a ratio of $\frac{1}{6}$?

26. **EXTENDED RESPONSE** If you double the numerator 8 in the proportion $\frac{8}{12} = \frac{2}{3}$, do you need to double the other three numbers as well? Explain.

Practice

Have students write a ratio comparing the number of girls in the class to the number of boys in the class. Then ask them to write a proportion using that ratio.

Discuss the vocabulary used in the word problems, such as *lasagna, orchestra, instruments, strings, brass, woodwinds,* and *percussion.* You may want to show students pictures of instruments or an orchestra.

Assignment Guide
■ Beginning 1–3, 7–17, 20–23, 26
■ Intermediate 1–7 odd, 8–24, 26
■ Advanced 2–8 even, 9–26

Notes on Exercises
Exercise 13 Discuss how students used mental math to tell if the ratios were equal. Ask students if $\frac{10}{16}$ and $\frac{20}{8}$ are equal (*no*).

Exercises 14–19 Remind students that each solution is an equation showing the value of the variable.

Exercise 20 Encourage students to use mental math to solve the problem before they write a proportion.

Exercises 23 and 24 Students should use the answer to Exercise 21 to solve these problems.

Exercise 26 Use this exercise to assess students' understanding of proportions.

Answers
Samples are given for Exercises 1–12.

1. $\frac{36}{24}, \frac{6}{4}, \frac{3}{2}$ **2.** $\frac{10}{16}, \frac{20}{32}, \frac{15}{24}$

3. $\frac{4}{1}, \frac{96}{24}, \frac{12}{3}$ **4.** $\frac{2}{3}, \frac{12}{18}, \frac{4}{6}$

5. $\frac{3}{9}, \frac{1}{3}, \frac{6}{18}$ **6.** $\frac{4}{10}, \frac{2}{5}, \frac{8}{20}$

7. Yes; $\frac{10 \div 5}{25 \div 5} = \frac{2}{5}$

8. Yes; $20 \times 30 = 600 = 12 \times 50$

9. No; $4 \times 6 = 24$, $5 \times 5 = 25$, and $24 \neq 25$

10. Yes; $54 \times 50 = 2{,}700 = 45 \times 60$

11. No; $0.5 \times 7 = 3.5$; $4 \times 0.8 = 3.2$, and $3.5 \neq 3.2$

12. No; $13 \cdot 81 = 1{,}053$, $39 \cdot 26 = 1{,}014$, and $1{,}053 \neq 1{,}014$

13. Sample: The first is less than 1, and the second is greater than 1; so they are not equal.

14. $n = 60$ **15.** $m = 6$
16. $x = 4$ **17.** $c = 150$
18. $a = 3$ **19.** $n = 0.9$
20. 32 lb **21.** 96 instruments
22. $\frac{4}{1}$ $\left(\frac{60}{15}\right)$ **23.** 27 woodwinds

See Additional Answers, page T40.

Program Resources
Practice Book Use page 58.

Teach Evaluating

- Remind students that *evaluate* has more than one meaning: "make a judgment about whether something meets certain criteria" and also "find the value of something."

- Have students work in pairs to complete the activity. In the ensuing class discussion, be sure students understand that there are often factors other than cost to consider when making decisions.

See Additional Answers, page T40.

Hands On

Encourage students to write at least one proportion describing their models. Check students' work.

Partner Practice

Let students work in pairs to write equal ratios. Check students' work.

Key Connection

One particular ratio, the Golden Ratio, has been used by artists and builders for centuries to design objects of beauty. The dimensions of the Great Pyramid in Giza, built almost 5,000 years ago, approximate this ratio. The legs of an isosceles triangle with a vertex angle of 36° are in a Golden Ratio to its base, that is any ratio that is equal to approximately 1.618 to 1.

Activities

Evaluating When you evaluate something, you determine its value. Here you will evaluate costs for renting theaters.

The Drama Club is looking for a theater to rent for its next play. There are four theaters large enough. Work with a partner to evaluate the theaters by deciding which one offers the best deal.

Local Theaters

Nugent	Liberty	Paramount	Tivoli
$220 for 400 seats	$300 for 520 seats	$150 for 250 seats	$200 for 300 seats

1. **Compute** Find the cost for one seat at each theater.

2. **Evaluate** Talk with your partner about which cost is the least and which theater offers the best deal.

3. **Explain** Tell how you made your decision.

4. **Discuss** Talk with your partner about which theater offers the best deal if you need only 225 seats.

▲ Theater

Hands On

Ratio Mania Work with a partner. Use counters in two colors. Display a ratio using counters. Have your partner make three ratios equal to your ratio. Talk about whether your partner's ratios are correct. Take turns making the first ratio.

Partner Practice

More Equal Ratios Work with a partner. Each of you should write a list of twelve ratios using numbers less than 25. Switch papers and write two ratios equal to each ratio in your partner's list. Use cross products to verify that the newly written ratios are correct. Talk about how you found the equal ratios.

Program Resources

Practice Book Use page 59.

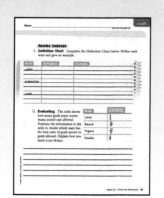

Assessment Book

Use page 45 to assess students' comprehension.

Activity: Be Consumer Reporters

Have pairs of students pretend they are consumer reporters, and have them compare two different brands of the same product, such as peanut butter.

Ask them to evaluate each product and find the better buy. Have them list each factor, such as taste, that influenced their decision.

Have them repeat the activity with a different product, such as milk.

Have students give their consumer reports to the class.

Understanding Percent

Big Idea A percent is a special kind of ratio in which a part is compared to one hundred. Percents are useful in making comparisons.

Building Background

▲ In South Africa, we have many art forms, like colorful woven baskets.

- Describe the picture.
- What do you think makes up the picture?
- What part of the picture is made up of the darkest color?

Key Concepts

Fractions, **decimals**, and **percents** are related. Any one of them can be changed to one of the other forms.

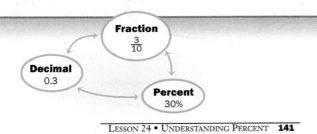

Fraction
$\frac{3}{10}$

Decimal
0.3

Percent
30%

LESSON 24 • UNDERSTANDING PERCENT **141**

 Activity: Decimals, Fractions, and Percents, Oh, My!

Have pairs of students cut out newspaper articles and advertisements that use fractions, decimals, or percents. Have them sort the examples by type and see if there are any patterns in how each form is used to explain data. For example, articles on the sports pages use decimals and percents more often than fractions.

 Resource Library

Math at Hand
Percent 020–022, 044, 185, 189–194

Math on Call
Percent 025–026, 441–442

Reader's Handbook (red)
Circle Graph 558

Reader's Handbook (yellow)
Circle Graph 427

Understanding Percent

STANDARDS CONTENT
Mathematics
- Write percents
- Relate fractions, decimals, and percents

Language
- Predict future events based on current percents

Materials
- 10-by-10 grids (Overhead Transparency 15)

Introduce the **Big Idea**

Ask students if they would go on a picnic if there were a 90% chance of rain (*probably not*). Then read aloud the Big Idea.

Begin **Building Background**

- On page 142, students are informed that the picture of Elvis Presley is made from pieces of toast.
- Ask students how they estimated what part of the picture is the darkest color.

Teach **Key Concepts**

- Discuss the terms. Ask students how they can write a fraction as a decimal. (*Divide the numerator by the denominator.*)
- Explain that a fraction, a decimal, and a percent can be used to name the same amount.

Warm-Up Review

Have students explain how to solve a proportion. (*Sample: Find cross products. Write an equation. Solve the equation.*)

Have students solve each proportion.

1. $\frac{40}{8} = \frac{a}{100}$ (a = *500*)
2. $\frac{16}{100} = \frac{4}{b}$ (b = *25*)
3. $\frac{70}{e} = \frac{7}{10}$ (e = *100*)
4. $\frac{15}{20} = \frac{75}{f}$ (f = *100*)
5. $\frac{100}{l} = \frac{1}{100}$ (l = *10,000*)

24

Look and Read

Teach Percent

- Ask students what decimal and what fraction are shown by each grid. Write the equations on the board: $19\% = 0.19 = \frac{19}{100}$, $40\% = 0.40 = \frac{40}{100}$, $85\% = 0.85 = \frac{85}{100}$.

- Ask students what other way they could use to find $\frac{3}{5} = \frac{n}{100}$. (*Find the ratio equal to $\frac{3}{5}$ with a denominator of 100; the numerator is 3×20, or 60.*)

- As another example, have a volunteer use the method shown to write $\frac{8}{15}$ as a percent ($53\frac{1}{3}\%$).

- Use Overhead Transparency 15 to shade in several different percents on the grid. Give students three possible answers for the percent shaded. Have them show thumbs up or thumbs down for each possible percent. You can also use the transparency to have students estimate the percent shaded.

Talk and Share

- Make sure that students understand how to read the information in the circle graph. Explain that Tori's graph shows her exact expenses, not what she expects to spend.

- Ask, *What do you need to do before you find each percent?* (*Find the sum of the three amounts.*)

Answers: Clothes, 40%; lunch, 27%; books, 33%; entire graph, 100%

Build VOCABULARY

Define *percent* as "per hundred." Explain that the word *cent* is from the Latin word *centum* meaning "hundred."

Percent

The picture of Elvis Presley on page 141 is made of toast. About 5 percent of the toast was burned to form the dark hair.

Percent means "per hundred," indicated by the symbol %. A percent is the number of hundredths that represents a part of a whole. So, 5% means 5 hundredths, or $\frac{5}{100}$.

Each hundredths grid shows a percent of squares shaded.

19 per hundred	40 per hundred	85 per hundred

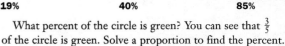

19%	40%	85%

What percent of the circle is green? You can see that $\frac{3}{5}$ of the circle is green. Solve a proportion to find the percent.

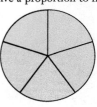

$$\frac{3}{5} = \frac{r}{100}$$
$$3 \times 100 = 5 \times r$$
$$300 = 5r$$
$$r = 60$$

Since $\frac{3}{5} = \frac{60}{100}$, 60% of the circle is green.

Talk and Share

Work with a partner. Find the percent of money that is spent on each item in the graph. Take turns explaining how you found each percent. What percent is represented by the entire graph?

Tori's Expenses

Clothes $24
Lunch $16
Books $20

VOCABULARY
percent—the number of hundredths representing a part of a whole

---

Differentiating Instruction

Beginning

Finding Percent Using a Grid Have students work individually to shade fifteen squares in a 10-by-10 grid (Overhead Transparency 15). Have them complete each phrase:

___ squares shaded (*15*)

___ per hundred (*15*) ___ % (*15*)

Intermediate

Writing a Percent Have pairs of students shade a 10-by-10 grid to show

$\frac{3}{10}$. Have them tell how to write a percent for the shaded portion ($\frac{3}{10} = \frac{30}{100} = 30\%$).

Advanced

Explaining Percents Have partners write sentences explaining how to write a fraction as a percent and then follow those steps to write $\frac{3}{25}$ as a percent. (*Sample: Write the fraction with a denominator of 100. Write the number in the numerator, followed by a percent sign; $\frac{3}{25} = \frac{3 \times 4}{25 \times 4} = \frac{12}{100} = 12\%$.*)

Fractions, Decimals, and Percents

To change among fractions, decimals, and percents, remember that a percent is a ratio of a number compared to 100.

You can write a percent as a fraction and as a decimal.

$20\% = \frac{20}{100} = \frac{1}{5}$ $\qquad$ $20\% = \frac{20}{100} = 0.20$, or 0.2

$38\% = \frac{38}{100} = \frac{19}{50}$ $\qquad$ $38\% = \frac{38}{100} = 0.38$

You can write a decimal as a fraction and as a percent.

$0.45 = \frac{45}{100} = 45\%$ $\qquad$ $0.09 = \frac{9}{100} = 9\%$

Here's another way to write a decimal as a percent. Multiply the decimal by 100 and write a % symbol.

$0.75 \rightarrow 0.75 \times 100 \rightarrow 0{.}75{.} \rightarrow 75\%$

Of the balloons shown, $\frac{2}{10}$ are orange. Write the fraction as a percent and as a decimal. When the denominator is a factor of 100, find an equivalent fraction.

$\frac{2}{10} = \frac{20}{100} = 20\% = 0.20$ $\qquad$ $\frac{11}{25} = \frac{44}{100} = 44\% = 0.44$

If the denominator is not a factor of 100, divide the numerator by the denominator.

$\frac{3}{8} = 0.375 = 37.5\%$

$\frac{2}{3} = 0.666\ldots \approx 66.7\%$

$$\begin{array}{r} 0.375 \\ 8\overline{)3.000} \\ -24 \\ \hline 60 \\ -56 \\ \hline 40 \\ -40 \\ \hline 0 \end{array}$$

$$\begin{array}{r} 0.666\ldots \\ 3\overline{)2.000} \\ -18 \\ \hline 20 \\ -18 \\ \hline 20 \\ -18 \\ \hline 2 \end{array}$$

0.375 is a **terminating decimal.** You also can write $37\frac{1}{2}\%$.

0.666 … is a **repeating decimal.** You also can write $66\frac{2}{3}\%$.

Talk and Share

Work with a partner. Use division to write $\frac{5}{16}$ and $\frac{5}{12}$ as decimals. Discuss with your partner whether the decimals are terminating or repeating decimals. Tell how you decided.

VOCABULARY
terminating decimal—a decimal with a fixed number of digits. It has an end.
repeating decimal—a decimal with a digit or group of digits that repeats forever

LESSON 24 • UNDERSTANDING PERCENT **143**

Teach Fractions, Decimals, and Percents

■ Point out that every fraction will be either a terminating or a repeating decimal. Explain that the repeating part may be one or many numbers.

■ Write $\frac{2}{3} = 0.666\ldots \approx 66.7\%$ and $\frac{2}{3} = 0.666\ldots = 66\frac{2}{3}\%$ on the board to show two ways to write a repeating decimal as a percent. Point out that an ellipsis (. . .) means that a number repeats and that the symbol $\approx$ means "is about equal to." A bar may be drawn to show the digits that repeat in a repeating decimal: $0.666\ldots = 0.\overline{6}$.

■ Have volunteers show how to write each of the numbers below:
  • 55% as a fraction and a decimal ($55\% = \frac{55}{100} = \frac{11}{20} = 0.55$)
  • 0.9 as a fraction and a percent ($0.9 = \frac{9}{10} = \frac{90}{100} = 90\%$)
  • $\frac{5}{6}$ as a decimal and a percent ($\frac{5}{6} = 0.833\ldots = 83\frac{1}{3}\%$)

Talk and Share

Ask students to use proper notation for repeating decimals in their quotients when needed.
Answers: $\frac{5}{16} = 0.3125$, *terminating;* $\frac{5}{12} \approx 0.41\overline{6}$, *repeating*

Build **VOCABULARY**

Use related words and meanings to help students remember the terms *terminating decimal* and *repeating decimal*. Point out that to *terminate* is to "end" and to *repeat* is to "do the same thing again."

Differentiating Instruction

Beginning
Modeling a Fraction, Decimal, and Percent Give students 10-by-10 grids. Have them shade 50 squares and write a fraction in simplest form, a decimal, and a percent for the amount shaded ($\frac{1}{2}$, 0.5, 50%). Ask, *Are the three numbers equal? How do you know?*

Intermediate
Writing a Fraction as a Decimal and a Percent Give students 10-by-10 grids. Have them shade the grid to show $\frac{2}{5}$. Have them write a decimal and a percent for the shaded amount (*0.4 or 0.40, 40%*). Then have them talk about how to write the decimal and the percent without using a model.

Advanced
Writing Percents as Fractions After students read the examples on page 143, have them find the fractions equivalent to 60%, 75%, and 62.5% ($\frac{3}{5}$, $\frac{3}{4}$, $\frac{5}{8}$). Have them show their work and tell a partner the steps they used.

Practice

Remind students that fractions, decimals, and percents all show parts of a whole. Have students write *28 out of 100* in each of those ways ($\frac{28}{100}$ or $\frac{7}{25}$, 0.28, 28%).

Assignment Guide

■ Beginning 1–4, 5–19 odd, 21–39, 40, 42, 43

■ Intermediate 1–19 odd, 21–43

■ Advanced 2–20 even, 21–43

Notes on Exercises

Exercises 21–24 Students need to round only those decimals that have four or more digits to the right of the decimal point. They are not required to rewrite a decimal that ends in tenths or hundredths as a decimal in thousandths.

Exercises 25–37 Encourage students to write any repeating decimals using fractions or rounding. Suggest that they save the tables to use as a reference in the next two lessons. You may want to have students extend the table to show $\frac{1}{10}$ through $\frac{9}{10}$ and to post a copy of the table for classroom use throughout the year.

Exercises 38–42 Students will need to compare and order percents to match the country with the section on the graph.

Practice

Tell what percent of each figure is shaded.

1. 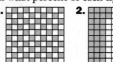 2. 3. 4.

Write each percent as a decimal and as a fraction in simplest form.

5. 90%   **6.** 65%   **7.** 4%   **8.** 87.5%

9. 72%   **10.** 39%   **11.** 100%   **12.** 15%

Write each decimal as a percent and as a fraction in simplest form.

13. 1.0   **14.** 0.8   **15.** 0.24   **16.** 0.7

17. 0.46   **18.** 0.025   **19.** 2.5   **20.** 0.05

Write each fraction as a decimal and as a percent. Tell whether each decimal is repeating or terminating. Round decimals to the nearest thousandth and percents to the nearest tenth. You may use your calculator.

21. $\frac{3}{4}$ **22.** $\frac{5}{6}$ **23.** $\frac{3}{11}$ **24.** $\frac{7}{7}$

Copy and complete the tables. Save the tables to use for reference.

	Fraction	Decimal	Percent
25.	$\frac{1}{2}$	?	?
26.	$\frac{1}{3}$	0.33 …	?
27.	$\frac{2}{3}$	?	?
28.	$\frac{1}{4}$	?	?
29.	?	?	75%
30.	$\frac{1}{5}$	?	?
31.	$\frac{2}{5}$	?	40%

	Fraction	Decimal	Percent
32.	?	0.6	?
33.	$\frac{4}{5}$	?	?
34.	$\frac{1}{8}$	?	12.5%
35.	$\frac{3}{8}$	?	?
36.	?	0.625	?
37.	?	?	87.5%

The circle graph shows the top 5 medal-winning countries in the 2000 Olympics. Match each country with its percent.

38. Australia, 58 medals

39. Russia, 88 medals

40. Germany, 56 medals

41. China, 59 medals

42. United States, 97 medals

16.5% 27.1%
15.6% 16.2%
24.6%

43. (**EXTENDED RESPONSE**) Find the sum of the percents in the graph. Explain why this sum makes sense.

Program Resources

Practice Book Use page 60.
Overhead Transparencies Use 15.

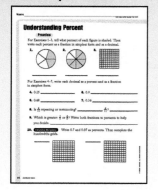

Answers

1. 50%   **2.** 32%

3. 75%   **4.** 33.3… %

5. 0.9, $\frac{9}{10}$ **6.** 0.65, $\frac{13}{20}$

7. 0.04, $\frac{1}{25}$ **8.** 0.875, $\frac{7}{8}$

9. 0.72, $\frac{18}{25}$ **10.** 0.39, $\frac{39}{100}$

11. 1.0, $\frac{1}{1}$ **12.** 0.15, $\frac{3}{20}$

13. 100%, $\frac{1}{1}$ **14.** 80%, $\frac{4}{5}$

15. 24%, $\frac{6}{25}$ **16.** 70%, $\frac{7}{10}$

17. 46%, $\frac{23}{50}$ **18.** 2.5%, $\frac{1}{40}$

19. 250%, $2\frac{1}{2}$ **20.** 5%, $\frac{1}{20}$

21. 0.75, 75%, terminating

22. 0.833, 83.3%, repeating

23. 0.273, 27.3%, repeating

24. 1.0, 100%, terminating

25. 0.5, 50%   **26.** $33\frac{1}{3}$%

27. 0.66…, $66\frac{2}{3}$%

28. 0.25, 25%   **29.** $\frac{3}{4}$, 0.75

30. 0.2, 20%   **31.** 0.4

32. $\frac{3}{5}$, 60%   **33.** 0.8, 80%

34. 0.125   **35.** 0.375, 37.5%

36. $\frac{5}{8}$, 62.5%   **37.** $\frac{7}{8}$, 0.875

See Additional Answers, page T40.

Activities

Predicting Remember that to predict means to make a judgment about a future event based on known information.

The graph shows the number of different types of hits Sammy Sosa of the Chicago Cubs had during the 1998 season. Work with a partner.

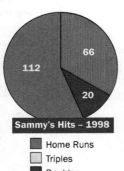

Sammy's Hits – 1998
- Home Runs
- Triples
- Doubles
- Singles

1. **Compute** Find what percent of the hits were home runs, triples, doubles, and singles.

2. **Explain** Find the sum of the percents. Does that make sense? Explain.

3. **Predict** Tell how many home runs, triples, doubles, and singles you might expect Sosa to have in a season of 189 hits. Explain how you made your prediction.

4. **Discuss** In 2003, Sosa had 144 hits. Of those hits, 44 were home runs. Discuss with your partner whether the percent of home runs was less than or greater than the 1998 percent.

Terminators or Repeaters? Work with a small group. Use your completed tables from Exercises 25–37 on page 144. Notice that the fractions with a denominator of 3 are repeating decimals. Fractions with a denominator of 5 or a power of 2 are terminating decimals. Use these patterns to predict whether the following fractions will be terminating or repeating decimals. Check with a calculator.

$$\frac{3}{32} \quad \frac{11}{18} \quad \frac{37}{64} \quad \frac{13}{99} \quad \frac{7}{150} \quad \frac{57}{128} \quad \frac{247}{300} \quad \frac{375}{1,000}$$

Partner Practice

Repeat That Please? Write $\frac{1}{9}, \frac{2}{9}, \frac{3}{9}$, and $\frac{4}{9}$ as decimals. Have your partner try to write $\frac{5}{9}, \frac{6}{9}, \frac{7}{9}$, and $\frac{8}{9}$ as decimals without computing. Have your partner write $\frac{1}{11}, \frac{2}{11}, \frac{3}{11}, \frac{4}{11}$, and $\frac{5}{11}$ as decimals. Try to write $\frac{6}{11}, \frac{7}{11}, \frac{8}{11}, \frac{9}{11}$, and $\frac{10}{11}$ as decimals without computing. Look for other groups of fractions with patterns in their decimal forms.

◄ Sammy Sosa

LESSON 24 • UNDERSTANDING PERCENT **145**

Teach Predicting

- Have pairs of students work through the activity. Suggest that students write all the percents to the nearest tenth.

- The third part of the activity prepares students for Lesson 25, Finding the Percent of a Number.

  Answers:
  1. *Home runs, 33.3%; triples, 0%; doubles, 10.1%; singles, 56.6%*
  2. *100%; Yes, the graph represents all hits.*
  3. *63 home runs, no triples, 19 doubles, 107 singles*
  4. *31%; less than*

Oral Language

All decimals in Exercises 5–20 on page 144 are terminating. You may wish to provide students with the denominators for those exercises: 2, 5, 8, 10, 20, 25, 50, 100.

Answers: Fractions with denominators that have a factor of 3 will be repeating decimals: $\frac{11}{18}, \frac{13}{99}, \frac{7}{150}, \frac{247}{300}$. Those with prime factors of only 2 and/or 5 are terminating decimals: $\frac{3}{32}, \frac{37}{64}, \frac{57}{128}, \frac{375}{1,000}$.

Partner Practice

Encourage students to look for all kinds of patterns, not just patterns like the ones for ninths and elevenths. Suggest they try sixths or sevenths.
See Additional Answers, page T40.

 Activity: Percent Patterns

Have pairs of students each create a design or picture by shading squares in a 10-by-10 grid. Have partners exchange grids and have the partner write a fraction, decimal, and percent for the shaded area.

 Assessment Book

Use page 46 to assess students' comprehension.

 Program Resources

Practice Book Use page 61.

Percent of a Number

STANDARDS CONTENT

Mathematics
- Find the percent of a number
- Explore percents less than 1% and greater than 100%

Language
- Recognize the meaning of the idiom *give 110%*
- Persuade someone that a given suggestion is the best

Introduce the Big Idea

Read aloud the Big Idea. Then talk about how a percent can be greater than 100%. Say, *Suppose a soccer player is expected to kick two goals per game. If he kicks three goals, this is more than, or 150% of, what was expected.*

Begin Building Background

Have students share how percents and decimals can be used in their favorite sports.

Teach Key Concepts

Read the percents shown above each model. Have students relate each percent to the number of shaded squares in the corresponding model.

Ask, *Why is the first model labeled 0.5%?* (Only half a small square is shaded and $\frac{1}{2} = 0.5$.) *What does the completely shaded large square in the third model mean?* (100%)

Warm-Up Review

Have students find each product.

1. 6×0.8 *(4.8)*
2. 12×0.03 *(0.36)*
3. 2.36×9 *(21.24)*
4. $\frac{1}{10} \times 50$ *(5)*
5. $\frac{1}{100} \times 230$ *(2$\frac{3}{10}$)*
6. $190 \times \frac{1}{10}$ *(19)*

Percent of a Number

Big Idea Percents can be less than 1% and greater than 100%. There are several ways to find a percent of a number.

Building Background

▲ My sister and I play soccer. My family goes to watch our games.

- What is happening in the picture?
- What sports are your favorites?
- Tell how percents and decimals might be used in soccer.

Key Concepts

0.5%	5%	105%
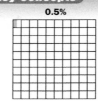		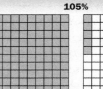
Less than 1%	From 1% to 100%	More than 100%

 Activity: Is It More or Less?

Have students use *less than 1%*, *from 1% to 100%*, or *more than 100%* to complete each sentence.

1. A model showing __ uses two or more grids (*more than 100%*).
2. A model showing __ has one grid with one or more squares shaded (*from 1% to 100%*).
3. A model that has only part of one square shaded shows __ (*less than 1%*).
4. An example of a percent __ is 98.2% (*from 1% to 100%*).

Resource Library

Math at Hand
Percent 193–194

Math on Call
Percent 443–444

Finding the Percent of a Number

One way to find the percent of a number is to use a proportion. Another way is to change the percent to a decimal or a fraction and multiply.

The U.S. Women's National Soccer Team scored 110 goals in the 2000 season. Mia Hamm kicked 10% of those goals. How many goals did Hamm kick?

Proportion

$\frac{10}{100} = \frac{g}{110}$

$100g = 1,100$

$g = 11$

Decimal

10% of $110 = 0.1 \times 110 = 11$

Fraction

$\frac{10}{100}$ of $110 = \frac{1}{10} \times 110 = 11$

Hamm kicked 11 of the team's goals.

You can use the same methods to find percents of large numbers.

▲ Mia Hamm

Artis Gilmore ▼

In 2004, Artis Gilmore was still the National Basketball Association's leader in field-goal percent. During his career, he made nearly 60% of the field goals he attempted. His attempts numbered 9,570. About how many field goals did he make? Let f stand for the number of field goals.

Proportion

$60\% = \frac{60}{100} = \frac{6}{10}$

$\frac{6}{10} = \frac{f}{9,570}$

$10f = 57,420$

$f = 5,742$

Decimal

$60\% = 0.6$

$0.6 \times 9,570 = 5,742$

Gilmore made about 5,742 field goals.

Talk and Share

Some people say that Mia Hamm gives 110% when she plays soccer. Ask your partner if that is possible and talk about what that means.

Language Notes

Idioms
This saying doesn't mean what it seems.

- give 110%
  work harder than people expect

Teach Finding the Percent of a Number

■ Ask, *How would you find $\frac{1}{4}$ of 4?* (*Multiply $\frac{1}{4}$ and 4.*) Explain that the word *of* also means "multiply" when finding the percent *of* a number.

■ Ask, *What does g in the proportion $\frac{10}{100} = \frac{g}{110}$ stand for?* (*the number of goals that Mia Hamm kicked*) Explain that percents are written as fractions with a denominator of 100 when used in a proportion.

■ Summarize the page by having students name the three ways to find the percent of a number. (*1. Write the percent as a decimal and multiply; 2. write the percent as a fraction and multiply; and 3. write and solve a proportion.*) Then have them find 25% of 80 (*20*).

Language Notes

Remind students that an *idiom* doesn't mean what it seems. Ask, *Did you ever "give 110%"? Tell us about it.*

Talk and Share

Point out that there is not a right or wrong answer to these questions. Have partners share their opinions with the class. *Giving 110%* means "going beyond what is minimally required."

Differentiating Instruction

Beginning

Finding Percent of a Number Mentally
Have pairs of students explain how they can use mental math to find 50% of 8 ($\frac{50}{100} = \frac{1}{2}$; $\frac{1}{2} \times 8 = 4$). Say, *Find 25% of 16 and 10% of 50 using mental math* (*4, 5*). *How did you do it?*

Intermediate

Finding Percent of a Number Say, *Use each way described on page 147 to find 75% of 40* (*30*). Have pairs of students talk about which method they prefer and why.

Advanced

Explaining Mental Math with Percents
After students read page 147, have small groups find 20% of 30, 25% of 12, 17% of 8, and 50% of 12. Have them write about which solutions were easy to find using mental math and why (*6, 3, 1.36, 6; sample: The only hard one was 17% of 8. For the others, I changed the percent to a fraction and then divided the number by the fraction denominator; for instance, $50\% = \frac{1}{2}$ and $12 \div 2 = 6$.*)

Activity: Tic-Tac Definitions

Have partners copy the diagram shown below. Have one student choose a word and give a definition or example of the word. If the partner agrees that the definition or example is correct, the first student takes the space. The first student to take three spaces in a row, column, or diagonal is the winner.

repeating decimal	percent	proportion
terminating decimal	rate	fraction
cross products	term	(students' choice)

Teach Percents Less Than 1% or Greater Than 100%

■ Discuss why the decimal point can be moved two places to the right when writing a decimal as a percent. Write $0.004 \times 100 = 0.4$ on the board to remind students that the decimal is multiplied by 100 to find the percent.

■ Stress that students can find percents less than 1% and greater than 100% using the same methods they use to find percents from 1% to 100%. Point out that they should find the number of parts per hundred and then write the fraction or decimal as a percent.

■ Be sure students know how to read percents less than 1% and percents greater than 100%.

Talk and Share

Have students work in pairs. If students ask, tell them that the abbreviation *APR* stands for "annual percentage rate." It is a special kind of interest rate that takes into account the fees and other costs of securing or processing a loan.

Answers: $\frac{9}{10}$ of a percent; it is less than 1%.

Percents Less Than 1% or Greater Than 100%

Meda's goal was to make 1,000 sock monkeys to give to a children's hospital. Meda made 4 sock monkeys as samples. Write 4 out of 1,000 as a percent.

Using a Fraction

$$\frac{4}{1,000} = \frac{4 \div 10}{1,000 \div 10}$$ ← Divide numerator and denominator by 10 to get 100 in the denominator.

$$= \frac{0.4}{100} = 0.4\%$$ ← Write as a percent.

Using a Decimal

$$\frac{4}{1,000} = 0.004$$ ← Write as a decimal.

$$0.004 \rightarrow 0.00.4 \rightarrow 0.4\%$$ ← Move the decimal point two places to the right. Then write %.

0.4% is read "four tenths percent." 0.4% is less than 1%. The 4 samples represent less than 1% of the goal.

At the end of six months, Meda had completed 1,200 sock monkeys. Write 1,200 as a percent of 1,000.

Using a Fraction

$$\frac{1,200}{1,000} = \frac{1,200 \div 10}{1,000 \div 10}$$ ← Divide numerator and denominator by 10 to get 100 in the denominator.

$$= \frac{120}{100} = 120\%$$ ← Write as a percent.

Using a Decimal

$$\frac{1,200}{1,000} = 1.20$$ ← Write as a decimal.

$$1.20 \rightarrow 1.20. \rightarrow 120\%$$ ← Move the decimal point two places to the right. Then write %.

120% is more than 100%. So Meda made more than her goal of 1,000 sock monkeys.

▲ Sock monkeys

ONLY **0.9%** APR!

Buy the Car of Your Dreams Today!

Talk and Share

Work with a partner. Read the sign on the right that tells how much a car dealer will charge you to borrow money to buy a car. Tell what the percent means. Tell how the percent compares to 1%.

 Activity: And the Goal Is . . .

Have small groups of students form two teams. One team states a ratio, such as 3 out of 1,000, and the second team writes that ratio as a fraction and as a percent. If correct, the second team scores 1 point. The teams take turns until one team reaches the goal of 10 points.

 Differentiating Instruction

Beginning
Understanding Large and Small Percents Say, *Joy's goal is to collect $100 for charity. She actually collected $105.* On the board, write $\frac{105}{100} = 105\%$. Say, *Joy's first contribution was 50¢.* On the board, write $\frac{0.5}{100} = 0.5\%$. Have students look back at the third and first models on page 146 and talk about how they relate to this situation.

Intermediate
Relating Fractions, Decimals, and Percents Put students in groups of

three and tell them: *Jan wants to collect 5,000 aluminum cans for his recycling project. He has 20.* Have students explain to each other how to find the fraction, decimal, and percent that represent the cans Jan has collected.

Advanced
What's Possible? Have small groups discuss how it is possible for there to be more than 100%. Students must use examples in their explanations.

Practice

Write each percent as a decimal and as a fraction in simplest terms.
1. 0.25%   **2.** 2.5%   **3.** 130%   **4.** 110%
5. 500%   **6.** 0.05%   **7.** 200%   **8.** 1.25%

Write each decimal or fraction as a percent.
9. 1.75   **10.** $\frac{3}{200}$ **11.** 0.006   **12.** $3\frac{1}{2}$
13. $\frac{8}{1,000}$ **14.** 2.4   **15.** 5   **16.** $\frac{29}{1,000}$

Find each percent.
17. 75% of 52   **18.** 60% of 70   **19.** 60% of 20
20. 87.5% of 72   **21.** $66\frac{2}{3}$% of 18   **22.** 59% of 200
23. 43% of 65   **24.** 3.5% of 36   **25.** 140% of 50
26. 275% of 100   **27.** 0.6% of 120   **28.** 0.02% of 3,000

Copy and complete each row of the table.

	Percent	0.5%	50%	100%	150%	200%	250%
29.	Number	0.24	?	48	?	96	?
30.	Number	?	?	240	?	480	600

Kurt Warner ▶

31. During one game in 2000, Kurt Warner completed about 71.42% of his 35 passes. How many passes did Warner complete?

32. From 1980 to 2000, the population of Iowa increased by only 0.41%. The 1980 population was about 2.914 million. What was the 2000 population?

33. In one day, a ruby-throated hummingbird eats 200% of its weight. If the bird weighs 0.11 ounce, how much does it eat?

 ◀ Ruby-throated hummingbird

34. (**EXTENDED RESPONSE**) Tell or show two ways to find 25% of 824. Tell which way you think is easier.

Practice

Have students explain how to find 150% of 4 and 0.15% of 40 (*Samples: 1.5 × 4 = 6; 0.0015 × 40 = 0.06*).

Assignment Guide
- Beginning 1–24, 29–31, 32, 34
- Intermediate 1–16, 17–27 odd, 29–34
- Advanced 1–16, 18–28 even, 29–34

Notes on Exercises
Exercises 29 and 30 Exercises 29 and 30 must be assigned together. Point out that the percents in the top row of the table label the columns. In Exercise 29, the number 48 is 100% of a number (*48*). From there, students can think, "What is 50% of 48?" (*24*) to find the entry for the second column. They can use similar reasoning to complete the table.

Exercise 32 This is a two-step problem. Students should find the increase and then add it to the 1980 population.

Answers

1. $0.0025; \frac{1}{400}$ **2.** $0.025; \frac{1}{40}$
3. $1.3; 1\frac{3}{10}$ **4.** $1.1; 1\frac{1}{10}$
5. $5; \frac{5}{1}$ **6.** $0.0005; \frac{1}{2,000}$
7. $2; \frac{2}{1}$ **8.** $0.0125; \frac{1}{80}$
9. 175%   **10.** 1.5%
11. 0.6%   **12.** 350%
13. 0.8%   **14.** 240%
15. 500%   **16.** 2.9%
17. 39   **18.** 42
19. 12   **20.** 63
21. 12   **22.** 118

23. 27.95   **24.** 1.26
25. 70   **26.** 275
27. 0.72
28. 0.6
29. 24, 72, 120
30. 1.2, 120, 360
31. 25 passes
32. about 2.926 million
33. 0.22 oz
34. Multiply 824 by $\frac{1}{4}$ or by 0.25. Sample: The first way is easier because I can do it in my head.

Program Resources
Practice Book Use page 62.

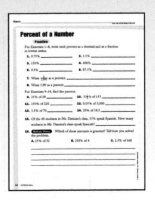

Teach Persuading

■ Ask students to give examples of when they attempted to *persuade* someone. You may want to start the discussion by modeling a situation. Say, *I tried to persuade my friend to go with me to run some errands. I told her how much fun it would be to get together and talk and explained that she could do some of her errands at the same time.*

■ Have pairs of students complete the activity. Then have the pairs try to persuade another pair that the batting order they chose is best.

See Additional Answers, page T40.

Partner Practice

■ You may wish to write the number of left-handed people in the class on the board or plan a time for students to survey one another.

■ Be sure students understand that there is nothing unlucky or "bad" about being left-handed. Point out the prominent and successful people pictured in the text: Mahatma Gandhi, Albert Einstein, and M. C. Escher.

Answers: 24 people; percents will vary.

Partner Practice

Encourage students to write at least one word problem.

Develop Language

Player	On Base/ Times at Bat	Hits/ Times at Bat
Suzi	36/60	30/60
Kimi	35/50	24/50
Wendy	32/64	24/64
Cassie	30/60	24/60
Teresa	45/75	35/75
Karen	50/75	36/75
Tonya	24/48	18/48
Debbie	27/45	25/45
Elena	45/72	40/72

Activities

Persuading When you persuade, you give reasons to make someone believe something. Many softball coaches find that data from games give persuasive reasons for setting up batting orders. For instance, coaches might want their first two batters to have high on-base percents. Then they might want the next three batters to be "power" hitters. That is, they have high hitting percents.

The table gives the on-base and hitting ratios for the Avoca Tigers softball team.

1. **Compute** Work with a partner to find the on-base and hitting percents for each player.

2. **Decide** Set up a batting order for these nine players.

3. **Persuade** Tell how you would persuade the Tigers' coach that your batting order is good.

Partner Practice

Lefty or Righty? It is estimated that 12% of the world's population is left-handed. In many cultures, it is considered unlucky to be left-handed. A "left-handed compliment" is really an insult. A "left-handed ship" is an unlucky one.

Work with a partner to answer these questions. How many people would you expect to be left-handed in a group of 200? Find the percent of people in your class who are left-handed. Is it close to 12%?

Famous Lefties

Gandhi ▲

Einstein ▶

Partner Practice

Big Percents Work with a partner. Each of you should write 8 problems to find a percent of a number. Use percents greater than 100%. Make several of the problems easy to do with mental math and several easy to do using fractions. Trade problems and solve. Check each other's work.

▲ Escher

Program Resources

Practice Book Use page 63.

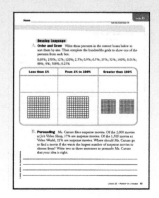

Assessment Book

Use page 47 to assess students' comprehension.

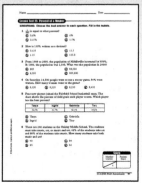

Activity: Be a Party Planner

Write *Decorations*, *Food*, *Music*, *Invitations*, and *Favors* on the board. Explain that each pair of students should imagine that they have $100 to spend on these party items. Have them decide what percent of the budget will be spent on each set of items and calculate the dollar amount.

After the budgets are prepared, have two groups meet. Each group should try to persuade the other group that their budget is better.

Applications of Percent

Talk and Explore

Big Idea Percents are used in many everyday situations. Discounts, sales tax, and interest earned on savings accounts all involve percents.

Building Background

▲ My family loves shopping when there is a sale!

CLEARANCE
40% OFF

- What is happening in the picture?
- What does the sign mean?
- How much would you pay for a $30 sweater at a 40% off sale?

Key Concepts

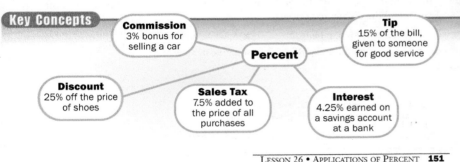

Commission 3% bonus for selling a car

Tip 15% of the bill, given to someone for good service

Percent

Discount 25% off the price of shoes

Sales Tax 7.5% added to the price of all purchases

Interest 4.25% earned on a savings account at a bank

LESSON 26 • APPLICATIONS OF PERCENT **151**

 Activity: What Percent?

Have small groups of students list the five ways to use percents given in the Web.

Have them discuss situations in which they would want the percent in each example to be a greater number and in which they would want it to be a lesser number. (*Answers will vary, but generally when paying money or offering a discount, you would like the least percent. When receiving money or buying a discounted item, you would like the greatest percent.*)

Resource Library

Math at Hand
Percent 193, 196–197, 449

Math on Call
Percent 443, 447–451

Applications of Percent

STANDARDS CONTENT
Mathematics
- Solve problems involving discounts and sales tax
- Solve problems involving simple interest

Language
- Recognize the meanings of *principal* and *principle*
- Summarize information about ratios by giving examples

Materials
- Webs (Overhead Transparency 33)

Introduce the Big Idea
Read the Big Idea. Ask students to describe times they have seen a percent used to calculate a money amount.

Begin Building Background
To supplement the discussion, you might give students newspapers and ask them to find ads with percent-off sales.

Answers: You won't pay full price; $18

Teach Key Concepts
- Have a volunteer describe the Web. Read aloud the words and examples in each oval. Except for *commission*, each boldface word is defined again later in the lesson. Define *bonus* as "an additional amount paid." If students have newspapers, have them try to find examples of the terms in the Web.

Warm-Up Review
Have students find the percent of each number.
1. 15% of 100 (*15*)
2. 60% of 50 (*30*)
3. 25% of 16 (*4*)
4. 3% of 21 (*0.63*)
5. 5% of 80 (*4*)
6. 10% of 95 (*9.5*)
7. 75% of 160 (*120*)
8. 6% of 13 (*0.78*)

Teach Discounts and Sales Tax

■ Ask, *Is a* <u>sale price</u> *greater or less than the regular price?* (*less than*) *Is the cost of an item with* <u>sales tax</u> *greater or less than the cost of the item?* (*greater than*)

■ After discussing the examples, ask students to find a sale price. Use jeans that cost $50, a discount of 20%, and sales tax of 8% (*$43.20*). Ask volunteers to explain each step in finding the sale price.

Talk and Share

Students should find each sale price individually and then discuss how they found each. Explain that a *bargain* is something that is sold for a low price.

Answers: Explanations will vary; tulip bulbs, $7.20; spading fork, $10; Carolina sweet shrub, $13.50; large mum plant, $4

Build VOCABULARY

Review the meanings of *discount*, *sales tax*, and *tip*. Have students add the terms and their definitions to their vocabulary word files.

Discounts and Sales Tax

Jacob is buying a pair of jeans. The regular price of the jeans is $40. The **discount** is 30%. What is the sale price of the jeans?

You need to do two things to find the sale price.

Find the discount.	30% of 40 = 0.3 × 40 = 12
Subtract the discount from the regular price.	40 − 12 = 28

The sale price of the jeans is $28.

You also need to use percents to find **sales tax** and tips. Find the total cost of a $14.50 CD if the sales tax is 7%.

Find the tax.

7% of 14.50 = 0.07 × 14.50 = 1.015 ≈ $1.02

Add the tax to the cost.   14.50 + 1.02 = $15.52

The total cost with tax is $15.52.

Elena's lunch, with tax, cost $6. She has $7. Does she have enough money if she wants to leave a 15% **tip?**

0.15 × 6 = 0.90   6 + 0.90 = 6.90 $6.90 < $7

Elena has enough money.

Talk and Share

Count the Discount The regular prices for items at Erika's Garden Shop are given below. The sign shows the discounts. Work with a partner to find each discounted price. Try to compute using mental math. Tell your partner how you found the discounted prices.

■ Package of 25 tulip bulbs, $8
■ Carolina Sweet Shrub, $18
■ Spading fork, $15
■ Large mum plant, $8

Erika's Blossoming Bargains

Plants   50% off
Tools $33\frac{1}{3}$% off
Shrubs   25% off
Bulbs   10% off

VOCABULARY

discount—an amount taken off the cost of an item
sales tax—an amount of money the government collects when something is sold
tip—a percent of a bill paid to someone who provides a service

152 UNIT 6 • RATIOS, PROPORTIONS, AND PERCENTS

Activity: Let's Eat Out

Have one student in a pair "order" a meal from a take-out menu and present a discount coupon to his or her partner, the server.

The server should prepare a check with the discount calculated and tax added. The customer should calculate the tip. Then students can switch roles and repeat the activity.

Differentiating Instruction

Beginning
Understanding Discount and Sales Tax
Have pairs of students find the final cost of a $25 vase that has a 20% discount and a 5% sales-tax rate (*$21*). Have them label their work with the terms *original price, discount, sale price, sales tax,* and *final cost.*

Intermediate
Using Another Way to Find Sale Price
After students read the first example on page 152, have pairs find the sale price of Jacob's jeans another way:

Subtract the discount rate from 100% and multiply the new rate by the regular price (*100% − 30% = 70%; 70% × $40 = $28*). Have them talk about which method they prefer.

Advanced
Finding Two Discounts After students read page 152, have pairs find the cost of a $50 coat that has been discounted twice, first at 20% and then at 10% (*$36*). Then have them reverse the order of the discounts. Ask, *Are the final costs the same?* (*yes*)

Simple Interest

When you put money into a savings account, you earn **interest.** When you borrow money, you pay interest.

Interest is money paid for the use of money. To calculate interest, you need to know 3 things: the principal, the rate, and the time. **Principal** is the amount of money you save or borrow. The **rate** tells what percent of interest will be paid or earned per year. The time is the number of years the money is saved or borrowed.

Simple interest is paid on only the principal. You can find simple interest using this **formula:** $I = p \times r \times t$

Interest = principal × yearly rate × time in number of years
$I \quad = \quad p \quad \times \quad r \quad \times \quad t$

Marci's savings account pays 1.5% simple interest. How much simple interest would $3,000 earn in 2 years?

$I = \quad p \; \times \; r \; \times t$
$I = 3,000 \times 0.015 \times 2 = 90$

In 2 years, $3,000 would earn $90 simple interest.

The Garcias wish to borrow $25,000 to start a small business. They can get a 3-year loan at 3.5% simple interest. How much will the Garcias pay back altogether?

$I = 25,000 \times 0.035 \times 3 = 2,625$
Total = $25,000 + 2,625 = 27,625$

The Garcias will pay back $27,625.

Talk and Share

With a partner, tell what each letter of the formula $I = p \times r \times t$ represents. Write the formula to find the simple interest for borrowing $4,000 at a rate of 6.25% for 6 months. Then find the interest.

VOCABULARY

interest—the money paid on a savings account or for borrowing money
principal—an amount of money borrowed or put in a savings account. It is separate from the interest paid or earned.

rate—the percent of interest paid or earned
simple interest—interest paid on only the amount saved or borrowed, not also on the interest earned
formula—an equation that states a rule

LESSON 26 • APPLICATIONS OF PERCENT **153**

Language Notes

Homophones
These words sound alike, but they have different spellings and meanings.

☐ **principal**
1. money on which interest is paid
2. chief

☐ **principle**
a basic truth or belief

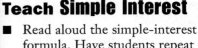

Teach Simple Interest

■ Read aloud the simple-interest formula. Have students repeat the words that the variables represent. Discuss how to substitute values in the formula.

■ Point out that the rate in the formula is in years.

■ Ask, *How can you find the total in the account?* (*Calculate the interest and add it to the principal.*)

Language Notes

Draw students' attention to the Language Notes. Pronounce each word and read each definition. Point out that because the words sound alike, they are easily confused.

Talk and Share

Have students work in pairs. As part of a class discussion, ask, *How can you find the total amount owed?* (*You can add the interest and principal.*)
Answers: I = *interest, dollars;* p = *principal, dollars;* r = *rate, percent;* t = *time, years;* I = *4,000 • 0.0625 •* $\frac{1}{2}$ = *$125*

Build VOCABULARY

Discuss the definitions of *interest, principal, rate, simple interest,* and *formula.* Have students write the formula for finding simple interest, with the words written above the variables.

Differentiating Instruction

Beginning
Using Fractions for Time Have students read the interest formula on page 153. Ask, *What number would you use if the time were 6 months?* ($\frac{1}{2}$) If needed, remind students that a year is 12 months. Have them find the numbers to use in the formula if the times are 1, 2, 3, 4, and 9 months. ($\frac{1}{12}$; $\frac{2}{12}$, or $\frac{1}{6}$; $\frac{3}{12}$, or $\frac{1}{4}$; $\frac{4}{12}$, or $\frac{1}{3}$; $\frac{9}{12}$, or $\frac{3}{4}$)

Intermediate
Comparing Interest and Sales Tax Have students talk about how finding simple interest and sales tax are alike and different. (*Alike: Both multiply percent and money. Different: Interest includes time in the calculation.*)

Advanced
Writing a Rule for Total Amount Have students discuss a rule for finding the total amount that the Garcias must pay in the problem on page 153. (*total amount = principal + (principal × rate × time)*).

Activity: Financial News

Give students financial sections of newspapers to find local interest rates (or provide three typical interest rates). Have students assume that the rates are simple-interest rates. Have them compare the total cost of a 1-year, $5,000 loan from banks with three different interest rates.

Practice

Have students name the different applications of percent presented in the lesson (*finding discounts, sales tax, tips, simple interest*).

Ask, *How can you find the total cost of an item with a sales-tax rate of $6\frac{1}{2}$%? (Multiply the cost of the item by 0.065 and add the product to the cost of item.)*

Assignment Guide
- Beginning 1–10, 12–15, 18, 20
- Intermediate 2–16, 18–20
- Advanced 2–20

Notes on Exercises
Exercises 1–4 Be sure students understand that the first number is the regular cost of an item and the second number is the percent of the discount.

Exercises 9–12 Review how to substitute values into the formula, and check that students are correctly changing percents to decimals.

Exercise 11 Students need to first rewrite 9 months as $\frac{9}{12}$, $\frac{3}{4}$, or 0.75.

Exercise 19 Discuss students' answers to this problem. Point out that the sale prices are different because the 50% discount was taken on a smaller selling price than the 60% discount, so the amount of the discount is less.

Practice

Find each sale price with the discount.
1. $25, 20% **2.** $8.99, 10% **3.** $75, $33\frac{1}{3}$% **4.** $80, 40%

Find each total price with the sales tax.
5. $25, 5% **6.** $36, 7.25% **7.** $1,200, 4.5% **8.** $18.99, 7%

Find the simple interest.
9. $5,000 at 5% for 4 years **10.** $1,000 at 7.25% for 10 years
11. $15,000 at 6% for 9 months **12.** $20,000 at 4.25% for 30 years

13. Kang opened a savings account with $2,000. The simple interest rate was 3.5%. How much simple interest would the account earn in 1 year? In 3 years?

14. If Kang makes no more deposits and does not withdraw any money from the account, how much will be in the account after 10 years?

15. Gary and Nancy went out for dinner and the amount of their bill was $42. Gary wanted to leave a 15% tip. Use the shortcut at the right to figure the amount of the tip. Is it the same as if you had found 15% of $42?

I know a shortcut. 15% is the same as 10% plus 5%. 10% is easy to find and 5% is half of that.

16. Peter works at a large car dealership. His monthly salary is $2,500 plus 2% of his monthly sales. In July, Peter's sales totaled $95,000. What was his July salary?

17. Cathy needed to borrow $8,000. The credit union offered her a 3% loan for 2 years. The bank offered her a 2.75% loan for 3 years. Which plan charges more interest?

18. The price of a certain car in 1960 was $1,700. The price of a comparable car in 2000 was 900% of that cost. What was the price in 2000?

19. (EXTENDED RESPONSE) Golf clubs had a price tag of $250. That price was slashed by 10% and dropped to $225. Now the discount is another 50% off. Is that the same sale price as 60% off the original price of $250? Explain.

20. (MULTIPLE CHOICE) Find the total amount in a savings account if $400 is deposited at a simple interest rate of 2.25% and left there for 8 years.
A. $1,300 **B.** $900 **C.** $472 **D.** $360

Program Resources
Practice Book Use page 64.

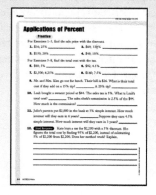

Answers
1. $20
2. $8.09
3. $50
4. $48
5. $26.25
6. $38.61
7. $1,254
8. $20.32
9. $1,000
10. $725
11. $675
12. $25,500
13. $70; $210

14. $2,700
15. $6.30; yes
16. $4,400
17. The 2-year plan costs more per year.
18. $15,300
19. $112.50; no, 60% off is $100.
20. C

Activities

Summarizing When you summarize, you pull together lots of information by pointing out the key parts. Use a Web to help you summarize information about ratios. Copy the one that has been started for you.

1. **Write** With a partner, write examples of fractions, percents, and rates in the ovals.

2. **Discuss** Talk with your partner about the similarities and differences among the three types of ratios.

3. **Summarize** Review with your partner how to change each type of ratio to the other two types.

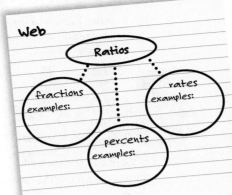

Web

Ratios

fractions examples:

rates examples:

percents examples:

Oral Language

Commission Mission Prepare five slips of paper, each with the price of a new car. Also have five slips of paper, each with a low percent written on it. Someone acting as a salesperson selects a paper of each type and goes to the manager. Role-play a situation like this.

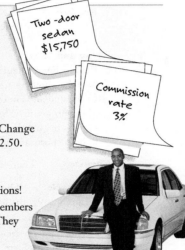

Two-door sedan $15,750

Commission rate 3%

Salesperson: I sold a car today for $15,750. My commission is 3%. Please give me my commission.

Manager: First, we need to compute your commission. Change 3% to 0.03 and multiply by $15,750. That comes to $472.50. Is that what you computed?

Salesperson: Yes. When will I get my check?

Manager: It will be with your next paycheck. Congratulations!

Take turns being Salesperson or Manager. Other class members should compute each commission to check the amounts. They may use a calculator.

Partner Practice

What's the Bottom Line? Discuss this with a partner. Cindy leaves the waiter a tip that is 15% of the entire bill. Tony leaves a 15% tip on the bill before tax. Who leaves a greater tip? Use examples to explain your answer.

Teach Summarizing

■ Remind students that to *summarize* is to "pull together information by pointing out the key parts." Ask students when they have summarized information (*Samples: describing steps in math calculations, writing book reports, describing the plot of a movie*).

■ Have students work in pairs to summarize what they have learned about the relationships among ratios, fractions, and percents. Have students share their summaries with the class.

Oral Language

■ Explain that a *commission* is a *bonus*, or an additional amount, paid to a salesperson. Suggest that students write commission rates less than 15%.

■ You may want to role-play this scenario with a volunteer and then have students complete the activity. Allow students to use calculators.

Partner Practice

Have students assume that Cindy and Tony ordered the same items at the same restaurant so each has the same food cost and tax amount.

Answers: Assuming the bills are the same, Cindy; $50 + 8% tax = $54; 15% (54) = $8.10. Tony would leave 15% (50) = $7.50. Because $8.10 > $7.50, Cindy leaves the greater tip.

Activity: Help a Friend

Have students summarize today's lesson as if for an absent classmate. Ask them to include an example for any new concepts that were taught. Encourage them to write a problem for that student to solve.

Assessment Book

Use page 48 to assess students' comprehension.

Program Resources

Practice Book Use page 65.
Overhead Transparencies Use 33.

Use Logical Reasoning

STANDARDS CONTENT

Mathematics
- Solve problems by using logical reasoning

Language
- Use the adjectives *some, any, many, every, each,* and *neither/nor*

Teach Use Logical Reasoning

- Introduce the strategy *use logical reasoning.* Point out that this strategy involves thinking clearly, organizing information, and drawing conclusions.

- Explain that an organizer helps to keep track of information as it is learned. Point out that students may use a Venn Diagram, a list, a table, or any other organizer of their choice.

Talk and Share

Explain that even though the diagram changes, there will still be 96 students. Because students may think that all Venn Diagrams have overlapping ovals, draw this diagram on the board to show the relationship.

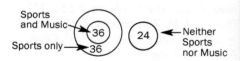

Sports and Music — 36
Sports only — 36
24 ← Neither Sports nor Music

Problem-Solving Skills

Use Logical Reasoning

When you solve a mystery, or a puzzle, you use logical reasoning. You decide how the facts are related and then work step by step toward a reasonable solution.

Problem: Each of the 96 students in seventh grade at Montclair Middle School is taking music, or sports, or both. There are 72 students out for a sport and 36 in music programs. How many students are taking both sports and music?

Read and Understand

Need to find: The number of students taking both sports and music

You know: There are 96 students in the seventh grade; 72 are in sports and 36 are in music.

Key fact: The number of students in sports and music adds to 108, which is 12 more than 96.

Plan and Solve

Draw a **Venn Diagram** to show how the numbers are related. Every student is in one or both of the programs. The overlap of 12 is the number of students in both sports and music.

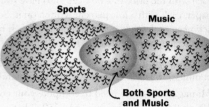

Sports

Music

Both Sports and Music

Answer
There are 12 students in both sports and music programs.

Look Back
The total number of students represented in the Venn Diagram is 96, the total number of students in seventh grade.

Talk and Share

Work with a partner to discuss how making a Venn Diagram helped you to solve the problem. Explain how the diagram would change if all 36 music students also were out for a sport.

VOCABULARY
Venn Diagram—an organizer that uses overlapping circles or rectangles to show what two or more sets have in common

---

Activity: Model a Strategy

Have pairs of students solve this problem:

Miguel, Ronna, Lyn, and Danny are in line. Miguel is not first. Ronna is behind Miguel but is not standing next to him. Danny is in front of Ronna. Lyn is neither first nor last. In what order are the people standing? (*Danny, Miguel, Lyn, Ronna*)

Discuss students' solving strategies as a class. Ask students to share any models they drew to help them organize the information.

Differentiating Instruction

Beginning
Modeling Have pairs of students model the problem using 72 blue counters to stand for students in sports and 36 red counters to stand for students in music. Have students stack one red and one blue counter to model a student in both sports and music.

Intermediate
Discussing the Diagram Have pairs of students discuss how to draw the Venn Diagram using the key facts. Encourage

them to discuss how they know how many marks are in the overlap and in each oval.

Advanced
Explaining the Diagram Have pairs of students discuss how to draw the Venn Diagram using the key facts. Ask them how they would draw a diagram if there were 70 students in sports. (*Explanations will vary. The diagram would have 10 students in the overlap, 60 in only sports, and 26 in only music.*)

Practice

Use the strategy *use logical reasoning.*

1. Suppose there are 16 students in both programs. How many students would be in only sports? In only music? In neither sports nor music?

2. Draw a Venn Diagram to show the situation in Exercise 1.

3. Ms. Hayes, Mr. Mesa, and Mrs. Salton are teachers. One teaches science, one teaches math, and one teaches English. No one teaches a subject with the same first letter as his or her name. Mrs. Salton does not teach math. Copy and complete the table to find who teaches which subject.

	Science	Math	English
Ms. Hayes			
Mr. Mesa			
Mrs. Salton		NO	

4. Use a table to find how Abby, Ben, Dave, and Ellie get to school. One person walks, one rides a bicycle, one takes the bus, and one rides in a car. Neither girl walks to school. Neither Ben nor Abby rides in a bus or car. Ben and the boy who rides the bus are brothers.

Grammar Spotlight

Adjectives: Using *some*, *any*, *many*, *every*, *each*, and *neither/nor*
These words are adjectives. They come before a noun to tell about how many.

Adjective	Example	What It Means
some	The students have *some* books.	They are not without books.
any	She doesn't have *any* books.	She has no books.
many	He has *many* books.	He has a lot of books.
every	*Every* book he has is old.	All his books are old.
each	She took *each* book off the shelf.	She took all the books off the shelf.
neither/nor	*Neither* Juan *nor* Carla has a new book.	Juan doesn't have a new book, and Carla doesn't have a new book.

Work with a partner to write sentences using *some*, *any*, *many*, *every*, *each*, and *neither/nor*. Explain why you chose the adjective you used in each sentence.

Practice

Refer students back to the Venn Diagram on page 156. Ask, *How would the Venn Diagram change if no music students were also in sports?* (*The overlapping region would be empty.*) *Can you think of another way to show this situation?* (*Draw two figures that do not overlap.*)

Assignment Guide
- Beginning 1–4
- Intermediate 1–4
- Advanced 1–4

Notes on Exercises
Exercises 1 and 2 To get students started, suggest that they subtract the 16 students in the overlap to find the number in sports only and music only.

Exercises 3 and 4 Students can use logic tables to solve problems. You may need to review how to list the possibilities and eliminate those that do not fit.

Grammar Spotlight

Discuss the meanings of *some*, *any*, *many*, *every*, *each*, and *neither/nor*. Point out that *any* also means "one or more." Say, *You may check out* any *library book you choose. Any* in the chart example means she has *no* books because the word *not* (*doesn't*) is in the sentence.

Answers

1. 56 sports only (72 − 16); 20 music only (36 − 16); 4 neither (96 − 56 − 20 − 16 = 4)

2.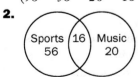

   Sports 56 | 16 | Music 20 | Neither Sports nor Music 4

3. Ms. Hayes, math; Mr. Mesa, science; Mrs. Salton, English

4. Abby, bike; Ben, walk; Dave, bus; Ellie, car

Activity: Modeling Adjectives

Have students work in pairs. Have one student use grid paper (Overhead Transparency 15) or counters to make a model. The partner uses one of the adjectives *some*, *any*, *many*, *every*, *each*, or *neither/nor* in a sentence describing the model. Have the first student change the model slightly, and have the partner make another sentence.

Have students switch roles.

A sample sentence is: Some *of the squares are shaded.*

Program Resources

Practice Book Use pages 66 and 67.

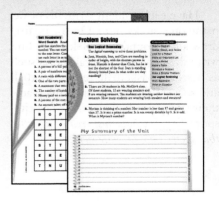

Organizing Data

STANDARDS CONTENT

Mathematics
■ Organize data in a frequency table
■ Display data using a line plot

Language
■ Distinguish between *choose* and *choice*
■ Ask questions to gather data

Introduce the Big Idea
Read aloud the Big Idea. Ask students to describe any kinds of graphs or charts they have seen.

Begin Building Background
■ If students cannot identify what is happening in the picture, ask, *What is printed on the overturned box at the upper left of the photo?* They should recognize that the people are trying to organize the results of a presidential election.

■ Invite students to talk about any experience they have had with an election, perhaps for a club office or a team captain. Ask, *How was the election conducted?*

Teach Key Concepts
Read aloud the Key Concepts paragraph. Ask, *Have any of you been questioned for a survey?* Tell students that *data* is just another word for "information." Point to the line plot and show how the numbers in the set of data have been used. Ask volunteers to tell what the line plot shows.

Warm-Up Review
Have each student write his or her name on a sticky note. On the board, draw a horizontal line. Below the line, write the names of several sports such as baseball, basketball, tennis, football, and soccer. Then have students place their sticky notes above their favorite sport. Say, *We have just created a picture that shows your favorite sports.*

Organizing Data

Big Idea We organize and show data in graphs, charts, and other kinds of pictures.

Building Background

▲ My club took a survey to find out what our members like to do.

■ **What do you think this person is doing?**
■ **When have you had to organize lots of information?**
■ **What information did you have to organize?**

Key Concepts

To take a **survey,** you ask questions to gather information. The information is **data.** A line plot is one way to show organized data.

 Who did you vote for?

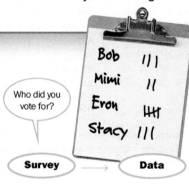

Bob |||
Mimi ||
Eron ||||
Stacy |||

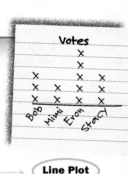

Votes

Survey → Data → Line Plot

Activity: Read the Picture
Tell students to look at the two displays of data on page 158. Ask, *How many votes did each person get?* (*Bob: 3 votes; Mimi: 2 votes; Eron: 5 votes; Stacy: 3 votes*) *How many votes were there in all?* (*13 votes*)

Resource Library

Math at Hand
Frequency Tables and Line Plots 268, 281–282

Math on Call
Frequency Tables and Line Plots 271–272, 286, 301

Reader's Handbook (red)
Tables 559–560

Frequency Tables

The photo on the previous page shows someone about to **organize** data. **Data** are facts and other information about a topic. For example, information about the temperature or how much rain falls is data about weather.

◀ Pizza

One way to collect data is to take a **survey.** To take a survey, you choose a topic and ask people a question, such as "What television shows do you like to watch?" or "What is your favorite take-out food?"

The data from a food survey can be organized in a frequency table like the one on the right. **Tally marks** are used as counters. Count the tally marks to find the **frequency.** In this table, each tally mark stands for one vote for a particular food.

Frequency Table

Favorite Take-out Food		
FOOD	TALLY	FREQUENCY
Hamburger	ǀǀ	2
Pizza	ǀǀǀǀ	4
Taco	ǀǀǀ	3
Fried rice	ǀǀǀǀ	4
Quesadilla	~~ǀǀǀǀ~~ ǀ	6

▲ Tacos

To organize data in a frequency table:

- List the choices in the first column.
- Make a tally mark for each vote in the second column.
- Write the frequency for each choice in the third column.

Fried rice ▶

Language Notes

Confusing Word Pairs
These words are easily mixed up.

- **choose:** decide or pick something
- **choice:** something you pick or decide

Talk and Share

Work with a partner. Ask 10 people to tell you their favorite colors. Together, make a frequency table for the data. Share your table and explain it to the class.

Favorite Color
Blue
Red
Purple
Green
Yellow
Brown

VOCABULARY

organize—put into working order; arrange
data—information. *Data* is a plural word.
survey—a set of questions used to collect data
tally marks—short marks used as counters
frequency—the number of times something happens within a given time period

Teach Frequency Tables

- Point out the frequency table. Tell students that *frequency* comes from the word *frequent*, which means "often." A frequency table tells how often something occurs.
- Probably most students have used a frequency table. Be sure they know that four marks with a slash represent a count of 5. Ask, *How does this system make it easier to count the tally marks?*
- After discussing the steps for making a frequency table, draw a blank frequency table titled *Favorite Snack* on the board. Have students one at a time make a tally mark for their favorite snack and use a diagonal slash for every fifth tally. Have volunteers write the totals for each snack.

Language Notes

Discuss the words *choose* and *choice.* Point out that *choose* is a verb and *choice* is a noun. Elicit from students that *what* they choose is their choice.

Talk and Share

Check that students have constructed their frequency tables correctly. Ask, *How useful is information from only ten people?*

Build VOCABULARY

Have students talk about how some of the vocabulary terms are represented in the Talk and Share activity. For example, students should say that the *data* are the *tally marks* that they marked in their *frequency* table.

Differentiating Instruction

Beginning

Demonstrating Tally Marks Distribute counters in several colors to students. On the board, list the colors. Have students come to the board and make tally marks for their counters in the appropriate rows. Demonstrate the slash that indicates five. Say, *You are making* tally marks *to count. This is a* frequency table. *It tells how many of each color counter there are.* Have volunteers total the marks for each color.

Intermediate

Discussing a Frequency Table After students read page 159, have groups make a frequency table to record their three favorite types of music. Have them exchange tables and tell what each shows.

Advanced

Planning a Survey Have students decide on a survey question, what questions will be asked, who will record responses, and so on. Have them share their ideas with the class.

Teach Line Plots

- On the board, copy the Favorite Take-out Food frequency table from page 159, but omit the tally marks. Poll the class and complete the table for students' favorite foods. Say, *We're going to make a line plot of the data. A line plot is similar to a frequency table. It uses Xs rather than tally marks, and the Xs are marked vertically (up and down) rather than horizontally (across).*

- Draw a line and write the names of the foods under it. Then have volunteers make an *X* above the appropriate food for each tally mark in the table. Ask, *How can you tell the favorite and least favorite foods?* Then discuss the Favorite Take-out Food line plot on page 160.

- Discuss the Math Quiz Scores line plot. Point out that each column represents a span of ten. Explain that the *range* is the difference between the least and greatest numbers in a set of data. Have students give the range for the Favorite Take-out Food plot on page 160 (*4*).

Talk and Share

Have students find the range of the data. There are 4 *it*s, 25 *the*s, 8 *of*s, and 11 *a*s, so the range is 21.

▲ Hamburger

Line Plots

Another way to organize data is to use a **line plot.** You use an X for each tally mark to show the frequency of the data. Below is a line plot of the favorite take-out food data.

Quesadillas ▼

Favorite Take-out Food				
				X
				X
	X		X	X
	X	X	X	X
X	X	X	X	X
X	X	X	X	X
Hamburger	Pizza	Taco	Fried rice	Quesadilla

A line plot shows the *shape* of the data. You quickly see that the quesadilla had the most votes because it has the most Xs. It also is easy to see that the hamburger had two votes. This next line plot is of the quiz scores shown on the left.

Math Quiz Scores
71, 81, 59, 90, 93, 100,
64, 65, 79, 74, 84, 84,
76, 87, 80, 82, 97, 93

Math Quiz Scores				
			X	
			X	X
		X	X	X
		X	X	X
	X	X	X	X
X	X	X	X	X
less than 60	60–69	70–79	80–89	90–100

The least score is 59, and the greatest is 100. The **range** is the difference between the least and the greatest numbers in a data set. Since $100 - 59 = 41$, the range of these data is 41.

Talk and Share

Work with a partner. Together, make a line plot to show the number of times the words *it*, *the*, *of*, and *a* are printed on this page. Explain your line plot to the class.

Times a Word
Is Used

it   the   of   a

VOCABULARY

line plot—a display of data that uses marks (such as Xs) in a vertical line to show frequency
range—the difference between the greatest and the least numbers in a data set

---

 Activity: Plot the Data

Have students poll the class to find out how many aunts and uncles each student has. Have them make a line plot of the data using these labels: 0, 1, 2, 3, 4, 5, 6, 7, 8, 9, 10, and *more*.

 Differentiating Instruction

Beginning
Making a Line Plot On the board, draw a line and write these labels underneath: *0, 1, 2, 3, 4, 5,* and *more*. Have each student make an *X* above the number that tells how many sisters and brothers he or she has. Say, *This is a line plot. What does it show?*

Intermediate
Comparing Plots and Tables After students have worked through the examples on page 160, have them make

a frequency table for the data in the Math Quiz Scores table. Have them talk about which display they prefer, and why.

Advanced
Exploring Shapes of Data Have students talk about how line plots give a visual picture of data. Ask, *How can you tell at a glance which value is greatest? Least? Can you make comparisons among values? Are there any values that are very different from the rest?*

Practice

1. How is a frequency table different from a line plot? How are they similar?

2. Make a line plot for these data. Each number tells the number of hours someone spent doing homework in one month.

4, 6, 10, 7, 6, 7, 4, 7, 10, 8, 9, 6, 8, 5, 6, 10, 9, 10, 10, 4

3. Find the range of the data set in Exercise 2.

4. How does the range of a set of data affect the line plot of the data?

5. What word belongs in the blanks?

a. When you make a _____, you list each different item of a data set and give the number of times each item occurs.

b. When you make a _____, you display a data set by writing Xs above each data value on a number line.

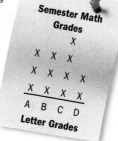

Semester Math Grades

X
X   X   X
X   X   X   X
X   X   X   X
A   B   C   D
Letter Grades

Use the line plot on the right for Exercises 6–8.

6. What information is displayed?

7. How many math grades are recorded?

8. How many students received an A or a B?

9. These data give the number of days in each of the 12 months of a year. Make a line plot for these data.

31, 28, 31, 30, 31, 30, 31, 31, 30, 31, 30, 31

10. Raul took a survey and organized his data. His frequency table had 17 tally marks. How many Xs are on his line plot? Explain.

11. (MULTIPLE CHOICE) The difference between the least and greatest numbers in a data set is called the

A. frequency.   **B.** range.   **C.** tally mark.   **D.** data.

12. (EXTENDED RESPONSE) Just for fun, a town on the Isle of Anglesey in Northern Wales, England, gave itself this unusually long Welsh name: Llanfairpwllgwyngyllgogerychwyrndrobwllllantysiliogogogoch. Make a line plot to show the number of times each letter in the name is used. Which letter is used most?

...YNGYLLGOGERYCHWYRNDROBWLLLLANTYSILIOGOGOGOCH

...quin-gill-go-ger-u-queern-drob-ooll-llandus-ilio-gogo-goch

Practice

Invite students to share their ideas about the advantages and disadvantages of frequency tables and line plots.

Assignment Guide
- Beginning 1–3, 5–12
- Intermediate 1–12
- Advanced 1–12

Notes on Exercises
Exercise 2 For extra practice, have students make a frequency table of the data in this exercise.

Exercise 12 You may want to have students work with a partner or in small groups to complete this exercise.

Answers
1. Sample: A frequency table uses tally marks and numbers; a line plot uses Xs and may give numbers or spans of numbers. Both show exact data if spans are not used.

3. 6

4. Sample: If the range is small, the line plot will not have many columns; if the range is great, the plot may have many columns.

5. a. frequency table   **b.** line plot

6. semester math grades

7. 12 math grades

8. 6 students

10. 17 Xs; Raul should mark an X for each tally mark.

11. B

12. Line plots should show: a, 3; b, 1; c, 2; d, 1; e, 1; f, 1; g, 7; h, 2; i, 3; l, 11; n, 4; o, 6; p, 1; r, 4; s, 1; t, 1; w, 4; y, 5. The l is used most.

For Exercises 2 and 9, see Additional Answers, page T40.

Program Resources
Practice Book Use page 68.

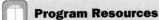

Teach Gathering Data

After students complete this activity, have pairs design a survey question that involves asking for an opinion. Have pairs share their questions with the class and discuss whether or not the questions are carefully written and will give good results. Then have them choose the best question, survey the class, and make a line plot of their data.

Partner Practice

Students should find that the English meaning of *range* closest to the mathematical meaning is "distance between certain limits."

Oral Language

Have students compare the shapes of their two line plots. Ask them to find the range for each plot. Ask someone to summarize what the plots show.

Key Connection

Another kind of data display closely related to a frequency table or a line plot is a *pictograph*. A pictograph uses symbols to represent countable data. One symbol can represent more than one of an item. For instance, in a pictograph showing favorite pets, one dog symbol might represent 100 or 1,000 dogs.

Have students make a pictograph of the Favorite Take-out Food line plot on page 160.

Develop Language

	Siblings	
Number	Tally	Frequency
0		
1		
2		
3		
4		
5		
6		

▲ Each of these babies has 6 siblings. They are septuplets.

Activities

Gathering Data When you take a survey, you ask a question to gather data. You ask many people the same question. Your question should be easy to understand.

Work with a partner to take a survey. Gather data by asking your classmates how many siblings (brothers and sisters) they have. Record the data in a frequency table like the one shown on the left.

1. **Draw** Make a line plot of your data.

2. **Explain** Tell how you made your line plot.

3. **Summarize** Write two sentences about what the data show.

Partner Practice

Range Rover With a partner, work to find several different ways the word *range* can be used. Use a dictionary. Write a sentence for each of the different meanings. Take turns reading the sentences aloud and explaining the use of *range*. Which English definition is closely related to the mathematics definition of *range?*

Oral Language

What's Your Time? Work as a whole class. Start by listing 30 minutes, 60 minutes, and 90 minutes on the blackboard. Each student must say the time that is closest to how long it takes him or her to get from home to school and back again. Then each student must make an X above that time. Use this information to complete a line plot.

Discuss what the plot shows. What does the total number of Xs equal? Which time has the most Xs? Why is that?

Repeat the activity using shorter times: 10 minutes, 20 minutes, 30 minutes, and 40 minutes. Discuss the results. Which times, if any, have no Xs? Does anyone have a travel time that is not close to one of the listed times? Which time has the most Xs? Talk about it.

Program Resources

Practice Book Use page 69.

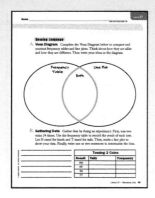

Assessment Book

Use page 49 to assess students' comprehension.

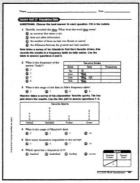

Activity: Culture Connection

Seventeen U.S. presidents had a popular vote of less than 50% of the votes cast, but their electoral college votes represented a majority. Some since 1900 include Woodrow Wilson, Harry Truman, John F. Kennedy, Richard Nixon, William Clinton, and George W. Bush in 2000.

Use this site to find the percent of the popular vote won by each of the presidents listed above: http://www.archives.gov/federal_register/electoral_college/electoral_college.html.

Analyzing Data

Big Idea There are many ways to display data. Stem-and-leaf plots are useful displays because they show how data fall into groups.

Building Background

▲ In my home country of Egypt, we vote for a new president every 6 years.

- **Here former United States President John F. Kennedy is delivering a speech. What kind of person would you like to have as president?**
- **How could you show the results of a presidential election?**

Key Concepts

A **stem-and-leaf plot** uses place value to display numbers and show their distribution. Each number is split between the tens place and the ones place. For instance, you split 63 as 6|3 and 107 as 10|7. The digits to the left of the vertical line form the **stem.** The digits to the right form the **leaf.** Stems are not repeated. 10|1 and 10|7 are written in the same row as 10|1 7.

The stem-and-leaf plot shown here displays these test scores in order: 63, 68, 68, 72, 78, 85, 101, and 107. Notice that the plot lists all possible stems for numbers 60 to 109.

Stem-and-Leaf Plot

Stem	Leaf
6	3 8 8
7	2 8
8	5
9	
10	1 7

Key: 10|1 is 101.

LESSON 28 • ANALYZING DATA **163**

Activity: Read the Picture

Have pairs of students each make a line plot of the data in Key Concepts. One line plot could have a separate column for each number, and another can use the spans 60–69, 70–79, 80–89, 90–99, and 100–109. Then have students discuss the plots and give advantages and disadvantages of each.

Resource Library

Math at Hand
Stem-and-Leaf Plots 284
Mean, Median, and Mode 257–263

Math on Call
Stem-and-Leaf Plots 303
Mean, Median, and Mode 273–276

Analyzing Data

STANDARDS CONTENT
Mathematics
- Make a stem-and-leaf plot to organize data
- Find mean, median, and mode to describe data

Language
- Recognize multiple meanings of *leaf* and *stem*
- Analyze data by finding the range, mean, median, and mode

Introduce the **Big Idea**

Read aloud the Big Idea. Tell the class that a *stem-and-leaf plot* is yet another type of data display.

Begin **Building Background**

Help students read the comment under the girl's picture. Invite students to tell what they know about presidential elections. Tell them they will learn different ways to show results of counting votes.

Teach **Key Concepts**

- Read the Key Concepts paragraph. Explain that just as a real stem can have many leaves, the stem in a stem-and-leaf plot can also have many leaves.
- Stress that the leaf column contains only the ones digits of the numbers and the stem column contains the remaining digits.

Warm-Up Review

Have students write the numbers in each exercise in order from least to greatest.

1. 87, 92, 76, 83, 79, 90, 88
(*76, 79, 83, 87, 88, 90, 92*)

2. 12, 8, 10, 9, 22, 18, 24, 15
(*8, 9, 10, 12, 15, 18, 22, 24*)

3. 33, 52, 50, 38, 29, 57, 36
(*29, 33, 36, 38, 50, 52, 57*)

4. 121, 104, 115, 119, 102, 110
(*102, 104, 110, 115, 119, 121*)

Teach Stem-and-Leaf Plots

- Have a volunteer read aloud the first two paragraphs. Then help volunteers construct the stem-and-leaf plot on the board.

- Point out the key at the bottom of each plot. Have a student tell its meaning.

- Direct students to the second plot. Ask, *Why is a 4 listed in the stem column even though there are no numbers in the 40s?*

Language Notes

Discuss the words *leaf* and *stem*. Ask, *Which meanings of* leaf *and* stem *are used in this lesson?*

Talk and Share

Students should be able to tell from the stem-and-leaf plot that there are more people in the $90–$98 category than in either of the other two groups.

Build VOCABULARY

Tape a 6-foot tape measure vertically to the wall with the zero point on the floor. Measure students and have them write their height, in inches, on the board. Then have the class work together to make a stem-and-leaf plot of their heights. Discuss the range of the data and which heights seem to be most common. Have students use the lesson vocabulary words in their discussion.

Look and Read

Stem-and-Leaf Plots

In the year 2000, George W. Bush won all the electoral votes from 29 U.S. states. The number of electoral votes in the nine largest states were 25, 13, 12, 11, 14, 21, 11, 32, and 13. Display the data in a **stem-and-leaf plot**.

A stem-and-leaf plot **displays** an ordered set of data. So first, put the data in order from least to greatest: 11, 11, 12, 13, 13, 14, 21, 25, 32. Then, split the data into leaves and stems. Each ones digit is a **leaf** and goes on the right in the plot. The rest of the digits in each number make up the **stem**. Stems go on the left in the plot. Last, give the plot a title and a key.

Order the stems.

Give a key or example.

Add a title.

Next to each stem, write the ones digits.

Number of Electoral Votes

Stem	Leaf
1	1 1 2 3 3 4
2	1 5
3	2

Key: 3|2 means 32 votes.

Language Notes

Multiple Meanings
These words have more than one meaning.

- **leaf**
  1. the ones or units digit of a data item in a stem-and-leaf plot
  2. the part of a plant that gathers sunlight
  3. quickly look through pages or sheets of paper

- **stem**
  1. all the digits except the ones or units digit of a data item in a stem-and-leaf plot
  2. the main trunk of a plant
  3. stop something

Refer to the stem-and-leaf plot at the right. It shows the number of phone calls made by 6 families in a week. The data are 24, 27, 28, 35, 39, and 57.

The plot makes it easy to see very small or very large values, such as 57.

Number of Calls

Stem	Leaf
2	4 7 8
3	5 9
4	
5	7

Key: 5|7 means 57 calls.

Talk and Share

Work with a partner. Read aloud all the numbers shown in the plot of wages. Which stem has the most leaves? Tell what this means.

Weekly Part-Time Wages

8	1 5 6 8
9	0 0 2 6 7 8
10	3 3 9 9

Key: 8|1 means $81.

VOCABULARY

stem-and-leaf plot—a diagram used to display and order a data set
displays—shows visually, as in a graph, chart, or store window
leaf—the ones or units digit of a data item
stem—all the digits except the ones or units digit of a data item

---

Differentiating Instruction

Beginning
Plotting Numbers on Number Cubes
After students have studied the examples on page 164, have partners use two number cubes to generate twelve 2-digit numbers. Have them complete a stem-and-leaf plot listing each number. Have them use words from page 164 Vocabulary to describe their plots.

Intermediate
Plotting Dates After students have studied the examples on page 164, have each student write on the board the day

of the month he or she was born. Then have partners work together to make a stem-and-leaf plot of the days. Remind students to use a zero in the stem column for those days from 1 to 9.

Advanced
Making a Stem-and-Leaf Plot After students have studied the examples on page 164, have them research the ages of the U.S. presidents when they took office. Have students make a stem-and-leaf plot of the data and share their displays with the class.

Mean, Median, and Mode

The stem-and-leaf plot on the right shows the number of games won by different basketball teams in a season. A **statistic** is a number used to describe a set of numbers. The **mean**, the **median**, and the **mode** are statistics, often called *measures of central tendency*.

> There are 11 leaves, or numbers, in the data set. The 6th, 53, is the *median*, or middle number.

> The number 59 occurs most often. It is the *mode*.

Number of Games Won

Stem	Leaf
1	0
2	
3	8
4	1 3 8
5	3 9 9 9
6	2 7

Key: 6|2 means 62 games won.

> The *mean* is 49.

There are two steps for finding the mean, or average. First, you add all the data. Then, you divide that sum by the number of data items in the set: 10 + 38 + 41 + 43 + 48 + 53 + 59 + 59 + 59 + 62 + 67 = 539. There are 11 numbers in the set, so divide 539 by 11. 539 ÷ 11 = 49. The mean is 49.

If the data are in numerical order, the median is the middle number. When the number of items in a data set is even, the median is the sum of the two middle numbers divided by 2. Here the median is 53. Finally, the mode is 59, because 59 occurs most often in the data set.

The number 10 is called an **outlier** for this plot because it is not close to the other numbers. When a data set has an outlier, the mean may not describe the data set very well. In the data set above, the mean is 49. Without the number 10, the mean would be greater: 529 ÷ 10 = 52.9, or about 53. When people analyze data, they may choose not to include outliers.

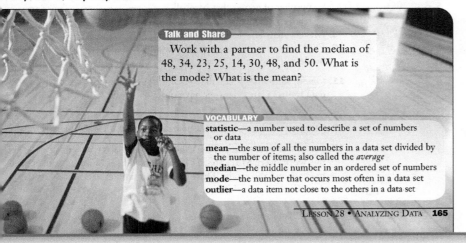

Talk and Share

Work with a partner to find the median of 48, 34, 23, 25, 14, 30, 48, and 50. What is the mode? What is the mean?

VOCABULARY

statistic—a number used to describe a set of numbers or data
mean—the sum of all the numbers in a data set divided by the number of items; also called the *average*
median—the middle number in an ordered set of numbers
mode—the number that occurs most often in a data set
outlier—a data item not close to the others in a data set

LESSON 28 • ANALYZING DATA **165**

Differentiating Instruction

Beginning
Exploring Mean, Median, and Mode
On the board, write all the data values from the first plot on page 164 in order. Ask, *What is the middle number? (13) How did you find it? This number is the* median. *Which occurs most? (11 and 13) These numbers are the* modes. Then show students how to find the *mean (about 17).*

Intermediate
Explaining Mean, Median, and Mode
Have pairs of students read aloud together the first three paragraphs on

page 165. Then have them talk about how they would find the mean, median, and mode for the Weekly Part-Time Wages plot on page 164.

Advanced
Finding Mean, Median, and Mode
Have pairs read page 165 and then find the mean, median, and mode, both with and without the number 57, for the Number of Calls plot on page 164. Ask, *Which is affected more by an outlier, the mean or the median?* (*See Additional Answers, page T40.*)

Teach Mean, Median, and Mode

- Ask students whether they are familiar with the term *statistics*. Many of them may know about sports statistics.

- Work through finding the mean, median, and mode. Tell students that *mean* is another name for *average*. Relate the term *median* to *middle* and the term *mode* to *most*.

- Ask, *Do you have to order the numbers to find the mean?(no)*

- Discuss the term *outlier* and have students connect the word to *out* and *lie*. Show them how an outlier *lies outside* most of the data.

- Ask, *How can you find the median of the stem-and-leaf data without the outlier?* With ten data values, students will need to find the mean of the middle two values, 53 and 59, which is 56.

Talk and Share

Students should order the numbers before they find the median. There are eight values, so the median is the mean of 30 and 34, or the number halfway between 30 and 34, 32. The mode is 48 and the mean is 34.

Build VOCABULARY

Write the vocabulary words on the board. Have volunteers use the words to complete these sentences:

- The number that occurs most often is the mode.
- The middle number is the median.
- A number that is not close to others in a set of data is an outlier.
- When you add the values in a set of data and divide by the number of values, you find the mean.
- Another name for average is mean.

Practice

Refer students to the data in Exercise 2, on page 161. Have them work in pairs to find the mean, median, and mode (*mean, 7.3; median, 7; mode, 10*).

Assignment Guide
- Beginning 1–10, 13
- Intermediate 2–13
- Advanced 1–13

Notes on Exercises

Exercises 9 and 10 Be sure students use 10 as a stem so that they have only single digits in the leaf column.

Exercise 11 Have students give an example of a set of data that has more than one mode (*Sample: 110, 184, 113, 125, 113, 110, 176*).

Look and Read

Practice

1. How is a stem-and-leaf plot useful?

2. Which do you think is better for large sets of data, a line plot or a stem-and-leaf plot? Explain why.

Number of Words	
Stem	Leaf
2	3 3 6 8
3	1 5 6
4	4

Key: 3|1 means 31.

Use the stem-and-leaf plot on the left for Exercises 3–5. It gives the numbers of words in each of the first eight sentences of *Harry Potter and the Order of the Phoenix.*

3. List the data items from the stem-and-leaf plot.

4. Find the mean and the mode of the data.

5. Since there are 8 data items, the median is the mean of the 4th and 5th data items. What is the median?

For Exercises 6–8, use the following information. Stan works part time delivering newspapers. Here are his earnings for each of the first 5 weeks he worked: $29, $44, $44, $33, $40.

6. Find the mean, the median, and the mode.

7. In week 6, Stan earned only $14. Find the mean, the median, and the mode for the 6 weeks of earnings.

8. Exercise 7 includes an outlier, $14. Which changed the most when you included the outlier—the mean, the median, or the mode?

For Exercises 9 and 10, use the table on the right. It shows the number of games that baseball teams won during the 2003 season.

9. Make a stem-and-leaf plot of the data.

10. Find the mean, the median, and the mode of the data.

Baseball Team	Games Won
Atlanta	101
San Francisco	100
Chicago Cubs	88
N.Y. Yankees	101
Minnesota	90
Oakland	96

11. (SHORT RESPONSE) If a data set has a mode, is it always one of the data items? Can a data set have more than one mode? Explain your thinking.

12. (SHORT RESPONSE) Is the mean usually one of the data items? Explain.

13. (EXTENDED RESPONSE) The Vanisi family's grocery bills for the last five weeks were $132, $68, $145, $150, and $138. Find the mean, the median, and the mode. Then tell which number best represents the data. Explain your thinking.

Program Resources

Practice Book Use page 70.

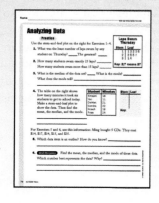

Answers

1. Sample: It's easy to find the median, the mode, and the range; all the exact data are shown.

2. Sample: A stem-and-leaf plot; it takes up less room.

3. 23, 23, 26, 28, 31, 35, 36, 44

4. mean, 30.75; mode, 23

5. 29.5

6. mean, $38; median, $40; mode, $44

7. mean, $34; median, $36.50; mode, $44

8. the mean

9. **Baseball Games Won**

Stem	Leaf
8	8
9	0 6
10	0 1 1

10. mean, 96; median, 98; mode, 101

11. Yes; yes; more than one value may occur the same number of times.

12. Sample: Usually not; the mean is a calculated value.

13. mean, $126.60; median, $138; no mode; the median, because the outlier 68 affects the mean too greatly

Activities

Analyzing When you analyze data, you study them to understand what they mean. Analyzing helps you learn important details about the data.

Work with a classmate to collect some data. For example, find out how many minutes per night each of your classmates studies. Or look up how many goals the top 10 soccer players scored in a season. Use a table like the one shown to record the data you collect.

Amount of Nightly Study Time

Name	Study Time (minutes)

1. Draw Make a stem-and-leaf plot of your data.

2. Explain Tell how you got the information.

3. Analyze Analyze the data by finding the range, mean, median, and mode.

4. Summarize Write two sentences about what your data show.

Partner Practice

Drum Up the Data Work with a partner to write two data sets of 5 numbers for each one of these requirements.

    a. The mean is 30.

    b. The mean is 30 and the range is more than 30.

    c. The mode is 9 and the mean is 7.

Take turns with your partner making up a requirement and finding a data set.

Oral Language

Rap It Write a rap to help you remember how to find the mean, the median, or the mode. Here is an example for finding range.

    To find the range
    Is not so strange.
    Find the high and the low
    And there you go.
    Find their difference, and then you'll know.

LESSON 28 • ANALYZING DATA **167**

Teach Analyzing

■ Refer students to almanacs or the Internet to get data for this activity.

■ If several pairs collect the same data, have them compare their results.

Partner Practice

As a follow-up to this activity, say, *Find a set of data in which the mean, median, and mode are the same number* (*Sample: 20, 30, 40, 40, 40, 40, 50, 60*).

Sample answers:

a. 30, 30, 30, 30, 30; 32, 31, 30, 29, 28

b. 8, 30, 30, 30, 52; 1, 30, 30, 30, 59

c. 9, 9, 9, 6, 2; 9, 9, 5, 8, 4

Oral Language

If students are having difficulty, suggest rhyming words such as *mean, green, lean; middle, fiddle, riddle; range, strange; mode, code, road, toad.*

 Activity: Culture Connection

John Fitzgerald Kennedy, pictured on page 163, was an influential president of the 20th century. During his administration, he established the U.S. Peace Corps and promoted sweeping legislation to enforce integration. Have students look on the Internet to find out and report on his progress with the space program.

 Assessment Book

Use page 50 to assess students' comprehension.

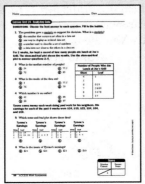

Program Resources

Practice Book Use page 71.

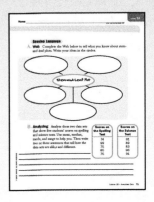

Bar and Line Graphs

STANDARDS CONTENT

Mathematics
- Make a bar graph
- Make a line graph

Language
- Recognize multiple meanings of *scale*
- Interpret data from a graph

Materials
- Grid paper (Overhead Transparency 15)

Introduce the Big Idea

Read aloud the Big Idea. Ask students if they know how to construct *bar graphs* or *line graphs*.

Begin Building Background

- Be sure students recognize that the students in the photo are standing under numbers representing their heights.
- Ask, *How many students are listed in the graph for each height?*

Teach Key Concepts

Read the Key Concepts paragraph. Students have seen many tables, so this one should not cause them difficulty. Ask students why the graph in the middle is a line graph and why the graph at the right is a bar graph. Ask, *What do the points and the bars represent?*

Warm-Up Review

Have students make a line plot for each set of data.

1. 87, 92, 86, 83, 89, 90, 88, 86, 89, 81, 83, 90, 92, 95, 90
2. As: 5, Bs: 8, Cs: 12, Ds: 2

Check students' line plots.

Talk and Explore

Bar and Line Graphs

Big Idea Graphs show trends and differences in data that tables do not show. Bar graphs can give a quick comparison of quantities. Line graphs can show how data change over time.

Building Background

▲ I am not the tallest person in my class, but I am the fastest runner.

Heights of 67 Students

- What does the picture show?
- Tell what you know from the graph.

Key Concepts

A table, a bar graph, and a line graph all display data. A **table** lists data. A **line graph** shows how data change over time. A **bar graph** uses the lengths of its bars to compare data.

Table

Game Attendance	
Game Date	Number
8/28	2,548
9/3	2,976
9/11	3,024
9/17	3,115
9/25	2,887
10/6	3,045

Line Graph

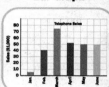
Bar Graph

Activity: Grid the Plot!

Have students make a line plot showing their favorite fruits. Then have them use grid paper (Overhead Transparency 15) and color in a square for each *X* in the line plot.

Favorite Fruits

Resource Library

Math at Hand
Bar and Line Graphs 269–273, 277–278

Math on Call
Bar and Line Graphs 288–289, 292, 297, 298

Reader's Handbook (red)
Bar and Line Graphs 537–554

Bar Graphs

A **bar graph** uses bars to display data. A bar graph gives a visual comparison of data. The graph of languages below shows how many people in the world speak each language. Which language is spoken by about 60 million people?

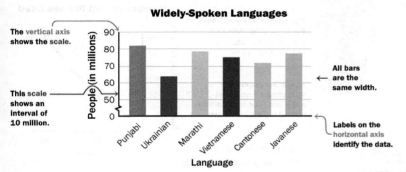

Widely-Spoken Languages

The vertical axis shows the scale.

This scale shows an interval of 10 million.

All bars are the same width.

Labels on the horizontal axis identify the data.

People (in millions)

Language

Punjabi · Ukrainian · Marathi · Vietnamese · Cantonese · Javanese

An **interval** is the amount from one number to the next on a scale. In the graph of languages, the interval is 10 million people. Since all data are more than 50 million, the scale jumps to 50 million to save space. The break (✦) in the scale shows that intervals were skipped.

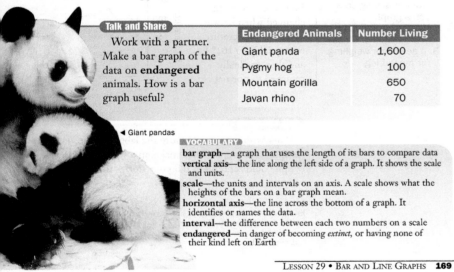

◄ Giant pandas

Talk and Share

Work with a partner. Make a bar graph of the data on **endangered** animals. How is a bar graph useful?

Endangered Animals	Number Living
Giant panda	1,600
Pygmy hog	100
Mountain gorilla	650
Javan rhino	70

VOCABULARY

bar graph—a graph that uses the length of its bars to compare data
vertical axis—the line along the left side of a graph. It shows the scale and units.
scale—the units and intervals on an axis. A scale shows what the heights of the bars on a bar graph mean.
horizontal axis—the line across the bottom of a graph. It identifies or names the data.
interval—the difference between each two numbers on a scale
endangered—in danger of becoming *extinct*, or having none of their kind left on Earth

LESSON 29 • BAR AND LINE GRAPHS **169**

Teach Bar Graphs

■ Read aloud the first paragraph. Ask, *Which language in the graph is spoken by the most people? (Punjabi) How can you tell?* Students should see that the bar for Punjabi is the longest. Ask, *How can you tell which language is spoken by about 70 million people? (Follow the horizontal line to the right of 70; the Cantonese bar is close to 70.)*

■ Point out the *vertical* and *horizontal* axes. Have students note that the vertical scale is in *millions* of people and the *interval* is 10 million. Then explain the break in the scale.

■ Ask volunteers to estimate the number of people that speak each language.

Talk and Share

Tell students to title their graph and to label both axes. Ask, *What would be a good interval for the scale?* Students should note that a graph gives a visual display, while a table gives exact numbers.

Build VOCABULARY

Tell students to look at the bar graph of heights on page 168. Ask, *What is the name of the heavy line that goes up and down? (vertical axis) What is the heavy line that goes across? (horizontal axis)* Ask, *What is the interval? (2)* Have them tell the label for each axis.

Differentiating Instruction

Beginning

Reading a Bar Graph Help students to read the graph on page 168. Ask:

• Which is the tallest height? The shortest?

• Which height group has the fewest students? The most?

Have students tell how they know.

Intermediate

Making a Bar Graph After students have worked through the example on page 169, have pairs make a bar graph

of the Game Attendance table on page 168.

Advanced

Making a Horizontal Bar Graph Have students work through the example on page 169. Then say, *In some bar graphs the bars are horizontal. They go across, rather than up and down. Work with a partner to make a horizontal bar graph for the data in the Widely-Spoken Languages graph on page 169.*

Teach Line Graphs

- Have volunteers point out the various parts of the first graph. To help them read the graph, say, *When a point is on a line, you can read the data from the axes.* Indicate the point at 70 million. Say, *When a point is between lines, you have to estimate.* Indicate the point for 1996. *The point for 1996 is between 40 and 50. What does this point represent? (about 45 million phones in 1996)*

- Read aloud the middle paragraph. Tell students that *trend* means general "direction." Ask them to describe the general direction of the line segments (*upward to the right*). Help them see that a graph like this shows an *increase* over time.

Language Notes

Point out how the word *scale* is used in the text. Have volunteers read aloud the meanings. Ask volunteers to describe experiences they have had with any one of these scales.

Talk and Share

Help students understand that the line of the graph should level out and remain around 98.6 °F.

Look and Read

Line Graphs

A **line graph** shows changes in data. Here is a line graph that shows how the number of cell phones used in the United States changed over the years 1992 to 1998.

The height of the point shows the value of the data item.
Each point is a data item representing a year.

As with bar graphs, you must choose a **scale** and a title and must label both the vertical and horizontal axes.

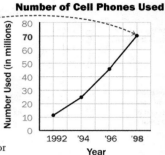

Number of Cell Phones Used

Start at the data point for 1992 and follow the graph line. Notice that it continues to rise. This shows a **trend** or pattern. The number of cell phones increased over time.

Language Notes

Multiple Meanings
This word has more than one meaning.

☐ scale
1. a set of numbers for measuring data on a graph
2. a small thin plate on the skin of a fish
3. a device for weighing or measuring

The graph on the right shows how Eugene's temperature changed when he was sick. His temperature rose quickly to 101° F and then gradually returned to normal.

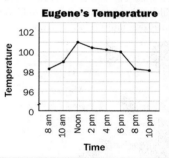

Eugene's Temperature

Talk and Share

Work with a partner. Ignore the labels on the temperature graph. Then make up a story that the line graph could represent. Tell your stories to the class.

VOCABULARY

line graph—a graph that uses line segments to connect pieces of data and show the direction of change
trend—a clear pattern in a line graph that suggests what future data might be

---

 Activity: From Lines to Bars

Have students choose one of the graphs on this page and construct a bar graph of the data. Then discuss with them whether they prefer a bar graph or a line graph. Ask, *Does a bar graph show trends?*

Differentiating Instruction

Beginning
Talking About Graphs Work with students to read aloud and discuss the information in the two graphs on page 171.

Intermediate
Making a Line Graph After students have worked through the examples on page 170, have partners research temperature or rainfall data and make a line graph of the data. An almanac is a good source of information. Ask, *Can you see any trend in the data?*

Advanced
Comparing Bar and Line Graphs After students have worked through the examples on page 170, have one student in a pair make a bar graph of the data in the Game Attendance Table on page 168 and the other student make a line graph of the data. Have them talk about which graph is easier for them to understand and which makes any trend more obvious.

Practice

For Exercises 1–5, use the bar graph at the right.
  1. What does the vertical axis tell?
  2. What interval was used for this graph?
  3. Who scored the most goals?
  4. Who scored the fewest goals?
  5. What is the difference in the number of goals scored by Choi and by Ueslei?
  6. When is a line graph better than a bar graph?
  7. When is a bar graph better than a line graph?

For Exercises 8 and 9, use the line graph.
  8. Does the line show an increase or decrease in the number of Americans aged 65 and older? How can you tell?
  9. If the trend continues, about how many Americans will be 65 or older in the year 2010?

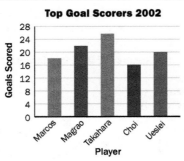

Top Goal Scorers 2002

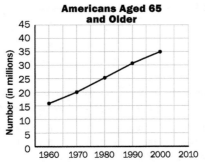

Americans Aged 65 and Older

  10. Make a line graph for the typical weights of iguanas.
    age 1: 1 lb   age 2: 3 lb
    age 3: 5 lb   age 4: 7 lb   age 5: 12 lb

◄ Iguana

  11. Make a bar graph that shows the amount of vitamin C in different fruits.
    apricot: 5 mg   avocado: 17 mg   pear: 4 mg
    cherry: 10 mg   grape: 3 mg

  12. (SHORT RESPONSE) Should you use a line graph or a bar graph to display the data on snack foods listed on the left? Explain your thinking.

Snack Foods Eaten During Super Bowl Football Game	
SNACK	**POUNDS**
Potato chips	12,000,000
Tortilla chips	9,000,000
Popcorn	4,000,000

◄ Tortilla chips and salsa

Practice

Have students read the bar graph and tell how many goals each player scored.

Assignment Guide
■ Beginning 1–11
■ Intermediate 1–12
■ Advanced 1–12

Notes on Exercises
Exercise 9 You might want to have students copy the graph onto grid paper. Then they can extend the line to get an estimate for 2010. Another strategy is to estimate that during each 10-year period, the number increased by about 5 million and add this amount to the figure for 2000.

Exercise 10 If students need help getting started, tell them that times (or ages) are usually given on the horizontal axis of a line graph.

Answers
  1. number of goals scored
  2. 4 goals   **3.** Takahara
  4. Choi   **5.** 4 goals
  6. Sample: when you want to show changes over time
  7. Sample: When you want to make comparisons; the tops of bars make it easy to compare data.
  8. Increase; the line rises from left to right.
  9. Sample: about 40 million
  12. Sample: A bar graph; it compares quantities, while a line graph compares changes over time.

  10.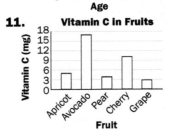

Weight of Iguanas

  11. Vitamin C in Fruits

Program Resources
Practice Book Use page 72.
Overhead Transparencies Use 15.

Teach Interpreting

- Remind students that to *interpret* means to "explain the meaning of."

- The graph shows a sharp decrease from 1991 to 1992. Ask, *What kinds of things might cause the number to drop so much? What year had the fewest immigrants?* (*1998*)

- Have students tell whether they think the numbers continue to increase.

Oral Language

You might want to supply students with copies of *USA Today*. This newspaper has very interesting graphs.

Partner Practice

From either graph, students should be able to see that ticket prices increased from $5 to $8 but that the second graph makes the increase seem greater. Have students compare the 2000 and 2004 prices on each graph and tell how the second one distorts the price increase. Have students redo the second bar graph but without the break in the scale. Ask, *Does the increase still seem so great?*

Develop Language

Activities

Interpreting When you interpret data from a graph, you study the graph to understand the data. Then you use your own words to describe what the graph shows.

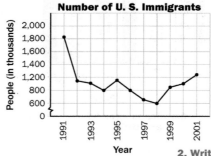

The line graph shows the number of people who moved, or immigrated, to the United States from 1991 through 2001. Notice that the numbers are in thousands. So, 1,600 on the scale represents 1,600,000. Work with a partner to interpret the data.

1. **Describe** Talk about the trend from 1991 to 2001. Did more people immigrate in 1991 or 2001? During what year did the fewest people immigrate to the United States?

2. **Write** Write (or tell) a story that the line graph could represent. Read aloud (or tell) your story to the class.

Oral Language

Graphs in the News Work with a partner. Look through newspapers and magazines to find a bar graph or a line graph. Discuss these details of the graph with your partner.

- What the graph is about
- The title and the labels
- The scale
- What you learned from the graph
- Any trend in the data

Present the graph and your findings to the class.

Partner Practice

Analyze This! Work with a partner to compare the two graphs on the right. Consider the following questions.

- How much did the ticket price increase from 2000 to 2004?
- Do both graphs show the same increase?
- Which graph makes the increase in price seem greater?
- How are the scales for the graphs alike? How are they different?

Write two or three sentences to sum up what you found. Trade sentences with your partner and see if you agree.

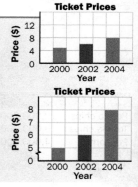

 Program Resources

Practice Book Use page 73.
Overhead Transparencies Use 15.

Assessment Book

Use page 51 to assess students' comprehension.

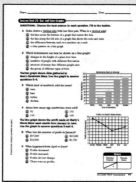

Activity: Culture Connection

Ask students to make a bar graph to compare these data of language families. Each is spoken by more than 200 million people.

Indo-European: 2,600,000,000

Sino-Tibetan: 1,200,000,000

Malayo-Polynesian: 275,000,000

Afro-Asian: 220,000,000

Japanese-Korean: 200,000,000

Dravidian: 200,000,000

Double Bar Graphs

Big Idea Graphs can show a comparison of two or more quantities. Some graphs can give false impressions. Be careful when you draw one. Be critical when you read one.

Building Background

▲ I've been to the zoo in Walsrode, Germany. It has a huge, cold house for penguins and polar bears.

- What do you know about penguins?
- About how many penguins do you see here?
- How could you show numbers of animals in a graph?

Key Concepts

The graph on the right is a **double bar graph**. A double bar graph compares information from two data sets on one graph.

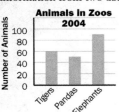

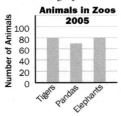

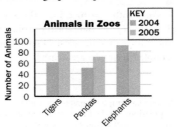

LESSON 30 • DOUBLE BAR GRAPHS **173**

Activity: Double Up!

On the board, list every student's name and age. Then have pairs of students make a double bar graph like the one in Key Concepts. They should use one color for girls and a different color for boys. Offer help if they are having difficulty. They should list ages on the horizontal axis and the number of students on the vertical axis.

Resource Library

Math at Hand
Double Bar Graphs 274

Math on Call
Double Bar Graphs 293
Misleading Graphs 290

Double Bar Graphs

STANDARDS CONTENT
Mathematics
- Read and make a double bar graph
- Recognize graphs that mislead
Language
- Recognize homophones
- Contrast data in a double bar graph
Materials
- Grids (Overhead Transparency 15)

Introduce the **Big Idea**

Read aloud the Big Idea. Discuss with students what it means "to be careful" when they draw a graph and "to be critical" when they read a graph.

Begin **Building Background**

Be sure students recognize the birds as penguins. Tell them that the seventeen species of penguins in the world live only south of the equator. They are found near the Galapagos Islands, New Zealand, Australia, South America, Africa, and Antarctica.

Teach **Key Concepts**

- Read aloud the Key Concepts paragraph. Point out how the data in the two graphs are combined in the third one. Ask, *Why is it important to use a different color for each year?*
- Ask, *Is it easier to compare the data by looking at the first two graphs or by looking at the third?*

Warm-Up Review

On the board, write the following information: *In Swallow School, there are 75 sixth graders, 82 seventh graders, and 72 eighth graders.* Then have volunteers help to draw a bar graph. Be sure they include all pertinent information.

Teach Double Bar Graphs

■ Read aloud the first two paragraphs. Tell the class that the state of Iowa is the leader in U.S. hog production, with one fourth of the country's output. China is the world leader in hog production, with more than 38 million head.

■ Discuss the four steps for making the double bar graph, and point out how the graph follows these steps. Ask, *Why is the key important?*

Talk and Share

The graph very clearly points out that in the years 1995, 1999, and 2003, North Carolina's hog population exceeded its human population. Students will probably recognize that general comparisons are easier with the graph than with the numbers in the table.

Build VOCABULARY

Students will probably connect *population* with people. Point out that *population* can refer to animals as well.

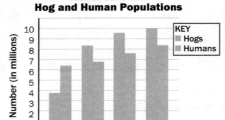

North Carolina Hog and Human Populations		
YEAR	HOGS	HUMANS
1991	3,700,000	6,389,000
1995	8,300,000	6,906,000
1999	9,500,000	7,490,000
2003	10,000,000	8,407,000

Sources: www.ncagr.com/stats, U.S. Census Bureau

North Carolina Hog and Human Populations

KEY
■ Hogs
■ Humans

Number (in millions) — Year

Talk and Share

Work with a partner. Read the graph. For which years did North Carolina have more hogs than humans? Discuss how double bar graphs are helpful.

VOCABULARY

double bar graph—a graph that compares two data sets
population—all the people and/or animals of the same kind that live in one area
key—a list that explains colors or symbols in a graph or map

174 Unit 7 • Data and Statistics

Double Bar Graphs

A **double bar graph** shows two sets of data on the same graph. Look again at page 173. You can easily compare the number of animals in zoos when the two separate graphs are combined into one double bar graph.

North Carolina is the second largest hog-producing state. To compare North Carolina's hog **population** to its human population, create a double bar graph. One set of bars will show the hog population. The other set will show the human population.

Step 1: Analyze the data to determine the interval for the graph. Since the data go from 3 million to 10 million, each horizontal line can stand for 1 million.

Step 2: Label the vertical and horizontal axes.

Step 3: Make a **key** to show which bars represent humans and which represent hogs. Use two different colors or shadings.

Step 4: Draw bars to the correct heights.

Activity: Who Likes What Better?

Have students poll the class to find out students' favorite sport. Have them work in pairs to make a double bar graph with one color for girls and another color for boys. Then have them discuss their graphs.

Differentiating Instruction

Beginning

Understanding the Bar Graph Review with students the terms *interval, vertical axis,* and *horizontal axis.* Have them identify each and talk about what the numbers mean in the graph on page 174. Have a volunteer read the title of the graph. If necessary, identify the state of North Carolina on a wall map. Ask, *Is there another name for hogs? (pigs) What is another name for humans? (people)*

Intermediate

Reading the Bar Graph Go slowly through the steps on page 174 to be sure students understand them. For instance, to analyze the data, they need to see that the vertical axis is labeled in *millions* and that the labels on the horizontal axis are four years apart.

Advanced

Explaining the Page Have partners take turns reading a paragraph on page 174 aloud. Have them stop and talk about each paragraph.

Misleading Graphs

Some graphs are confusing or **misleading**. In the graph below on the left, the Light Rider has a bar that is twice as high as the Sliderboard bar. That makes it appear to cost twice as much as the Sliderboard. One problem is that the scale has a break in it, so you see only the top portions of two bars. Also, the small intervals make the differences seem greater. This graph is *misleading*.

The graph below on the right has a more reasonable scale and shows all of the two bars. This graph is *accurate*. You can see that the Light Rider costs only $20 more than the Sliderboard. The prices are close.

The two graphs below show the same data about DVD rentals. Why does the one on the right make the growth in DVDs rented seem so much greater?

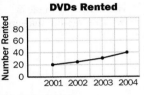

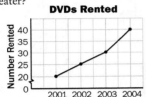

Brazilian skateboarder Sandro Dias is a master of best trick contests. ▶

Talk and Share

Talk with a partner about the two graphs on DVDs rented. Use the words *slow* and *fast* to describe growth shown by the graphs. Explain why you might want to show data in each of these ways.

VOCABULARY
misleading—suggesting something that is not true

Teach Misleading Graphs

■ Read aloud the first sentence. Ask students to talk about the difference between *confusing* and *misleading*. Explain that *confusing* graphs can mix people up and that *misleading* graphs can make people think the wrong thing. This lesson deals with *misleading* graphs.

■ Call students' attention to the two graphs. Then discuss the differences in the vertical axes and the intervals.

Language Notes

Point out how *break* is used in the reading. Then discuss the meanings of *break* and *brake*. Discuss the meaning of *homophones*.

Talk and Share

■ To help students understand the terms *slow* and *fast* as they relate to the two line graphs, draw two "hills" on the board. Make one very steep and the other very gently sloping. Tell students to imagine they are sledding down the hills. Ask, *On which hill will they go faster? Slower?* Relate the speeds to the two graphs.

■ Students should identify the left graph as the one showing slow growth and the one on the right as showing fast growth.

Differentiating Instruction

Beginning
Understanding Misleading Graphs
Tell students, *The first two graphs on this page both show the same information. They show the prices of two skateboards.* Ask, *How are the graphs different?* Invite responses. Point to the break, if no one suggests it. Then repeat with the lower graphs. Introduce *accurate* and *misleading*. Ask students to point to the graphs and use these terms to demonstrate understanding.

Intermediate
Explaining Misleading Graphs Have pairs take turns reading the paragraphs on page 175 aloud. The listening partner then explains what the paragraph read means. Provide explanations as needed.

Advanced
Talking About Misleading Graphs
Have partners in turn read a paragraph silently and then tell what it means. After completing the Talk and Share, have them present their ideas about why people might create a misleading graph.

Activity: Mislead Me, Please!

Have pairs of students use the information below and make two line graphs or bar graphs, one that is accurate and one that misleads. Have them share their graphs with the class. Suggest that they use different scales and have them compare their graphs with other pairs'.

Average temperatures in Bismarck, North Dakota: January, 7 °F; April, 43 °F; July, 70 °F; October, 46 °F

Practice

On the board, write this set of data: *88, 42, 70, 72, 82, 84, 84, 78.* Have students find the mean, median, and mode. Then have them tell which of the three numbers is most representative and why. (*mean: 75; median: 80; mode: 84; the median is probably most representative, as there is an outlier, 42, and more numbers in the 80s than 70s.*)

Assignment Guide
- Beginning 1, 2, 5–9
- Intermediate 1–8
- Advanced 1–9

Notes on Exercises
Exercise 3 Be sure students know that the notation $3.1 million means $3,100,000. Give them other examples of numbers in this format to translate to standard form.

Exercise 6 Ask, *How will you redraw the fish for the pictograph?*

Exercise 7 Ask volunteers to explain how to find mean, median, and mode for the data.

Practice

1. Why do we use different colors in double bar graphs?

2. Tell one or two things that can make graphs misleading.

3. The mean of the salaries on the right is $3.1 million. How could that fact be misleading? How well does the mean represent the salaries in the list?

Salaries of Company Presidents
$9,400,000
$2,500,000
$1,700,000
$1,100,000
$800,000

The graph on the left is a *pictograph*. It is similar to a bar graph. Use it for Exercises 4–6.

4. Are there more pikes or more minnows in the lake?

5. What makes this graph misleading?

6. Redraw the graph so that it is not misleading.

Fish in the Lake

Pike
Minnow
Bass

KEY:
Each picture = 10 fish

7. (EXTENDED RESPONSE) Pat scored 100, 100, 90, 70, and 60 on his five tests. Which will make his grade seem higher, the mean or the median? Which would show Pat that he needs to study harder for the next test? Make a bar graph to compare the mean, the median, and the mode of Pat's test scores.

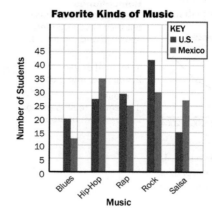

Favorite Kinds of Music

KEY
■ U.S.
■ Mexico

(bar graph: Number of Students vs Music — Blues, Hip-Hop, Rap, Rock, Salsa)

For Exercises 8 and 9, use the double bar graph on the left.

8. (MULTIPLE CHOICE) Which kinds of music in this group are liked by more Mexican students than U.S. students?
   A. Blues and rock
   B. Hip-hop and salsa
   C. Rap and rock
   D. Hip-hop and rap

9. (MULTIPLE CHOICE) How many more U.S. students in the group like rock than rap?
   A. 7   B. 27   C. 13   D. 18

Program Resources
Practice Book Use page 74.
Overhead Transparencies Use 15.

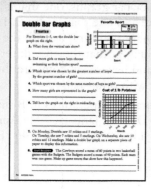

Answers
1. Sample: so the two separate sets of data are clearly visible
2. Sample: different scales, breaks in the vertical scale
3. Sample: The mean is higher than four of the five salaries. The mean is unusually high because of the outlier, $9.4 million; the mean does not represent the data well.
4. more minnows
5. the sizes of the fish
8. B   9. C

6. Sample: **Fish in the Lake**

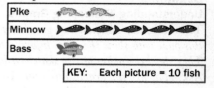

Pike
Minnow
Bass

KEY: Each picture = 10 fish

7. the median; the mean

Pat's Tests

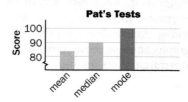

(bar graph: Score vs mean, median, mode)

Activities

Contrasting When you contrast, you tell how things differ. Work with a partner to analyze the graph on the right.

1. **Explain** Tell how the lengths of class periods differ at King School. Which period is the longest? The shortest?

2. **Explain** Tell how the lengths of class periods differ at Lincoln School. Which period is the longest? The shortest?

3. **Contrast** Write two or three sentences to describe how the class periods at the two schools differ. Share your writing with the class.

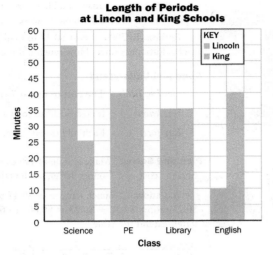

Length of Periods at Lincoln and King Schools

KEY
Lincoln
King

(y-axis) Minutes
(x-axis) Class: Science, PE, Library, English

 Partner Practice

Is It or Isn't It? With your partner, make a list of ways that graphs can be misleading. Think about the scale and the intervals. Look in newspapers or magazines for graphs that mislead. Talk about how these graphs are misleading.

Hands On

How's the Weather? Work in a small group to collect weather data for two towns in different parts of the country for a week. You may want to use the Internet. Decide what data to use, such as daily low temperatures or amount of rain. Make a double bar graph to compare the data for the two towns. Make a display that includes a table of the data and the graph.

LESSON 30 • DOUBLE BAR GRAPHS **177**

Teach Contrasting

Tell students that to *contrast* is to "tell how things are different" and to *compare* is to "tell how things are alike."

Partner Practice

Invite students to share their lists and graphs with the class. Have them talk about why the various graphs are misleading and why they might have been drawn that way.

Hands On

An almanac is a good source of information for the data suggested in this activity. Be sure to check students' displays.

Key Connection

Another type of graph that students have probably encountered is a *circle graph*. A circle graph is used to show how parts of a set of data relate to the whole set. Sketch this circle graph on the board, and discuss its meaning with the class.

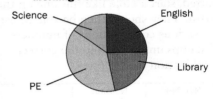

Morning Periods at King School

Science, English, Library, PE

 ### Activity: Culture Connection

North Carolina raises more turkeys than any other state and is a leading chicken-producing state. Have students find the number of hogs, turkeys, and chickens raised in North Carolina each of the last two years. Then have them draw a double bar graph to compare the numbers.

You may prefer to use production numbers of other items that North Carolina produces, such as textiles, furniture, or peanuts.

 ### Assessment Book

Use page 52 to assess students' comprehension.

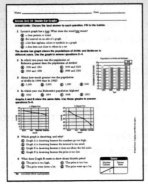

 ### Program Resources

Practice Book Use page 75.
Overhead Transparencies Use 15.

Make a Table

STANDARDS CONTENT

Mathematics
- Solve problems by making a table

Language
- Recognize count and noncount *nouns*

Teach Make a Table

- Have a volunteer read aloud the first paragraph. Ask, *How much did a first-class stamp cost in 2004?*

- Discuss the three parts of Read and Understand.

- Copy the beginning of the table on the board. Have volunteers fill in the table for each extra ounce of a letter until they reach 7 ounces. Be sure that they know to add 23¢ for each additional ounce.

- Ask, *Do you think a guess, check, and revise strategy would make sense to check the problem in this situation? Why or why not?*

Talk and Share

If students have problems getting started, start a table like this one on the board. They should then be able to list the various combinations of numbers of stamps until they find the correct combination of stamps.

Number at 23¢	Number at 37¢	Total
5	1	$1.52

Problem-Solving Skills

Make a Table

Use the strategy make a table to organize information. Then look for a pattern and extend the table to solve the problem.

Problem: In 2004, it cost $0.37 to mail a 1-ounce letter. It cost $0.23 for each additional ounce. How much did it cost to mail a 7-ounce letter?

Read and Understand

Need to find:	The cost to mail a 7-ounce letter
You know:	It cost $0.37 to mail a 1-ounce letter.
Key fact:	Each additional ounce cost $0.23.

Plan and Solve
Make a table of values to solve the problem. You must find the cost of a 7-ounce letter, so the table should have 7 columns.

You know a 1-ounce letter cost $0.37 to mail. A 2-ounce letter cost $0.23 more: $0.37 + $0.23 = $0.60. To find the cost to mail a 7-ounce letter, extend the table.

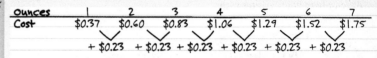

Ounces	1	2	3	4	5	6	7
Cost	$0.37	$0.60	$0.83	$1.06	$1.29	$1.52	$1.75

+ $0.23 + $0.23 + $0.23 + $0.23 + $0.23 + $0.23

Answer
It cost $1.75 to mail a 7-ounce letter in 2004.

Look Back
Check your answer by solving the problem a different way. Each extra ounce cost $0.23, and a 7-ounce letter includes 6 extra ounces. So the total cost was $0.37 + $0.23 × 6 = $0.37 + $1.38 = $1.75. The answer is correct.

Talk and Share
Work with a partner. Tai bought 23-cent stamps for postcards and 37-cent stamps for letters. His total was $1.94. How many of each kind did he buy?

Activity: Table It Another Way

Remind students that they learned in Unit 1 to evaluate expressions by using a table. Give them the expression $37 + 23n$. Tell them that this expression will give the same results as those in the table. Have them set up a table and verify that the values agree with those on page 178.

Differentiating Instruction

Beginning
Understanding the Table On the board, write *Cost for 1 ounce, Cost for each ounce over 1, Total number of ounces.* Ask, *What is the cost for 1 ounce?* (37¢) *For each ounce over 1 ounce?* (23¢) *How many ounces are there altogether?* (7 ounces) Then have a volunteer copy the table on page 178 and show how the three numbers are represented.

Intermediate
Using a Table to Explain Have students use the table on page 178 as a guide to explain the solution to this problem: Late in 1975, first-class rates were 13¢ for the first ounce and 11¢ for each additional ounce. How much did it cost to mail a 10-ounce letter? (*$1.12*)

Advanced
Solving a Riddle Have pairs solve this problem by using a table: A farmer had some chickens and cows. He counted 12 heads and 38 legs. How many of each kind of animal did he have? (*5 chickens, 7 cows*) Have students explain their solutions.

1. In 2004, how much did it cost to mail an 8-ounce letter?

2. How much would it cost to mail a 7-ounce letter if it cost $0.62 to mail a 1-ounce letter and $0.25 for each additional ounce?

Use the strategy *make a table*.

3. Trina will start working at a fruit stand on Saturday. She will earn $4.15 the first day. Her pay will increase by $1 every Saturday she works. If she works 9 Saturdays, how much money will she earn in all?

4. A sunflower plant is 3 feet 8 inches tall. It is growing at a rate of 3 inches per week. How tall will it be in 7 weeks?

5. Tam has 10 coins in her pocket. Some are nickels and some are dimes. The coins are worth $0.70. How many of each coin does she have?

Choose a strategy and solve the problem.

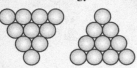

6. In three moves, change the first set of circles to look like the second set. Move only one circle at a time.

Grammar Spotlight

Using Numbers with Nouns There are two types of nouns, *count* and *noncount*. Count nouns are nouns that we can describe with a number. *Hat* is a count noun. We can say 1 hat, 3 hats, or 16 hats. Count nouns have a singular and a plural form.

Noncount nouns are nouns that we cannot count. For example, *water* is a noncount noun because we cannot say 3 waters or 8 waters. Noncount nouns have only one form.

Common Nouns		Nouns in This Lesson	
Count	*Noncount*	*Count*	*Noncount*
1 car	some hay	a letter	money
4 oranges	much time	7 weeks	pay

Work with a partner. Take turns making up a sentence with a count noun and then with a noncount noun. Say it out loud and have your partner write it down. Check to see if your partner wrote it correctly. Then switch roles. Write the sentence as your partner says it.

MAKE A TABLE   **179**

Give students this problem to solve by using a table: *For shipping and handling, a mail-order company charges $2.50 for the first pound of merchandise and $1.50 for each additional pound. Find the cost of shipping and handling for a 6-lb order ($10).*

Assignment Guide

■ Beginning 1–6
■ Intermediate 1–6
■ Advanced 1–6

Notes on Exercises

Exercise 3 Students will need to add the weekly amounts to find the total amount. Encourage students to check their weekly amounts by using the Look Back step on page 178.

Exercise 4 Remind students that there are 12 inches in 1 foot.

Exercise 5 Students can use a table similar to that in Talk and Share on page 178.

Exercise 6 Allow students to work in pairs and to use round markers to help.

Grammar Spotlight

■ Read aloud the two paragraphs. Be sure students can identify nouns as *count* and *noncount*. Give them a variety of examples, such as milk, shoes, girls, and rain.

■ Talk about the nouns in the table.

Answers

1. $1.98
2. $2.12
3. $73.35
4. 5 ft 5 in.
5. 4 dimes, 6 nickels
6.

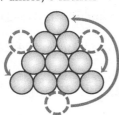

Activity: Culture Connection

Invite interested students to research the people shown on the stamps on page 178. Other students can check http://library.thinkquest.org/ 10320/USstamps.htm to find out how individuals are chosen to be featured on stamps.

Program Resources

Practice Book Use pages 76 and 77.

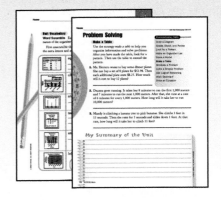

Lines and Angles

STANDARDS CONTENT

Mathematics
- Identify points, lines, planes, rays, segments, and pairs of lines
- Identify, measure, and draw angles

Language
- Recognize verb phrases
- Classify triangles

Materials
- Protractors

Introduce the **Big Idea**

Read aloud the Big Idea. Ask students to tell what they know about lines and angles.

Begin **Building Background**

Ask students to point to lines and angles in the picture.

Teach **Key Concepts**

- Discuss the terms in the table. Explain that *point*, *line*, and *plane* are basic concepts in geometry on which most other geometric terms are based. Point out how the diagrams and the symbols illustrate the terms.

- Have students point out things in the classroom that represent the terms in the table.

Warm-Up Review

Review with students the concept of number lines and points on a number line. Draw a number line on the board, pointing out that the line extends in both directions. Graph several points on the number line, stressing that the points are *locations* on the number line.

Talk and Explore

Lines and Angles

Big Idea Lines and angles are all around you. They form the basic shapes of many things.

Building Background

▲ This reminds me of a train station back in Mexico.

- **What kind of place is pictured here?**
- **Describe the shapes and figures that you see.**
- **What shapes and figures do you see every day?**

Key Concepts

Term	Description	Diagram	Name and Symbol	
point	a location in space	•A	A	Use a capital letter.
line	a straight path of points that continues in both directions	B C	$\overleftrightarrow{BC}$	Use any two points on the line.
ray	a part of a line that has one endpoint and continues in one direction	E D	$\overrightarrow{ED}$	Name the endpoint first.
line segment	a part of a line that has two endpoints	F G	$\overline{FG}$	Name the endpoints.
plane	a flat surface that continues without end	m	m	Use a lowercase letter.

 Activity: Get the Point?

Give students newspapers and magazines. Have them cut out pictures that show uses of points, lines, and planes. Then have them create a collage of the pictures, labeling the points, lines, and planes and telling how they are used in some of the pictures.

 Resource Library

Math at Hand
Points, Lines, and Planes 334–339
Pairs of Lines and Angles 340–341, 345–347

Math on Call
Points, Lines, and Planes 315–317, 321–323
Pairs of Lines and Angles 324–325, 330–331

▲ The lines in the sign are intersecting lines.

▲ The short bars are parallel line segments.

▲ The two bars are skew line segments.

Pairs of Lines

You can describe pairs of lines by talking about how the two lines are **related**. Lines that cross are **intersecting lines.** **Parallel lines** lie in the same plane but never cross. Two lines that do not lie in the same plane are called **skew lines.**

Intersecting lines meet at one point. $\overleftrightarrow{NM}$ and $\overleftrightarrow{PQ}$ intersect at point O. Intersecting lines are in the same plane.

Parallel lines never meet. They are in the same plane. $\overleftrightarrow{RS} \parallel \overleftrightarrow{TU}$ means $\overleftrightarrow{RS}$ is parallel to $\overleftrightarrow{TU}$.

Skew lines never meet. They are never in the same plane. $\overleftrightarrow{VW}$ and $\overleftrightarrow{XY}$ are skew lines.

Pairs of rays and line segments also may be intersecting, parallel, or skew.

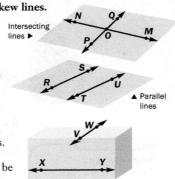

Intersecting lines ▶

▲ Parallel lines

▲ Skew lines

Talk and Share

With a partner, look at the New Zealand road sign on the right.

Name or point out a pair of lines or rays for each word: *intersecting, parallel,* and *skew.* Tell how you made your decisions. How are intersecting lines and parallel lines alike? How are they different?

VOCABULARY
related—having something in common
intersecting lines—lines in the same plane that meet at one point
parallel lines—lines in the same plane that never cross
skew lines—lines that lie in different planes

LESSON 31 • LINES AND ANGLES **181**

Teach Pairs of Lines

- Ask, *When have you used the terms* point *and* line? Students should recall plotting points on number lines.

- Provide students with simple maps. Have them think of the map as a plane and point to *points, lines, rays,* and *segments.*

- Be sure that students understand the vocabulary terms. You can use two pencils or straws to demonstrate *parallel, intersecting,* and *skew lines.*

- Help students see that both intersecting lines and parallel lines are necessarily in the same plane, while skew lines never are.

- Invite students to point out parallel and intersecting lines on their maps.

Talk and Share

Discuss the road sign in the picture. Be sure students can identify the three pairs of lines, and ask them to find examples in the classroom.

Sample answers: intersecting, $\overleftrightarrow{AB}$ *and* $\overleftrightarrow{AE}$; *parallel,* $\overleftrightarrow{AB}$ *and* $\overleftrightarrow{CD}$; *and skew,* $\overleftrightarrow{CD}$ *and* $\overleftrightarrow{EF}$

Build VOCABULARY

Read aloud the definitions of terms describing pairs of lines. Relate the terms to the Key Concepts.

Differentiating Instruction

Beginning
Talking About Pictures Have less fluent learners focus on the pictures on page 181. Encourage students to work in small groups. Have them use the vocabulary words to talk about the three small pictures on the left-hand side of page 181.

Intermediate
Describing Geometric Concepts Have students work in small groups to talk about things in the classroom or everyday items that represent the terms in Key Concepts and Vocabulary.

Advanced
Defining Geometric Terms Have students work in pairs and take turns defining in their own words the mathematical terms in Key Concepts and Vocabulary. Have them draw examples to illustrate their definitions.

Activity: Web the Lines

Have students work in small groups to make a Web (Overhead Transparency 33) using one of the terms in the lesson. Have them present their Web to the class. An example is given here.

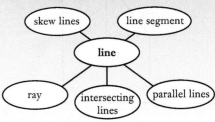

Teach Types of Angles

- Demonstrate how to read a protractor and discuss the four types of angles.

- Ask students to draw various size angles. Then have them measure each angle. Their concepts of *acute* and *obtuse* should help them read the correct scale on the protractor.

- Point out that the symbols for *angle*, *right angle*, and *perpendicular* are descriptive. Discuss how an angle is named.

Language Notes

Discuss how the red phrase *line up* is used in the reading. A common phrasal verb used in mathematics is *add up*, which has nothing to do with direction. Another is *figure out*, which has nothing to do with *out* or *in*. Have students volunteer other phrasal verbs.

Talk and Share

Ask pairs to describe how they estimated the angle measures.

Answers: ∠RQU, *90°*; ∠RQT, *130°*; ∠RQP, *180°*; ∠UQT, *40°*; ∠UQP, *90°*; ∠UQS, *130°*; ∠TQP, *50°*; ∠TQS, *90°*; ∠PQS, *40°*; ∠RQS, *140°*

Build VOCABULARY

Have students write in their own words definitions of *acute, obtuse, right,* and *straight angle* and include a drawing for each.

Look and Read

Types of Angles

Look at the diagram on the left. If you drive from point *D* to point *C*, you could turn toward point *A* or point *B*.

Each turn is an **angle.** The turn toward *B* is easier because angle *DCB* is the wider angle. Angle *DCB* is written ∠*DCB*.

∠*ACB* has sides $\overrightarrow{CA}$ and $\overrightarrow{CB}$. Its vertex is the intersection of the two rays. The vertex is the middle letter in the angle name.

Language Notes

Verb Phrases
These phrases have special meanings.

- **line up:** make straight or put in the right position
- **make up:** form or compose

A **protractor** is used for measuring angles. It is divided into units called **degrees.** Place the center mark on the **vertex** of the angle. One **side** of the angle should line up with zero. Read the degrees where the second side crosses that scale.

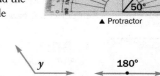

▲ Protractor

acute angle
$0° < x < 90°$

right angle
exactly 90°

obtuse angle
$90° < y < 180°$

straight angle
exactly 180°

The symbol ⌐ indicates a right angle. The sides of a right angle are **perpendicular.** The symbol ⊥ is read "is perpendicular to." On the left below, $\overrightarrow{QU} \perp \overrightarrow{PR}$.

Talk and Share

Estimate the measures of four of the angles in the diagram on the left. Share your estimates with your partner. Trace the diagram and extend the lines. Then use a protractor to find the measures. How close are your estimates?

VOCABULARY

angle—two rays with a common endpoint

protractor—a tool for measuring angles

degrees—the units for measuring angles

vertex—the common endpoint of two rays of an angle

side—in an angle, one of its two rays

perpendicular—meeting to form a right angle

 Activity: Fold and Guess

Have pairs of students fold sheets of paper as shown to create angles of various sizes. Have them measure and identify one angle of each type shown on page 182.

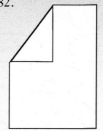

Differentiating Instruction

Beginning

Hunting for Angles After discussing types of angles, refer students to the photo at the top of page 182. Ask them to name or describe an *acute angle* (∠ACB or ∠ACD) and an *obtuse angle* (∠BCD).

Intermediate

Finding Angles in Time After discussing types of angles, refer students to the classroom clock. Have them write times for which the clock hands form *acute angles, obtuse angles,*

right angles, and *straight angles.* When possible, students should give several examples of each.

Advanced

Comparing English and Math Definitions Have pairs of students choose one of the following terms: *acute, obtuse, right, straight.* Have them use their dictionaries to find the definitions and share with the class the similarities and differences between the English and mathematical meanings.

Practice

State whether each is a line, a ray, or a segment.

1.   **2.**   **3.** **4.**

State whether each is a point, a line, a ray, a segment, or a plane.

5. pencil point **6.** laser beam **7.** floor **8.** desktop

Use the photo of the car for Exercises 9–12.

9. Name an obtuse angle, a right angle, an acute angle, and a straight angle.

10. Which lines appear to be parallel?

11. Give another name for ray FG.

12. Name two different rays with endpoint G.

Describe the relationship between the lines, rays, and segments.

13.   **14.**   **15.**  **16.**

17. How are a ray and a line segment alike? How are they different?

18. Tell how you know that the vertex of $\angle XYZ$ is Y.

19. Name the sides of $\angle XYZ$.

20. Draw two parallel lines. Label the lines CD and EF. Draw a new line that is parallel to $\overleftrightarrow{CD}$. Will the new line cross $\overleftrightarrow{EF}$?

21. Find a picture that shows several pairs of lines. Show it to your class. Point out pairs of lines. Tell which pairs of lines are intersecting, parallel, or skew.

22. Ted and Paolo are walking in the same direction and at the same speed on parallel streets. If they are 0.5 km apart when they begin, how far apart will they be 20 minutes later? Explain.

23. (**EXTENDED RESPONSE**) Trace $\angle ABC$ and $\angle CBD$ in the boat photo. Extend the lines so that you can measure each of the angles. What is the sum of their measures? Why does this sum make sense?

Practice

On the board, write *point, line, segment, ray, angle, parallel lines,* and *intersecting lines.* Have students copy the list and sketch an example of each term. Have them label each drawing and give its symbolic name, such as $\overrightarrow{AB}$.

Assignment Guide
- Beginning 1–12, 13–19 odd, 22
- Intermediate 1–23 odd
- Advanced 2–22 even, 23 odd

Notes on Exercises
Exercise 12 Students should note that there are five possible rays with endpoint G.

Exercise 21 Other textbooks are good sources for pictures.

Exercise 22 Ask two students to role-play the situation involving Ted and Paolo to enhance their thinking.

Answers

1. line **2.** ray
3. segment **4.** ray
5. point **6.** ray
7. plane **8.** plane
9. Samples: $\angle FGC$; $\angle BGF$; $\angle CGD$; $\angle FGD$
10. $\overleftrightarrow{AF}$ and $\overleftrightarrow{CG}$
11. ray FD
12. Samples: $\overrightarrow{GC}$, $\overrightarrow{GF}$
13. perpendicular **14.** parallel
15. intersecting
16. parallel

17. Both are parts of lines. Rays have one endpoint; segments have two.
18. Y is the middle letter.
19. $\overrightarrow{YZ}$ and $\overrightarrow{YX}$
20. 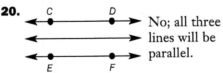 No; all three lines will be parallel.

21. Check students' pictures.
22. 0.5 km; parallel lines are the same distance apart everywhere.
23. 180°; $\overleftrightarrow{ABD}$ is a straight line.

Program Resources
Practice Book Use page 78.

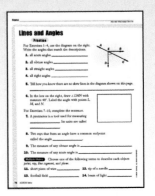

Teach Classifying

■ Draw a table with a column for each month. Fill in the table with the number of students whose birthdays are in each month. Say, *We have* classified, *or sorted, the students in this class by their birthday month. The classifying table on page 184 can help you sort the types of triangles.*

■ Ask students to identify the two angles in each triangle that are *not* the largest angles. The remaining angles are always *acute* angles.

See Additional Answers, page T40.

Partner Practice

Remind students that pairs of line segments or rays can be *parallel, intersecting, perpendicular,* or *skew.* The segments are on a flat sheet of paper, so none of them can be skew.

Hands On

You may wish to have students prepare ten or twelve cards picturing all sizes of angles for their partners to sort and classify.

Key Connection

Discuss the word *geometry,* which means "earth measure." *Geo-* means "earth" and *-metry* means "measure." Have volunteers find other words that begin with the prefix *geo-.*

Develop Language

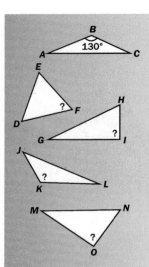

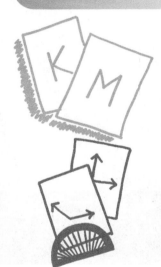

Activities

Classifying The figures on the left are triangles. You can classify or sort triangles by the size of their angles. The size of the largest angle determines whether the triangle is acute, right, or obtuse. Copy the table below to record your findings.

1. **Classify** Use a protractor to measure the largest angle of each triangle shown. Then write the measure of that angle and the name of each triangle in the table to classify it as acute, right, or obtuse.

2. **Draw** Draw an acute triangle, a right triangle, and an obtuse triangle. Ask a partner to classify your triangles.

3. **Explain** Tell how you decided to classify each triangle.

Acute Triangle	Right Triangle	Obtuse Triangle
		$130° \triangle ABC$

Partner Practice

Find Those Pairs With a partner, place a set of cards with capital letters facedown on a table. Take turns choosing a card. For your letter, point to or name all segments that are parallel, intersecting, or perpendicular. For example, the letter K has three pairs of intersecting line segments. The letter Q has no line segments. Check each other's work. Why are there no letters with skew segments?

Hands On

All Sorts of Angles Work with a partner. Start with a set of cards showing angles of different sizes. Take turns sorting the cards into groups of right, acute, obtuse, and straight angles. To check angle sizes, measure the angles with a protractor. Your partner must agree that the cards are sorted correctly.

Program Resources

Practice Book Use page 79.

Assessment Book

Use page 53 to assess students' comprehension.

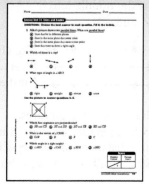

Activity: Culture Connection

Gestalt psychologists use geometry and related puzzles in their study of human perception. Give students the diagram below, without red answers. Have students try to move only two line segments to change from five squares to four squares.

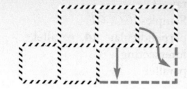

Talk and Explore

Angles and Triangles

Big Idea A triangle has three angles and three sides. Triangles are used in building such things as bridges and roller coasters.

Building Background

▲ The longest steel roller coaster in the world is in Mie, Japan.

■ Point out triangles in the photo.
■ Where else might triangles be used?

Key Concepts

Complementary Angles
Sum of measures is 90°.
35° + 55° = 90°

35°
55°

Supplementary Angles
Sum of measures is 180°.
62° + 118° = 180°

62°   118°

Vertical Angles
Opposite angles have equal measures.
48° = 48°

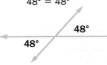

48°
48°

LESSON 32 • ANGLES AND TRIANGLES **185**

Activity: It Takes Two to Angle

Give pairs of students magazines and newspapers. Have them find pictures illustrating the three kinds of angle pairs defined in Key Concepts. Have them make posters using the pictures and highlight and label the various pairs. You can display the posters or have students share their posters with the class.

Resource Library

Math at Hand
Angles and Triangles 348–351, 353–354, 358–363

Math on Call
Angles and Triangles 333–335, 337, 348, 351–352

Angles and Triangles

STANDARDS CONTENT

Mathematics
■ Identify angle pairs as complementary, supplementary, or vertical
■ Classify triangles by angles or sides

Language
■ Recognize multiple meanings of *acute*, *right*, and *obtuse*
■ Describe figures by providing details

Materials
■ Protractors, index cards

Introduce the **Big Idea**

Read aloud the Big Idea. Ask, *Can you think of any other uses of triangles in building things?*

Begin **Building Background**

■ Encourage students to describe roller coasters that they have seen or experienced.
■ Invite and help students to trace with their fingers triangles of different shapes and sizes in the picture.

Teach **Key Concepts**

■ Read aloud the Key Concepts terms and sentences. Ask whether either of two complementary angles can be obtuse and whether supplementary angles can both be acute. Have students explain their reasoning.
■ Help students find the measures of the unmarked pair of vertical angles (*132°*).

Warm-Up Review

Have students use a protractor to draw each angle.

1. right angle *ABC*
2. obtuse angle *DEF*
3. acute angle *GHK*
4. angle *MNO* with measure 45°
5. angle *PQR* with measure 90°
6. angle *XYZ* with measure 120°

Check students' drawings.

Teach **Angle Pairs**

- Help students to see that *supplementary, complementary,* and *vertical* describe *pairs* of angles. We then say that one angle is the *complement* or *supplement* of another.

- Draw a pair of nonadjacent complementary and supplementary angles on the board labeled with their measures. Explain that the angles do not have to share a side to be complementary or supplementary.

- Ask students to identify the type of angles in the picture marked with red arcs and tell whether they appear to be the same size (*vertical; yes*). Then ask them to identify the type of angles *without* red arcs and whether they appear to be the same size (*vertical; yes*).

Talk and Share

Have students describe the relationships among the angles. They should see that ∠1 is a supplement of ∠2, so its measure is 180° −110°, or 70°. Because ∠3 and ∠1 are vertical angles, the measure of ∠3 is also 70°. Finally, ∠4 and ∠2 are vertical angles, so the measure of ∠4 is 110°.

Build **VOCABULARY**

Write the vocabulary terms on the board. Then have students provide the correct terms for these sentences:

Two angles with measures 55° and 35° are <u>complementary</u> angles.

Two angles with measures 45° and 45° are <u>complementary or congruent</u> angles.

Opposite angles formed by intersecting lines are <u>vertical</u> angles.

Vertical angles are <u>congruent</u> angles.

Two angles with measures 120° and 60° are <u>supplementary</u> angles.

Angle Pairs

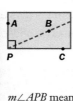

Each corner of an index card is a 90° angle. Fold a card so that point *P* is an angle vertex. ∠*APB* and ∠*BPC* are **complementary angles** because the sum of their measures is 90°. Each angle is the *complement* of the other.

m∠*APB* means "the measure of angle *APB*." Suppose *m*∠*APB* is 65°. What is *m*∠*BPC*? Let $x = m\angle BPC$.

$$x + 65 = 90$$
$$x + 65 - 65 = 90 - 65 = 25$$
$$m\angle BPC = 25°$$

On another card, mark point *Q* on the bottom edge. Fold the card so that *Q* is a vertex. ∠*MQN* and ∠*NQR* are **supplementary angles** because the sum of their measures is 180°. Each angle is a *supplement* of the other.

If $m\angle RQN = 80°$, what is $m\angle NQM$? Let $x = m\angle NQM$.
$$80 + x = 180$$
$$80 - 80 + x = 180 - 80 = 100$$
$$m\angle NQM = 100°$$

Fold a card twice so that the folds intersect. The angles opposite each other are **vertical angles.** ∠1 and ∠3 are a pair of vertical angles. So are ∠2 and ∠4. Vertical angles have the same measure and therefore are **congruent (≅) angles.** You write ∠1 ≅ ∠3 and ∠2 ≅ ∠4.

Talk and Share

Work with a partner. If $m\angle 2$ is 110° in the diagram above, what are $m\angle 1$, $m\angle 3$, and $m\angle 4$? Tell how you know.

▲ Vertical angles are marked in this picture. They are also congruent.

VOCABULARY

complementary angles—two angles whose measures add to 90°

supplementary angles—two angles whose measures add to 180°

vertical angles—opposite angles formed by intersecting lines. They are always congruent.

congruent angles—angles with the same measure

186 UNIT 8 • GEOMETRY

Differentiating Instruction

Beginning

Understanding Pairs of Angles On the board, draw right ∠ABC and ray BD inside the angle. Ask, *What is the measure of* ∠ABC? (90°) *If the measure of* ∠ABD *is 40°, what is the measure of* ∠DBC? (50°) *These two angles are* complementary *angles because the sum of their measures is 90°.*

Intermediate

Finding Measures in Pairs of Angles Have each student in a pair repeat the three activities in the explanation on

page 186. Have them use a protractor to measure one of the angles on each card and then tell each other how to find the measure of the other angle.

Advanced

Demonstrating Pairs of Angles Have small groups demonstrate what they know about the three types of angle pairs. Have them draw examples and explain them to others in their group.

Triangles

A triangle has three angles and three sides. Triangles may be classified by their angles.

Language Notes

Multiple Meanings
These words have more than one meaning.

☐ **acute**
1. measuring less than 90°
2. sharp

☐ **right**
1. measuring 90°
2. correct

☐ **obtuse**
1. measuring more than 90°
2. blunt

Acute triangle	Right triangle	Obtuse triangle
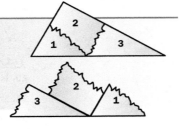		
3 acute angles	1 right angle	1 obtuse angle

A triangle also may be classified by its sides. The tick marks on the sides indicate sides that have the same length, or are **congruent** ($\cong$) **sides.**

Equilateral triangle	Isosceles triangle	Scalene triangle
all sides $\cong$	2 sides $\cong$	no sides $\cong$

Talk and Share

With a partner, draw a large triangle. Label the angles. Cut out the triangle. Tear it into three pieces. Rearrange the pieces so that the vertices are together. What seems to be true about the sum of the angle measures? Do your results match your classmates' results?

Triangle-Sum Rule: The sum of the measures of the angles of any triangle is 180°. So, $m\angle 1 + m\angle 2 + m\angle 3 = 180°$.

VOCABULARY

acute triangle—has 3 acute angles
right triangle—has 1 right angle
obtuse triangle—has 1 obtuse angle
congruent sides—sides with the same length

equilateral triangle—has 3 congruent sides
isosceles triangle—has 2 congruent sides
scalene triangle—has no congruent sides

LESSON 32 • ANGLES AND TRIANGLES **187**

Teach Triangles

- Have a volunteer read the first paragraph. Ask students to describe *acute*, *right*, and *obtuse* angles. Ask, *Why is the first triangle an* acute *triangle? The second triangle a* right *triangle? The third triangle an* obtuse *triangle?*

- Have a volunteer read the second paragraph. Point out that the symbol for *is congruent to* is a combination of an equal sign (=) and a similarity sign (~). Discuss how congruence includes both same size (=) and same shape (~).

- Tell students that the names for the first two triangles in the second table come from the prefixes *iso-* and *equi-*, meaning "equal," and the suffix *-lateral*, meaning "sides."

Language Notes

Students can think of an *acute* angle as having a "sharp" point and an *obtuse* angle as having a "dull" point.

Talk and Share

Have students draw several more triangles of different shapes and follow the steps described to verify the relationship. Also have them measure the angles to verify that this relationship is true for every triangle.

Answer: The sum of the angle measures is 180°.

Differentiating Instruction

Beginning

Matching Triangles with Types After discussing the types of triangles, give partners a diagram of each and two sets of cards labeled *acute*, *right*, *obtuse*, *equilateral*, *isosceles*, and *scalene*. Have them match the cards with the appropriate triangles.

Intermediate

Describing and Naming Triangles After students study the tables on page 187, give pairs diagrams of the six types of triangles. Have them take

turns describing and naming each type with two different names.

Advanced

Building Triangles Provide groups of students with straws cut into 1-, 2-, 3-, 4-, and 5-in. lengths, three of each length, and short pieces of pipe cleaner. Have them make a triangle of each type on page 187. Ask, *Are there any three straws that will not make a triangle? (2-, 3-, 5-in. straws; two sides together have to measure more than the third in order to form an angle.)*

Activity: How Are They Related?

Give students copies of all six types of triangles shown. Have partners study the diagrams. Ask, *Can you see any relationship between the largest angle and longest side of a triangle?* They should see that sides opposite largest angles are longest, sides opposite smallest angles are shortest, and sides opposite congruent angles are congruent.

Practice

Have volunteers draw a triangle of each type. Have the class check whether the drawings are correct, and tell why or why not.

Assignment Guide
- Beginning 1–18, 22–24
- Intermediate 1–24
- Advanced 1–24

Notes on Exercises
Exercises 4–11, 16–19 If students are having difficulty determining angle measures, help them set up equations similar to those on pages 186 and 187 and then have them solve those equations.

Exercises 20–23 Allow students to work together on these exercises.

Exercise 24 Students can use the equation $m\angle M + m\angle L + m\angle N = 180°$ to help them find the correct answer.

Key Connection

The American engineer and inventor Buckminster Fuller invented large lightweight enclosures that he called "geodesic domes." They are made of polygonal units that are self-supporting and have no internal supports. Part of one is shown on pages 186 and 187. Find a picture of the famous dome *Spaceship Earth* at Walt Disney World® Epcot Center in Florida, and have students tell what shapes are used.

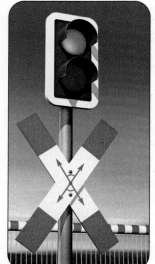

▲ Traffic signal for a railroad crossing

Practice

Classify each triangle as *acute*, *obtuse*, or *right*.
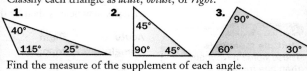
1. 40° 115° 25° **2.** 45° 90° 45° **3.** 90° 60° 30°

Find the measure of the supplement of each angle.
4. 155° **5.** 60° **6.** 130° **7.** 10°

Find the measure of the complement of each angle.
8. 45° **9.** 27° **10.** 75° **11.** 10°

12. What kind of angle pair is made by the red lines in the photo on the left?

Use the figure below on the right for Exercises 13–16.
13. Name a pair of supplementary angles.
14. Name a pair of complementary angles.
15. Name a pair of vertical angles.
16. Find $m\angle FBC$, $m\angle ABF$, and $m\angle DBE$.

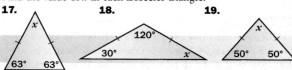

Find the value of x in each isosceles triangle.
17. x 63° 63° **18.** 120° 30° x **19.** x 50° 50°

20. Is an equilateral triangle also isosceles? Explain.

21. Is an isosceles triangle also equilateral? Explain.

22. (SHORT RESPONSE) Do you think every isosceles triangle has two congruent angles? Draw and measure several to check.

23. (SHORT RESPONSE) Do you think every equilateral triangle has three congruent angles? Draw and measure several to check.

24. (MULTIPLE CHOICE) What is $m\angle N$?
A. 135° **B.** 45° **C.** 25° **D.** 60°

Program Resources
Practice Book Use page 80.

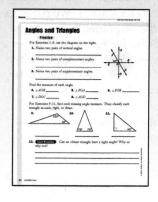

Answers
1. obtuse
2. right
3. right
4. 25° **5.** 120°
6. 50° **7.** 170°
8. 45° **9.** 63°
10. 15° **11.** 80°
12. vertical angles
13. Sample: $\angle DBE$ and $\angle EBF$
14. Sample: $\angle ABD$ and $\angle DBE$
15. Sample: $\angle ABD$ and $\angle CBF$
16. 40°; 140°; 50°

17. 54° **18.** 30°
19. 80°
20. Yes; any two of its sides are congruent.
21. No; it does not necessarily have 3 congruent sides.
22. Yes; the congruent angles are always opposite the congruent sides.
23. Yes; there are 3 congruent sides so there are also 3 congruent angles.
24. B

Acute isosceles ▶
triangle

Activities

Describing When you describe a figure, you provide details that help someone else visualize the figure. A good description can help you organize the details.

Term: acute isosceles triangle

Definition An acute isosceles triangle is both acute and isosceles.	**Characteristics** All three angles are acute. Two sides are congruent. Two angles are congruent.
Examples	**Nonexamples**

not acute

not acute, not isosceles

1. **Describe** Draw an example and a nonexample of a kind of triangle. Describe your example to a partner.

2. **Write** In one or two sentences, explain your nonexamples.

Oral Language

What's Your Angle? Everyone gets a card with an angle on it. Use a protractor to measure your angle. Talk with other students to find someone with an angle that is supplementary to yours. You might ask: *What is the measure of your angle? Do the measures of our two angles add to 180°?*

When everyone has matched supplementary angles, start over. Now look for a complementary angle. Will every angle have a complement? Explain.

Hands On

Can You Draw It? Triangles can be classified by sides or by angles. This means triangles may have more than one classification. Draw a triangle for each description. If no triangle can be drawn, write "impossible" and explain why. See if your drawings match your partner's drawings. Talk about it.

obtuse isosceles	right equilateral	scalene acute
scalene right	right isosceles	obtuse scalene

Teach Describing

- Have students recall that to *describe* means to "talk about."
- Have a volunteer read aloud the definition of *acute isosceles triangle*. Point out the two examples. Then have another volunteer read aloud the characteristics. After discussing the nonexamples, ask, *Can anyone think of another nonexample?* (Sample: *a right isosceles triangle*)
- Give students the term *obtuse scalene triangle* to define and show with examples and nonexamples.

Oral Language

Prepare a set of cards with angles measuring 20°, 25°, 30°, 35°,..., 160°, with two each of 45° and 90°. Review with students the definitions of *complementary* and *supplementary*. Students will be able to find all matching supplementary angles but will find no complementary angles for angles with measures 90°–160°. Have them explain why this is the case.

Hands On

Students will be able to draw every triangle but the right equilateral triangle. Ask, *Why is this triangle impossible to draw?* (It has three congruent angles, and three right angles make a sum of 270°.) Ask, *What other triangle, not listed, is also impossible to draw?* (obtuse equilateral)

Activity: Extend the Lesson

Have students draw two parallel lines *m* and *n* and a third line *t*, called a *transversal*, that crosses both lines but is not perpendicular to them. Have students measure each angle and tell which pairs are congruent, vertical, and supplementary.

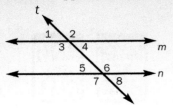

Assessment Book

Use page 54 to assess students' comprehension.

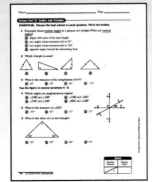

Program Resources

Practice Book Use page 81.
Overhead Transparencies Use 8.

Polygons

STANDARDS CONTENT

Mathematics
- Classify polygons by number of sides
- Identify and classify quadrilaterals

Language
- Recognize multiple meanings of *figure* and *regular*
- Synthesize information about polygons

Materials
- Protractors, rulers

Introduce the Big Idea

Read aloud the Big Idea. Tell students that the figures discussed in this lesson are *plane*, or flat, figures. Ask them to point out some four-sided plane figures in your classroom.

Begin Building Background

Students should recognize some four-sided figures such as *kites* or *parallelograms*.

Teach Key Concepts

- Read the Key Concepts paragraph. Explain that the word *polygon* comes from the Greek word meaning "many angles." Draw this figure on the board. Ask why it is *not* a polygon. (*Sample: The line segments do not meet.*)

- Discuss the terms in the table. Draw a four-sided figure on the board. Have volunteers identify the parts.

Warm-Up Review

Have students sketch an example of each geometric figure.

1. acute angle *CDE*
2. obtuse angle *PQR*
3. right angle *ABC*
4. right triangle *DEF*
5. equilateral triangle *KLM*

Check students' drawings.

Polygons

Big Idea Plane figures can have three or more straight sides. Some four-sided figures have shapes that you have seen many times.

Building Background

▲ My family came to the United States from China, where the very first kites were made and flown.

- **What shapes do you recognize in this picture?**
- **What kind of kite would you like to fly?**
- **Point out some shapes in your classroom.**

Key Concepts

A **polygon** is a closed figure made up of line segments that meet only at their endpoints. Polygons, angles, and sides are important ideas in the study of geometry.

Part	How to Name It
Polygon	List all the vertices in order around the figure: *PQXYZ* and *YXQPZ* are examples.
Side	Use the endpoints: $\overline{PQ}$, $\overline{QX}$, $\overline{XY}$, $\overline{YZ}$, and $\overline{ZP}$.
Angle	Use the angle vertex: $\angle P$, $\angle Q$, $\angle X$, $\angle Y$, and $\angle Z$; $\angle X$ is the same as $\angle QXY$.
Vertex	The vertex is a corner. Only the letter is needed: *P, Q, X, Y, Z.*

Activity: Polygon Trade

Have pairs of students each draw and label a five- or six-sided polygon. Have them exchange drawings and identify and name the polygon, the sides, the angles, and the vertices.

Resource Library

Math at Hand
Polygons and Quadrilaterals 356–357, 364–366

Math on Call
Polygons and Quadrilaterals 345, 362–364

Polygons

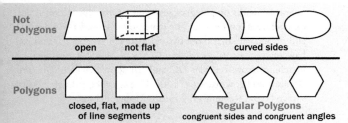

Not Polygons
open   not flat   curved sides

Polygons
closed, flat, made up of line segments

Regular Polygons
congruent sides and congruent angles

The figures in the top row are *not* **polygons.** One figure is open, one is not flat, and the others have curves. The figures in the second row are polygons because they are closed and have line segments for sides. Each segment intersects two others, one at each endpoint. Polygons are flat, meaning that all their points lie in the same plane.

The last three figures in the second row are regular polygons because each is a polygon with all sides congruent and all angles congruent. An equilateral triangle is an example of a **regular polygon.**

You can classify a polygon by the number of its sides. This table names some polygons and tells the number of sides.

> **Language Notes**
>
> **Multiple Meanings**
> These words have more than one meaning.
>
> ☐ figure
> 1. an outline or a shape
> 2. find out
>
> ☐ regular
> 1. a figure with all sides congruent and all angles congruent
> 2. normal or usual

Triangle 3 sides	Quadrilateral 4 sides	Pentagon 5 sides	Hexagon 6 sides	Octagon 8 sides

Talk and Share

Work with a partner and tell which shapes are used for the traffic signs shown. Draw some other signs you have seen and tell their shapes.

VOCABULARY
polygons—closed plane figures whose sides are line segments
regular polygon—a polygon with all sides congruent and all angles congruent

---

Differentiating Instruction

Beginning
Identifying Polygons Say, *A polygon is a closed plane figure made up of line segments.* Then draw a variety of polygons and nonpolygons on the board. Have students tell which figures are polygons and which are not and explain why.

Intermediate
Classifying Polygons After discussing the pictures at the top of page 191, have partners take turns drawing polygons and regular polygons for each other. Have them trade drawings, classify each figure by the number of sides, and tell whether the polygon is a regular polygon.

Advanced
Creating Drawings After discussing page 191, have pairs of students work together to draw two quadrilaterals, one with congruent sides and noncongruent angles and the other with noncongruent sides and congruent angles. Then have them draw two hexagons using the same criteria.

Teach Polygons

- Direct students' attention to the figures in the top row. Ask, *Why is the first figure an open figure?*

- The second group of figures all contain curves. Draw some straight and curved lines on the board, and have students tell whether they are straight or curved.

- Point out that the figures in the second row meet the criteria given in Key Concepts for polygons. Be sure students recognize that *regular* polygons must have congruent angles as well as congruent sides.

- Read the first two paragraphs aloud. Then discuss the last paragraph and the table.

Language Notes

- Ask, *Which meaning of* figure *is used on this page?*

- When discussing *regular,* be sure students know the meaning of *congruent.*

Talk and Share

- After students identify the three traffic-sign shapes (*slow, quadrilateral; yield, triangle; stop, octagon*), ask, *Are the shapes regular polygons?* (*yes*)

- If students are unable to think of other road signs, draw a school crossing sign, a no-passing-zone sign, and a circular railroad-crossing sign on the board. Have students identify the figures and tell whether each is a regular polygon.

Build **VOCABULARY**

Discuss the names of the various polygons. Triangle comes from *tri-,* meaning "three," and *angle.* Quadrilateral comes from *quadri-,* "four," and *-lateral,* "sides." *Pentagon, hexagon,* and *octagon* all have the suffix *-gon,* meaning "angles." Their prefixes come from "five," "six," and "eight," respectively.

Have volunteers name other English words with the given prefixes.

Teach Quadrilaterals

- As you discuss the quadrilateral at the top of the page, be sure students know what tick marks are. Point out all of the markings that indicate pairs of congruent parts and pairs of parallel lines. Then review the symbols used in the notations.

- Work through the diagram of the quadrilaterals. Ask volunteers to describe all characteristics of each figure. Ask students to classify quadrilateral *ABCD* (*trapezoid*) and their book cover (*rectangle*).

- Work through the development of the angle-measure sum. Have students each draw a random quadrilateral and measure the angles to verify the relationship.

Talk and Share

Students should find that $\angle A \cong \angle C$ and $\angle B \cong \angle D$. They should also find that $m\angle A + m\angle B = 180°$, $m\angle B + m\angle C = 180°$, $m\angle C + m\angle D = 180°$, and $m\angle D + m\angle A = 180°$, so the angles in these last four pairs are supplementary.

Build VOCABULARY

Have students identify each figure as you read these descriptions aloud:

- My four sides are congruent (*rhombus, square*).

- My four angles are congruent (*rectangle, square*).

- I have four sides (*quadrilateral, parallelogram, trapezoid, rectangle, rhombus, square*).

- I have two pairs of parallel sides (*parallelogram, rectangle, rhombus, square*).

- I am a parallelogram with four right angles (*rectangle, square*).

- I have only one pair of parallel sides (*trapezoid*).

- My four angles are right angles and my sides are congruent (*square*).

Quadrilaterals

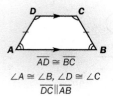

$$\overline{AD} \cong \overline{BC}$$
$$\angle A \cong \angle B, \angle D \cong \angle C$$
$$\overline{DC} \parallel \overline{AB}$$

Special marks on polygons give you information. Look at the **quadrilateral** on the left. The matching tick marks on sides *AD* and *BC* indicate that those two sides are congruent. $\angle D$ and $\angle C$ have matching arcs, so $\angle D \cong \angle C$. Also, $\angle A \cong \angle B$. Finally, the matching arrows on sides $\overline{DC}$ and $\overline{AB}$ show that sides *DC* and *AB* are parallel, written $\overline{DC} \parallel \overline{AB}$. Five special quadrilaterals are shown below. Remember, $\parallel$ means "is parallel to."

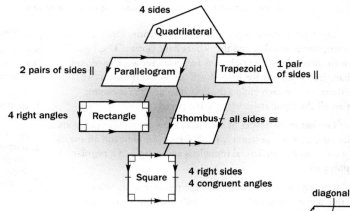

Talk and Share

You and your partner each should draw a parallelogram. Label the vertices *A*, *B*, *C*, and *D*. Measure each angle. Tell what you can conclude about each angle pair: $\angle A$ and $\angle B$, $\angle A$ and $\angle C$, $\angle A$ and $\angle D$, $\angle B$ and $\angle C$, $\angle B$ and $\angle D$, $\angle C$ and $\angle D$. Talk about it.

Notice that a **diagonal** separates a quadrilateral into two triangles. So, the sum of the angle measures in a quadrilateral is 360°. Find the measure *x* of the fourth angle in the diagram.

$$120° + 80° + 125° + x = 360°$$
$$325° + x = 360°$$
$$x = 35°$$

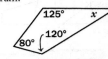

VOCABULARY
quadrilateral—a polygon with 4 sides
parallelogram—a quadrilateral with 2 pairs of parallel sides
trapezoid—a quadrilateral with only 1 pair of parallel sides
rectangle—a parallelogram with 4 right angles
rhombus—a parallelogram with 4 congruent sides
square—a parallelogram with 4 right angles and 4 congruent sides
diagonal—a segment in a polygon that connects 2 vertices but is not a side

---

Differentiating Instruction

Beginning
Classifying Quadrilaterals On the board, draw an example of each type of quadrilateral pictured on page 192. Have students come to the board one at a time and tell as much as they can about each one. Label each with its name.

Intermediate
Identifying Polygons
Give pairs of students enlarged copies of this tangram pattern. Have

them identify each polygon. Then have them use all the pieces and try to make other polygons or fanciful figures such as birds or boats.

Advanced
Making a Mobile of Quadrilaterals
Give pairs of students string, construction paper, and scissors, and have them make a mobile of the quadrilateral diagram. Each shape should be accurate and labeled with its name.

Practice

Use Figure 1 for Exercises 1–5.

1. How many sides does the figure have?

2. Based on the number of sides, what kind of polygon is it?

3. Do the sides appear to be congruent?

4. Do all the angles appear to be congruent?

5. Is the figure a *regular* polygon?

6. Repeat Exercises 1–5 for Figure 2.

7. Name three special types of parallelograms.

8. Draw a rhombus with all right angles. What is another name for this rhombus?

9. Draw a hexagon and an octagon. Tell how many sides each one has.

10. Look at the five signs. Which signs are quadrilaterals? Describe the signs that are not quadrilaterals.

11. Three angle measures in a quadrilateral are 65°, 100°, and 75°. What is the measure of the fourth angle?

Figure 1

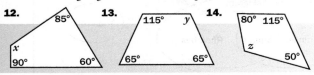

Figure 2

Find the missing angle measure in each quadrilateral.

12. (quadrilateral with angles 85°, x, 90°, 60°)

13. (quadrilateral with angles 115°, y, 65°, 65°)

14. (quadrilateral with angles 80°, 115°, z, 50°)

15. **MULTIPLE CHOICE** Two angles in a parallelogram have a measure of 70° each. If the other two angles are congruent, what is the measure of each?
   A. 140°   **B.** 110°   **C.** 30°   **D.** 20°

LESSON 33 • POLYGONS   **193**

Practice

Review the ideas in this lesson by having students draw an example of each polygon as you name it. Encourage volunteers to name all the properties of each.

Assignment Guide
■ Beginning 1–10, 12, 15
■ Intermediate 1–13, 15
■ Advanced 1–15

Notes on Exercises
Exercise 6 Students will probably note that some of the sides and some of the angles appear to be congruent. However, not *all* sides and angles are congruent.

Exercise 10 Ask, *Are any of the figures regular polygons?* (*the intersection sign*) Then ask, *Is the railroad crossing sign a polygon?* (*yes*) *How many sides does it have?* (*12 sides*)

Exercises 12–14 You may want students to write an equation for each quadrilateral.

Exercise 15 Be sure students account for all four angles in the quadrilateral.

Answers
1. 6 sides
2. hexagon
3. yes
4. yes
5. yes
6. 6 sides; hexagon; no; no; no
7. rectangle, rhombus, square
8. 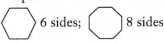 square
9. Samples: ⬡ 6 sides; ⯃ 8 sides
10. Camping, intersection, speed limit; the pedestrian-crossing sign is a pentagon; the railroad-crossing sign has 12 sides.
11. 120°
12. 125°
13. 115°
14. 115°
15. B

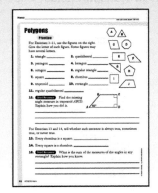

Teach Synthesizing

■ Tell students that sometimes a table helps to *synthesize* or "pull together" many bits of information.

■ Ask students to explain the meaning of *opposite* as used in the table. Draw several quadrilaterals on the board, and have volunteers point out opposite sides and opposite angles.

See Additional Answers, page T40.

Oral Language

Extend this activity by including some or all of these terms: *triangle, isosceles triangle, right triangle, equilateral triangle, hexagon,* and *octagon*.

Partner Practice

Review with students the uses of Venn Diagrams (Overhead Transparency 31).

Answers: rhombus: parallelogram, quadrilateral; rectangle: parallelogram, quadrilateral; square: rhombus, rectangle, parallelogram, quadrilateral

Key Connection

Invite students to investigate properties of the diagonals of a rhombus, a rectangle, a square, and a kite. (*rhombus—perpendicular, bisect each other; rectangle—congruent, bisect each other; square—congruent, perpendicular, bisect each other; kite—perpendicular, one bisects the other one.*)

Activities

Synthesizing   When you synthesize, you pull together information from several places. Synthesize the information you learned about quadrilaterals by copying and completing this table. Work with a partner. Draw the quadrilaterals and measure as needed.

Quadrilateral	How many pairs of sides are ‖ ?	Are opposite sides ≅ ?	Are all sides ≅ ?	Are opposite angles ≅ ?	Are all angles right angles?
trapezoid	1 pair	sometimes	no	no	no
parallelogram	2 pairs	yes	sometimes	yes	sometimes
rectangle	?	?	?	?	?
rhombus	?	?	?	?	?
square	?	?	?	?	?

Oral Language

Tell All   Work in small groups. The group should have five cards. Each card has one of these words: *parallelogram, trapezoid, square, rectangle,* and *rhombus*. Each student selects a card. Say and draw the figure named on the card. Then tell all you know about the figure.

Partner Practice

Name It   The Venn Diagram below shows how quadrilaterals are related. Work with a partner. Give all the other names for each of these three figures: rhombus, rectangle, and square.

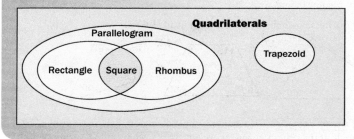

Program Resources

Practice Book Use page 83.
Overhead Transparencies Use 31.

Assessment Book

Use page 55 to assess students' comprehension.

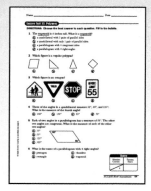

Activity: Culture Connection

With its origin in China more than 2,000 years ago, the kite is the oldest form of aircraft. It is named after a graceful bird, the kite. Benjamin Franklin used a kite to prove that lightning is electricity. The U.S. Weather Bureau used kites to measure the weather for many years.

For more information, refer students to:

• http://www.kites.org/zoo

• http://www.aloha.net/~bigwind/20kidskites.html

Congruent Figures

Talk and Explore

Big Idea Often when figures are congruent, they fit together. Many objects and designs are made from congruent polygons.

Building Background

▲ People in my grandfather's village made beautiful tiles. He helped paint and bake the tiles.

■ **What do you see in the picture?**

■ **Name one shape that you see repeated in the tiling design.**

■ **Which tiles look as if they have the same size and shape?**

Key Concepts

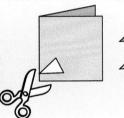

The triangle on the left was drawn on a folded sheet of paper and then cut out, giving two triangles exactly the same shape and same size. These two triangles are **congruent**. When you place one of the triangles on top of the other, the sides that match up are **corresponding sides**. The angles that match up are **corresponding angles**.

LESSON 34 • CONGRUENT FIGURES **195**

Activity: A Cut Above

Have students create their own congruent figures using scissors and folded paper. Encourage them to cut a quadrilateral or some other polygon. Then have them label the corresponding pairs of sides using lower-case letters (*a*, *b*, *c*) and corresponding pairs of angles using numbers (*1*, *2*, *3*). Alternatively, they can draw and trace a polygon and label both figures.

Resource Library

Math at Hand
Congruent Figures 372–374

Math on Call
Congruent Figures 381–383

Congruent Figures

STANDARDS CONTENT

Mathematics
■ Identify congruent figures
■ Find missing angle or side-length measures in congruent figures

Language
■ Recognize multiple meanings of *corresponding*
■ Summarize information about congruent figures

Materials
■ Protractors, rulers

Introduce the **Big Idea**

Read aloud the Big Idea. Review the meaning of *congruent*. Ask, *When have you worked with congruent sides and angles?*

Begin **Building Background**

Let the students know that this is a close-up of part of the Alhambra, a fourteenth-century palace-citadel in Granada, Spain. Help students point out patterns and repeated shapes that are exactly the same size.

Teach **Key Concepts**

■ Read the Key Concepts paragraph. Stress that *congruent figures* have the *same shape* and the *same size*.

■ The word *corresponding* used here means "matching." Ask students to draw two triangles of the same size and same shape. Have them point to the corresponding pairs of angles and the corresponding pairs of sides.

Warm-Up Review

Have students sketch an example of each geometric figure.

1. triangle, two congruent sides
2. triangle, two congruent angles
3. quadrilateral, two congruent angles
4. quadrilateral, four congruent angles
5. quadrilateral, two congruent sides
6. quadrilateral, four congruent sides

Check students' drawings.

Teach Congruent Figures

- Read aloud the first paragraph. Then copy the two triangles on the board without the tick and angle marks. Ask, *Which angle is congruent to ∠A?* (∠D) Draw a single arc on ∠A and ∠D. Repeat with the other two angles in *ABC*, noting, *Double and triple arcs are used for the other two pairs of congruent angles.* Repeat the procedure with the triangles' sides. Then write the congruence statement △ABC ≅ △DEF. Point out that the symbol for *triangle* is a triangle.

- Have volunteers read the angle- and side-congruence statements.

- Work through the corresponding- parts table after students identify the pairs of congruent parts.

Talk and Share

- Say, *Remember that the vertices of any two congruent polygons match up in the order they are listed.* Suggest that students sketch two congruent pentagons labeled *BXQRE* and *ACMNT* to better see the correspondence.

- With or without diagrams, students should identify the following congruences: $\overline{BX} \cong \overline{AC}$; $\overline{XQ} \cong \overline{CM}$; $\overline{QR} \cong \overline{MN}$; $\overline{RE} \cong \overline{NT}$; $\overline{BE} \cong \overline{AT}$; ∠B ≅ ∠A; ∠X ≅ ∠C; ∠Q ≅ ∠M; ∠R ≅ ∠N; ∠E ≅ ∠T

Congruent Figures

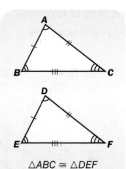

△ABC ≅ △DEF

Figures are congruent if they have the same shape and the same size. If two figures are **congruent figures**, then their corresponding angles and corresponding sides are congruent.

The symbol for triangle is △. △*ABC* and △*DEF* at the left are congruent triangles. This is written △*ABC* ≅ △*DEF*. Congruent triangles have congruent corresponding angles.

∠A ≅ ∠D, ∠B ≅ ∠E, ∠C ≅ ∠F

Also, the corresponding sides are congruent.

$\overline{AB} \cong \overline{DE}$, $\overline{AC} \cong \overline{DF}$, $\overline{BC} \cong \overline{EF}$

You can list all the **corresponding parts** for any two congruent polygons. When you write names for congruent polygons, you must list corresponding vertices in the same order for both polygons.

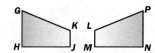 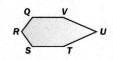 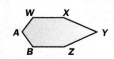

If GHJK ≅ PNML, then	
∠G ≅ ∠P	$\overline{GH} \cong \overline{PN}$
∠H ≅ ∠N	$\overline{HJ} \cong \overline{NM}$
∠J ≅ ∠M	$\overline{JK} \cong \overline{ML}$
∠K ≅ ∠L	$\overline{KG} \cong \overline{LP}$

If QRSTUV ≅ WABZYX, then			
∠Q ≅ ∠W	∠T ≅ ∠Z	$\overline{QR} \cong \overline{WA}$	$\overline{TU} \cong \overline{ZY}$
∠R ≅ ∠A	∠U ≅ ∠Y	$\overline{RS} \cong \overline{AB}$	$\overline{UV} \cong \overline{YX}$
∠S ≅ ∠B	∠V ≅ ∠X	$\overline{ST} \cong \overline{BZ}$	$\overline{VQ} \cong \overline{XW}$

Talk and Share

Work with a partner. Suppose you know that pentagon *BXQRE* is congruent to pentagon *ACMNT*. Work together to list each pair of congruent corresponding sides and each pair of congruent corresponding angles.

VOCABULARY

congruent figures—figures that have the same size and same shape. Their corresponding parts also are congruent.

corresponding parts—parts that match up when you place a figure on top of a congruent figure

Activity: Make Them Congruent

Ask partners to draw four identical triangles on grid paper (Overhead Transparency 15). Have them cut out the triangles and stack them to make sure they are identical.

Challenge partners to arrange the four triangles with no overlap, to form one large triangle that has the same shape as the smaller ones.

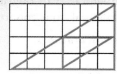

Differentiating Instruction

Beginning
Exploring Congruence After discussing congruent figures, have partners each draw a triangle and a quadrilateral on grid paper, with one side along a grid line. Then have them exchange papers and draw figures congruent to those on their paper.

Intermediate/Advanced
Drawing Congruent Polygons After discussing congruent figures, have partners each draw and label a triangle and quadrilateral on grid paper with one side along a grid line. Then have them exchange papers and draw and label figures congruent to those on their paper. Have them write congruence statements for the figures.

Missing Measures

A carpenter is building a closet under a staircase. The outline of the door is congruent to the outline of the opening.

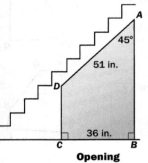

Opening

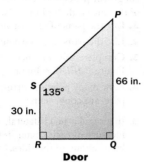

Door

$ABCD \cong PQRS$

For the door, the measure of $\angle S$ is 135°. In the opening, $m\angle A$ is 45°. What is $m\angle P$? What is $m\angle D$? To answer, remember the definition of congruent figures: *If two figures are congruent, then their corresponding sides and corresponding angles are congruent.*

Because $ABCD \cong PQRS$, $\angle A \cong \angle P$ and $\angle D \cong \angle S$.

So $m\angle P = 45°$ and $m\angle D = 135°$.

The *length* of a segment is indicated without the segment symbol. So the length of $\overline{AB}$ is AB. What are the lengths DC, AB, SP, and RQ?

$DC = SR = 30$ inches $AB = PQ = 66$ inches

$DA = SP = 51$ inches $CB = RQ = 36$ inches

Talk and Share

Work with a partner to draw $\triangle XYZ$. Make it isosceles, and make the angle formed by the two congruent sides 42°. Then draw $\triangle PQR$ so that it is congruent to $\triangle XYZ$. Work with your partner to find the measures of the three angles of $\triangle PQR$.

Teach Missing Measures

■ Read the first paragraph aloud. Sketch the opening and the door on the board. Ask for the congruence statement for the two figures (ABCD ≅ PQRS).

■ Read the second paragraph, stressing the definition of congruent figures. Have volunteers write on the board congruence statements for all the angles and sides of the two figures.

■ Ask, *What are the measures of ∠C and ∠B? (90°) How do you know?* If they are not sure, point out the right-angle symbol with each angle.

■ Read the last paragraph. Point out that the statements students wrote on the board correspond to the statements in the last paragraph on the page. Ask, *What is different here? (The segment names do not have symbols and the sign is* equals.)

Language Notes

Have a volunteer read the two meanings of *corresponding*. Ask, *Do any of you* correspond *with a friend?*

Talk and Share

Students can measure the angles in $\triangle PQR$. But they should also use the fact that the sum of the angle measures in a triangle is 180° to verify that the angle measures are 42°, 69°, and 69°.

Differentiating Instruction

Beginning
Finding Missing Measures in Triangles
On the board, draw $\triangle ABC \cong \triangle DEF$. Draw the triangles so that all the parts are of obviously different sizes. Write the congruence statement underneath the triangles. Have volunteers point out congruent angles and congruent sides. Write in several measures of angles and sides in $\triangle ABC$. Have volunteers write the corresponding measures in $\triangle DEF$.

Intermediate/Advanced
Finding Missing Measures in Quadrilaterals Have partners each draw a quadrilateral $ABCD \cong$ quadrilateral $EFGH$ and write the congruent statement underneath the figures. Have them label two angle sizes and two side lengths in $ABCD$ and angle sizes and side lengths for the remaining corresponding parts in $EFGH$. Have them exchange papers, list the congruent angles and sides, and fill in the missing measures.

Activity: Pretty Patterns

Have pairs of students work together to make designs similar to the wall design on page 195. Tell them to use several different polygons in their designs. Have them color their designs, or give them scissors, paste, and several colors of construction paper to glue their designs onto another sheet of paper. Display their designs on the bulletin board.

Practice

Have students measure the sides and angles in the figures for Exercises 1–4 to verify that they are congruent.

Assignment Guide
- Beginning 1–6, 9–13
- Intermediate 1–13
- Advanced 1–13

Notes on Exercises

Exercises 1–4 Some students may not recognize the congruence in the two pentagons because they are mirror images of each other. Suggest that they flip one of the figures or use the results from measuring.

Exercise 5 Review the term *regular polygon.* Ask, *What is the sum of the angle measures in any quadrilateral?* (360°)

Exercise 7 Ask, *What would happen to the roof if the trusses in the picture were not all congruent?*

Exercise 9 Be sure students give the correct correspondence before answering Exercise 10.

▲ The space shuttle *Endeavour* was launched on May 7, 1992.

Practice

The space shuttle has fins that look like congruent pentagons. Use the diagrams of the fins on the right for Exercises 1–4.

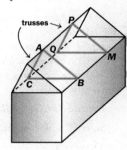

1. List the pairs of congruent angles.
2. List the pairs of congruent sides.
3. Complete this sentence: Figure *BAEDC* ≅ Figure _____.
4. How many pairs of corresponding parts are congruent?
5. In a regular quadrilateral, what is the measure of each angle? Tell what you know about all the sides.
6. What is another name for a regular quadrilateral?

The diagram at the right shows trusses. They are the triangular supports that hold up the roof of a building. Use the diagram for Exercises 7–10.

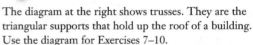

7. Why is it important for all the triangles formed by trusses to be congruent?
8. If $m\angle C = 72°$, what is $m\angle Q$? Tell how you know.
9. Complete this statement: $\triangle CBA \cong \triangle$____ .
10. Which vertices correspond in the two labeled triangles?
11. Find x, y, and z.   **12.** Find r, s, and t.

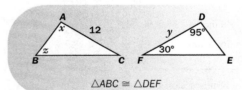

$\triangle ABC \cong \triangle DEF$

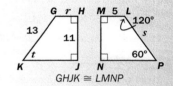

$GHJK \cong LMNP$

13. (SHORT RESPONSE) A farmer is testing different seeds on two triangular fields. She labeled the fields $\triangle OLD$ and $\triangle NEW$. If $\triangle OLD \cong \triangle NEW$, list the pairs of congruent parts. Tell how you know which vertices correspond.

Program Resources

Practice Book Use page 84.

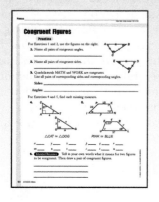

Answers

1. $\angle A \cong \angle G$; $\angle B \cong \angle K$; $\angle C \cong \angle J$; $\angle D \cong \angle I$; $\angle E \cong \angle H$
2. $\overline{AB} \cong \overline{GK}$; $\overline{BC} \cong \overline{KJ}$; $\overline{CD} \cong \overline{JI}$; $\overline{DE} \cong \overline{IH}$; $\overline{EA} \cong \overline{HG}$
3. *KGHIJ*
4. 10 pairs
5. 90°; all four sides are congruent.
6. square
7. Sample: If the trusses were not congruent, the roof line would not be straight.

8. 72°; $\triangle ABC \cong \triangle PMQ$
9. *QMP*
10. C, Q; B, M; A, P
11. $x = 95°$, $y = 12$, $z = 55°$
12. $r = 5$, $s = 13$, $t = 60°$
13. $\angle O \cong \angle N$; $\angle L \cong \angle E$; $\angle D \cong \angle W$; $\overline{OL} \cong \overline{NE}$; $\overline{LD} \cong \overline{EW}$; $\overline{OD} \cong \overline{NW}$; vertices are given in the order of their correspondence.

Activities

Summarizing When you summarize, you organize information and talk about the main points. Work with a partner to summarize what you know about two congruent figures.

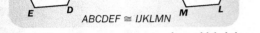

1. Identify Copy and complete the table for the two congruent hexagons. Identify all pairs of congruent sides and all pairs of congruent angles.

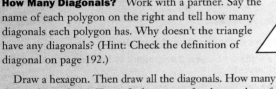

ABCDEF ≅ IJKLMN

2. Draw Draw two congruent triangles and label the vertices.

3. Summarize Tell your partner which pairs of sides and pairs of angles in the triangles are congruent. Tell how you know.

Hands On

How Many Diagonals? Work with a partner. Say the name of each polygon on the right and tell how many diagonals each polygon has. Why doesn't the triangle have any diagonals? (Hint: Check the definition of diagonal on page 192.)

Draw a hexagon. Then draw all the diagonals. How many diagonals are there? Try to find a pattern for the number of diagonals in a polygon. Order your data by the number of sides. See if you can predict the number of diagonals a heptagon (7-sided polygon) has. Draw it to see if you are right.

Oral Language

Long May It Wave Work with a partner. Tell which parts of the flag of the United States are congruent. Choose a different country and look up its flag. Draw the flag and then tell which parts are congruent. Share your drawings and findings with the class.

LESSON 34 • CONGRUENT FIGURES **199**

Teach Summarizing

■ Ask, *What word do you know that is similar to* summarize? If they say "sum," connect this to the idea that to summarize is to cover all the major parts.

■ To extend the activity, you might ask students to repeat Exercises 2 and 3 using quadrilaterals.

Answers: ∠A ≅ ∠I; ∠B ≅ ∠J; ∠C ≅ ∠K; ∠D ≅ ∠L; ∠E ≅ ∠M; ∠F ≅ ∠N; $\overline{AB}$ ≅ $\overline{IJ}$; $\overline{BC}$ ≅ $\overline{JK}$; $\overline{CD}$ ≅ $\overline{KL}$; $\overline{DE}$ ≅ $\overline{LM}$; $\overline{EF}$ ≅ $\overline{MN}$; $\overline{FA}$ ≅ $\overline{NI}$

Hands On

■ Suggest that students make a table with two rows, like the one below. They might be better able to discern the pattern.

	Triangle	Quadrilateral
Sides	3	4
Diagonals	0	2

■ They should find that a hexagon has 9 diagonals and a heptagon has 14 diagonals. Ask students to describe the pattern. (*Add 2, add 3, add 4, add 5, ...*)

Oral Language

The stars in the United States flag are congruent, as are all the short stripes and all the long stripes.

Activity: Culture Connection

The Alhambra was built around 1300 by the Moors in Granada, Spain. The Moors were Muslims from North Africa. Their religion forbids showing *living* things on the walls of a house of worship, so the Alhambra has abstract designs. For more Alhambra patterns, have students go to:

• http://www.GreatBuildings.com/buildings/The_Alhambra.html
• http://weasel.cnrs.humboldt.edu/~spain/alh

Assessment Book

Use page 56 to assess students' comprehension.

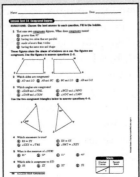

Program Resources

Practice Book Use page 85.

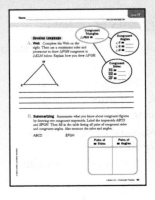

Similar Figures

STANDARDS CONTENT

Mathematics
- Identify similar figures
- Apply properties of similar figures

Language
- Recognize multiple meanings of *model*
- Identify properties of similar figures

Materials
- Grid paper (Overhead Transparency 15)

Introduce the [Big Idea]

Read aloud the Big Idea. Ask, *Do you know what it means for two things to be* similar? On the board, draw two triangles that are similar but of different sizes. Students should see triangles that look alike but are not the same size.

Begin [Building Background]

Invite students to share information about dollhouses or model airplanes, trains, or cars.

Teach [Key Concepts]

- Read the Key Concepts paragraph. Review the concept of *proportion*.
- Ask, *Why are the corresponding angles of the two triangles shown congruent?* Remind students that the Triangle-Sum Rule says that the sum of the angle measures in a triangle is 180°.
- Ask, *Why are the corresponding sides of the two triangles proportional?* Students should see that the ratio of each side length of △ABC to the corresponding side length of △FED is 3 to 6.

Warm-Up Review

Have students sketch an example for each exercise.

1. two congruent squares
2. two congruent nonsquare rectangles
3. two congruent nonsquare rhombuses
4. two congruent trapezoids

Similar Figures

[Big Idea] You can draw a figure that is the same as another figure in all ways but size. The new figure will be similar to the original. The new size may be easier to work with.

Building Background

▲ In my native country, making dollhouses is an art.

- Describe the furniture in the tiny room shown above.
- What likenesses are there between the furniture in the tiny room and the furniture in a real house?
- How would you draw two things that are the same shape but different sizes?

Key Concepts

Equilateral triangles are good examples of **similar figures.** They come in all sizes, but their shapes always are the same. All the angles measure 60°, so pairs of corresponding angles are congruent. The sides of one equilateral triangle are **proportional** to the sides of the other equilateral triangle.

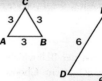

Similar Triangles

Congruent Corresponding Angles
$\angle A \cong \angle D$, $\angle B \cong \angle E$, $\angle C \cong \angle F$

Proportional Corresponding Sides
$\frac{AB}{DE} = \frac{3}{6}$, $\frac{AC}{DF} = \frac{3}{6}$, and $\frac{BC}{EF} = \frac{3}{6}$

 Activity: Toon In

Provide students with cartoon figures from newspapers or magazines. Have them tape a figure to $\frac{1}{4}$-in. grid paper (Overhead Transparency 15) and draw the grid lines over the cartoon. Then have them copy the cartoon, square by square, onto $\frac{1}{2}$-in. or 1-in. grid paper. Have them compare the original cartoon and their reproductions and give the ratio of the large figure to the small one.

Resource Library

Math at Hand
Similarity 369–371

Math on Call
Similarity 376, 378–379

Similar Figures

A decorator drew two models of a triangle that was formed by the refrigerator, sink, and stove in a kitchen. Triangles *ABC* and *XYZ* are **similar figures** because they have exactly the same shape. This is written $\triangle ABC \sim \triangle XYZ$. The symbol $\sim$ means "is similar to."

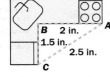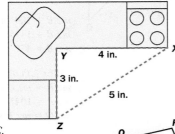

If you measure the angles, you find that $\angle A \cong \angle X$, $\angle B \cong \angle Y$, and $\angle C \cong \angle Z$. So the corresponding angles are congruent. The sides of $\triangle ABC$ are 2 inches, 1.5 inches, and 2.5 inches. In $\triangle XYZ$, the sides are 4, 3, and 5 inches. Each side of $\triangle XYZ$ is twice as long as its corresponding side in $\triangle ABC$.

$$\frac{XY}{AB} = \frac{4}{2} = \frac{2}{1}, \frac{ZY}{CB} = \frac{3}{1.5} = \frac{2}{1}, \text{ and } \frac{XZ}{AC} = \frac{5}{2.5} = \frac{2}{1}$$

If ratios of corresponding sides are equal, the sides are **proportional**. With congruent corresponding angles and proportional corresponding sides, the figures are similar.

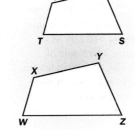

If $QRST \sim XYZW$, then we can list the congruent pairs of angles and the proportions of the corresponding sides.

$$\angle Q \cong \angle X, \angle R \cong \angle Y, \angle S \cong \angle Z, \angle T \cong \angle W,$$
$$\frac{QR}{XY} = \frac{RS}{YZ} = \frac{ST}{ZW} = \frac{TQ}{WX}$$

Work with a partner. Look at $\triangle ABC$ and $\triangle XYZ$ at the top of the page. They are similar, but are they also congruent? Draw a pair of congruent triangles. Are they also similar triangles? Explain your thinking.

VOCABULARY

similar figures—figures having the same shape but not necessarily the same size. The corresponding angles of similar figures are congruent and corresponding sides are proportional.

proportional—*a* and *b* are proportional to *c* and *d* if $\frac{a}{b} = \frac{c}{d}$ ($b \neq 0$ and $c \neq 0$).

Language Notes

Multiple Meanings
This word has more than one meaning.

☐ model
1. something done or made to illustrate a problem
2. a smaller version
3. a good example

Teach Similar Figures

- Have a volunteer read the first paragraph. Talk with students about what a decorator does. Tell them that these diagrams are plans for part of a kitchen. Have students identify each appliance in the diagram. Ask students to measure the angles in the two triangles to verify that corresponding pairs are indeed congruent (*90°, 58°, 32°*).

- Write the side-length proportions on the board. If students don't recognize that the second and third ratios are 2 to 1, have them verify using cross products.

- Point out that the congruence and proportion statements follow from the order of the vertices in the similarity statement.

Talk and Share

- Students should see that $\triangle ABC$ and $\triangle XYZ$ are *not* congruent, as corresponding lengths are not equal.

- Have students give the ratios of the side lengths in their congruent triangles (*1 to 1*). So, the triangles are similar as well as congruent.

Language Notes

The first definition is the one used on the page. The kitchen diagrams are *models*. Ask students to share what they know about *model*, as in the remaining definitions.

Differentiating Instruction

Beginning
Finding Similarities Have partners draw a right triangle and a rectangle on grid paper, right angles along grid lines, and exchange papers. Have the partner draw triangles and rectangles with side lengths twice as long. Ask, *Are the new figures similar to the originals?* (*yes*)

Intermediate
Using Diagonals Have students draw several rectangles on grid paper, sides along grid lines. Have them draw and

extend a diagonal and then form at least one new rectangle using the same diagonal. Ask, *Are the rectangles similar?* (*yes*) They can count or measure to check the proportions.

Advanced
Drawing Similar Triangles Have students draw several triangles on grid paper, one side along a grid line. Tell them to draw a line in each triangle parallel to that side. Ask, *Are the two triangles similar?* (*yes*)

Activity: Make Them Similar

Give students each a sheet of grid paper. Have them draw two or three simple triangles and rectangles on their papers. Have them exchange papers with a partner, and have the partner draw a figure similar to each. Students can measure angles to verify their congruence and measure sides to verify the proportionality.

Teach Applying Similarity

- In this part of the lesson, students will learn to find missing measures in similar figures. On the board, work through finding the missing angle measures. Ask, *How is this like finding missing angle measures in congruent figures?* They should remember that corresponding angles in both congruent and similar figures are congruent.

- Ask, *What is true about side lengths in similar figures?* (*They are proportional.*) Then write the proportions on the board, and work through finding the missing side length.

- Finally, sketch the last two diagrams on the board. Ask, *Why are the two triangles similar? How do you know?* Then work through the solution. Ask, *Does it make sense that the tree's height is 15 feet?* (*Yes; trees are usually taller than people.*)

Talk and Share

Students can think of this problem in two ways. One involves the fact that the vertices of the similar triangles are given in corresponding order, so $\overline{TE}$ corresponds with $\overline{PS}$. Another idea is that $\overline{PS}$ is the shortest side in the smaller triangle, and the shortest side in the larger triangle is $\overline{TE}$.

Look and Read

Applying Similarity

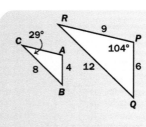

Given that $\triangle PQR < \triangle ABC$, you can use the definition of similar figures to find $m\angle Q$, $m\angle R$, $m\angle A$, and $m\angle B$, and side length AC. Here's how you can do that.

For $\triangle ABC$, $m\angle C = 29°$ ← Given in diagram
$m\angle A = m\angle P = 104°$ ← ∠P and ∠A are corresponding angles of similar triangles.
$m\angle B + 104° + 29° = 180°$ ← Sum of the angle measures in a triangle is 180°.
$m\angle B + 133° = 180°$ ← Simplify.
$m\angle B = 47°$ ← Subtract 133 from both sides.

For $\triangle PQR$,
$m\angle R = m\angle C = 29°$ ← ∠R and ∠C are corresponding angles.
$m\angle P = 104°$ ← Given in diagram
$m\angle Q = m\angle B = 47°$ ← ∠Q and ∠B are corresponding angles.

To find AC, use the proportions of corresponding sides: $\frac{PQ}{AB} = \frac{PR}{AC} = \frac{QR}{BC}$. The diagram shows the lengths PQ and AB, and AC is what you need. So use the first two ratios.

$\frac{PQ}{AB} = \frac{PR}{AC}$ ← Corresponding sides are proportional.
$\frac{6}{4} = \frac{9}{AC}$ ← Substitute the known lengths.
$6 \cdot AC = 36$ ← Find the cross products.
$AC = 6$ ← Solve for AC.

Talk and Share

Look at the diagrams below. Tell how you know which side of $\triangle TRE$ corresponds with $\overline{PS}$. Talk about it with your partner.

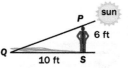

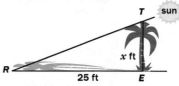

Here is another way to use similar triangles. A man drew similar triangles to find the height of a tree. He used a proportion based on lengths he could measure: his height, 6 feet; his shadow, 10 feet; tree's shadow, 25 feet.

$\triangle PQS \sim \triangle TRE$, so $\frac{PS}{TE} = \frac{QS}{RE}$ and $\frac{6}{x} = \frac{10}{25}$.

Because the triangles are similar, the corresponding sides are proportional. Then the cross products are equal: $10x = 150$ and $x = 15$. The tree's height is 15 feet.

Activity: Model a Room

Give students grid paper and have them work in pairs to design a model room. They might need to measure a room and furniture in order to make a sensible drawing. They should use a given number of units per foot to make the drawing as large as possible. Have them show windows, doors, and furniture and be creative with drawings and color. Display completed drawings.

Differentiating Instruction

Beginning
Finding Missing Measurements
On the board, draw the following diagram. Have volunteers identify corresponding parts in the similar triangles. Then help them find the missing measures (e = 5, f = 3, x = 58°, y = 32°, z = 90°).

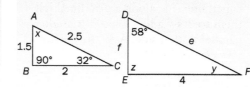

Intermediate/Advanced
Explaining the Process Give students this diagram showing similar triangles. Have them find the height of the airplane 150 meters from takeoff and explain how they found it (*75 meters; sample:* $\frac{50}{150} = \frac{25}{h}$; *h = 75*).

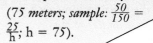

Practice

1. Suppose $\triangle ABC \sim \triangle DEF$. List all three pairs of congruent angles and list the proportions of the corresponding sides.

2. The rectangles on the right show two sizes for class photos: 7 inches by 5 inches and 10 inches by 8 inches. Are the two shapes similar? Tell why or why not.

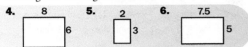

7 in.

5 in.

10 in.

8 in.

3. List three sizes of photographs that are similar to a 6-inch-by-8-inch photograph.

For Exercises 4–6, tell whether each rectangle is similar to the green rectangle at the left.

12

8

4. 8

6

5. 2

3

6. 7.5

5

7. $STUV \sim WXYZ$. Find the five missing angle measures and the two missing side lengths.

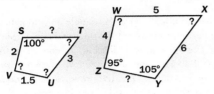

8. Use the figure below. Points D, E, and F separate $\overline{AB}, \overline{AC},$ and $\overline{BC}$ into congruent segments. List the triangles that appear to be congruent. Use the $\cong$ symbol. Then list the triangles that appear to be similar. Use the $\sim$ symbol.

◄ This U.S. Air Force chapel is made up of many congruent triangles.

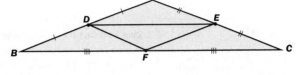

9. Tell whether congruent polygons also are similar polygons. Are similar polygons also congruent polygons? Explain.

10. (SHORT RESPONSE) Suppose $\triangle PQR \sim \triangle STU$ with $PQ = 5$, $ST = 10$, $PR = 13$, and $TU = 30$. Find the two missing side lengths. Which pairs of angles are congruent?

LESSON 35 • SIMILAR FIGURES   **203**

Practice

Ask, *What kind of triangles are similar, even if they are different sizes?* They should recall the Key Concepts diagrams of equilateral triangles. Ask, *Can you think of any other figures that are all similar to each other?* If they do not offer square and circle, draw examples of the shapes on the board. Some students might also suggest regular hexagons and octagons.

Assignment Guide
- Beginning 1–2, 4–8, 10
- Intermediate 1–8, 10
- Advanced 1–10

Notes on Exercises
Exercise 1 It may help students to visualize the similarity if they draw and label the two similar triangles given.

Exercise 8 You may want students to measure side lengths and angles to verify that the four small triangles are congruent and similar to the large triangle.

Exercise 10 If students have difficulty with this exercise, have them sketch the two triangles.

Answers
1. $\angle A \cong \angle D$, $\angle B \cong \angle E$, $\angle C \cong \angle F$,
$\dfrac{AB}{DE} = \dfrac{BC}{EF} = \dfrac{AC}{DF}$

2. No; $\dfrac{7}{10} \neq \dfrac{5}{8}$

3. Samples: 3-by-4-inch; 12-by-16-inch; 24-by-32-inch

4. no   **5.** yes   **6.** yes

7. $m\angle V = 95°$; $m\angle U = 105°$; $m\angle T = 60°$; $m\angle W = 100°$; $m\angle X = 60°$; $ST = 2.5$; $YZ = 3$

8. $\triangle BDF \cong \triangle DAE \cong \triangle FEC \cong \triangle EFD$; $\triangle BDF \sim \triangle DAE \sim \triangle FEC \sim \triangle EFD \sim \triangle BAC$

9. All pairs of congruent figures are also similar because corresponding angles are congruent and corresponding side lengths are proportional (*1 to 1*). All pairs of similar figures may or may not be congruent, as they have congruent corresponding angles, but the side lengths are proportional and not necessarily equal.

10. $SU = 26$, $QR = 15$; $\angle P$ and $\angle S$, $\angle Q$ and $\angle T$, $\angle R$ and $\angle U$

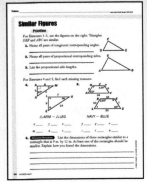

Teach Identifying

- Have volunteers read the four properties given in the Web. Ask volunteers to tell what each property means.

- The property that is *not* necessarily true for similar figures is "same size." Similar figures simply have to have the same shape.

Partner Practice

Students will find their calculations easier if they draw one or two sides of their triangles along grid lines.

Hands On

Students could use grid paper to help them create interesting halves. If the halves fit, they are congruent and thus also similar.

Key Connection

Display a picture of Mount Rushmore. Ask, *Have any of you seen Mount Rushmore? Who are the men whose faces are carved there?* (*George Washington, Thomas Jefferson, Theodore Roosevelt, and Abraham Lincoln*) If students cannot identify the four presidents, explain their significance in United States history. Ask, *Where else have you seen these men's pictures used?* (*U.S. coins and bills*) Explain that Gutzon Borglum, the sculptor who designed the carving, made a model in which 1 inch represented 12 inches on the face of the mountain.

Develop Language

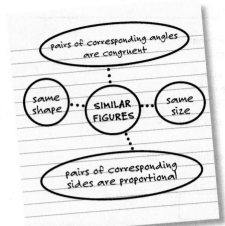

Activities

Identifying You can identify a statement or property by selecting it from a list of statements.

Work with a partner to identify the properties of similar figures. Use the Web on the left.

1. **Identify** There is an error in the Web. One of the properties is not always true. Which one is it?

2. **Explain** Tell your partner why the property you selected is *not* always true.

3. **Explain** Tell how you know the other properties *are* always true.

Partner Practice

Are They Similar? Draw a triangle on grid paper. Work with a partner to measure the sides and angles. Sketch a second triangle that is similar but not congruent to the first triangle. Label all angle measures. Measure only one side of the second triangle. Then use proportions to *calculate* the lengths of the other two sides. Finally, measure the sides of the second triangle to check your calculations. If they match, you did a great job of drawing similar figures.

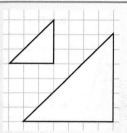

Hands On

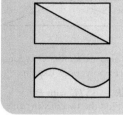

Can You Cut It? Work in small groups. Each group should have 6 rectangular sheets of paper. With each sheet, find a new way to divide the rectangle in half. Two samples are shown. Describe the shapes of your halves. Cut out the halves and see if one half fits exactly on top of the other. If the two halves match, are they similar, congruent, or both? Share your results with the class.

Program Resources

Practice Book Use page 87.
Overhead Transparencies Use 33.

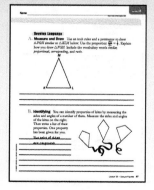

Assessment Book

Use page 57 to assess students' comprehension.

Activity: Culture Connection

Dollhouses were first built for adults in the 1500s. They were 6 feet tall and contained fine furnishings. A very famous one was built in the 1930s for the silent-film star Colleen Moore. For a tour of her dollhouse, visit www.msichicago.org/exhibit/fairy_castle/Fc_home.htm.

Have students solve this problem: The floor size of a model is 12 in. by 15 in. One inch represents 50 ft. What is the floor size of the actual building? (*600 ft by 750 ft*)

Transformations

Transformations

Big Idea Geometry studies shapes and sizes. It also studies movement. This lesson explores ways to move a figure.

Building Background

▲ Some of Escher's pictures remind me of crowds.

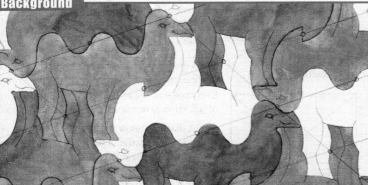

- The artist M.C. Escher created many patterns like this one. He said this type of drawing is a "regular division of a plane." What do you think he meant?

- What would you have to do to move one horse onto another? Would you turn it? Flip it? Slide it?

- How does the picture suggest movement?

Key Concepts

A **transformation** is the movement of a figure in a plane. The figure that you start with and move around is called the **pre-image**. The figure resulting from the movement is called the **image**.

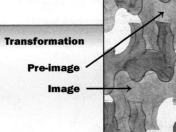

Transformation

Pre-image

Image

LESSON 36 • TRANSFORMATIONS **205**

Activity: Move It!

Give pairs an index card and scissors. Have each student cut out a figure from the card, trace it onto regular paper, and label it *pre-image*. Then have them slide, flip, or turn it and trace it again, labeling the new figure *image*. Have them exchange papers, and have the partner describe the move that was made. If both modeled the same transformation, have them model the other two.

Resource Library

Math at Hand
Transformations 375–377, 379
Tessellations 381

Math on Call
Transformations 384–386, 388
Tessellations 391

Transformations

STANDARDS CONTENT

Mathematics
- Explore three kinds of transformations
- Use transformations to identify and create tessellations

Language
- Explain results of a step-by-step procedure

Materials
- Index cards, scissors

Introduce the **Big Idea**

Read aloud the Big Idea. Cut a large triangle out of cardboard. Ask volunteers to come to the board to demonstrate how they might move the triangle and trace the end result. If none flip or rotate it, show those two moves. Name the moves *slide*, *flip*, and *turn*. Ask, *How does the second triangle compare with the original triangle?* (*It is congruent.*)

Begin **Building Background**

- Ask, *Have any of you seen pictures like this?* Discuss what a *regular division of a plane* means.

- To move from one camel to another, turn it, slide it, or both.

Teach **Key Concepts**

- Read the Key Concepts paragraph. Tell students that the word *transformation* comes from *transform*, meaning to "change."

- Ask a volunteer to explain the difference between *image* and *pre-image*.

Warm-Up Review

Have students draw an example for each exercise. You may want to provide them with grid paper.

1. two congruent right triangles
2. two congruent squares
3. two congruent rectangles
4. two congruent trapezoids
Check students' drawings.

Teach Translations, Reflections, and Rotations

- Have students look again at the picture on page 205. Ask, *Did the size of the camel change?* (*no*) *Are the camels congruent?* (*yes*)

- If students did the activity on page 205, ask, *Are your images and pre-images congruent?* (*yes*)

- Work through the three examples of transformations.

Talk and Share

- Suggest students draw their transformations on grid paper.

- Have students label their drawings with the terms *pre-image, image, translation, reflection, line of reflection, rotation,* and *center of rotation.* Check that they have labeled their drawings correctly.

- Students' images should all be congruent to their pre-images.

Build VOCABULARY

Discuss with students the various meanings of the three terms *translation, reflection,* and *rotation.* Ask if they know another meaning for *translation* (as in *language* translation) and *reflection* (as in *mirror* reflection). Point out the reflection of the Taj Mahal at the bottom of page 206. Ask, *Do you know of anything that* rotates? (*Samples: Earth, windmills*)

Translations, Reflections, and Rotations

A **transformation** of a figure is a change in its **position** or size. In this lesson, we explore three transformations that change only the position of a figure.

The diagram on the right shows a **translation.** Every point of the pre-image is slid the same distance and in the same direction.

Translation (slide)

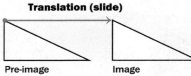

Pre-image   Image

On the left is a **reflection.** The pre-image is flipped over the line, putting the image on the opposite side of the line. Every point of the image is the same distance from the line of reflection as its corresponding pre-image point.

Reflection (flip)

Pre-image   Image
Line of Reflection

The diagram below shows a **rotation.** One point is chosen as the *center of rotation.* The image is turned using that point as the center of the turn. Notice that under these three transformations, images are congruent to their pre-images.

Rotation (turn)

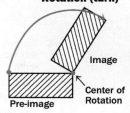

Image
Center of Rotation
Pre-image

Talk and Share

Work with a partner. Draw a translation, a reflection, and a rotation of a shape you choose. Explain what you did.

VOCABULARY

transformation—a change in the position or size of a figure
position—the place where something is located
translation—a change in the position of a figure by sliding it along a straight path

reflection—a change in the position of a figure by flipping it over a line. The line is called the *line of reflection.*
rotation—a change in the position of a figure by turning it around a point. The point is called the *center of rotation.*

Reflection pool at the Taj Mahal in Agra, India ▼

Activity: Slide, Flip, and Turn

Give students grid paper, an index card, and scissors. Have them cut out a triangle or some other polygon from the card. Next have them trace the figure onto the grid paper, with one side along a grid line. Then have them slide the figure along the grid line and trace again. Have them copy their figure and repeat with a flip and a turn. Then have them label their drawings *translation, reflection,* and *rotation.*

Differentiating Instruction

Beginning

Transforming Letters Have pairs of students write simple lower-case and capital letters of the alphabet. Ask them to list any of the letters that might produce another letter if flipped or turned (*Samples: b to d, flipped; b to q, turned; d to p, turned; M to W, flipped or turned; N to Z, turned*).

Intermediate

Discussing Transformations Give pairs of students samples of wallpaper or gift-wrapping paper that illustrate

various transformations. Have them talk with their partners about which transformations, *slide, flip,* and *turn,* are shown.

Advanced

Creating a Pattern Have pairs work together to draw the footprints of a person walking barefoot on the sand. Ask what combination of transformations would create this pattern (*translation and reflection*). Say, *This transformation is called a* glide reflection.

Tessellations

A **tessellation** is a design created by repeating shapes that fit together with no spaces in between. Tilings of floors and walls are examples of tessellations.

Which regular polygons could you use to tile a floor or to create a tessellation? You could use equilateral triangles, squares, or regular hexagons. You could not use regular pentagons because they do not fit together without spaces.

▲ This floor tiling is made with congruent squares.

Equilateral Triangles **Squares** **Regular Hexagons** **Regular Pentagons**

You can create a tessellation with any quadrilateral. Here are two samples.

Sometimes you can use more than one kind of polygon to create a tessellation. The tessellation below is made from squares and regular octagons.

▲ M.C. Escher (1898–1972) used a lizard-like shape for this tessellation.

Talk and Share

Work with a partner. Look at the tessellation above, created with a square and a regular octagon. Could you create a tessellation using only a regular octagon? Talk about it and explain your answer.

VOCABULARY
tessellation—a design created by repeating shapes that fit together with no spaces in between

Teach Tessellations

- Have a volunteer read the first paragraph. Then ask, *Is the camel design on page 205 a tessellation? Why or why not?*

- Discuss the remainder of the page and point out the Escher lizard design. If you can, display more of Escher's tessellations, or have students research his work and bring examples to share with the class.

- Ask, *Do the blue and gold regular pentagons form a tessellation? Why or why not?* (The pentagons alone *leave gaps, so they do* not *form a tessellation. However, the pentagons and rhombuses (white) together do* form a tessellation *using two different polygons.*)

Talk and Share

Students will see that the squares in the tessellation would represent gaps if there are only regular octagons in the design.

Differentiating Instruction

Beginning
Creating a Tessellation Give students an index card and scissors. Have them draw and cut out any type of triangle and use it to create a tessellation. Have them color their drawings and share them with the class.

Intermediate
Describing Transformations Have students follow directions for the Beginning activity, using any type of quadrilateral. Then have them describe their transformations.

Advanced
Testing Polygons Give pairs several index cards and scissors. Have them cut out from the cards an equilateral triangle, a square, a regular pentagon, a regular hexagon, and a regular octagon. (See examples on pages 191 and 192.) Have them rotate each figure around a given point to see if it tessellates and if they see a pattern. (*The pentagon does not tessellate; the angle measures of each other polygon are factors of 360°; the sums of angle measures around a point are 360°.*)

 Activity: Round and Round

Give pairs of students index cards and scissors. Then have them create a tessellation using isosceles triangles with angle measures 30°, 75°, and 75°. They should start by rotating the triangle around a point, with the 30° angle at the point. Then they can add triangles around the edges for one or more rows.

For fun creating tessellations, have students go to this site: http://library.thinkquest.org/16661/mosaics.html.

Practice

Try to display various tessellations created by Escher. They are available on many websites. Then have students describe the transformations used in each one.

Assignment Guide
■ Beginning 1–5, 7–9, 11, 12
■ Intermediate 1–12
■ Advanced 1–13

Notes on Exercises
Exercises 5–7 Have students trace and cut out each figure to help them with their drawings.

Exercises 11 and 12 Students who don't understand these exercises may place a mirror along the line of reflection. The mirror should face the side with the writing.

Practice

In Exercises 1–3, complete the sentence.
1. Translations, reflections, and rotations are 3 types of ___?___.
2. A change in position resulting from a turn is called a ___?___.
3. A ___?___ is a design created by repeating a shape that fits together with no spaces.

4. On the right, triangle 1 is the pre-image. Tell whether each of triangles 2, 3, and 4 is a *translation*, a *reflection*, or a *rotation* of triangle 1.

For Exercises 5–7, tell if the figure can be used to create a tessellation. Make a drawing to show your answer.

5.   **6.**   **7.**

8. Describe each transformation as a *translation*, a *reflection*, or a *rotation*. The pre-images are green, and the images are purple.

Transformation 1   Transformation 2   Transformation 3

9. Look at the Escher picture of fish on the right. Tell which transformation you could use to move fish A onto fish B.

10. Look at the Escher picture of birds on the left. Tell which transformation you could use to move bird X onto bird Y.

In Exercises 11 and 12, trace the figure. What word results from a reflection of the figure over the red line?

11.   **12.**

13. (SHORT RESPONSE) Find the sum: ∠m1 + ∠m2 + ∠m3 + ∠m4. Explain your answer.

Program Resources
Practice Book Use page 88.

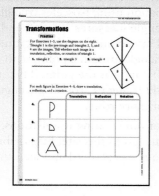

Answers
1. transformations
2. rotation   **3.** tessellation
4. 2, reflection; 3, reflection; 4, rotation
5. no

6. yes

7. yes

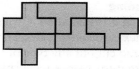

8. rotation; translation; reflection
9. translation   **10.** rotation
11. OH   **12.** WOW
13. 360°; the sum of the angle measures in any quadrilateral is 360°, so $m\angle 1 + m\angle 2 + m\angle 3 + m\angle 4 = 360°$.

Activities

Explaining You can explain a process by carefully describing each step. Work with a partner. You will need a sheet of grid paper and an index card. Cut a figure from your index card.

1. **Rotate** Trace your figure onto grid paper. Rotate the figure 90°. Write *rotation* on the image.

2. **Reflect** Trace your figure and draw a line next to it. Reflect the figure over the line. Write *reflection* on the image.

3. **Translate** Trace your figure. Translate the figure 2 units down and 3 units right. Write *translation* on the image.

4. **Explain** Pick one of the transformations. Explain to your partner step-by-step how you performed the transformation.

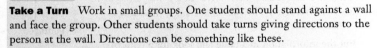

▲ To move from bird A to bird B in this Escher tessellation, reflect A to the right and translate it down.

Oral Language

Take a Turn Work in small groups. One student should stand against a wall and face the group. Other students should take turns giving directions to the person at the wall. Directions can be something like these.

■ *Reflect (flip) over the line at the side of the chalkboard.* (If the line is 3 feet away, the student should end up 3 feet on the other side of the line, facing the wall.)

■ *Translate (slide) 4 steps to the left.*

Take turns being the student who moves. Talk together about whether the move was correct.

Partner Practice

A Perfect Fit With a partner, carefully trace the shape shown at the right onto paper. Cut out the shape. Use your cutout to tessellate a sheet of paper. When you are done, trim the cutout by drawing and cutting along $\overline{DC}$. What shape do you get if you rearrange the resulting two parts? Discuss with your partner how you might make your own shapes that will tessellate.

Develop Language

Teach Explaining

■ Each student should perform every transformation.

■ Be sure that all three transformations are explained and that each partner has a turn at explaining.

Oral Language

Be sure that students also do rotations. You might help them to position themselves at a point on the floor and have them rotate, for instance, 90° in a clockwise direction or 180° in a counterclockwise direction.

Partner Practice

Have pairs create their own original tessellations using the method shown. Then have them share their work with the rest of the class and explain how they made the patterns.

Key Connection

Maurits C. Escher (1898–1972) was a Dutch artist who created lithographs and woodcuts of intricate designs. His colored prints frequently showed tessellations. His black-and-white prints showed impossible situations such as circular waterfalls that are complex optical illusions.

Have students read and report on the *Mathematical Art of M. C. Escher*: http://www.mathacademy.com/pr/minitext/escher/index.asp.

Activity: Extend the Lesson

A *dilation* is another type of transformation that involves enlarging or reducing a figure while maintaining similarity. The number ratios involved in these size changes are called *scale factors*.

Have students solve this problem: How long should a model train car be if the original train car is 50 ft long and the scale factor is 1 in. to 5 ft? *(10 in.)*

Assessment Book

Use page 58 to assess students' comprehension.

Program Resources

Practice Book Use page 89.

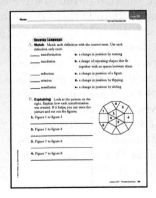

Solve a Simpler Problem

STANDARDS CONTENT

Mathematics
- Solve problems by solving a simpler problem

Language
- Recognize imperatives

Teach Solve a Simpler Problem

- Read aloud the first paragraph. If students do not remember what a hexagon is, refer them to the table in the middle of the page, and review all the polygon names and definitions. Relate the prefixes and suffixes to the number of angles or sides.

- Begin the problem, stressing the three parts of Read and Understand. Continue to work through the problem, focusing on the remaining steps.

Talk and Share

Provide ten pennies and a ruler to each pair or small group. Students can find the height of ten pennies and then multiply by 10 to find the height of 100 pennies. If they wish to verify the computed height, they can measure 25 pennies and multiply by 4 or measure 50 pennies and multiply by 2.

Problem-Solving Skills

Solve a Simpler Problem

Sometimes you can understand how to solve difficult problems by solving a simpler problem first.

Problem: Find the sum of the measures of the angles in a hexagon.

Read and Understand

Need to find: Sum of the measures of the angles in a hexagon
You know: There are six sides and six angles in a hexagon.
Key fact: The sum of the angle measures in a triangle is 180°.

Plan and Solve Solve a simpler problem first. Find the sum of the measures of the angles in a quadrilateral and in a pentagon. Then look for a pattern.

Draw a diagonal of the quadrilateral to divide it into two triangles. The sum of the angle measures is $2 \times 180° = 360°$.

Draw two diagonals from a vertex of a pentagon to divide it into three triangles. The sum of the angle measures is $3 \times 180° = 540°$.

Put the information in a table and look for a pattern.

	Triangle	Quadrilateral	Pentagon	Hexagon
Number of sides	3	4	5	6
Number of triangles	1	2	3	4
Sum of angle measures	$1 \times 180° =$ 180°	$2 \times 180° =$ 360°	$3 \times 180° =$ 540°	?

Answer The sum of the angle measures in a hexagon is $4 \times 180° = 720°$.

Look Back The pattern in the table shows that the sum of the angle measures is (number of sides − 2) × 180°. Then $(6 − 2) \times 180° = 4(180°) = 720°$.

Talk and Share
Work with a partner. Explain how you could solve a simpler problem to help you find the height of a stack of 100 pennies.

Activity: Some Sum!

Have students work together to find the sum of the first ten odd numbers. Remind them that the odd numbers are 1, 3, 5, ... The "sum" of the first odd number is 1, of the first two odd numbers is 4, and of the first three odd numbers is 9. Ask, *What do you notice about these numbers? (They are the squares of 1, 2, and 3.) What is the sum of the first ten odd numbers? (10^2, or 100) The sum of the first 100 odd numbers? (100^2, or 10,000).*

Differentiating Instruction

Beginning
Using a Table to Find Sums Provide diagrams of a triangle, quadrilateral, pentagon, and hexagon. Have students find the sum of angle measures in each and create a table with the sum of the measures. Help them to see that the sum increases by 180° as the number of sides increases by 1.

Intermediate
Explaining the Sums of Angle Measures Follow the directions for the Beginning activity, but have these students *explain why* the sum increases by 180° as the number of sides of the polygon increases by 1.

Advanced
Expressing the Sum of Angle Measures Have students draw a triangle, a quadrilateral, a pentagon, and a hexagon and find the sum of the angle measures in each polygon. Then have them try to write an expression for the sum of the angle measures in *any* polygon ($(n − 2) \cdot 180$).

1. If the sum of the angle measures of a figure is 540°, what kind of figure is it?

2. What is the sum of the angle measures of a square?

3. Find the sum of the angle measures of a decagon (a 10-sided figure).

Use the strategy *solve a simpler problem.*

4. Find the sum of the whole numbers 1 through 50.

5. The seats in a theater are numbered 1 through 200. How many seats have a 3 in the number?

6. Six volleyball players on a team all shake hands with one another. How many handshakes take place?

Choose a strategy and solve each problem.

7. Juan is drawing a border around his bedroom walls using the pattern shown. Will the 36th figure be a triangle or a square?

8. Half of Nadine's books are about candle making. One-fourth of her books are about sailing. The remaining two books are about birds. How many books does she have?

9. For lunch, you choose a meat, a vegetable, and a fruit from the menu on the right. How many different lunches are possible?

~LUNCH MENU~
* Jerk Chicken
* Mongolian Beef
* Red Beans
* Black-eyed Peas
* Banana
* Mango
* Orange

Grammar Spotlight

Imperatives Imperatives are verbs that express a command or a request. They sometimes are followed by exclamation points.

Common Imperatives	Imperatives in This Lesson
Go at once!	*Find* the sum.
Please *do* it now!	*Solve* a simpler problem.
Tell me why you were late.	*Look* for a pattern.
Wash your hands before dinner.	*Choose* a strategy.

1. Think of a sentence with an imperative. Say it aloud and have your partner write it down. Check to see if your partner wrote it correctly.

2. Write down an imperative sentence as your partner speaks one. Have your partner check to see if you wrote it correctly.

3. Talk with your partner about times when imperatives often are used.

SOLVE A SIMPLER PROBLEM **211**

On the board, draw a large circle. Draw a segment joining two points of the circle. Ask, *How many regions are formed?* (2). Then draw another segment, intersecting the first *not* at an endpoint, and ask, *How many regions are formed?* (4) Start a table and have volunteers draw another segment each time, trying to get the maximum number of regions. Have them use the pattern to predict how many regions will be formed by five and six segments (*16 and 22*).

Assignment Guide
■ Beginning 1–5, 7
■ Intermediate 1–6, 8
■ Advanced 1–6, 9

Notes on Exercises
Exercise 2 Have students think of another way to solve the problem (*Sample: Each angle in a square measures 90°; 4 × 90 = 360°*).

Exercise 4 Be sure students include 1 and 50.

Exercise 5 Encourage students to start a list of the numbers.

Exercise 8 Students can work backward to solve this problem.

Grammar Spotlight

Read the paragraph aloud. Have students note that each example has a verb. The subject, *you*, is understood.

Answers
1. pentagon
2. 360°
3. 1,440°
4. 1,275
5. 38 seats
6. 15 handshakes
7. square
8. 8 books
9. 18 combinations

Activity: Real-world Connection

Talk to students about the U.S. fighter plane known as the "stealth bomber." If possible, show them a picture of it. Tell students that its triangular wings enable the plane to fly at speeds as fast as 750 miles per hour. It has been designed to be nearly invisible to radar. Ask students to search the Internet for other devices that benefit from their triangular shape (*Samples: windmills, bridge supports*).

Program Resources
Practice Book Use pages 90 and 91.

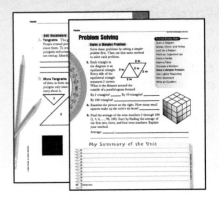

Perimeter and Area

STANDARDS CONTENT

Mathematics
- Find the perimeter of a polygon
- Find the area of a polygon

Language
- Recognize multiple meanings of *base*
- Connect the ideas of perimeter and area for rectangles

Materials
- 1-in. grid paper (Overhead Transparency 15), scissors

Introduce the Big Idea

Read aloud the Big Idea. On the board, draw a random triangle or quadrilateral. Ask a volunteer to point out the distance around it. Have another volunteer point out the space inside.

Begin Building Background

Ask, *Does anyone know what kind of dinosaur is in the photo?* (*Tyrannosaurus Rex*) Then ask, *Why has the area been roped off?*

Teach Key Concepts

Read the Key Concepts paragraph. Ask volunteers to point out the perimeter and the area of the figure you drew on the board.

Build VOCABULARY

Tell students that the prefix of *perimeter* is *peri-*, meaning "around." Ask if anyone can think of the meaning of *-meter* in this context (*measure*).

Warm-Up Review

Have students evaluate each expression for $x = 5$ and $y = 8$.

1. $4x$ *(20)*
2. $x + y$ *(13)*
3. $2x + 2y$ *(26)*
4. $x \cdot y$ *(40)*
5. x^2 *(25)*

Perimeter and Area

Big Idea There are two measurements that relate to plane figures. One is the distance around. The other is the space inside.

Building Background

▲ One summer, my job was to make sure no one stepped inside a fenced-off area at the museum.

- **What do you see in the picture?**
- **Why is a section closed off?**
- **How would you find the total length of the fence for the closed-off section?**

Key Concepts

Perimeter tells you the distance around something. In the picture on the right, the length of the fence is the perimeter. **Area** tells you how much space is inside the figure. The area of the garden is a measure of the space inside the fence.

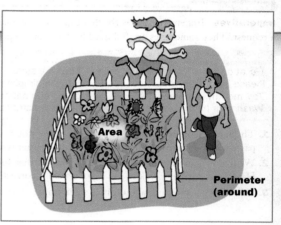

Area

Perimeter (around)

Activity: Measure It

Give students rulers and square tiles. Have them find the distance around the covers of several books and their desktops. Have them give each measure in inches or centimeters. Ask, *What do you call this measure?* (*perimeter*) Then have students pool their tiles and cover a desktop with no gaps and no overlapping. Have them count the tiles and give the measure in terms of tiles. Ask, *What do you call this measure?* (*area*)

Resource Library

Math at Hand
Perimeter and Area 295–297, 299–304

Math on Call
Perimeter and Area 346–347, 354, 356–357, 365–368

Reader's Handbook (red)
Reading Math 117–131

Perimeter

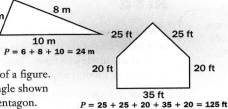

The **perimeter** of a figure is the sum of its side lengths. We use P to represent the perimeter of a figure. $P = 24$ meters for the triangle shown and $P = 125$ feet for the pentagon.

$P = 6 + 8 + 10 = 24$ m

$P = 25 + 25 + 20 + 35 + 20 = 125$ ft

A **formula** is an equation that describes a pattern in math. The opposite sides of a rectangle always are congruent. We use ℓ for length and w for width, so we can write the formula for the perimeter of a rectangle.

$P = \ell + \ell + w + w$	Add the measures of the 4 sides.
$P = 2 \cdot \ell + 2 \cdot w$	$\ell + \ell = 2 \cdot \ell$ and $w + w = 2 \cdot w$.
$P = 2\ell + 2w$	Remember $2w$ means "2 times w."

Rectangle

A square is a rectangle with four congruent sides. This is a formula for the perimeter of a square.

$P = 4s$ $\qquad\qquad s + s + s + s = 4s$.

Square

Find the perimeters of Enrico's house and garage.

House		**Garage**
$P = 2\ell + 2w$	Write the formula.	$P = 4s$
$= 2 \cdot 110 + 2 \cdot 50$	Substitute values.	$= 4 \cdot 45$
$= 220 + 100$	Compute.	$= 180$ meters
$= 320$ meters		

Talk and Share

Work with a partner. A park near Andrew's house is 205 feet long and 415 feet wide. Find the distance Andrew will run if he runs around the park 4 times. Start by drawing a picture of a rectangular park and then label it.

VOCABULARY
perimeter—the distance around a figure
formula—an equation that describes a rule or pattern

LESSON 37 • PERIMETER AND AREA **213**

Teach Perimeter

- Read aloud the first paragraph. Sketch another triangle and a quadrilateral on the board, labeling sides with measures. Have volunteers explain at the board how to find the perimeter of each figure.

- Then draw a rectangle on the board, labeling the sides ℓ and w. Work through the development of the formula for the perimeter. You might want to start with the statement $P = \ell + w + \ell + w$ and progress to the first statement in the text. Review with students the Commutative and Associative properties.

- Repeat this process to develop the formula for the perimeter of a square. Then work through the examples involving Enrico's house and garage.

Talk and Share

Suggest that students label each side of their diagrams with its measure. Have one student in each pair use the formula and the other add the measures. Note that Andrew will run 4 times around the park.

Answer: The perimeter of the park is 1,240 ft; the total distance Andrew will run is 4,960 ft.

Build VOCABULARY

Write *perimeter* on the board and review its meaning. Ask, *Do you know of any other words that end in* -meter? Write their suggestions on the board and elicit the meanings of the words. If no one offers a word, write some of these: *centimeter, kilometer, speedometer, thermometer.* Then ask, *What does each word refer to? (measure)*

⬜ Differentiating Instruction

Beginning
Finding Perimeter Have partners each draw two different figures on grid paper (Overhead Transparency 15), keeping all sides on grid lines. Have partners exchange papers and find the distance around each figure. Say, *You are finding* perimeters.

Intermediate
Explaining How to Find Perimeter
Have partners each draw two different figures on grid paper, keeping all sides on grid lines. Then have them exchange papers, find the perimeters of the figures, and briefly explain how they found their answers.

Advanced
Finding Perimeter Formulas Have students find a perimeter formula for an equilateral triangle in terms of a side length ($P = 3s$). Have them explain their reasoning and then write formulas for the perimeter of a regular hexagon and octagon (P = 6s, P = 8s).

Teach Area

- Read the first paragraph. Ask volunteers to describe a *square inch*, a *square meter*, and a *square foot*.

- Discuss finding the area of the lake and the two rectangles. Then draw a rectangle on the board, with $\ell = 10$ and $w = 5$. Say, *There are no small squares in my drawing. How can you find the area?* Elicit from the students the formula, $A = 5 \times 10 = \ell w$. Follow the same procedure with a square, labeling two adjacent sides $s = 8$. Elicit the formula $A = 8 \times 8 = s^2$.

- Point out that m^2 is shorthand for "square meters."

Language Notes

- Ask, *How does the first definition of* base *relate to the term as it is used on this page?*

- Discuss the second definition of *base*. Ask, *Can anyone see an example of this meaning on the page?* (s^2 *in the square area formula*)

Talk and Share

Give students grid paper and scissors. Have them copy the diagrams and cut out and move the triangle to verify that the area of the parallelogram is 18 units^2.

Build VOCABULARY

Help students understand the term *base*. Refer them to the base of a lamp, a statue, or a trophy, each of which is the *lowest* part.

Then have them think about the word *height*. Draw two segments from the bottom to the top of the board, one perpendicular to the bottom of the board, the other making an angle other than 90° with the bottom of the board. Ask, *Which segment should you measure to get the height of the board?* (*the one perpendicular to the bottom of the board*)

Look and Read

Language Notes

Multiple Meanings
This word has more than one meaning.

- base
1. the bottom of an object
2. a number raised to a power

Parallelogram

$h = 3$ m

$b = 6$ m

h

b

Talk and Share

Work with a partner. If you cut the triangle from the left side of the parallelogram and add it to the right side, what new polygon is formed? What is the area?

Area

A **square unit** is a square with a side length of 1 unit. The **area** (A) of a figure is the number of square (sq) units needed to cover the inside of a figure. For example, a square with side measures of 1 foot is a *square foot*.

Count the square units each figure covers to estimate or to find the area of each figure below.

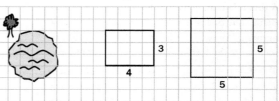

3
4
5
5

The lake covers about 10 whole square units and parts of 4 more. The area is about 14 sq units.

There are 3 rows of 4 squares each. The area is 12 sq units.

There are 5 rows of 5 squares each. The area is 25 sq units.

For the lake, you can only estimate the area. For the rectangle, you quickly can count 3 rows of 4 squares by multiplying 3 times 4. This is the same as length (ℓ) times width (w) of the rectangle. So the formula for the *area of a rectangle* is $A = \ell w$.

The length and width of a square are the same, so the formula for the *area of a square* is $A = s^2$.

Any side of a parallelogram can be the **base** (b). The **height** of a figure is the distance between the top and the bottom. In a parallelogram, the height (h) is the length of a segment drawn perpendicular to the base from the opposite side.

The *area of a parallelogram* is $A = bh$. If $b = 6$ m and $h = 3$ m, then $A = bh = 6 \cdot 3 = 18$ sq meters, or 18 m^2.

w
ℓ

s
s

VOCABULARY

square unit—a square with a side length of 1 unit
area—the number of square units needed to cover the inside of a figure
base—any side of a figure; usually the bottom side
height—in a parallelogram, the length of a segment drawn perpendicular to the base from the opposite side

---

Differentiating Instruction

Beginning
Finding Area Have partners each draw two different figures on grid paper keeping all sides on grid lines. Have partners exchange papers and find the area of each figure. Have them talk about how they did it.

Intermediate
Using an Area Formula Have partners follow the directions for the Beginning activity, but draw a rectangle and a square. Have partners label the lengths of the sides of the figures and discuss how to use a formula to find each area. Areas can be verified by counting squares.

Advanced
Finding Areas of Parallelograms Have partners follow the directions for the Beginning activity, but draw two nonrectangular parallelograms. Have partners label the base and height of the parallelograms and show how to use a formula to find each area. Areas can be verified by counting squares.

Practice

Estimate the area of each figure.

1.

2.

3.

Find the perimeter and the area of each figure.

4. 12 cm, 4.5 cm

5. 11 cm

6. 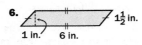 $1\frac{1}{2}$ in., 1 in., 6 in.

For Exercises 7–9, use the diagram on the right.

7. Find the area of each of the rectangles marked A, B, and C.

8. Find the area of the large rectangle with length 17 cm and width 10 cm.

9. Find the area of the colored section.

10. Find the perimeter and area of D. All angles in D are right angles.

Each row in the table below is missing some measures for a rectangle. Copy the table and fill in the missing measures. Then use a ruler and carefully draw each rectangle.

	Rectangle	Length	Width	Perimeter	Area
11.	E	3.5 in.	2.5 in.	?	?
12.	F	?	4 in.	?	10 in.^{2}
13.	G	4 in.	?	16 in.	16 in.^{2}
14.	H	5 in.	x in.	?	$5x$ in.^{2}

15. Find the area of a parallelogram if the base measures 12 inches and the height is one-third as long as the base.

16. (SHORT RESPONSE) Does 46 square yards represent a perimeter or an area? Explain.

Diagram (Exercises 7–9)
5 cm, 4 cm, 10 cm, B: 1.5 cm, A, C: 1.5 cm, 5 cm, 17 cm

Diagram (Exercise 10)
D, 6 ft

Practice

Review the ideas in this lesson by having students find the perimeter and the area of labeled rectangles, squares, and parallelograms you sketch on the board. Have volunteers explain how they found each measure.

Assignment Guide
- Beginning 1–12, 15, 16
- Intermediate 1–16
- Advanced 1–16

Notes on Exercises
Exercises 4–6 You may need to remind students of the significance of the tick marks on the sides of the rectangles.

Exercise 9 Students will need to find the total area of rectangles A, B, and C and subtract the sum from the area of the largest rectangle.

Exercise 10 Students can add the measures of the sides or multiply the measure of one side by 12 to find the perimeter. They should multiply the area of one square by 5 to find the area.

Exercises 11–14 Students may benefit from drawing each rectangle. They can then fill in the formulas with the known measures to find the missing measures.

Exercise 16 Ask, *Why do we use units to give measures of length and square units to give measures of area?*

Answers
1. 8 units^2
2. about 14 units^2
3. 11 units^2
4. 33 cm; 54 cm^2
5. 44 cm; 121 cm^2
6. 15 in.; 6 in.^{2}
7. A: 16 cm^2; B: 7.5 cm^2; C: 7.5 cm^2
8. 170 cm^2
9. 139 cm^2
10. 72 ft; 180 ft^2
11. 12 in.; 8.75 in.^{2}
12. 2.5 in.; 13 in.
13. 4 in.
14. $(10 + 2x)$ in.
15. 48 in.^{2}
16. An area; area is measured in square units, while perimeter is measured in units.

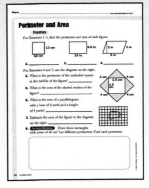

Teach Connecting

- Tell students that to *connect* also means to "join two things together." In this activity, students will connect the ideas of area and perimeter.

- You might want students to use square tiles rather than have them cut squares from grid paper.

- Be sure students find the remaining two rectangles for their table. The measures are: 28 in., 24 in.²; 3 by 8, 22 in., 24 in.²; 4 by 6, 20 in., 24 in.² The area stays the same because 24 squares were used each time. From their table, students will see that as the length and width become closer in size, the perimeter decreases.

Have partners role-play the situation for a path that is $3\frac{1}{4}$ ft by 16 ft and find the number of bags needed and the cost (*13 bags, $195*).

Answer: Seven bags of gravel cover only 28 ft².

Hands On

Because the triangles are congruent, each one has an area equal to half the area of the parallelogram. If students are not convinced, have them actually count the squares and partial squares. The formula, then, is $A = \frac{1}{2}bh$.

Activities

Connecting When you connect ideas, you tell how the ideas are related. Work with a partner to see how area and perimeter are related.

1. **Create** Form rectangles using 24 squares cut from 1-inch grid paper. You should be able to form four rectangles of different sizes.

2. **Compute** Find and record the perimeter and area of each rectangle. Tell why the area is the same for each rectangle.

3. **Connect** Connect by completing this summary sentence: The perimeter decreases as the length and the width _____.

Rectangles Formed of 24 1-inch Squares

Length × Width	Perimeter	Area
24 by 1	50 in.	24 in.²
12 by 2	?	?
?	?	?
?	?	?

Partner Practice

Planning a Path

Customer: I need gravel for a rectangular path that is $2\frac{1}{2}$ feet by 15 feet. That area is $37\frac{1}{2}$ ft². How much will it cost?

Clerk: One bag of gravel covers 4 ft². So for 37 ft² you need 10 bags. At $15 a bag, the cost is $150.

Customer: That's more than I can spend for the project.

Clerk: Well, why not make the path narrower?

Customer: If the path is only 2 feet wide, then the area is 30 ft². I'll need 8 bags of gravel and pay $120. That's better.

Work with a partner. Check the math in the problem. Why does the customer need 8 bags to cover 30 ft²? Share your findings with the class.

▲ A garden with a gravel path

Hands On

Rectangles to Triangles Work with a partner. Draw a rectangle on grid paper. Label the base and the height. Find the area. Cut out the rectangle, and then cut along one diagonal. Show that the triangles formed are congruent by matching one on top of the other. Talk with your partner about what you think the area of each triangle is. Try to write a formula for the area of a triangle based on the area of a rectangle. Test your formula with other triangles.

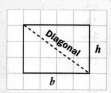

Program Resources

Practice Book Use page 93.
Overhead Transparencies Use 15.

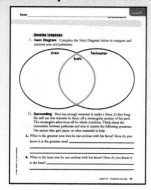

Assessment Book

Use page 59 to assess students' comprehension.

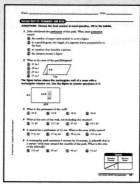

Activity: Real-world Connection

On the board, write this practical problem. *What is the least amount of fencing needed to enclose a given area?* Have students use grid paper to find which type of rectangle has the least perimeter for an area of 16 square units and of 36 square units. They might use the table in Connecting on page 216 as a guide. (*A 4-by-4 square and a 6-by-6 square give the least perimeters.*)

Circles

Big Idea A circle is a special shape with no straight sides. It is a set of points in a plane that are the same distance from the center point. There are special formulas related to circles.

Building Background

▲ Before I went to Hawaii, I didn't know why those hoops were called "hula hoops."

- **What are these people doing?**
- **What games have you played with hoops?**
- **How could you find out the amount of tubing needed for a hoop?**

Key Concepts

Draw a shape using a tack, a pencil, and a string as shown. It's a **circle.** The pencil traces a set of points that are all the same distance from the tack, or a point called the **center.** The length of the string is the **radius,** or the distance from the center to the circle.

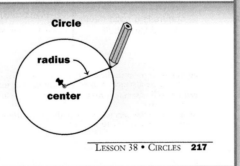

Circle

radius

center

LESSON 38 • CIRCLES **217**

Activity: Circle Around

Give students string and a push pin. Have them use the method shown in the Key Concepts to draw circles of different sizes. Tell them that they are using a simple *compass.* Have them mark the center of one of their circles and then draw a radius. Then have them draw a line segment through the center of the circle with its endpoints on the circle. Ask, *How does this segment compare with the radius?* (*It is twice as long as the radius.*)

Resource Library

Math at Hand
Circles 298, 305, 367

Math on Call
Circles 370, 372–373, 375

Circles

STANDARDS CONTENT

Mathematics
- Find the circumference of a circle
- Find the area of a circle

Language
- Identify confusing word pairs
- Organize information relating to circles

Materials
- String, large and small paper plates, circular paper coaster, scissors, ruler

Introduce the **Big Idea**

Read aloud the Big Idea. On the board, draw a circle and an oval, or egg shape. Ask, *Does either figure have straight sides?* Ask, *Which one is a circle?*

Begin **Building Background**

Ask, *Have any of you ever used a hula hoop? How does the name* hula hoop *relate to Hawaii?*

Teach **Key Concepts**

- Read the Key Concepts paragraph. Use string taped to the board and a piece of chalk at the other end of the string to draw a circle on the board. Have volunteers identify each part and write the name.
- Students can draw their own circles using a simple compass as shown on page 217, or using a paper clip instead of string.

Warm-Up Review

Have students find each product. Remind them of the different ways to indicate multiplication.

1. 4×3.14 (*12.56*)
2. $\frac{1}{2}(8.2)$ (*4.1*)
3. $5 \cdot 5 \cdot 3.14$ (*78.5*)
4. $(\frac{22}{7})(21)$ (*66*)
5. 3.14×32 (*100.48*)
6. $3\frac{1}{7} \times 70$ (*220*)

Teach Circumference of a Circle

- Read aloud the first paragraph. Have students refer back to the drawing of a circle on page 217. Ask, *How is the circumference of a circle similar to a perimeter of a polygon? (It is the distance around.) How is it different? (Circumference has no straight parts.)*

- If necessary, help students as they use string to measure each object.

- Allow students to use their calculators to find $C \div d$. Have them round to the nearest tenth. Copy the table on the board and have volunteers supply numbers.

- The two values given for π are approximate, so computations involving π will also be approximate. Have students use the formula to check that table numbers match their computations.

Language Notes

Have volunteers read the definitions of *circle* and *sphere*. Then show students a circle cut from heavy paper or cardboard and a ball. Ask, *Which of these is a plane figure? (the paper figure) Which is not? (the ball)* Then ask, *Which is a circle? (the paper one) Which is a sphere? (the ball)*

Talk and Share

Students should use the formula $C = \pi d$ (*131.88 in.*). Have them recalculate the circumference using $\frac{22}{7}$ (*132 in.*).

Build VOCABULARY

Write the Vocabulary terms on the board. Then draw a circle with a center, a radius, and a diameter. Label the radius 5 and the diameter 10. Underneath the circle, write $C = 2\pi r \approx 31.4$. As you read each definition, have a volunteer write the term at the appropriate place on your drawing.

Circumference of a Circle

A circle is a set of points in a plane that are the same distance from a point called the **center**. The **radius** is the distance from every point on the circle to the center. The **diameter** is a line segment through the center that joins two points of the circle. The diameter is twice as long as a radius: $d = 2r$. The **circumference** is the distance around a circle.

Activity

Work with a partner. Copy the table on the left for recording.

1. Cut string to match the distance around each: a large paper plate, a small paper plate, and a paper coaster.
2. Use a ruler to measure each piece of string. Record the measure under *circumference (C)* in the table.
3. Fold each object in half and measure across the fold. Record those measures under *diameter (d)*.
4. Now find $C \div d$ for each. Share your results.

For *all* circles, the quotient $C \div d$ is the same, a little more than 3. The symbol π (pronounced pī) represents the exact value of the quotient. The digits in π never end or repeat, so **approximate values** of π, 3.14 and $\frac{22}{7}$, are commonly used. You can use $C \div d = \pi$ to find formulas for the circumference.

$$C \div d = \pi, \text{ so } C = \pi d \text{ and } C = 2\pi r.$$

Talk and Share

Work with a partner. Find the circumference of a hula hoop with a diameter of 42 inches. Use 3.14 for the value of π.

Language Notes

Confusing Word Pairs These words are easily mixed up.

- circle: a set of points in a *plane* that are all the same distance from the center. A circle is a plane, or flat, figure.
- sphere: a set of points in *space* that are all the same distance from the center. A sphere is a solid figure shaped like a ball.

VOCABULARY

center—the point in the exact middle of a circle. It is the same distance from every point on the circle.
radius—a line segment from any point on a circle to its center
diameter—a line segment through the center from one point on a circle to another
circumference—the distance around a circle
π pi; a symbol for the circumference of a circle divided by its diameter
approximate values—values that are close to exact values

Differentiating Instruction

Beginning
Finding Circumference After students complete the activity on page 218, draw several circles on the board, with diameter lengths labeled. Let students work in pairs to find the circumference of each circle.

Intermediate
Explaining Computations of Circumference After students complete the activity on page 218, have partners each draw four circles. Two should be labeled with radius length and two with

diameter length. Have partners exchange papers, find the circumferences, and explain their computations.

Advanced
Choosing a Value for π After students complete the activity on page 218, give them these four numbers as radii of a circle: 5, 2.4, 28, and 67. Ask them to tell which value of π, 3.14 or $\frac{22}{7}$, they would use to find each circumference and why. (*Sample: 3.14 with 5, 2.4, and 67; $\frac{22}{7}$ with 28; reasons will vary.*)

Area of a Circle

Imagine a circle cut into wedges. Then think about how you could **arrange** the wedges into a figure that looks like a parallelogram.

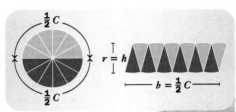

The base of the parallelogram is half the circumference. So $b = \frac{1}{2}C = \frac{1}{2}(2\pi r) = \pi r$.

Also, the height of the parallelogram is the same as the radius of the circle ($h = r$). The circle and the parallelogram are made up of the same wedges, so they have the same area.

Area of the parallelogram: $A = bh$

$A = (\pi r)(r)$ **Substitute πr for b and r for h.**

$A = \pi r^2$ **Simplify.**

So the formula for the area of a circle is $A = \pi r^2$.

A field is watered by a large sprinkler. The watering pipe is 10 meters long. What is the area that is watered? Use the formula $A = \pi r^2$ and use 3.14 for π.

$A = \pi r^2 = (3.14)(10^2)$
$= 3.14(100) = 314 \text{ m}^2$

The area watered by the sprinkler is about 314 square meters.

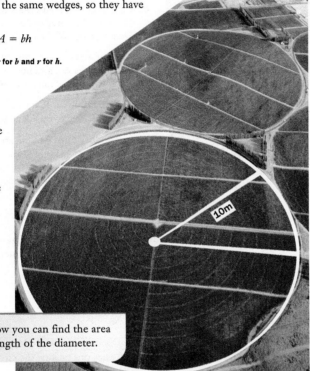

Talk and Share

Talk with a partner. Tell how you can find the area of a circle if you know the length of the diameter.

VOCABULARY
arrange—change the position

Teach Area of a Circle

■ Work through the development of the formula for the area of a circle. Call students' attention to the equation in the second paragraph. Ask, *Why does the equation say that $\frac{1}{2}$C equals $\frac{1}{2}(2\pi r)$?* Then discuss with them why $\frac{1}{2}(2\pi r)$ equals πr. Be sure students understand the substitutions and simplification.

■ Have students trace the circle onto grid paper (Overhead Transparency 15). Have them count square units to estimate the area of the circle. Then have them measure the radius and use the formula for the area. Their two areas should be close in value.

■ After discussing the sprinkler example, give students several other examples, some with radii given, some with diameters given. Have them find each area.

■ Remind students that the value of π is an *irrational* number. When written as a decimal, an irrational number never ends nor repeats.

Talk and Share

Suggest that students draw a circle and label the diameter with a measure. They should realize that they need to find the radius before they can apply the area formula.

Differentiating Instruction

Beginning
Using Different Processes After developing the circle area formula, have students trace a paper plate onto grid paper and count grid squares to find the circle's area. Then have them measure the diameter, divide by 2, and use the area formula to find the area.

Intermediate
Comparing Formulas After developing the circle area formula, have students trace a paper plate onto grid paper. Then have them cut the plate into eight congruent sections and arrange them into a parallelogram as on page 219. Have them find the area using $A = bh$ and $A = \pi r^2$ and compare results.

Advanced
Evaluating Estimates Have advanced students follow the directions for the Intermediate activity and talk about the method (counting, parallelogram formula, circle formula) that gives the most accurate measure and why.

Activity: Calculate It!

Have students use their calculators to find the circumference and the area of a circle with radius 8. You may need to help them find the appropriate keys. Give students these key sequences:

- $\boxed{\pi}$ $\boxed{\times}$ 2 $\boxed{\times}$ 8 $\boxed{=}$
- $\boxed{\pi}$ $\boxed{\times}$ 8 $\boxed{x^2}$ $\boxed{=}$

For some students' calculators, these sequences might not work. Help these students to find sequences that work.

Practice

Sketch a large circle on the board, labeling the radius 6. Review the ideas in this lesson by having students identify the parts of the circle. Then have them find the circumference and the area, with volunteers explaining how they found each measure (*37.68 units; 113.04 units²*).

Assignment Guide
■ Beginning 2–10 even, 11
■ Intermediate 2–12 even
■ Advanced 1–11 odd, 12, 13

Notes on Exercises

Exercise 6 If students don't know what a *discus* is, have them find the definition in their dictionary. Interested students might want to do further research to learn how the discus is used in competition.

Exercise 8 Explain that the prefix *semi* means "half." Relate this prefix to the term *semiannual*.

Exercises 9–12 Students will need to perform more than one operation in each of these exercises.

Exercise 13 Suggest that students work together and investigate these ideas by using actual measures for radii. Each student should use a different measure.

Look and Read

▲ Bicycles have two wheels and often are called *bikes*. This has three wheels and is called a *tricycle*.

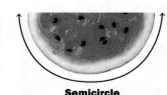

Semicircle

Practice

For Exercises 1–4, find the circumference and the area of each object. Use 3.14 for π and round answers to the nearest tenth.
1. A bicycle wheel with a radius of 14 inches
2. The top of a coffee cup with a diameter of 9 centimeters
3. A tomato slice with a diameter of 3 inches
4. A circular garden with a radius of 6 meters
5. A circular patio has a circumference of 20π feet. Find the
   a. diameter.   b. radius.   c. area.
6. A member of a men's track team practices with a discus that has a diameter of 22 centimeters. What is the circumference of the discus?
7. A bag of gravel covers an area of 4 square feet. A circular drainage area has a radius of 3 feet. How many bags of gravel would you need to cover the drainage area?
8. Another name for half a circle is *semicircle*. Find the length of the semicircle if its diameter is 14 inches. Use $\frac{22}{7}$ for π.

In Exercises 9 and 10, find the area of each colored region. Use 3.14 for π. Round answers to the nearest square unit.

9.  4 in. 2 in.

10. 7 m

In Exercises 11 and 12, each figure has congruent semicircles and a rectangle. Find the perimeter and the area of each figure.

11. 12 cm

12. 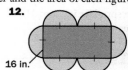 16 in.

13. (**EXTENDED RESPONSE**) If the radius of a circle is doubled, how does this change the circumference? The area?

Program Resources

Practice Book Use page 94.

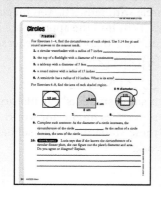

Answers
1. 87.9 in.; 615.4 in.²
2. 28.3 cm; 63.6 cm²
3. 9.4 in.; 7.1 in.²
4. 37.7 m; 113.0 m²
5. **a.** 20 ft   **b.** 10 ft   **c.** 314 ft²
6. about 69.1 cm
7. 8 bags   8. 22 in.
9. 38 in.²   10. 42 m²
11. about 75 cm; about 370 cm²
12. about 151 in.; about 1,115 in.²
13. The circumference is doubled; the area is multiplied by 4.

 Activity: Extend the Lesson

Have students investigate these interesting problems:

- By how much is the circumference of a circle with radius 10 ft increased if the radius is increased by 1 ft? (*about 6.28 ft*) A circle with radius 1,000 ft? (*about 6.28 ft*)

- How much larger would a belt around the earth's equator need to be if the radius is increased by 1 ft? Use 3,963 miles for the radius (*about 6.28 ft*).

Activities

Organizing When you organize information, you show how the details are related. The diagram below shows one way to organize details about a circle. It shows how each pair of terms is related by a formula.

Circles

circumference	diameter	radius	area
$C = \pi d$	$d = 2r$		$A = \pi r^2$

1. **Organize** Draw a Web like the one on page 25 to organize the information about circles.

2. **Explain** Tell what each symbol means in the formula $C = \pi d$. Tell how the formula organizes some details about a circle.

3. **Explain** Tell what each symbol means in the formula $A = \pi r^2$. Tell how the formula organizes some details about a circle.

Partner Practice

How Big Is the Bull's-Eye? The archery target shows 5 circles, each with the same center. The measures are in centimeters. Work with a partner to find the radius of each circle.

Find the area of the entire target and of the yellow region, or *bull's-eye*. What percent of the target is yellow? Find the area of each colored ring. (To find the area of the *red ring*, for example, find the area of the outer circle around the red ring and subtract the area of the yellow region.) What percent of the target is each color? (The total of your percents should be about 100%.) Think about how much area each ring takes up. Then tell how many points you think each colored area should be worth and why.

Hands On

Round and Around Work with a partner. Each of you should draw or trace two circles of different sizes. Measure the *diameter* of one circle and label it. Measure the *radius* of the other circle and label it. Trade circles with your partner and find the circumference and area of each. Use 3.14 for π. Check to see if your answers are reasonable by rounding π to 3 and using mental math.

Teach Organizing

Discuss with students how the parts of the diagram show how terms are related.

Sample answer:

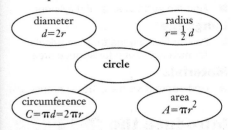

Partner Practice

- You may want students to use their calculators for this activity. Explain how to use the π key.

- Have pairs share their point systems. The center circle should offer the most points because it has the least area.

Answers: The radii of the concentric circles are 6, 14, 22, 30, and 38 cm. Using 3.14 for π, the areas of the circle and rings are 113.04, 502.40, 904.32, 1,306.24, and 1,708.16 cm². The area of the entire target is 4,534.16 cm². The percents of the entire target are approximate: yellow, 2.5%; red, 11.1%; blue, 19.9%; black, 28.8%; white, 37.7%.

Hands On

Suggest that students fold the circles in half to find the diameters.

Activity: Culture Connection

The same Eratosthenes who devised the *sieve* for finding prime numbers also calculated the radius and circumference of Earth using shadows and distances between two Egyptian cities around 240 B.C. He estimated that the radius and circumference were about 4,213 and 26,458 miles, respectively. Have students find out how these measurements compare with the actual radius and circumference.

Assessment Book

Use page 60 to assess students' comprehension.

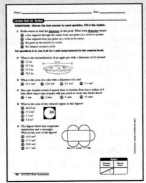

Program Resources

Practice Book Use page 95.
Overhead Transparencies Use 33.

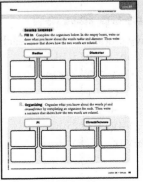

Surface Area

STANDARDS CONTENT

Mathematics
- Find the surface area of a prism
- Find the surface area of a cylinder

Language
- Persuade someone that a particular formula is the one for surface area

Materials
- Grid paper (Overhead Transparency 15)

Introduce the **Big Idea**

Read aloud the Big Idea. Ask students to describe types of packages or containers they know. They might name boxes, bottles, cans, and cones.

Begin **Building Background**

- Ask, *What might be stored in a barn?* (*hay*) *In a silo?* (*grain*)
- Help students to see that to find the amount of paint needed for any structure, they need to find the areas of all the sides. Ask, *What shapes are the sides of the barn?* (*rectangles and rectangles combined with triangles*)

Teach **Key Concepts**

- Read the Key Concepts paragraph. Ask, *What is the difference between plane and solid figures?* (*A plane figure is flat; a solid figure is not.*)
- Point out the three parts of the solid figure pictured. Then pass around models of solid figures (or boxes, cans, balls, and so on), and have volunteers identify each *face*, *vertex*, and *edge*.

Warm-Up Review

Have students evaluate each expression, using 3.14 for π.

1. $6(25) + 2(9)$ (*168*)
2. $6(5^2)$ (*150*)
3. $5(3 + 4 + 5)$ (*60*)
4. $2(\pi)(4)(5)$ (*125.6*)
5. $2(\pi)10^2$ (*628*)

Talk and Explore

Surface Area

Big Idea Packages and containers come in many different shapes. Sometimes you need to find the total area of all the outside surfaces of a package or container.

Building Background

▲ My cousin's farm has buildings that look like the ones in this picture.

- **What shapes do you see in the picture?**
- **How could you determine the amount of paint needed for the barn?**

Key Concepts

A **solid figure** is a 3-dimensional figure, such as a pyramid. Diagrams of solid figures often have dotted lines to show the hidden parts.

An **edge** is a line segment where 2 faces meet.

A **vertex** is where 3 or more edges meet.

Solid Figure

The flat surfaces are **faces**.

Activity: Euler, Not Oiler

Tell students that a famous mathematician, Leonhard Euler, discovered a special relationship among the faces (F), vertices (V), and edges (E) of any solid figure formed of polygons. Have students make a table listing the number of faces, vertices, and edges of the figures shown on pages 222, 223, and 225 to see if they can discover the relationship (*The sum of the numbers of faces and vertices minus the numbers of edges is 2*; $F + V - E = 2$).

Resource Library

Math at Hand
Solid Figures and Surface Area
307–308, 382–385, 387–391

Math on Call
Solid Figures and Surface Area
400–401, 403, 406, 409–412, 416

Reader's Handbook (**red**)
Reading Diagrams 552–553

Surface Area of a Prism

Solid figures are not flat and do not lie in a plane. The **faces, bases, edges,** and **vertices** of a box are shown in the diagram labeled rectangular prism.

A **prism** is a solid figure with two parallel and congruent faces that are polygons. These faces are the bases. The name of a prism depends on the polygon that forms its bases.

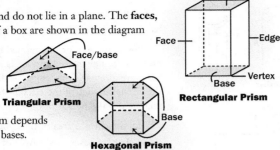

Triangular Prism
Hexagonal Prism
Rectangular Prism

The **surface area** (*SA*) of a figure is the sum of the areas of all the faces of the figure. If you cut apart a solid figure and lay the pieces flat, you have a **net**. A net can help you find the surface area.

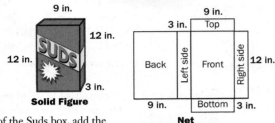

Solid Figure

Net

To find the surface area of the Suds box, add the areas of all the rectangles in the net.

$$
\begin{array}{cccccc}
\text{Top} + \text{Bottom} + \text{Front} + \text{Back} + \text{Left} + \text{Right} \\
3(9) + 3(9) + 12(9) + 12(9) + 3(12) + 3(12) = \\
27 + 27 + 108 + 108 + 36 + 36 = 342 \text{ in.}^2
\end{array}
$$

The surface area of the box is 342 square inches.

Talk and Share

A **cube** is a special rectangular prism. All 6 of its faces are congruent squares. Work with a partner to find the surface area of the cube on the right.

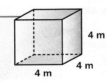

4 m
4 m
4 m

VOCABULARY

solid figure—a figure that is not flat and does not lie in a plane
face—each flat surface of a solid figure
base—the top or bottom face of a prism
edge—a line segment where two faces meet
vertex—a point where three edges meet. The plural is *vertices*.

prism—a solid figure with faces that are polygons; bases are congruent and parallel
surface area—the sum of the areas of all the faces of a solid figure
net—the unwrapped form of a solid figure
cube—a rectangular prism whose faces are congruent squares

LESSON 39 • SURFACE AREA **223**

Teach Surface Area of a Prism

- Point out that *vertices* is the plural form of *vertex*.

- Point out the nonrectangular prisms. Ask, *What shapes form the sides of the triangular and hexagonal prisms?* (*rectangles*) *What shapes form the bases?* (*triangles, hexagons*) Be sure students realize that the bases are congruent. Have volunteers explain the meaning of each label.

- Display a box, such as a cereal box, and point out all the faces. Then cut along the seams to create a net for the box.

- Discuss the computation of the surface area of the box. Then sketch on the board the net of the box you created, including dimensions. Have students calculate the surface area of the box.

- If time allows, you might elicit this formula from the students: $SA = 2\ell w + 2\ell h + 2wh$.

Talk and Share

- Students can find the area of one face ($16\ m^2$) and add 6 such areas or multiply the area by 6 ($96\ m^2$).

- Have students try to find a formula for the surface area of a cube in terms of an edge length e ($6e^2$).

Differentiating Instruction

Beginning

Understanding Surface Area Show students an empty box, such as a cereal box. Say, *You learned how to find the area of a rectangle. This box is a* prism. As you point to the six faces, say, *Its* surface area *includes all six sides, or faces.* Ask, *How can you find its surface area?* Help students see that the surface area is the sum of the areas of the six sides.

Intermediate

Finding Surface Area Show students an empty box. Say, *This box is a*

rectangular prism *because its* faces *are* rectangles. Have volunteers measure each face, find its area, and write the area on the board. Total the areas and say, *This sum is the surface area of the box.*

Advanced

Explaining How to Find Surface Area Give pairs of students an empty box. Say, *Your box is a* rectangular prism. *Its* surface area *includes the areas of all the sides, or faces. Tell another pair how you would find the surface area.*

Activity: Cube It!

Have students use 1-in. grid paper and draw and cut out nets for cubes. See if they can find all eleven of them. One is shown here.

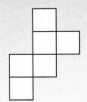

Lesson 39 • Surface Area **223**

Teach Surface Area of a Cylinder

■ After you discuss the first two paragraphs, ask students to tell the differences and similarities between prisms and cylinders.

■ Work through the computation of the surface area of a cylinder. You might illustrate the rectangular part by removing the label from a can and having students determine the two measures involved.

■ To help students better visualize finding the surface area of the potato chip can, you might cut a sheet of wrapping paper into a rectangle that just covers the curved surface of the potato chip can and two circles that match the top and bottom.

■ Bring several different-sized cans to class, and have students use the formula to find the total area of tin in each.

Talk and Share

■ Without computing, students should recognize that the size of the circles is way too large for the rectangular portion of the net.

■ Mathematically, students should note that the length of the rectangle is $2\pi r$, which is π times the diameter of the circle.

Build VOCABULARY

Have students describe the similarities among various prisms and cylinders. They should recall that prisms have congruent bases and rectangular faces, while a cylinder has congruent bases and a curved "face."

Surface Area of a Cylinder

A **cylinder** is a solid figure with two congruent, parallel bases that are circular. A can is an example of a cylinder.

Look at the net, or unwrapped form, of the cylinder on the left. The curved surface is a rectangle and the bases are circular. The length of the rectangle matches the circumference of the circular base. The width of the rectangle is the height of the cylinder.

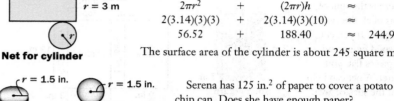

Cylinder

Net for cylinder

$h = 10$ m
$r = 3$ m

Find the surface area of the cylinder. Use 3.14 for π.

Area of bases	+	Area of rectangle	=
$\pi r^2 + \pi r^2$	+	ℓw	=
$2\pi r^2$	+	$(2\pi r)h$	$\approx$
$2(3.14)(3)(3)$	+	$2(3.14)(3)(10)$	$\approx$
56.52	+	188.40	≈ 244.92 m^2

The surface area of the cylinder is about 245 square meters.

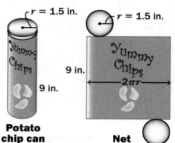

Serena has 125 in.^{2} of paper to cover a potato chip can. Does she have enough paper?

Use the net on the left to find the surface area.

Area of bases	+ Area of rectangle =
$2\pi r^2$	$(2\pi r)h$ =
$2(3.14)(1.5)(1.5)$	$+ 2(3.14)(1.5)(9)$ =
14.13	$+ \quad 84.78 \quad = 98.91$ in.^{2}

$r = 1.5$ in. $r = 1.5$ in.

9 in.

9 in.

Potato chip can   **Net**

To cover the potato chip can, she needs about 99 square inches of materials. Serena has enough paper because $99 < 125$.

Talk and Share

Look at the net on the right. Discuss with a partner why the net cannot be folded into a cylinder. Explain your reasons.

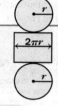

$2\pi r$

VOCABULARY
cylinder—a solid figure with two congruent, parallel circular regions as bases and a curved surface as the side of the figure

---

Differentiating Instruction

Beginning

Finding Areas of Can Labels Give pairs of students several cans with labels. Have them remove the labels carefully, measure them, and find each area. Then have them measure the diameter of each can and use h for the height and πd for the other dimension and recalculate the area.

Intermediate

Constructing a Net for a Cylinder Give each pair of students a cylindrical container, string, and tape. Have them

use the string to measure diameter, circumference, and height. Then have them use the measures to draw a net for the box. Have them calculate the surface area using the net. They can then reconstruct the container.

Advanced

Modeling Cylinder Area Give students a compass, scissors, and tape. Have them draw a net for a cylinder with radius 5 cm and height 10 cm, find the surface area (*471 cm²*), construct the cylinder, and explain their work.

Practice

Name each prism and tell the number of faces it has.

1.

2.

3.

4.

For Exercises 5 and 6, find the surface area of each prism *without* either base.

In Exercises 7–9, find the surface area of each solid.

5. 6 cm 4 cm
6 cm
6 cm   4 cm
4 cm

6. 3 in. 4 in.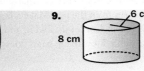
4 in.
5 in.

7. 7 in.
7 in. 2 in.

8. 8 cm
8 cm

9. 6 cm
8 cm

Before a pencil is sharpened and the eraser is attached, a pencil is a long, thin hexagonal prism. For Exercises 10 and 11, find the surface area. Do not include the bases.

10. The height of the pencil is 180 millimeters and the width of each side of the base is 6 millimeters.

11. For a large display pencil, the height is 32 inches and the width of each side of the base is 2.5 inches.

12. (SHORT RESPONSE) Andrea wants to wrap the box on the right. Find the total surface area that she has to cover. Explain how you found it.

12.5 cm
10 cm   8 cm

LESSON 39 • SURFACE AREA   **225**

Practice

Review the ideas in this lesson by having students complete sentences such as these:

- A rectangular prism has <u>two</u> bases and four rectangular faces.
- A <u>triangular</u> prism has two <u>triangular</u> bases and three rectangular faces.
- A <u>cylinder</u> has two circular bases but no faces.

Assignment Guide

- Beginning 1–10, 12
- Intermediate 1–12
- Advanced 1–12

Notes on Exercises

Exercise 3 Students may need help counting the sides in the base of this prism. There are three dashed segments and five solid, so the base is octagonal.

Exercises 10 and 11 You might tell students that the surface area will tell the amount of surface to be painted.

Exercise 12 Ask a volunteer to tell how he or she computed the amount of paper to use. Then ask, *Did anyone do it another way?* Some students might have added the six areas. Others might have found the area of one of each size face, multiplied by 2, and added the products.

Answers

1. rectangular prism; 6 faces
2. pentagonal prism; 7 faces
3. octagonal prism; 10 faces
4. triangular prism; 5 faces
5. 144 cm^2
6. 48 in.^{2}
7. 154 in.^{2}
8. 301.44 cm^2
9. 527.52 cm^2
10. 6,480 mm^2
11. 480 in.^{2}

12. 610 cm^2; Sample: I multiplied the length times the width times 2, the length times the height times 2, and the width times the height times 2; then I added the three products.

Program Resources

Practice Book Use page 96.
Overhead Transparencies Use 15.

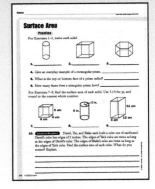

Teach Persuading

Tell students that the word *persuade* comes from the Latin *per*, meaning "thoroughly," and *suadere*, meaning "to urge." Here they will try to persuade their partner that their plan for finding the surface area of the post will work. Have volunteers present their plans to the class for discussion.

Answer:

3. *about 5.6 ft²*

■ Provide students with $\frac{1}{4}$-in. or $\frac{1}{2}$-in. grid paper to make their copies (Overhead Transparency 15). They can count squares and then use a compass or string and pin to draw both the quarter circle and the small circle on grid paper.

■ The net given is for a *cone*. Ask, *Where have you seen cone-shaped figures? (Sample: ice-cream cones)*

Hands On

Be sure that students' nets form the *square pyramid* shown. Ask, *Where might you see a pyramid? (Samples: Egypt, Peru, Mexico City)*

Language Notes

Discuss the three meanings of the word *net*. Ask volunteers to describe nets they have seen (*Samples: basketball nets, volleyball nets, tennis nets*).

Develop Language

Activities

Scratching post ▶

$r = \frac{1}{3}$ ft

$h = 2\frac{1}{2}$ ft

Persuading When you want to persuade someone, you give that person reasons to agree with your opinions.

Angie wants to buy fabric to cover a scratching post for her cat. The post is a cylinder. The bottom will not be covered. Work with a partner to find the amount of fabric needed.

1. Draw Draw a net for the cylinder and decide on a plan for finding the area to be covered.

2. Persuade Explain your plan to your partner. Persuade your partner that your plan will work. Use words such as *cover, top, bottom, curved surface, net, rectangle,* and *circles.* Go back and look at examples in the lesson to help you.

3. Compute Find how many square feet of fabric are needed to cover the post.

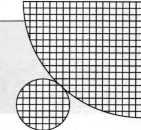

Partner Practice

You Form It Work with a partner. Discuss the net shown. Try to decide what solid figure you can form from the net. Make a larger copy on grid paper. Cut it out, fold it, and tape it. Were you right? How many bases does the shape have?

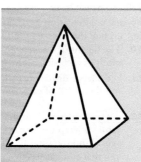

Language Notes

Multiple Meanings
This word has more than one meaning.

■ **net**
1. the unwrapped form of a solid figure
2. an open fabric made of knotted string
3. catch or capture

Hands On

Can You Cut It? Work with a partner. On grid paper, draw a large net for the solid shown. Think about the shape of the base and the shape of the other faces. Cut out your net, fold it, and tape it. Does your net form a pyramid like the one shown? Discuss the results. Try to determine what changes you need to make to your net, if any.

 Program Resources
Practice Book Use page 97.

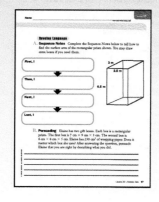

 Assessment Book
Use page 61 to assess students' comprehension.

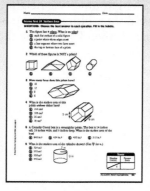

 Activity: Extend the Lesson

A solid figure formed of polygons, such as a prism or pyramid, is called a *polyhedron*. The faces of a *regular polyhedron* are congruent polygons. Five regular polyhedrons, described in detail by Plato around 400 B.C., are called "Platonic solids." Have interested students research these polyhedrons and make a poster or straw models of them. Students may use this website: http://www. enchantedlearning.com/math/ geometry/solids/index.shtml.

Volume

Talk and Explore

Big Idea Volume is a measure of how much space a solid takes up. That measure is based on the dimensions of the solid.

Building Background

▲ Some of my fish are as colorful as birds.

- What pet fish have you seen?
- About how large do you think this tank is?
- How could you figure out how much water is needed to fill this tank?

Key Concepts

Volume is the amount of space *inside* a solid figure. Volume is given in cubic units. A **cubic unit,** such as a cubic inch, is a cube with all edges measuring 1 unit.

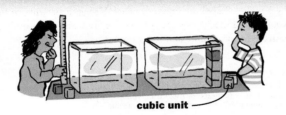

cubic unit

LESSON 40 • VOLUME **227**

Activity: Fill 'Er Up!

Give each small group of students an open box and enough inch or centimeter cubes to fill the box. Have students tell which boxes they think have the greatest and least volume. Then have each group find the volume of their box by filling it with the cubes. Have them check if their predictions were correct. Ask volunteers to tell why this method of finding the volume is limited.

Resource Library

Math at Hand
Volume of Prisms 309–312

Math on Call
Volume of Rectangular Prisms and Cylinders 402, 413

Volume

STANDARDS CONTENT

Mathematics
- Find the volume of a prism
- Find the volume of a cylinder

Language
- Recognize multiple meanings of *volume*
- Compare and contrast the steps for finding volume

Materials
- Cylindrical containers, tape, rice or sand

Introduce the Big Idea

Read aloud the Big Idea. On the board, draw a line segment, a rectangle, and a rectangular prism. Point out that we use *length* (*cm*) to measure segments, *area* (*cm²*) to measure the flat space inside plane figures, and *volume* (*cm³*) to measure how much a solid holds.

Begin Building Background

Ask volunteers to tell about their fish or any other pets they have.

Teach Key Concepts

Read aloud the Key Concepts paragraph. In the picture, one person is measuring the dimensions of the tank so she can compute the volume. The other person is finding volume by counting the cubic units the tank will hold. Ask, *Which method do you think is better?*

Warm-Up Review

Have students evaluate each expression, using 3.14 for π.

1. $6 \times 25 \times 2$ *(300)*
2. $4(5)(8)$ *(160)*
3. 6^3 *(216)*
4. $\pi(2)(2)(5)$ *(62.8)*
5. $\pi(10^2)(4)$ *(1,256)*

Teach Volume of a Prism

- After students count the unit cubes in the prism and you discuss the first three paragraphs, write the formula $V = \ell wh$ on the board. Have volunteers replace the variables with the numbers shown in the diagram and verify that the volume is 60 cubic units.

- Before discussing the general formula for the volume of a prism, ask students to give an expression for the area of the base of any rectangular prism (ℓw). They can use this idea to understand the formula $V = Bh$. Stress that the capital B in this volume formula stands for "area," not "length" as in the area formulas.

- Finally, discuss the problem relating to the fish tank. Point out that $in.^3$ stands for "cubic inches."

Language Notes

Discuss the three meanings of the word *volume*. Ask, *What does it mean to* turn down the volume?

Talk and Share

- Students should find that the volume of the gift box is 455 in.^{3} and the surface area is 382 in.^{2}

- Students must use *cubic* units for volume and *square* units for area.

Look and Read

Rectangular Prism

2 in. 5 in. 6 in.

1 in. 1 in.

Language Notes

Multiple Meanings
This word has more than one meaning.

■ volume
1. the amount of space inside a solid object
2. the loudness of a sound
3. a book that is part of a set

$V = Bh$

Volume of a Prism

The **volume** of a solid figure is the number of **cubic units** needed to fill the space inside the figure. The units are cubic units because the figure is 3-dimensional. Find the volume of the prism on the left by counting the cubic units.

Each layer has 5 rows of 6 cubes, or 30 cubes. With 2 layers, the volume is 2(30), or 60 cubic units.

Notice that to find the volume, we found the area of one layer, the *base*, and multiplied by the number of layers, or the *height*. For a rectangular prism, the area of the base is ℓw. So, a formula for the volume of a rectangular prism is $V = \ell wh$.

$V = \ell wh$

Use a formula to find the volume of a fish tank. It is a rectangular prism. Use the dimensions shown in the diagram.

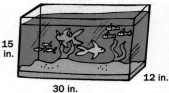

15 in.
30 in.
12 in.

$$V = \ell wh$$
$$= (12)(30)(15) = 5{,}400$$

The volume is 5,400 cubic inches or 5,400 in.^{3}

You can use $V = \ell wh$ to write a formula for the volume of any prism. Let B be the area of the base and h be the height. Then the *volume of any prism is* $V = Bh$.

Talk and Share

Working with a partner, draw a sketch of a gift box that is 13 by 7 by 5 inches. Label the measurements. Use your drawing to find the volume and the surface area of the box. Talk about the different units used for volume and for surface area.

 VOCABULARY
volume—the amount of space inside a solid figure
cubic units—the units for measuring volume. A cubic inch is a cubic unit with all edges measuring 1 inch.

Gift boxes ▶

Activity: Do It Another Way

Ask partners to work together to find other ways to find the volume of the cube prism at the top of the page. If no one volunteers, point out that they could have found the number of cubes on the front and multiplied by the number of rows. A third way is to find the number of cubes on the right end and multiply by the number of columns. Show the products $10 \times 6 = 60$ and $12 \times 5 = 60$ to verify that each way is correct.

Differentiating Instruction

Beginning
Modeling Volume Display a box, such as a small shoebox. Label the dimensions *length*, *width*, and *height*. As students watch, fill the box with cubes and ask, *How many cubes are in one layer? How many layers are there? How many cubes are there in all?* Ask, students how they found the total number of cubes. Say, *This number is the* volume. *It tells how many cubes the box holds.*

Intermediate
Building Prisms and Finding Volume After developing the volume formula, have one partner pick three small numbers, and have the other build a rectangular prism with those dimensions. Have partners find the volume by counting with the formula.

Advanced
Writing About Volume Have students discuss page 228. Give them a small box and have them describe in writing how they would find its volume.

Volume of a Cylinder

The formula $V = Bh$ works for **cylinders** as well as for prisms. Remember that B is the area of the base and h is the height of the cylinder. The **base of a cylinder** is circular. Use $A = \pi r^2$ for the area of the base, B. Then the formula for the volume of a cylinder is $V = \pi r^2 h$.

Which of the two cylinders below do you think has a greater volume?

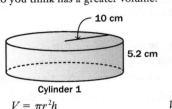

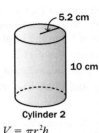

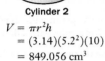

Cylinder 1

$V = \pi r^2 h$
$\quad = (3.14)(10^2)(5.2)$
$\quad = 1{,}632.8 \text{ cm}^3$

Cylinder 2

$V = \pi r^2 h$
$\quad = (3.14)(5.2^2)(10)$
$\quad = 849.056 \text{ cm}^3$

Base $\quad B = \pi r^2$

$V = B\,(h)$
$V = (\pi r^2)h$

The volume of the first cylinder is greater. This is because it has the greater radius, 10, which is squared in the formula.

Talk and Share

Work with a partner. A container is a cylinder with a radius of 2 inches and a height of 7 inches. Find the volume of the container. Use $\frac{22}{7}$ for π. Now double the radius and the height. How is the volume changed?

VOCABULARY

cylinder—a solid figure with circular bases. The side of a cylinder is a curved surface.
base of a cylinder—one of the two flat surfaces of a cylinder. The base of a cylinder is circular.

Teach Volume of a Cylinder

- Work through the development of the formula for the volume of a cylinder. Stress that the volume of any cylinder or prism is given by the general formula $V = Bh$. Ask a volunteer to explain what each letter stands for.

- Call students' attention to Cylinders 1 and 2. Ask, *Which cylinder do you think has greater volume?* They may think the volumes are equal because the dimensions are the same numbers.

- Then have students work through the two computations to find that the cylinder with the greater radius has greater volume. Students will see that Cylinder 1 has an extra factor of 10, while Cylinder 2 has an extra factor of 5.2.

- Have the students test this relationship by finding the volumes of two other cylinders: one with height 8 and radius 7 and one with height 7 and radius 8. Have them use $\frac{22}{7}$ for π (*1,232 and 1,408 cubic units*).

Talk and Share

The volume of the container is 88 in.^{3} When radius and height are both doubled, the volume is 8 times the original, 704 in.^{3}

Differentiating Instruction

Beginning
Understanding Volume of a Cylinder
Refer students to the second formula for volume of a prism, $V = Bh$. Say, *This formula can be used to find the volume of any prism or cylinder. What does B stand for?* (the area of the base) Ask, *What is the area of the base?* ($A = \pi r^2$) Show how to use the base area and the height to find the volume formula ($V = \pi r^2 h$).

Intermediate
Finding Volume of Cylinders After students study the examples on page 229, have partners find the volume of two cans you supply and talk about how they computed.

Advanced
Comparing Cylinders' Volume After reading and discussing page 229, students should write several sentences explaining how to tell, without computing, which cylinder has greater value: radius 12 and height 8 or radius 8 and height 12. (*The first; it has an extra factor of 12, while the other has an extra factor of 8.*)

Activity: A Cylinder Works Best

Give groups of students newspapers and magazines. Have them find pictures of cylindrical containers and make a poster of the pictures. At the bottom of their posters, have them list the types of things that typically are packaged or stored in cylinders. Have them try to find a great variety, including water tanks, silos, and tin cans.

Practice

To review the ideas in this lesson, display a can and a box, and have students point out the base and the height of each. Then give them the dimensions of each, and have them find the volume of each. Ask volunteers to tell how they computed the volume.

Assignment Guide
■ Beginning 1–4, 6, 7, 10, 11
■ Intermediate 2, 4–12
■ Advanced 1, 4–12

Notes on Exercises

Exercise 5 Students will need to recall that a cube's edges are all the same length. They can draw and label a diagram if they need to visualize a cube.

Exercise 7 Ask, *What formula can you use to find the volume of the box?* (V = Bh)

Exercise 9 Have students draw a diagram and label each edge *s*. They can substitute *s* in the formula and arrive at $V = s^3$.

Build VOCABULARY

Point out that the *-al* suffix in *hexagonal* and *cylindrical* means "shaped like."

Look and Read

Practice

Find the volume of each rectangular prism by counting the cubes.

1.   2.   3.

Find the volume of each figure in Exercises 4–8. Use 3.14 for π and round your answer to the nearest tenth when needed.

4. A straw with radius of 3 mm and height of 180 mm

5. A storage cube with an edge of 11 in.

6. A cylindrical water pipe with radius of 3 m and height of 2.8 m

7. A hexagonal box (prism) with a base area of 25.6 cm² and height of 5 cm

8. A cylindrical oil drum with a diameter of 3 ft and a height twice the diameter

9. A cube is a rectangular prism with all edges the same length (*s*). Write a volume formula for a cube with side *s*.

10. A hole with a diameter of 10 mm is drilled through a cube whose edge is 25 mm. What is the volume of the cube minus the volume of the hole?

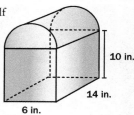

11. (MULTIPLE CHOICE) A large cylindrical fish tank has a radius of 13.9 feet and a height of 32 feet. What is its approximate volume in cubic feet?
   A. 600 ft³   B. 1,300 ft³   C. 6,200 ft³   D. 19,400 ft³

12. (EXTENDED RESPONSE) The bottom of the mailbox below is a rectangular prism. The top is half of a cylinder.
   a. Look at the semicircle near the top of the mailbox. What is its diameter? What is its radius? Find the area of the semicircle.
   b. Find the volume of the half cylinder that forms the top of the mailbox.
   c. What is the volume of the mailbox without the half cylinder?
   d. What is the total volume of the mailbox?

Program Resources

Practice Book Use page 98.

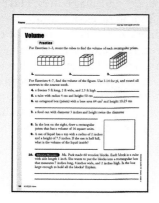

Answers
1. 84 units³   2. 45 units³
3. 30 units³   4. 5,086.8 mm³
5. 1,331 in.³   6. 79.1 m³
7. 128 cm³   8. 42.4 ft³
9. $V = s^3$ 10. 13,662.5 mm³
11. D
12. a. 6 in.; 3 in.; 14.13 in.²
    b. 197.82 in.³
    c. 840 in.³
    d. 1,037.82 in.³

Activity: Extend the Lesson

Students might be interested in knowing formulas for the surface area and the volume of a sphere. They are, respectively, $SA = 4\pi r^2$ and $V = \frac{4}{3}\pi r^3$. You might have them find the radius of a tennis ball or basketball and then calculate its surface area and volume.

Activities

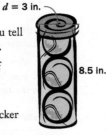

d = 3 in.

8.5 in.

Comparing and Contrasting When you compare and contrast, you tell how things are alike and how they are different. Work with a partner.

1. **Tell** Explain to your partner how to find the volume of the can of tennis balls in the picture. Write the formula for the volume of a cylinder and find the volume.

2. **Tell** Have your partner explain how to find the volume of the cracker box. Your partner should give the formula and find the volume.

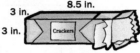

8.5 in.

3 in.

3 in.

Crackers

3. **Compare and Contrast** Tell how the formulas and the steps needed are the same. Tell how they are different. Which container has the greater volume?

Hands On

Cylinder   Cone

What Part Is It? Work with a partner. Start with an empty cylinder. Then make a cone out of paper. The cone must have the same size circular base and the same height as the cylinder.

Tell which figure you think has the greater volume. Tell how the volumes might be related. Fill the cone with sand or rice. Pour the rice or sand into the cylinder. Repeat until the cylinder is full. Discuss your results. How do the volumes of the cylinder and the cone compare?

Partner Practice

My Oh My, We Love Pi

The value of π is the value of the circumference of any circle divided by its diameter: 3.14159265…. No fraction can give the exact value of π, but this table has some early approximations. Use your calculator to find a decimal value for each. Whose decimal value is closest to 3.14159265?

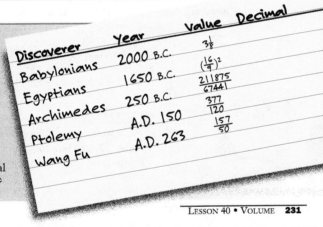

Discoverer	Year	Value Decimal
Babylonians	2000 B.C.	$3\frac{1}{8}$
Egyptians	1650 B.C.	$(\frac{16}{9})^2$
Archimedes	250 B.C.	$\frac{211875}{67441}$
Ptolemy	A.D. 150	$\frac{377}{120}$
Wang Fu	A.D. 263	$\frac{157}{50}$

Teach Comparing and Contrasting

- Remind students that to *compare* means to tell how things are alike and to *contrast* means to tell how things are different.

- In both cases, students can multiply the area of the base by the height to find the volume. The difference is that the base of the can is a circular region and the base of the box is rectangular.

- The can's volume is about 60.1 in.[3], and the box's volume is 76.5 in.[3] Because the heights are the same, they need compare only the areas of the two bases.

Hands On

- Oatmeal or salt boxes work well for this experiment. Students may need help making the cones.

- Students will find that it takes 3 cones to fill the cylinder, so the volume of the cone is $\frac{1}{3}$ the volume of the cylinder.

- Ask students to try to write a formula for the volume of a cone ($V = \frac{1}{3}\pi r^2 h$).

Partner Practice

The values for π are: Babylonians, 3.125; Egyptians, 3.16049. . . ; Archimedes, 3.14163. . . ; Ptolemy, 3.14167; Wang Fu, 3.14. Archimedes' was the closest.

 Activity: Real-world Connection

A problem encountered by manufacturers is to minimize packaging while maintaining volume. Have groups work together to find which type of rectangular prism has the least surface area for a given volume. Give each group one of these volumes: 8, 27, 64, or 125 cubic units. Have them try various combinations of length, height, and width. For 8, they can use 8, 1, 1; 4, 2, 1; and 2, 2, 2. Each group should find that a cube has the least surface area for a given volume.

 Assessment Book

Use page 62 to assess students' comprehension.

 Program Resources

Practice Book Use page 99.

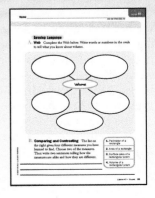

Draw a Diagram

STANDARDS CONTENT

Mathematics
- Solve problems by drawing a diagram

Language
- Clarify when to use *fewer than* and *less than*

Teach Draw a Diagram

- Have a volunteer read aloud the first two paragraphs. To help students understand what the picture backing is, you might bring in a framed picture and point out the paper on the back that seals in the picture to keep out moisture.

- Work through the steps of the problem solution, and copy the diagram on the board. You might also label the left side and the bottom of the frame to reinforce the idea that the width of the frame must be added *twice* to the dimensions of the picture.

Talk and Share

Have partners draw a diagram representing the situation.

Answer: They will see that they must add 4 to both the length and the width of the backing, for an area of 168 in.²

Problem-Solving Skills

Draw a Diagram

For some problems it is useful to draw a diagram. A diagram can help you understand information given in problems.

Problem: Francine is cutting the backing for a picture and its frame. The picture is 8 inches by 10 inches. Its frame is $1\frac{1}{2}$ inches wide. What is the area of the backing she needs?

Read and Understand

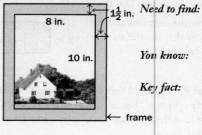

Need to find: The area of the backing. It must be large enough to go behind the picture and the frame.

You know: The picture is 8 inches by 10 inches. The frame is $1\frac{1}{2}$ inches wide.

Key fact: The width of the frame has to be added to each side, that is, twice to the length and twice to the width.

Plan and Solve Draw a diagram to show the total length and total width needed. Find the area.

The total length is $8 + 1\frac{1}{2} + 1\frac{1}{2} = 11$ inches.
The total width is $10 + 1\frac{1}{2} + 1\frac{1}{2} = 13$ inches.
Use the formula $A = \ell w$.

Answer $A = \ell w = 11(13) = 143$ in.² The area of the backing is 143 square inches.

Look Back The backing for the photo has an area of $8 \times 10 = 80$ in.² Then $143 - 80$ leaves 60 in.² for the backing of the frame portion. The answer of 143 in.² is reasonable.

Talk and Share

Work with a partner. Suppose the width of the frame is 2 inches. Discuss how the diagram you draw will change. Find the total area for a backing with the same picture in its new frame.

232 UNIT 9 • AREA AND VOLUME

Activity: Can You Dig It?

Have students solve this problem by drawing a diagram or by acting it out using counters: Gary plans to build a fence around his backyard. He must dig holes for posts to support the fence. His backyard measures 120 feet by 48 feet. He wants the posts to be 12 feet apart. How many holes must he dig? (*28 holes*) Suppose he wants the posts to be only 8 feet apart. How many holes must he dig? (*42 holes*)

Differentiating Instruction

Beginning
Diagramming Heights Give students this problem: *Nora is taller than Kim. Meg is taller than Jane. Meg's height is the only one between Nora's and Kim's.* Have students draw a diagram of the heights and name the girls in order, tallest first (*Nora, Meg, Kim, Jane*).

Intermediate
Arranging Tables Have pairs of students draw all the ways 16 square tables can be arranged in a solid rectangle and tell which way seats

the most people, one person to a side (*1 by 16, 34; 2 by 8, 20; 4 by 4, 16*).

Advanced
Diagramming a Race Give students this problem: In a marathon, Jim is 2.5 km behind Pedro, who is 3.5 km ahead of Tim. Tim is 1.25 km behind Carl, and Carl is 5.75 km behind Mike. Have students draw a diagram to find the distance between the first and last runners (*7 km*).

1. A rectangular swimming pool measures 20 feet by 35 feet. A 3-foot-wide walkway surrounds the pool. You want to cover the pool and the entire walkway with a protective cover. What is the area of the cover?

2. You cut away 1 inch from all four sides of an $8\frac{1}{2}$-inch-by-11-inch piece of paper. What is the area of the paper that is left?

Use the strategy *draw a diagram*.

3. A patio is a rectangle 11 feet by 7 feet. You want to place 1-square-foot tiles around the patio. How many tiles do you need?

4. A room is 12 feet by 16 feet. Make a scale drawing of the room using the scale $\frac{1}{2}$ inch equals 1 foot. Use your drawing to find the length of a diagonal of the room.

Choose a strategy and solve each problem.

5. You buy 25 tickets at an amusement park. You use 4 tickets for rides and 6 tickets for ice cream. After you give some tickets to a friend, you have 4 tickets left. How many tickets did you give to your friend?

6. List the different ways to pay a 30-cent toll using nickels, dimes, and quarters.

Grammar Spotlight

Fewer Than/Less Than These phrases signal comparisons. You use *fewer* with count nouns and *less* with noncount nouns.

Comparisons with Count Nouns	Comparisons with Noncount Nouns
There are fewer dimes than nickels. (You can count dimes and nickels.)	We have less money today than yesterday. (We don't say 2 money or 3 money.)
There are fewer people than desks in the room.	There is less gas in the tank than I thought.

Think of ways to use *fewer than* and *less than*. Share ideas with your partner. Together write a sentence using each term and share your sentences with the class.

DRAW A DIAGRAM **233**

Give students practice in drawing diagrams by giving them problems similar to those in the Activity and Differentiating Instruction on page 232. Have volunteers draw appropriate diagrams on the board. Discuss the diagrams. You might ask for just the diagrams, not the solutions.

Assignment Guide
- Beginning 1–6
- Intermediate 1–6
- Advanced 1–6

Notes on Exercises
Exercise 4 You might want to give students $\frac{1}{4}$-in. grid paper (Overhead Transparency 15) to use for their diagrams.

Exercise 6 Discuss where students might have encountered having to pay tolls. Encourage students to make a table to solve this problem, listing all the possible combinations for 30¢.

Grammar Spotlight
- Give students other examples, such as *water, hats, milk, sand,* and *shoes,* and have them tell whether to use *fewer than* or *less than*.

- Have volunteers offer other examples, and have the class decide which phrase to use.

Answers
1. 1,066 ft^2
2. $58\frac{1}{2}$ in.^{2}
3. 40 tiles
4. Check students' drawings; 20 ft
5. 11 tickets
6. 1 quarter, 1 nickel; 3 dimes; 6 nickels; 2 nickels, 2 dimes; 4 nickels, 1 dime

Activity: Real-world Connection

Tolls are fees levied by local and national governments to build and maintain roads and bridges. The tolls are paid by those who use the roads. Tolls were first charged by three counties in England in 1663 to maintain their roads.

Have students find the cost to travel through the same 40¢ toll twice a day, 5 days a week, for 52 weeks (*$208*). Students can check if their state has a toll system at http://www.fhwa.dot.gov/programadmin/toll_Rds.html.

Program Resources
Practice Book Use pages 100 and 101.

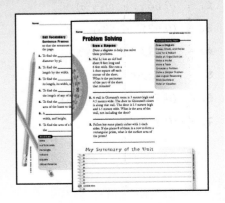

What Is Probability?

STANDARDS CONTENT

Mathematics
- Find the probability that an event will happen
- Identify certain, impossible, and possible events

Language
- Recognize the meanings of *chance* and *change*
- Interpret the results of an experiment

Materials
- Colored and silver paper clips, circles divided into sixths

Introduce the **Big Idea**

Read aloud the Big Idea. Explain that an *event* is something that happens. Discuss how knowing *probability*, or the chances of something happening, can help you prepare for events such as multiple births or various weather events.

Begin **Building Background**

Ask, *What games have you played in which you used a spinner?*

Teach **Key Concepts**

Ask, *Would the probability of winning paints still be $\frac{1}{8}$ if the CD prize were replaced with a volleyball prize? (Yes; paints is still one of eight equally likely outcomes.)*

Warm-Up Review

Have students write each fraction as a decimal and as a percent.

1. $\frac{1}{2}$ *(0.5, 50%)*
2. $\frac{2}{3}$ *(0.66 . . . , $66\frac{2}{3}$%)*
3. $\frac{5}{8}$ *(0.625, 62.5%)*
4. $\frac{5}{6}$ *(0.833 . . . , $83\frac{1}{3}$%)*
5. $\frac{4}{20}$ *(0.2, 20%)*
6. $\frac{7}{12}$ *(0.5833 . . . , $58\frac{1}{3}$%)*
7. $\frac{4}{5}$ *(0.8, 80%)*

What Is Probability?

Big Idea Before an event happens, you may be able to measure how likely it is to occur. That measure is called the *probability* of the event.

Building Background

▲ Every year, my neighborhood has a big party with food, music, and games where you can win prizes.

- **What is happening here?**
- **What items are the prizes?**
- **What chance do you think a player has of winning?**

Key Concepts

For the spinner above, each section shows a prize, a possible **outcome,** or result. The set of all possible outcomes is an **event.** If each outcome has the same chance of happening, then the outcomes are **equally likely outcomes.** The 8 outcomes are equally likely, so the **probability,** or chance, of winning any one prize is $\frac{1}{8}$.

> **Event:** spin and land on a prize
>
> **Outcomes:** any one result of a spin
>
> **Equally likely outcomes:** CD, backpack, lock, shirt, tickets, paints, brushes, easel
>
> **Probability** of winning paints = P(paints) = $\frac{1}{8}$

Activity: Equally Likely

Show students one yellow and one red chip. Place the chips in an opaque bag. Elicit that when selecting a chip without looking, a person is equally likely to draw a yellow chip or a red chip. Repeat with two yellow and two red chips. Ask, *How are the two situations alike? (Both have equal numbers of each color chip.)*

Have groups use spinners or chips to design two events that have equally likely outcomes and then share their work with the class.

Resource Library

Math at Hand
Probability 285–287

Math on Call
Probability 461, 465

Reader's Handbook (red)
Reading Math 117–131

Reader's Handbook (yellow)
Reading Math 88–100

Introduction to Probability

Meda will use a spinner to determine her prize. What do you think is her **probability**, or chance, of winning paints?

The probability of an **event**, written $P(E)$, is this ratio:

$$\frac{\text{number of favorable outcomes}}{\text{number of possible outcomes}}$$

Meda wants to win paints, so "paints" is a **favorable outcome**. The number of favorable outcomes is 1. The spinner has 8 sections, so the number of possible outcomes is 8.

$$P(\text{winning the paints}) = \frac{\text{number of favorable outcomes}}{\text{number of possible outcomes}} = \frac{1}{8}$$

Suppose you want to know the probability of winning any item related to painting. Then there are 3 favorable outcomes—the paints, the brushes, and the easel.

$$P(\text{winning paints, brushes, or easel}) =$$
$$\frac{\text{number of favorable outcomes}}{\text{number of possible outcomes}} = \frac{3}{8}$$

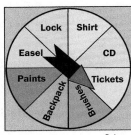
▲ Spinner

A number cube has six faces numbered 1 through 6. The probability of rolling a 2 is written $P(2)$. It is $\frac{1}{6}$, because only one face shows a 2 and there are six faces in all. Look at these probabilities.

Cube: $P(2) = \frac{1}{6}$ $P(\text{even number}) = \frac{3}{6}$ $P(2, 3, 4, 5, \text{or } 6) = \frac{5}{6}$

A coin has two faces, heads and tails.

Coin: $P(\text{heads}) = \frac{1}{2}$ $P(\text{tails}) = \frac{1}{2}$ $P(\text{heads or tails}) = \frac{2}{2} = 1$

▲ Number cube

Talk and Share

Suppose the numbers 1 through 6 on the cube are written as words. Work with a partner to find the probability of rolling a number with the letter "o" in it.

▲ Quarter

VOCABULARY
probability—the chance that an event will occur; the number of favorable outcomes divided by the number of possible outcomes
event—one outcome or the set of all possible outcomes
favorable outcome—an outcome that is wanted

LESSON 41 • WHAT IS PROBABILITY? **235**

Language Notes
Confusing Word Pairs
These words are easily mixed up.
- chance: the likelihood that something will happen
- change: make different

Teach Introduction to Probability

- On the board, draw a circle showing fourths. Label each section a different color. Ask, *What are the possible outcomes if this circle were a spinner?* (*each of the four colors*) Ask students to find the probability of spinning one color ($\frac{1}{4}$) and then the probability of spinning one of two colors, such as red or green ($\frac{1}{2}$).
- Point out that the notation $P(2)$ means "the probability of spinning a 2." The parentheses here enclose the outcome and do not indicate multiplication.
- Review definitions of *odd* and *even* numbers. Show students a coin on the overhead or use play money to show *heads* and *tails*.

Language Notes
The word *change* is not printed in the lesson. Ask, *How would the probability of winning the paints change if the easel were removed from the prize list and replaced with paints?* ($P(paints) = \frac{2}{8}$, or $\frac{1}{4}$)

Talk and Share
You may want to have volunteers write the word form for the numbers 1–6 on the board. The probability of rolling a number with the letter "o" is $\frac{3}{6}$, or $\frac{1}{2}$.

Build VOCABULARY
Review the vocabulary words as often as possible. Have students add them to their vocabulary card file.

Differentiating Instruction

Beginning
Understanding Probability Give each student a number cube. Ask, *What numbers are on the number cube?* (1, 2, 3, 4, 5, 6) *Tossing one of the numbers is* an outcome. *What fraction of the time would you toss 1 ($\frac{1}{6}$), 4 ($\frac{1}{6}$), a number less than 4 ($\frac{3}{6}$, or $\frac{1}{2}$)? Each fraction is the probability of tossing that particular number or numbers.*

Intermediate
Writing Probabilities Have students take turns reading one of the number-cube probabilities on page 235, and have their partner explain what the probability means. Then have them take turns using the form $P(E)$ to write and explain the number-cube probabilities.

Advanced
Creating a Game of Chance To show comprehension, have partners design and write directions for a game of chance. The game can utilize a spinner, number cubes, or coins. Have them share games with other pairs and discuss probabilities.

Teach Impossible or Certain?

- Ask, *What is another way the marble example could say* P (*not green*)? (P(*yellow or red*))

- Have students compare the probability for selecting a red marble, $\frac{2}{12}$, and the probability for selecting a yellow marble, $\frac{7}{12}$. Ask, *Which event is more likely to happen?* Have them explain their answers (*selecting a yellow marble because* $\frac{7}{12} > \frac{2}{12}$).

- Ask, *Can a probability be a mixed number?* (*No; a probability cannot be greater than 1, while a mixed number is greater than 1.*)

Talk and Share

Be sure students understand that the sum of the probabilities for the possible outcomes is 1 because all of the possible outcomes are also the favorable outcomes.

Answers: Odd: 1, 3, 5; even: 2, 4, 6; P(*odd*) $= \frac{3}{6}$, P(*even*) $= \frac{3}{6}$; *the probability should be 1 because* P(*odd*) *and* P(*even*) *together cover all possibilities.*

Build VOCABULARY

Introduce the terms in the table. Have students name the terms with opposite meanings (*unlikely/likely* and *impossible/certain*).

Impossible or Certain?

There are 12 marbles in a bag: 3 green, 7 yellow, and 2 red. Suppose you select a marble without looking. What is the probability that

- the marble is yellow? $P(\text{yellow}) = \frac{7}{12}$
- the marble is red? $P(\text{red}) = \frac{2}{12} = \frac{1}{6}$
- the marble is green? $P(\text{green}) = \frac{3}{12} = \frac{1}{4}$
- the marble is *not* green? $P(\text{not green}) = \frac{9}{12} = \frac{3}{4}$
- the marble is blue? $P(\text{blue}) = \frac{0}{12} = 0$
- the marble is *not* blue? $P(\text{not blue}) = \frac{12}{12} = 1$

▲ Marbles

An event E that *cannot* happen is an **impossible event**: $P(\text{E}) = 0$. The bag has no blue marbles, so it is impossible to select a blue one and $P(\text{blue}) = \frac{0}{12} = 0$.

An event F that *has* to happen is a **certain event**: $P(\text{F}) = 1$. The probability of selecting a marble that is *not* blue is 1. $P(\text{not blue}) = \frac{12}{12} = 1$.

A probability is always a number from 0 to 1. It may be written as a fraction, a decimal, or a percent.

	Impossible	Unlikely	Likely to occur half the time	Likely	Certain
Fraction:	0	$\frac{1}{4}$	$\frac{1}{2}$	$\frac{3}{4}$	1
Decimal:	0.0	0.25	0.5	0.75	1.0
Percent:	0%	25%	50%	75%	100%

Talk and Share

Work with a partner. Which of the 6 numbers on the number cube are odd and which are even? Find P(roll an odd number) and find P(roll an even number). Tell why $P(\text{odd}) + P(\text{even})$ should equal 1.

VOCABULARY

impossible event—an event that cannot happen. Its probability is 0.
certain event—an event that has to happen. Its probability is 1.

Activity: In Any Event

Give each pair of students a handful of chips in several colors. Have pairs write four different events and list the *possible outcomes*, *favorable outcomes*, and the *probability* for each event.

Have pairs classify each probability as *certain, likely, unlikely,* or *impossible*. There should be at least one event in each classification.

Differentiating Instruction

Beginning

Making Up Events Have pairs of students use data from the marble example on page 236 to write a different impossible event and a different certain event. (*Samples:* P(*pencil*) *= 0;* P(*marble*)*= 1*)

Intermediate

Designing a Spinner Ask pairs to draw a six-section spinner labeled with each letter in the word "banana." Have them give the probability of spinning each letter (P(*b*) $= \frac{1}{6}$, P(*a*) $= \frac{3}{6}$, P(*n*) $= \frac{2}{6}$).

Then have them describe an *impossible* event, a *certain* event, and three events that have a sum of 1 using the six letters. (*See Additional Answers, page T40.*)

Advanced

Describing Events Give small groups five cards labeled *impossible, unlikely, likely, half the time, likely,* and *certain.* Have students take turns drawing a card and describing an event with that probability.

Practice

Use the spinner for Exercises 1–4.

1. How many sections does the spinner have? How many ways are there to spin 1? To spin 2?

2. What is the probability of spinning 1? Of spinning 2?

3. What is the probability of spinning a 1 or a 2?

4. What is the probability of spinning a 5?

Use a number cube labeled 1 through 6 for Exercises 5–8.

5. What is the probability of rolling a number less than 2?

6. What is the probability of rolling a number greater than 4?

7. What is the probability of rolling a whole number?

8. What is the probability of rolling a prime number?

In Exercises 9–13, tell if each event is *certain*, *impossible*, or *likely* (might happen).

9. It will rain this afternoon.

10. Your desk will walk out of the room by itself.

11. The sun will rise tomorrow.

12. Four students will be absent from school on Tuesday.

13. You will choose a purple ball from a bag that has only purple balls.

There are 10 cards in a hat, labeled 1 through 10. You choose a card without looking. For Exercises 14–17, find each probability and write it as a fraction, a decimal, and a percent.

14. *P*(your number is greater than 9)

15. *P*(you have an odd number)

16. *P*(you have a multiple of 3)

17. *P*(you have a number less than 20)

18. Use the 10 cards described above. Give examples of an outcome that is impossible and an outcome that is certain.

19. If $P(\text{event}) = \frac{9}{9}$, what do you know about the event?

20. Event A has a probability of $\frac{1}{3}$ and event B has a probability of $\frac{2}{3}$. Which event is more likely to happen? Explain.

21. **(MULTIPLE CHOICE)** A gumball machine has 14 red balls, 15 white balls, and 11 green balls. When you turn the handle, the machine releases one ball. What is the probability of getting a green ball on your first turn of the handle?

A. $\frac{1}{40}$ **B.** $\frac{29}{40}$ **C.** $\frac{11}{40}$ **D.** $\frac{40}{40}$

LESSON 41 • WHAT IS PROBABILITY? **237**

Practice

Have eight students stand. Ask, *What is the probability of choosing someone wearing a red shirt if all of you have the same chance of being selected?* Then have students use the set of eight students to give examples of *certain*, *impossible*, and *likely* events. (*Sample:* P(*boy or girl*) = 1; P(*person over 80*) = 0; *likely events will vary by class.*)

Assignment Guide

■ Beginning 1–17 odd, 18, 19, 21

■ Intermediate 2–18 even, 19–21

■ Advanced 1–21

Notes on Exercises

Exercise 3 Be sure students understand that spinning a 1 and spinning a 2 are both favorable outcomes.

Exercise 8 Review the definition of a prime number as a number with only two factors, 1 and itself.

Exercises 9–13 Have a volunteer read the direction line. Review the terms *certain*, *impossible*, and *likely*.

Exercises 14–17 Suggest that students list the outcomes and mark the favorable outcomes to help them write each probability. Remind them to write the probability in three different ways.

Answers

1. 6 sections; 1 way for 1 and 1 way for 2

2. $\frac{1}{6}, \frac{1}{6}$

3. $\frac{2}{6}$, or $\frac{1}{3}$

4. $\frac{1}{6}$

5. $\frac{1}{6}$

6. $\frac{2}{6}$, or $\frac{1}{3}$

7. 1

8. $\frac{3}{6}$, or $\frac{1}{2}$

9. likely

10. impossible

11. certain

12. likely

13. certain

14. $\frac{1}{10}$, 0.1, 10%

15. $\frac{5}{10}$, 0.5, 50%

16. $\frac{3}{10}$, 0.3, 30%

17. $\frac{10}{10}$, 1, 100%

18. Sample: impossible: to draw a number greater than 10; certain: to draw a whole number less than 11

19. It is certain to happen.

20. event B, because $\frac{2}{3} > \frac{1}{3}$

21. C

Program Resources

Practice Book Use page 102.

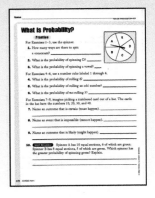

Teach Interpreting

- This activity is a preview to Lesson 42. Have students describe any experiments they have done.

- Point out that the table is a frequency table. Review how to use tally marks to record data. Have a volunteer write tallies for the numbers 1–5 on the board. Point out the diagonal mark used to show 5.

- As students will write sentences as part of the activity, you may want to pair students with a stronger command of English with less fluent speakers. Be sure to check students' work.

Hands On

Demonstrate how to construct the spinner. A simple spinner can be made using a partially straightened paper clip and a pencil tip.

Answer: Expected probability is what is expected to occur over time; few repetitions may have different results.

Partner Practice

Demonstrate the activity by writing the names *Mark* and *Juan* on the board. Ask students to find the probability of choosing an *M* and the probability of choosing an *A* (P(*M*) = $\frac{1}{8}$; P(*A*) = $\frac{1}{4}$). Students do not need to actually make cards as part of the activity.

Develop Language

Activities

Interpreting When you interpret, you explain the meaning of something. Here you will interpret the results of an experiment. For the experiment, you will select two paper clips from a box without looking. The box should have two colored paper clips and two silver ones.

Event	Tally	Number of occurrences ÷ 20
2 colored paper clips		
1 colored and 1 silver paper clip		
2 silver paper clips		

1. **Predict** Write a sentence to predict which of the 3 events listed in the table is most likely to occur.

2. **Select** Copy the table shown. Then select two paper clips from the box. Use a tally mark to record the result in your table. Replace the paper clips. Select and record again 19 more times. Complete the last column.

3. **Interpret** Interpret the results by writing two sentences that describe the results. Compare your predictions with the results.

Hands On

Making Spinners Each of three students should have a card with one of the fractions $\frac{1}{6}$, $\frac{2}{6}$, or $\frac{3}{6}$. Write your names on sections of a spinner so that the probability of landing on your name is equal to your fraction. Spin the spinner 18 times and record the result of each spin. Compare the *number of times the spinner landed on your name divided by 18* with your original fraction. Tell why the two numbers might not match.

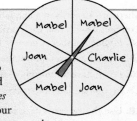

Partner Practice

Your Name or Mine? Suppose each letter of your first name and of your partner's first name is written on a card and put into a hat. Write the probability of choosing each letter from the hat. Tell which letters have the best chance and which have the least chance of being chosen. Explain why.

Program Resources

Practice Book Use page 103.

Assessment Book

Use page 63 to assess students' comprehension.

Activity: Extend the Lesson

Copy the figure below on the board. Tell students that a chip can land on any part of the figure. Have them find the probability that a chip will land on the shaded area.

Suggest that students use area formulas to help them solve the problem (P(*shaded*) = $\frac{8}{10}$, or $\frac{4}{5}$). Challenge them to write and solve a similar problem.

Making Predictions

Talk and Explore

Big Idea When a game or an experiment involves probability, you can gather and use data to help you make a prediction.

Building Background

▲ Sometimes I let my younger brother win games, but I predict that someday he will win on his own!

- How are you supposed to play the Ring-A-Bottle game?
- What other games might you play at a fair?
- How can keeping track of successes help you make predictions?

Key Concepts

An **experiment** is an activity you can repeat many times to gain information. One experiment is trying to ring a bottle. Each time you toss a ring, you are performing one **trial** of the experiment. Getting a ring around a bottle is a **success** for the experiment.

trial

success

LESSON 42 • MAKING PREDICTIONS **239**

Activity: Collect Ring-Toss Data

Provide small groups with cut-out cardboard or canning-jar rings and 2-liter soda bottles to play a ring-toss game. Have students make rules, such as the distance between the player and the bottle, for the game.

Have groups write a brief description of the experiment, define the trials and the successes in the experiment, and record the results. Have them share their results and find and compare the experimental probabilities after reading page 240.

Resource Library

Math at Hand
Probability 285–287

Math on Call
Probability 466–470

Reader's Handbook (red)
Focus on Word Problems 143–154

Reader's Handbook (yellow)
Focus on Word Problems 101–107

Making Predictions

STANDARDS CONTENT
Mathematics
- Find experimental probabilities
- Use data to make a prediction

Language
- Predict a likely outcome for an event

Materials
- Brown socks, blue socks, opaque bag

Introduce the Big Idea

Read aloud the Big Idea. Ask, *How might you use probability to predict how many times a coin toss will land heads when tossed two times?* Most students will predict *one time*, but *no times* and *two times* are acceptable answers.

Begin Building Background

Ask, *Why couldn't you use equally likely outcomes to find the probability of getting a ring on the bottle?* (Sample: *I cannot tell what makes up an equally likely outcome.*)

Teach Key Concepts

- Discuss the diagram. Ask, *Why is the oval for* Successes *inside the oval for* Trials? (Sample: *Each success is one of the trials.*)
- Have students name the trials and successes for any carnival games they mentioned while discussing the picture.

Warm-Up Review

Have students find each product.

1. $\frac{1}{2} \times 6$ (*3*)
2. $\frac{3}{8} \times 24$ (*9*)
3. $\frac{3}{4} \times 20$ (*15*)
4. $\frac{1}{3} \times 81$ (*27*)
5. $\frac{4}{5} \times 80$ (*64*)
6. $\frac{3}{10} \times 100$ (*30*)

Teach **Experimental Probability**

- Explain that in the second example a *match* is a game; for this example, it is also a trial.

- Ask students to find the sum of the probability of winning and the probability of not winning (*1*).

- Write this on the board: *Blokes 16 wins, 2 losses, 2 ties.* Ask, *Are* P(*not winning*) *and* P(*losing*) *the same?* (*No; the probability of not winning includes losing matches and tie matches.*)

- Ask students to use their data from the activity on page 239 to find the experimental probability of ringing a bottle. Encourage them to write the probability as a fraction, a decimal, and a percent.

Talk and Share

Ask, *Would the experimental probability increase, decrease, or remain the same if Stan lost the 26th game?* (*increase, $\frac{11}{26} \approx 42.3\%$*)

Answer: $\frac{11}{25}$, or 44%

Build **VOCABULARY**

Discuss the meanings of these words in the reading: *basket, trial, match,* and *table.*

Look and Read

▲ Free-throw game

Experimental Probability

Yesterday Jalika tried to make 10 free throws. She made 6 of them. Each attempt was a **trial**, so there were 10 trials. Each basket she made was a **success**, so there were 6 successes. She used her data to find the **experimental probability** of making a free throw.

$$\text{Experimental Probability} = \frac{\text{number of successes}}{\text{number of trials}} = \frac{6}{10} \text{ or } 60\%$$

Below is a record of wins and losses for three rugby teams. Complete the last column of the table.

Team	Number of wins	Number of losses	Number of matches	Winning %: wins/matches
Mates	14	6	20	$\frac{14}{20} = ?\%$
Enders	12	8	20	$\frac{12}{20} = ?\%$
Hawks	10	10	20	$\frac{10}{20} = ?\%$

The last column of the table tells you the winning percent, which is the experimental probability. Who has a better chance of winning a match between the Enders and the Hawks?

$P(\text{Enders winning}) = \frac{12}{20} = 60\%$ $P(\text{Hawks winning}) = \frac{10}{20} = 50\%$

The Enders are more likely to win the match.

Talk and Share

Stan and Leon played 25 games of checkers. Stan won 14 games. Work with a partner to find the experimental probability that Leon will win the next game. Express the probability as a percent.

VOCABULARY
trial—an attempt during an experiment
success—a desired result
experimental probability—in an experiment, the number of successes divided by the number of trials

 Activity: Flipping Out

Ask pairs to predict the number of times a coin will land heads when tossed twenty times. Have them use the vocabulary words *trial, success,* and *experiment* to create and perform an experiment to gather the data. Ask them to find the experimental probability for tossing heads.

 Differentiating Instruction

Beginning
Making Up Data Have volunteers explain the meaning of the vocabulary words. Ask students to practice using the vocabulary by making up new data for wins and losses of the rugby teams. Then have them choose an event and write the experimental probability.

Intermediate
Using Words in Different Ways Have pairs of students choose a word from Build Vocabulary and find the different ways that the word is defined in the

dictionary. Have them write two sentences that use the word in different ways. Allow them to share their research with the class.

Advanced
Supporting an Opinion Tell pairs that Suzi believes that doing an experiment more than once always gives the same experimental probability. Have them use the vocabulary words to explain why they agree or disagree. Have them include numerical data in their explanations.

Making Predictions from Data

This jar has 6 blue marbles and 12 red marbles. So, $P(\text{blue}) = \frac{6}{18} = \frac{1}{3} =$ and $P(\text{red}) = \frac{12}{18} = \frac{2}{3}$.

Suppose you select a marble, record its color, and return the marble to the jar 60 times. How many times should you expect to select a red marble?

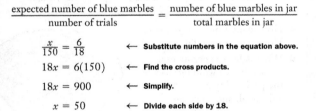

$$P\left(\begin{array}{c}\text{red for}\\\text{each trial}\end{array}\right) \times \left(\begin{array}{c}\text{number}\\\text{of trials}\end{array}\right) = \begin{array}{c}\text{number of red}\\\text{marbles expected}\end{array}$$

$$\frac{2}{3} \qquad\times\qquad 60 \qquad=\qquad 40$$

You should expect, or predict, that you will select a red marble about 40 times out of 60 trials.

If you have 150 trials, how many times should you expect to select a blue marble? Now, use a proportion to solve the problem. Let x be the expected number of blue marbles.

$$\frac{\text{expected number of blue marbles}}{\text{number of trials}} = \frac{\text{number of blue marbles in jar}}{\text{total marbles in jar}}$$

$$\frac{x}{150} = \frac{6}{18} \qquad \leftarrow \textbf{Substitute numbers in the equation above.}$$

$$18x = 6(150) \qquad \leftarrow \textbf{Find the cross products.}$$

$$18x = 900 \qquad \leftarrow \textbf{Simplify.}$$

$$x = 50 \qquad \leftarrow \textbf{Divide each side by 18.}$$

The prediction is that you will select a blue marble 50 times out of 150 trials.

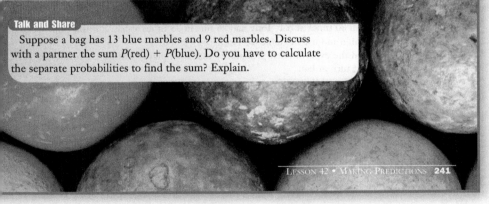

Talk and Share

Suppose a bag has 13 blue marbles and 9 red marbles. Discuss with a partner the sum $P(\text{red}) + P(\text{blue})$. Do you have to calculate the separate probabilities to find the sum? Explain.

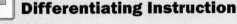

Differentiating Instruction

Beginning

Predicting a Letter On the board, write PROBABILITY. Ask, *How many letters are in this word?* (11) Ask, *What fraction of the letters are ls?* $(\frac{1}{11})$ *How many times do you think you will draw an l if you make 22 picks?* (2 times) *How do you know?* Repeat with the other letters. Relate this to page 241.

Intermediate

Talking About Predicting Have students talk about the two ways to predict probability. Ask them to use the ways to predict how many times they would get a number greater than 2 when tossing a number cube 120 times (80 times).

Advanced

Predicting Without Computing Follow the directions for the Beginning activity. Ask students if they need to find the probabilities to predict whether they will select more *B*s than *I*s or more *B*s than *R*s. (See *Additional Answers, page T40*.)

Teach Making Predictions from Data

■ Briefly discuss why students should suppose each marble is returned to the bag (*so that all trials have the same probability*).

■ Have one volunteer solve this problem using multiplication and another solve it using proportions:

A company tested 500 toy trucks, and 54 of them failed the test. How many of the 20,000 toy trucks made would you expect to fail the test? ($\frac{54}{500} \times 20,000 = 2,160$ *or* $\frac{54}{500} = \frac{x}{20,000}$, $x = 2,160$; *2,160 toy trucks*)

■ Ask, *Is a prediction always correct?* (*no*) Stress that a *prediction* is an "educated guess" about what will happen; it is not a fact.

Talk and Share

■ Point out that the bag has only the marbles listed in the problem.

■ Extend the exercise by asking students to find how many times they would expect to select a red marble out of 110 picks if each selected marble is returned to the bag (*45 times*).

Answers: The P(*red*) + P(*blue*) *is 1 because it is certain that any marble selected will be either red or blue. It is not necessary to calculate the individual probabilities to know the sum.*

Build VOCABULARY

Have a volunteer explain what it means to make a prediction (*tell what you think will happen*).

Explain that the prefix *pre-* means "before," so that to *predict* means to "tell what may happen before it happens." Have small groups list other words that have the prefix *pre-* and write short definitions for the words (*Samples: precede, come before; prehistoric, before recorded history*).

Practice

Have students explain how to find experimental probability. (*Sample: Repeat a trial many times, recording the results. Write the results as the fraction* $\frac{number\ of\ successes}{number\ of\ trials}$.)

Ask students to name two ways to use probability to make predictions. (*Multiply the probability times the number of trials, or solve this proportion:*

$$\frac{expected\ number}{number\ of\ trials} = \frac{\begin{array}{c}number\ of\\favorable\ outcomes\end{array}}{\begin{array}{c}number\ of\\possible\ outcomes\end{array}} .)$$

Assignment Guide
- Beginning 1–5, 7
- Intermediate 1–8
- Advanced 1–8

Notes on Exercises
Exercises 1–3 Ask a volunteer to name the vowels in the alphabet.

Exercises 4–6 Students need to read the introductory paragraph to work through these exercises. You may want students to work in pairs to make sure that everyone understands the data.

Point out that in this problem the word *basket* is a "woven container" and that a *disk* is a "thin, circular object."

Exercises 7 and 8 Let pairs construct the table using the data from the paragraph. Then have students solve the problems independently.

Practice

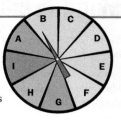

Use the spinner on the right for Exercises 1–3.
1. What is P(spinning a vowel)?
2. What is the probability of spinning a consonant?
3. What is the sum of the probabilities in Exercises 1 and 2? Tell why you should get that sum.

▲ A Mandan woman

The Mandan people play a game with disks and a basket. One side of each disk is decorated and the other side is plain. In a game, Jen won if the disk she tossed landed inside the basket, plain side up. Here are the results for Jen's tosses. Use the table for Exercises 4–6.

Jen's tosses	In the basket	Out of the basket
Plain side up	12 times	14 times
Decorated side up	16 times	8 times

4. How many times did Jen win? How many times did Jen lose?
5. What is Jen's experimental probability of winning? Write the probability as a fraction, a decimal, and a percent.
6. What is Jen's experimental probability of losing? Write the probability as a fraction, a decimal, and a percent.

During part of the baseball season, Tim had 15 hits in 60 times at bat. Tom had 20 hits in 80 times at bat. Tony had 25 hits in 75 times at bat. Put this information into a table and use the table for Exercises 7 and 8.

7. Find the experimental probability that each player will have a hit during his next turn at bat.
8. (EXTENDED RESPONSE) Over the summer, Tim, Tom, and Tony will have a contest. Tim will try 100 times to get a hit. Tom and Tony each will try 120 times. Use each player's experimental probability of getting a hit to predict the number of times each will be successful during the contest. Explain or show how you found your answers.

Program Resources
Practice Book Use page 104.

Answers
1. $\frac{1}{3}$
2. $\frac{2}{3}$
3. 1, because it is certain that the spinner will land on a vowel or a consonant
4. 12 times, 38 times
5. $\frac{12}{50}$, or $\frac{6}{25}$; 0.24; 24%
6. $\frac{38}{50}$, or $\frac{19}{25}$; 0.76; 76%
7. Tim, $\frac{15}{60}$, or $\frac{1}{4}$; Tom, $\frac{20}{80}$, or $\frac{1}{4}$; Tony, $\frac{25}{75}$, or $\frac{1}{3}$
8. Tim, 25 hits; Tom, 30 hits; Tony, 40 hits; I multiplied each player's experimental probability by his number of times at bat.

Aties

Pr When you predict an outcome for an event, you tell which will happen. You use results from past events. Work with. Put four brown and two blue socks into a bag.

1. Predict which is more likely: drawing n socks or drawing one brown and

2. Draw two socks from the bag without Record the results. Return the socks g. Repeat this activity 19 times.

3. Tell how your predictions e with the results.

4. Find the experimental probabilities for each event.

Event	Frequency	Experimental probability
2 brown	?	$\frac{?}{20}$
1 brown, 1 blue	?	$\frac{?}{20}$
2 blue	?	$\frac{?}{20}$

gain Work with a small group. Discuss the meanings of *trials, successes,* and *experimental probability*. Then conduct an t. Give someone 15 paper wads to shoot into a wastebasket. ter should stand in the same spot for every shot. Predict the of times the shooter will get a paper wad in the basket. Then number of shots the shooter makes in 15 trials.

experimental probability and explain how to find it. Express the ity two other ways. Using the results of this experiment, tell how nes you expect the same person to make a basket in 50 trials.

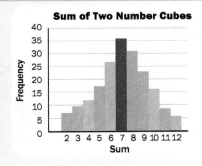

It The bar graph on the right he results of rolling two number cubes es. After each roll, the numbers g on the two cubes were added and ed. With a partner, find and tell the mental probability of rolling each sum. bout the results. Why was a sum of 7 most often? Why aren't sums of 0 and d? Would the probabilities change if you rolled the cubes 200 more times?

Sum of Two Number Cubes

(bar graph: Frequency on vertical axis 0–40, Sum on horizontal axis 2 3 4 5 6 7 8 9 10 11 12)

LESSON 42 • MAKING PREDICTIONS **243**

Develop Language

Teach Predicting

■ Students may use chips or cubes in different colors instead of socks.

■ Explain that students can use data to make predictions about what will happen. Point out that marketing and advertising executives often use data from a small group, a *sample*, to predict how a large group will react to a new product or advertising campaign.

■ Discuss why students' results may differ.

Hands On

Review the three ways to express probability: as a fraction, as a percent, and as a decimal. Then have a volunteer demonstrate how to shoot baskets for the experiment. Be sure to check students' work.

Oral Language

Read the graph as a class so that all students have the same data.

Answers: 2, $\frac{7}{200}$; 3, $\frac{9}{200}$; 4, $\frac{17}{200}$; 5, $\frac{20}{200}$; 6, $\frac{27}{200}$; 7, $\frac{36}{200}$; 8, $\frac{31}{200}$; 9, $\frac{23}{200}$; 10, $\frac{16}{200}$; 11, $\frac{8}{200}$; 12, $\frac{6}{200}$

There are more pairs of numbers with a sum of 7 than with any other sum. Because each number cube has the numbers 1–6, the least sum is 2 (1 + 1). In the next 200 rolls, the probabilities should not change significantly.

Activity: Ups and Downs

Have students perform this eriment: Drop a paper cup from e same height 20 times; record the mber of times the cup lands on its le, on its top, and on its bottom, d write the experimental probability.

Before they perform the eriment, students should predict w many times the cup will land ch way. After students compare the ults with their predictions, combine class data and find the experimental obability.

Assessment Book

Use page 64 to assess students' comprehension.

Program Resources

Practice Book Use page 105.

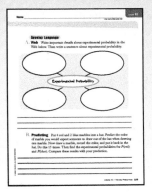

Counting

STANDARDS CONTENT

Mathematics

- Draw a tree diagram to find all possible ways an event can happen
- Use the counting principle to find the number of possible outcomes

Language

- Use signal words to order events
- Persuade a person by giving convincing reasons

Introduce the Big Idea

Read aloud the Big Idea. Say, *Suppose you toss three number cubes. How many outcomes are possible in each cube? (6 outcomes) How many possible outcomes are there altogether for tossing three number cubes?* Tell students that they will learn how to find the answer in this lesson.

Begin Building Background

Have volunteers tell about activities in which they participate, such as dance and sports. Ask, *What special clothes do you wear?* The third question is answered in detail in Key Concepts.

Teach Key Concepts

- Have students match the name and picture for each article of clothing.
- Ask, *How are tree diagrams and factor trees alike and different? (Sample: Both have branches from a starting point. A factor tree starts with one number. A tree diagram starts with two or more words or phrases.)*

Warm-Up Review

Have students draw a factor tree for each number.

1. 240 $(2 \times 2 \times 2 \times 2 \times 3 \times 5)$
2. 150 $(2 \times 3 \times 5 \times 5)$
3. 462 $(2 \times 3 \times 7 \times 11)$
4. 60 $(2 \times 2 \times 3 \times 5)$

Check students' factor trees. Products list the prime factors of each number.

Talk and Explore

Counting

Big Idea You can use special methods to find a nt all possible outcomes. The methods are useful for find ₃e number or only a small number of outcomes.

Building Background

▲ When I was very young, my grandmother sewed my dance costumes.

- Describe the outfits the boys are wearing in the photo.
- When might you wear a special outfit?
- How many different outfits are possible when you have two sw nd two pairs of pants to choose from?

Key Concepts

A **tree diagram** is an organized list that shows all possible ways to combine things. You can count all the possibilities once you have the list. This tree diagram shows that there are four possible ways to combine two sweaters and two pairs of pants.

Tree Diagram

Sweaters	Pants	Possible Co ns
pullover	straight leg	pullover and leg
	flared leg	pullover and g
cardigan	straight leg	cardigan and leg
	flared leg	cardigan and g

straight leg   flared leg

pullover sweater   ca sw

244 UNIT 10 • PROBABILITY

Activity: A Shoe Tree

On the board, draw the tree diagram from Key Concepts. Show how to add shoe choices of sneakers and loafers.

Sweaters	Pants	Shoes	Poss. Comb.
pullover	straight	sneakers	PSS
	flared	loafers	PSL
cardigan	straight		
	flared		

Have pairs copy and complete the diagram and list the possible combinations. (*See Additional Answers, page T40.*)

Resource Library

Math at Hand
Tree Diagrams and the Counting Principle 291–292

Math on Call
Tree Diagrams and the Counting Principle 459, 464

Tree Diagrams

The members of the Flag Squad get lunch on days of long practices. Each lunch offers three choices.

First, pick a drink: white milk or chocolate milk
Next, pick a sandwich: turkey or tomato
Finally, pick chips: corn, potato, or cheese

A **compound event** is an event that involves making more than one choice. You can make a **tree diagram** to list all the possible combinations in a compound event.

Language Notes

Signal Words:
Time Order
These words are clues to the order in which things happen.

☐ first
☐ next
☐ finally

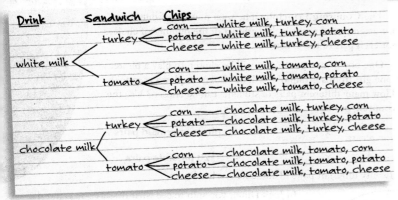

To find the number of different ways to select a drink, a sandwich, and chips, count the combinations from the last column of the tree diagram. There are 12 combinations.

On the left is a tree diagram that shows all four possible outcomes from the toss of a penny and a dime.
H = heads and T = tails.

$P(\text{2 heads}) = P(\text{HH}) = \frac{1}{4}$

$P(\text{2 tails}) = P(\text{TT}) = \frac{1}{4}$

$P(\text{1 head and 1 tail}) = P(\text{H and T}) = \frac{1}{2}$

Talk and Share

With a partner, make a tree diagram to show all the ways of choosing a bass player (Jeb or Lon) and a guitar player (Toshie or Amy) for a band. Explain your diagram to the class.

VOCABULARY
compound event—a combination of two or more single events
tree diagram—an organized list showing all possible outcomes

Teach Tree Diagrams

■ Ask two volunteers to draw the lunch tree diagram on the board. One volunteer should start with sandwich choices; the other volunteer should start with chip choices. Have students compare the tree diagrams. (*Sample: They have the same combinations, but the order of the choices is different.*)

■ Ask, *Why is the probability of tossing heads once and tails once* $\frac{1}{2}$*?* Elicit that the outcomes HT and TH are both favorable outcomes. The two other possible outcomes are HH and TT, so the probability is $\frac{2}{4}$, or $\frac{1}{2}$.

Language Notes

Have students read the words and explain how each tells order. Encourage them to use each word in a sentence.

Talk and Share

Encourage students who drew the diagrams in different ways to share their work with the class.

Answer:

Bass	Guitar	Combinations
Jeb	Toshie	Jeb, Toshie
	Amy	Jeb, Amy
Lon	Toshie	Lon, Toshie
	Amy	Lon, Amy

Build VOCABULARY

Explain that *compound* is an adjective meaning "parts put together."

Differentiating Instruction

Beginning
Drawing a Tree Diagram After discussing the tree diagram on page 245, have pairs of students use the signal words *first, next,* and *last* to explain how to draw a tree diagram that shows the possible combinations of colors and shapes for *red, blue, green* and *square, circle, triangle.* Have them use the colors and shapes to draw the tree diagram and list the possible combinations (*Check students' tree diagrams; RS, RC, RT, BS, BC, BT, GS, GC, GT*).

Intermediate/Advanced
Explaining a Tree Diagram After discussing the tree diagram on page 245, have pairs make up an event with three colors, three styles of hats, and three sizes. Have them draw a tree diagram to show the possible combinations. Encourage students to use signal words to explain their work. (*Check students' tree diagrams. There are 27 possible combinations.*)

Activity: Compounded
Define a compound word as one made up of two or more words. Point out that *outcome* is made up of the words *out* and *come.* Have pairs find the compound words on pages 237, 238, 242, and 243 (*afternoon, itself, percent, gumball, something, without, baseball, someone, outcome, wastebasket*).

Teach The Counting Principle

- Stress that the counting principle is used only to find *how many* different outcomes are possible for a compound event. Ask, *How could you find the possible outcomes?* (*Make an organized list; draw a tree diagram.*)

- Help students use the tree diagram on page 245 to see the twelve combinations. Explain that the word *combos* means combinations.

- Have the class write an organized list of the dessert outcomes on the board to show that the probability of spinning two brownies is $\frac{1}{16}$. (*BB, BI, BF, BP, IB, II, IF, IP, FB, FI, FF, FP, PB, PI, PF, PP; BB is $\frac{1}{16}$ of the total number of combinations.*)

Talk and Share

Have pairs share their explanations with the class. Discuss possible ways to show each person, such as making up names for the boys and girls, or using a different letter to identify each person.

Sample answer: List choices for pirates and then for mermaids.

Build **VOCABULARY**

Ask students the meaning of the word *principle* (*a rule*). Have them write the counting principle and give an example of it in their math journal.

The Counting Principle

To find out *how many* different outcomes are possible for a compound event, you can use the counting principle.

For lunch, there are 2 drink choices, 2 sandwich choices, and 3 chip choices. The total number of choices can be found by multiplying.

drink choices	×	sandwich choices	×	chip choices	=	lunches
2	×	2	×	3	=	12 combos

The **Counting Principle:** The total number of outcomes for a compound event is the product of the number of choices for each part of the event.

One boy from a group of 4 will be chosen to play a pirate. One girl from a group of 5 will be chosen to play a mermaid. How many different pairs of students can be chosen? Use the counting principle.

choices for pirate	×	choices for mermaid	=	pirate/mermaid pairs
4	×	5	=	20 possible pairs

Twenty different pairs of students can be chosen.

▲ The spinner at Joe's Diner

In Joe's Diner, you spin to see what dessert you can order. Use the counting principle to find the probability of spinning "Brownie" two times in a row.

Number of possible outcomes = choices first spin × choices second spin = 4 × 4 = 16

There is only one way to land on Brownie both times, so P(Brownie and Brownie) = $\frac{1}{16}$.

Talk and Share

Work with a partner. Tell how you can make a tree diagram to show the possible pairs of pirates and mermaids from above.

VOCABULARY
counting principle—the idea that the total number of outcomes for a compound event is the product of the number of choices for each part

---

 Activity: Count Me In

Have pairs use menus or catalogs to create a compound event and then find how many outcomes are possible.

If necessary, provide suggestions such as different salads and sides to help get students started.

Differentiating Instruction

Beginning
Understanding Compound Events On the board, draw two spinners. Label one *A, B, C, D* and the other *1, 2, 3, 4*. Ask volunteers to help you list the combinations if the spinners are spun together. Ask, *How many outcomes are on each spinner?* (*4 outcomes*) *How many combinations did we list?* (*16 combinations*) *What is 4 times 4?* (*16*)

Intermediate
Creating a Compound Event Have pairs use a number cube and a spinner to create a compound event with 12 possible number combinations. Have them talk about how they decided on the spinner. (*The spinner should show halves.*)

Advanced
Explaining a Compound Event Have pairs create a compound event that has 20 possible outcomes and share how they decided on the number of choices for each event (*Sample: a spinner showing tenths and a coin*).

Practice

In Exercises 1–5, use this tree diagram of the toss of a number cube labeled 1 through 6 and the toss of a coin.

Cube	Coin	Outcome
1	H	1H
	T	1T
2	H	2H
	T	2T
3	H	3H
	T	3T
4	H	4H
	T	4T
5	H	5H
	T	5T
6	H	6H
	T	6T

1. Tell how many outcomes there are. Tell how you could use the counting principle to be sure you have all possible outcomes listed.

2. How many of the outcomes have heads? Tails?

3. Find P(heads). Find P(tails).

4. What do you notice about the two probabilities in Exercise 3?

5. How many outcomes have a 6? Find P(heads and a 6).

6. A high school band has 12 sophomores, 15 juniors, and 10 seniors. Use the counting principle to calculate how many ways the band teacher can select a group of 3 students, one from each grade.

7. A 7-digit phone number cannot start with 0 or 1. Digits may be repeated. How many different phone numbers are possible?

8. (MULTIPLE CHOICE) A deli sells 8 kinds of bagels and 6 kinds of cream cheese. How many different combinations of a bagel and a cream cheese are possible?
   A. 14   **B.** 8   **C.** 6   **D.** 48

A restaurant's sandwich special can be on wheat bread, rye bread, or pita bread. It can have chicken or turkey, and it can be topped with mustard, relish, or hummus.

9. Use the counting principle to find how many combinations are possible for the sandwich. Then make and label a tree diagram that lists all the combinations.

10. (SHORT RESPONSE) If all choices are equally likely, what is the probability that a sandwich is on pita bread with turkey and hummus? What is the probability that a sandwich has chicken?

LESSON 43 • COUNTING **247**

Practice

Have students explain how to use the counting principle to find the number of combinations that can be made using five different car body colors and three different colors for seats (*Find 5 × 3 = 15; 15 combinations*).

Ask, *How could you find what color of car and what color of seat make up each combination?* (*Sample: Make a tree diagram or make an organized list.*)

Assignment Guide
■ Beginning 1–6, 8–10
■ Intermediate 1–10
■ Advanced 1–10

Notes on Exercises
Exercise 7 Ask, *What digits can be used in the phone number?* (0, 1, 2, 3, 4, 5, 6, 7, 8, 9) Encourage them to write the number of different digits that can be used for each digit in the phone number before they use the counting principle.

Exercises 9 and 10 Ask a volunteer to read the introductory paragraph, or have students work in pairs to solve Exercise 9. Suggest that students list the choices for the sandwich specials before completing the exercises.

Answers
1. 12 outcomes; multiply 6 and 2.
2. 6 outcomes; 6 outcomes
3. $\frac{6}{12}$, or $\frac{1}{2}$; $\frac{6}{12}$, or $\frac{1}{2}$
4. They are equal.
5. 2 outcomes; $\frac{1}{12}$
6. 1,800 ways

7. 8 • 10 • 10 • 10 • 10 • 10 • 10 = 8,000,000 numbers
8. D
9. 18 combinations

For tree diagram, see Additional Answers, page T41.

10. $\frac{1}{18}$; $\frac{9}{18}$, or $\frac{1}{2}$

Program Resources
Practice Book Use page 106.

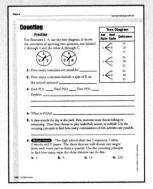

Teach Persuading

- Have students talk about how they persuaded a friend to do something. For example, did they promise to do a favor for the person?

- If you need to clarify the problem, tell students that each player in this two-person game has a 30% probability of winning, so there is a 40% probability that either the game will end in a tie or there will be no winner. Point out that a game like tic-tac-toe sometimes has no winner. They could expect a win 6 times.

- As a class, discuss why the game results may be different from the predictions. (*Experimental probability may vary, especially in experiments with few trials.*)

Answer:

2. *6 wins*

Oral Language

You may want to have four students at a time role-play the activity in front of the class. Have the clerk for each group change the menu by erasing or adding choices.

Partner Practice

Point out that the juice choices do not need to be added to the diagram.

Answers: For tree diagram, see Additional Answers, page T41; 72 smoothies

---

Activities

▲ What games do you play with your family? How often do you win?

Persuading When you persuade, you give reasons to convince someone to accept your opinion. How would you persuade a friend to accept your predictions?

The probability of winning a game is 30%. Suppose you and a friend will play the game 20 times.

1. **Predict** Before you start playing, tell how many games you think you and your friend will each win.

2. **Compute** Calculate your predictions with this equation.

$$P(winning) \times number\ of\ games = expected\ number\ of\ wins$$

3. **Persuade** Convince your partner that you are correct by explaining your calculation.

4. **Compare** Play the game and count the wins. Compare the game results with your predictions.

Oral Language

What'll It Be? Four students choose roles and act out this scene. The clerk writes the "Healthy Smoothies" menu choices on the board.

Clerk: Here is our menu. You can choose a fruit, a cream, and a booster for your smoothie.

Student 1: How many different smoothies are there?

Student 2: I know how to find out. Find the number of choices for each category. Then find the product of those numbers.

Student 3: That means there are $3 \times 4 \times 2$, or 24 different types of smoothies. I know what kind I want.

Clerk: Give me your orders, and I'll have them in a jiffy.

Healthy Smoothies		
Fruit	Cream	Booster
strawberries	yogurt	wheat
mango	milk	germ
papaya	soy milk	vitamins
	ice cream	

Partner Practice

Smoothie Tree Work with a partner. Make a tree diagram that lists all the smoothies from the "Healthy Smoothies" menu. Talk about how you know if your tree diagram is complete. Discuss how the number of smoothies would change if you added three juices to the other choices.

Program Resources

Practice Book Use page 107.

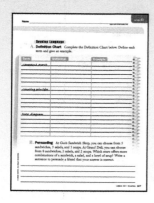

Assessment Book

Use page 65 to assess students' comprehension.

Activity: Internet Connection

Have students access these sites for more practice making and reading tree diagrams, finding probability, and using probability vocabulary:

- http://regentsprep.org/Regents/math/math-topic.cfm?TopicCode=tree

- http://www.bbc.co.uk/education/mathsfile/shockwave/games/fish.html

- http://www.mathgoodies.com/puzzles2004/puzzles/iprobability

Arrangements

Talk and Explore

Big Idea When you list the outcomes for a compound event, the way you order them may be important.

Building Background

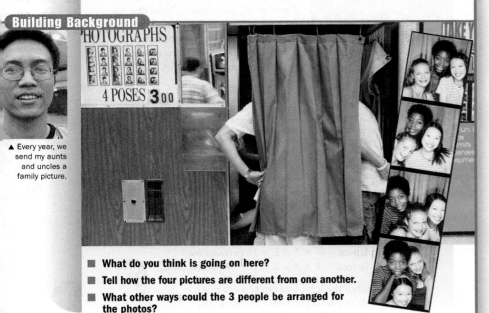

▲ Every year, we send my aunts and uncles a family picture.

- What do you think is going on here?
- Tell how the four pictures are different from one another.
- What other ways could the 3 people be arranged for the photos?

Key Concepts

An **arrangement** of things in a *particular order* is called a **permutation**. When the *order does not matter*, the arrangement is just a group and is called a **combination**.

Arrangements

Permutation	Combination
Order matters, as with the digits of a phone number.	Order does not matter, as with the names of people on a committee.
Example: *I think Sean's phone number is 897-1234. Or is it 897-4321?*	**Example:** *Terrie, Melanie, and Mae are on the decorating committee.*

LESSON 44 • ARRANGEMENTS **249**

Activity: Undercover Work

Say, *Pretend that you are detectives. Name some ways that you could change your appearance.* List the categories and characteristics on the board. For example, *facial hair* might be a category, with *mustache, beard,* and *no hair* as characteristics.

Have students list all the possible *disguises* they could make with three choices. Have them select a disguise and persuade their partner why that disguise is the one to use.

Resource Library

Math at Hand
Combinations 291

Math on Call
Permutations and Combinations 457–460

***Reader's Handbook* (red)**
Focus on Word Problems 143–154

Arrangements

STANDARDS CONTENT
Mathematics
- Find and count permutations
- Find and count combinations

Language
- Use signal words to order events
- Clarify the meaning of *permutation* and *combination*

Introduce the **Big Idea**

Read aloud the Big Idea. Ask, *Does it matter which item you list first when you want to find the number of combinations for three jackets and four hats?* (*no*)

Begin **Building Background**

Have three students—A, B, and C—show the different ways they could stand in a row to have their picture taken (*ABC, ACB, BCA, BAC, CAB, CBA*).

Teach **Key Concepts**

- Have a volunteer draw a Web (Overhead Transparency 33) showing the relationship between the terms *arrangement, permutation,* and *combination. Sample:*

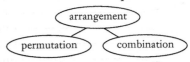

- Ask, *Does the order of the three students posing for the pictures matter?* (*yes*) *Is the arrangement a permutation or a combination?* (*permutation*)

Warm-Up Review

Have students tell the possible outcomes for each event.

1. tossing a number cube (*1, 2, 3, 4, 5, 6*)
2. selecting a marble from a group of 1 blue and 2 red marbles (*blue, red, red*)
3. tossing a coin (*heads, tails*)
4. tossing a coin and a number cube (*H1, H2, H3, H4, H5, H6, T1, T2, T3, T4, T5, T6*)

Teach Permutations

- Use counters in four colors to demonstrate how the number of choices decreases for each subsequent runner. Tell students that each color stands for one runner. Show that if one color is used for the first choice, then there are three colors remaining for the next choice, and so on, until there is only one color left.

- Have students use the counting principle to check that all the ways to arrange three people in a row are listed ($3 \times 2 \times 1 = 6$).

Language Notes

Point out that all the words tell the order numerically, so that the word *first* names step 1, *second* names step 2, and so on. Have students match other counting numbers with the order words.

Talk and Share

Ask pairs to explain why the arrangement TDH and HDT are not different when the students are on a cleanup committee. (*The order does not matter for a committee.*)

Answer:

1st	2nd	3rd	Order
T	D	H	TDH
	H	D	THD
D	T	H	DTH
	H	T	DHT
H	T	D	HTD
	D	T	HDT

Look and Read

Permutations

Runners A, B, C, and D are in a race. On the right is a list of all possible ways they can finish in first and second place. There are 12 possibilities. Note that AB means A is first and B is second. So AB and BA are different **permutations**. When the order of the items matters, each **arrangement** is called a permutation.

12 Permutations

AB	AC	AD
BA	BC	BD
CA	CB	CD
DA	DB	DC

How many ways are there for all four runners to finish the race? We can use the counting principle.

4 choices for first place		3 choices for second place		2 choices for third place		1 choice for fourth place		number of permutations
4	×	3	×	2	×	1	=	24

Just as the word *was* is different from the word *saw*, the letter arrangements ABCD and DCBA are different. Suppose you have 4 letters to use and letters can't be repeated.

Find the number of permutations that use
2 letters: $4 \times 3 = 12$ permutations
3 letters: $4 \times 3 \times 2 = 24$ permutations
4 letters: $4 \times 3 \times 2 \times 1 = 24$ permutations

List all the ways you can arrange three people in a row. Let Tom (T), Dana (D), and Harriet (H) stand for the three people.

TDH	DTH	HDT
THD	DHT	HTD

Language Notes

Signal Words: Time Order
These words are clues to the order in which things happen.
- first
- second
- third
- fourth

Talk and Share

Work with a partner.
Draw a tree diagram to show the six permutations of Tom, Dana, and Harriet. If the three of them were on a cleanup committee, would it matter how you listed them?

VOCABULARY
permutations—arrangements of items in a particular order
arrangement—the way things are organized or put together

Activity: Order Counts

Have small groups write the twenty-four 4-letter permutations for the letters *A, B ,C,* and, *D.* Then have them take turns using a signal word for order and telling which group of letters is in that position (*ABCD, ABDC, ACBD, ACDB, ADCB, ADBC, BACD, BADC, BCDA, BCAD, BDCA, BDAC, CABD, CADB, CBDA, CBAD, CDAB, CDBA, DABC, DACB, DBAC, DBCA, DCAB, DCBA*).

Differentiating Instruction

Beginning
Understanding Permutations Ask volunteers to come to the board and write a 3-digit number using the numbers *1, 2,* and *3.* Ask, *Does the order of the digits matter?* (*yes*) *How many different numbers did you write?* (6) Say, *These six numbers are called permutations because the order matters.* Show them how to use the counting principle to find the number of permutations.

Intermediate/Advanced
Finding Permutations Ask pairs to list all the 3-digit numbers possible using the digits *1, 2, 3,* and *4* (24). Ask, *Does the order of the digits matter?* (*yes*) *Your numbers are called* permutations *because the order matters.* Have them talk about how the counting principle could be used to find the number of permutations.

Combinations

Four cars are entered in a soapbox derby. Their names are Atlas (A), Brody (B), Cagey (C), and Dingy (D). The top two finishers will enter the final race. The list at the right shows all the possible pairings for the top two finishers. In this situation, AB and BA represent the same pair. The paired letters are combinations. If you change the order of the items in a **combination,** you do not get a new combination.

AB	AC
AD	BC
BD	CD

Monique is selecting two skirts out of four to take on a trip. How many combinations of the skirts can she choose? Represent the skirts with the letters R, S, T, and U. Start by listing all two-letter permutations. There will be 4 × 3, or 12, of them.

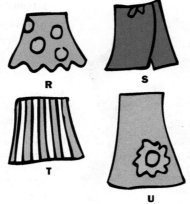

R

S

T

U

Permutations			Combinations		
RS	RT	RU	RS	RT	RU
SR	ST	SU	~~SR~~	ST	SU
TR	TS	TU	~~TR~~	~~TS~~	TU
UR	US	UT	~~UR~~	~~US~~	~~UT~~

Notice that RS and SR are the same two skirts. So cross out SR. Finish by crossing out all the others that are repeats. Monique can choose from six combinations of pairs of skirts.

Talk and Share

Work with a partner. You are planning to have 8 people over for a party. You have the 8 names listed on a piece of paper. If you switch the order of the 8 names, will you get a new group? Is the list of 8 people a permutation or a combination?

VOCABULARY

combination—a group of items. If you change the order of the items in the group, you do *not* get a new combination.

Guest List

Jennifer	Sudhir
Todd	Rosa
Jamal	Hiromi
Katie	Miguel

Teach Combinations

■ Have students look at the picture. Ask, *What do you think happens at a soapbox derby?*

■ Ask, *Why doesn't the order matter for the derby finishers?* (Because both the first and the second place finishers will race again, the order of the top two finishers does not matter. If they were winning medals or prizes for placing first or second, then the order would *matter.*)

■ Have students look at the two organized lists. Ask, *Why are the number of permutations and the number of combinations different?* (Order matters for permutations, but not for combinations. So RS and SR are both listed as permutations, but not as combinations.)

Talk and Share

Have students explain their answers. Ask, *Why are the eight people a combination and not a permutation?*

Answers: No; combination; the same people will attend the party, regardless of their place on the list.

Build VOCABULARY

Stress that the math and everyday meanings of the word *combination* differ. A combination is also the result of joining two or more items.

Differentiating Instruction

Beginning
Acting Out Combinations Have small groups find as many different combinations of four people as they can from five people. Have them label group members and then arrange themselves in the combinations (*5 combinations: ABCD, ABCE, ABDE, ACDE, BCDE*).

Intermediate
Using Manipulatives Have pairs follow the directions for in the Beginning activity, except have them use five different-colored chips, counters, or paper squares to find all the combinations of four items. (*See answer to Beginning activity.*)

Advanced
Listing Combinations Have pairs of students list all the two-letter combinations they can, using the letters *A, B, C, D, E,* and *F.* Then have them write explaining how they found the combinations (*AB, AC, AD, AE, AF, BC, BD, BE, BF, CD, CE, CF, DE, DF, EF*).

Activity: Concentration

Have pairs prepare two cards for each vocabulary term in Unit 10, one card listing the term and the other card listing the definition.

Have pairs mix the cards and lay them facedown. Have pairs alternate turning over two cards, keeping any cards that match. When all the cards are gone, the winner is the student with more cards.

Practice

Ask, *Is a license-plate number a combination or a permutation? (It is a permutation because the order of the numbers and letters matters.)*

You may want to have students complete the Clarifying activity on page 253 before assigning the Practice exercises. The activity can help them differentiate between permutations and combinations.

Assignment Guide
- Beginning 3–8, 10, 11, 13, 14
- Intermediate 2–6 even, 7, 9–14
- Advanced 1–7 odd, 8–14

Notes on Exercises
Exercise 7 Discuss students' answers as a class.

Exercise 10 Have students work in groups or use a computer anagram program to find the real 5-letter words. There are 120 arrangements of the letters to test.

Exercises 11 and 12 Point out that the two exercises are different: The two digits in Exercise 11 cannot be used more than once; but in Exercise 12, the three digits can be used more than once.

Look and Read

Practice

For Exercises 1–6, tell if order matters in each situation. Explain your answers.
1. Describing 6 pigeons sitting on a bench
2. Selecting 3 numbers to open a lock
3. Choosing 3 scoops of ice cream for a banana split
4. Choosing a 7-letter password
5. Selecting 5 students to sing in a chorus
6. Arranging 14 stuffed animals on your bed
7. Suppose you find all permutations of the letters GHI. Then you find all the combinations of GHI. Will you find more permutations or more combinations? Tell how you know.
8. At a big meeting, 6 people will give special talks. In how many different orders can the 6 people give their talks?
9. How many ways can you choose from 9 violin players for first-chair, second-chair, and third-chair positions?
10. Use the letters in the word PARTY. How many 5-letter permutations can be made? How many 4-letter permutations can be made? How many are real words?

Use the digits 0, 1, 2, and 3 for Exercises 11 and 12.
11. How many different 2-digit numbers can you make? Use each digit no more than once in each number. The first digit of the 2-digit numbers cannot be 0. List all of the 2-digit numbers you can make.
12. If you can use each digit as many times as you like, how many 3-digit numbers can you make? The first digit of the 3-digit numbers cannot be 0.
13. How many ways can you choose 3 different ice cream toppings if 5 toppings are offered? List all the different ways.
14. (MULTIPLE CHOICE) How many different ways can you show one of these shapes inside one of the other shapes?
A. 6   B. 4   C. 3   D. 1

Program Resources
Practice Book Use page 108.

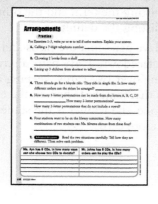

Answers
1. yes   2. yes
3. no   4. yes
5. no   6. yes
7. More permutations; there are 6 permutations and only 1 combination.
8. 720 orders   9. 504 ways
10. 120 five-letter permutations; 120 four-letter permutations; sample real words: part, tarp, trap, rapt, pray, tray, arty, party
11. 9 numbers; 10, 12, 13, 20, 21, 23, 30, 31, 32
12. 48 numbers: 100, 101, 102, 103, 110, 111, 112, 113, 120, 121, 122, 123, 130, 131, 132, 133, 200, 201, 202, 203, 210, 211, 212, 213, 220, 221, 222, 223, 230, 231, 232, 233, 300, 301, 302, 303, 310, 311, 312, 313, 320, 321, 322, 323, 330, 331, 332, 333
13. 10 ways: ABC, ABD, ABE, ACD, ACE, ADE, BCD, BCE, BDE, CDE
14. C

Activities

Clarifying When you clarify, you give details and examples to make the meaning clear. You might tell how an item is like or different from other items. Work with a partner to clarify the meanings of *permutation* and *combination*.

1. **Clarify** Tell why the different ways of arranging 4 pictures on a wall are permutations. Give other examples of permutations.

2. **Clarify** Tell why the different ways of arranging 12 roses in a vase are combinations. Give other examples of combinations.

3. **Explain** Tell how a *permutation* and a *combination* are alike. Tell how they are different.

Partner Practice

Ready to Wear All the students on the soccer team start the year with these pieces of clothing for their uniforms.

   shirts: long sleeve, short sleeve
   shorts: striped, solid
   pants: black, red, white

Work with a partner to make a tree diagram for all the possible choices for shirts, shorts, and pants. How many different outfits are possible?

Oral Language

What's the Story? Work in a small group. List all possible arrangements of the letters A, P, S, and T. How many arrangements should you have altogether? Which of the arrangements form real words? Use a dictionary if you are not sure. Take turns saying sentences with these words. Together, make up a short story that uses one of the words. Are the arrangements you found permutations or combinations? Explain how you know.

Teach Clarifying

■ Invite students to write a sentence and draw a picture that tells about a favorite pastime. Have them answer simple questions about their pastimes. Explain that by answering questions and showing pictures, they can *clarify* what the pastimes are like.

■ You may want to discuss pairs' answers to Exercises 1 and 2 to make sure students understand the concepts before having them complete Exercise 3.

See Additional Answers, page T41.

Partner Practice

This is a review of Lesson 43. Have pairs share their diagrams with the class and discuss how they labeled them. Ask, *Did any of you draw pictures instead of using words or did you use abbreviations? If you used abbreviations, tell us how you decided on each abbreviation.*

See Additional Answers, page T41.

Oral Language

Suggest that less fluent students use pictures where needed to help them write the story or have them find the words in other printed materials.

See Additional Answers, page T41.

 Activity: Phone Me

Have each student in a pair write down a phone number, leaving out two digits. Ask students to find the number of permutations needed to find the two missing digits. Remind them that the numbers may be repeated (*10 × 10 = 100 ways*).

Have students give their partners clues to help them identify the missing numbers. You may want to suggest, *The first digit is an even number, and it is divisible by 3.*

 Assessment Book

Use page 66 to assess students' comprehension.

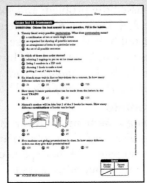

Program Resources

Practice Book Use page 109.

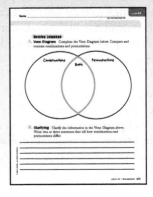

Simulate a Problem

STANDARDS CONTENT

Mathematics
■ Solve problems by using a simulation

Language
■ Determine how to use *who* and *what*

Materials
■ Coins, number cubes, spinner materials (circle models, paper clips)

Teach Simulate a Problem

■ Have students explain why they will toss three coins to simulate the births. (*Each coin will stand for 1 birth.*) Ask, *Would you use three coins to simulate five births?* (*No; 5 coins are needed to show 5 births.*)

■ Ask, *How would you record a toss that showed "tails, tails, tails?"* (*Put 1 tally mark in the table in the row for 3 boys.*)

■ Have students work in pairs to perform the simulation. Discuss why their probabilities may be different from those in the Answer step. (*Sample: Experimental probabilities may vary, especially when there are not many trials.*) You may want to have several pairs combine their data for the Look Back step.

Talk and Share

Encourage pairs to use math vocabulary to talk about how they made their predictions.

Problem-Solving Skills

Simulate a Problem

When you simulate something, you make something that acts like it. Simulation is useful for experiments you can't actually do. You can't have dozens of babies just to find out the chances of having a boy or a girl. However, you can simulate dozens and dozens of births by tossing coins.

Problem: A couple has 3 children. What is the probability that they have 2 girls and 1 boy?

Read and Understand

Need to find: The experimental probability of 2 girls and 1 boy

You know: For each birth, there are two equally likely outcomes: a boy or a girl. The probability of having a girl and the probability of having a boy is $\frac{1}{2}$ in each case.

Type of Births		
Possibilities	Tally	Frequency
3 boys		
2 boys, 1 girl		
2 girls, 1 boy		
3 girls		

Key fact: When you toss a coin, there are two equally likely outcomes: heads or tails. The probability of each is $\frac{1}{2}$. So tossing coins is a good model for simulating births.

Plan and Solve
Let heads stand for a girl and let tails stand for a boy. Toss 3 coins. Use a table like the one shown to record the results from each toss. Toss the 3 coins at least 20 times.

Answer
Show the experimental probability of 2 girls and 1 boy as a fraction. Suppose "2 girls and 1 boy" occurred on 9 tosses. Then your experimental probability is $\frac{9}{20}$, or about 45%. Research shows that the combination of 2 girls and 1 boy is expected to occur about 38% of the time with 3 births.

Look Back
For any simulation problem, the more data you have, the more reasonable your results. Toss the 3 coins another 20 times and combine your data. Are your results about the same for 40 tosses as for the first 20 tosses?

Talk and Share
Work with a partner. Use your data to predict the probability of 3 girls. Talk about it.

Activity: I Got the Spirit

Give students this problem to solve: On spirit day, $\frac{5}{6}$ of the students pinned school buttons to their backpacks and $\frac{3}{6}$ of the students wore school shirts. What is the probability that a student is wearing both a button and a school shirt?

Have small groups use two number cubes of different colors to create and perform a simulation and then find the experimental probability. (*See Additional Answers, page T41.*)

Differentiating Instruction

Beginning
Spinning a Simulation After the class has discussed the problem and solution on page 254, have pairs of students show or tell how they could use spinners to simulate the three births. (*Sample: Make three spinners, each with half labeled* girls *and half labeled* boys.)

Intermediate
Describing a Simulation After the class has discussed the problem and solution on page 254, have pairs of students talk about other ways to simulate the births. Ask them to draw or describe one of the other methods.

Advanced
Writing About a Simulation After the class has discussed the problem and solution on page 254, have pairs of students list other ways to simulate the births. Have them write several sentences explaining why they would use one method rather than others.

1. Suppose each student in your class tossed 3 coins 20 times. Which results would you believe, the results based on all students' data or the results based on your data? Explain.

Use the strategy *simulate a problem*.

2. For a bowler, the probability of knocking down all 10 pins with one ball is 60%. A spinner has 10 sections. Explain how you can label the spinner to simulate the bowler's probability of knocking down all 10 pins with one ball.

3. A quiz has 3 true-false questions. If you fill in the answer sheet without thinking, what is the probability that you will get all wrong answers? Explain how to simulate the problem. Then find an answer.

Choose a strategy and solve each problem.

4. A football team has 30 players. They count off by 3s (3, 6, 9, 12, . . .). All the players with numbers that are divisible by 5 go to the locker room. How many players go to the locker room?

5. A sock drawer has 10 black socks and 8 red socks. What is the least number of socks you have to take out to be sure that you have a matching pair of socks to wear? Explain your answer.

Grammar Spotlight

Who or What *Who* and *what* questions are questions about the subject of the sentence.

Uses	Examples	Answers
Use *who* to ask about a person.	**Who wakes you?**	My little brother wakes me.
Use *what* to ask about a thing.	**What wakes you?**	My alarm clock wakes me.

Talk with your partner about the differences between *who* and *what* questions. Take turns asking a *who* question and a *what* question. Say your questions aloud and have your partner answer.

Ask, *Can you think of a time when you might use the strategy* simulate a problem? (*Sample: when it is hard to collect the data in other ways*)

Ask, *Why are the probabilities found in a simulation experimental probabilities?* (*A simulation is a type of experiment that uses probability to predict an outcome, so the expected probability is experimental.*)

Assignment Guide
- Beginning 1–5
- Intermediate 1–5
- Advanced 1–5

Notes on Exercises
Exercise 2 You may want to ask, *Who has bowled? How is the game played?*

Exercise 3 Suggest that students work in pairs to create and conduct the simulation.

Exercise 4 You may want to review how to find multiples and the divisibility rule for 5.

Grammar Spotlight

For Spanish-speaking students, point out that the word *who* is often used in place of the word *quién* and the word *what* is often used in place of the word *qué*.

Answers
1. results based on all students' data, because the data include more trials
2. Label 6 sections "success" and 4 sections "nonsuccess."
3. Sample: Use 3 coins. Toss them 20 times. Use H to represent a wrong answer. Record how many times HHH comes up. $P(\text{HHH}) \approx 13\%$
4. 6 players
5. 3 socks; if the first 2 socks don't match, the third sock will match one of them.

 Activity: Social Interviews

Have students interview a person whom they do not know well to find out about that person's likes and dislikes. Encourage students to ask *who* and *what* questions, such as *Who is a friend of yours?* and *What is your pet's name?*

Ask students to write a sentence sharing something interesting they found out about the other person.

Allow students to record the interviews, reminding them to first ask permission from the other person.

 Program Resources
Practice Book Use pages 110 and 111.

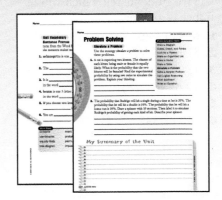

What Are Integers?

STANDARDS CONTENT

Mathematics
■ Graph integers on a number line
■ Compare and order integers

Language
■ Recognize signal words for positive and negative values
■ Recognize multiple meanings of *positive* and *negative*
■ Identify number relationships

Materials
■ Number lines (Overhead Transparency 28)

Introduce the Big Idea

Read aloud the Big Idea. Ask, *How do you think you could write a negative number?*

Begin Building Background

■ Have students describe some of the ice sculptures in the picture.

■ Ask, *How cold must it be before water will freeze?* (32 °F or 0 °C)
Sample answer: a number below zero

Teach Key Concepts

■ Discuss the terms in the illustration. Point out the symbol for a negative number and model how to read the five negative numbers on the number line.

■ Stress that the sign of a negative number is always read as *negative*, not *minus*. *Minus* indicates subtraction.

Warm-Up Review

Have students tell which whole number is greater.

1. 608 or 680 (*680*)
2. 57 or 75 (*75*)
3. 123 or 23 (*123*)
4. 19 or 15 (*19*)
5. 486 or 685 (*685*)
6. 350 or 349 (*350*)

Talk and Explore

What Are Integers?

Big Idea Many situations cannot be represented by whole numbers. You may need negative numbers to show a loss, a temperature below zero, or an opposite direction.

Building Background

▲ In my home city in Norway, we make ice sculptures for the winter carnival every year.

■ How cold does it get where you live?
■ How cold do you think it is where these ice sculptures were made?
■ What kind of number might you use to express a temperature at the South Pole?

Key Concepts

Integers are the counting numbers, their opposites, and zero. The counting numbers are the **positive integers**. Their opposites are the **negative integers**. The diagram shows what these numbers are.

Integers

··· −5 −4 −3 −2 −1 0 1 2 3 4 5 ···

Negative integers   **Positive integers**

0 (zero) is neither positive nor negative.

 Activity: Drawing the Line

Have pairs of students look at the pattern of numbers in the number line on page 256. Challenge them to copy and extend the line so it shows −10 to 10.

Have one student give directions on how to move on the number line, such as start at 0 and move 3 units to the left. Then have the partner name the number at that location, negative 3.

Have students take turns describing moves and naming points.

Resource Library

Math at Hand
Integers 045–048, 199–200

Math on Call
Integers 46–47, 50–51, 53

Reader's Handbook (red)
Reading Math 117–131

Integers on a Number Line

Mount Everest, in Nepal, is the highest mountain in the world. Its highest point is 29,035 feet above sea level, or +29,035 feet. This number is read as *positive 29,035*. Temperatures there can reach 70 degrees below zero, or −70 °F. This number is read as *negative 70*.

The number +29,035 is a **positive integer.** Positive integers usually are written without a sign. They are always to the right of 0 on a number line.

The number −70 is a **negative integer.** Negative integers are always to the left of 0 on a number line. Zero (0) is *neither* positive *nor* negative.

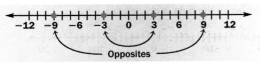

The distance on a number line from an integer to zero is its **absolute value.** The absolute value of −7 is 7. This is written, |−7| = 7. The absolute value of 7 is 7. This is written |7| = 7. Why does |−7| = |7|? They are the same distance (7 units) from 0 on the number line.

Pairs of integers with the same absolute value are called **opposites.** The opposite of −10 is 10. The opposite of 3 is −3. Zero is its own opposite.

Talk and Share

Work with a partner. The inside temperature of an ice palace is about −6 °C. Describe another situation that could be represented by −6. Tell how 6 and −6 are alike. Tell how they are different.

VOCABULARY

positive integer—any of the counting numbers: 1, 2, 3, and so on
negative integer—any of the opposites of the counting numbers: −1, −2, −3, and so on
absolute value—the distance a number is from zero on a number line
opposites—two integers with the same absolute value

▲ Climbing Mt. Everest

Language Notes

Signal Words: Positive/Negative
These words signal positive values.

- above
- up
- increase
- gain

These words signal negative values.

- below
- down
- decrease
- loss

Teach Integers on a Number Line

Ask, *Is the opposite of a number a positive or a negative number?* (*The opposite of a positive number is a negative number. The opposite of a negative number is a positive number.*) *What about absolute values?* (*Absolute values are always positive or zero.*)

Language Notes

Discuss how the words *above* and *below* are used in the reading. Then ask students if these words signal a positive or a negative number: *over, forward, profit.* (*All signal positive.*) Have volunteers give their opposites (*under, backward, loss*).

Talk and Share

After pairs complete the exercise, ask, *Is what you found about 6 and −6 true for all opposites?* (*Yes; the distance from zero to the numbers in each pair is the same.*)

Answers: 6 and −6 are both 6 units away from zero. 6 is greater than zero and −6 is less than zero.

Build VOCABULARY

Define the vocabulary words on page 257. Copy and distribute the crossword puzzle at http://www.mathgoodies.com/puzzles/2002/puzzles/Integerslimited. Have pairs solve the puzzle.

Differentiating Instruction

Beginning
Naming Opposites Have pairs of students take turns using a number line, pointing to and naming positive and negative integers and their opposites.

Intermediate
Explaining Opposites Have pairs of students name opposites for all the points on the number line shown on page 257. Have them explain how they know that numbers in each pair are opposites (*−12 and 12, −11 and 11, . . .,*

−1 and 1; they are the same distance from 0).

Advanced
Writing About Opposites Have pairs of students follow the directions for the Intermediate activity. Then ask them to write a sentence explaining how they found the opposites. (*Sample: We changed the sign and kept the same digit.*)

Activity: What's the Signal?

Have students work in pairs. One student uses a signal word from Language Notes to describe a situation, such as *five feet above sea level.* The partner writes, then reads, the number 5. Have students alternate roles and repeat the activity several times.

Teach Comparing and Ordering Integers

You may want to display a thermometer as another example of a vertical number line with positive and negative integers.

Language Notes

Discuss the multiple meanings of *positive* and *negative*. Point out how the words shown in red are used in the reading. Explain that each word also has other meanings not listed.

Talk and Share

Extend the discussion by asking students to tell how to compare two negative numbers. (*Sample: Compare absolute values. The negative number with the greater absolute value is the lesser number.*)

Answers: Zero is greater than any negative integer; it is to the right of any negative integer on a number line. Any negative integer is less than any positive integer; it is to the left of any positive integer on a number line. $-15 > -20$; $12 > -12$; $-32 < 4$; $-50 < -40$

Build VOCABULARY

Discuss the two definitions of *vertical* and of *horizontal*. Have volunteers give sentences, each using one of the words in a sentence.

Mt. Everest, Nepal — 29,035 ft
Mt. McKinley, Alaska — 20,320 ft
Mt. Rainier, Washington — 14,410 ft
Sea Level — 0
Puerto Rico Trench, Atlantic Ocean — −28,374 ft
Mariana Trench, Pacific Ocean — −36,198 ft

Language Notes

Multiple Meanings
These words have more than one meaning.

positive
1. greater than zero
2. sure of something

negative
1. less than zero
2. disagreeable

Comparing and Ordering Integers

You can use a **vertical** number line to compare heights and depths. For any two integers on the vertical number line on the photos, the number farther up is greater. Mount Rainier is above the Mariana Trench. That relationship can be expressed as $14,410 > -36,198$. The Mariana Trench is below Mount Rainier, so you can write $-36,198 < 14,410$.

From least to greatest, the integers are:

$$-36,198 \quad -28,374 \quad 14,410 \quad 20,320 \quad 29,035$$

For any two integers on a **horizontal** number line, the integer farther to the right is greater.

(horizontal number line marked: −20, −14, −10, −9, −2, 0, 8, 10, 19, 20)

The following integers are in order from least to greatest.

$$-14 \quad -9 \quad -2 \quad 0 \quad 8 \quad 19$$

In the game of golf, *par* is the number of times a good player is expected to hit the ball in one game. Hits above and below par are scored as positive and negative numbers. The fewer the hits, the better the score. Gary's score was 3 under par, Carol's was 4 over par, Erle's was 1 under par, and Bill's was 2 over par. List the scores from best to worst.

Scores ordered: $-3, -1, +2, +4$. Gary had the best score.

Talk and Share

Work with a partner. Tell how zero compares with any negative number. Tell how any negative integer compares with any positive number. Then use < or > to compare the integers in each pair.

$$-15 \ \blacksquare \ -20 \qquad 12 \ \blacksquare \ -12 \qquad -32 \ \blacksquare \ 4 \qquad -50 \ \blacksquare \ -40$$

VOCABULARY
vertical—running up and down
horizontal—running straight across

 Activity: From Negative to Positive

Have small groups make a poster showing different situations where positive and negative numbers can be used. Have them include data from newspapers or other references and order all of the numbers from least to greatest at the bottom of the poster.

 Differentiating Instruction

Beginning
Ordering Integers Draw a number line from −20 to 20, labeled by 5s (Overhead Transparency 28). Have volunteers circle the numbers 15, −15, 0, −5, and 5. Then have students order the numbers and explain how they did it (*−15, −5, 0, 5, 15*).

Intermediate
Telling Steps for Ordering Integers
Refer students to the number line on page 258. Then have pairs talk about the steps they would follow to order 16, −16, 0, −3, and 3 from least to greatest. (*Sample: Group negative numbers, group positive numbers, and separate zero. Order negative numbers. Write zero. Order positive numbers −16, −3, 0, 3, 16.*)

Advanced
Writing Steps for Ordering Integers
Follow the directions for the Intermediate activity, but have pairs of students write the steps. (*Sample: Draw a number line. Mark and label the five points. Then list the numbers in order from left to right.*)

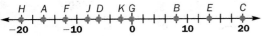

Practice

Write an integer to describe each situation.

1. a profit of $500

2. a decrease of 59 cities

3. 89°F

4. a loss of 12 yards

Use the number line for Exercises 5 and 6.

```
 H  A   F  J D   K G      B     E     C
←+◆+◆+┼+◆+◆┼+◆◆┼┼┼┼◆┼┼┼┼◆┼┼┼┼◆→
 -20     -10      0       10      20
```

5. Name the integer for each point.
  a. A   **b.** B   **c.** C   **d.** D

6. Name the point for each integer.
  a. −12   **b.** 14   **c.** 0   **d.** −2

Find the absolute value and the opposite of each integer.

7. 15   **8.** −20   **9.** 48   **10.** −16

11. −38   **12.** 2   **13.** 30   **14.** 0

Find each absolute value.

15. $|-17|$ **16.** $|0|$ **17.** $|12|$ **18.** $|-12|$

Use < or > to compare the integers in each pair.

19. 41 ▧ −17   **20.** 12 ▧ −24   **21.** −30 ▧ 8   **22.** −2 ▧ −20

Write the integers in order from least to greatest.

23. −23, 48, −50, 22, −12   **24.** −3, 8, −16, 25, −30

25. 18, −18, 0, 36, −6   **26.** −40, −62, −53, −18, −75

27. The table on the right gives the lowest temperatures for six places. List them in order of their temperatures from warmest to coldest.

28. (EXTENDED RESPONSE) Tell if each sentence is *always*, *sometimes*, or *never* true. Explain your choices.
  a. The absolute value of a negative integer is greater than the absolute value of a positive integer.
  b. The absolute values of a pair of opposites are equal.

Antarctica	−129 °F
Argentina	−27 °F
Australia	−9 °F
Canada	−81 °F
Morocco	−11 °F
Russia	−96 °F

Practice

Review the vocabulary words *positive integers*, *negative integers*, *absolute value*, and *opposites*.

Ask, *How is comparing two negative numbers like comparing two positive numbers?* (Sample: Compare distance from zero on a number line.) *How is it different?* (*A negative number with a greater absolute value is less than one with a lesser absolute value, while a positive number with the greater absolute value is the greater number.*)

Assignment Guide
■ Beginning 1–24, 27, 28
■ Intermediate 1–28
■ Advanced 1–28

Notes on Exercises
Exercises 5 and 6 Point out that the points are on the number line above the exercises.

Exercises 7–14 Point out that students need to give two answers for each exercise, the absolute value and the opposite.

Exercise 27 Students should list the *names*, not *temperatures*.

Exercise 28 Suggest that students give examples to support their decisions.

Answers

1. 500   **2.** −59

3. 89   **4.** −12

5. a. −16   **b.** 8
   c. 20   **d.** −6

6. a. F   **b.** E
   c. G   **d.** K

7. 15, −15   **8.** 20, 20

9. 48, −48   **10.** 16, 16

11. 38, 38   **12.** 2, −2

13. 30, −30   **14.** 0, 0

15. 17   **16.** 0   **17.** 12

18. 12   **19.** >   **20.** >

21. <   **22.** >

23. −50, −23, −12, 22, 48

24. −30, −16, −3, 8, 25

25. −18, −6, 0, 18, 36

26. −75, −62, −53, −40, −18

27. Australia, Morocco, Argentina, Canada, Russia, Antarctica

28. a. Sometimes; if the negative number is farther from zero, its absolute value will be greater.
   b. Always; the two opposites are the same distance from zero.

Program Resources
Practice Book Use page 112.
Overhead Transparencies Use 28.

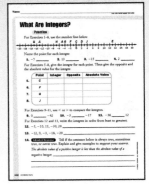

Teach Identifying

- Read aloud the names of the number sets: *real numbers, irrationals, rationals, integers, whole numbers,* and *counting numbers.* To make sure students understand the organizer, ask, *Are all rational numbers also real numbers?* (*yes*) *Are all real numbers also rational numbers?* (*no*)

- Before having pairs complete Exercise 1, discuss the example explaining how to identify −5.

  Answers:
  1. a. *rational, real*
     b. *whole, integer, rational, real*
     c. *counting, whole, integer, rational, real*
     d. *rational, real*

Oral Language

Encourage students to speak in complete sentences and use this lesson's vocabulary words during the activity. For example, Student 3 might say, *The opposite of six is negative six.*

Partner Practice

- If students wonder how they could lose more money than they found, point out that they could have had money before they found or lost any money.

- Review the signal words in the activity (*found—positive, lost—negative*).

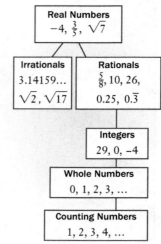

Develop Language

Number Sets

Real Numbers
$-4, \frac{3}{5}, \sqrt{7}$

Irrationals
3.14159...
$\sqrt{2}, \sqrt{17}$

Rationals
$\frac{5}{8}, 10, 26,$
$0.25, 0.\overline{3}$

Integers
29, 0, −4

Whole Numbers
0, 1, 2, 3, ...

Counting Numbers
1, 2, 3, 4, ...

What's the Result?
I found **7** dollars.
I lost **18** dollars.
Altogether, I **lost**
more than I found.
I can write the total
as an integer: **−11.**
I found **30** dollars.
I lost **25** dollars.
Altogether, I **found**
more than I lost.
I can write the total
as an integer: **5.**

Activities

Identifying To identify a number, you need to know what number set it belongs to. The diagram on the left shows examples of numbers in each set. The number line below shows where these kinds of numbers are placed.

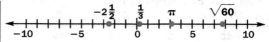

$-2\frac{1}{2} \quad \frac{1}{3} \quad \pi \quad \sqrt{60}$
−10   −5   0   5   10

1. **Identify** Tell a partner which number sets contain each number below. Here is an example.
   −5: *The integer, rational, and real number sets contain* −5.
   a. $-3\frac{1}{2}$ **b.** 0   **c.** 8   **d.** 0.25

2. **Explain** Tell a partner how you made your decisions.

Oral Language

Working on the Line Work in a group of four students. Draw a number line and label it from −12 to 12.

- Student 1 names an integer from −12 to 12.
- Student 2 says the integer aloud and points to the integer on the number line.
- Student 3 says the *opposite* of the number and points to the opposite on the number line.
- Student 4 repeats the integer and its opposite and then tells the absolute value of each.
- Switch roles and name other integers.

Partner Practice

What's the Result? Copy the four sentences below. Fill in whole numbers for the first two sentences. Trade papers with a partner and complete the last two sentences. Check each other's work. Repeat this activity four times with new numbers. Samples are shown at the left.

I found _____ dollars. I lost _____ dollars. Altogether, I _____ more than I _____. I can write the total as an integer: _____.

 Program Resources

Practice Book Use page 113.
Overhead Transparencies Use 28.

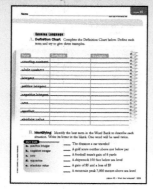

 Assessment Book

Use page 67 to assess students' comprehension.

Activity: Culture Connection

Refer students to the photo of the ice sculptures on page 256. Say, *Ice has even been used to make hotels.* In 2003, the first ice hotel in the United States, the Aurora Ice Hotel, opened in Alaska.

Ask students to find and compare the coldest temperatures in Sweden, Finland, and Alaska.

Adding and Subtracting
Integers

Big Idea You can add or subtract integers by modeling the operations with colored chips or by using rules.

Building Background

▲ The game called football in Brazil is called soccer in the United States.

■ What game is being played here?

■ If a football team gained 10 yards and then lost 4 yards, how far forward did the team move?

■ How many ways could you figure out the answer?

Key Concepts

Use colored chips to **model** or show operations with negative numbers. You can use a yellow chip to stand for +1 and a red chip to stand for −1. One yellow chip and one red chip together form a **zero pair** because they represent a sum of zero.

Using Chips to Model Addition and Subtraction

 Represents 1

 Represents −1

 Represents 0 because
$1 + (-1) = 0$

Zero Pair

LESSON 46 • ADDING AND SUBTRACTING INTEGERS **261**

Adding and Subtracting Integers

STANDARDS CONTENT

Mathematics
■ Add integers
■ Subtract integers

Language
■ Summarize rules for adding and subtracting integers

Materials
■ Yellow and red chips or counters in two colors

Introduce the **Big Idea**

Read aloud the Big Idea. Ask students to describe situations where they might need to add or subtract positive or negative integers.

Begin **Building Background**

Ask, *How could a team have two plays but be farther from the goal line than when they started?* (Samples: *They could lose more yards than they gain. They could lose yards on both plays.*)

Answers: football; 6 yards

Teach **Key Concepts**

Discuss the terms *model* and *zero pair*. Ask, *Why is the term* zero pair *a good way to describe the matching of the yellow and the red chips?* (Sample: *The chips stand for 1 and −1. I can think of gaining 1 and losing 1 for a total move of zero.*)

 Activity: Making Zero Pairs

Supply each student with yellow and red chips. Have one student take a handful of chips and make as many pairs of one red and one yellow chip as possible. Have the partner describe the process. You may wish to model a description: *Lee started with 7 red chips and 3 yellow chips. Now he has 3 zero pairs and 4 red chips.*

Resource Library

Math at Hand
Adding and Subtracting Integers
201–209

Math on Call
Adding and Subtracting Integers
108, 136

Reader's Handbook (red)
Focus on Word Problems 143–154

Warm-Up Review

Have students find each sum or difference.

1. $13 + 8$ (*21*)
2. $13 - 8$ (*5*)
3. $5 + 6$ (*11*)
4. $6 - 5$ (*1*)
5. $21 + 18$ (*39*)
6. $32 - 4$ (*28*)
7. $62 - 0$ (*62*)
8. $16 + 12$ (*28*)

Teach Adding Integers

- Help students use colored chips to model each example.

- You might demonstrate how to use a number line to show the addition of integers (Overhead Transparency 28). Find the first number on the line. To add a positive number, move to the right. To add a negative number, move to the left.

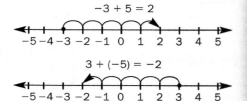

$-3 + 5 = 2$

$3 + (-5) = -2$

- Ask, *Why is the addend −5 in Example B written in parentheses?* (*so the negative sign is not read as a minus sign*)

Talk and Share

- Have students who used mental math share the ways they found each sum.

- Have students write what they found about the sum of an integer and zero and the sum of an integer and its opposite in their math journals.

  Answers: integer + 0 = integer; integer + opposite = 0; 0, −15, 6, −8

Look and Read

Adding Integers

You can use colored chips to help you add integers. Use a yellow chip for 1 and use a red chip for −1.

A. Find $3 + 5$.

Show 3 yellow chips.
Add 5 yellow chips.
There are 8 yellow chips,
so $3 + 5 = 8$.

B. Find $-3 + (-5)$.

Show 3 red chips.
Add 5 red chips.
There are 8 red chips,
so $-3 + (-5) = -8$.

In **A** and **B**, the integers added are either both positive or both negative. In **C** and **D**, one integer is positive and one is negative, so use **zero pairs**. A yellow chip and a red chip form a zero pair because the sum of 1 and −1 is 0. You do not change the sum when you remove or insert a zero pair.

C. Find $-3 + 5$.

Show 3 red chips.   Remove zero pairs.
Add 5 yellow chips.   Two yellow chips remain, so $-3 + 5 = 2$.

D. Find $3 + (-5)$.

Show 3 yellow chips.   Remove zero pairs.
Add 5 red chips.   Two red chips remain, so $3 + (-5) = -2$.

Talk and Share

Work with a partner. Tell the sum of any integer and zero. Tell the sum of any integer and its opposite. Then use colored chips or mental math to find each sum. $5 + (-5)$ $-12 + (-3)$ $10 + (-4)$ $-8 + 0$

VOCABULARY
zero pair—a pair of opposite integers. Their sum is 0.

 Activity: Calculator Addition

Show students how to enter a negative number on a calculator by using the plus/minus key. Then show how to find $1 + (-1)$: Press 1 ⊞ 1 ⊬ ⊟.

Have pairs name two 1-digit addends. Have one student use chips and the other use a calculator to find the sum. Have each student explain his or her work. Encourage students to take turns and repeat the activity several times.

 Differentiating Instruction

Beginning
Modeling Integer Addition Have pairs of students use colored chips to model $-8 + 1$ and $8 + (-1)$. Have them talk about how to find each sum and why the zero-pair chips are removed to find the sum. (*−7; 7; zero-pair chips are removed because zero does not affect the sum.*)

Intermediate
Adding Zero Pairs After students study the examples on page 262, have pairs write a sentence telling when they need to form zero pairs to add integers. (*Sample: We need to form zero pairs when there are both positive and negative integers as addends.*)

Advanced
Explaining Adding Zero Pairs After students study the examples on page 262, have pairs write a paragraph explaining why zero pairs are helpful in showing addition of positive and negative integers. (*Sample: Each zero pair has no value, so the remaining chips represent the sum.*)

Subtracting Integers

You can use colored chips to help you subtract integers.

A. Find $5 - 3$.

Show 5 yellow chips.
Take away 3 yellow chips.
Two yellow chips remain, so $5 - 3 = 2$.

B. Find $-5 - (-3)$.

Show 5 red chips.
Take away 3 red chips.
Two red chips remain, so $-5 - (-3) = -2$.

Use zero pairs to subtract integers with different signs.

C. Find $-5 - 3$.

Start by showing 5 red chips. You want to take away 3 yellow chips, but you don't have any. So insert 3 zero pairs.

Show 5 red chips.
Insert 3 zero pairs.
Take away 3 yellow chips.

Eight red chips remain, so $-5 - 3 = -8$.

D. Find $5 - (-3)$.

Show 5 yellow chips.
Insert 3 zero pairs.
Take away 3 red chips.

Eight yellow chips remain, so $5 - (-3) = 8$.

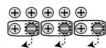

Work with a partner to find each sum. How do these sums compare with the differences in the examples above?

$$5 + (-3) \qquad -5 + 3 \qquad -5 + (-3) \qquad 5 + 3$$

Find $8 - 12$ and $8 + (-12)$. Then find $13 - (-2)$ and $13 + 2$. What appears to be true about subtracting an integer and adding its opposite?

LESSON 46 • ADDING AND SUBTRACTING INTEGERS **263**

Teach Subtracting Integers

- Help students use colored chips to model each example.

- Stress that adding zero pairs does not change the difference.

- Ask, *How do you know how many zero pairs to add?* (*Add the same number as the absolute value of the number being subtracted.*)

- A number line can be used to show subtraction. Because subtraction is the *opposite* of addition, move the *opposite* direction that you would move to add.

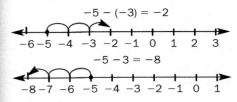

$$-5 - (-3) = -2$$

$$-5 - 3 = -8$$

Talk and Share

Point out that the first four problems add opposites of the problems in the examples. On the board, write $-6 - 2$. Ask, *How could you use the fact that subtracting an integer is the same as adding its opposite to find the difference?* ($-6 - 2 = -6 + (-2) = -8$)

Answers: 2; −2; −8, 8; −4, −4; 15, 15; they are the same.

Build **VOCABULARY**

Ask, *What does it mean to insert a zero pair?* (*Insert a yellow chip and a red chip.*)

Differentiating Instruction

Beginning
Modeling Integer Subtraction Have pairs of students describe how to use colored chips to model Example C. Ask, *How do you know how many zero pairs to insert?* Help students model $-2 - 3$ with colored chips. (*Check students' models; $-2 - 3 = -5$*)

Intermediate
Sketching Integer Subtraction After students study the examples on page 263, have them sketch a picture to show $2 - (-8)$ and talk about why

their pictures are correct. If they have difficulty, refer them to Example D. (*Check students' drawings; $2 - (-8) = 10$*)

Advanced
Writing Steps for Subtracting Integers After students study the examples on page 263, have pairs write the steps needed to find $-5 - 7$. (*Sample: Draw 5 circles labeled with −. Insert 7 zero pairs. Then cross out the 7 circles labeled with +. There are 12 circles labeled with −, so $-5 - 7 = -12$.*)

Activity: Insert the Signs

Ask pairs to complete each number sentence by inserting a plus, minus, positive, or negative sign and to explain their choices.

$$6 \blacksquare (-3) = 9 \ (\textit{minus sign})$$

$$\blacksquare 8 + (-3) = 5 \ (\textit{positive sign})$$

Have students write missing-sign problems for their partners to solve.

Practice

Ask, *If you remove zero pairs, are you adding or subtracting?* (*adding*) *If you insert zero pairs, are you adding or subtracting?* (*subtracting*)

Assignment Guide
- Beginning 1–12, 14–16, 19–24
- Intermediate 1–17, 19–25
- Advanced 1–25

Notes on Exercises
Exercise 13 Remind students that sea level is considered zero. Ask a student to define *depth* for the class (*distance below the surface*).

Exercises 19–21 Suggest that students add or subtract any numbers with *like* signs first.

Exercise 21 Point out that the *total* rating is the sum of the ratings for the three games, not the average rating for the three games.

Exercises 22 and 23 Suggest that students use the examples in the reading as references to help them write other problems. Point out that they do not have to write a word problem.

If students have difficulty, suggest that they use the strategy *guess, check, and revise* to write the problems.

Look and Read

Practice

Find each sum or difference. Use colored chips or mental math.

1. $8 + 13$ **2.** $-8 + 13$ **3.** $8 - 13$ **4.** $-8 - (-13)$
5. $-19 + 12$ **6.** $20 - 27$ **7.** $-25 + (-16)$ **8.** $15 - (-22)$
9. $18 + (-9)$ **10.** $-55 - 55$ **11.** $68 + (-79)$ **12.** $-34 - (-34)$

13. A diver is at 64 feet below sea level. The diver rises 16 feet. What integer tells the depth of the diver?

14. To find $7 - (-3)$ by using chips, you start with 7 yellow chips. Tell how many zero pairs you need to insert. Explain how you know.

Use what you know about adding and subtracting integers to find each sum or difference.

15. $8\frac{3}{4} - (-3\frac{1}{4})$ **16.** $12 - 15.5$ **17.** $-2\frac{1}{5} + 3\frac{4}{5}$ **18.** $10.4 + (-15)$

19. In 3 plays, the Trevians football team gained 8 yards, lost 5 yards, and then gained 16 yards. What was the team's total gain or loss?

20. Lee played four rounds of golf. His scores were 2 below par, 1 above par, 3 above par, and 2 above par. What was his total score for the four rounds?

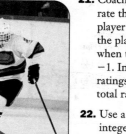

▲ Ice hockey

21. Coach Karlov has a plus/minus system to rate the players on his hockey team. If a player is on the ice when the team scores, the player gets 1. If a player is on the ice when the other team scores, the player gets -1. In three hockey matches, Ivan had ratings of -1, 4, and -7. What was his total rating for the three games?

22. Use a positive integer and a negative integer to write an addition problem whose sum is
   a. positive.   **b.** negative.   **c.** zero.

23. Use a positive integer and a negative integer to write a subtraction problem whose difference is
   a. positive.   **b.** negative.   **c.** zero.

24. (SHORT RESPONSE) Explain how to find $-21 + 45$.

25. (SHORT RESPONSE) Explain how to find $-21 - 45$.

Program Resources
Practice Book Use page 114.

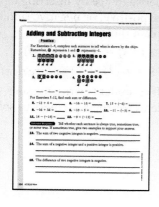

Answers
1. 21   **2.** 5   **3.** -5
4. 5   **5.** -7 **6.** -7
7. -41 **8.** 37   **9.** 9
10. -110 **11.** -11 **12.** 0
13. -48
14. 3 zero pairs; I need to have 3 negative chips so I can remove them.
15. 12   **16.** -3.5
17. $1\frac{3}{5}$ **18.** -4.6
19. gain of 19 yd
20. 4 above par   **21.** -4

22. Samples: **a.** $8 + (-4)$
   b. $-12 + 2$ **c.** $5 + (-5)$
23. Samples: **a.** $5 - (-9)$
   b. $-13 - 2$ **c.** $-9 - (-9)$
24. Find difference of absolute values, $45 - 21 = 24$; use positive sign; 24
25. Add the opposite of 45, $-21 + (-45) = -66$; -66

Activities

Summarizing When you summarize, you pull information together and tell the main points.

1. Summarize Give the main points for adding integers by completing the last column of this table.

Adding Two Integers	Sample	Sign of Sum	Rule
When both are positive	$2 + 5 = 7$	positive	Add the two numbers. The sign of the sum is _____?_____.
When both are negative	$-2 + (-5) = -7$	negative	Add absolute values of the two numbers. The sign of the sum is _____?_____.
When one is positive and one is negative	$-2 + 5 = 3$ $-9 + 2 = -7$	positive negative	Find the *difference* of absolute values. The sum takes the sign of the integer that has _____?_____.

2. Summarize Summarize by completing this rule for subtracting integers:
To subtract an integer, _____.

Hands On

It's in the Chips You will need colored chips and 11 cards: 5 cards with different positive integers, 1 card with 0, and 5 cards with different negative integers. Mix up the cards.

- With a partner, take turns drawing 2 cards.
- Model each number using chips: yellow chips for a positive number and red chips for a negative number.
- Find the sum of the 2 numbers by removing all zero pairs and telling what is left.
- Write a number sentence for the sum.

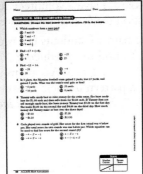

The sum is −1.
$-4 + 3 = -1$

When school started, the temperature was 5°F. By noon, the temperature had dropped 8°. What was the temperature at noon? Answer: 5 − 8 = −3 The temperature at noon was −3°F.

Oral Language

Time for a Story Work in a small group. Each of you should tell a simple story with a problem that can be solved by adding or subtracting integers. Use words that are opposites, such as *up, down, above, below, gain,* and *lose.*

Take turns saying aloud a story. Others listen carefully and write a number sentence to solve the problem. Someone then reads aloud his or her number sentence and explains the solution. Continue until you have told and solved all the stories.

LESSON 46 • ADDING AND SUBTRACTING INTEGERS **265**

Teach Summarizing

- Ask, *How could summarizing information help you to study for tests? (Sample: The most important ideas are listed.)*
- You could have students copy the table and the sentence in Exercise 2 to help reinforce the rules in their minds and provide a reference to use when adding or subtracting integers.
- Students can work individually or in pairs to complete the activity.
  Answers:
  1. *positive, negative, the greater absolute value*
  2. *Add its opposite.*

Hands On

- You might want to demonstrate how students are to complete this activity. Work through one example, with volunteers explaining each step.
- Extend the activity by changing the operation to subtraction.

Oral Language

- For their stories, have students brainstorm topics such as temperature changes, altitude changes, or comparisons of sports statistics.
- Less fluent speakers can either tell their stories to another student who then translates it into English or use pictures in place of words.

Activity: Family Ties

Write these number sentences on the board: $7 - 2 = 5$, $7 - 5 = 2$, $5 + 2 = 7$, $2 + 5 = 7$. Elicit that these are related number sentences, or a *fact family*. Have small groups write similar sets of four number sentences using positive and negative numbers. Have them summarize how the four related number sentences are alike and how they are different. (*Sample: They have the same numbers but in different order. Two sentences involve addition, and two involve subtraction.*)

Assessment Book

Use page 68 to assess students' comprehension.

Program Resources

Practice Book Use page 115.

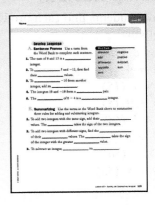

Multiplying and Dividing Integers

STANDARDS CONTENT

Mathematics
- Multiply integers
- Divide integers

Language
- Recognize the meaning of the idiom *on the right track*
- Organize information to find rules for multiplying and dividing integers

Introduce the Big Idea

Read aloud the Big Idea. Ask, *When might you use negative integers to multiply or divide?* (*Sample: to find the change in temperature when the temperature drops 3 °F during each of 3 hours*)

Begin Building Background

Have students share any stories or pictures about tarantulas or snails to supplement the discussion of the picture and the related questions.

Answers: A tarantula; answers will vary; 4 in. down

Teach Key Concepts

Ask, *How do the red chips show $4 \times (-2) = -8$?* (*The 4 groups of 2 red chips show 8 red chips in all.*) Have a volunteer tell how to use chips to show $4 \times 2 = 8$. (*Show 4 groups of 2 yellow chips each.*) Then, ask, *Could you use chips to show $-4 \times (-2) = 8$?* (*no*). Explain that they will use patterns to help them find the product of -4 and (-2).

Warm-Up Review

Have students find each product or quotient.

1. 6×8 *(48)*
2. $72 \div 4$ *(18)*
3. 5×3 *(15)*
4. $45 \div 9$ *(5)*
5. 9×7 *(63)*
6. $49 \div 7$ *(7)*
7. 8×7 *(56)*
8. $90 \div 3$ *(30)*

Multiplying and Dividing Integers

Big Idea In many real-life situations, you need to multiply or divide with negative integers. Often patterns will help you discover rules and keep you on the right track.

Building Background

▲ I like tarantulas better than snails because tarantulas make good pets. There are tarantulas in Mexico.

▲ Tarantula   ▲ Snail

- Which creature moves faster, a tarantula or a snail?
- Describe how a tarantula or a snail moves.
- In one hour, a snail moves 3 inches up the side of an aquarium but slides back down 4 inches. After 4 hours, how many inches and in what direction has the snail moved?

Key Concepts

To multiply and divide integers, look for **patterns** and then learn the rules. Use colored chips to help you get started.

Using Chips to Model Multiplication

4 groups of 2 red chips is 8 red chips.

$4 \times (-2) = -8$

 Activity: Repeat to Find a Pattern

Write $2 \times (-3) = -3 + (-3) = ?$ on the board. Have a volunteer replace the question mark with the answer, -6.

Have pairs of students use repeated addition to find the products $2 \times (-2)$, $2 \times (-1)$, . . . , 2×3. Ask them to describe a pattern in their answers. (*$-4, -2, 0, 2, 4, 6$; the products increase by 2.*)

 Resource Library

Math at Hand
Multiplying and Dividing Integers
210–211

Math on Call
Multiplying and Dividing Integers
164, 193

Multiplying Integers

You can use colored chips to help you multiply integers.

A. Find 3×4.
Show 3 groups of 4 yellow chips.
There are 12 yellow chips, so $3 \times 4 = 12$.

B. Find $3 \times (-4)$.
Show 3 groups of 4 red chips.
There are 12 red chips, so $3 \times (-4) = -12$.

C. Find -3×4.
By the Commutative Property,
you know that $-3 \times 4 = 4 \times (-3)$.
Show 4 groups of 3 red chips.
There are 12 red chips, so $-3 \times 4 = -12$.

D. Find $-3 \times (-4)$.
Use this pattern to find the product.

$-3 \times 4 = -12$ **This is known from part C above.**
$-3 \times 3 = -9$ **The product increases by 3 each time.**
$-3 \times 2 = -6$
$-3 \times 1 = -3$
$-3 \times 0 = 0$
$-3 \times (-1) = 3$ **Continue the pattern.**
$-3 \times (-2) = 6$
$-3 \times (-3) = 9$
Then, $-3 \times (-4) = 12$.

Rules for Multiplying Integers

The product of two positive or two negative integers is *positive*. | The product of a positive integer and a negative integer is *negative*.

Language Notes

Idioms
These words don't mean what they seem.

■ **on the right track**
on the way to a goal

Talk and Share

Work with a partner to solve this problem. Harry withdrew $15 from his savings account each week for 4 weeks. Explain why you can express the total change in his account as $4 \times (-15)$.

Teach Multiplying Integers

■ After working through Example D, have students find 5×10, $5 \times (-10)$, -5×10, and $-5 \times (-10)$ ($50, -50, -50, 50$). Write each problem as a number sentence on the board. Ask students to compare the number sentences to discover the rules for multiplying integers, which are printed on the page.

■ Ask students to copy the rules for multiplying integers and write two examples for each rule in their math journals.

Language Notes

■ Draw students' attention to the idiom in Language Notes. Then read aloud the Big Idea on page 266 to show the idiom in context.

■ Ask, *What does the idiom mean in the Big Idea?* (*Sample: The rules will help you to multiply and divide integers correctly.*)

Talk and Share

You may have to explain the term *withdraw*. Have pairs find the total withdrawal for the four weeks and give an integer to express the change in his account balance (*$60 in withdrawals, -$60*).

Answer: -15 means a $15 withdrawal, which Harry made 4 times.

Differentiating Instruction

Beginning
Modeling Multiplication of Integers
Have pairs of students use colored chips to model 5×2, $5 \times (-2)$, and -2×5 ($10, -10, -10$). Have them show how they found each product. Then, on the board, work through the pattern of products -2×4 through $-2 \times (-5)$ (10).

Intermediate
Comparing and Contrasting Integer Products Have pairs of students compare and contrast the four examples and then use the rules for multiplying integers to classify each example (*Sample: Like: Absolute values are the same; different: signs*).

Advanced
Explaining How to Multiply Integers
Have pairs of students use the rules for multiplying integers to classify each example. Then ask them to write a sentence explaining how the patterns and rules for multiplying integers keep them *on the right track*.

 Activity: Multiplication Mix-Up
Have students write each of the integers -6 through 6 on thirteen cards. Have them mix the cards and place them facedown. Have partners take turns drawing two cards and explaining how to multiply the integers. Cards should be replaced after each turn.

Teach **Dividing Integers**

- Remind students that *inverse operations* "undo" each other, so multiplication and division are inverse operations. Ask, *What other operations are inverse operations?* (*addition and subtraction*)

- You may want to show related multiplication sentences in Examples A and B to prepare students for the more abstract applications in Examples C and D.

  A. Find $12 \div 3$. Since $3 \times 4 = 12$, $12 \div 3 = 4$.

  B. Find $-12 \div 3$. Since $3 \times (-4) = -12$, $-12 \div 3 = -4$.

- Have students copy the rules for dividing integers and add two examples for each rule in their math journals.

Talk and Share

Have pairs share their observations with the class.

Answer: If two integers have the same sign, their product or quotient is positive. If two integers have opposite signs, their product or quotient is negative.

Build **VOCABULARY**

Ask, *What do you think* inverse *means?* (*opposite*) Have students define *inverse operations* (*opposite operations; operations that undo each other*).

Look and Read

Dividing Integers

You also can use colored chips to help you divide integers.

A. Find $12 \div 3$.
Show 12 yellow chips. Separate them into 3 equal groups. Each group has 4 yellow chips, so $12 \div 3 = 4$.

B. Find $-12 \div 3$.
Show 12 red chips. Separate them into 3 equal groups. Each group has 4 red chips, so $-12 \div 3 = -4$.

Remember that division and multiplication are **inverse operations.** So you can use a related product to find a quotient.

C. Find $12 \div (-3)$.
You know that $-3 \times (-4) = 12$, so $12 \div (-3) = -4$.

D. Find $-12 \div (-3)$.
You know that $-3 \times 4 = -12$, so $-12 \div (-3) = 4$.

E. Find $0 \div 5$.
You know that $5 \times 0 = 0$, so $0 \div 5 = 0$.

Can you find $5 \div 0$? There is no answer because $0 \times$ any number $= 0$, not 5.

Rules for Dividing Integers

Divide as with whole numbers. The quotient of two positive or two negative integers is *positive.*
Divide as with whole numbers. The quotient of a positive integer and a negative integer is *negative.*

Talk and Share

Work with a partner. Compare the rules for dividing integers with the rules for multiplying integers.

VOCABULARY
inverse operations—operations that undo one another

 Activity: Using Inverse Ops

Have one student in a pair use a calculator to multiply two integers and then write the multiplication sentence. Have the partner write a related division sentence and tell how he or she used inverse operations to write the division sentence.

 Differentiating Instruction

Beginning
Modeling Division of Integers Have pairs of students use colored chips to model $15 \div 3$ and $-15 \div 3$ (5, -5). Have paired students talk about how they found each quotient. Then, on the board, work through the concept of inverse operations to find $15 \div (-3)$ and $-15 \div (-3)$ (-5, 5). Elicit from the students the rules for dividing integers.

Intermediate
Explaining Inverse Operations Have pairs of students write a sentence

explaining how inverse operations can be used to find $18 \div (-3)$. (*Sample: The inverse of division is multiplication; $-3 \times (-6) = 18$, so $18 \div (-3) = -6$.*)

Advanced
Writing About Inverse Operations Have pairs of students write a definition for inverse operations and show how they can be used to find $-16 \div (-8)$. (*Sample: Inverse operations undo each other. $-8 \times (2) = -16$, so $-16 \div (-8) = 2$.*)

Practice

Tell whether each result will be positive or negative. Then find each product or quotient.

1. 10×14 **2.** -4×15 **3.** $-45 \div (-3)$

4. $56 \div (-14)$ **5.** $-12 \times (-7)$ **6.** $\frac{-40}{-4}$

7. $-16(5)$ **8.** $\frac{72}{-4}$ **9.** $-87 \div 3$

10. $22 \times (-4)$ **11.** $-50 \div 2$ **12.** $-23(-2)$

13. -9×11 **14.** $-51 \div 17$ **15.** $-30 \times (-4)$

16. What is the product of any integer and zero?

Write each expression in expanded form and then evaluate.

17. $(-5)^2$ **18.** $(-3)^3$ **19.** $(-2)^4$ **20.** $(-2)^5$ **21.** $(-4)^4$

22. Refer to Exercises 17–21. When the exponent was even, was the expression positive or negative? When the exponent was odd, was the expression positive or negative?

Use what you know about integers to help you find each product or quotient.

23. $-1.25 \times (-8)$ **24.** $7\frac{1}{2} \div (-3)$

25. $-9.6 \div 0.16$ **26.** $-\frac{3}{4}(-24)$

Evaluate each expression. Remember to use the correct order of operations.

27. $(-6)^2 + 7(-2)$ **28.** $8(-8) - (-4)^2$

29. $2^3 - (4 - 6)$ **30.** $(-8)^2 \div (-20 + 4)$

31. Over 5 days, the value of a share of a stock dropped 16.5 points. What was the average change per day?

32. If Michelle's scores for 4 rounds of golf were $+5$, -2, $+3$, and -2, what was her mean score for the 4 rounds?

33. Use two integers to write a division problem whose quotient is

  a. positive.   **b.** negative.   **c.** zero.

34. (MULTIPLE CHOICE) The product of a negative integer and a positive integer is
  A. greater than either integer.   **C.** less than either integer.
  B. equal to zero.   **D.** unknown.

▲ Professional golfer Michelle Wie began golfing at the age of 4.

LESSON 47 • MULTIPLYING AND DIVIDING INTEGERS   **269**

Practice

Review the rules for multiplying and dividing integers. Then discuss with students why they cannot divide by zero. (*There is no related multiplication sentence for division by zero, because zero times any number is zero.*)

Assignment Guide
- Beginning 1–12, 16–22, 23–33 odd, 34
- Intermediate 1–15 odd, 16–34
- Advanced 2–16 even, 17–34

Notes on Exercises
Exercises 17–21 You may want to review how to write an expression with exponents in expanded form.

Exercises 27–30 Students may need to review the order of operations.

Exercises 31 and 32 If necessary, review the mathematical definitions of *average* and *mean* and how to find each.

Exercise 33 Suggest that students use the examples on page 268 to help them write the division problems. Remind them that they do not need to write a word problem.

Answers
1. 140   **2.** -60

3. 15   **4.** -4

5. 84   **6.** 10

7. -80 **8.** -18

9. -29 **10.** -88

11. -25 **12.** 46

13. -99 **14.** -3

15. 120   **16.** zero

17. 25   **18.** -27

19. 16   **20.** -32

21. 256

22. Even powers are positive; odd powers are negative.

23. 10   **24.** $-2\frac{1}{2}$

25. -60 **26.** 18

27. 22   **28.** -80

29. 10   **30.** -4

31. -3.3 points   **32.** 1

33. Samples: **a.** $-12 \div (-3)$
  b. $18 \div (-6)$ **c.** $0 \div (-17)$

34. D

Program Resources
Practice Book Use page 116.

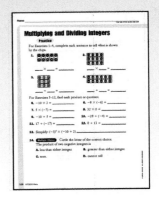

Teach Organizing

- Ask, *What does the word* organize *mean?* (*to arrange in order*)
- If students are concerned about which integer is the First Integer and which is the Second Integer, you could explain that it doesn't matter for this activity or you could have the class decide which factor is the First Integer and whether the dividend or the divisor is the First Integer.

Answers:

1. *positive, positive, negative, negative*

2.–3. *Check students' work.*

Partner Practice

Students use related multiplication and division sentences to decide the sign of the quotient. If they have not worked with related multiplication and division sentences, you may want to have them first compare the sentences in the first row.

Answers: $-40 \div 8 = -5$, *negative;* $-40 \div (-8) = 5$, *positive;* $40 \div (-8) = -5$, *negative*

Oral Language

Ask students to identify the *diagonals* of the square verbally or by sketching the magic square on the board and having a student show the diagonals.

See Additional Answers, page T41.

Activities

Organizing You can organize the rules for multiplying and dividing integers in a table like this.

First Integer	Second Integer	Product or Quotient
positive	positive	
negative	negative	
positive	negative	
negative	positive	

1. **Organize** Copy the table and complete the last column.

2. **Explain** Tell a partner how the chart is organized.

3. **Summarize** Write a sentence or two explaining how to tell whether a quotient of two integers is positive or negative.

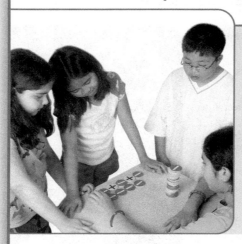

Partner Practice

Relatives Work with a partner to show how the rules for multiplying integers can help you divide integers. Copy and complete each related division sentence. Then tell whether the quotient is positive or negative. The first one is done for you.

Multiplication	Related Division	Quotient
$8 \times 5 = 40$	$40 \div 8 = 5$	+
$8 \times (-5) = -40$	$-40 \div 8 = ?$	?
$-8 \times 5 = -40$	$-40 \div (-8) = ?$	?
$-8 \times (-5) = 40$	$40 \div (-8) = ?$	?

Oral Language

Magic Square Work with a partner to copy and complete the magic square. The square is magic because the sum of each row, column, and diagonal is the same. Tell what that sum will be. Take turns finding one of the missing numbers and telling how you found the number.

		−3
	−2	−4
−1		

Program Resources

Practice Book Use page 117.

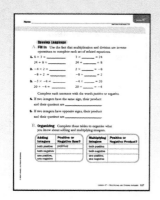

Assessment Book

Use page 67 to assess students' comprehension.

Activity: Quiz Each Other!

Have small groups of students write a short math quiz to cover the information in this unit. Have them provide headings to group similar problems.

Encourage students to discuss why each topic should or should not be covered in the quiz.

Invite groups to exchange quizzes and complete another group's quizzes.

The Coordinate Plane

Talk and Explore

Big Idea A coordinate plane helps to show how an area is laid out. Integers can be used to locate points on the plane.

Building Background

▲ I want to move to a city when I get older.

■ Have you ever been to a city? Where?

■ How did you find your way around?

■ What else is laid out in a grid?

Key Concepts

A vertical number line called the **y-axis** and a horizontal number line called the **x-axis** separate a plane into 4 parts. You use a pair of numbers, or **coordinates,** to locate or graph any point in the plane. The *x*-coordinate is always first in the pair.

A Coordinate Plane

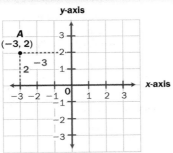

Activity: Label the Points

Have students copy the coordinate plane on page 271 or label a blank grid (Overhead Transparency 15). Explain that *all* points are found by starting at the point where the *x*-axis and *y*-axis meet (zero). Model directions to locate (4, −2): *Move right 4 units; move down 2 units.* Have students in small groups each write directions to locate a point. Have other group members copy the directions and then use their fingers to show the movement, mark the point, and label it with a letter.

Resource Library

Math at Hand
The Coordinate Plane and Linear Equations 244–245, 265–266

Math on Call
The Coordinate Plane and Linear Equations 245–247, 318–320

The Coordinate Plane

STANDARDS CONTENT
Mathematics
■ Identify and graph points on a coordinate plane
■ Graph linear equations

Language
■ Recognize multiple meanings of *coordinate* and *graph*
■ Explain the likenesses and differences among graphs

Materials
■ Coordinate grids (Overhead Transparency 15)

Introduce the **Big Idea**

Read aloud the Big Idea. On the board, sketch a simple coordinate grid. Ask, *How do you think we could show positive and negative numbers?*

Begin **Building Background**

Have students share stories about large cities they have visited. Ask, *How could you direct a classmate to a certain place in the city?*

Teach **Key Concepts**

■ Point out that the coordinates of point *A* tell the distance of the point from the *x*-axis and *y*-axis.

■ Have students locate (3, −3) by using their finger to start at point (0, 0), move 3 units right on the *x*-axis, and then move down 3 units.

Warm-Up Review

Draw these two number lines on the board. Have students name the position of each point. (A: −3, B: 2, C: 0, D: −8, E: −4, F: 3, G: 9)

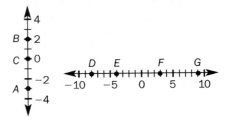

Teach Points on a Coordinate Plane

- Suggest that students remember the order of the coordinates in an ordered pair by thinking that *x* comes before *y* in the alphabet, so the *x*-coordinate comes first.

- Have volunteers explain their answers for these additional examples: Give the ordered pair for point *T* (*6*, −*7*). Tell which point is at (*5, 4*) (*U*).

Language Notes

Discuss the multiple meanings of *coordinate* and *graph*. Stress that even though *coordinate* is spelled the same for both meanings, the pronunciation is different. Provide pronunciation.

Talk and Share

Make sure that students write the coordinates in the proper order.

Answers: V(−*7*, −*2*), *W*(*7, 0*); (*0, 2*): *start at the origin, move 2 units up;* (−*5*, −*2*): *start at the origin, move 5 units left and 2 units down.*

Build VOCABULARY

Discuss the vocabulary on page 272. Have students sketch a coordinate plane or use a blank grid. Have them label it using the vocabulary words. Tell students that *axes* is the plural form of *axis*.

Language Notes

Multiple Meanings
These words have more than one meaning.

☐ coordinate
1. a number that locates a point
2. help to work together

☐ graph
1. a diagram or chart that shows relationships
2. make a diagram or chart
3. plot points

Talk and Share

Work with a partner to name the coordinates of points *V* and *W* on the coordinate plane above. Explain how to graph these points: (0, 2) and (−5, −2).

Points on a Coordinate Plane

A **coordinate plane** is a grid with two perpendicular number lines called the ***x*-axis** and the ***y*-axis.** The *axes* intersect at the **origin** (0, 0) and split the plane into four **quadrants,** labeled I, II, III, and IV.

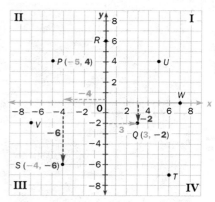

Point *P* is in quadrant II. The **ordered pair** of numbers (−5, 4) locates *P*. The first coordinate is the ***x*-coordinate,** −5. It tells that the point is 5 units to the *left* of the origin. The second coordinate is the ***y*-coordinate,** 4. It tells that the point is 4 units *above* the origin.

Find the coordinates of point *Q*. Start at the origin and count units. *Q* is 3 units to the right (3) and 2 units down (−2). The coordinates of point *Q* are (3, −2).

Find the point with coordinates (−4, −6). Start at the origin. For −4 units, count 4 units to the *left*. For −6, count 6 units *down*. The point located at (−4, −6) is point *S*.

VOCABULARY

coordinate plane—a grid with two perpendicular number lines
x-axis—the horizontal number line
y-axis—the vertical number line
origin—the point (0, 0) where the x-axis and y-axis intersect
quadrants—four sections of a coordinate plane formed by two intersecting number lines

ordered pair—two numbers that locate a point on a plane
x-coordinate—the first number in an ordered pair
y-coordinate—the second number in an ordered pair

 Activity: Coordinate the Points

Have one student choose a point. Have his or her partner ask questions about it, such as *Is the x-coordinate greater than 4?*, to find the point. Have students take turns and repeat the activity several times.

Differentiating Instruction

Beginning
Defining the Origin Have pairs of students give the ordered pair that names the origin (*0, 0*). Explain that *origin* means beginning. Have the pair talk about why that is a good name for the point. (*Sample: To find points on a coordinate plane, I begin at the origin.*)

Intermediate
Defining Ordered Pairs Have pairs of students tell what is *ordered* about an *ordered pair* and how the two numbers are ordered (*The coordinates are ordered;*

the x-coordinate comes before the y-coordinate.*)

Advanced
Naming Points in Quadrants Have students name several ordered pairs in each quadrant. (*Samples: I, (5,8), (3,2); II, (−3,5), (−6, 1); III, (−2,−4), (−8, −6); IV, (3, −8), (4, −7)*)

Graphing Linear Equations

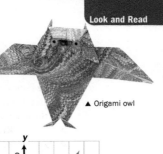

▲ Origami owl

Origami is the Japanese art of folding paper. Miyoko made a variety of origami animals to sell at the school fair. She paid $6 to rent a table. She plans to charge $2 for each animal. How much profit (*y*) will she make? The answer depends on how many animals (*x*) she sells.

You can use an equation and its graph to show Miyoko's profit. Use *x* for the number of animals and *y* for the profit. The equation $y = 2x - 6$ shows how *x* and *y* are related. Pick a value for *x* and substitute it for *x* in the equation to find *y*. The table shows 4 sets of values for *x* and *y*. Graph the ordered pairs and connect the points.

$y = 2x - 6$
For $x = 0$, $y = 2(0) - 6 = -6$
For $x = 2$, $y = 2(2) - 6 = -2$
For $x = 5$, $y = 2(5) - 6 = 4$
For $x = 6$, $y = 2(6) - 6 = 6$

x	y	Ordered Pair
0	−6	(0, −6)
2	−2	(2, −2)
5	4	(5, 4)
6	6	(6, 6)

The points lie in a straight line, so the equation is a **linear equation.** You can extend the line in both directions.

The line contains all points that are solutions to the equation. The point (3, 0) is on the line. Is this point a solution? Substitute 3 for *x* and 0 for *y*: $0 = 2(3) - 6 = 0$, so the point is a solution.

The point (3, 0) tells you that if Miyoko sells 3 animals, she will make no profit. The point (4, 2) is on the line. It tells us that if Miyoko sells 4 animals, she will make $2.

Talk and Share

Work with a partner. Find the point (8, 10). Is it on the line? What does it tell you about Miyoko's profit? Is the point (10, 8) on the line? Tell why or why not.

VOCABULARY

linear equation—an equation whose graph is a straight line

Teach Graphing Linear Equations

■ Ask, *In the equation for Miyoko's profit, why is the cost to rent the table subtracted?* (*Miyoko must pay for the table, no matter how many animals she sells.*)

■ Point out that any number can be chosen for *x* when making the table.

■ Ask, *What does the point (2, −2) tell about Miyoko's profit?* (*If she sells only 2 animals, she will lose $2.*) Have students explain why she will lose money if she sells 2 animals. (*She paid $6 for the table and $4 − $6 = −$2.*)

Talk and Share

Encourage students to trace and extend the graph to find the point (8, 10). Ask students if there is another way to tell if the point (8, 10) is on the line. (*Substitute 8 for* x *in the equation and then simplify to see if the y-value is 10.*)

Answers: Yes, if Miyoko sells 8 animals, her profit is $10. No, the values for x *and* y *do not make the equation true: 2 • 10 − 6 = 14 ≠ 8.*

Build VOCABULARY

Explain that *linear* is an adjective meaning "in a straight line," so a *linear equation* is an equation with a graph that is a straight line.

Differentiating Instruction

Beginning
Graphing a Line Show students how the equations and the table on page 273 help to graph $y = 2x - 6$. Then help them make a table and graph for the equation $y = x + 3$. (*See Additional Answers, page T42.*)

Intermediate
Extending the Table Have pairs of students use other values of *x* to extend the table on page 273 to include *x*-values of −3 and 12. Have them verify that the points are on the graph ((−3, −12),

(12, 18); $-12 = 2(-3) - 6$ and $18 = 2(12) - 6$).

Advanced
Explaining How to Graph After students study the example on page 273, have pairs explain in writing how to graph an equation. They should include an equation, its table, and its graph. (*Sample: Make a table; substitute values for* x *in the equation to find* y*; write ordered pairs; graph the ordered pairs; connect points with a line. Check students' work.*)

Activity: Graph an Equation

Have pairs of students discuss how to graph the equation $y = -4x$. Then have each student graph the equation and then compare their graphs. Ask, *Is the graph of a linear equation?* (*yes*) (*See Additional Answers, page T42.*)

Practice

Write (−5, 4) on the board. Have students identify the *x*-coordinate and the *y*-coordinate and tell how to graph the point. (*−5; 4; from (0, 0), move 5 units left and 4 units up.*)

Have students identify each quadrant on the coordinate plane (*quadrant I: upper right, quadrant II: upper left, quadrant III: lower left, quadrant IV: lower right*).

Assignment Guide
- Beginning 1–12, 15, 16, 18–21
- Intermediate 1–10, 13–17, 10–21
- Advanced 1–10, 13–21

Notes on Exercises
Exercises 1–6 Explain that all coordinates will be integers and should be given as an ordered pair.

Exercises 7–10 Point out that students should tell in which quadrant or on which axis the point is located.

Exercise 11 Have students add this information to their math journals.

Exercise 18–21 Students may refer to the example on page 273 for the facts about Miyoko's sale of her animals.

Exercise 21 Include this exercise as part of a classroom discussion. It is important that students distinguish between mathematically possible answers and situation-sensible answers.

Look and Read

Practice

Use the coordinate plane on the right for Exercises 1–11.
Give the coordinates for each point.
1. *A*   **2.** *B*   **3.** *C*
4. *D*   **5.** *E*   **6.** *F*

Name the point with the given coordinates. Tell in which quadrant or on which axis each point is located.
7. (2, −4)   **8.** (0, 5)
9. (−3, −5)   **10.** (−3, 2)

11. Tell the signs of the coordinates of a point from each quadrant.

Copy and complete the table of values for each equation.
12. $y = x - 5$ **13.** $y = 2 - x$ **14.** $y = 3x + 2$ **15.** $y = 5x - 4$

x	y
−2	
−1	
0	
1	
2	

x	y
−2	
−1	
0	
1	
2	

x	y
0	
1	
2	
3	
4	

x	y
−1	
0	
2	
4	
6	

For Exercises 16 and 17, pick four values for *x* and find the *y* value for each. Then graph the ordered pairs and connect the points to draw the line.
16. $y = x - 6$ **17.** $y = 2x + 5$

For Exercises 18–21, use the graph on the left, which shows Miyoko's profit.

18. Explain what the point (0, −6) means.

19. Tell the least number of animals Miyoko has to sell to make a profit.

20. How many origami animals does Miyoko have to sell to earn $8 profit?

21. (EXTENDED RESPONSE) The point (−2, −10) is on the line, but it does not make sense in terms of the situation. Explain why.

▲ Origami dogs

Program Resources
Practice Book Use page 118.
Overhead Transparencies Use 15.

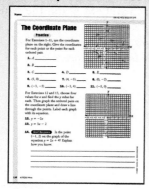

Answers
1. (3, 0)   **2.** (3, −5)
3. (−4, −2)   **4.** (−4, 2)
5. (−5, 5)   **6.** (6, 4)
7. *H*; quadrant IV
8. *M*; *y*–axis
9. *J*; quadrant III
10. *G*; quadrant II
11. I: *x* and *y* both positive
  II: *x* negative, *y* positive
  III: *x* and *y* both negative
  IV: *x* positive, *y* negative

12. −7, −6, −5, −4, −3
13. 4, 3, 2, 1, 0
14. 2, 5, 8, 11, 14
15. −9, −4, 6, 16, 26

For Exercises 16 and 17, see Additional Answers, page T42.

18. Before Miyoko sells any animals, she has to pay $6 to rent a table.
19. 4 animals
20. 10 animals
21. Miyoko cannot sell fewer than zero animals.

Activities

Explaining The graphs on the coordinate plane on the right are labeled with their equations. Work with a partner to explain the likenesses and differences among the graphs.

1. **Explain** Tell how the graphs are alike and tell how they are different.

2. **Explain** Tell how the equations for the graphs are alike and tell how they are different.

3. **Write** In a sentence or two, describe any pattern you notice.

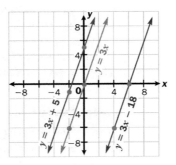

Oral Language

Tell It Like It Is Work in a small group. Each group should have a set of cards and a coordinate grid labeled like the one below. Each card has one of these terms on it: *coordinate plane, quadrant, origin, x-axis, y-axis, ordered pair.*

Take turns choosing a card, reading the word aloud, pointing to that item on the grid, and telling what the word means. If you choose the card *ordered pair,* you think of an ordered pair, such as (−3, 1), and tell someone else how to locate it on the grid: *Start at the origin. Move 3 units to the left. Now move 1 unit up. What is my ordered pair?* Check one another's work.

Hands On

What's My Polygon? Draw a polygon on a coordinate plane and name the points (ordered pairs) at the vertices of the polygon. Your partner must graph the points on another grid and connect the points in order to form and name the polygon. Compare polygons and then switch roles to play again. A sample triangle with vertices *A, B,* and *C* is shown.

LESSON 48 • THE COORDINATE PLANE **275**

Teach Explaining

Ask, *What are the equations of the three graphs at the top of the page?* (y = 3x + 5, y = 3x, y = 3x − 18) Discuss pairs' comparisons as a class.

Answers:

1. *They all rise from left to right and are parallel to each other. They pass through different points.*

2. *The equations all have 3x as a term; the numerical terms are different.*

3. *Sample: Graphs of equations in which x is multiplied by the same number are parallel. When a number is added to the x term, the graph of the equation is to the left of the graph of the equation with only an x term; when a number is subtracted, the graph is to the right.*

Oral Language

You may want to extend the activity by having students who draw cards other than "ordered pairs" ask other students to point out specific examples. For example, a student drawing the *quadrant* card could ask someone to locate quadrant III.

Hands On

Review the terms *polygon* and *vertices.* (*A polygon is a closed plane figure with straight lines as sides. Vertices are points formed by intersecting sides.*)

Activity: Reading Map Coordinates

Provide small groups with copies of street maps. Discuss how to read the maps, and have students use the key to locate three streets.

Ask, *How are a street map and a coordinate plane alike and how are they different?* (*Sample: Both use two coordinates to locate points or places. A map has one quadrant and labels the areas between lines. A coordinate plane has four quadrants and labels the points.*)

Assessment Book

Use page 70 to assess students' comprehension.

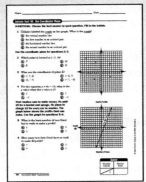

Program Resources

Practice Book Use page 119.
Overhead Transparency Use 15.

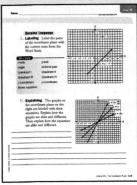

Write an Equation

STANDARDS CONTENT

Mathematics

■ Solve problems by writing an equation

Language

■ Recognize how to use *more, less, fewer,* and *than* to compare numbers or amounts

Teach Write an Equation

■ Stress that the strategy *write an equation* is a *tool* to help solve a problem and that the equation is usually not the answer.

■ Have students give examples of track events or describe a relay race.

■ Ask, *How are equations and expressions alike and how are they different?* (*Sample: Both equations and expressions may have numbers, variables, and operations. Equations are sentences stating equality; expressions are phrases.*)

Talk and Share

As a class, discuss what students need to find, what they know, and the key facts in the problem. Then have pairs write an equation. (*Find: the amount of money in Amal's account before the withdrawal; Know: withdrawal of $103.45; Key fact: The balance after the withdrawal is $967.67.*)

Sample answer: x − 103.45 = 967.67, $1,071.12

Problem-Solving Skills

Write an Equation

You can organize information by writing an equation. The equation becomes your tool for solving the problem.

Problem: In 1928, the first year for women's track-and-field events in the Olympic Games, the Canada team won the 400-meter relay in 48.4 seconds. This time was 6.2 seconds longer than the winning time of the Bahamas team in 2000. What was the winning time of the Bahamas team?

Read and Understand

Need to find: Winning time of the Bahamas team

You know: The Canada team's time was 48.4 seconds.

Key fact: The Bahamas team's time plus 6.2 is the Canada team's time.

Plan and Solve   To solve this problem, write and solve an equation. Translate the key fact into an equation. Let B be the variable, the time of the Bahamas team.

Time of Bahamas team	plus	more time	equals	Time of Canada team
B	$+$	6.2	$=$	48.4

$$B + 6.2 = 48.4$$
$$B + 6.2 - 6.2 = 48.4 - 6.2 \quad \leftarrow \text{Subtract 6.2 from both sides of the equation.}$$
$$B = 42.2 \quad \leftarrow \text{Simplify.}$$

Answer   The time of the Bahamas team was 42.2 seconds.

Look Back   The time of the Bahamas team was less than that of the Canada team, so the answer makes sense.

Talk and Share

Work with a partner. Amal withdrew $103.45 from his savings account. That left $967.67 in the account. Write an equation to find how much money was in his account before the withdrawal.

◀ Runners in the 1928 Olympic Games

Activity: Write an Equation

Have pairs of students write an equation to help them solve this problem: Wood fencing is sold in 6-ft sections. Franz bought 132 feet of wood fencing. How many sections did he buy? (*Let f stand for each fence section; 6 × f = 132, f = 22; 22 sections*)

Discuss students' equations as a class. Invite students to share any models they drew to help them organize the information.

Differentiating Instruction

Beginning

Organizing to Model a Problem

Show students how to use an organizer to model the problem on page 276. Have small groups examine how the same facts are shown in the problem, the organizer, and the equation $B + 6.2 = 48.4$.

48.4	
B	6.2

Intermediate

Explaining Data   Have pairs of students explain how the data in Read and Understand are used to define a variable and to write an equation. (*The "Need to Find" is the variable. The "You Know" is one side of the equation. The "Key Fact" gives information for both sides of the equation.*)

Advanced

Writing an Equation   Have students follow the directions for the Intermediate activity, but challenge them to change one fact in the problem and to write a new equation to help them solve the new problem.

1. Tell why the equation for the Olympics problem contains a plus sign.

Use the strategy *write an equation*.

2. The Panama Canal opened to traffic in 1917. It took 36 years to build the canal. When did work begin on the canal?

3. The first modern Olympic Games were in Athens, Greece, in 1896. Thomas Burke of the United States won the 100-meter dash with a time of 12 seconds. This was 1.2 times Bob Hayes's winning time in 1964. Write an equation to find Bob's time.

4. In 1906, the first Olympic javelin throw was won by Eric Lemming of Sweden. His distance of $176\frac{5}{6}$ feet was $112\frac{5}{12}$ feet less than the distance of Jan Zelezny of the Czech Republic in 1996. Write an equation to find the distance of Zelezny's throw.

▲ Olympic Games in Athens, Greece

Choose a strategy and solve each problem.

5. Sammy has 9 coins with a total value of 45¢. What are the 9 coins? (There may be more than one correct answer.)

6. Kareem's lunch bill was $22.50. What would Kareem pay if he left an 18% tip?

More, Less, Fewer, and Than When you want to compare numbers or amounts, you use the words *more*, *less*, or *fewer* before the noun. You use *than* after the noun.

Comparing Words	Numbers	Amounts
more	I have more CDs than you have.	The recipe for bread calls for more flour than sugar.
less		A desert gets less rain than a grassland.
fewer	Abdul has fewer books than Sari has.	

Write a sentence using each term. Read your sentences aloud to a partner.

WRITE AN EQUATION **277**

Ask, *Why it is important to check that your answer makes sense?* (*Sample: to make sure the equation is correct, and that it was solved correctly*)

Discuss the vocabulary words *canal*, (100-meter) *dash*, and *javelin* used in the problems (*canal: manmade waterway; dash: short, fast running race; javelin: wooden or metal spear*).

Assignment Guide
- Beginning 1, 3–6
- Intermediate 1–6
- Advanced 1–6

Notes on Exercises
Exercise 5 Have students find as many answers as they can. Ask what strategy they used to solve the problem.

- Point out that *more* is used with both numbers and amounts, while *less* is used only with amounts and *fewer* is used only with numbers. You may want to discuss the difference between an amount and a number. (*A number is countable. An amount is not countable.*)

- Explain that *than* is a function word used to show a comparison.

- Have students work in pairs to complete the exercise. Be sure to check their work.

Answers
1. Because the Canada time was greater than that of the Bahamas time
2. $C + 36 = 1917$; 1881
3. $1.2 \cdot B = 12$; 10 seconds
4. $Z - 112\frac{5}{12} = 176\frac{5}{6}$; $289\frac{1}{4}$ ft
5. 1 quarter, 3 nickels, 5 pennies; 4 dimes, 5 pennies; or 9 nickels
6. $26.55

Activity: Is It *More, Less, or Fewer?*

Explain that the words *fewer* and *less* are often misused. Have small groups of students look through their other textbooks to find sentences with *more*, *less*, or *fewer*. Have them talk about whether or not the words are used correctly.

Program Resources

Practice Book Use pages 120 and 121.

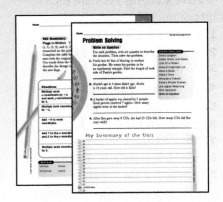

Solving Equations

STANDARDS CONTENT

Mathematics
- Review solving simple equations
- Solve two-operation equations

Language
- Recognize the different spellings and meanings of *way* and *weigh*
- Justify steps taken to solve an equation

Materials
- Algebra tiles

Introduce the [Big Idea]

Read aloud the Big Idea. Ask, *How much change will you get back from $1.00 if you buy two pencils that cost 40¢ each?* *(20¢)* Explain that it took two steps to find the answer and that some equations take two or more steps to solve.

Begin [Building Background]

Have a volunteer explain how to use a balance scale. (*Put the object to be weighed on one side. Add weights to the other side until the two sides are level*).

Teach [Key Concepts]

- Ask, *How are the two equations different?* (*The two-operation equation has different numbers and* x *is multiplied by 3.*)
- Ask, *What does it mean to* undo *an operation?* (*Sample: Reverse it or use an inverse operation.*)

Warm-Up Review

Have students evaluate each expression.

1. $x + 2$ for $x = 3$ *(5)*
2. $n - 6$ for $n = 4$ *(−2)*
3. $3a$ for $a = -6$ *(−18)*
4. $\frac{d}{10}$ for $d = 120$ *(12)*
5. $3f + 2$ for $f = 2$ *(8)*
6. $g + 2 - 8$ for $g = -3$ *(−9)*
7. $10 - 5k$ for $k = 2$ *(0)*
8. $8 \div 2 \times p$ for $p = 4$ *(16)*
9. $r + 6 \div 2$ for $r = 3$ *(6)*

Solving Equations

[Big Idea] Sometimes it takes more than one step to solve an equation, even if it has only one variable.

Building Background

▲ It takes the same weight on both sides to make a scale balance.

- **What is shown here?**
- **When might you use a balance scale?**
- **How could you use a balance scale to help you solve the equation** $x + 8 = 23$?

Key Concepts

To solve an equation, you use basic operations $(+, -, \times, \div)$ to find all the numbers that make the equation true. To solve a **simple equation**, you need to undo only one operation. To solve a **two-operation equation**, you need to undo two operations.

Simple Equation

$$n - 13 = 8$$
$$n - 13 + 13 = 8 + 13 \quad \leftarrow \text{Add 13 to undo subtraction.}$$
$$n = 21$$

Two-operation Equation

$$3x - 5 = 16$$
$$3x - 5 + 5 = 16 + 5 \quad \leftarrow \text{Add 5 to undo subtraction.}$$
$$3x = 21$$
$$\frac{3x}{3} = \frac{21}{3} \quad \leftarrow \text{Divide by 3 to undo multiplication.}$$
$$x = 7$$

Activity: One Operation or Two?

On the board, write the equations below. Have pairs classify the equations as *simple* or *two-operation* and tell which operation(s) will undo the operation(s) in the equation (*simple: 1 and 3; two-operation: 2 and 4*).

1. $x + 10 = 15$ *(subtraction)*
2. $\frac{n}{5} - 2 = 8$ *(addition and multiplication)*
3. $0 = d + (-5)$ *(subtraction)*
4. $18 = 3y + 2$ *(subtraction and division)*

Resource Library

Math at Hand
Solving Equations 240–243

Math on Call
Solving Equations 241–242

Reader's Handbook (red)
Focus on Word Problems 143–154

Reader's Handbook (yellow)
Focus on Word Problems 101–107

Solving Simple Equations

▲ Dufflebag

Before solving equations with two operations, you need to review solving simple equations.

Eron's dufflebag weighed 45 pounds. After he added books to the bag, it weighed 62 pounds. How much did the books weigh?

You can solve problems like this by writing and solving an equation. Let w be the weight of the books.

weight of bag	plus	weight of books	equals	total weight
45	+	w	=	62

Think of the equation as a balance scale. You must do the same thing to both sides to maintain equality. You want the **variable** alone on one side of the equation. Then the **solution** will be on the other side.

$$45 + w = 62 \qquad \leftarrow \text{The variable is } w.$$
$$45 + w - 45 = 62 - 45 \qquad \leftarrow \text{Subtract 45 from both sides.}$$
$$w = 17 \qquad \leftarrow \text{The solution is 17.}$$

The books weighed 17 pounds.

Solve $\frac{x}{7} = \frac{5}{8}$. Use cross products or the Multiplication Property of Equality.

$$\frac{x}{7} = \frac{5}{8}$$
$$8x = 35 \qquad \leftarrow \text{Use cross products.}$$
$$\frac{8x}{8} = \frac{35}{8} \qquad \leftarrow \text{Divide both sides by 8.}$$
$$x = 4\frac{3}{8} \qquad \leftarrow \text{Simplify.}$$

$$\frac{x}{7} = \frac{5}{8}$$
$$\frac{(7)x}{7} = \frac{(7)(5)}{8} \qquad \leftarrow \text{Multiply by 7.}$$
$$x = \frac{35}{8} = 4\frac{3}{8} \qquad \leftarrow \text{Simplify.}$$

Talk and Share

Work with a partner. Tell how to solve each equation. Check your work.

$$n - \frac{1}{8} = \frac{7}{8} \qquad 4.5m = 18 \qquad \frac{c}{5} = -15$$

VOCABULARY

variable—a quantity that can change. It usually is written as a letter, often x or y.
solution—a number that makes an equation true

Teach Solving Simple Equations

■ Ask, *Will the variable always be on the left side of the equal sign?* (*No, it can be on either side.*)

■ An alternate approach is to have students use counters (or algebra tiles) to model equations. For example, to model $45 + w = 62$, they should show 45 counters and one variable strip in one section and 62 counters in the other section. To solve for w, they should remove 45 counters from each section.

■ Stress the importance of checking a solution by substituting the value for the variable and simplifying.

■ Ask, *Why can you use cross products to solve $\frac{x}{7} = \frac{5}{8}$?* (*It is a proportion, and using cross products is one way to solve a proportion.*)

Talk and Share

As part of the class discussion, have students explain how they could use mental math to solve each equation.

Answers: addition, n = *1; division*, m = *4; multiplication*, c = −*75*

Build **VOCABULARY**

Review the properties of equality for addition, subtraction, multiplication, and division. Have students explain how they might use each property to solve an equation.

Differentiating Instruction

Beginning
Solving Simple Equations Have pairs talk about how to solve each equation by undoing the operation.

$a + 2 = 8$ (a = *6, subtraction*)
$5c = 10.5$ (c = *2.1, division*)
$\frac{d}{11} = 3$ (d = *33, multiplication*)
$b - 6 = 12$ (b = *18, addition*)

Intermediate
Explaining How to Solve Equations
Have pairs write four equations that have one operation, identify the operation that can be used to solve each equation, and then solve the equation. Have them choose one equation and tell a word problem that could be solved by the equation.

Advanced
Writing a Word Problem Have pairs write one of the four properties of equality and then write an equation that can be solved using that property. Have them create and write a word problem that can be solved using one of the equations.

Activity: "Ion"ization

Write *solve* and *solution* on the board. Explain that the base word *solve* is a verb and that when the suffix *-ion* is added, the new word is a noun.

Have small groups list other base words and the related *-ion* noun. Encourage students to use math terms (*add/addition; subtract/ subtraction; etc.*).

Teach Two-Operation Equations

- Review the order of operations. Explain that because addition and subtraction are *done last*, these operations are *undone first*.

- Have students use algebra tiles to model other two-operation equations such as $2x + 5 = 11$ and $4x + 6 = 14$ (x = 3; x = 2).

Language Notes

Discuss the words in Language Notes. Tell students that another confusing word pair is *fare*, which means "a charge," and *fair*, which can mean "all outcomes are equally likely."

Talk and Share

Make sure students justify each step.
Answers:

$2a - 3 + 3 = 41 + 3$ *Add 3 to both sides.*

$2a = 44$ *Simplify.*

$2a \div 2 = 44 \div 2$ *Divide both sides by 2.*

$a = 22$ *Simplify.*

$2 \cdot 19 - 3 = 35 \neq 41$

Build VOCABULARY

Have students use the words *way*, *weigh*, *fare*, and *fair* in sentences. Ask for other confusing word pairs (*Samples: some, sum; by, bye; ate, eight*).

Look and Read

Language Notes

Homophones
These words sound alike, but they have different spellings and meanings.

- ☐ way: method
- ☐ weigh: measure by weight

Two-Operation Equations

Mr. Perez took a taxi home. The fare was $2 to start plus $3 a mile. He paid $11. How many miles did he travel?

Write a **two-operation equation** to solve this problem. You will have to undo two operations. Let x be the number of miles.

Base cost	plus	fare times number of miles	equals	total cost
2	+	$3 \cdot x$	=	11

The equation is $2 + 3x = 11$. Solve it with algebra tiles.

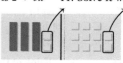
$2 + 3x = 11$

First operation: Remove 2 tiles from each side.

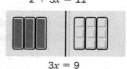
$3x = 9$

Second operation: Divide each side into 3 equal groups.

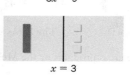
$x = 3$

Solution.

Another way to solve the equation is to use properties of equality. This method will save time later when the equations are more complicated.

$2 + 3x = 11$
$2 + 3x - 2 = 11 - 2$ ← **Subtract 2 to undo the addition.**
$3x = 9$ ← **Simplify.**
$\frac{3x}{3} = \frac{9}{3}$ ← **Divide each side by 3 to undo the multiplication.**
$x = 3$ ← **Simplify.**

Check: $2 + 3(3) = 11$. Mr. Perez rode 3 miles.

Talk and Share

Work with a partner. Show how to solve $2a - 3 = 41$. Have your partner check your work. Tell why $a = 19$ is *not* a solution.

VOCABULARY
two-operation equation—an equation that you solve with two operations

Activity: Write It Out

Have one student write a two-operation equation in words, such as *five times x plus three equals eighteen*. Then have his or her partner use symbols to write the equation, $5x + 3 = 18$. Have partners work together to solve the equation (x = 3). Have them take turns and repeat with several other two-operation equations.

Differentiating Instruction

Beginning
Modeling a Solution Process After working through the algebra-tile example on page 280, have pairs of students use algebra tiles to solve $2x + 4 = 10$. Have them talk about each step as they find the solution (x = 3).

Intermediate
Explaining a Solution After students have studied the second solution method on page 280, have pairs of students use properties of equality to solve $3x - 2 = 10$. Have them show and explain each step as they find the solution (x = 4).

Advanced
Writing an Equation After discussing the solution methods on page 280, ask students to solve $3x - 2 = 10$ (x = 4). Challenge them to write another two-operation equation that has the same solution, and explain how to solve that equation (*Sample*: $\frac{x}{2} + 2 = 4$, x = 4).

Practice

Solve each equation. Check your solutions.

1. $12x + 6 = 42$ **2.** $20 = 5z - 20$ **3.** $\frac{t}{7} - 8 = 14$

4. $11 = \frac{c}{6} + 4$ **5.** $75 = 10a - 15$ **6.** $12 = 9c + 12$

7. $27 = \frac{n}{2} + 11$ **8.** $21 = \frac{x}{5} - 9$ **9.** $7c + 9\frac{3}{4} = 23\frac{3}{4}$

10. $\frac{a}{4} - 2\frac{1}{2} = 3$ **11.** $\frac{n}{10} - 4 = 5.5$ **12.** $2.5x + 10 = 30$

13. $8y - 4 = 0$ **14.** $\frac{m}{5} + 7 = 5$ **15.** $\frac{c}{8} + 6 = 9\frac{1}{2}$

16. Solve the proportion $\frac{x}{8} = \frac{7}{4}$.

Cricket ▼

How fast a snowy tree cricket chirps is related to the air temperature. The warmer the air, the faster the cricket chirps. The relationship is given by the equation $F = \frac{n}{4} + 40$, where F is the temperature in degrees Fahrenheit and n is the number of chirps. Find the temperature or the number of chirps.

17. $n = 40$ **18.** $n = 160$

19. $F = 60°$ **20.** $F = 40°$

21. What does your answer to Exercise 20 tell you about a cricket's chirping?

22. Daisy has 60 feet of fencing to enclose part of the yard for her dog. She wants the section to be 20 feet long. How wide can it be? Write and solve an equation.

23. Rico is going to Mexico City. He thinks airfare will be $800 and living expenses will be $40 a day. How many days can Rico stay in Mexico City if he has $1,120 to spend? Write and solve an equation.

24. The monthly charge for Damon's long-distance telephone service is $4.95 plus $0.07 for each minute of long-distance calls. Last month, Damon's long-distance bill was $8.80 without tax. How many long-distance minutes did Damon use? Write and solve an equation.

25. (EXTENDED RESPONSE) Tell how the equations $15x = 180$ and $15x - 30 = 180$ are alike and different. Tell how solving $15x - 30 = 180$ is different from solving $15x = 180$.

26. (MULTIPLE CHOICE) Solve the equation $16 + \frac{n}{5} = 4$.
A. $n = 100$ **B.** $n = 36$ **C.** $n = 4$ **D.** $n = -60$

LESSON 49 • SOLVING EQUATIONS   **281**

Practice

Ask students to compare solving simple and two-operation equations. (*Sample: Both use properties of equality to get the variable alone on one side of the equation. Simple equations have one operation, one undo, and one simplify step. Two-operation equations have two operations, two undos, and two simplify steps.*)

Have students explain how to undo each operation. (*Undo addition by subtraction, subtraction by addition, multiplication by division, and division by multiplication.*)

Assignment Guide
- Beginning 1–8, 13–17, 20–23, 25, 26
- Intermediate 1–8, 11–17, 20–23, 25, 26
- Advanced 6–26

Notes on Exercises
Exercises 17–21 For these problems, the number of chirps is counted in 1-minute intervals.

Exercise 22 Tell students to assume that the section will be rectangular.

Exercise 25 Have students solve both equations as part of their answers ($15x = 180$, $x = 12$; $15x - 30 = 180$, $x = 14$).

Answers
1. $x = 3$ **2.** $z = 8$
3. $t = 154$ **4.** $c = 42$
5. $a = 9$ **6.** $c = 0$
7. $n = 32$ **8.** $x = 150$
9. $c = 2$ **10.** $a = 22$
11. $n = 95$ **12.** $x = 8$
13. $y = 0.5$ **14.** $m = -10$
15. $c = 28$ **16.** $x = 14$
17. $50\,°F$ **18.** $80\,°F$
19. 80 chirps   **20.** 0 chirps

21. It stops chirping at 40 °F.
22. $2w + 2(20) = 60$, $w = 10$; 10 ft
23. $800 + 40d = 1,120$, $d = 8$; 8 days
24. $4.95 + 0.07m = 8.80$, $m = 55$; 55 min
25. Both have $15x$ and 180; one has 30 subtracted from $15x$. With $15x - 30 = 180$, you have to add 30 to both sides before dividing by 15.
26. D

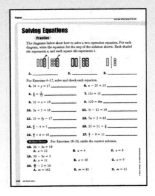

Teach Justifying

Read the first sentence aloud. Ask, *Did you ever have to justify your actions to someone else?*

Answers:

1. *Subtraction Property of Equality; Simplifying; Multiplication Property of Equality; Simplifying*

Hands On

If algebra tiles are not available, pairs can use same-sized colored rectangles to represent the variables and counters for the numbers.

Answers: x = 3; x = 2; x = 5; x = 0

Oral Language

Begin by solving the example as a class. Tell students that *x* represents the number.

Answer: 3x + 12 = 27; x = 5

Key Connection

Invite students (ages 9–12) to read *The Cricket in Times Square*, by George Selden. Chester is a cricket who winds up in New York City, where he is adopted and makes friends with Tucker the mouse and Harry the cat.

Have students give a book report or make a chart giving formulas for number of chirps per minute for different kinds of crickets. They can check this website: http://www.insecta-inspecta.com/crickets/field.

Activities

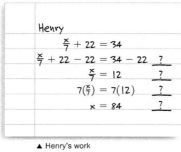

$$\frac{x}{7} + 22 = 34$$
$$\frac{x}{7} + 22 - 22 = 34 - 22 \quad \underline{\quad ?\quad}$$
$$\frac{x}{7} = 12 \quad \underline{\quad ?\quad}$$
$$7(\tfrac{x}{7}) = 7(12) \quad \underline{\quad ?\quad}$$
$$x = 84 \quad \underline{\quad ?\quad}$$

▲ Henry's work

Justifying To justify is to give the reasons for comments you make or for the steps you take. A *justification* in math is often a rule or a property.

Look at Henry's work for solving an equation. Talk with your partner about the justification for each step in the solution. Choose your reasons from this list: *Addition Property of Equality, Subtraction Property of Equality, Multiplication Property of Equality, Division Property of Equality,* and *Simplify.*

1. Justify Give the reasons for the steps.

2. Explain Explain to your partner how you chose the reasons.

3. Justify Write a two-operation equation. Trade equations with your partner and solve. Justify your steps.

Hands On

Modeling Equations Work with a partner to solve these equations. Take turns using algebra tiles or pencil and paper. Check each other's work.

$3x + 4 = 13$
$7 + 4x = 15$
$11 = 1 + 2x$
$8 = 8 + 3x$

Oral Language

What's My Number? Work with a partner. Take turns giving each other riddles involving two operations such as this: *If I multiply my number by 3 and then add 12, I get 27. What's my number?*

For each riddle, write and solve an equation. Then tell your partner how you solved the equation.

Program Resources

Practice Book Use page 123.

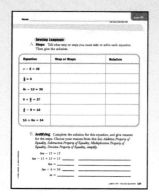

Assessment Book

Use page 71 to assess students' comprehension.

Activity: Is It Fair?

Have students work in pairs to set up a fee schedule similar to the one shown for taxi fares on page 280 to use in a tutoring business.

Point out that they should have a base rate and a charge for each specific time period. Have them write an expression to calculate how much to charge for each tutoring session and an equation to find the charge for one half-hour session.

Have pairs justify their rates.

Inequalities

Talk and Explore

Big Idea Many times you need to compare two quantities that are not equal. You can use mathematical sentences to make these comparisons.

Building Background

▲ I remember when I wasn't tall enough to go on the ride. I could only watch and wait for my brother.

You must grow as tall as I am to ride.

■ **What does the sign tell you?**

■ **How does this girl know if she is tall enough to go on the ride?**

Key Concepts

A **mathematical sentence** is a sentence that uses operations, variables, and numbers to state a relationship. When the sentence states an equality, the sentence is an **equation**. When the sentence states that two quantities are not equal, the sentence is an **inequality**.

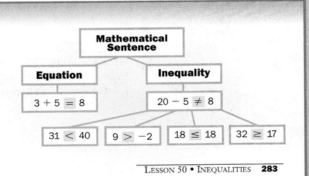

Mathematical Sentence

Equation

$3 + 5 = 8$

Inequality

$20 - 5 \neq 8$

$31 < 40$ $9 > -2$ $18 \leq 18$ $32 \geq 17$

LESSON 50 • INEQUALITIES   **283**

Activity: I'm the Greatest!

Have each student in a pair toss two number cubes and write a 2-digit number. Then have partners use the symbol $>$, $<$, or $=$ to write a mathematical sentence comparing the two numbers. Have them repeat the activity several times.

Resource Library

Math on Call
Inequalities 257–260

MATH ON CALL

Inequalities

STANDARDS CONTENT

Mathematics
■ Graph inequalities on a number line
■ Solve inequalities

Language
■ Recognize multiple meanings of *solution*
■ Compare inequalities

Materials
■ Number lines (Overhead Transparency 28)

Introduce the **Big Idea**

Read aloud the Big Idea. Ask, *Would you rather score 5 points or 10 points on a quiz?* Point out that they compared two quantities that were not equal. Ask them to use symbols to show the relationship ($5 < 10$ or $10 > 5$).

Begin **Building Background**

Have students tell which amusement-park rides are their favorites. Ask, *Do any of those rides have a height limit?*

Answers: How tall a person must be to go on the ride; compare her height to the height of the sign.

Teach **Key Concepts**

■ Review how to read the math symbols $=$, $\neq$, $<$, $>$, $\leq$, and $\geq$.

■ Ask a volunteer to explain the diagram and to read aloud each mathematical statement.

Warm-Up Review

Present the number line (Overhead Transparency 28) below to the class.

Have students identify the coordinate of each point.

1. A (-3) **2.** B (-1)
3. C (3) **4.** D (5)

Ask volunteers to plot point E at -5, point F at 0, and point G at 2.

Teach Exploring Inequalities

Stress that most inequalities have many solutions. Ask, *How many numbers are greater than 1?* (*an unlimited number*) Point out that the number of solutions to the inequality $x > 1$ is unlimited.

Language Notes

You may want to dissolve a packet of drink mix in water to show students an example of a solution.

Talk and Share

Suggest that students use numbers that are multiples of 7 to label points on the graph. Ask, *Will any negative values be needed?* (*no*) Ask students to graph $x < 42$ so that each student can explain one graph. Encourage them to give one solution for each inequality (*Samples:* x ≥ 42, x = 49; x < 42, x = 35).

Answer:

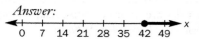

Build VOCABULARY

Define *inequality*. Have students add the symbols and meanings from the table on page 284 to their math vocabulary card file. Have them write an example using each symbol.

Look and Read

Language Notes

Multiple Meanings
This word has more than one meaning.

☐ solution
1. an answer to a problem
2. an explanation
3. a mixture formed by dissolving one ingredient into another

People on a roller coaster ▼

284 Unit 12 • MORE ALGEBRA

Exploring Inequalities

An **inequality** is a sentence that compares two quantities that are not equal. Inequalities contain one of these symbols.

Symbol	Meaning
≠	is not equal to
<	is less than
>	is greater than
≤	is less than or equal to
≥	is greater than or equal to

Solutions to an inequality are numbers that make the inequality true. Most inequalities have many solutions.

The graph of an inequality helps you see all the solutions. An open circle shows that the starting point *is not* a solution. A closed circle shows that the starting number *is* a solution.

Today's temperature will be less than 7°.

$t < 7$ 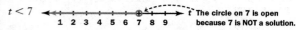 The circle on 7 is open because 7 is NOT a solution.

You can tell if a number is a solution to $t < 7$ by checking if it is on the red part of the ray. 8 is not a solution, but 2 is.

Mari spends $4 or more on her daily lunches.

$m \geq 4$ 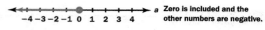 The circle on 4 is closed because 4 IS a solution.

The inequality for the graph below is $a \leq 0$.

Zero is included and the other numbers are negative.

Talk and Share

The inequality for how tall someone must be to ride the roller coaster is $x \geq 42$ inches. Graph this inequality on a number line. Tell your partner how you did it.

VOCABULARY
inequality—a statement that says two quantities are *not* equal

---

Activity: Open or Closed?

Read aloud each inequality shown below. For each sentence, have students move their index finger and thumb apart if the graph described will have an open circle and move them together if the graph will have a closed circle.

1. $x < 4$ (*open*)   **2.** $y \geq -15$ (*closed*)
3. $z \leq 9$ (*closed*)   **4.** $a > -2$ (*open*)

Have volunteers give at least one solution for each inequality (*Samples: 1.* x = 0; 2. y = −3; 3. z = 9; 4. a = 2).

Differentiating Instruction

Beginning/ Intermediate
Graphing Inequalities on a Number Line On the board, draw a simple number line from −5 to 5, labeled *x*. Ask volunteers to come to the board and shade circles for the numbers greater than 0. Ask, *What about all the fractions and decimals between the circles?* Shade in a heavy line between 0 and 5. *What about numbers greater than 5?* Shade in a heavy arrow to the right of 5. *Is zero included?* (*no*) Draw an empty circle on zero. Write x > 5 and say, *We have graphed* x > 5. Repeat with other inequalities.

Advanced
Explaining How to Graph Inequalities
Have pairs of students talk about when to use an open circle and when to use a closed circle to graph an inequality. Then have them try to graph the inequality 5 < x < 10 and talk about how they did it. (◄––○––○►x; 0 5 10 *Sample: We drew open circles on 5 and 10, because* x *is not equal to either number. Then we drew a heavy line between the circles because* x *is greater than 5 but less than 10.*)

Solving Inequalities

Annika needs to sell at least 200 boxes of cookies to break her club's record for cookie sales by one person. She has sold 137 boxes. How many more boxes must she sell?

You can write an inequality to solve this problem. Let n be the number of boxes Annika still needs to sell.

boxes sold	plus	boxes needed	is more than or equal to	total sold
137	+	n	$\geq$	200

$137 + n \geq 200$

$137 + n - 137 \geq 200 - 137$ ← **Subtract 137 from both sides.**

$n \geq 63$ ← **Simplify.**

Annika needs to sell at least 63 more boxes of cookies.

You can check your solution by substituting numbers in the inequality.

$137 + n \geq 200$

$137 + 63 \geq 200$ ← **Substitute 63.**

$200 = 200$ ← **It checks.**

The inequality $n \geq 63$ tells you that 63 and any number greater than 63 are solutions.

To solve inequalities, use the properties of inequalities.

▲ Clubs sometimes have bake sales to raise money. What would you make to sell at a bake sale?

Properties of Inequalities

Addition/Subtraction If two quantities are not equal, adding or subtracting the same number from both quantities does not change the inequality.

Multiplication/Division If two quantities are not equal, multiplying or dividing both quantities by the same positive number does not change the inequality.

Talk and Share

Work with a partner. Tell how to solve each inequality. Then solve each and check your solutions.

$x - 15 < 25$ $n + 40 > 8$ $5c \leq 45$ $\frac{a}{3} \geq 12$

LESSON 50 • INEQUALITIES   **285**

Teach Solving Inequalities

- After reading aloud the cookie problem, ask, *How do you know that an inequality should be written to solve the problem?* (*The phrase* at least *signals that the sentence should be an inequality.*)

- Ask, *Does 64 or 20 solve the inequality* $137 + n \geq 200$? (*64 does; 20 does not.*)

- While discussing the properties of inequalities, explain that *does not change the inequality* means that the inequality symbol stays the same. Stress that the Multiplication and Division Properties of Inequality will *not* change the inequality symbol *if* you multiply or divide by a *positive* number.

Talk and Share

Have students graph the solutions on a number line.

Answers: Add 15 to both sides, $x < 40$; *subtract 40 from both sides,* $n > -32$; *divide both sides by 5,* $c \leq 9$; *multiply both sides by 3,* $a \geq 36$.

Build VOCABULARY

Explain that the prefixes *in-*, *im-*, *il-*, and *ir-* all mean *not*. The prefix *il-* is used with words starting with *l* (*illegal*); *im-* with *b*, *m*, or *p* (*impeach*); *ir-* with *r* (*irrational*); and *in-* with all other letters (*inequality*).

🔲 Differentiating Instruction

Beginning

Exploring Solving Inequalities

Review with students the properties of equality and how they are used to solve equations. Say, *You can use properties like these to solve inequalities.* On the board, write inequalities like those on page 285, and have volunteers solve them, telling how they found each solution. Do not include negative factors or divisors.

Intermediate

Graphing Solutions to Inequalities

Give students inequalities such as

$x + 5 \geq 10$ and $3y > 9$. Have them solve one of the inequalities and then graph the solution on a number line. Have them talk about how their graph shows the solution.

Advanced

Checking Solutions to Inequalities

Give students several simple inequalities to solve. Then have them choose several numbers in each solution and verify that those numbers do satisfy the inequality and explain why.

🎲 Activity: Inequality Races

Write an inequality on the board for teams to solve. The first team with the correct answer scores 1 point. Play continues until a team has 10 points.

Practice

Ask, *How would you graph the inequality* x > 6? (*Draw a number line. Put an empty circle on 6. Darken the line to the right of 6 and put an arrow on the end.*) *How would you change the graph to show* x ≥ 6? (*Shade in the circle.*)

Ask, *Which property of inequality would you use to solve* a + 2 ≥ 4? (*Subtraction Property of Inequality*) Then have students solve the inequality (a ≥ 2).

Assignment Guide
- Beginning 1–16, 20–24 even
- Intermediate 1–10, 15–24
- Advanced 1–16, 20–24

Notes on Exercises

Exercises 1–4 Point out the variable at the right end of each graph. Explain that students should use this variable when writing the inequality.

Exercises 7–10 Remind students to check that the numbers on each graph are solutions to the inequality.

Exercises 22 and 23 Remind students that to solve each problem, they need to write and solve an inequality.

Exercise 24 Discuss students' answers as a class to make sure everyone recognizes the need to change the inequality symbol when multiplying or dividing by a negative number.

Look and Read

Practice

Write the inequality that is graphed on each number line.

1. ⟵⊕–6–5–4–3–2–1 0 1 2⟶ x   **2.** ⟵–4–3–2–1 0 1 2̶ 3 4⟶ y

3. ⟵–2–1 0 1 2 3 4 5 6⟶ k   **4.** ⟵–5–4–3–2̶–1 0 1 2 3⟶ n

5. Graph *n* > 4 and *n* < 4 on the same number line. Then tell what you notice.

6. Graph *n* > 4 and *n* ≥ 4 on separate number lines. Then tell how the solutions are different.

Write each inequality. Then graph it on a number line.

7. 10 is greater than *s*.   **8.** *n* is less than or equal to 0.

9. *y* is greater than 3.   **10.** *c* is greater than or equal to −4.

Solve each inequality. Check two solutions for each exercise.

11. $n + 5 < 23$ **12.** $7m > 42$ **13.** $\frac{x}{12} < 3$

14. $a - 14 \geq 8$ **15.** $d + 9 \leq 16$ **16.** $\frac{b}{3} \geq 15$

17. $n - 5 > -13$ **18.** $11 < 3 + x$ **19.** $12 \geq m - 4$

▲ A busy street in India

20. In India, you must be at least 18 years old to get a driver's license. Write an inequality to show how old you must be.

21. In some places, you cannot drive faster than 55 miles per hour. Write an inequality to tell how fast you can drive.

22. At the Cozy Cafe, the cost for lunch per person is $12. How many people can Cathy invite if she wants to spend no more than $150?

23. Antoine wants to give some of his baseball cards to 4 friends. How many cards must he give away so that each friend gets at least 18 cards?

24. (EXTENDED RESPONSE) The properties for dividing and multiplying inequalities are only for positive numbers. Multiply or divide both sides of these inequalities by a negative number, such as −3. What happens to each inequality?

$$3 > -12 \qquad 15 < 21 \qquad -9 < 36$$

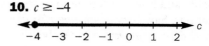

Program Resources

Practice Book Use page 124.
Overhead Transparencies Use 28.

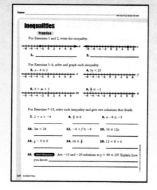

Answers

1. $x > -5$ **2.** $y < 2$

3. $k \geq 4$ **4.** $n \leq -1$

5. Together they include all numbers except 4.

6. $n > 4$ has an empty circle at 4; $n \geq 4$ has a solid circle at 4.

7. $10 > s$

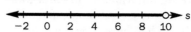
⟵ –2 0 2 4 6 8 10⟶ s

8. $n \leq 0$

⟵ –3 –2 –1 0 1 2 3⟶ n

9. $y > 3$

⟵ –6 –3 0 3 6 9 12⟶ y

10. $c \geq -4$

⟵ –4 –3 –2 –1 0 1 2⟶ c

11. $n < 18$ **12.** $m > 6$ **13.** $x < 36$
14. $a \geq 22$ **15.** $d \leq 7$ **16.** $b \geq 45$
17. $n > -8$ **18.** $8 < x$ **19.** $16 \geq m$
20. $a \geq 18$ **21.** $m \leq 55$
22. no more than 12 people
See Additional Answers, page T42.

Activities

Comparing Work with a partner to compare the inequalities listed below. First match each inequality with its graph. Then compare the inequalities by telling how they are alike and how they are different.

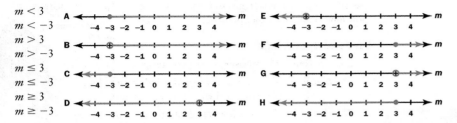

$m < 3$
$m < -3$
$m > 3$
$m > -3$
$m \leq 3$
$m \leq -3$
$m \geq 3$
$m \geq -3$

1. **Read** With your partner, take turns reading aloud each inequality.

2. **Match** Match each inequality with its graph. Explain how you made your choices.

3. **Compare** Pick an inequality and have your partner pick another. Talk about how the two inequalities are alike and how they are different.

4. **Write** Take turns making up a story to go with one of the inequalities. Try to guess the inequality your partner used in his or her story.

 Oral Language

The Number Hold-up Work with a partner. Prepare 21 cards, each containing a different integer from −10 to 10. Say an inequality and have your partner hold up all the cards from the pile whose numbers are solutions to the inequality. Take turns saying the inequalities and checking your partner's solutions.

Partner Practice

Two Ways to Check Work with a partner. Take turns saying an inequality such as $3x \leq 45$. Have your partner write the inequality and solve it by graphing or by using properties of inequality. Check your partner's work.

Teach Comparing

Remind students that they have had to compare many different math ideas this year. In this activity, they will compare two different inequalities.

Answers:

2. m < 3, D; m < −3, E; m > 3, G; m > −3, B; m ≤ 3, H; m ≤ −3, C; m ≥ 3, F; m ≥ −3, A

Oral Language

Encourage students to identify several integers in each solution. Suggest that for the inequality $x + 2 \leq -3$ they say, *The solution to the inequality* x + 2 ≤ −3 *includes* −5, −6, −7, −8, −9, and −10.

Partner Practice

Point out that students should graph some of the inequalities. Encourage them to give some numbers that are in the solution to check their work.

Key Connection

The age requirements for getting a driver's license vary by state and by country. Suggest that students visit Internet sites to learn more about the driving requirements in different states and other countries. Ask students to make a list of inequalities to share results. One site to try is http://members.aol.com/learnanliv/learner.html.

 Activity: Extend the Lesson

Have students solve two-operation inequalities. Write $2x + 6 < 8$ on the board. Write each step as students respond. Ask students what they would do first to solve the inequality. (*Subtract 6 from each side.* 2x + 6 − 6 < 8 − 6, 2x < 2.) Then ask what they would do next. (*Divide each side by 2.* 2x ÷ 2 < 2 ÷ 2, x < 1.) Have students solve $3a - 5 \geq 22$ and $\frac{c}{6} + 2 \leq 4$ (a ≥ 9, c ≤ 12). Have them watch for negative multipliers or divisors.

Assessment Book

Use page 72 to assess students' comprehension.

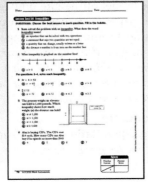

 Program Resources

Practice Book Use page 125.
Overhead Transparencies Use 28.

Make a Model

STANDARDS CONTENT

Mathematics
■ Solve problems by making a model

Language
■ Identify when to use *some* and *any*

Materials
■ Scissors, tape, grid paper (Overhead Transparency 15)

Teach Make a Model

■ Explain that a model may be an actual construction or a picture that shows the problem.

■ Stress that the ratio 2:1 is the ratio of the 36-in. piece of wood to the 18 units shown for that piece in the model.

Talk and Share

Remind students that the possible models must be different. Have them recall that models that can be folded into solid shapes are called *nets*. Suggest that they turn each net to make sure it is not identical to any other.

Answers:

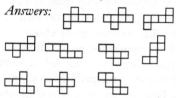

Problem-Solving Skills

Make a Model

A problem is always easier to solve if you can see it. To help you see a problem, it is a good strategy to make a model.

Problem: Yuko wants to make a kite like the one shown. She has two thin pieces of wood that are 36 inches long. If she keeps one piece 36 inches long, how long should the other piece be?

shorter piece of wood

longer piece of wood

Read and Understand

Need to find: The measure of the shorter piece of wood

You know: The basic shape of a kite and that the longer piece of wood will be 36 inches long

Key fact: The kite should look like the one on the right.

Plan and Solve
Use grid paper and draw a kite similar to the one above. Make the longer piece of wood 18 units. Each unit stands for 2 inches on the kite. If you estimate the proportions of the pattern shown above, you will see that the shorter piece of wood is about 12 units.

The ratio of the longer piece of wood to the longer length in the model is 2 to 1. So the ratio of shorter pieces also will be 2 to 1. Then 2(12) = 24 inches for the shorter piece of wood.

Answer
The shorter piece of wood will be 24 inches long.

Look Back
Use a proportion to check the lengths.

$$\frac{36}{18} = \frac{n}{12} \quad \leftarrow \text{actual length}$$
$$\phantom{\frac{36}{18} = \frac{n}{12}} \leftarrow \text{grid length}$$
$$18 \times n = 36 \times 12$$
$$18n = 432$$
$$n = 24$$

Talk and Share
With a partner, draw on grid paper all possible models that you can fold to make a cube. Cut them out and fold them to be sure that they are correct. One net is shown. There are 11 different models in all. Try to find at least 5 others.

 Activity: Post It

Have pairs of students solve this problem: Hector is building a square pen for his dog. He will use 400 ft of chain-link mesh for the fence and put a post every 10 ft. Make a model to find how many posts he will need to make the pen (*40 posts*).

Ask, *What other strategy could you use to solve the problem?* (*Sample: Act it out.*)

Differentiating Instruction

Beginning
Drawing a Model Have pairs draw a smaller model of the kite on page 288 on grid paper (Overhead Transparency 15), using 12 units for the longer piece of wood. Ask, *What is the length of the short piece in this model?* (*8 units*) *What is the ratio of the length in the actual kite to the lengths in this model?* (*3:1*)

Intermediate
Finding Equal Ratios Ask, *What is the ratio of the lengths of the two pieces of*

wood in the model on page 288? ($\frac{18}{12}$, *or* $\frac{3}{2}$) *Find the ratio of the lengths in the kite* ($\frac{36}{24}$, *or* $\frac{3}{2}$). *Are the ratios the same?* (*yes*)

Advanced
Explaining a Model Follow the directions for the Beginning activity. Ask, *What proportion shows that your lengths are correct?* (*Sample:* $\frac{36}{12} = \frac{24}{8}$)

---

1. Suppose Yuko had used only 9 units on the grid to represent the longer piece of wood. Would the answer have been the same? Explain.

Use the strategy *make a model*.

2. Draw a net for the triangular prism shown on the right. Think about which faces are rectangles and which are triangles. Then cut out the net and fold it to make a model.

3. Work in a small group. Make differently-sized open boxes. Use an $8\frac{1}{2}$-inch-by-11-inch sheet of paper. Use a ruler and scissors to mark off and then cut squares from each corner of the paper. One of you should use 1-inch squares; another, 2-inch squares; a third person, 3-inch squares; and a fourth person, 4-inch squares. Fold the paper as shown and find the volume of each box. Which box has the greatest volume? Describe its shape.

9 in.

1 in.

$6\frac{1}{2}$ in.

Grammar Spotlight

Some* and *Any   The words *some* and *any* are adjectives that refer to *how much* or *how many*. You can use the words with plural nouns, both count and noncount. Use them when the number is not known or is not important.

Use *some* in statements or in a question when you are offering something. Use *any* in negative statements.

Examples	Explanations
Affirmative Statements *Jane has some books. She has some money.*	Use *some* in affirmative statements with plural count and noncount nouns.
Negative Statements *Dick doesn't have any books. He doesn't have any money.*	Use *any* in negative statements with plural count and noncount nouns.
Questions *Does Sally have any books? Would you like some fruit?*	Use *any* in questions with plural count and noncount nouns. Use *some* when you offer something.

Take turns with your partner coming up with your own examples of each type of sentence in the table. Have your partner write each example. Check your partner's written sentences.

Ask, *Does anyone build models? How do the models compare with actual items?*

Assignment Guide
- Beginning 1–3
- Intermediate 1–3
- Advanced 1–3

Notes on Exercises
Exercise 1 Suggest that students write a proportion to solve the problem.

Exercise 2 Discuss the relative sizes of edges to help students draw the net.

Exercise 3 Model how the first person's sheet of paper will look with 1-in. squares cut out of each corner. Review how to find the volume of a box: $V = \ell \cdot w \cdot h$.

Grammar Spotlight

- Review the definitions of *plural count nouns* and *noncount nouns*. (*A count noun is a noun that can have a number placed in front of it. A noncount noun usually cannot.*) In the examples, the word *books* is a plural count noun and *money* is a noncount noun.

- Point out that negative statements are those using the word, or a form of the word, *not*.

Answers
1. Yes; the proportion would have been $\frac{36}{9} = \frac{n}{6}$, and $n = 24$.

2.

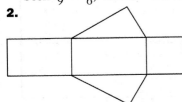

3. $6\frac{1}{2} \cdot 9 \cdot 1 = 58\frac{1}{2}$; $4\frac{1}{2} \cdot 7 \cdot 2 = 63$;
$2\frac{1}{2} \cdot 5 \cdot 3 = 37\frac{1}{2}$; $\frac{1}{2} \cdot 3 \cdot 4 = 6$;
$4\frac{1}{2} \cdot 7 \cdot 2$; check descriptions.

Activity: Language Hunt

Have students go on a language hunt to find how the words *some* and *any* are used in daily conversation. Have them record the usage for one week and share sample sentences, correct or incorrect, in class.

Students may practice their own usage at this website:
- http://a4esl.org/q/h/vm/someanyno.html

Program Resources

Practice Book Use pages 126 and 127.
Overhead Transparencies Use 15.

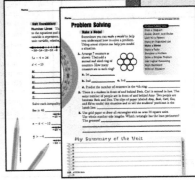

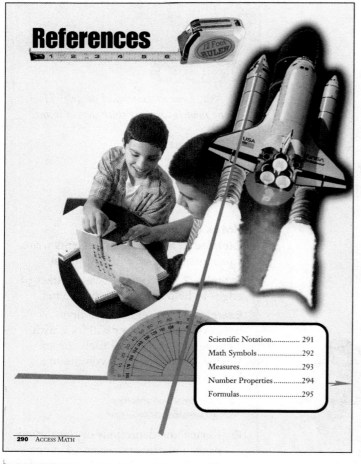

References

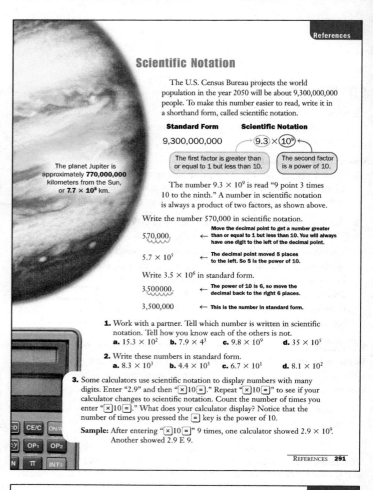

Scientific Notation

The U.S. Census Bureau projects the world population in the year 2050 will be about 9,300,000,000 people. To make this number easier to read, write it in a shorthand form, called scientific notation.

The planet Jupiter is approximately **770,000,000** kilometers from the Sun, or **7.7 × 10⁸** km.

Standard Form	Scientific Notation
9,300,000,000	9.3×10^9

The first factor is greater than or equal to 1 but less than 10.

The second factor is a power of 10.

The number 9.3×10^9 is read "9 point 3 times 10 to the ninth." A number in scientific notation is always a product of two factors, as shown above.

Write the number 570,000 in scientific notation.

5.70,000. ← Move the decimal point to get a number greater than or equal to 1 but less than 10. You will always have one digit to the left of the decimal point.

5.7×10^5 ← The decimal point moved 5 places to the left. So 5 is the power of 10.

Write 3.5×10^6 in standard form.

3.500000. ← The power of 10 is 6, so move the decimal back to the right 6 places.

3,500,000 ← This is the number in standard form.

1. Work with a partner. Tell which number is written in scientific notation. Tell how you know each of the others is not.
   a. 15.3×10^2 **b.** 7.9×4^3 **c.** 9.8×10^9 **d.** 35×10^5

2. Write these numbers in standard form.
   a. 8.3×10^3 **b.** 4.4×10^5 **c.** 6.7×10^1 **d.** 8.1×10^2

3. Some calculators use scientific notation to display numbers with many digits. Enter "2.9" and then "×10=." Repeat "×10=" to see if your calculator changes to scientific notation. Count the number of times you enter "×10=." What does your calculator display? Notice that the number of times you pressed the = key is the power of 10.

Sample: After entering "×10=" 9 times, one calculator showed 2.9×10^9. Another showed 2.9 E 9.

Math Symbols

+	plus (addition)
−	minus (subtraction)
×, •	times (multiplication)
÷, ⟌	divided by (division)
=	is equal to, equals
≠	is not equal to
≟	Is the statement true?
>	is greater than
≥	is greater than or equal to
<	is less than
≤	is less than or equal to
≈	is approximately equal to
≅	is congruent to
~	is similar to
( )	parentheses for grouping
...	and so on
°	degrees
°C	degrees Celsius
°F	degrees Fahrenheit
5^6	5 raised to the 6th power
−8	the opposite of 8
$\frac{1}{3}$	reciprocal of 3
|7|	absolute value of 7
8 : 5	ratio of 8 to 5
%	percent

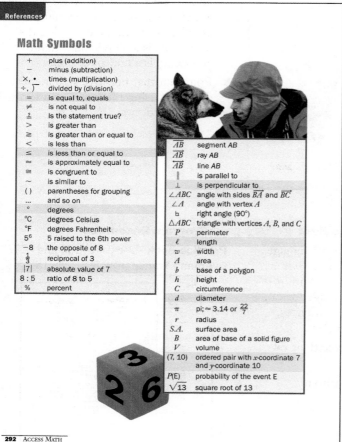

$\overline{AB}$	segment AB
$\overrightarrow{AB}$	ray AB
$\overleftrightarrow{AB}$	line AB
∥	is parallel to
⊥	is perpendicular to
$\angle ABC$	angle with sides $\overrightarrow{BA}$ and $\overrightarrow{BC}$
$\angle A$	angle with vertex A
∟	right angle (90°)
$\triangle ABC$	triangle with vertices A, B, and C
P	perimeter
ℓ	length
w	width
A	area
b	base of a polygon
h	height
C	circumference
d	diameter
π	pi; ≈ 3.14 or $\frac{22}{7}$
r	radius
$S.A.$	surface area
B	area of base of a solid figure
V	volume
(7, 10)	ordered pair with x-coordinate 7 and y-coordinate 10
$P(E)$	probability of the event E
$\sqrt{13}$	square root of 13

Measures

Metric	United States Customary	Equivalents
LENGTH	**LENGTH**	**LENGTH**
10 millimeters (mm) = 1 centimeter (cm)	12 inches (in.) = 1 foot (ft)	1 in. = 2.54 cm
100 cm = 1 meter (m)	36 in. = 1 yard (yd)	1 m ≈ 39.37 in.
1,000 mm = 1 meter	3 ft = 1 yard	1 m ≈ 1.09 yd
1,000 m = 1 kilometer (km)	5,280 ft = 1 mile (mi)	1 mi ≈ 1.61 km
	1,760 yd = 1 mile	
AREA	**AREA**	
100 square millimeters (mm²) = 1 square centimeter (cm²)	144 square inches (in.²) = 1 square foot (ft²)	
10,000 cm² = 1 square meter (m²)	9 ft² = 1 square yard (yd²)	
1 square kilometer (km²) = 1,000,000 m²	4,840 yd² = 1 acre	
VOLUME	**VOLUME**	
1,000 cubic millimeters (mm³) = 1 cubic centimeter (cm³)	1,728 cubic inches (in.³) = 1 cubic foot (ft³)	
1,000,000 cm³ = 1 cubic meter (m³)	27 ft³ = 1 cubic yard (yd³)	
MASS	**MASS**	**MASS**
1,000 milligrams (mg) = 1 gram (g)	16 ounces (oz) = 1 pound (lb)	1 oz ≈ 28.35 g
1,000 g = 1 kilogram (kg)	2,000 lb = 1 ton (t)	1 kg ≈ 2.2 lb
		1 metric ton (t) ≈ 1.102 tons (T)
LIQUID CAPACITY	**LIQUID CAPACITY**	**LIQUID CAPACITY**
1,000 milliliters (mL) = 1 liter (L)	8 fluid ounces (fl oz) = 1 cup (c)	1 L ≈ 1.06 qt
1,000 L = 1 kiloliter (kL)	2 c = 1 pint (pt)	1 gal ≈ 3.79 L
	2 pt = 1 quart (qt)	
	4 qt = 1 gallon (gal)	

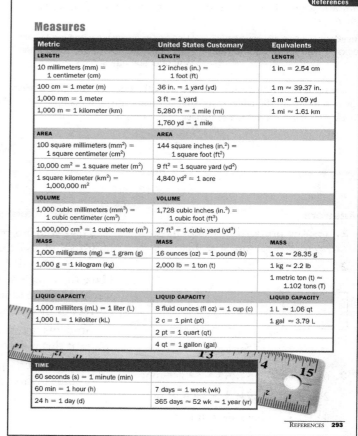

TIME	
60 seconds (s) = 1 minute (min)	
60 min = 1 hour (h)	7 days = 1 week (wk)
24 h = 1 day (d)	365 days ≈ 52 wk ≈ 1 year (yr)

Number Properties

Associative Properties	
Addition	$(a + b) + c = a + (b + c)$
Multiplication	$(a \cdot b) \cdot c = a \cdot (b \cdot c)$

Commutative Properties	
Addition	$a + b = b + a$
Multiplication	$a \cdot b = b \cdot a$

Addition of Opposites
$a + (-a) = 0$ and $-a + a = 0$

Multiplication of Reciprocals
$a \cdot \frac{1}{a} = 1$ and $\frac{1}{a} \cdot a = 1 \ (a \neq 0)$

Distributive Properties
$a(b + c) = ab + ac$
$a(b - c) = ab - ac$

Cross Products
If $\frac{a}{c} = \frac{b}{d}$, then $ad = bc$ $(c \neq 0, d \neq 0)$.

Properties of Equality	
Addition	If $a = b$, then $a + c = b + c$.
Subtraction	If $a = b$, then $a - c = b - c$.
Multiplication	If $a = b$, then $a \cdot c = b \cdot c$.
Division	If $a = b$ and $c \neq 0$, then $\frac{a}{c} = \frac{b}{c}$.

Properties of Inequality	
Addition	If $a > b$, then $a + c > b + c$.
	If $a < b$, then $a + c < b + c$.
Subtraction	If $a > b$, then $a - c > b - c$.
	If $a < b$, then $a - c < b - c$.
Multiplication	If $a > b$ and c is positive, then $ac > bc$.
	If $a < b$ and c is positive, then $ac < bc$.
Division	If $a > b$ and c is positive, then $\frac{a}{c} > \frac{b}{c}$.
	If $a < b$ and c is positive, then $\frac{a}{c} < \frac{b}{c}$.

Formulas

$P = 2\ell + 2w$, or $P = 2(\ell + w)$
$A = \ell w$
Rectangle

$P = s + s + s + s$, or $P = 4s$
$A = s^2$
Square

$A = bh$
Parallelogram

$A = \frac{1}{2}bh$
Triangle

$C = 2\pi r$, or $C = \pi d$
$A = \pi r^2$
Circle

$V = Bh$, or $V = \ell wh$
Surface Area (S.A.) =
$2\ell w + 2\ell h + 2wh$
Rectangular Prism

$V = Bh$, or $V = \pi r^2 h$
Surface Area (S.A.) =
$2\pi r^2 + \pi dh$
Cylinder

SELECTED ANSWERS

Unit 1, Lesson 1, PAGE 19
1. thousands; 5,000 **3.** ones; 5
5. hundreds; 500 **7.** nine hundred two
9. eighty-three thousand, one hundred twenty
11. eight hundred thousand, four hundred forty
13. 402,871 **15.** 650,000,098
17. < **19.** 98,905; 99,850; 101,962; 110,359
21. one thousand, nine hundred eighty-nine
23. one thousand, three hundred sixteen
25. 13,000,000,000

Unit 1, Lesson 2, PAGE 24
1. 57,000 **3.** 400,000 **5.** 804,000
7. 400,000 **9.** 300,000 **11.** 300,000
13–15.

```
       59          375  501          848
|----|----|----|----|----|----|----|----|----|
0  100 200 300 400 500 600 700 800 900
```

13. 400 **15.** 100
17. Samples: 385,421; 384,862
19. $18 \times 22 = 396$; Juan should plan to stop for gas before the end of the trip. 396 is very close to 390, and he should not risk running out of gas.

Unit 1, Lesson 3, PAGE 29
1. 8^5 **3.** 100^3 **5.** 16×16
7. $7 \times 7 \times 7 \times 7 \times 7 \times 7 \times 7$
9. 343 **11.** 8,000
13. That number; the number is used as a factor only once.
15. 3^3; 9 **17.** $3 \times 3 \times 3 \times 3$; 3^4; 81
19. $3 \times 3 \times 3 \times 3 \times 3 \times 3$; 3^6; 729
21. $32.79

Unit 1, Lesson 4, PAGE 34
1. 12; Assoc., Mult. **3.** 5; Distr. Prop
5. 268; Distr. Prop
7. 662; Comm., Assoc., Add.
9. 837 **11.** 496 **13.** 445 **15.** 2,300
17. Sample: $(3 \times 12) \times 5$ or $3 \times (12 \times 5)$; 180 in.
19. Yes; $8 \times (10 - 7) = (8 \times 10) - (8 \times 7) = 24$
21. No; sample: $100 \div 4 = 25$; $4 \div 100 = 0.04$

Unit 1, Problem-Solving Skills, PAGE 37
1a. Amy's and Bret's ages
b. The sum of the ages is 22 years; Bret is 4 years older than Amy.
c. Amy's age: 9 years; Bret's age: 13 years.
3. Marta's total score was 93 points.

Unit 1, Lesson 5, PAGE 41
1. 31 **3.** 99 **5.** 0 **7.** 36
9. s minus 20; s decreased by 20

11. 16 divided by n; the quotient of 16 and n
13. $a + 32$ **15.** $\frac{y}{9}$ **17.** $\frac{18}{n}$
19. $5 + 4 \times (6 - 3) = 17$
21. $(8 + 5) \times (6 - 3) = 39$
23. the number of dollars in c cents
25. m mugs increased by 100 **27.** C

Unit 2, Lesson 6, PAGE 46
1. 45, 37, 28, 3 **3.** 12, 18, 40, 72
5. Multiply by 5; $5a$ **7.** Subtract 13; $y - 13$
9. Add 5; 25, 30, 35
11. Multiply by 4; 512; 2,048; 8,192
13. Add 1, then 3, then 5, and so on; 37, 50, 65; no, the rule is not the same for each step.
15. Add 4, then subtract 2; 9, 13, 11; no, the rule is not the same for each step.
17. $\frac{5}{16}$ **19.** $\frac{p}{2000}$

Unit 2, Lesson 7, PAGE 51
1. No; $18 + 53 = 71$, not 35
3. No; $28 + 14 = 42$, not 28
5. Add 8 to both sides.
7. Add 21 to both sides.
9. $b = 63$ **11.** $p = 9$ **13.** $n = 44$ **15.** $n = 160$
17. $n + 10 = 23$; $n = 13$
19. $23 + n = 76$; $n = 53$
21. $141 - x = 129$; \$12

Unit 2, Lesson 8, PAGE 56
1. No; $1 + 8 = 0.125$, not 1
3. Yes; $35 \div 35 = 1$
5. Divide both sides by 8.
7. Divide both sides by 4.
9. DPE, $s = 13$ **11.** MPE, $t = 105$
13. MPE, $a = 162$ **15.** DPE, $n = 34$
17. $5n = 45$; divide by 5; $n = 9$
19. $5x = 85$; \$17
21. Sample: I would think, "84 divided by what number equals 7?" Then I would try various numbers and find that 12 works.

Unit 2, Problem-Solving Skills, PAGE 59
1. 49 sequins **3.** 15 games **5.** 204 squares

Unit 3, Lesson 9, PAGE 63
1. 1.09 **3.** 1.1 **5.** 10 tens **7.** 10 tenths
9. 100 thousandths **11.** tenths, 235.1
13. thousandths, 0.355 **15.** thousandths, 2.100
17. 1 **19.** \$0.35 **21.** \$0.11

Unit 3, Lesson 10, PAGE 68
1. 0.4, 0.04; 0.4 > 0.04

3. < **5.** > **7.** =
9. St. Louis Cardinals
11. Milwaukee Brewers
13. hundredths place; potassium

Unit 3, Lesson 11, PAGE 73
1. \$122.61 **3.** 303.209 **5.** 1,237.236
7. 2.5 **9.** 0.123 **11.** \$36.16
13. Sample: He added 8 tenths and 5 tenths and wrote the answer as 13 hundredths. He should have regrouped the tenths to get 1.3.
15. 50.67 m
17. 39.87 units; 42.8 units; 2.93 units

Unit 3, Lesson 12, PAGE 78
1. 38.482 **3.** 1,500
5. 205, 1,640, 166.05 **7.** 12,222, 2716, 393.82
9. 3.4 **11.** 2,308.5 **13.** 8.1796
15. 600 oz **17.** \$150.50

Unit 3, Problem-Solving Skills, PAGE 81
1. 5 weeks **3.** 23 ft, 19 ft **5.** 226 ft

Unit 4, Lesson 13, PAGE 85
1. 1, 2, 3, 4, 6, 12 **3.** 1, 5, 25
5. 1, 2, 3, 4, 5, 6, 10, 12, 15, 20, 30, 60
7. 8 is a factor of 32. 32 is a multiple of 8. 32 is divisible by 8.
9. 5 is a factor of 45. 45 is a multiple of 5. 45 is divisible by 5.
11. Yes; the ones digit is 0.
13. No; $2 + 1 + 6 + 3 = 12$ and 12 is not divisible by 9.
15. No; $2 + 2 + 2 + 2 + 2 = 10$ and 10 is not divisible by 3.
17. 2, 3, 9 **19.** 2, 3, 5, 9, 10 **21.** 5
23. $3 + 4 = 7$ and 7 is not divisible by 3.

Unit 4, Lesson 14, PAGE 90
1. prime **3.** composite **5.** prime
7. 2; all other even numbers have at least three factors: 1, 2, and the number itself.
9. $3^2 \cdot 5$ **11.** $2^3 \cdot 7$ **13.** $2^3 \cdot 3^2$ **15.** $2^5 \cdot 3$
17. $2^3 \cdot 3 \cdot 5$ **19.** $2^4 \cdot 3^2$ **21.** $2 \cdot 3 \cdot 5^2 \cdot 7$
23. Yes; the squares match up by sides and you can always make a row of single squares.
27.

```
            112
        4        28
      2   2    4    7
            2    2
```

29. C

Unit 4, Lesson 15, PAGE 95
1. 1, 3 **3.** 1, 3 **5.** 1, 3
7. 1, 2, 3, 4, 6, 12 **9.** 1, 2, 3, 6
11. 1, 3, 9 **13.** 2 **15.** 1

17. 9 **19.** 6 **21.** 1 **23.** 12
25. 9 in. by 9 in. **27.** \$13
29. Sample: The greatest factor a number can have is the number itself.
31. 1; A prime number has only itself and 1 as a factor.

Unit 4, Lesson 16, PAGE 100
1. 19, 38, 57 **3.** 20, 40, 60
5. 50, 100, 150 **7.** 33, 66, 99
9. 30, 60, 90 **11.** 72, 144, 216
13. 20 **15.** 120 **17.** 60 **19.** 36
21. 16, 32, 48; 48 is the LCM; It is the least multiple of 16 that is also a multiple of 6 and 8.
23. 31 students **25.** $2^2 \cdot 3^3 \cdot 5 = 540$

Unit 4, Problem-Solving Skills, PAGE 103
1. 120 words **5.** \$45

Unit 5, Lesson 17, PAGE 107
1. $\frac{4}{8}$ or $\frac{1}{2}$ **3.** $\frac{3}{8}$ **5.** $\frac{10}{16} = \frac{5}{8}$ **7.** $\frac{3}{16}$
9. Sample: $\frac{10}{12}, \frac{15}{18}, \frac{20}{24}$ **11.** Sample: $\frac{5}{8}, \frac{50}{80}, \frac{75}{120}$
13. 20 **15.** 40 **17.** $\frac{1}{3}$ **19.** $\frac{7}{9}$
21. $\frac{2}{3}$ **23.** $\frac{5}{9}$ **25.** $\frac{5}{7}$ **27.** $\frac{2}{9}$
29. $\frac{1}{2}$ **31.** Yes; $\frac{2}{3} = \frac{2 \times 2}{3 \times 2} = \frac{4}{6}$

Unit 5, Lesson 18, PAGE 112
1. $1\frac{3}{4}; \frac{7}{4}$ **3.** $1\frac{5}{8}$ **5.** $1\frac{4}{5}; \frac{5}{4}$ **7.** $1\frac{1}{3}$
9. $4\frac{1}{5}$ **11.** 7 **13.** $2\frac{2}{5}$ **15.** $\frac{13}{2}$
17. $\frac{37}{5}$ **19.** $\frac{3}{1}$ **21.** $\frac{67}{8}$
23. Samples: $\frac{10}{1}, \frac{24}{2}$ **25.** $1\frac{1}{2}$ c
27. Kurasawa; he has $1\frac{1}{4}$ lb which is more than Morito's $\frac{10}{8}$ lb.

Unit 5, Lesson 19, PAGE 117
1. > **3.** = **5.** < **7.** <
9. > **11.** < **13.** > **15.** <
17. $\frac{2}{5}, \frac{1}{2}, \frac{3}{5}$ **19.** $\frac{3}{5}, \frac{5}{8}, \frac{5}{6}$
21. 0.375, $\frac{5}{8}, \frac{7}{10}, \frac{3}{4}$ **23.** Ayisha
25. $\frac{1}{2}$ **27.** $\frac{1}{10}$
29. No; you need to compare only the whole numbers.
31. Sample: $\frac{3}{16}$ in.; On a ruler, $\frac{3}{16}$ in. is between $\frac{1}{8}$ in. and $\frac{1}{4}$ in.

Unit 5, Lesson 20, PAGE 122
1. $\frac{7}{10} + \frac{9}{10} = \frac{16}{10} = 1\frac{3}{5}$ **3.** $\frac{4}{5}$ **5.** $\frac{7}{15}$
7. $1\frac{5}{24}$ **9.** $9\frac{5}{8}$ **11.** $10\frac{1}{2}$ **13.** $5\frac{3}{4}$

15. $45\frac{4}{9}$ in. **17.** Albuquerque, Houston, Mobile
19. Write $\frac{5}{6}$ as $\frac{10}{12}$ and $\frac{1}{4}$ as $\frac{3}{12}$; $\frac{10}{12} + \frac{3}{12} = \frac{13}{12} = 1\frac{1}{12}$. Yes; the answer in simplest form will be the same regardless of the common denominator used.

Unit 5, Lesson 21, PAGE 127
1. $\frac{9}{10} - \frac{3}{10} = \frac{6}{10} = \frac{3}{5}$ **5.** $\frac{7}{24}$
7. $\frac{11}{24}$ **9.** $2\frac{5}{8}$ **11.** $\frac{1}{2}$ **13.** $5\frac{1}{2}$
15. stag, unicorn, click **17.** $\frac{1}{2}$ in.
19. $\frac{11}{16}$ in. **21.** B

Unit 5, Lesson 22, PAGE 132
1. $\frac{4}{15}$ **3.** $\frac{6}{12} = \frac{1}{2}$ **5.** $1\frac{1}{2}$ **7.** $\frac{1}{9}$
9. $6\frac{4}{7}$ **11.** $2\frac{2}{3}$ **13.** 6 **15.** <
17. $1\frac{1}{2}$ **19.** $\frac{7}{14}$ **21.** $3\frac{1}{3}$ **23.** $\frac{3}{10}$
25. $1\frac{1}{4}$ **27.** $\frac{1}{4}$ **29.** $\frac{7}{10}$
31. is greater than **33.** is less than
35. is greater than
37. 56 in. wide; 84 in. long; multiplied the width and length of each square by the number of squares: $3\frac{1}{2} \times 16 = 56$, $3\frac{1}{2} \times 24 = 84$

Unit 5, Problem-Solving Skills, PAGE 135
1. $5 for watering plants **3.** 85 cards
5. June, July, and August—that's when the most rain falls.

Unit 6, Lesson 23, PAGE 139
1-5. Answers may vary.
1. $\frac{36}{24}$, $\frac{4}{3}$ **3.** $\frac{4}{7}$, $\frac{96}{24}$, $\frac{12}{}$ **5.** $\frac{3}{1}$, $\frac{6}{18}$
7. Yes; $\frac{10 \div 5}{15 \div 5} = \frac{2}{3}$
9. No; $4 \times 6 = 24$; $5 \times 5 = 25$; $24 \neq 25$
11. No; $0.5 \times 7 = 3.5$; $4 \times 0.8 = 3.2$; $3.5 \neq 3.2$
13. Sample: The first is less than 1, and the second is greater than 1, so they are not equal.
15. $m = 6$ **17.** $c = 150$ **19.** $n = 0.9$
21. 96 instruments **23.** 27 woodwinds
25. 1 staff member

Unit 6, Lesson 24, PAGE 144
1. 50% **3.** 75% **5.** 0.9, $\frac{9}{10}$
7. 0.04, $\frac{1}{25}$ **9.** 0.72, $\frac{18}{25}$ **11.** 1.0, $\frac{1}{1}$
13. 100%, $\frac{1}{1}$ **15.** 24%, $\frac{6}{25}$ **17.** 46%, $\frac{23}{50}$
19. 250%, $2\frac{1}{2}$ **21.** 0.75, 75%, terminating
23. 0.273, 27.3%, repeating
25. 0.5, 50% **27.** 0.66..., $66\frac{2}{3}$%
29. $\frac{3}{4}$, 0.75 **31.** 0.4 **33.** 0.8, 80%

35. 0.375, 37.5% **37.** $\frac{7}{8}$, 0.875
39. Russia, blue, 24.6% **41.** China, green, 16.5%
43. 100%; the graph represents the entire number, or all, of the medals for the top five countries.

Unit 6, Lesson 25, PAGE 149
1. 0.0025; $\frac{1}{400}$ **3.** 1.3; $1\frac{3}{10}$ **5.** 5.0; $\frac{5}{1}$
7. 2.0; 2 **9.** 175% **11.** 0.6% **13.** 0.8%
15. 500% **17.** 39 **19.** 12 **21.** 11.9
23. 27.95 **25.** 70 **27.** 0.72
29. 24, 72, 120 **31.** 25 passes **33.** 0.22 oz

Unit 6, Lesson 26, PAGE 154
1. $20 **3.** $50 **5.** $26.25 **7.** $1,254
9. $1,000 **11.** $675
13. $70; $210 **15.** $6.30; yes
17. The 2-year plan costs more per year. The 3-year plan costs more if you keep the loan for 3 years.
19. $112.50; no; $112.50 > $100.

Unit 6, Problem-Solving Skills, PAGE 157
1. 56 sports only $(72 - 16)$; 20 music only $(36 - 16)$; 4 neither $(96 - 56 - 20 - 16 = 4)$
3. Ms. Hayes, math; Mr. Mesa, science; Mrs. Salton, English

Unit 7, Lesson 27, PAGE 161
1. Sample: A frequency table uses tally marks and numbers; a line plot uses Xs and may use numbers or spans of numbers. Both show exact data if spans are not used.
3. 6
5a. frequency table
b. line plot
7. 12 math grades
11. B

9. Days in Months of Year
(line plot) — Number of Days: 28 29 30 31

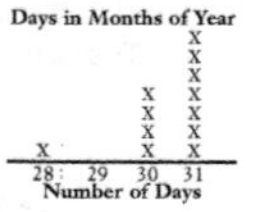

Unit 7, Lesson 28, PAGE 166
1. Sample: First to find the median, the mode, and the range; and all the exact data are shown.
3. 23, 23, 26, 28, 31, 35, 36, 44 **5.** 29.5
7. mean, $34; median, $36.50; mode, $44

9. Baseball Games Won

Stem	Leaf
8	8
9	0 6
10	1

Key: 8|8 means 88 games

11. yes; yes; a set of data can have any number of the same number
13. mean, $126.60; median, $138; no mode; the median because the outlier 68 affects the mean too greatly.

Unit 7, Lesson 29, PAGE 171
1. number of goals scored **3.** Takahara **5.** 4 goals
7. Sample: When you want to make comparisons, the tops of bars make it easy to compare data.

---

9. Sample: about 40 million
11. Vitamin C in Fruits (bar graph)
Vitamin C (mg): 0–18 — Apricot, Avocado, Pear, Cherry, Grape

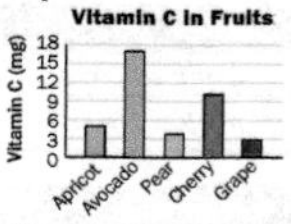

Unit 7, Lesson 30, PAGE 176
1. Sample: so the two separate sets of data are clearly visible.
3. Sample: It implies a typical salary, which is higher than 4 of the 5 salaries. The mean is unusually high because of the outlier, $9.4 million; the mean does not represent the data very well.
5. the sizes of the fish **7.** the median; the mean
9. C

Unit 7, Problem-Solving Skills, PAGE 179
1. $1.98 **3.** $73.35 **5.** 4 dimes, 6 nickels

Unit 8, Lesson 31, PAGE 183
1. line **3.** segment **5.** point **7.** plane
9. Samples: $\angle FGC$; $\angle BGF$; $\angle CGD$; $\angle FGD$
11. ray $\overrightarrow{FD}$ **13.** perpendicular
15. intersecting
17. Both are parts of lines; rays have one endpoint, while segments have two.
19. $\overline{YZ}$ and $\overline{YX}$
23. 180°; ABD is a straight line.

Unit 8, Lesson 32, PAGE 188
1. obtuse **3.** right **5.** 120° **7.** 170°
9. 63° **11.** 80°
13. Sample: $\angle DBE$ and $\angle EBF$
15. Sample: $\angle ABD$ and $\angle CBF$
17. 54° **19.** 80°
21. No; it does not necessarily have 3 congruent sides.
23. Yes; there are 3 congruent sides so there are also 3 congruent angles.

Unit 8, Lesson 33, PAGE 193
1. 6 sides **3.** yes **5.** yes
7. rectangle, rhombus, square
9. Samples: (hexagon) 6 sides (hexagon) 8 sides
11. 120° **13.** 115° **15.** B

Unit 8, Lesson 34, PAGE 198
1. $\angle A$, $\angle G$; $\angle B$, $\angle K$; $\angle C$, $\angle J$; $\angle D$, $\angle I$; $\angle E$, $\angle H$
3. KGHIJ **5.** 90°; the sides are all congruent.
7. Sample: If the trusses are not congruent, the roof line will not be straight.
9. QMP **11.** $x = 95°$, $y = 12$, $z = 55°$

13. $\angle O \cong \angle N$; $\angle L \cong \angle E$; $\angle D \cong \angle W$; $\overline{OL} \cong \overline{NE}$; $\overline{LD} \cong \overline{EW}$; $\overline{OD} \cong \overline{NW}$. Vertices are given in the order of their correspondence.

Unit 8, Lesson 35, PAGE 203
1. $\angle A \cong \angle D$, $\angle B \cong \angle E$, $\angle C \cong \angle F$; $\frac{AB}{DE} = \frac{BC}{EF} = \frac{AC}{DF}$
3. Samples: 3-by-4 inch; 12-by-16 inch; 24-by-32 inch
5. yes
7. $m\angle V = 95°$; $m\angle U = 105°$; $m\angle T = 60°$; $m\angle W = 100°$; $m\angle X = 60°$

Unit 8, Lesson 36, PAGE 208
1. transformations **3.** tessellation
5. No **7.** Yes 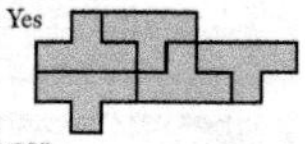
9. translation **11.** OH

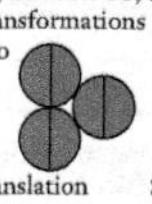

Unit 8, Problem-Solving Skills, PAGE 211
1. pentagon **3.** 1,440° **5.** 36 seats
7. square **9.** 12 combinations

Unit 9, Lesson 37, PAGE 215
1. 8 units² **3.** 11 units² **5.** 44 cm; 121 cm²
7. A: 16 cm²; B: 7.5 cm²; C: 7.5cm²
9. 139 cm² **11.** 12 in.; 8.75 in.²
13. 4 in. **15.** 48 in.²

Unit 9, Lesson 38, PAGE 220
1. 87.9 in.; 615.4 in.² **3.** 9.4 in.; 7.1 in.²
5a. 10 ft **b.** 75 ft²
7. 8 bags **9.** 38 in.²
11. about 75 cm; about 370 cm²
13. The circumference is doubled; the area is multiplied by 4.

Unit 9, Lesson 39, PAGE 225
1. rectangular prism; 6 faces
3. octagonal prism; 10 faces
5. 144 cm² **7.** 154 in.²
9. 527.5 cm² **11.** 480 in.²

Unit 9, Lesson 40, PAGE 230
1. 84 units³ **3.** 30 units³ **5.** 1,331 in.³
7. 128 cm³ **9.** $V = s^3$ **11.** D

Unit 9, Problem-Solving Skills, PAGE 233
1. 1,066 ft² **3.** 40 tiles **5.** 11 tickets

Unit 10, Lesson 41, PAGE 237
1. 6 sections; 1 way for 1 and 1 way for 2
3. $\frac{2}{5}$ or $\frac{2}{5}$ **7.** 1
9. likely **11.** certain **13.** certain
15. $\frac{5}{10}$, 0.5, 50% **17.** $\frac{10}{10}$, 1, 100%

---

19. It is certain to happen. **21.** C
Unit 10, Lesson 42, PAGE 242
1. $\frac{1}{3}$
3. 1, because it is certain that the spinner will land on a vowel or a consonant.
5. $\frac{12}{50}$ or $\frac{6}{25}$, 0.24, 24%
7. Tim: $\frac{15}{50}$ or $\frac{3}{10}$, Tom: $\frac{20}{80}$ or $\frac{1}{4}$; Tony: $\frac{25}{75}$ or $\frac{1}{3}$
Unit 10, Lesson 43, PAGE 247
1. 12 outcomes; Multiply 6 and 2.
3. $\frac{6}{12}$ or $\frac{1}{2}$; $\frac{6}{12}$ or $\frac{1}{2}$ **5.** 2 outcomes; $\frac{1}{12}$
7. $8 \cdot 10 \cdot 10 \cdot 10 \cdot 10 \cdot 10 = 8,000,000$ numbers
9. 18 combinations
Unit 10, Lesson 44, PAGE 252
1. no **3.** no **5.** no
7. More permutations; there are 6 permutations and only 1 combination.
9. 504
11. 10, 12, 13, 20, 21, 23, 30, 31, 32; 9 numbers
13. 10 ways: ABC ACD BCD CDE
ABD ACE BCE
ABE ADE BDE
Unit 10, Problem-Solving Skills, PAGE 255
1. results based on all students' data because it is based on more trials
3. Sample: Use 3 coins. Flip them 20 times. Use H to represent a wrong answer. Record how many times HHH comes up. P(HHH) ≈ 13%.
5. 3 socks; If the first two socks don't match, the third sock will match one of them.
Unit 11, Lesson 45, PAGE 259
1. 500 **3.** 89
5a. −16 **b.** 8 **c.** 20 **d.** −6
7. 15, −15, 48, −48, 11, 38, 38
13. 30, −30 **15.** 17 **17.** 12
19. > **21.** <
23. −50, −23, −12, 22, 48
25. −18, −6, 0, 18, 36
27. Australia, Morocco, Argentina, Canada, Russia, Antarctica
Unit 11, Lesson 46, PAGE 264
1. 21 **3.** −5 **5.** −7 **7.** −41
9. 9 **11.** −11 **13.** −48 **15.** 12
17. $1\frac{3}{5}$ **19.** Gain of 19 yd **21.** −4
23. Samples:
a. 5 − (−9) **b.** −13 − 2
c. 4 − (−9)
25. −21 + (−45) = −66; use a negative sign

Unit 11, Lesson 47, PAGE 269
1. 140 **3.** 15 **5.** 84 **7.** −80
9. −29 **11.** −25 **13.** −99 **15.** 120
17. 25 **19.** 16 **21.** 256 **23.** 10
25. −60 **27.** 22 **29.** 10
31. −3.3 points
33. Sample answers are given.
a. −12 ÷ (−3) **b.** 18 ÷ (−6)
c. 0 ÷ (−17)
Unit 11, Lesson 48, PAGE 274
1. (3, 0) **3.** (−4, −2) **5.** (−5, 5)
7. H; quadrant IV **9.** J; quadrant III
11. I. x and y are both positive;
II. x negative; y positive;
III. x and y are both negative;
IV. x positive, y negative
13. 4, 3, 2, 1, 0 **15.** −9, −4, 6, 16, 26
19. 4 animals
21. Miyoko cannot sell fewer than 0 animals.
Unit 11, Problem-Solving Skills, PAGE 277
1. Because the Canada team's time was greater than the Bahamas team's time
3. $1.2 \cdot B = 12$; 10
5. one quarter, 3 nickels, 5 pennies; 4 dimes, 5 pennies; or 9 nickels
Unit 12, Lesson 49, PAGE 281
1. $x = 3$ **3.** $t = 154$ **5.** $a = 9$ **7.** $n = 32$
9. $c = 2$ **11.** $n = 95$ **13.** $y = 0.5$ **15.** $c = 28$
17. 50°F **19.** 80 chirps
21. It stops chirping at 40 °F.
23. $800 + 40d = 1,120$, $d = 8$; 8 days
Unit 12, Lesson 50, PAGE 286
1. $x > -5$ **3.** $k \geq 4$
5. Together they include all numbers except 4.
7. $10 > s$ (number line)
9. $y > 3$ (number line)
11. $n < 18$ **13.** $x < 36$
15. $d \leq 7$ **17.**
19. $16 \geq m$ **21.** $m \leq 55$
23. at least 72 cards
Unit 12, Problem-Solving Skills, PAGE 289
1. Yes; the proportion would have been $\frac{16}{9} = \frac{n}{6}$.
3. $6\frac{1}{2} \times 9 \times 1 = 58\frac{1}{2}$; $4\frac{1}{2} \times 7 = 2 \times 63$;
$2\frac{1}{2} \times 5 \times 3 = 37\frac{1}{2}$; $\frac{1}{2} \times 3 \times 4 = 6$;
The greatest volume is 63 in.³

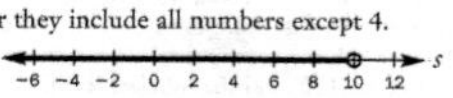

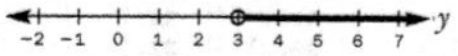

GLOSSARY

Pronunciation Key

ă pat	ī pit	oi boy	th thin
ā pay	ī pie	ou out	th this
âr care	îr pier	ŏŏ took	hw whoop
ä father	ŏ pot	ŏŏ boot	zh vision
ĕ pet	ō toe	ŭ cut	ə about
ē be	ô paw	û urge	N *French* bon

< a symbol showing that the first number is less than the second. (p. 18)
≈ a symbol that means "is about equal to." (p. 62)
> a symbol showing that the first number is greater than the second. (p. 18)
π (pi) a symbol that stands for the result of dividing the circumference of any circle by its diameter. The value of *pi* is about 3.14. (p. 218)

A
absolute value *n.* the distance a number is from 0 on a number line. (p. 257)
acute triangle *n.* a triangle that has 3 angles that each measure less than 90°. (p. 187)
add (ăd) *v.* combine two or more numbers to find their total. *When I* **add** *7 and 4, I get 11.*
Addition Property of Equality *n.* a property that says adding the same number to both sides of an equation does not change the equality. (p. 48)

Addition Property of Equality
If $a = b$, then $a + c = b + c$.

algebraic expression *n.* a phrase containing variables as well as numbers and operation symbols. (p. 40)

angle (ăng' gəl) *n.* two rays with a common endpoint. *The corner of my paper forms an* **angle**. (p. 182) 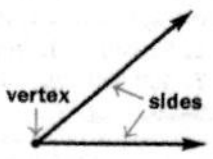
approximate value *n.* a value that is close to the exact value. (p. 218)
area (âr' ē ə) *n.* the measure of how much surface is covered inside a figure. *Area* is measured in square units. *The* **area** *of the top of my desk is 1,440 square inches.* (p. 212)
arithmetic expression *n.* an expression with numbers and operation symbols. (p. 40)
arrange (ə rānj') *v.* change the position of one or more objects. *In a combination, you can* **arrange** *the items in any order.* (p. 219)
arrangement (ə rānj' mənt) *n.* the way things are organized or put together. (p. 249)
Associative Properties *n.* properties that say changing the grouping of addends or factors in an expression does not change the sum or the product. (p. 32)

Associative Properties
$8 + (7 + 31) = 46$ and $(8 + 7) + 31 = 46$
$15 \times (5 \times 4) = 300$ and $(15 \times 5) \times 4 = 300$

average *n.* see *mean*.

average speed *n.* the approximate speed that something moves over a period of time. (p. 61)

B

balance (băl′ əns) **1.** *n.* an equality; the state of being equal. *The two sides of an equation are in **balance**.* **2.** *v.* make an equation true. *Juan will **balance** the equation by doing the same operation on both sides.* (p. 48)

bar graph *n.* a graph that uses the lengths of its bars to compare data. (p. 168)

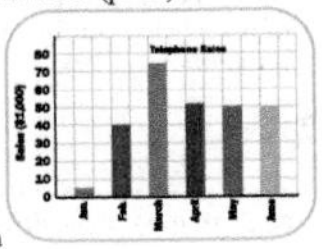

base (bās) **1.** *n.* a number raised to a power. (p. 27) **2.** *n.* the top or bottom face of a prism. (p. 214)

base of a cylinder *n.* one of the two flat surfaces of a cylinder. *The **bases of a cylinder** are circular.* (p. 229)

C

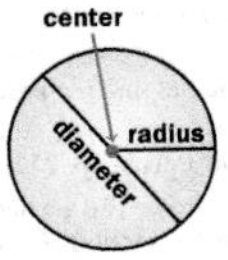

center (sĕn′ tər) *n.* a point in the middle of a circle. *The **center** is the same distance from every point on the circle.* (p. 217)

certain event *n.* an event that has to happen. Its probability is 1. (p. 236)

circle (sûr′ kəl) *n.* a plane figure in which all points are the same distance from the center point. *A **circle** is a closed curve.* (p. 217)

circumference (sər kŭm′ fər əns) *n.* the distance around a circle. *She drew a circle so large you could not walk around its **circumference**!* (p. 218)

code (kōd) *n.* a system of secret writing. *You need a computer to break a really difficult **code**.* (p. 88)

combination (kŏm′ bə nā′ shən) *n.* a group of items arranged in no particular order. *If you change the order of the items in the group, you do not get a new **combination**.* (p. 249)

commission (kə mĭsh′ ən) *n.* a fee or percentage of a sale paid to a salesperson. *My sister gets a 3% **commission** on every car she sells.* (p. 151)

common denominator *n.* a denominator that is the same for two or more fractions. (p. 119)

common factor *n.* a factor that two or more numbers share. (p. 92)

common multiple *n.* a number that is a multiple of two or more numbers. (p. 97)

Commutative Properties *n.* properties that say changing the order of addends or factors does not change a sum or product. (p. 32)

Commutative Properties

$13 + 24 = 37$ and $24 + 13 = 37$

$6 \times 9 = 54$ and $9 \times 6 = 54$

compare (kəm pâr′) *v.* examine quantities in order to find out which is the greater. *If you **compare** $\frac{7}{22}$ and $\frac{1}{5}$, you see that $\frac{1}{5}$ is greater.* (p. 114)

compatible numbers *n.* pairs of numbers that can be computed easily. (p. 33)

compensation (kŏm′ pən sā′ shən) *n.* something that makes up for a difference. *You use **compensation** to make up the difference between an easy number used in mental math and the actual number in a problem.* (p. 31)

complementary angles *n.* two angles whose measures add to 90 degrees. (p. 185)

composite number *n.* a whole number with more than two factors. (p. 87)

compound event *n.* a combination of two or more single events. (p. 245)

congruent (≅) (kən grōō′ ənt) *adj.* having the same measure. *All four angles in a square are **congruent**.* (p. 195)

congruent angles *n.* angles with the same measure. (p. 186)

congruent figures *n.* figures that have the same size and same shape. (p. 196)

congruent sides *n.* sides with the same length. (p. 187)

convert (kən vûrt′) *v.* change, switch, or trade. *To **convert** money from one country's currency to that of another, you must know the exchange rate.* (p. 76)

coordinate plane *n.* a grid with two perpendicular number lines. (p. 272)

coordinates (kō ôr′ dn ĭtz) *n.* a pair of numbers that describes the location of a point on a graph. *The **coordinates** locate a point on a graph. The first number tells the point's distance left or right of the origin, and the second number tells distance up or down from the origin.* (p. 271)

corresponding parts *n.* the parts that match up when you place a figure on top of a congruent figure. (p. 196)

counting principle *n.* the idea that the total number of outcomes for a compound event is the product of the number of choices for each part. (p. 246)

cross products *n.* in a proportion, the products of the first term of one ratio and the second term of the other ratio. (p. 138)

cube (kyōōb) **1.** *v.* raise to the third power. (p. 28) **2.** *n.* a rectangular prism with faces that are congruent squares. (p. 223)

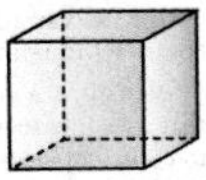

cubic unit *n.* the unit for measuring volume. *A cubic inch is a **cubic unit** with all edges measuring 1 inch.* (p. 227)

currency (kûr′ ən sē) *n.* money. *Dollars are the **currency** of the United States.* (p. 75)

cylinder (sĭl′ ən dər) *n.* a solid figure with two congruent, parallel circular regions as bases and a curved surface on the side of the figure. (p. 224)

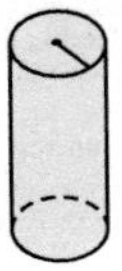

D

data (dā′ tə) *n.* facts; information. *Maria used **data** she collected to persuade the principal that we need new books.* (p. 25)

decimal (dĕs′ ə məl) *n.* an expression used to show a quantity that is part of a whole or part of a set of items. *The **decimal** 0.50 has the same value as $\frac{1}{2}$.* (p. 104)

decimal number *n.* a number written with digits and a decimal point. (p. 60)

decimal part *n.* the part of a number that follows the decimal point. (p. 61)

decimal point *n.* the symbol in a decimal number that separates the whole-number part from the decimal part. (p. 60)

decode (dē kōd′) *v.* solve a code to read a message. *Please **decode** the message Pia wrote in code and tell me what it says.* (p. 88)

degrees (dĭ grēz′) *n.* the units for measuring angles. *A right angle measures 90 **degrees**.* (p. 182)

denominator (dĭ nŏm′ ə nā′ tər) *n.* the number below a fraction bar. *The **denominator** tells the number of objects or equal parts in all.* (p. 105)

diagonal (dī ăg′ ə nəl) *n.* a segment that connects two vertices of a polygon and is not a side. (p. 192) *A line that crosses the room from one corner to another corner is a **diagonal**.*

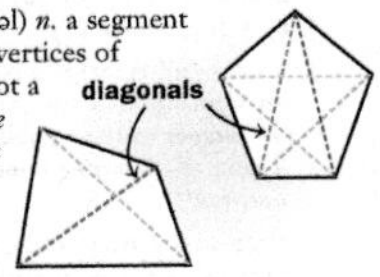

diameter (dī ăm′ ĭ tər) *n.* the distance from one side of a circle to the other through the center. *The **diameter** of Earth is about 12 thousand kilometers.* (p. 18)

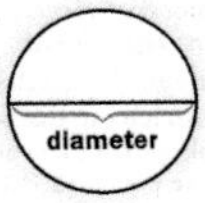

difference (dĭf′ ər əns) *n.* the result of subtracting. *The **difference** of 13 and 5 is 8.* (p. 40)

digit (dĭj′ ĭt) *n.* any value of these 10 symbols used to write numbers: 0, 1, 2, 3, 4, 5, 6, 7, 8, 9. *By changing one **digit**, the clerk ordered 5,000 pens instead of 1,000.* (p. 17)

discount (dĭs′ kount′) *n.* an amount taken off the cost of an item. *Haille went shopping with a coupon that gave him a 10% **discount** on anything he bought that day.* (p. 151)

display (dĭ splā′) *v.* show visually, as in a graph, chart, or store window. (p. 164)

Distributive Property *n.* a property that says numbers can be broken into smaller numbers for calculating. (p. 32)

Distributive Property

$7 \times (12 + 2) = 98$ and $(7 \times 12) + (7 \times 2) = 98$

divide (dĭ vīd′) *v.* separate a quantity into equal groups. *Let's **divide** the number of donuts by the number of students so everyone gets the same amount.*

dividend (dĭv′ ĭ dĕnd′) *n.* the number being divided. *In the fraction $\frac{3}{4}$, the number 3 is the **dividend**.* (p. 77)

divisibility rule *n.* a quick way to tell when one number is divisible by another number. (p. 84)

divisible (dĭ vĭz′ ə bəl) *adj.* able to be divided without a remainder. *10 is **divisible** by 5 because 10 ÷ 5 is 2 with no remainder.* (p. 82)

Division Property of Equality *n.* a mathematical property that says if two quantities are equal, dividing both quantities by the same nonzero number does not change the equality. (p. 53)

Division Property of Equality

If $a = b$ and $c \neq 0$, then $\frac{a}{c} = \frac{b}{c}$.

divisor (dĭ vī′ zər) *n.* the number by which another number, the dividend, is to be divided. *In the fraction $\frac{3}{4}$, the number 4 is the **divisor**.* (p. 77)

double bar graph *n.* a graph that compares two data sets. (p. 173)

E

edge (ĕj) *n.* a line segment where 2 faces meet. *Kim measured one **edge** of the pyramid to find its length.* (p. 222)

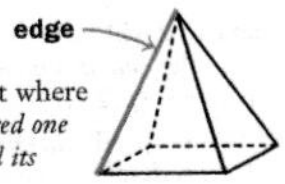

endangered (ĕn dān′ jərd) *adj.* in danger of becoming *extinct*, or having none of their kind left on Earth. *The blue whale is an **endangered** animal.* (p. 125)

equally likely outcomes *n.* outcomes that have the exact same chance of happening. (p. 234)

equation (ĭ kwā′ zhən) *n.* a mathematical sentence that states that two mathematical expressions are equal. *In an **equation**, the expressions on both sides of the equals sign (=) have the same value.* (p. 48)

equilateral triangle *n.* a triangle that has 3 congruent sides. (p. 187)

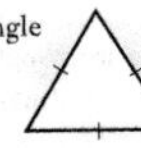

equivalent fractions *n.* fractions that name the same amount. (p. 106)

eruption (ĭ rŭp′ shən) *n.* a sudden, violent outburst. *During the **eruption** of a volcano, hot, melted rock pours down the side of a mountain.* (p. 22)

estimate **1.** (ĕs′ tə mĭt) *n.* an approximate value. **2.** (ĕs′ tə māt′) *v.* give an approximate value. (p. 21)

evaluate (ĭ văl′ yōō āt′) *v.* **1.** find the value of. ***Evaluate** the expression 2y + 6 for y = 9; 2(9) + 6 = 24.* (p. 44) **2.** make a judgment. (p. 47)

event (ĭ vĕnt′) *n.* an outcome or the set of all outcomes of an experiment or situation. *When something happens, that is an **event**.* (p. 234)

exact number *n.* a number that can be counted. (p. 21)

expanded form *n.* a number written as a product of factors. *The **expanded form** of 7^3 is 7 × 7 × 7.* (p. 26)

experiment (ĭk spĕr′ ə mənt) *n.* an activity that is repeated many times in order to gain information. *Javier designed an **experiment** to find the probability of the teacher's calling on a boy, not a girl.* (p. 239)

experimental probability *n.* in an experiment, the number of successes divided by the number of trials. (p. 240)

exponent (ĕk′ spō′ nənt) *n.* a number that tells how many times another number (the base) is used as a factor. *When you square a number, the **exponent** is 2, as in 3^2.* (p. 27)

exponential form *n.* a number written with an exponent. *The **exponential form** of 16 is 2^4.* (p. 26)

expression (ĭk sprĕsh′ ən) *n.* a mathematical phrase with numbers and operation symbols. *In the equation 3y × 2 = 9, both 3y × 2 and 9 are **expressions**.* (p. 39)

F

face (fās) *n.* each flat surface of a 3-dimensional figure. *You could find the area of each **face** on the pyramid.* (p. 222)

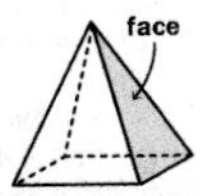

factor (făk′ tər) *n.* **1.** a whole number that divides another whole number with no remainder. (p. 27) **2.** a number that is multiplied. (p. 76)

factor tree *n.* a diagram showing the prime factors of a number. (p. 87)

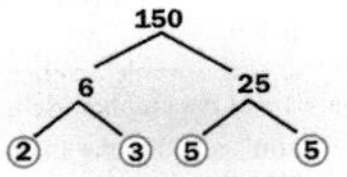

favorable outcome *n.* an outcome that is wanted. (p. 235)

formula (fôr′ myə lə) *n.* an equation that states a rule. *Marek knows that the **formula** for finding the area of a rectangle is A = lw.* (p. 153)

fraction (frăk′ shən) *n.* a number that shows or describes part of something. *$\frac{3}{4}$ is the **fraction** represented by the decimal 0.75.* (p. 104)

fraction model *n.* a model that shows how to divide or separate something into fraction measurements. (p. 129)

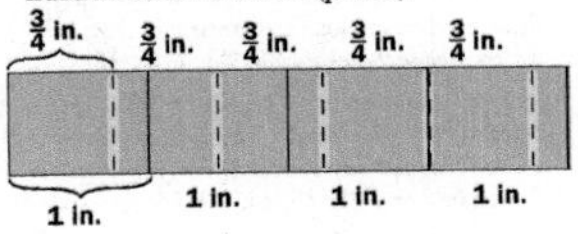

frequency (frē′ kwən sē) *n.* the number of times something happens within a given period. *The **frequency** of a full moon in a year is 12.* (p. 159)

frequency table *n.* a table showing the number of times an item was chosen. (p. 159)

G

greatest (grāt′ əst) *adj.* largest. *The **greatest** number of 10, 50, and 75 is 75.* (p. 114)

greatest common factor (GCF) *n.* the largest factor common to two or more numbers. (p. 92)

grid (grĭd) *n.* a pattern of evenly spaced lines running both across and up and down. *The streets of cities are often set up in a **grid** pattern.* (p. 61)

H

height (hīt) *n.* the distance from the top to the bottom of an object. *The tallest girl in class has a **height** of 5 feet 10 inches.* (p. 214)

horizontal (hôr′ ĭ zŏn′ tl) *adj.* running straight across. *A shelf is **horizontal**.* (p. 258)

horizontal axis *n.* the line across the bottom or the center of a graph. It identifies the data. (p. 169)

hundredth (hŭn′ drĭdth) *n.* 1 of 100 equal parts. (p. 61)

I

image (ĭm′ ĭj) *n.* a figure produced by a transformation. *Look in the mirror to see an **image** of yourself.* (p. 205)

impossible event *n.* an event that cannot happen. Its probability is zero. (p. 236)

improper fraction *n.* a fraction whose numerator is greater than or equal to its denominator. (p. 109)

inequality (ĭn′ ĭ kwŏl′ ĭ tē) *n.* a mathematical statement that says two quantities are not equal. *To express the **inequality** that says* a *is less than* b, *you use the symbol* < *and write* a < b. (p. 283)

inequality symbol *n.* > or <. It shows that two numbers are not equal. (p. 18)

insurance money *n.* the money an insurance company pays to people affected by a disaster. (p. 23)

integer (ĭn′ tĭ jər) *n.* a counting number, the opposite of a counting number, or zero. *An **integer** can be a counting number, the opposite of a counting number, or zero, but not a decimal.* (p. 256)

interest (ĭn′ trĭst) *n.* the amount earned on a savings account or paid for borrowing money. *Save your money in a bank, and the **interest** will make your money increase.* (p. 151)

intersecting lines *n.* two lines in the same plane that meet at one point. (p. 181)

interval (ĭn′ tər vəl) *n.* the difference between a number and the next number on a scale. *On a ruler, the main **interval** is one inch.* (p. 169)

inverse operations *n.* operations that undo each other. *Addition and subtraction are **inverse operations**.* (p. 50)

isosceles triangle *n.* a triangle that has two congruent sides. (p. 187)

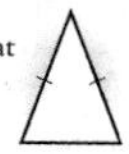

K

key (kē) *n.* a list that explains colors or symbols on a graph or map. *The **key** on the graph tells what the colors stand for.* (p. 174)

L

leaf (lēf) *n.* the ones digit of each data item on a stem-and-leaf plot. *You can tell how many pieces of data were collected by counting each **leaf** on a stem-and-leaf plot.* (p. 163)

least (lēst) *adj.* smallest. *Among 14, 8, and 22, 8 is the **least** number.* (p. 114)

least common denominator (LCD) *n.* the smallest common multiple of the denominators of two or more fractions. (p. 115)

least common multiple (LCM) *n.* the smallest multiple common to two or more numbers. (p. 97)

line (līn) *n.* a straight path of points that continues in both directions. (p. 180)

line graph *n.* a graph that uses line segments to connect pieces of data and show the direction of change. (p. 168)

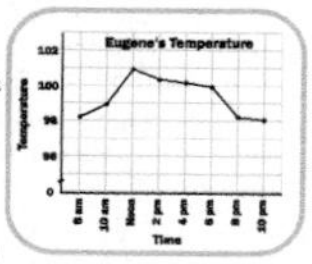

line plot *n.* a display of data that uses Xs to show frequency. (p. 158)

line segment *n.* a part of a line. It has two endpoints. (p. 180)

linear equation *n.* an equation with a graph that is a straight line. (p. 273)

M

mathematical sentence *n.* a sentence that uses operations, variables, and numbers to state a relationship. (p. 283)

mean (mēn) *n.* the sum of all the numbers in a data set divided by the number of items. *The **mean** is also called the* average. (p. 165)

median (mē′ dē ən) *n.* the middle value of an ordered set of numbers. *In the set 2, 4, 6, 8, 10, the **median** is 6.* (p. 165)

mental math *n.* solving problems in your head without using a calculator, pencil and paper, or a computer. ***Mental math** is done using only your brain.* (p. 31)

misleading (mĭs lē′ dĭng) *adj.* suggesting something that is not true. *I was angry because the committee used my data to make a **misleading** graph.* (p. 175)

mixed number *n.* a number greater than 1 with a whole-number part and a fraction part. (p. 109)

mode (mōd) *n.* the number that occurs most often in a data set. *We looked at the ages of all the students in Sara's class, and the **mode** was 12 years and 4 months.* (p. 165)

model (mŏd′ l) **1.** *n.* an object or drawing used to explain something. (p. 129) **2.** *v.* demonstrate or make an example. (p. 261)

multiple (mŭl′ tə pəl) *n.* the product of a factor and a whole number greater than zero. *35 is a **multiple** of 7.* (p. 82)

multiply (mŭl′ tə plī′) *v.* add a number to itself any given number of times. *When you **multiply** 7 times 3, you get 21.*

Multiplication Property of Equality *n.* a property that says if two quantities are equal, multiplying both quantities by the same nonzero number does not change the equality. (p. 55)

Multiplication Property of Equality

If $a = b$, then $ac = bc$.

N

negative integers *n.* any of the opposites of the counting numbers: −1, −2, −3, and so on. (p. 256)

net (nĕt) *n.* the unwrapped form of a solid figure. *You make a **net** of a solid figure in order to easily find its surface area.* (p. 223)

numerator (no͞o′ mə rā′ tər) *n.* the number above the fraction bar that tells the number of parts being considered. *In $\frac{54}{7}$, 54 is the **numerator**.* (p. 105)

O

obtuse triangle *n.* a triangle that has one angle of more than 90°. (p. 187)

operation (ŏp′ ə rā′ shən) *n.* a thing done to a number according to certain rules. *The 4 basic **operations** are addition, subtraction, multiplication, and division.* (p. 32)

opposites (ŏp′ ə zĭtz) *n.* two integers with the same absolute value. *−8 and 8 are **opposites**.* (p. 257)

order of operations *n.* a set of rules for simplifying numerical expressions. (p. 38)

ordered pair *n.* numbers that locate a point on a plane. (p. 272)

organize (ôr′ gə nīz′) *v.* put into working order; arrange. *Data are just a bunch of numbers until you **organize** them to make them mean something.* (p. 159)

origin (ôr′ ə jĭn) *n.* the point (0, 0) where the two axes on a graph intersect. (p. 272)

outcome (out′ kŭm′) *n.* one of a set of possible events. *We all waited for the **outcome** as Jenna spun the giant spinner.* (p. 234)

outlier (out′ lī′ ər) *n.* a data item not close to the others in a data set. *This **outlier** is so much greater than the rest of the data that including it makes the average much higher.* (p. 165)

P

parallel lines *n.* lines in the same plane that never cross. *The rails on a railroad track are **parallel lines**.* (p. 181)

parallelogram (păr′ə lĕl′ ə grăm′) *n.* a quadrilateral with 2 pairs of parallel sides. *A rectangle is one kind of **parallelogram**.* (p. 192)

parentheses (pə rĕn′ thĭ sēz′) *n.* two curved lines used to enclose a quantity. *In 2 × (3 + 1), the **parentheses** enclose 3 + 1.* (p. 38)

pattern (păt′ ərn) *n.* a group of numbers related by a given rule. *Sophia was pleased when she found this **pattern**: every multiple of 5 ends in 0 or 5 (5, 10, 15, 20, 25, …).* (p. 45)

percent (pər sĕnt′) **1.** *n.* a ratio in which a number is compared to 100. (p. 141) **2.** *n.* the number of hundredths representing a part of a whole. *Forty-eight **percent** of our classmates are girls.* (p. 141)

perimeter (pə rĭm′ ĭ tər) *n.* the distance around a figure. *Jan jogged around the **perimeter** of the football field, and Asok measured it.* (p. 212)

period (pîr′ ē əd) *n.* a group of 3 number places. *Each **period** of three digits is separated from the others by a comma: 3,529,407.* (p. 17)

permutation (pûr′ myo͞o tā′ shən) *n.* an arrangement of items in a particular order. *If you change the order of the items in an arrangement, you get a new **permutation**.* (p. 249)

perpendicular (pûr′ pən dĭk′ yə lər) *adj.* meeting to form a right angle. *The two lines that make the letter* T *are **perpendicular**.* (p. 182)

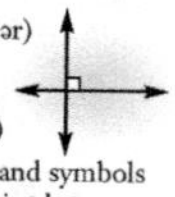

phrase (frāz) *n.* a group of words and symbols with meaning. *A **phrase** has a subject but no verb or* = *sign.* (p. 40)

pi π (pī) *n.* the result of dividing the circumference of any circle by its diameter. *The value of **pi** is about 3.14.* (p. 218)

place (plās) *n.* the position of a digit in a number. *In the number 584, the **place** of the 8 is the tens place.* (p. 17)

plane (plān) *n.* a flat surface that continues without end. *Figures on a **plane**, like a square or a circle, do not have any thickness.* (p. 180)

plot (plŏt) *v.* place a point on a number line or other graph. *Please **plot** your data on a graph to show me what they mean.* (p. 23)

point (point) *n.* a location in space. *A **point** can be anywhere, so we need ways to describe where it is.* (p. 180)

polygon (pŏl′ ē gŏn′) *n.* a closed plane figure whose sides are line segments. *A **polygon** has at least 3 sides.* (p. 190)

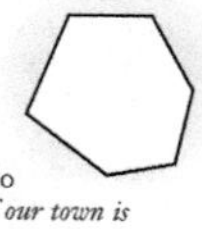

population (pŏp′ yə lā′ shən) *n.* all the people and/or animals who live in an area. *The **population** of our town is 36,000.* (p. 20)

position (pə zĭsh′ ən) *n.* the place where something is located. *If you slide a figure to the right, you change its **position**.* (p. 206)

positive integers *n.* the counting numbers: 1, 2, 3, and so on. (p. 256)

power (pou′ ər) *n.* the number of times a number or expression is used as a factor, as shown by an exponent. *When you cube a number, you raise it to the third **power**. For example, 10^3 is 1,000.* (p. 27)

pre-image *n.* the figure that is being moved in a transformation. (p. 205)

prime factorization *n.* a product of prime numbers. (p. 89)

prime number *n.* a whole number whose only factors are 1 and the number itself. (p. 87)

principal (prĭn′ sə pəl) *n.* the amount of money on which interest is paid. *My records show that the **principal** I invested was $400, and I've received $60 in interest so far.* (p. 153)

prism (prĭz′ əm) *n.* a solid figure with faces that are polygons; bases are congruent and parallel. *A cube is an example of a rectangular **prism**.* (p. 223)

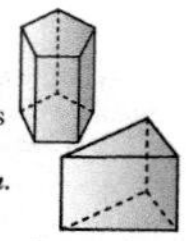

probability (prŏb′ ə bĭl′ ĭ tē) *n.* the chance that an event will occur. ***Probability** is the number of favorable outcomes divided by the number of possible outcomes.* (p. 234)

product (prŏd′ əkt) *n.* the result of multiplying. *The **product** of 3 and 20 is 60.* (p. 40)

proper fraction *n.* a fraction less than 1 with a numerator that is less than its denominator. (p. 109)

property (prŏp′ ər tē) *n.* a special quality of something. *One **property** of numbers is that when they are multiplied by 1, they remain the same. 3 × 1 = 3.* (p. 32)

proportion (prə pôr′ shən) *n.* a statement that two ratios are equal. (p. 136)

proportional (prə pôr′ shə nəl) *adj.* having the same ratio. *Values* a *and* b *are **proportional** to* c *and* d *if* $\frac{a}{b} = \frac{c}{d}$, with $b \neq 0$ and $c \neq 0$. (p. 200)

protractor (prō trăk′ tər) *n.* a tool for measuring angles. (p. 182)

pygmy (pĭg′ mē) *adj.* very small; tiny. (p. 125)

Q

quadrant (kwŏd′ rənt) *n.* a section of a coordinate plane formed by two intersecting number lines. *On graphs, the coordinates of points in the upper right **quadrant** are positive numbers.* (p. 272)

quadrilateral (kwŏd′ rə lăt′ ər əl) *n.* a polygon with 4 sides. (p. 192)

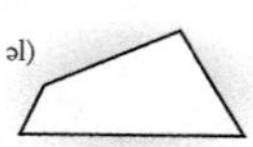

quilt (kwĭlt) *n.* a kind of blanket for a bed. *A **quilt** has a soft pad in the middle and many designs made with stitches.* (p. 130)

quotient (kwō′ shənt) *n.* the result of dividing. *In the sentence 12 ÷ 6 = 2, the **quotient** is 2.* (p. 40)

R

radius (rā′ dē əs) *n.* a line segment from any point on a circle to its center. *In any circle, the **radius** is half the length of the diameter* (p. 217)

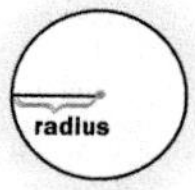

range (rānj) *n.* the difference between the greatest and the least numbers in a data set. *The **range** of ages among the children in my family is 6 years, because I'm 12 and my youngest brother is 6.* (p. 160)

rate (rāt) **1.** *n.* a ratio with different units of measure. (p. 136) **2.** *n.* the percent of interest per year. (p. 153)

ratio (rā′ shē ō′) *n.* a pair of numbers compared by division. *The **ratio** of students to teachers in my school is 24 to 1.* (p. 136)

ray (rā) *n.* a part of a line that has one endpoint and continues in one direction. (p. 180)

reciprocal (rĭ sĭp′ rə kəl) *n.* one of two numbers with a product of 1. *I know that $\frac{2}{3}$ is a **reciprocal** of $\frac{3}{2}$, because when I multiply them, I get 1.* (p. 131)

rectangle (rĕk′ tăng′ gəl) *n.* a parallelogram with 4 right angles. *A square is one kind of **rectangle**.* (p. 192)

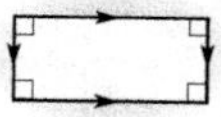

reflection (rĭ flĕk′ shən) *n.* the change in the position of a figure that comes from flipping it over a line, called the line of reflection. *The **reflection** of a tree that you see in a pond is upside down.* (p. 206)

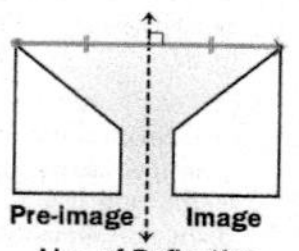

regroup (rē gro͞op′) *v.* write a number as a sum of different numbers. *You can **regroup** 42 as 3 tens and 12 ones.* (p. 70)

regular polygon *n.* polygon with all sides congruent and all angles congruent. (p. 191)

related (rǐ lā' tǐd) *adj.* having something in common. (p. 181)

remainder (rǐ mān' dər) *n.* the amount left after division. *When you divide 7 by 2, you get 3 with a remainder of 1.* (p. 83)

rename (rē nām') *v.* write numbers in a different way. (p. 119)

repeating decimal *n.* a decimal with a digit or group of digits that repeats forever. (p. 143)

rhombus (rŏm' bəs) *n.* a parallelogram with 4 congruent sides. (p. 192)

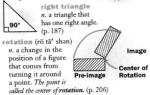

right triangle *n.* a triangle that has one right angle. (p. 187)

rotation (rō tā' shən) *n.* a change in the position of a figure that comes from turning it around a point. *The point is called the center of rotation.* (p. 206)

Image
Center of Rotation
Pre-image

round (round) *v.* change to give an estimated value. *Because it's easier to compute with tens or fives, I always round numbers when I'm doing mental math.* (p. 21)

rule (rōōl) *n.* an algebraic expression that tells you what to do with, say, a variable. *A rule is a statement that tells you how to do something.* (p. 43)

sales tax *n.* an amount of money the government collects when a product is sold. *A sales tax is expressed as a percent of the price of the product.* (p. 151)

scale (skāl) *n.* on a graph, the units and intervals on an axis. (p. 169)

scalene triangle *n.* a triangle that has no congruent sides. (p. 187)

sentence (sěn' təns) *n.* a group of words or symbols that express a complete idea. *An equation is a kind of mathematical sentence.* (p. 49)

set (sět) *n.* a group of items. (p. 105)

short-word form *n.* a number written with both digits and words. *The number 26,000,000 is written in short-word form as 26 million.* (p. 16)

side (sīd) *n.* one of two rays in an angle. (p. 182)

similar figures *n.* figures that have the same shape but not necessarily the same size. *The corresponding angles of similar figures are congruent and the corresponding sides are proportional.* (p. 200)

simple equation *n.* an equation that requires only one operation to solve. (p. 278)

simple interest *n.* interest paid only on the amount saved or borrowed. (p. 153)

simplest form *n.* a way of writing a fraction so that the numerator and denominator have no common factor other than 1. (p. 106)

skew lines *n.* lines that lie in different planes. (p. 181)

solid figure *n.* a figure that is not flat and does not lie in a plane. (p. 223)

solution (sə lōō' shən) *n.* a number that makes an equation true. *The solution is the answer to a problem or exercise.* (p. 279)

solve the equation *v.* find values that make the equation true. (p. 49)

square (skwâr) **1.** *v.* raise to the second power. (p. 28) **2.** *n.* a parallelogram with 4 right angles and 4 congruent sides. (p. 192)

square unit *n.* a square with a side length of 1 unit. (p. 214)

---

standard form *n.* a way of writing a number using only digits and with commas between periods. *The number 8,425,115 is written in standard form.* (p. 16)

statistic (stə tǐs' tǐk) *n.* a number used to describe a set of numbers or data. (p. 165)

stem (stěm) *n.* the part of a stem-and-leaf plot that shows all the digits except the ones, or units of a data item. (p. 163)

stem-and-leaf plot *n.* a diagram used to display and order a data set. (p. 163)

strategy (străt' ə jē) *n.* a plan for how to do something. *Heidi's strategy for deciding if she likes a book is to read the chapter titles.* (p. 33)

subtract (səb trăkt') *v.* find the difference of two numbers. *When you subtract 7 from 10, you get 3.*

Subtraction Property of Equality *n.* a property that says subtracting the same number from both sides of an equation does not change the equality. (p. 49)

Subtraction Property of Equality
If $a = b$, then $a - c = b - c$.

success (sək sěs') *n.* a favorable result for a trial. *When a baby is learning to walk, each little step is a success.* (p. 239)

sum (sŭm) *n.* the result of adding. *The sum of 23 and 2 is 25.* (p. 60)

supplementary angles *n.* two angles whose measures add up to 180 degrees. (p. 185)

surface area *n.* the sum of the areas of all the faces of a solid figure. (p. 223)

survey **1.** (sûr' vā) *n.* a set of questions used to collect data. (p. 158) **2.** (sěr vā') *v.* ask questions to collect data.

table (tā' bəl) *n.* a format used to list data. *Tron showed us his data about motorcycles in a table.* (p. 168)

tally mark *n.* a short mark used as a counter. (p. 159)

term (tûrm) **1.** *n.* a number, variable, product, or quotient in an expression. *Terms are separated by a plus or minus sign.* (p. 45) **2.** *n.* one of the two parts of a ratio. (p. 137)

terminating decimal *n.* a decimal with a fixed number of digits. (p. 143)

tessellation (těs' ə lā' shən) *n.* a design created from repeating shapes that fit together with no spaces in between. (p. 207)

tip (tǐp) *n.* a percent of a bill paid to someone who provides a service. *Dad usually gives a waiter a 15 percent tip.* (p. 151)

transformation (trăns' fər mā' shən) *n.* a change in the position or size of a figure; the movement of a figure in a plane. (p. 205)

translation (trăns lā' shən) *n.* a change in the position of a figure that comes from sliding it along a straight path. (p. 206)

Pre-image
Image

trapezoid (trăp' ǐ zoid') *n.* a quadrilateral with only one pair of parallel sides. (p. 192)

tree diagram *n.* an organized list showing all possible outcomes. (p. 244)

trend (trěnd) *n.* a clear pattern in a graph that suggests what future data might be. *The graph of the ages at which people get married shows a trend toward marrying later in life.* (p. 170)

trial (trī' əl) *n.* an attempt of an activity or experiment. *Each trial in the experiment gave the same result.* (p. 239)

two-operation equation *n.* an equation that you solve using two operations. (p. 278)

---

value (văl' yōō) *n.* the quantity represented by a digit based on its position. *A digit has a different value in the ones place from its value in the tens place.* (p. 17)

variable (vâr' ē ə bəl) *n.* a quantity, usually a letter, that can change. *The expression for finding the perimeter of a square, 4s, has the variable s in it because the length of the side (s) may vary or be different for each square.* (p. 40)

Venn diagram *n.* an organizer that uses overlapping circles or rectangles to show what two or more sets have in common. (p. 92)

vertex (vûr' těks') *n.* the common endpoint of two rays, two sides, or three edges. The plural is *vertices.* (p. 182)

vertices

vertical (vûr' tǐ kəl) *adj.* running up and down. *A tree is vertical unless it is leaning over.* (p. 258)

vertical angles *n.* opposite angles with equal measures formed by intersecting lines. (p. 185)

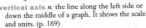

vertical axis *n.* the line along the left side or down the middle of a graph. It shows the scale and units. (p. 169)

volume (vŏl' yōōm) *n.* the amount of space inside a solid figure. *If I know the volume of this pitcher, I know how much lemonade I can put in it.* (p. 227)

whole number *n.* a number in the set (0, 1, 2, 3, 4, ...). (p. 17)

word form *n.* a way of writing a number using only words. *The number ten is written in word form.* (p. 16)

x-axis *n.* the horizontal number line. (p. 271)

x-coordinate *n.* the first number in an ordered pair. (p. 272)

y-axis *n.* the vertical number line. (p. 271)

y-coordinate *n.* the second number in an ordered pair. (p. 272)

zero pair *n.* the pair of a yellow chip (+1) and a red chip (−1). Their sum is 0. (p. 261)

INDEX

SKILLS AND FEATURES

Grammar Spotlight
Adjectives: Using some, any, many, every, each, and neither/nor, 157
Fewer than/less than, 233
Imperatives, 211
More, less, fewer, and than, 277
Phrasal Verbs, 59
Simple Sentence, 135
Singular and Plural Nouns, 37
Some and any, 289
Using too and very, 81
Who or what, 255
The Word the, 103

Language Notes
Confusing Word Pairs, 62, 153, 159, 218, 235, 280
Homophones, 153, 175, 280
Idioms, 94, 147, 267
Multiple Meanings, 18, 22, 27, 32, 45, 89, 110, 120, 137, 164, 170, 187, 191, 197, 201, 214, 226, 228, 258, 272, 284
Signal Words
  Compare/Contrast, 67
  Importance, 99
  Location, 105
  Positive/Negative, 257
  Time Order, 39, 245, 250
Verb Phrases, 182

Problem-Solving Skills
Draw a Diagram, 232
Guess, Check, and Revise, 80
Look for a Pattern, 58
Make a Model, 288
Make a Table, 178
Make an Organized List, 102
Simulate a Problem, 254
Solve a Simpler Problem, 210
Use Logical Reasoning, 156
Use a Problem-Solving Guide, 36
Work Backward, 134
Write an Equation, 276

Develop Language Skills
Analyzing, 86, 167
Choosing an Operation, 42
Clarifying, 133, 253
Classifying, 184
Comparing, 20, 118, 287
Comparing and Contrasting, 123, 231
Connecting, 216
Contrasting, 177
Demonstrating, 79, 128
Describing, 52, 91, 113, 189
Evaluating, 47, 140
Explaining, 35, 57, 209, 275
Gathering Data, 162
Identifying, 64, 204, 260
Interpreting, 25, 108, 172, 238
Justifying, 282
Organizing, 69, 221, 270
Persuading, 101, 150, 226, 248
Predicting, 30, 145, 243
Responding, 94
Summarizing, 74, 155, 199, 265
Synthesizing, 194

Oral Language
And the LCM is . . ., 101
Are You Close?, 79
Commission Mission, 155
Distribute the Whole, 133
Graphs in the News, 172
The Great Fraction Divide, 113
How Close Is It?, 25
Keeping All Things Equal, 57
Long May It Wave, 199
Lots of Language, 30
Magic Square, 270
Make It Simplest, 108
Meet Our Pet, 42
Move That Point!, 64
The Number Hold-up, 287
Prime Time, 91
Rap About It, 35
Rap It, 167
"Sum" Differences, 74
Sum of It, 243
Take a Turn, 209
Tell All, 194
Tell It Like It Is, 275
Terminators or Repeaters?, 145
Time for a Story, 265
Very Variable, 52
What'll It Be?, 248
What's My Number?, 86, 282
What's the Story?, 253
What's Your Angle?, 189
What's Your Time?, 162
Which Is Greatest?, 20
Words Have Roots, 47
Working on the Line, 260

SKILLS AND FEATURES

Partner Practice
Analyze This!, 172
Are They Similar?, 204
Big Percents, 150
Drum Up the Data, 167
Express Yourself, 42
Factor It In, 86
Find Those Pairs, 184
How Big Is the Bull's-Eye?, 221
How Does It Work?, 74
Is It or Isn't It?, 177
It Takes Teamwork!, 96
Lefty or Righty?, 150
More Equal Ratios, 140
My Oh My, We Love Pi, 231
My Story, 52
Name It, 194
Name That Property, 35
Order in the Library, 69
Paychecks, 108
People, People, Everywhere!, 20
A Perfect Fit, 209
Planning a Path, 216
Pony Express, 79
Range Rover, 162
Ready to Wear, 253
Relatives, 270
Repeat That Please?, 145
Round and Round, 64
Round and Tell, 25
Sift Them Out, 91
Smoothie Tree, 248
Test Me, 123, 128
Tic-Tac-Math, 47
Two Ways to Check, 287
What's in a Label?, 118
What's the Bottom Line?, 155
What's the Difference?, 30
What's the Result?, 260
You Form It, 226
Your Name or Mine, 238

Hands On
All Sorts of Angles, 184
Calculate It, 133
Can You Cut It?, 204, 226
Can You Draw It?, 189
Come to Order!, 118
Diagram It, 96
Find the Least, 101
How Many Diagonals?, 199
How's the Weather?, 177
It's in the Chips, 265
Line 'Em Up!, 69
Making Spinners, 238
Model That, 52
Modeling Equations, 282
Ratio Mania, 140
Rectangles to Triangles, 216
Round and Around, 221
Try, Try Again, 243
Use a Ruler, 128
Use the Ruler, 123
What Part Is It?, 231
What's My Number?, 57
What's My Polygon?, 275
What's the Rule(r)?, 113

Unit 1

Lesson 4, Page 33, Talk and Share

$(200 \times 5) \times 36 = 1,000 \times 36 = 3,600$; $(25 + 75) + 634 = 100 + 634 = 734$; $352 - 49 = (352 + 1) - (49 + 1) = 353 - 50 = 303$

Lesson 4, Page 33, Differentiating Instruction

Intermediate/Advanced: Samples: $(4 \times 25) \times 31 = 100 \times 31 = 3,100$; $(200 \times 5) \times 16 = 1,000 \times 16 = 16,000$; $(398 + 2) + (56 - 2) = 400 + 54 = 454$; $(572 - 1) + (99 + 1) = 571 + 100 = 671$; $8 \times (30 + 9) = (8 \times 30) + (8 \times 9) = 240 + 72 = 312$; $7 \times (60 + 3) = (7 \times 60) + (7 \times 3) = 420 + 21 = 441$; $(81 + 2) - (58 + 2) = 83 - 60 = 23$; $(492 + 1) - (179 + 1) = 493 - 180 = 313$

Lesson 4, Page 34, Practice

21. No; sample: $100 \div 4 = 25 \neq 4 \div 100 = 0.04$
22. No; sample: $(75 - 25) - 10 = 40 \neq 75 - (25 - 10) = 60$; $(200 \div 20) \div 4 = 2.5 \neq 200 \div (20 \div 4) = 40$

Unit 4

Lesson 13, Page 85, Practice

15. No; $2 + 2 + 2 + 2 + 2 = 10$ and 10 is not divisible by 3.
16. Yes; $1 + 8 + 3 + 6 = 18$ and 18 is divisible by 9.
17. 2, 3, 9   **18.** 2, 3
19. 2, 3, 5, 9, 10   **20.** 2, 3, 5, 10
21. 5   **22.** 2, 3, 9
23. $3 + 4 = 7$ and 7 is not divisible by 3.
24. 3-inch, 6-inch, and 12-inch tiles
25. 10, 20, 30, 40, 50, 60, 70; if the ones digit is zero, the number is divisible by 10.
26. Because 9 is divisible by 3
27. Not always; the number is divisible by 10 and by 5 if the ones digit is 0. It is divisible by 5 but not by 10 if the ones digit is 5.
28. A team of 20 can be arranged in more ways because 20 has more factors than 25.

Lesson 14, Page 90, Practice

25.

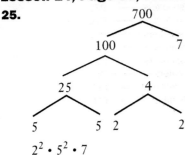

$2^2 \cdot 5^2 \cdot 7$

26.

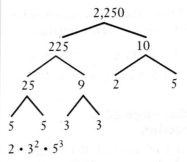

$2 \cdot 3^2 \cdot 5^3$

27. Sample:

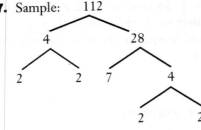

$2^4 \cdot 7$

28. Not necessarily; the composite number 143 has factors of 1, 11, 13, and 143.
29. C

Lesson 14, Page 91, Partner Practice

Prime numbers to 100: 2, 3, 5, 7, 11, 13, 17, 19, 23, 29, 31, 37, 41, 43, 47, 53, 59, 61, 67, 71, 73, 79, 83, 89, 97

Samples: The multiples of 2 take out five columns; the multiples of 5 take out the column of 5s and 10s; the multiples of 11 are all in one diagonal.

Unit 5

Lesson 17, Page 104, Activity: Coin Fractions

Coin	Number of Cents	Decimal Part of $1	Fraction Part of $1
Penny	1	0.01	$\frac{1}{100}$
Nickel	5	0.05	$\frac{5}{100}$, or $\frac{1}{20}$
Dime	10	0.10	$\frac{10}{100}$, or $\frac{1}{10}$
Quarter	25	0.25	$\frac{25}{100}$, or $\frac{1}{4}$
Half dollar	50	0.50	$\frac{50}{100}$, or $\frac{1}{2}$

Lesson 22, Page 132, Practice

36. 8 squares
37. 84 in. long and 56 in. wide; I multiplied the width of each square by the number of squares: $3\frac{1}{2} \times 24 = 84$, $3\frac{1}{2} \times 16 = 56$.

38. This method is useful only when the whole number is divisible by the denominator of the fraction.

$$\frac{2}{3} \times 9 \rightarrow 9 \div 3 = 3, 3 \times 2 = 6; \frac{2}{3} \times 9 = \frac{18}{3} = 6$$

$$\frac{2}{5} \times 15 \rightarrow 15 \div 5 = 3, 3 \times 2 = 6; \frac{2}{5} \times 15 = \frac{30}{5} = 6$$

Problem-Solving Skills, Page 134, Differentiating Instruction

Advanced: $5 for plants is $\frac{1}{6}$ of the total. Berries are twice plants because $\frac{1}{3} = 2 \times \frac{1}{6}$. So earnings are $2 \times \$5$, or $10. Plants and berries together are $\frac{1}{2}$ of the total ($\frac{1}{6} + \frac{1}{3}$), so mowing, as the other half, is equal to the sum of plants and berries: $5 + $10 = $15.

Unit 6

Lesson 23, Page 139, Practice

24. 2 percussion instruments
25. 1 staff member
26. No, you need to double just 12; the ratio is $\frac{16}{24}$, which is $\frac{2}{3}$.

Lesson 23, Page 140, Evaluating

1. Nugent: $0.55, Liberty: ≈ $0.58, Paramount: $0.60, Tivoli: ≈ $0.67
2. $0.55, Nugent
3. Answers will vary.
4. Even though the Nugent's rate per seat is least, the overall cost of the Paramount is better.

Lesson 24, Page 144, Practice

38. Australia, yellow   **39.** Russia, blue
40. Germany, orange   **41.** China, green
42. United States, red
43. 100%; the graph represents the entire number, or all, of the medals for the top five countries.

Lesson 24, Page 145, Partner Practice

Answers have been given with bars to show repeating numbers. $0.\overline{11}$, $0.\overline{22}$, $0.\overline{33}$, $0.\overline{44}$, $0.\overline{55}$, $0.\overline{66}$, $0.\overline{77}$, $0.\overline{88}$; $0.\overline{09}$, $0.\overline{18}$, $0.\overline{27}$, $0.\overline{36}$, $0.\overline{45}$, $0.\overline{54}$, $0.\overline{63}$, $0.\overline{72}$, $0.\overline{81}$, $0.\overline{90}$

Lesson 25, Page 150, Persuading

1. Suzi: 60%, 50%   Karen: ≈ 66.7%, 48%
Kimi: 70%, 48%   Tonya: 50%, 37.5%
Wendy: 50%, 37.5%   Debbie: 60%, ≈ 55.6%
Cassie: 50%, 40%   Elena: 62.5%, ≈ 55.6%
Teresa: 60%, ≈ 46.7%
2–3. Answers will vary.

Unit 7

Lesson 27, Page 161, Practice

2. Homework Time

```
              x
       x      x
x   x x      x
x   x x x x x
x x x x x x x
4 5 6 7 8 9 10
    Hours
```

9. Days in Months of Year

```
                    x
                    x
                    x
              x   x
              x   x
              x   x
     x     x   x
    28  29  30  31
         Days
```

Lesson 28, Page 165, Differentiating Instruction

Advanced: With 57: mean, 35; median, 31.5; no mode. Without 57: mean, 30.6; median, 28; the mean

Unit 8

Lesson 31, Page 184, Classifying

60°, △DFE, acute; 90°, △HGI, right; 120°, △JKL, obtuse; 90°, △MON, right

Lesson 33, Page 194, Synthesizing

rectangle, 2, yes, sometimes, yes, yes; rhombus, 2, yes, yes, yes, sometimes; square, 2, yes, yes, yes, yes

Unit 10

Lesson 41, Page 236, Differentiating Instruction

Intermediate: Samples: P(number 1) = 0; P(letter b, a, or n) = 1; P(letter b) + P(letter a) + P(letter n) = 1

Lesson 42, Page 241, Differentiating Instruction

Advanced: There are equal numbers of Bs and Is, so I would expect to select each letter the same number of times. There are fewer Rs than Bs, so I would expect to select more Bs.

Lesson 43, Page 244, Activity: A Shoe Tree

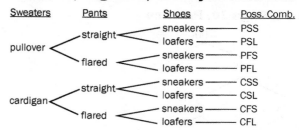

Lesson 43, Page 247, Practice

9.

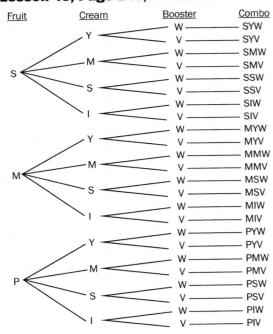

Lesson 43, Page 248, Partner Practice

Lesson 44, Page 253, Clarifying

1. Sample: The order matters because each arrangement is a different picture; sample: loading five CDs into a CD player to be played in sequence
2. Sample: The order does not matter because the flowers are grouped in the arrangement, not in a sequence; sample: selecting five CDs to take to a party
3. Sample: Alike: They are types of arrangements; different: There are more permutations because they rely on order. Order is not important for combinations.

Lesson 44, Page 253, Partner Practice

12 outfits

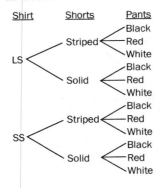

Lesson 44, Page 253, Oral Language

24 arrangements

APST	PAST	SAPT	TAPS
APTS	PATS	SATP	TASP
ASPT	PSAT	SPAT	TPAS
ASTP	PSTA	SPTA	TPSA
ATSP	PTAS	STAP	TSAP
ATPS	PTSA	STPA	TSPA

Real words are past, pats, spat, taps, and in some locales, PTAs; permutation; order makes a difference.

Problem-Solving Skills, Page 254, Activity: I Got the Spirit

Sample simulation: Let five faces on one number cube, such as the numbers 1–5, stand for students who pinned school buttons to their backpacks. On the other number cube, let three faces, such as odd numbers, stand for students who wore a school shirt. Toss the two cubes together 20 times and record the results. A success is the number 1, 2, 3, 4, or 5 on the first cube and an odd number on the second cube. Answers will vary.

Unit 11
Lesson 47, Page 270, Oral Language

Sum: −6

−5	2	−3
0	−2	−4
−1	−6	1

Lesson 48, Page 273, Differentiating Instruction

Beginning:

Sample table:

x	y	Ordered Pair
0	3	(0, 3)
1	4	(1, 4)
2	5	(2, 5)
3	6	(3, 6)

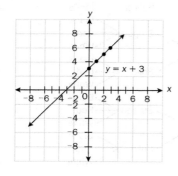

Unit 12

Lesson 50, Page 286, Practice

23. at least 72 cards

24. Samples:

$3 \times (-3) = -9$, $-12 \times (-3) = 36$, $-9 < 36$;

$15 \div (-3) = -5$, $21 \div (-3) = -7$, $-5 > -7$;

$-9 \div (-3) = 3$, $36 \div (-3) = -12$, $3 > -12$

If you divide or multiply both sides of an inequality by a negative number, you must reverse the inequality symbol to get a true statement.

Lesson 48, Page 273, Activity: Graph an Equation

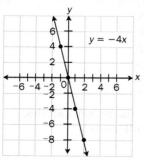

Lesson 48, Page 274, Practice

16. Sample:

x	y
-1	-7
0	-6
1	-5
2	-4

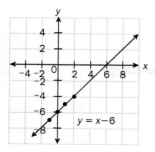

17. Sample:

x	y
-1	3
0	5
1	7
2	9

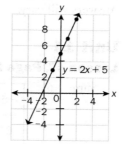

Acknowledgments

PHOTOS AND ILLUSTRATIONS

Lê/CORBIS **280** ©Hurewitz Creative/CORBIS **281** *top*
©Johnathan Smith; Cordaiy Photo Library Ltd./CORBIS
281 *bottom* ©Creatas **282** ©Eileen Ryan Photography, 2004
283 *left* ©John Schaefer, Director, Children's Media Workshop
283 *center* ©Tony Freeman/PhotoEdit, Inc. **284** ©James
Marshall/CORBIS **285** ©Eileen Ryan Photography, 2004
287 *left* ©The Image Bank/Getty Images **287** *right* ©Chase
Swift/CORBIS **287** ©Eileen Ryan Photography, 2004
288 ©Creatas **289** ©John Schaefer, Director, Children's Media
Workshop **T32 (290** *left* ©Eileen Ryan Photography, 2004 **290**
right ©Courtesy of NASA **290** *bottom* ©Stockbyte/Royalty Free
292 *top* ©Paul A. Souders/CORBIS **293** *top* ©Getty Images)
Front Cover *Foreground:* Photodisc/Getty Images; *Background:*
Photodisc/Getty Images; BrandX/Getty Images; Based on a
system of labeling the columns A through J and the rows 1 through
18, the following background images were taken by the following
photographers: A2, A5, A6, A15, A17, A18, B13, B14, B16, C1, C6,
C7, C16, D2 D5, D13, D15, E1, E3, E4, E6, E8, E9, E16, E17,
E18, F1, F4, F8, F9, F13, F15, F18, H1, H2, H4, H9, H13, H17, I1,
I3, I5, I7, I8, I10, I12, I14, I15, J3, J4, J8, J9, J13, J15: Philip
Coblentz/Getty Images; B3: Spike Mafford/Getty Images; E5: Albert
J Copley/Getty Images; F5, J7: Steve Allen/Getty Images; F12: Sexto
Sol/Getty Images

Illustrations on the following pages: **47, 105, 152, 212, 227, 227,
228, 231, 237, 239** and **242** are by Sean O'Neill

TEXT
301 Pronunciation Key, Copyright ©2003 by Houghton Mifflin
Company. Reproduced by permission from the American Heritage
Student Dictionary.

*The editors have made every effort to trace the ownership of
all copyrighted selections found in this book and to make full
acknowledgment for their use. Omissions brought to our
attention will be corrected in a subsequent edition.*